Reinterpreting Criminal Complicity and Inchoate Participation Offences

In *Reinterpreting Criminal Complicity and Inchoate Participation Offences*, Dennis J. Baker argues that the mental element in complicity is one of intention, that recklessness alone is not sufficient. This is demonstrated by showing that the ancient and modern authorities on complicity required intention. The book argues the 'causal participation' element in complicity means that the conduct element can only be established when there is intentional encouragement on the part of the accessory. As the Accessories and Abettors Act 1861, like most of the statutory provisions found in the United States, deems that both perpetrator and accessory are perpetrators for the purpose of punishment and crime labelling, limiting the mental element in complicity to intentional participation is, the author argues, the only way to reconcile these provisions with the requirements of proportionate punishment and fair labelling. As some forms of reckless encouragement and assistance will not be criminalised if the mental element in complicity is intention only, the author suggests that the solution is to amend section 45 of the Serious Crime Act 2007 to criminalise reckless participation. In addition, the author argues that standard complicity and joint enterprise complicity have the same mental and conduct elements and thus joint enterprise complicity is not a distinct form of complicity.

Dennis J. Baker is Professor of English Law and Head of the School of Law at the University of Surrey, UK.

Reinterpreting Criminal Complicity and Inchoate Participation Offences

Dennis J. Baker

Routledge
Taylor & Francis Group
LONDON AND NEW YORK

First published 2016 by Routledge

2 Park Square, Milton Park, Abingdon, Oxfordshire OX14 4RN
711 Third Avenue, New York, NY 10017

Routledge is an imprint of the Taylor & Francis Group, an informa business

First issued in paperback 2018

British Library Cataloguing in Publication Data
A catalogue record for this book is available from the British Library

Library of Congress Cataloging-in-Publication Data
Names: Baker, Dennis J., author.
Title: Reinterpreting criminal complicity and inchoate participation offences / Dennis J. Baker.
Description: New York, NY: Routledge, 2016. | Includes bibliographical references and index.
Identifiers: LCCN 2015050395 | ISBN 9781138675568 (hbk) | ISBN 9781315560649 (ebk)
Subjects: LCSH: Accomplices—Great Britain. | Accomplices. | Inchoate offenses—Great Britain. | Criminal liability—Great Britain.
Classification: LCC KD7910 .B35 2016 | DDC 345.41/03—dc23
LC record available at http://lccn.loc.gov/2015050395

ISBN: 978-1-138-67556-8 (hbk)
ISBN: 978-1-138-61425-3 (pbk)

Typeset in ITC New Baskerville Std
By Swales & Willis Ltd, Exeter, Devon, UK

Contents

Foreword

I had a copy of the manuscript of this book when examining the issues raised in R v Jogee [2016] UKSC 8, and it was helpful to me. Professor Baker's arguments on the point, which was of central importance in that case, that foresight is evidence from which intention may be inferred, but no more than evidence, and that secondary liability for a criminal offence requires intent to encourage or assist its perpetration, were well researched and cogent. The same applies to his writing about the need for there to be actual assistance or encouragement, and about the nature of intent, which may be conditional. All in all, Professor Baker's book is a valuable contribution to the understanding of an important and sometimes confusing part of the criminal law.

The Right Hon Lord Toulson, Justice of The Supreme Court of the United Kingdom

Table of cases

In this Table of Cases R.; Com.; D.P.P.; Ex parte; People; re.; State; U.S. are ignored for sorting purposes.

Preface

In this monograph, I try to tackle the problem of complicity in criminal law. The law of complicity has been in a confused state for many years and it has not been systematically and analytically unpacked by academics. Academics have pointed to the obvious injustices caused by labelling a person as a murderer when she was merely reckless in assisting or encouraging another to perpetrate a murder, but beyond that the claim that there is a form of complicity that does not require assistance or encouragement has gone fairly well unchallenged by academics.

In this work I shall try to demonstrate that what is orthodoxly known as common purpose or joint enterprise complicity is not a distinct form of complicity. Academics and courts have routinely assumed that common purpose/joint enterprise complicity does not require an act of encouragement or assistance and therefore is a distinct form of complicity. I argue that the mental element in complicity is intention and that the *actus reus* for complicity is assistance and/or encouragement – nothing less. In addition, I argue that the foresight rule as expounded in the joint enterprise cases of the last three decades is merely a maxim of evidence. Foresight arose predominantly as an issue in cases that involved the conceptual issue of conditional intention, and evidence of foresight was only ever meant to be used to infer intention or conditional intention. This issue is currently before the Supreme Court in *R. v. Jogee*. I have sent a full manuscript of this monograph not only to counsel but to the Lords sitting in that case. It is hoped that they will reinterpret complicity as requiring nothing less than intention. The ancient and modern precedents involving conditional intention issues and 'encouragement by implied authorization' support such an interpretation of the law. In the 2015 edition of the *Glanville Williams Textbook of Criminal Law* at para 17-069, I cite this manuscript and summarize the thesis in Chapter 2 as follows: 'Until the decision in the House of Lords in *R. v. Powell* changed the law, the foresight of possibility rule (i.e. the accessory's foresight of the collateral crime as a possible incident of the underlying joint enterprise), like the probable and natural consequences maxim, was a mere maxim of evidence for inferring that the common purpose extended to the collateral crime.' I have no right to act as *amicus curiae* in Britain, so all I can do is give the Supreme Court and counsel access to my research; whether it will influence them to hold that foresight is mere evidence of intention is beyond my control.

In this monograph, I try to show that common purpose complicity is made out only under the *actus reus* requirement set out in the *Accessories and Abettors Act 1861* when an integral part of the co-perpetrator of an underlying crime such as a bank robbery is an act of intentional encouragement. Hence, the very act of jointly perpetrating the underlying robbery must have the double effect of being an act of encouragement. It must encourage the joint perpetrator of robbery to perpetrate some collateral crime such as the murder of a security guard. The double effect (encouragement) must also be intended.

When *A* is reckless as to the double effect of the joint enterprise (i.e. the effect that by joining the robbery *A* will send *P* a message of encouragement apropos certain foreseen collateral crimes – such as the need to kill a guard), then *A* should be charged with some lesser independent offence such as one of those found in the *Serious Crime Act 2007*.

When the act of joining the underlying robbery does not have the effect of *encouraging* the perpetrator to perpetrate the murder of the security guard etc., then the joint perpetrator of the robbery should be liable for the robbery only. In such a case, the conduct element required by the *Act of 1861* is not made out, because there is no encouragement and therefore there can be no derivative liability. Similarly, there can be no liability under the *Serious Crime Act 2007*, because there is no act that is capable of encouraging the perpetrator to perpetrate the collateral crime. The conduct element cannot and should not be constructed from some thin account of agency theory or vicarious liability based on association and foresight.

DJB
London

1 Introduction

Abstract

In this monograph, I shall argue that no doctrinal nor conceptual distinction can be drawn between what is orthodoxly known as standard complicity and what is orthodoxly known as joint enterprise/common purpose complicity. I shall argue that both have the same mental element and that the conduct element for both is either assistance or encouragement pursuant to section 8 of the Accessories and Abettors Act 1861 *(hereinafter the* Act of 1861*). Because I argue that the conduct element of all complicity has to come within section 8 of the* Act of 1861, *I shall not dedicate a separate chapter to the topic of standard complicity. I shall explain the way in which contemporary scholars and courts have divided the two forms of complicity, but overall my examination of the conceptual problems with the conduct and mental elements in complicity does not rest on demonstrating that joint enterprise/common purpose complicity is a distinct doctrine.*

I shall argue that the mental element in complicity is one of intention. It is submitted that recklessness is not sufficient. This will be demonstrated by showing that the ancient and modern authorities on complicity required intention. Coupled with this, it shall be argued that complicity's 'conduct element' element can only be made out in the common purpose complicity scenario when there is intentional encouragement *on the part of the accessory. Since the* Act of 1861, *like most of the statutory provisions found in the United States, deems that both the perpetrator and accessory are perpetrators (principals) for the purpose of punishment and crime labelling, limiting the mental element in complicity to intentional participation is the only way to reconcile these sorts of provisions with the requirements of proportionate punishment and fair labelling. It is true that some forms of reckless encouragement and assistance will not be criminalised if the mental element in complicity is intention only, but the solution is to amend section 45 of the* Serious Crime Act 2007 *to criminalise reckless* remote *participation, because that provision allows for fair labelling and proportionate punishment.*

I. The scope of this monograph

This monograph is divided into six chapters. The first chapter raises the core issues and provides some background on the theory and doctrine. The last chapter brings together the different theses considered in the earlier chapters and summarises them into a conclusive whole, reconciling them with the overall theme of fair labelling and proportionate punishment. In Chapter 2, the law of common purpose complicity is examined to support the claim that the mental element in complicity requires nothing less than intention. It will be argued that the English authorities dating back to the mid-sixteenth century support the theory that common purpose complicity requires intentional factual encouragement. It will be argued that common purpose liability as a form of complicity liability rests on the participants' mutual intentions – that is, their common purpose. The jury has to be able to infer that the common *purpose* extended to the particular collateral crime. It can do this by inferring that the accessory conditionally or directly intended the collateral crime to be perpetrated for the purpose of making the underlying joint enterprise succeed.

Furthermore, it will be argued that the *foresight of possibility* maxim proposed by the High Court of Australia in *Johns v The Queen*[1] was not proposed as a substantive fault doctrine for complicity liability, but was used as an evidential maxim. I shall argue that the Lords in *R v Powell*[2] mistook the evidential maxim that is used for inferring conditional intention to be a substantive fault element for common purpose complicity. I argue that the maxim can be used to allow the jury to infer that the accessory conditionally intended to encourage the perpetrator to perpetrate the anticipated collateral crime, if the facts show that the accessory knew that the perpetrator intended to perpetrate the collateral crime should certain conditions arise, such as a security guard confronting them during the course of a robbery.

In Chapter 3, the recent decision of the Supreme Court of the United Kingdom in *R v Gnango*[3] is examined. It is argued that the joint perpetrator theory adopted by some of the judges in that case was not applicable on the facts, because the facts clearly showed that 'Bandana Man' (BM) was the perpetrator and Gnango the encourager. It is argued that the jury should have been given a direction with respect to Gnango obliquely intending to encourage BM to kill himself. Coupled with this, the jury should have been given a direction with respect to mutual combats, because some perceived combats are genuine cases of self-defence. I also argue that the provocative act murder doctrine was not applicable in that case. It was not a case of provocative act murder, because BM was merely encouraged; BM was not forced to engage in the gunfight, nor was he an intervening instrument[4]

1 [1980] 143 C.L.R. 108.
2 [1999] 1 A.C. 1.
3 [2012] 1 A.C. 827.
4 He was not even close to falling within the concept of an innocent agent.

(a justified agent or an excused agent who was acting under duress of circumstances). His actions were voluntary and unnecessary; therefore, the provocative act murder doctrine was inapplicable.

The final point that I raise in Chapter 3 concerns the exclusion of the exempt party/victim rule. That rule holds that a victim cannot be liable for complicity for encouraging another to perpetrate a crime against her. Hence, if *X* encourages *Y* to chop off *X*'s finger, *X* should not be liable under section 8 of the *Accessories and Abettors Act 1861* as a perpetrator for the assault against herself. Only *Y* should be liable. I also argue that the victim rule is not applicable in cases where the real victim is a third party. In *R. v. Gnango*, Gnango was not the victim, so the victim rule did not cover him. If Gnango had been a joint victim with Magda Pniewska (the innocent passer-by who was killed in the crossfire from Gnango and BM, who were trying to kill each other as parties to a mutual gunfight in a London car park), Gnango being wounded and Pniewska being killed, the victim rule still would have been excluded as far as the third party was concerned. If Gnango had been the actual victim and the *only* victim, the victim rule, as a matter of policy, would not have been excluded.

In Chapter 4, I examine the *Serious Crime Act 2007*. The independent facilitation offences found in sections 44 and 45 of the *Serious Crime Act 2007* have improved the law in some respects, because those offences distinguish the perpetrator of the anticipated target crime from the facilitator. The facilitator is not treated as a perpetrator of the anticipated target crime, but is convicted of an independent participation offence. However, if we accept the thesis presented in this monograph that section 8 of the *Act of 1861* only criminalises intentional assistance or encouragement, there will be a *lacuna* in the law. My thesis supports criminalising reckless assistance/encouragement, but I shall argue that this can be done fairly only by enacting an independent offence.

If *D* sells a gun and is suspicious that *P* might misuse it, *D* should not be liable for murder under section 8 of the *Act of 1861*, but instead should be liable for an independent participation offence similar to the one found in section 45 of the *Serious Crime Act 2007*, since that type of offence criminalises *D* at a lower level and allows for fair labelling and proportionate punishment. Nonetheless, as we shall see in Chapter 4, section 45 criminalises only oblique intentional assistance/encouragement and thus is too narrow to cover reckless assistance/encouragement more generally. *Consequently, section 45 should be amended so that its mental element is recklessness, not oblique intention.*

In Chapter 5, I examine the defence of withdrawal and its application to the law of complicity. I also examine the defence of abandonment and its application to the law of attempted participation under the *Serious Crime Act 2007*. It seems reasonable to allow for a defence where the encourager or assister has taken steps to render her encouragement and assistance wholly ineffective. If the secondary party retrieves a gun that she has attempted to supply to *P* before *P* gets a chance to sight the gun, then she should be able to raise the defence of abandonment. Such a case is not a case of failed attempt, but a case where the assister has had a complete change of heart and has taken reasonable steps to try to do the right thing. The defence of abandonment would provide such defendants with an incentive for neutralising their attempted assistance and encouragement before it has a chance to facilitate the perpetrator's crime. As the facilitator often will be in the best position to neutralise her attempted participation, it makes sense to provide her with an incentive to do so.

II. Overview

Why a book on the criminal law of complicity.[5] One would have thought after almost a thousand years the English law of complicity would be well settled,[6] but the fact is that the English law of criminal complicity is in a shambles. It cannot be reconciled with a normative reading of the basic human rights that emerged in the later part of the twentieth century.[7] Increasingly, twenty-first-century courts are taking the human rights developed in the twentieth century seriously, but we have a long way to go.[8] Coupled with this, the law of criminal complicity, as interpreted by the courts of the last few decades, cannot be reconciled with the modern and ancient authorities. Parliament created further complexity when it enacted the *Serious Crime Act 2007*. The *Serious Crime Act 2007* not only introduced new personal liability offences to criminalise consummated encouragement and assistance, but also criminalised attempted participation.[9] The complexity and incongruity of some of the provisions found in the *Serious*

5 There are three books that have tackled the law of complicity in the past. Peter Gillies, *The Law of Criminal Complicity* (Sydney: Law Book Co., 1980); Gordon Rose, *Parties to an Offence* (Toronto: Carswell Co, 1982); K.J.M. Smith, *A Modern Treatise on the Law of Criminal Complicity* (Oxford: Clarendon Press, 1991). Alas, I was unable to obtain a copy of Gordon Rose's book in any British library; therefore, I have not had a chance to read it.

6 In our own law, it dates back at least 800 years. See the *Principal and Accessory Act 1275* (1275 (3 Edw. 1) C A P. XIV); Sir William Staunford, *Les Plees del Coron* (London: by Rychard Tottel, 1567) at 41; Bracton recognised the doctrine of complicity before the year 1268. See Henrici de Bracton, *De Legibus et Consuetudinibus Angliae* (Cambridge MA: Belknap Press of Harvard University Press, 1968) Vol. II at 392.

7 See for example, Ronald Dworkin, *Freedom's Law: The Moral Reading of the American Constitution* (Cambridge MA: Harvard University Press, 1996).

8 For a recent decision based a normative reading of a Bill of Rights, rather than a literal reading, see the decision of the Supreme Court of Canada in *Carter v. Canada* (Attorney General) [2015] S.C.C. 5.

9 Attempted encouragement was already covered by the common law offence of incitement. The new provisions cover attempted assistance as well as attempted encouragement.

Crime Act 2007 is such that I have dedicated a lengthy chapter to the interpretive and conceptual problems it raises.

A part of the reason that the law of complicity remains in a shambolic state is attributable to the fact that constructive liability has survived in our modern criminal law. Recent judicial interpretations[10] of the scope of the common purpose complicity doctrine have made it impossible to reconcile that doctrine with a person's moral right not to be punished disproportionately and the moral right not to be unfairly criminalised.[11] The use of 'recklessness' as a fault standard for inculpating accessories, when the perpetrator has perpetrated a specific intent crime such as murder, is contrary to justice.[12]

There would be nothing wrong with having a lesser personal liability rather than derivative liability offence of reckless assistance or encouragement,[13] but it is unjust to label and punish reckless *participation* as intentional *perpetration.* The new offences found in the *Serious Crime Act 2007* only criminalise intentional and oblique intentional assistance or encouragement, but under that Act the assister/encourager is convicted of a separate offence and thus is not labelled and punished as a perpetrator of the anticipated target offence. For example, if a person intentionally assists or encourages a murder she can be prosecuted under section 44 of the *Serious Crime Act 2007*, where her assistance and/or encouragement will be labelled and punished as a breach of section 44.

If the courts were to interpret the law of complicity under section 8 of the *Accessories and Abettors Act 1861* as requiring intentional assistance or encouragement there would be a *lacuna* in the law, because reckless participation is not covered under the *Serous Crime Act 2007.* The solution is for Parliament to amend section 45 of the *Serious Crime Act 2007* to make it a crime of reckless participation rather than one of oblique intentional participation. Little is gained by underwriting the intentional participation offence found in section 44 of the *Serious Crime Act 2007* with an oblique intentional participation offence. It should be underwritten with a reckless participation offence. It shall be argued in this monograph,

10 *R. v. Powell* [1999] 1 A.C. 1; *contra, Clayton v. The Queen* (2006) 168 A. Crim. R. 174 at 228–229, *per* Kirby, J. dissenting.

11 These rights have not been fully recognised by the courts, but I have argued elsewhere that a normative interpretation of our existing human rights shows that it is open to the courts to recognise that they do exist. Dennis J. Baker, *The Right Not to Be Criminalized: Demarcating Criminal Law's Authority* (Farnham: Ashgate Publishing, 2011).

12 *Clayton v. The Queen* (2006) 168 A. Crim. R. 174 at 228–229 *per* Kirby, J.

13 For an academic discussion of rationale for distinguishing reckless complicity from intentional complicity, see Sanford H. Kadish, 'Reckless Complicity' (1997) 87 *J. Crim. L. & Criminology* 369; Daniel G. Moriarty, 'Dumb and Dumber: Reckless Encouragement to Reckless Wrongdoers' (2010) 34 *S. Ill. U. L.J.* 647.

complicity at common law and under section 8 of the *Accessories and Abettors Act 1861* criminalised intentional participation only. Furthermore, it shall be argued that the courts ought to reinterpret the mental element in complicity to require nothing less than intention for the purposes of establishing the mental element under section 8. It is true that this would exclude reckless participants from being deemed perpetrators and from being punished on that basis, but any gap in the law could be plugged by amending section 45 of the *Serious Crime Act 2007*, which would allow reckless participation (encouragement/assistance) to be fairly labelled and punished proportionately.

III. The conduct element: *Accessories and Abettors Act 1861*

In this chapter, I use '*A*' to refer to the accessory or putative accessory/secondary party and '*P*' to refer to the perpetrator. Derivative liability differs from personal liability in that it extends liability beyond the perpetrator to those who participate by encouraging or assisting the perpetrator.[14] Participators differ from perpetrators, because they do not perpetrate or jointly perpetrate[15] a crime. Instead, they remotely participate in another's perpetration by providing antecedent assistance or encouragement. They make an indirect physical contribution to the perpetrator's crime, either by providing physical assistance or by using encouragement[16] to stimulate the perpetrator's thinking which in turn influences the perpetrator when she is deliberating about whether to perpetrate the anticipated target crime. The perpetrator is both a participant and a perpetrator, but the accessory is only an indirect participant. The accessory might participate by giving the perpetrator a gun, but the act of supplying a gun is not the same as the perpetrator's act of using that gun to murder another human being.

Both the perpetrator and the accessories are regarded by law as participants in the crime, and are treated as perpetrators for the purposes

14 Glanville Williams, *Criminal Law: The General Part* (London: Stevens & Sons, 2nd edn, 1961) at Chap. 9.

15 A joint perpetrator is a perpetrator *simpliciter*. If *P1* grabs *V*'s feet and *P2* grabs *V*'s hands with *P1* and *P2* simultaneously throwing *V* from a cliff, *P1* and *P2* are joint perpetrators of the act of throwing *V*. If *P1* encourages *P2* to push *V* over the cliff, *P2* is the perpetrator and *P1* a participant by encouragement.

16 The word 'abet' comes from Old French *abeter* to lure on, entice, from *beter* to bait. Thus, in the older authorities it was used to refer to encouragement. In *People v. Terman* (1935) 4 Cal.App.2d 345 at 347, Pullen, J. said: '"Abet" is a French word combined of two words "a" and "beter", – to bait or excite an animal. The word "aid" does not imply guilty knowledge or felonious intent, whereas the word "abet" includes knowledge of the wrongful purpose of the perpetrator and counsel and encouragement in the crime.' More recently the English courts have used it interchangeably with 'aid'. In this book, it will be used to refer to encouragement only.

of conviction and punishment.[17] The perpetrator is an accomplice of the accessories, and they are accomplices of the perpetrator and of each other. Section 8 of the *Accessories and Abettors Act 1861* provides: 'Whosoever shall aid, abet, counsel, or procure the commission of any offence] . . . shall be liable to be tried, indicted, and punished as a principal offender.' In modern terminology, we can say that the conduct element is established by showing that the accessory assisted and/or encouraged the perpetrator to perpetrate the anticipated target crime. The conduct element in complicity always requires an act of assistance and/or an act of encouragement, because that is expressly stated in section 8. The conduct might be that the accessory supplies a gun that is used by the perpetrator to perpetrate a murder. If the perpetrator does not use the gun supplied by the accessory to kill the victim, but uses a gun supplied by another person, then the accessory has only attempted to participate in the murder and thus is not liable under section 8 of the *Act of 1861*. Instead, she should be prosecuted under section 44 or 45 of the *Serious Crime Act 2007*, if the mental element for either of those offences is made out.

Likewise, where the accessory attempts to participate in the perpetrator's anticipated target crime by trying to encourage her, she is not derivatively liable under section 8 of the *Act of 1861*. Derivative liability supposes a physical link between *A*'s conduct and *P*'s act of perpetration. *A*'s liability has to derive from a crime perpetrated by another and it can only derive from such a crime if *A* was a culpable participant in that crime. *A* need only be an indirect participant (an encourager or assister), but she must consummate her participation for her liability to derive from another's crime. Liability cannot derive from merely hoping or trying – there must be a physical connection otherwise the concept of 'derivative' is vacuous.

Suppose *X* tries to e-mail an assassin, *Y*, to offer to pay *Y* £1 million to kill a political rival, *V*. Unbeknown to *X*, *Z* has already paid *Y* to kill *V* and the assassination is carried out before *Y* reads *X*'s e-mail offer. *X* cannot encourage *ex post facto*. *X* only attempts to encourage *Y* and thus is not liable under the *Accessories and Abettors Act 1861*. This example of attempted intentional encouragement is straightforward. However, the determination is far more complex in the common purpose/joint enterprise complicity scenarios, because some of those cases have been decided on what seems to be a presumption of factual encouragement rather than on factual encouragement itself.

Section 8 of the *Accessories and Abettors Act 1861* makes it clear that, regardless of the scenario that gives rise to complicity liability, there must be factual participation by way of assistance (aid) or encouragement (abet, council or procure). Section 8, unlike the provisions found in section 44–46 of the *Serious Crime Act 2007*, does not criminalise inchoate participation. The courts have made it clear that there must be factual participation in the anticipated

17 Section 8 of the *Accessories and Abettors Act 1861*.

target crime.[18] It is not enough to show that the accessory attempted to assist or encourage the perpetrator by trying to send her a gun; the gun must actually reach the perpetrator and be used by the perpetrator to kill.

The courts have been less cautious when the conduct element in complicity involves encouragement via entering into a criminal joint enterprise. Juries have been let infer encouragement in many cases where there was no evidence of encouragement and where the question should have been withdrawn from the jury. In *R. v. Lam*, in the Supreme Court of Victoria, Redlich, J. said:

> No causal connection is required between the act of aiding and abetting and the offence committed. The authors of Smith and Hogan suggest that it is unnecessary that the principal offender be influenced in any way by the principal in the second degree. They argue that the natural meaning of the terms of aiding and abetting does not imply a causal element. If the acts of the secondary participant were ignored . . . secondary participation would have been established.[19]
>
> . . .
>
> [I]t would be 'manifest nonsense' to require proof that the principal offenders were aware of the encouragement provided by each accused or that there had to be a causal connection between the acts of the secondary participant and the commission of the offence.[20]

I take the view that it would be manifest nonsense not to prove factual participation beyond reasonable doubt. The law of complicity under section 8 of the *Accessories and Abettors Act 1861*, unlike the *Serious Crime Act 2007* offences, requires factual influence and assistance, even if that influence or assistance is of a minor nature.[21] Glanville Williams has argued that factual influence must also be purposive.[22] The perpetrator has to be in fact influenced by the perpetrator's act of encouragement, even if it is only one of several factors influencing her decision to perpetrate the anticipated target crime.

18 *The Queen v. Coney* (1881–82) L.R. 8 Q.B.D. 534, *per* Denman, J., Huddleston, B., Manisty, Hawkins, Lopes, Stephen, Cave, and North, J.J.; *R. v. Jogee* [2013] EWCA Crim. 1433 at paragraph 23 *per* Laws, L.J.

19 (2005) 159 A. Crim. R. 448 at paragraph 60 citing J.C. Smith and Brian Hogan, *Criminal Law* (London: Butterworths, 7th edn, 1992) at 145.

20 *R. v. Lam* (2005) 159 A. Crim. R. 448 at paragraph 62.

21 *R. v. Giannetto* (1997) 1 Cr. App. R. 1 at 13; *Wilcox v. Jeffery* [1951] 1 All E.R. 464.

22 See Glanville Williams, 'Complicity, Purpose and the Draft Code: Part 1' [1990] Crim. L.R. 4 at 10; Glanville Williams, 'Complicity, Purpose and the Draft Code: Part 2' [1990] *Crim. L.R.* 98 at 99.

A. There must be an antecedent act of facilitation or encouragement

The perpetrator must perpetrate or attempt[23] to perpetrate the anticipated target crime under the accessory's influence.[24] To put it another way, the perpetrator must perpetrate the anticipated target crime partly 'in consequence'[25] of the accessory's encouragement. Where there is no influence, the accessory's liability has to be for engaging in inchoate conduct, not for consummating an act of assistance or encouragement. If the encouragement has reached *P*'s mind, it is no defence for *A* to assert that *P* was already intent on killing *V*, because a reasonable jury could infer that *A*'s encouragement was an additional factual influencer that pushed *P* over the edge.[26] Alternatively, the jury would be entitled conclude that *A*'s encouragement was too trivial to have made a factual contribution to *P*'s crime. It might infer that the encouragement was so trivial that it was not a factor that had any real influence on *P*'s decision to perpetrate the anticipated target crime. So even where encouragement has reached the mind of the perpetrator, it might be held to be insufficient to have made a factual contribution. This is an evaluative question for the jury.

In *R. v. Lam*, Redlich, J. goes on to assert:[27]

> Legal texts recognise that in criminal trials in which the secondary participant is not said to be acting pursuant to an agreement with the

23 *R. v. Dunnington* [1984] Q.B. 472; *R. v. Hapgood* (1870) L.R. 1 C.C.R. 221; *R. v. Clayton* (1843) 1 Car. & K. 128; *R. v. Williams* (1844) 1 Car. & K. 589.

24 *The Queen v. Coney* (1881–82) L.R. 8 Q.B.D. 534, *per* Denman, J., Huddleston, B., Manisty, Hawkins, Lopes, Stephen, Cave, and North, J.J. (Lord Coleridge, C.J., Pollock, B., and Mathew, J., dissenting); *R. v. Allen* [1965] 1 Q.B. 130 *per* Edmund Davies, J. (Marshall and Lawton J.J. concurring); *R. v. Clarkson* [1971] 1 W.L.R. 1402 *per* Megaw L.J. (Geoffrey Lane and Kilner Brown J.J. concurring); *R. v. Jones* (1977) 65 Cr. App. R. 250 at 252. In *Hutt v. R.* [1989] T.A.S.S.C. 27 at paragraph 53, Cox, J. (Underwood, Crawford, J.J. concurring) said: 'In the circumstances of this case an error of law occurred by reason of the omission to tell the jury that . . . there had to be proof to the requisite degree that the principal offender was in fact encouraged by the conduct of the accused to commit the crime.' In *State v. Bennett* (2013) 307 Conn. 758 at 770, Harper, J. said: 'Mere presence as an inactive companion, passive acquiescence, or the doing of innocent acts which may in fact aid the one who commits the crime must be distinguished from the criminal intent and community of unlawful purpose shared by one who knowingly and wilfully assists the perpetrator of the offence in the acts which prepare for, facilitate, or consummate it.'

25 James Fitzjames Stephen, *A History of the Criminal Law of England* (London, Macmillan & Co. 1883) vol. I at 501–502.

26 Cf. *State v. Tally* (1894) 15 So. 722. Kadish writes: 'The secondary party may be liable if the principal is aware of the proffered aid, since knowledge of the efforts of another to give help may constitute sufficient encouragement to hold the secondary actor liable.' Kadish, *op. cit. infra*, note 78 at 359 citing *State v. Tazwell* (1878) 30 La.Ann. 884; George P. Fletcher, *Rethinking Criminal Law* (Boston: Little, Brown, 1978) at 677–682.

27 *R. v. Lam* (2005) 159 A. Crim. R. 448 at paragraph 61 citing Peter Gillies, *The Law of Criminal Complicity* (Sydney: Law Book Co., 1980) at 54–55.

> principal offender, it would be unrealistic and most often impossible to establish that the principal offender knew of the secondary participant's act and was influenced by it to commit the crime. Gillies suggests that it is sufficient if the accessory's act, viewed objectively, is considered by the jury to be reasonably capable of having encouraged or assisted the principal offender. It need not do so in fact.

This passage highlights a fundamental error of application that has emerged in the complicity cases. The difficulty of proving this element does give judges *carte blanche* to convert section 8 of the *Accessories and Abettors Act 1861* into an inchoate offence. Nor does it give judges a permission to apply a presumption of encouragement. The jurors have to consider all the evidence and can infer factual encouragement only when there are strong facts in support of such an inference. The facts would have to be sufficient for the jury to infer that the encouragement reached the mind of the perpetrator and had some influence on her decision to perpetrate the anticipated target crime.

B. Common purpose scenarios giving rise to complicity liability

Establishing the conduct element is particularly important in the common purpose complicity cases where encouragement is presumed from the fact that the accessory participated jointly in some underlying crime. (Most commentators argue that joint enterprise is a different form of complicity that has a different conduct element that is not provided for in section 8 of the *Act of 1861*,[28] but I take the view that joint enterprise complicity's conduct element is found in section 8 of the *Act of 1861*. An independent and distinct conduct element is not used to criminalise the complicit encouragement that is the wrongful conduct found in the joint enterprise/common purpose complicity scenarios.)

To understand this better, we need to understand what is orthodoxly meant by common purpose complicity or joint enterprise complicity.[29] Under section 8 of the *Act of 1861* there is one doctrine of complicity. We have just seen there are two ways of performing its conduct element. Those two ways are outlined in section 8 of the *Act of 1861* as acts of assistance and/or encouragement. *A* assists *P* to perpetrate a murder when *A* gives *P* a gun and *P* uses the gun *A* has supplied to kill *V*. *A* encourages *P* to perpetrate a murder when *A* pays *P* £1 million to kill *V* and this influences *P* to kill *V*. Complicity liability hinges simply on acts of assistance or encouragement. The conduct

28 Andrew Ashworth, *Principles of Criminal Law* (Oxford: Oxford University Press, 2006) at 410 *et seq.*; Andrew Simester *et al.*, *Simester and Sullivan's Criminal Law: Theory and Doctrine* (Oxford: Hart Publishing, 2013) at 201 *et seq.*; David Ormerod and Karl Laird, *Smith and Hogan's Criminal Law* (Oxford: Oxford University Press, 2015) at 213–238.

29 Scholars and courts use the terms 'common purpose complicity' and 'joint enterprise complicity' interchangeably.

and fault elements under section 8 are the same regardless of the factual scenario that gives rise to complicity liability. Complexity has crept into the law, because in common purpose complicity scenarios the courts have not been cautious in identifying the conduct that makes it possible to convict the accessory under the *Act of 1861*. To understand this, we need to consider a typical example of complicity involving a common purpose scenario.

Common purpose/joint enterprise complicity liability arises when an accessory encourages another to perpetrate a crime by jointly perpetrating an underlying crime with the perpetrator. For example, *X* and *Y* jointly perpetrate a robbery and during the robbery *Y* perpetrates a second crime such as murder of a security guard. The murder of the security guard is a collateral crime. The underlying crime is the robbery, which *X* and *Y* jointly perpetrate. *X* and *Y* are directly liable for the robbery, because they jointly perpetrate it. They are joint perpetrators so their liability for the robbery is direct rather than derivative. Since the murder of the guard is perpetrated by *Y* alone, *X* can be liable for the murder of the guard, if at all, only as an accessory. Hence, any liability for *X* as far as the murder is concerned will be derivative, not direct.

If there is active encouragement or assistance during the robbery, then complicity is easy to apply.[30] Suppose that *X* and *Y* jointly perpetrate a robbery. *X* and *Y* are in the bank and *X* is at one end of the counter with a gun at a bank teller's head, while *Y* is at the other end of the counter filling a sack with money. *X* is armed with a gun, but *Y* is unarmed. A passing police officer notices the robbery, stands in the only exit to the bank and starts to fire bullets at *X*, because the officer fears *X* is about to kill the bank teller. *X* and *Y*, who are on opposite sides of the room, jump behind the nearest pieces of furniture to take refuge from the officer's shots. Only *X* has a gun, but *X* is in a blind spot and cannot get a clear aim at the police officer. *Y*, who is on the other side of the bank, can get a clear shot at the police officer, but *Y* does not have a gun. *Y* yells out to *X*, 'Kick the gun across the floor to me because I can get a clear shot.' *X* kicks the gun across to *Y* and yells out: 'Make sure you kill her, because she has seen our faces.' *Y* receives the gun and uses it to kill the police officer. Even though the murder of the police officer was collateral to the underlying joint enterprise, there is no need to determine whether *X*'s participation in the underlying joint enterprise *encouraged* *Y* to kill the police officer, because during the robbery

30 See *R. v. Jogee* [2013] EWCA Crim. 1433 at paragraph 20 where it is accepted that *A* actively encouraged *P* during a joint assault, because '[*A*] knew that *P* could get hold of a knife at the house and that he realised that *P* might use the knife with intent to kill or cause *V* serious bodily harm, and nevertheless, with that knowledge, participated in the attack on *V* by encouraging *P*. That encouragement took the form of verbal encouragement to harm *A*; threatening serious violence towards *V* himself when threatening to smash a brandy bottle over *V*'s head; deliberately damaging *V*'s car in close proximity to where *P* was attacking *V*, and being close at hand to lend support.'

X actively encouraged and assisted *Y* to kill the police officer. *X* uttered words of encouragement ('kill her, because she has seen our faces') and also actively assisted *Y* by providing her with a gun.

The need to infer encouragement via participation in the underlying unlawful joint enterprise in itself arises only when there is no active assistance or encouragement of the collateral crime during the unlawful joint enterprise. Compare the above scenario with the following scenario. Suppose *X* and *Y* have just been released from prison and are short of money so jointly perpetrate a burglary. During the burglary they are confronted by an occupant and without encouragement or assistance, *Y* produces a gun from her pocket and shoots the occupant dead. In this scenario *X* has not supplied *Y* with a gun, nor has *X* spoken words of encouragement. *Y* has acted without any encouragement or assistance. *X* can be derivatively liable under section 8 only if she assists or encourages *Y*'s murder of the occupant.

The accessory can be liable only for the intended target crime if she has assisted or encouraged. To establish encouragement in the common purpose/joint enterprise complicity cases, the courts have in the past operated on a presumption of implied encouragement. The presumption works like this: *A* jointly perpetrated a robbery with *P*, realising that during the burglary *P* might kill an occupant, therefore *A*, by joining the underlying lawful enterprise (e.g. the burglary) encouraged *P* to perpetrate the collateral crime (e.g. the murder of the house occupant). It is presumed that *A* simply by joining the underlying joint enterprise sends a message of encouragement to *P* that *P* has *A*'s support to perpetrate any collateral crime that *A* foresees that *P* might perpetrate.

The accessory's putative direct perpetration of the murder is fictitiously constructed from acts of assistance and encouragement. There is no moral equivalence between the accessory's acts and those of the perpetrator, but much of the injustice in deeming both to be perpetrators could be dampened by requiring equal fault. I shall try to show that the conduct element is made out in the joint enterprise scenarios only when the accessory intends to encourage by her conduct of joining the underlying unlawful joint enterprise.[31] It will be argued that historically it was necessary for *A* to imply by her conduct a message of approval of *P*'s anticipated collateral crimes, and thus *A* could not be liable where (s)he simply foresaw *P*'s potential collateral crime, especially when *A* had expressly forbidden *P* from perpetrating the potential collateral crime, but could only be liable if (s)he had at least obliquely intended to encourage *P* by implying from her conduct of joining the underlying enterprise that she approved of the collateral crime. I argue that this narrower interpretation of the conduct element supports a narrower interpretation of the mental element. A person cannot recklessly authorise, so if the

31 Cf. *R. v. Bristow* [2013] EWCA Crim. 1540.

conduct element requires the accessory to have encouraged the collateral crime as something she consented, authorised and approved the perpetrator committing, then the mental element can be nothing less than intention.

In many of the gang violence cases that have caused great controversy, there was ample evidence for inferring intentional encouragement. For example, in *R. v. Rajakumar*[32] there was ample evidence for a jury to infer that the accessories encouraged the perpetrator to use great violence, which resulted in *V*'s death. In that case, a gang went armed with cricket bats and poles to attack a rival group. One of the participants, *P2*, struck a rival gang member, *V2*, so hard that his cricket bat broke in half when it hit *V2*'s arm. Thereafter, the perpetrator of the murder, *P1*, beat *V1* repeatedly on the head with a pole and killed him by splitting his head wide open.[33] Given that the gang members were using the same sorts of weapons and given that they all went to attack with a shared intention of inflicting serious injury on their victims, it is hard to see how by their conduct they did not send a clear message of encouragement to each other. There was no escalation in violence, because they intended to inflict grievous bodily harm with the exact kind of weapons as the perpetrator used to kill. They intended to encourage the perpetrator to inflict grievous bodily harm and it was that act of GBH that caused *V*'s death.[34] If the perpetrator is constructively liable for murder then so too are the accessories. As we will see in the next chapter, it does not matter that the perpetrator might have formed a secret intention to kill, since her act was not outside of what had been authorised and encouraged by the other participants.[35]

However, encouragement might be difficult to infer from a minor joint attack on *V* in which *A* participated as joint perpetrator, which then escalated so that *P* commits a much more serious offence, e.g. a stabbing leading to *V*'s death. Suppose *X* and *Y* agree to handcuff *V* and cut off her ponytail, because *V* has slept with *Y*'s boyfriend. As they are wrestling with *V* in an attempt to handcuff her, *V* kicks *Y* in the mouth in an attempt to escape. This causes *Y* to get very angry and *Y* stabs *V* with the scissors that were brought merely to cut off *V*'s ponytail. *V* dies as a result of the stab wound. The question then is whether the co-perpetrator of the initial joint attack against *V* can be liable for the escalation of violence because (s)he was involved in the initial attack. This is not an instance in which the collateral crime can be described as one which must be committed in order for the purpose of the main underlying unlawful enterprise to succeed. The

32 [2014] 1 Cr. App. R. 168.

33 It is reported in the judgment that: 'Those who came onto the scene shortly after to assist him described how brain matter protruded from obvious skull fractures, along with extensive bleeding – a savage assault indeed.' *R. v. Rajakumar* [2014] 1 Cr. App. R. 168 at 173.

34 *R. v. Rajakumar* [2014] 1 Cr. App. R. 168 at 178 *per* Davis, L.J.

35 Cf. *R. v. Gamble* [1989] N.I. 268; *R. v. Carpenter* [2012] Q.B. 722; *R. v. Yemoh* [2009] EWCA Crim. 930; *R. v. Day* [2001] EWCA Crim. 1594. See also *R. v. Michaud* (2000) 144 C.C.C. (3d) 62.

attack on *V* could have succeeded without it becoming more serious. The complexity here is that there is a spontaneous escalation rather than any kind of conditional plan. Again, the starting point is to consider whether the stabbing was encouraged in accordance with the conduct element set out in section 8 of the *Accessories and Abettors Act 1861*.

Suppose that *X* knew that *Y* was a very violent woman and believed that should *V* get the better of *Y* in the struggle to handcuff *V*, *Y* might use the scissors to stab *V*. The fact that *X* engaged in an unlawful enterprise and foresaw that *Y* might stab *V* with the scissors if things got out of hand should not be enough to make *X* equally liable for the murder.[36] These cases will turn on the finest distinctions, but the jury should not convict unless the evidence shows that the accessory intended to encourage the collateral crime. There should be strong evidence demonstrating that the accessory believed that the collateral crime *would be* (not might be) perpetrated should certain conditions arise during the joint perpetration of the underlying unlawful joint enterprise.

If a person foresees that a person will perpetrate a collateral crime as a matter of virtual certainty, should certain conditions arise during the perpetration of the underlying joint enterprise such as the victim getting the better of the perpetrator in a struggle, then a jury could infer that by joining the underlying joint enterprise the accessory intentionally sent a message of encouragement to the perpetrator. Where the accessory only foresees that the perpetrator might perpetrate the collateral crime, the courts seem to take the view that by joining the joint enterprise that preceded the perpetration of the collateral crime, the accessory recklessly sent a message of support and therefore recklessly performed an act of encouragement by joining the underlying joint enterprise.[37]

It is true that if *P* was in fact encouraged (even if only partly) to perpetrate the collateral crime because she felt emboldened by having *A* present, that would be an act of encouragement for the purposes of section 8 of the *Accessories and Abettors Act 1861*, because *P* has in fact been encouraged to perpetrate the collateral crime by *A*'s participation in the underlying joint enterprise. However, if the mental element in complicity under section 8 of the *Act of 1861* requires intention, then reckless acts of encouragement should not be sufficient.

C. Change of normative position theory: the missing remote participation requirement

Derivative liability can be established only if the conduct element as provided for in section 8 of the *Act of 1861* is satisfied. *Per contra*, Simester argues

36 The House of Lords has suggested that not much more is needed. *R. v. Powell* [1999] 1 A.C. 1.

37 *R. v. Powell* [1999] 1 A.C. 1.

that the wrongful conduct requirement in joint enterprise complicity is made out without any encouragement or assistance from the accessory.[38] According to Simester it is enough that *A* changed her normative position by joining the underlying criminal enterprise with foresight of the fact *P* might perpetrate a collateral crime. Simester's change of normative position claim does not provide a normative explanation of the fairness of holding a person liable for unintended collateral crimes stemming from an underlying joint enterprise. Horder and Hughes[39] fall for the appeal of Simester's idea, but they too fail to explain why constructive liability based on mere foresight and association is fair when the accessory is being held equally liable for a crime perpetrated by another. Horder and Hughes do not provide any supporting arguments for their change of normative position justification for joint enterprise complicity, so it is difficult to critique their assertions. Simester, Horder and Hughes invoke the change of normative position rationale not only to justify recklessness as the fault element for 'murder by complicity' (among other crimes), but also as a justification for dispensing with the conduct element set out in section 8 of the *Act of 1861*. In this monograph, it is argued that the conduct element (assistance or encouragement) supplies a key normative ingredient. It is *A's intentional indirect physical contribution to P's harmful conduct* that makes it fair to hold *A* liable for *P*'s act of criminal perpetration. This does not mean *A* and *P* need to be held equally liable when there has been only reckless encouragement/assistance on the accessory's part. The reckless accessory should be charged with an independent lesser offence for personal wrongdoing rather than derivative wrongdoing.

Bad conduct (factual assistance or encouragement) is a part of the normative wrongness of complicit conduct. The unlawfulness of the underlying joint enterprise adds little normative value if it is association and foresight that is doing the normative work. If *A* and *P* go shopping together with *A* knowing her friend *P* has a history of shoplifting and is a borderline kleptomaniac, *A* associates with *P* with foresight of the fact that *P* might perpetrate theft. If it is just foresight and association that is doing the normative work, *A* is liable for shoplifting.

Also, Simester seems to assert that the unlawfulness of the underlying joint enterprise adds normative value to the association and foresight prongs. Simester's argument is that a person changes her normative position by joining a criminal enterprise as opposed to a lawful enterprise and therefore should be liable for the autonomous independent crimes of her associates, even if she made no indirect physical contribution (assisted or encouraged) to those crimes. Horder and Hughes also assert that

38 A. P. Simester, 'The Mental Element in Complicity' (2006) 122 *L.Q.R.* 578 at 598–599.

39 Jeremy Horder and David Hughes, 'Joint Criminal Ventures and Murder: The Prospects for Law Reform' (2009) 20 *King's L.J.* 379 at 398.

change of normative position theory provides an explanation for complicity liability when a person has joined an underlying criminal enterprise. What all three authors fail to explain is why it is fair to hold the accessory liable for a specific intention crime such as murder which she did not intend the perpetrator to perpetrate, simply because she was acting wrongly by joining the underlying joint enterprise. They give no explanation of why punishment for the underlying crime itself if not sufficient punishment for the putative accessory for changing her normative position.

If *D*'s culpable change of normative position was limited to jointly perpetrating the underlying criminal enterprise, then her change of normative position was limited to that wrong and her liability and punishment should be limited to punishing her for her joint perpetration of the underlying joint enterprise only. If it can be shown that she also intentionally encouraged *P* to perpetrate the collateral crime, then there should be additional liability for that as well – because her change of normative position then extends to that crime. If a change of normative position rests on doing wrong, then it cannot extend to putative wrongdoing (i.e. it cannot be extended to non-existent doing). *D* takes a normative position by joining the underlying joint enterprise, but she takes no new normative position with respect to *P*'s collateral crime, if she does not assist or encourage it. *D*'s change of normative position is limited to the wrongs that she assists or encourages.

If *D* recklessly encouraged *P* to perpetrate the collateral crime, her change of normative position extends to *P*'s collateral crime, but even here fairness and justice requires that she should be charged with some new independent reckless participation offence for her personal wrongdoing. Her personal wrongdoing was that she recklessly encouraged *P* to perpetrate the collateral crime. In the foregoing hypothetical, *D*'s change of normative position was not one where she *intentionally* encouraged *P* to perpetrate the anticipated target offence – *D*'s change of normative position was her decision to risk encouraging *P* (i.e. it was a case of reckless encouragement). *The change of normative position theory simply explains why D's act of reckless encouragement (i.e. D's extended change of normative position) is a wrong, but it does not supply the tools for deeming it is fair to constructively label reckless encouragement as intentional encouragement, nor does it supply any justification for punishing reckless encouragement as intentional encouragement.*

Normative position theory is not even a plausible theory for justifying constructive liability involving unintended consequences flowing from personal acts of wrongdoing, let alone for explaining and justifying holding a person liable for the unintended autonomous wrongdoing of another person. It is a theory that is often used to try to justify constructive liability so that people can be held strictly liable for the unintended consequences of their personal acts, but it fails because it only explains the wrongness of the base act, not its unintended consequences.

The missing ingredient in Simester's theory is the conduct element, that is, an act of assistance or encouragement. When Gardner[40] originally used this sort of reasoning in an attempt to explain that constructive liability is normatively fair, it was only applied to scenarios involving a causal link between *D*'s wrongful conduct and the unintended harmful consequences. The theory aimed to fill a fault gap that occurred when a person *caused* greater harm than she intended or foresaw. Hence, it has been used to *assert* that an element of strict liability is fair when it is connected to some wrongdoing, but it fails to explain why. The simple notion is that *D* was acting wrongly when she caused the greater harm than she intended or foresaw, so she should take the casual consequences of her wrongdoing. Her normative position is extended in a causal sense, because it has unintended causal consequences. Nonetheless, this theory is vacuous, because it cannot be used to extend *D*'s normative position in a culpable sense.

The normative position theory simply fails to explain the normative fairness of incorporating a strict liability element into constructive crimes. It is also incongruous that a crime label and sentence discount is given in the law of attempts, when a person had fault for the consequences she tried to cause, but she is fully liable for unintended consequences she has caused under the doctrine of constructive liability. In one case fault is present but causation is missing and in the other causation is present but fault is missing. *D*'s fault does not extend beyond the wrong and harm she intended simply because she was acting wrongly when she caused the harm. The proponents of strict liability based on the change of normative position theory are yet to make their case convincing.

I am not able to provide a full critique of change of normative position theory in this work on complicity, so I will limit my concluding remark on this point to the joint enterprise complicity scenario where there might not be any factual link between *A*'s wrongdoing (jointly perpetrating the underlying joint enterprise) and *P*'s wrongdoing (perpetrating the collateral crime).[41] In some cases there will be an indirect contribution in that *A* has in fact encouraged *P* to perpetrate the collateral crime, but they are not the cases that Simester has in mind when he suggests change of normative position theory as the rationale for joint enterprise complicity. Simester writes:

> Through entering into a joint enterprise, S changes her normative position. She becomes, by her deliberate choice, a participant in a group action to commit a crime. Moreover, her new status has moral significance: she associates herself with the conduct of the other members of the group in a way that the *mere aider or abettor*, who remains *an independent character throughout the episode*, does not. *Whereas aiding*

40 John Gardner, *Offences and Defences* (Oxford: Oxford University Press, 2007) at 41–42.
41 Simester, *op. cit. supra*, note 38 at 598–599.

> *and abetting doctrines are grounded in S's contribution to another's crime, joint enterprise is grounded in affiliation.* S voluntarily subscribes to a co-operative endeavour, one that is identified by its shared criminal purpose. As such, joint enterprise doctrines impose a form of collective responsibility, predicated on membership of the unlawful concert [emphasis added].

For Simester there is no need to show that there was a shared purpose that extended to the collateral crime or that *A* intentionally encouraged *P* to perpetrate the collateral crime or even that *A* recklessly encouraged *P* to perpetrate the collateral crime by joining the underlying joint enterprise. It is enough to show that *A* and *P* had a shared purpose with respect to the underlying joint enterprise. It is this shared purpose and *A*'s participation in the underlying joint enterprise that changes her normative position and thus makes her liable for *P*'s collateral crime, even though she did not encourage it or intend that *P* perpetrate it. Simester does not require any factual assistance or encouragement. Merely joining a joint enterprise in circumstances where co-perpetrator (an autonomous human agent) makes an autonomous choice to perpetrate some collateral crime, absent of any factual encouragement, cannot be said to be a (indirect) cause of that person's wrongdoing. There is no normative link between the two wrongs and liability has to be ring-fenced so that each party is held liable only for their personal wrongdoing.

If a person tries to rape another person he changes his normative position, but if he merely tries to have consensual intercourse his normative position is not wrongful.[42] The simple problem is that when a person does not intend or recklessly encourage or assist a collateral crime that is perpetrated during a joint enterprise, she takes no normative position with respect to that collateral crime and thus is not morally liable for it. If anything, a properly *re*conceptualised account of change of normative position theory is an argument against constructive and strict liability, not one for it.

D. Common purpose complicity is not vicarious liability

There has been a scholarly debate over the scope of joint enterprise complicity. If joint enterprise complicity does not require the accessory to make any causal contribution to the perpetrator's crime, and merely requires foresight as the mental element, then it collapses into a form of reckless vicarious liability. The distinguished scholar, Professor Michael Moore, observes:[43]

42 Cf. Heidi M. Hurd, 'The Moral Magic of Consent' (1996) 2(2) *Legal Theory* 121.

43 Moore, *op. cit. infra*, note 83 at 400. Moore goes on to write: '[I]n most states, complicity requires more than mere agreement or group membership; one has to aid the commission of a crime to be an accomplice, and in such states the aiding required cannot be reduced to mere group membership or general agreement.'

> Consider first the assimilation to vicarious liability. The often-expressed idea is that complicity, like conspiracy, is an agency form of vicarious liability. *For this form of liability, one needn't have contributed in any way toward the occurrence of some legally prohibited result; one only need be a member of some group or combination, the other member(s) of which does cause some legally prohibited result to occur.* On this view, an accomplice stands as the principal liable for the action of his 'agents' (i.e. the perpetrator) . . . [A] number of states make one liable as an accomplice not only for crimes that one agrees should be committed but for all crimes committed by any member of the group, so long as the commission of such crimes was foreseeable to the accomplice. If one puts these doctrines together, a form of vicarious liability results: merely by joining a group, but doing nothing else oneself, one is liable as an accomplice for all the crimes of that group's members that are foreseeably incident to those crimes that may have motivated the group's formation to begin with [emphasis added].

Moore's assessment fits the approach taken by many judges in recent years in England and Wales,[44] but the conduct element as expressed in section 8 of the *Act of 1861* requires more than mere association or group membership and foresight. It requires factual participation by use of encouragement or assistance.

The issue here is not whether reckless encouragement is sufficient for making *A* liable, but whether non-encouragement is sufficient for making *A* liable merely because she changed her normative position by joining the underlying joint criminal enterprise. If the common purpose/joint enterprise scenarios result in complicity liability being based on foresight and association, then the accessory's liability does not rest on the concept of derivative liability but instead is vicarious liability. It cannot be derivative liability when *A* is liable when she makes no indirect contribution by way of encouragement or assistance. If there is no normative connection between *A* and *P*'s crime, then her liability cannot be derivative. Otherwise, any thought crime or remote attempt to encourage/assist would give rise to derivative liability, without any factual assistance or encouragement being established. Remote acts that have no indirect physical connection with the perpetrator's conduct may be wrongs in themselves, but they are independent wrongs. The secondary party's liability for the perpetrator's wrong cannot derive from independent wrongs – it has to derive from the perpetrator's wrong and it can do so only if the secondary party has made a remote physical contribution to that wrong by way of antecedent encouragement or assistance.

What the common purpose cases show is that *A* is often held liable regardless of whether her act of participating in the underlying joint enterprise encouraged *P* to perpetrate the collateral crime. In many

44 See the cases cited in Chapter 2.

cases, encouragement might be inferred where the evidence shows that *A* expressly or tacitly agreed with *P* that the collateral crime should be perpetrated, if necessary, to make their underlying joint enterprise succeed.[45] If that cannot be established, then *A* should not be *deemed* to be a perpetrator under section 8 of the *Act of 1861*. In the case of a joint enterprise where *P* perpetrates a collateral crime that *A* foresees as a possible incident of the enterprise, but where *A* has instructed *P* not to perpetrate it, it can hardly be said that *A* joining the underlying enterprise *per se* intends to send *P* a message of encouragement.

E. Is common purpose/joint enterprise complicity a distinct doctrine of complicity?

Simester argues that joint enterprise complicity can be distinguished from standard complicity because it has a different mental element.[46] I disagree. Simester seems to take the view that the mental element in both forms of complicity is different, but his analysis of the 'knowledge' cases is not convincing. Simester argues that in the standard complicity cases of assistance or encouragement there was no need for the courts 'to borrow from joint enterprise doctrine and abandon the requirement of knowledge'.[47] This analysis overlooks the fact that the 'knowledge doctrine' belongs to the general part of the criminal law and is applicable to both forms of complicity.[48] Knowledge itself can also be used to infer intention.[49] Beyond that knowledge generally has no application outside of offences that require fault as to the attendant circumstances. A putative accessory cannot know what the perpetrator will do in the future, so the alternative way to obtain a conviction is to establish that she intended by her current assistance or encouragement to assist or encourage *P* to do crime *X* in the future.

45 See *Com. v. Adams* (1993) 416 Mass. 558.

46 Simester, *op. cit. supra*, note 38 at 585 *et seq.*

47 *Id.* at 586.

48 For some examples of knowledge being an issue in joint drug enterprise cases, see *Com. v. Sabetti* (1992) 585 N.E.2d 1385; *Com. v. James* (1991) 570 N.E.2d 168.

49 '"[O]ne who aids, commands, counsels, or encourages commission of a crime while sharing with the principal the mental state required for the crime is guilty as a principal . . . The jury may infer the requisite mental state from the defendant's knowledge of the circumstances and subsequent participation in the offence" . . . The defendant argues that the Commonwealth did not show that the defendant knew that Hamilton had a gun. In *Commonwealth v. Fickett* (1988) 403 Mass. 194, 197, and *Commonwealth v. Watson* (1983) 388 Mass. 536, 544, we held that it was essential for a finding of guilt of murder in the course of the commission of armed robbery that the defendant knew that the killer had a gun, and it was held in those cases that the evidence did not warrant such a finding. "When, as here, knowledge is an essential element of an offence, it may be, and generally is, proved by circumstantial evidence; and it may be inferred from a great variety of circumstances."' *Com. v. Pope* (1990) 406 Mass. 581 at 585–586.

Common purpose complicity does not exist outside of section 8 of the *Accessories and Abettors Act 1861*.[50] Simester argues that it is 'difficult to see how any account of joint enterprise liability can plausibly be assimilated within conventional forms of aiding, abetting, counselling, or procuring.'[51] In Chapter 2, I argue there can be no greater encouragement than by forming a common purpose – that is, an agreement that the collateral crime should be perpetrated, if necessary to make the underlying joint enterprise succeed. I do not share the view that the change of normative position theory,[52] which in the context of complicity is used to justify it as a form of constructive vicarious liability, should be invoked to obtain convictions where there was no assistance or encouragement from the defendant. Nor do I share the view that such an approach should be accepted because it would be difficult to prove that *P* was encouraged by *A*'s tacit encouragement of the collateral crime.

Some jurisdictions have enacted statutes that recognise common purpose complicity as a distinct form of complicity. Some jurisdictions have even made it a crime of negligence, but in England and Wales the law is to be found in section 8 of the *Accessories and Abettors Act 1861*.[53] It is true that the type of encouragement found in the joint enterprise cases relates to special factual scenarios involving joint criminal enterprises, but there is a line of cases going back 500 years that discuss that mode of entry, and none of the old cases suggest it is vicarious liability rather than a from of derivative liability. In *Giorgianni v. The Queen*,[54] Gibbs C.J. said: 'Section . . . 8 of the *Accessories and Abettors Act 1861* (U.K.) . . . as has often been said, was only declaratory of the common law on the subject.'

As I shall try to demonstrate in Chapter 2, this must be correct if common purpose complicity is to be something more than an extremely unjust form of constructive vicarious liability. Even if it is based on reckless encouragement as opposed to reckless association, it raises serious issues concerning human rights. A doctrine of reckless murder through remote participation would be a harsh doctrine. The normative interpretation that I argue our existing human rights should be given would not allow a person to be convicted of murder under a theory of reckless remote participation liability. I shall argue that there is no injustice in not convicting a person as a party to a collateral crime when she has not done something to encourage

50 Cf. Lord Hobhouse, 'Agency and the Criminal Law' in *Lex Mercatoria: Essays in Honour of Francis Reynolds* (London: Informa Law from Routledge, 2000).

51 Simester, *op. cit. supra*, note 38 at 593.

52 *Id.* at 599–600.

53 For an overview of the dozen or so U.S. states with such provisions see John F. Decker, 'The Mental State Requirement for Accomplice Liability in American Criminal Law' (2009) 60 *S.C.L. Rev.* 237. New Zealand and Canada as well as some of the Code states in Australia have similar provisions. See Chapter 2 of this monograph.

54 (1985) 156 C.L.R. 473 at 479–480.

the collateral crime. There is no injustice in not holding such people liable for the collateral crime, because they will already be convicted for the role they played in the underlying criminal joint enterprise. A conviction for their proportionate (equal) perpetration of the underlying criminal joint enterprise is sufficient, when they have not made a remote contribution to the perpetrator's collateral crime. Coupled with that, they could also be liable under section 44 or 45 of the *Serious Crime Act 2007* for inchoate assistance and encouragement.

F. Participation by remote involvement

In some cases it has been held that a person can be liable for causing a person to perpetrate the *actus reus* of a crime.[55] A person might cause an innocent agent to perpetrate an offence, but strictly speaking this is a very direct form of derivative liability, because the causer will be liable as a perpetrator even where the innocent agent is not liable for any offence. In some cases, both the causer and the innocent agent will be liable, because the causer causes the innocent agent to perpetrate a strict liability offence. When an offence requires *mens rea*, only the causer will have the requisite fault for the offence and, therefore, only the causer should be liable. In such a case, the causer's liability does not derive from that of the innocent agent's non-culpable perpetration of the *actus reus* of the particular offence, but from her personal fault and her use of the innocent agent to perpetrate the offence. These cases will not be dealt with further in this monograph.

IV. The mental element

The ancient law required that it be proved beyond reasonable doubt that the accessory '*maliciously and feloniously* counselled, commanded, procured, and abetted'.[56] In *U.S. v. Peoni*,[57] that great jurist, Learned Hand, J., drawing on centuries of English law[58] when interpreting a provision with wording almost verbatim to section 8 of the *Accessories and Abettors Act 1861*, held:

> It will be observed that all these definitions have nothing whatever to do with the probability that the forbidden result would follow upon the accessory's conduct; and that they all demand that he in some sort associate himself with the venture, that he participate in it as in

55 *Attorney-General's Reference (No. 1 of 1975)* [1975] Q.B. 773.

56 *Parker's Case* (1559) 2 Dyer 186a at 186b.

57 100 F.2d 401 at 402.

58 Learned Hand, J. draws on *Parker's Case* (1559) 2 Dyer 186a and the leading institutional writers including Coke, Foster, Hale, Hawkins and Blackstone.

> something that he wishes to bring about, that he seek by his action to make it succeed. All the words used – even the most colourless, 'abet' – carry an implication of purposive attitude towards it.

In *Rosemond v. U.S.*,[59] Kagan, J. (delivering the majority opinion in the Supreme Court of the United States) said:

> The federal aiding and abetting statute, 18 U.S.C. § 2, states that a person who furthers – more specifically, who 'aids, abets, counsels, commands, induces or procures' – the commission of a federal offence 'is punishable as a principal.' That provision derives from (though simplifies) common-law standards for accomplice liability. ('The substance of [§ 2's] formula goes back a long way'). And in so doing, § 2 reflects a centuries-old view of culpability: that a person may be responsible for a crime he has not personally carried out if he helps another to complete its commission.
>
> . . .
>
> And the canonical formulation of that needed state of mind – later appropriated by this Court and oft-quoted in both parties' briefs – is Judge Learned Hand's: To aid and abet a crime, a defendant must not just 'in some sort associate himself with the venture,' but also 'participate in it as in something that he wishes to bring about' and 'seek by his action to make it succeed.'[60]

Kagan, J. goes on to state:[61]

> We have previously found that intent requirement satisfied when a person actively participates in a criminal venture with full knowledge of the circumstances constituting the charged offence . . . *So for purposes of aiding and abetting law, a person who actively participates in a criminal scheme knowing its extent and character intends that scheme's commission* [emphasis added].
>
> . . .

59 (2014) 134 S.Ct. 1240 at 1245. Kagan, J., delivered the opinion of the Supreme Court of the United States, in which Roberts, C.J., and Kennedy, Ginsburg, Breyer and Sotomayor, J.J., joined, and in which Scalia, J., joined in all but footnotes 7 and 8. Alito, J., filed an opinion concurring in part and dissenting in part, in which Thomas, J., joined. Like Learned Hand, J., Kagan, J. draws on the common law. See generally, Michael G. Heyman, 'Clinging to the Common Law in an Age of Statutes: Criminal Law in the States' (2014) 99 *Minn. L. Rev.* 29.

60 *Rosemond v. U.S.* (2014) 134 S.Ct. 1240 at 1248.

61 *Rosemond v. U.S.* (2014) 134 S.Ct. 1240 at 1248–1249.

> For all that to be true, though, the § 924(c) defendant's knowledge of a firearm must be advance knowledge – or otherwise said, knowledge that enables him to make the relevant legal (and indeed, moral) choice. When an accomplice knows beforehand of a confederate's design to carry a gun, he can attempt to alter that plan or, if unsuccessful, withdraw from the enterprise; *it is deciding instead to go ahead with his role in the venture that shows his intent to aid an armed offence.*[62]

Kagan, J. took the view *A*'s advanced knowledge of *P*'s planned crime could be used to infer that *A* intended to further *P*'s crime. 'A defendant manifests that greater intent, and incurs the greater liability for [a collateral crime or aggravated form of the underlying offence], when he chooses to participate in a drug transaction knowing it *will* involve a firearm; but he makes no such choice when that knowledge comes too late for him to be reasonably able to act upon it.'[63]

Basically, Kagan, J. held that it is not possible to *infer that a person intended* to encourage or assist a collateral crime or some aggravated form of an underlying joint enterprise, if she did not know in advance the relevant circumstances that would make the planned crime an aggravated form of the underlying unlawful joint enterprise[64] or if she did not know the relevant circumstances that would make the assisted or encouraged act a crime. In the case of an aggravated form of the underlying joint enterprise, the accomplice must have a state of mind extending to the aggravated form of the crime. Likewise, where the act's criminality depends on circumstances,

62 *Rosemond v. U.S.* (2014) 134 S.Ct. 1240 at 1249. 'Of course, if a defendant continues to participate in a crime after a gun was displayed or used by a confederate, the jury can permissibly infer from his failure to object or withdraw that he had such knowledge. In any criminal case, after all, the fact finder can draw inferences about a defendant's intent based on all the facts and circumstances of a crime's commission.' *Ibid.*

63 *Rosemond v. U.S.* (2014) 134 S.Ct. 1240 at 1251.

64 For example, the offence in *Rosemond v. U.S.* (2014) 134 S.Ct. 1240 was an aggravated offence of drug trafficking. To aid and abet the offence of using a firearm during a federal drug-trafficking offence (the drug-trafficking offence being the underlying unlawful enterprise in its non-aggravated from), the defendant must know beforehand that one of his confederates will carry a gun (the use of the gun during the drug-trafficking offence is the aggravated form of the offence). In effect, the use of the gun can also be conceptualized as a collateral criminal wrong. Gun use during certain other crimes is treated as an aggravating feature as it results in a greater sentence, but not a separate conviction. See 18 U.S.C.A. § 924(c)(1)(A) which provides: '(Except to the extent that a greater minimum sentence is otherwise provided by this subsection or by any other provision of law, any person who, during and in relation to any crime of violence or drug trafficking crime (including a crime of violence or drug trafficking crime that provides for an enhanced punishment if committed by the use of a deadly or dangerous weapon or device) for which the person may be prosecuted in a court of the United States, uses or carries a firearm, or who, in furtherance of any such crime, possesses a firearm, shall, in addition to the punishment provided for such crime of violence or drug trafficking crime'

the accomplice must have a state of mind extending to the circumstances that make the act she encourages or assists criminal. A person cannot participate in another's crime as *something that she wishes to bring about, that she seek by her action to succeed*, if she does not know what is planned or does not know the relevant circumstances that make the perpetrator's planned act a crime.

A long line of strong English authorities supports this interpretation of the mental element in complicity.[65] Kagan, J. simply expounds that it would be difficult for a jury to infer that a person intended to assist or encourage another to use a gun during the course of a violent crime or some drug-trafficking crime, if that person had no advance knowledge of any plan for a gun to be used and/or if that person had no knowledge of the fact that the other participant was carrying a gun.

The important aspect of the decision is that it states the mental element in complicity for the Federal offence in the United States is intention and nothing less.[66] Both Learned Hand, J. and Kagan, J. are right to conclude that 18 U.S.C.A. § 2 of the Federal Criminal Code[67] varies little from the common law as stated in England for centuries. Notably, section 8 of the *Accessories and Abettors Act 1861* is substantively identical. The United States provision used the words 'aids, abets, counsels, commands, induces or procures its commission', while the *Accessories and Abettors Act 1861* uses the words, 'aid, abet, counsel, or procure the commission of any offence'. These provisions have essentially the same conduct element. Likewise, both provisions left it to the judges to state the mental element by drawing on the common law precedents.

65 See *Wilcox v. Jeffery* [1951] 1 All E.R. 464 at 466 *per* Lord Goddard, C.J. (Humphreys and Devlin, J.J. concurring.) See also *Thomas v. Lindop* [1950] 1 All E.R. 966 at 968, where Lord Goddard, C.J. (Morris and Finnemore, J.J. concurring) said: 'It is, of course, not necessary to show that the person knew that it was an offence, because he cannot plead ignorance of the law, but where anyone is charged with aiding and abetting a person to commit an offence, it must, at least, be shown that he knew what that person was doing. A person who does not know of the acts which another person is doing cannot be charged with aiding and abetting him because he does not know that he is doing acts which amount to an offence.' Lord Goddard, C.J. reiterated this in *Davies, Turner & Co. Ltd v. Brodie* [1954] 1 W.L.R. 1364 at 1368. A jury could infer that the accessory knew and intended to assist a rape where the evidence is that the accessory held a gun on a victim while she was raped by several other men. See *People v. Garner* (1993) 593 N.Y.S. 2d 620. Similarly, a jury could infer that a mother intended to assist or encourage the sexual violation of her 12-year-old son when she fails to prevent him from having sexual intercourse with a 30-year-old woman, because the mother has present knowledge of the fact that her son is underage and that he is unable to consent, because she herself gave birth to him 12 years before. See *State v. Ainsworth* (1993) 426 S.E.2d 410. The mother cannot make a mistake as to her son's present age, because she has present knowledge of his age.

66 The majority of state criminal codes in the United States also require intention. See *Wilson-Bey v. U.S.* (2006) 903 A. 2d 818 at 831–832 *per* Schwelb, J.

67 For example, it provides: 'Whoever commits an offense against the United States or aids, abets, counsels, commands, induces or procures its commission, is punishable as a principal.'

English law hovered between requiring intention[68] and oblique intention,[69] but slowly adopted a recklessness standard. In the next chapter, I shall draw on a long line of complicity cases involving common purpose/joint enterprise complicity scenarios to show that Learned Hand, J.'s and Kagan, J.'s (with Roberts, C.J., and Kennedy, Ginsburg, Breyer and Sotomayor, Scalia, J.J. concurring) interpretation of the mental element in complicity as requiring nothing less than intention is what was required in English law until the late 1990s. Not only do the common purpose complicity cases support interpreting the mental element in complicity as requiring nothing less than intention, but so too do the knowledge cases. What is important about Learned Hand, J.'s and Kagan, J.'s decisions is that they are based on a literal and natural interpretation of the words 'aid', 'abet', 'counsel' and 'procure'. Hence, the U.S. courts have not given the mental element a narrow interpretation for policy reasons (after all in the U.S. any gap in the law might be filled by other expansive doctrines like depraved heart murder offence and the felony murder rule), but simply because the ancient English authorities and the wording of the analogous statutory provision strongly supported interpreting the mental element in complicity as requiring nothing less than intention.

Knowledge is used for inferring intention. (If mere recklessness were required then the only advanced knowledge required would be the secondary's party's present awareness of the risk that *P* might perpetrate the collateral crime.) The jury would not be asked to consider whether: *A* knew the circumstances would exist, or whether *P* would perpetrate the collateral crime upon certain conditions arising, if mere foresight of possibility is all that is required. The requirement would be 'believe', not 'know', if recklessness were all that were required. This again is a way of inferring intention: a person cannot recklessly know; she either knows something or she does not. Nor can a person know the future, but she can know the present. She can intend the future.

A. Inferring intention from knowledge of circumstances v. unintended results

A strict intention requirement would have no bearing on constructive liability, because the law merely requires *A* to have it as her purpose that *P* perform the conduct constituting the offence and share whatever mental state *P* requires as to its result elements. Therefore, if *A* drives *P*, a kick-boxer, to *V*'s house because *A* wants to assist *P* to inflict grievous bodily harm on *V*, *A* will be liable for murder if *P* accidentally kills *V* as a result of *P* (unjustifiably) inflicting GBH upon *V*. However, constructive fault does

68 *R. v. Fretwell* (1862) Le. & Ca. 161; *Gillick v. West Norfolk and Wisbech AHA* [1986] A.C. 112.
69 *National Coal Board v. Gamble* [1959] 1 Q.B. 11.

not apply to unintended circumstances, because a person cannot intend to assist or encourage a crime if she is intending to assist or encourage an innocuous act. Suppose *A* assists *P* to have consensual sexual intercourse with *V* (a 15-year-old) believing *V* is 17. It could hardly be said *A* was intending to assist *P* to rape a child. There would be no need to require that a person *know* or *intend* the relevant circumstances to exist at the time that *P* does the conduct element of the anticipated offence, if all that was required were mere recklessness as to whether that act of assistance or encouragement would assist or encourage *P* to do the act that forms the conduct element of the target crime.

X can be liable for complicity liability if she intends to assist *Y* to rape *V*. She might have no way of knowing for sure that *V* will not consent, but if she intends to assist or encourage a rape, then she is liable as an accessory if *Y* rapes *V*. (If *V* consents, even though *X* intended the sexual intercourse to take place in circumstances where *V* would not be consenting, then *X* and *Y* will be equally liable for the attempt). *X*'s knowledge of the relevant circumstances need not be used to infer she intended to assist or encourage *Y* to rape *V*, if other evidence comes forward (such as a conversation caught on CCTV) showing *X* in fact intended to assist or encourage that crime. The knowledge enquiry becomes superfluous, since intention is established by examining other evidence.[70] The thing to keep in mind is that knowledge of the circumstances or of the planned collateral crimes is an important factor for inferring that the accessory intended to assist or encourage the perpetrator.

B. The mental element in contemporary English law

What is the current law in England and Wales? The current law is in a state of flux. The current law seems to be contrary to justice because it merely requires a person to assist or encourage and be reckless as to whether her act of assistance or encouragement might assist or encourage the perpetrator to perpetrate the anticipated target crime. In *R. v. Bryce*,[71] Potter, L.J. said that:

> [I]t is not necessary to show that the secondary party intended the commission of the principal offence and that it is sufficient if the secondary party at the time of his actions relied on as lending assistance or encouragement contemplates the commission of the offence, that is knows that it will be committed or realises that it is a real possibility that it will be committed.

70 *R. v. Saik* [2007] 1 A.C. 18 (a conspiracy case).
71 [2004] 2 Cr. App. R. 592 at 607.

Potter, L.J. cites *R. v. Rook*[72] as authority for the above reminting of the mental element in complicity, but *R. v. Rook* was a case where there was ample evidence for a jury to infer that Rook intended to encourage the anticipated target offence. The other authorities cited by Potter, L.J., as I aim to show in the next chapter, support interpreting the mental element in complicity as requiring nothing less than intention. However, in *R. v. Powell*,[73] Lord Hutton said: '[I]t is sufficient to found a conviction for murder for a secondary party to have realised that in the course of the joint enterprise the primary party might kill with intent to do so or with intent to cause grievous bodily harm.' Hence, the House of Lords in *R. v. Powell* held that a person can be liable for a crime (including a specific intention crime as serious as murder) if she does something to assist or encourage that person and is reckless as to whether her act of assistance or encouragement might assist or encourage the perpetrator to perpetrate the anticipated target crime. If a person sells a gun in her gunsmith and is suspicious that the person buying it might use it to perpetrate a murder, she also will be liable for murder and subject to a mandatory life sentence. In this monograph, I not only argue that such results are unjust and unfair, but also that the ancient and modern authorities provide a solution, since they support reinterpreting the law of complicity as having a mental element of intention and nothing less. They also support a narrowing of the conduct element, so that only those who have in fact provided some sort of encouragement will be equally liable under section 8 of the *Accessories and Abettors Act 1861*. The ancient and modern (by modern authorities I am referring to the authorities dating from the 1960s through to the 1990s) are strong enough to give the Supreme Court of the United Kingdom sufficient room to reinterpret the law.

C. Innocent participation

In some cases, there will be factual encouragement or assistance without fault such as where *A* innocently gives *P* a gun, which *P* uses to kill, or where *A* innocently tells *P* about his wife having an affair and this has the unintended and unforeseeable consequence of provoking *P* to find his wife and her lover and kill them. In both cases there is indirect physical involvement. (The accidental encouragement reaches *P*'s mind and makes his mind think in a certain way. The gun is in *P*'s hand and allows him to kill with it). In the above hypotheticals the participatory acts are not culpable, they are bare acts of factual facilitation and encouragement. Likewise, there can be fault without any physical encouragement or assistance. Complicity is only made out where the remote participation is the result of culpable conduct.

72 [1993] 1 W.L.R. 1005.
73 [1999] 1 A.C. 1 at 27.

Physical involvement (remote participation) without fault is not sufficient, and nor is fault without physical involvement (remote participation).

There is also a fundamental difference between *A* foreseeing that *P* might perpetrate a collateral crime and in *A* foreseeing that her participation in the underlying joint enterprise might send *P* a message of encouragement. If *P*'s participation in the underlying joint enterprise does in fact have the unintended effect of sending *P* a message of encouragement and *A* foresaw that it might have this effect, then she has engaged in reckless encouragement. *A* has recklessly encouraged *P*'s collateral crime, because there is a remote factual participation by way of encouragement and *A* foresaw that she might encourage *P* by jointly perpetrating the underlying crime. If *P* has perpetrated a murder during the course of a robbery, she can be liable only if she intended to kill or cause *V* serious injury, so *A* should not be liable unless she also intended to assist and encourage *P* to inflict GBH upon *V*.

A further complication in the law of complicity is that any crime that is perpetrated is not only contingent on assister/encourager's conduct, but also on the independent choices of the anticipated perpetrator of the target crime. It is a remote harm and as such it has a different moral content than that of direct perpetration.[74] Assistance and encouragement is innocuous in itself; it only becomes harmful if it is presented to a perpetrator who already has a propensity for perpetrating the target criminality. Therefore, there is no moral parity between the harmfulness of acts of assistance and encouragement and the perpetrator's acts of direct perpetration. Supplying a gun is an act with a very different moral content to the act of using a gun to kill. The intervening choice of a fully autonomous human agent distances the assister/encourager's wrongful acts from the end harm and makes them less dangerous, even if they have masterminded the crime.

A mastermind's ideas are harmless unless acted upon by others; if they are acted upon others who are not under duress, it is those perpetrators who are directly dangerous to society. A mastermind might influence many to perpetrate crimes if she is the head of a crime syndicate, but this does not convert her many acts of encouragement into acts of perpetration – the harm of the acts of perpetration are contingent on the culpable choices of others. Hence, even a mastermind's acts of encouragement are innocuous until an autonomous agent (or agents) act on them. They are once removed from the end harm and have a different normative dimension to direct perpetration. Recidivism or multiple acts of encouragement over many years are an aggravating feature for sentencing purposes, not a rationale for criminalising remote harm-doing as direct harm-doing. The sentence might not be too different in serious cases, but the criminal label ought to be.

74 Dennis J Baker, 'The Moral Limits of Criminalizing Remote Harms' (2007) 10 *New Crim. L. Rev.* 370; Dennis J Baker, 'Collective Criminalization and the Constitutional Right to Endanger Others' (2009) 28 *Crim. Just. Ethics* 168.

Thus, there is a case for arguing that the accessory's contribution is remote and that too provides a justification for labelling her conduct as an independent direct liability offence (i.e. section 44 or 45 of the *Serious Crime Act 2007*), rather than as an act of (derivative) perpetration under section 8 of the *Act of 1861*.[75] In this monograph, I will resist developing a theory for demonstrating that assistance and encouragement is morally less harmful and less wrong than perpetrating the anticipated target crime, because I do not think the moral difference makes a tangible difference where there is equal fault. Suppose *A* holds *V* down while *P* rapes *V*. Also suppose *A* intends to assist *P* to rape *V*. In such a case there is little injustice in labelling the secondary party as a rapist and also punishing him for rape.

Any theory explaining why perpetration is normatively more wrong and harmful than remote assistance/encouragement would have to contradistinguish the special case of the dictator who motivates many to perpetrate war crimes for her, because it is an exemplar that has special moral features that takes it out of the domain of the normal accessory and perpetrator problem. The dictator exemplar also falls outside the purview of my remote harms theory. The remote harm theory rests on the idea that harm that is contingent on the autonomous and informed choices of an intervener is less wrong, less dangerous and morally less reprehensible than harm that is direct. State crimes perpetrated by a collective of people enfolded in a social situation that prevents them from acting fully autonomously is conceptually distinct to the problem that is being dealt with in this monograph.

When duress or innocent agency is involved the remote harms theory does not apply, because the harm is not contingent on the fully informed, autonomous and morally voluntary choices of an intervening direct harm-doer. Innocent agency involves direct wrongdoing, because the innocent agent is a mere instrument in the remote party's hands. Duress also involves quasi-direct perpetration, since the party under duress is partly an instrument in the remote party's hands. The perpetrator who acts under duress is not acting fully voluntarily. *The remote party manifests not only direct culpability for the end harm, but culpably makes a choice to force another person to physically perpetrate a crime with full knowledge of the fact that duress is the key ingredient. When duress is involved the remote party's role is morally no different from that of a direct physical perpetrator.*

D. Punishment and labelling for independent facilitation offence

Are causal wrongs the only ones the criminal law should concern itself with? Lawmakers have long recognised the advantage of applying the criminal

75 See the discussion in George P. Fletcher, *Basic Concepts of Criminal Law* (New York: Oxford University Press, 1998) at 197 *et passim*. Fletcher observes that the German Code makes a distinction between perpetrators and indirect participants in the criminal harm.

law to conduct that has failed to cause harm or remotely make a contribution to another's attempt to harm. Inchoate offences have the advantage of deterring people from continuing with their attempts and also incapacitating them before any harm is done. However, non-causal wrongs tend to be punished less and labelled as less serious offences. A retributive theory of justice supports drawing a distinction between causal and non-causal wrongs. The issue of punishing inchoate participation as a lesser crime is raised only in Chapter 4, because the new facilitation offences found in the *Serious Crime Act 2007* fail to distinguish attempted participation from consummated (assistance/encouragement) participation, but the *Act of 2007* does create independent facilitation offences, and those offences do allow the sentencing judge the normal discretion in sentencing. Hence, while sections 44, 45 and 46 of the *Serious Crime Act 2007* label attempted participation no differently than consummated participation, proportionate punishment is provided for because the sentencing judge has the normal discretion. Fair labelling is also provided for more generally in that the assister/encourager is only labelled as having perpetrated a facilitation/encouragement offence under section 44, 45 or 46 of the *Serious Crime Act 2007*, not with the perpetrator's crime.

It is true that section 58 of the *Act of 2007* requires the assister/encourager's offence to be proportionate with the reference offence that she has assisted or encouraged, but in practice the assister/encourager will receive a sentence much lower than that received by the perpetrator. (Hence, under the *Act of 2007*, *D* will receive a much higher sentence for assisting or encouraging murder than she will for assisting or encouraging shoplifting – even though in both cases she will be labelled as having perpetrated an independent facilitation offence, rather than with shoplifting or murder, as would be the case if she had been convicted under the *Act of 1861*.) So if *D* assists or encourages *P* to perpetrate a murder, and if *D* is charged under the *Act of 2007* instead of the *Act of 1861*, *P* might receive a life sentence, but such a sentence would not be mandatory. Furthermore, she might receive a much lower sentence, because *D*'s sentence will depend on whether she provided substantial or trivial assistance or encouragement.

Judges, to justify labelling and punishing those who recklessly assist or encourage a crime as though they intentionally perpetrated the perpetrator's crime, routinely put forward a utilitarian justification. For example, in *R. v. Powell*, Lord Hutton said:

> My Lords, I recognise that as a matter of [justice] there is force in the argument advanced on behalf of the appellants, and that on one view it is anomalous that if foreseeability of death or really serious harm is not sufficient to constitute *mens rea* for murder in the party who actually carries out the killing, it is sufficient to constitute *mens rea* in a secondary party. But the rules of the common law are not based solely on logic but relate to practical concerns and, in relation to crimes committed in

> the course of joint enterprises, to the need to give effective protection to the public against criminals operating in gangs.[76]

The problem with this rationale for failing to distinguish reckless encouragement from intentional participation is threefold. (1) There is no empirical evidence to support the claim that punishing and labelling reckless encouragement as an intentional perpetration can achieve greater deterrence. (The same deterrence is likely to be achieved by convicting the reckless encourager of an independent encouragement/incitement offence and calibrating her sentence with the gravity of the wrong she has recklessly encouraged/assisted or tried to encourage/assist.) (2) Treating all remote participants as equal wrongdoers, regardless of their level of fault, cannot be reconciled with the just deserts theory that is central to modern penal systems. (3) The same rule has been applied in cases where there has been no gang violence.

Labelling is a conventional or linguistic factor: the term 'murder' could be used to refer to 'tennis' (a game involving a ball), rather than an act of unjustifiable or inexcusable killing of another human. Nonetheless, a label has real meaning when it attaches to wrongs by convention, because it sends the message that a particular conventional wrong was done. Therefore, crime labels should be applied consistently. It is unfair to apply the 'murder' label to reckless assistance or encouragement that helps or encourages another to kill, because that label normally applies only to intentional (unjustifiable or inexcusable) killing or to a killing that results from intentionally inflicting grievous bodily harm upon another.

A core issue regarding proportionate punishment and fair labelling arises in the second chapter with respect to complicity liability under section 8 of the *Act of 1861*, since that Act deems that assisters/encouragers are to be labelled and punished as perpetrators. Technically, a remote perpetrator (assister/encourager) should be punished less than a direct perpetrator (doer), because any harm is contingent on the autonomous choice of the doer – the doer is the perpetrator of the anticipated target crime and she need not be persuaded by the encourager's encouragement. Furthermore, she need not offend even when the accessory has provided her with physical assistance (e.g. supplied her with a gun) or with great encouragement (e.g. an offer of £1,000,000 to assassinate another). The direct chain of causation is broken by the perpetrator's autonomous decision to use the gun to kill or by her autonomous decision to accept the money to kill. The accessory's contribution is remote and thus it is fair to punish it as a separate wrong, which is the approach taken in the *Serious Crime Act 2007*.

My proposal in Chapter 2 is modest. I am simply arguing for the law of complicity under the *Act of 1861* to be reinterpreted by the judges so that

76 [1999] 1 A.C. 1 at 25. See also *Clayton v. The Queen* (2006) 168 A. Crim. R. 174 at 207.

the mental element in complicity is nothing less than intention, because the authorities support such an interpretation. If a secondary party is only reckless as to whether the perpetrator will use the gun she has supplied to kill, then she should not be liable for murder. Her fault is not sufficient to warrant labelling her as a murderer. In the latter situation, her conduct should be criminalised as reckless assistance or encouragement and be labelled and punished at that level. For that to be achieved, Parliament will be required to amend the facilitation offence found in section 45 of the *Serious Crime Act 2007* to make it a crime of reckless (remote) participation, instead of one of oblique intentional perpetration.

V. The conduct element: omissions and causation in complicity

Empress Car Company (Abertillery) Ltd. v. National Rivers Authority[77] is a superlative case for demonstrating the distinction between perpetration and remote participation by omission. In that case, by a negligent omission the company assisted a third party to perpetrate an act of environmental vandalism. The court did not treat it as a complicity case, and nor could it have, because negligence is not sufficient *mens rea* for complicity. Instead the Lords held the company caused the third party to perpetrate the act of criminal damage by being negligent in not preventing the third party from perpetrating her act of environmental damage. The reasoning in the case is fundamentally flawed, because the company was not a direct or indirect cause of the act of perpetration. To be a direct cause the company itself would had to have released the oil into the river or directly caused it to run into the river by not shutting the tap properly and so on. The fact was that the tap was shut and there was no act or omission by the company that was causing oil to leak. An independent and autonomous human agent intervened and released the oil into the river. Indirect causes do not involve autonomous human agents intervening. For example, if *D* fires a bullet at a mountain thereby causing an avalanche, which in turn kills a skier, *D* is an indirect cause of the skier's death. Or if *D* is speeding and hits a stationary car at a pedestrian crossing thereby causing that car to fly forward and kill a pedestrian, *D* is the indirect cause of *V*'s death – the direct cause is the other driver's car hitting *V*. *D*'s car itself does not come into contact with the pedestrian and thus is only an indirect cause, but in law it would be a legally imputable cause. There is no intervening act and this is a pure case of indirect causation.

Complicity liability is used to inculpate those who have contributed to the perpetrator's personal wrongdoing. It is about holding people responsible for personally contributing to the wrongs of others. John Gardner is on the

77 [1999] 2 A.C. 22.

right track in arguing: 'I think that aiding, abetting, and counselling are all straightforward ways of making a causal contribution to the wrongs that are aided, abetted, or counselled (as the case may be).'[78] However, the term 'causal contribution' seems to be the wrong terminology, because it suggests that the accessory is an indirect cause of the end harm. The accessory is not a cause at all, because the perpetrator breaks the chain of causation when she decides to misuse the accessory's assistance or allows herself to be partly persuaded to perpetrate the anticipated crime. Gardner asserts that 'any adequate analysis of causality must respect the transitivity of causality'. He proposes the following transitivity axiom:

> If *x* makes a causal contribution to *y* and *y* makes a causal contribution to *z* then *x* makes a causal contribution to *Z*.[79]

Gardner's reasoning is conceptually hollow. Thereafter, Gardner expounds:[80]

> *D2* (as an accomplice) sometimes makes a different kind of causal contribution from that made by *D1* (as the principal), and thereby commits a different causal wrong, even though both wrongs have, in the end, the same result, *r1* . . . *D2* (as an accomplice) sometimes makes a different causal contribution from that made by *D1* (as the principal) precisely because *D2* makes his contribution through *D1*.
>
> . . .
>
> Consider the revised premises that it forces upon us:
>
> (1) *D1* commits a causal wrong (as a principal) by making a causal contribution *c1* to result *r1*.
> (2) *D2* commits a wrong (as an accomplice) by making a causal contribution *c2* to result *r2* (where *r2* is *D1*'s making a causal contribution *c1* to result *r1*).
> (3) If *D2* makes a causal contribution to *D1*'s making a causal contribution to result *r1*, then *D2* also makes a causal contribution to result *r1*.
>
> . . .
>
> In particular, this framework preserves the possibility that *D2*'s causal wrong is a wrong of indirect causal contribution to *r1*, whereas D1's is a

78 John Gardner, 'Moore on Complicity and Causality,' (2008) 156 *U. Pa. L. Rev. PENNumbra* 432 at 436. See also Sanford Kadish, *Blame and Punishment: Essays in the Criminal Law* (New York: Macmillan Publishers, 1987) at 162 *et passim*; John Gardner, *Offences and Defences* (Oxford: Oxford University Press, 2007) at 68 *et passim*.

79 *Ibid.*

80 *Id.* at 437–438.

> wrong of direct causal contribution to *r1*, where the indirectness of *D2*'s causal contribution to *r1* lies precisely in the fact that *D2*'s only relevant direct causal contribution is to *r2*, which is the result that *D1* makes a direct causal contribution to *r1*.

When a person chooses to perpetrate a killing she makes the personal choice to perpetrate a serious crime and thus will be personally liable for it.[81] When a secondary party (accessory) chooses to assist or encourage another to perpetrate a killing she chooses to make a remote factual contribution to the perpetrator's wrong. Her direct wrongdoing is limited to her wrongful act of assistance/encouragement, but her remote wrongdoing extends to the wrong that she has assisted/encouraged. She is derivatively liable because her independent wrong (assistance/encouragement) made a remote contribution to a wrongful act perpetrated by another. (Whether she should be held liable for the same crime as the perpetrator or for some lesser crime is a question that should depend on her level of fault. If her contribution results from recklessness, then it would be fairer to convict her of some lesser independent offence).

In this monograph, I argue that conceptually complicity is only distinguishable from vicarious or agency liability, if we accept that its justification rests on the theory that the accessory is liable because she made a remote contribution (or under the *Serious Crime Act 2007* attempted to make a remote causal contribution) to *P*'s target crime. Assistance and encouragement is not an indirect contribution, but rather a remote wrong that underwrites the perpetrator's wrongdoing. It has a remote causal impact in that but for *A* assisting *P* by giving *P* a gun, *P* would not have been able to kill with the particular gun at the particular point in time. Similarly, but for *A* persuading *P* to perpetrate the crime, *P* might not have chosen to perpetrate the crime. However, since there is no coercion any direct or indirect causal link is broken by *P*'s independent choice to use the assistance or to be persuaded by the encouragement. Nonetheless, the remote wrongdoing involved in providing assistance and encouragement does give us a solid justification for criminalising complicity. The case law recognises that there must be a remote act of encouragement or assistance for derivative liability to be made out.[82]

81 See *R. v. Mendez* [2011] Q.B. 876 at 882–883 *per* Toulson, L.J. (as he then was); *R. v. Carpenter* [2012] Q.B. 722 at 731 *per* Richards, L.J.; *R. v. Anderson* [1966] 2 QB 110 at 120 *per* Lord Parker, C.J. See also Lord Toulson, 'Sir Michael Foster, Professor Williams and Complicity in Murder' in Dennis J. Baker *et al.* (eds), *The Sanctity of Life and the Criminal Law: The Legacy of Glanville Williams* (Cambridge: Cambridge University Press, 2013) at 230 *et seq.*

82 An example is given in a civil case (*Herrly v. Muzik* (1984) 355 N.W.2d 452 at 454) from Minnesota, where Wozniak, J., said: 'The rationale for complicity is that, in enforcing the dual purposes of the *Act*, a wrongdoer is not among those persons to whom the legislature

The only residual issue is whether complicity by omission comes within this rationale for complicity liability. I do not share Michael Moore's suggestion that complicity by omission can never rest on a remote factual wrong.[83] A bare 'failure to prevent' can have the effect of 'encouraging' the perpetrator and thus it is a remote wrong that causes the perpetrator to have a reason for perpetrating a crime. Being caused to have a reason to act does not mean that the perpetrator is forced to pay attention to that reason, so there is no causal connection between the remote omission and *P*'s end harm. The chain of causation is broken by *P*'s independent choice to follow the encouragement.

Moore argues:

> If there are no negative events that can be effects of some cause, surely there can be no negative events that can be causes of certain effects. 'Nothings' cannot cause 'somethings' any more than 'somethings' can cause 'nothings.' Absent events cannot serve as relata (of either kind) of the singular causal relation.[84]

But an omission is something that can have a causal effect on the perpetrator's thinking. It can send her a message of encouragement. When *P* observes *A*'s omission it might communicate to her a message that *A* in fact supports what she is doing. This message by omission physically operates on *P*'s mind and sends signals to her brain, which can cause *P* to have a reason to act, and that is enough to justify complicity liability. It does not matter whether that reason to act caused *P* to perpetrate the end crime as long as it has some influence on her decision.[85] A person is not liable as an accessory for allowing or permitting another to perpetrate a crime, unless she has a duty to prevent that person form perpetrating that crime.[86] In the permitting or allowing cases liability can hinge on a combination of derivative liability and on the defendant breaching a duty to prevent the perpetrator from perpetrating the anticipated target crime.

Direct encouragement might be implied from omissions. If *A* is a security guard in a store, she has a duty to ensure that customers do not shoplift. If by chance *A* sees her sister, *P*, shoplifting and fails to tell *P* to stop, or fails to report *P*, and *P* carries out further acts of shoplifting because of *A*'s continuing omission, *A* encourages by her intentional omission. On these facts, it

intended to provide a remedy.' In *Turk*, the Supreme Court noted that 'a person who buys drinks for an obviously intoxicated person . . . is at least as much the cause of the resulting or continued intoxication as the bartender who served the consumer illegally."

83 Michael S. Moore, 'Causing, Aiding, and the Superfluity of Accomplice Liability' (2008) 156 *U. Pa. L. Rev.* 395 at 426–430.

84 *Id.* at 428.

85 *The Queen v. Coney* (1881–82) L.R. 8 Q.B.D. 534; *R. v. Clarkson* [1971] 1 W.L.R. 1402.

86 Dennis J. Baker, *Glanville Williams Textbook of Criminal Law* (London: Sweet & Maxwell, 2015) at Chapter 10.

could be argued that the shoplifter is encouraged to carry out further acts of shoplifting, not only because of the circumstantial fact that the security guard on duty happens to be her sister, but also because of her sister's intentional omission. The accessory in this type of case cannot be liable as a perpetrator, because she is not the perpetrator of the theft. Therefore, a combination of derivative liability and omission liability has to be used to ground a conviction.

The accessory has a duty to prevent *P* from stealing and she also makes a remote contribution to *P*'s further acts of shoplifting by encouraging her by omission. This is a case of intentional encouragement by omission. Omission liability and complicity liability is needed, because the accessory is not a perpetrator and because there is no general duty to prevent others from stealing. A fellow shopper would not have been liable as an accessory had she failed to report *P* or had she failed to stop *P* from stealing. Nor would she be liable if she merely stood by and watched *P* stealing, even if her omission (failure to report *P*) had the incidental and indirect effect of encouraging *P* to continue shoplifting. Arguably, the omission of the soldiers in *R. v. Clarkson*[87] who stood by and watched a woman being raped without doing anything to try to prevent the rape had the effect of encouraging the rapist to continue raping, but since there is no general duty to police such crimes their bare omission was not enough to make them liable.[88] Their encouragement was at least reckless encouragement by omission.

In *R. v. Clarkson,*[89] Megaw, L.J. said:

> [I]f there was here aiding and abetting by the defendants Clarkson or Carroll it could only have been on the basis of inferences to be drawn that, by their very presence they, each of them separately as concerns himself, encouraged those who were committing rape.

Megaw, L.J. seems to take the view that encouragement by omission had to be intentional to inculpate accessories. Megaw, L.J. quotes the famous passage from *R. v. Coney,*[90] where Hawkins, J. said:

> Non-interference to prevent a crime is not itself a crime. But the fact that a person was voluntarily and purposely present witnessing the commission of a crime, and offered no opposition to it, though he might reasonably be expected to prevent and had the power to do so or at least to express his dissent, might, under some circumstances, afford cogent evidence upon which a jury would be justified in finding that he wilfully encouraged and so aided and abetted.

87 [1971] 1 W.L.R. 1402.
88 *R. v. Clarkson* [1971] 1 W.L.R. 1402.
89 [1971] 1 W.L.R. 1402 at 1405.
90 (1882) 8 Q.B.D. 534 at 557.

The above passage makes it clear that complicity liability might be made out where the jury is able to infer that there was a deliberate and intentional effort to encourage by omission. In *R. v. Clarkson*, the soldiers were let off the hook because they had not intentionally encouraged by omission. Megaw, L.J. took the view that direct intention makes a difference in complicity by omission cases. He said:

> It is not enough, then, that the presence of the accused has, in fact, given encouragement. It must be proved that the accused intended to give encouragement; that he wilfully encouraged. In a case such as the present, more than in many other cases where aiding and abetting is alleged, it was essential that that element should be stressed; for there was here at least the possibility that a drunken man with his self-discipline loosened by drink, being aware that a woman was being raped, might be attracted to the scene and might stay on the scene in the capacity of what is known as a voyeur; and, while his presence and the presence of others might in fact encourage the rapers or discourage the victim, he, himself, enjoying the scene or at least standing by assenting, might not intend that his presence should offer encouragement to rapers and would-be rapers or discouragement to the victim; he might not realise that he was giving encouragement; so that, while encouragement there might be, it would not be a case in which, to use the words of Hawkins J., the accused person 'wilfully encouraged'.

It is important to distinguish the conduct element from the mental element in such cases. Firstly, is the conduct (the omission) one of the reasons for *P*'s decision to continue raping *V*? If so, then the omission makes a causal contribution to *P*'s rape. It is no different from *A* standing nearby and yelling out: 'This is a good show, rape her more.' The positive act of uttering those gross words of encouragement would have the same causal effect as the omission – it would cause the perpetrator to have a reason for acting – but it would have no secondary causal effect of causing *P* to act on that reason. Arguably, they could give *P* a more than negligible reason for continuing his rape.

The reason why Clarkson and Carroll should have been found not guilty should not have rested simply on whether they directly[91] intended by their omission to encourage the rapist to continue raping, but also on the limited scope of omission liability. There is no general duty in England and Wales to

91 The courts have since held that in both standard complicity and common purpose complicity cases reckless participation is sufficient for grounding criminal liability. See *R. v. Gnango* [2012] 1 A.C. 827; *R. v. Rahman* [2009] 1 A.C. 129; *R. v. Bryce* [2004] 2 Cr. App. R. 592; *R. v. Powell* [1999] 1 A.C. 1. It doubtful the courts will hold that complicity by omission requires direct intention, given the movement towards adopting recklessness as an alternative fault element for complicity.

prevent others from perpetrating crimes. Thus, all those who fail to report or prevent the crimes of others are not liable simply because their omissions might have the unintended effect of encouraging the perpetrators to continue perpetrating their crimes. Omission liability would not come into the equation, if intentional encouragement by omission could have been made out on its own.

In cases where the omitter has a duty to act she may be liable as an accessory, if she encouragers by her omission. In *R. v. Russell*[92] a father stood by and watched as his wife drowned their children and thereafter drowned herself. The court held that he was liable for their murders because he had a duty to take reasonable steps to protect his children and he could easily have overpowered his wife and thus saved his children.[93] Nonetheless, if a neighbour had been present, she would not have been liable for failing to act to save the children because (1) she would not have had a duty to save them; and (2) it is doubtful a neighbour's intentional omission would be sufficient for a jury to infer it was deliberate and intentional encouragement by omission of such a nature as to have had some causal impact on the mother's decision to continue to drown the children.

The law of complicity comes into play in a case like *R. v. Russell*, because there was a perpetrator and secondary party involved. In *R. v. Russell*, the perpetrator was Russell's wife: she perpetrated the murder of their children by deliberately drowning them. If one of Russell's children had fallen into a shallow puddle by accident, then the law of complicity would not have been relevant because there is no perpetrator causing the child's death. Rather, the cause of the child's death is the fact that the child has accidentally fallen headfirst into a shallow puddle. In such a case, the father's liability would be for his personal omission only[94] and would not depend on derivative liability.

One version of the facts presented in *R. v. Russell* was that the father deliberately failed to act and that the wife could see that he was failing to act and was encouraged to continue with the murders and her own suicide partly because of her husband's omission. Her husband's omission was allegedly one of the factors playing on her mind when she continued with the murders. It was remote participation because it was one of the reasons

92 [1933] V.L.R. 59.

93 *R. v. Russell* [1933] V.L.R. 59.

94 When a person ought to have a duty to act is a controversial question that is beyond the scope of this book on complicity. A number of control cases that have been held to give rise to a duty to act seem controversial. See *Du Cros v. Lambourne* [1907] 1 K.B. 40; *R. v. Webster* [2006] R.T.R. 19; *State v. Travis* (1993) 497 N.W.2d 905. Cf. *R. c. Rochon* (2011) 357 D.L.R. (4th) 391, where *D* discovered that her son had been growing marijuana on her property. The Quebec Court of Appeal (*per* Duval Hesler, C.J.Q., Dalphond, and Kasirer, J.J.A.) held that *D* had no duty to report her son to the police or to control his criminal activities on her property. Nor was she liable for concealing his crime from the police.

for her continuing. If Russell had been hiding in the trees without his wife being aware of his omission, then it would not have been possible for the court to infer factual encouragement (i.e. Russell encouraged the perpetrator's murders by encouraging her by his overt omission). If there had been no encouragement, then according to the theory presented in this book there could be no liability on derivative principles.

Assuming no defences (e.g. insanity) were available to Russell's wife, had she not committed suicide by also throwing herself in the river, she would have been convicted of murder since she perpetrated the murder of their two children. Assuming also that Russell was hiding in the trees and that his wife was oblivious of his failure to act to rescue the children, then what is the role of law of complicity? If there is no factual encouragement by omission or assistance by omission, then the law of complicity has no role to play. On these facts, Russell could only be liable for his personal wrongdoing under the law of omission liability. It appears his wife's fully informed and independent conduct breaks the chain of causation and therefore there is no crime on his part.[95]

However, in *R. v. Russell*[96] McArthur, J. said:

> This is an example of a case in which two different persons, each committing a separate and distinct crime, may be held guilty of manslaughter for killing the same person . . . I have no hesitation in saying in the present case that the neglect of the [father] to make any effort to save his children is not too remote a cause, but may, as a matter of law, be relied upon as a direct cause of the children's death.

McArthur, J. held that the parental duty extended to protecting children from the 'wrongful or criminal acts of a third party'.[97] It appears that the courts might hold that both parties are independently liable for their personal wrongdoing in such cases.[98] Such a case involves independent instances of personal liability, not a case of personal liability and a case of derivative liability.[99] *In such cases concurrent causation would have to be present*

95 *R. v. Kennedy (No. 2)* [2008] 1 A.C. 269.

96 [1933] V.L.R. 59 at 82–83.

97 *R. v. Russell* [1933] V.L.R. 59 at 81. *Per contra, Com. v. Raposo* (1992) 413 Mass. 182.

98 Cf. section 5 of the *Domestic Violence, Crime and Victims Act 2004*. If Russell's wife had lived, she would have been liable for murder (assuming she was not excused on grounds of insanity), but Russell himself could have been independently liable for gross negligence manslaughter without any need to resort to derivative liability. See *Palmer v. State* (1960) 223 Md. 341.

99 'Principals cause, accomplices encourage (or otherwise influence) or help. If the instigator were regarded as causing the result he would be a principal, and the conceptual division between principals (or, as I prefer to call them, perpetrators) and accessories would vanish. Indeed, it was because the instigator was not regarded as causing the crime that the notion of accessories had to be developed. This is the irrefragable argument for

for each party to be held liable for the end harm. The decision in *R. v. Russell* is distinguishable, because there was factual encouragement by omission in that case and thus derivative liability was an available option. In that case, the wife was not oblivious to Russell's omission; she was aware of the fact he was watching and was able to draw a message of encouragement from his omission.

A. Omissions that are not causal encouragement

Under Gardner's indirect causation theory[100] it could be argued that Russell makes an indirect causal contribution by failing to act to try to stop his wife from killing the children and therefore under the law of complicity should share liability for the perpetrator's act. Gardner[101] asserts that failure to prevent a crime 'is straightforwardly causal. It is an adequacy-condition of any analysis of causality that it shows how one can make causal contributions by failing to act, including by failing to prevent actions by others.' I am not convinced that Gardner is correct, because uncausing and preventing a future cause is not causing it. If the omission does not have the effect of assisting or encouraging the perpetrator, but instead is a failure to uncause an act of perpetration that is already in progress, then it does not make an indirect causal contribution. Similarly, failing to act pre-emptively to prevent a future act of perpetration is not a cause of that act of perpetration when it is done. It is conceptually wrong to assert that a person makes a causal contribution to an act and its consequences when it is already being caused by others, simply because she fails to do some other act to uncause what is in progress. What she does, is fail to make a direct causal contribution to an *act* that might uncause the *perpetrator's act* of perpetration and its consequences. The act of uncausing the act of perpetration is independent and distinct to the act of perpetration. It can make a casual difference, but it does not indirectly or otherwise make a causal contribution to the act of perpetration.

In such a case there would be no factual encouragement and thus no remote factual participation in the perpetrator's crime for the purposes of establishing complicity liability. In such cases the act of perpetration has

recognising the *novus actus* principle as one of the bases of our criminal law. The final act is done by the perpetrator, and his guilt pushes the accessories, conceptually speaking, into the background. Accessorial liability is, in the traditional theory, "derivative" from that of the perpetrator. (I do not say that no other way of constructing a system of criminal law would be possible; what I do say is that, apart from some necessary adjustment, this is the foundation upon which the present law of complicity rests.)' Glanville Williams, 'Finis for Novus Actus?' [1989] *Cambridge L.J.* 391 at 392. This theory of the distinction between derivative and personal liability was accepted as correct by Lord Bingham in *R. v. Kennedy (No. 2)* [2008] 1 A.C. 269. Cf. *State v. McFadden* (1982) 320 N.W.2d 608.

100 Gardner, *op. cit. supra*, note 78 at 443.

101 *Ibid.*

been put into progress without *D*'s assistance or encouragement. If Russell had not encouraged his wife by his overt omission, the only culpability nexus he would have had with the murders would have been based in omission liability for failing to uncause what was causing their deaths when he had a duty to take reasonable steps to try and reverse the cause. This is a failure to uncause the act of perpetration, not an indirect causal contribution to the actions that are causing their deaths. The cause of the deaths was the fully autonomous and voluntary actions of Russell's wife.

If Russell had acted to prevent his wife from drowning their children he would have made a causal difference to the outcome by annulling or reversing the contributory causes, but his reversal itself is not a contributory cause of his wife's act of perpetration. *Thus, he would not be liable on derivative principles, because participation requires factual encouragement or assistance of the act of perpetration.* For example, suppose *P* injects *V* with poison and *D* has an antidote but fails to use it to prevent *P*'s act of poisoning from killing *V*. All *D* does is assist *P* not to have her criminal act reversed – *D* does not assist *P* to inject the poison or encourage her to inject it, so she does not assist the act of poisoning. She assists *P* to not have the act of poisoning's consequences prevented, but that is all. Any liability for this sort of failure to uncause what is casually in motion is to be found in the law of omission liability, not in the law of complicity. A person is only liable for omissions that result in her preventing some harm that she has a duty to prevent.[102] The harm in omission situations is normally caused by some event, rather than the voluntary intervening action of another human being, because voluntary independent (uninfluenced) human action normally breaks the chain of causation.

Compare this case to *R. v. Evans*,[103] where a woman was held liable for gross negligence manslaughter because she assisted her sister to create a dangerous situation for herself. Evans supplied her sister with drugs. Evans's sister self-injected the drugs and died as a result of a self-inflicted drug overdose. Evans assisted her sister's dangerous act, because she supplied her with the drugs. Evans did not perpetrate the dangerous act, but her act of supply meant she assisted her sister to perform a dangerous act upon herself. The sister's act was not an act of self-murder,[104] nor an

102 *R. v. Salmon* (1880–81) L.R. 6 Q.B.D. 79; *People v. Flayhart* (1988) 72 N.Y.2d 737; *People v. Abbott* (1981) 84 A.D.2d 11. Cf. *State v. Etzweiler* (1984) 125 NH 57.

103 [2009] 1 W.L.R. 1999.

104 Cf. *R. v. Fretwell* (1862) Le. & Ca. 161, where the question was whether *D* assisted *P*'s self-murder (which at the time was a crime) by supplying her with an abortifacient. Erle, C.J., (Martin, B., Channell, B., Blackburn, J. and Keating, J. concurring) held that, even if *P* were *felo de se*, *D* could not be convicted of murder, either as a principal or as an accessory because he had not administered the poison to *P*, nor had he caused *P* to take it. See also *R. v. Kennedy (No. 2)* [2008] 1 A.C. 269; *Burns v. The Queen* (2012) 246 C.L.R. 334. Section 1 of the *Suicide Act 1961* provides: 'The rule of law whereby it is a crime for a person to

attempt to commit suicide,[105] so the law of complicity was not applicable.[106] Because the sister did not perpetrate a crime, Evans could not be liable for her sister's death on derivative principles. Accessorial liability cannot derive from a non-existent crime.

Merely supplying a person with drugs, or a gun, or some other dangerous equipment is not an act that creates a dangerous situation.[107] It is not drugs or guns that *cause* harm to people, but people who *cause* harm to people. It is the fully autonomous human misuse of the drug or gun that results in harm. This is where the law of complicity cuts in. It criminalises remote contributions that result from prior assistance or encourage. Glanville Williams expounded:[108]

> The *novus actus* doctrine is at the root of the law of complicity. If one person instigates another to commit murder, the philosophy of autonomy teaches that the instigator does not cause the death, responsibility for causation being confined to the person who does the deed, and who is therefore the latest actor in the series. In order to bring in the instigator and helpers, bypassing this restriction on the law, the judges invented the doctrine of complicity, distinguishing between principals and accomplices. Principals [directly] cause, accomplices encourage (or otherwise influence) or help. If the instigator were regarded as [directly] causing the result he would be a principal, and the conceptual division between principals (or, as I prefer to call them, perpetrators) and accessories would vanish.

B. The double prevention cases

Moore[109] asserts that double preventions are non-causal. I think proving causation will be very difficult in many of the double prevention cases, but this problem can be overcome by prosecuting them as inchoate crimes under the *Serious Crime Act 2007*.[110] Nonetheless, where the proof of causation is not

commit suicide is hereby abrogated.' The victim in Fretwell was not attempting suicide, but was merely risking her life with the ulterior aim of aborting her foetus.

105 If Evans had intended to assist her sister to commit suicide, then she would have been liable under section 2 of the *Suicide Act 1961*.

106 Evans might have been convicted of a drug-supply offence. Likewise, her sister might have been convicted of a drug possession offence, but there is no offence of self-injecting drugs. See sections 4 and 5 of the *Misuse of Drugs Act 1971*.

107 If a person intends to encourage another to commit suicide, then they would be liable under section 2 of the *Suicide Act 1961*. But mere supply without any *mens rea* for any offence should not be sufficient to make a person liable for an offence as serious as manslaughter.

108 Glanville Williams, 'Finis for Novus Actus' (1989) 48 *Cambridge L.J.* 391 at 397–398.

109 Moore, *op. cit. supra*, note 83 at 426–428.

110 *State v. Tally* (1894) 102 Ala. 25 (to the extent that McClellan, J. suggests in his judgment in *State v. Tally*, that unused assistance is sufficient, his opinion is wrong. For *D* to be said

problematic, the double prevention cases seem to come within the purview of the remote participation by factual assistance and encouragement justification for complicity liability.

Take the example of two armed people chasing *V* towards *D*'s bulletproof motor car. The pursuit is in an open field and there are no other cars, trees, buildings or shelter of any kind in the field. *V* is in the open and *D*'s car is the only available shelter. *V* is just out of their firing range and has time to safely jump into *D*'s car to avoid being killed. As *V* attempts to enter *D*'s car, *D* hits her central locking system to prevent *V* from entering the car. This gives the gunpersons enough time to get *V* within firing range and they fire and kill *V*. Clearly, *D* assists the assassins by preventing *V* from escaping. *D*'s positive act helps the gunpersons get their target and is a concurrent cause. This is causally very different from the situation where *D*'s car is already locked and she simply omits to unlock it to rescue *V*, because she is scared the gunpersons will shoot her too. The latter situation is akin to there being no car there at all. I think Moore's non-causal theory covers the omission cases where *D* fails to rescue *V*, but not cases involving positive acts that are designed to assist the perpetrators by preventing the victim from escaping or sheltering from an attack.[111]

Moore cites the old case of *State v. Tally*[112] as a double prevention case. The issue in that sort of case seems to be one of proof of factual assistance or encouragement, not one of causation *per se*. In that case, *D* prevented a warning from being sent to *V*. There was no way of knowing whether if the warning had been sent it would have been effective in helping *V* to make a timely escape. It was all guesswork, because even if the warning had reached *V*, the killers might still have killed him before he was able to make a timely escape or seek police protection. Thus, the issue in that sort of case is a question of proof: did the prevention of the warning in fact assist? It is one thing to argue that it was an attempt to assist, but another to show that it did in fact assist. In the hypothetical above, it was clear that *D* by locking *V* out of her bulletproof car made a concurrent causal contribution. 'But for' *D* locking *V* out when she did, *V* would have lived. The same cannot be said in a case such as *State v. Tally*, so where consummated factual encouragement or assistance cannot be proved, the prosecution should charge the inchoate form of complicity found in the *Serious Crime Act 2007*.

In conclusion, the law of complicity's *raison d'être* is to criminalise remote participation by encouragement or assistance. This is a remote from of

to have factually participated in *P*'s crime, *P* must use *D*'s assistance. It is true that *P* need not be aware of factual assistance for *D* to factually participate, but unused assistance is no participation at all. The dissenting opinion of Head, J. in *State v. Tally* is the correct view as far as ineffectual assistance is concerned.

111 See *State v. Tally* (1894) 102 Ala. 25 cited by Moore as a double prevention case. See Moore, *loc. cit. supra*, note 83.

112 (1894) 102 Ala. 25.

participation, because it assists or encourages the perpetrator to perpetrate the anticipated target crime, but it does not make a direct concurrent causal contribution. The other rationale that has been put forward to justify complicity liability has been the widely disputed agency theory.[113] Agency theory is so widely disputed as a rationale for complicity liability that I will not dedicate space to revising those critiques. What is important for present purposes is to keep in mind that if there is no encouragement or assistance, the conduct element under section 8 of the *Accessories and Abettors Act 1861* collapses into an inchoate requirement.

113 'Punishment of accomplices is currently justified euphemistically by the civil doctrines of agency or, more candidly, by a concept of forfeiture of personal identity. These doctrines conflict with the morality of and focus upon individual culpability that underlie the common-law rules of crimes. Penal systems would be more morally justifiable and more coherent if guilt and punishment of accomplices were proportionate to the degree of participation in the crime, their degree of control or hegemony over others, or the harm they actually caused.' Joshua Dressler, 'Reassessing the Theoretical Underpinnings of Accomplice Liability: New Solutions to an Old Problem' (1985) 37 *Hastings L. J.* 91 at 140. See also Luis E. Chiesa, 'Reassessing Professor Dressler's Plea for Complicity Reform: Lessons from Civil Law Jurisdictions' (2014) 40 *New Eng. J. on Crim. & Civ. Confinement* 1; Robert Weisberg, 'Reappraising Complicity' (2000) 4(1) *Buffalo Criminal Law Review* 217.

2 The mental element in complicity requires intention

Abstract

I shall argue that the common purpose complicity doctrine as expounded by Sir Robin Cooke in Chan Wing-Siu v. The Queen *(and since adopted by the Lords) cannot be reconciled with a consistent line of authorities going back 500 years. Historically it was necessary for D2 to authorise D1's actions. Thus D2 could not be liable where (s)he simply foresaw D1's actions, especially when D2 had expressly forbidden those actions. D2 could only be liable if (s)he had at least obliquely intended to encourage the perpetrator by impliedly authorising any collateral crimes. Collateral crimes are normally conditional – they depend on what happens while the joint enterprise is being carried out. 'Foresight' was only ever meant to pertain to D2's knowledge of any planned collateral crime that would be perpetrated where necessary to make the underlying joint enterprise succeed. It was not meant to supplant the requirement that any criminal response to the contingencies of a joint enterprise be intended and authorised. (D2's implied authorisation forms the conduct element because it is factual encouragement.) If judges were to accept this interpretation, it would result in a radical narrowing of the doctrine as laid down in* Chan Wing-Siu v. The Queen. *Such a change, in practical terms, could raise concern that it would remove protection for society. However, this concern could be addressed by amending the* Serious Crime Act 2007 *to criminalise reckless participation. The advantage of amendment to the 2007 Act's offences is that it allows for fair labelling and proportionate punishment.*

I. Introduction

> Most emphatically the progressive tendency has been to repudiate the imposition of severe penalties where bare chance results in an unsought harm.[1]

1 Jerome Hall, *General Principles of Criminal Law* (Indianapolis: Bobbs-Merrill, 1947) at 455.

> It is not correct to say that a person may be convicted of aiding, abetting, counselling or procuring the commission of an offence simply because he has acted *recklessly*.[2]

Standard complicity (that is, assistance and/or encouragement not involving an underlying joint enterprise) normally involves a person providing direct assistance or encouragement. For example, *D* assists *P* by supplying *P* with a gun to assist *P* to kill *V*. Alternatively, *D* might pay *P* £100,000 to encourage *P* to kill *V*.[3]

A. The mental element in standard complicity

In *R. v. Bryce*, Potter, L.J. expounded the fault element for standard complicity as follows:[4]

> We are of the view that, outside the Powell and English situation (violence beyond the level anticipated in the course of a joint criminal enterprise), where a defendant, *D*, is charged as the secondary party to an offence committed by *P* in reliance on acts which have assisted steps taken by *P* in the preliminary stages of a crime later committed by *P* in the absence of *D*, it is necessary for the Crown to prove intentional assistance by *D* in the sense of an intention to assist (and not to hinder or obstruct) *P* in acts which *D* knows are steps taken by *P* towards the commission of the offence. Without such intention the *mens rea* will be absent whether as a matter of direct intent on the part of *D* or by way of an intent sufficient for *D* to be liable on the basis of 'common purpose' or 'joint enterprise'. Thus, the prosecution must prove:
>
> (a) an act done by *D* which in fact assisted the later commission of the offence,
> (b) that *D* did the act deliberately realising that it was capable of assisting the offence,

2 *Giorgianni v. The Queen* (1985) 156 C.L.R. 473 at 487 *per* Gibbs, C.J. In *Beatty v. Gillbanks* [1882] 9 Q.B.D. 308. it was held that the Salvation Army had acted lawfully in congregating in Weston-super-Mare even though its officers knew from past experience that this might encourage an opposing organisation, the Skeleton Army, to attack them. Similarly, in *Redmond-Bate v. D.P.P.* [2000] H.R.L.R. 249, Ms Redmond-Bate, the Wakefield preacher, foresaw the possibility that her sermons on the steps of the cathedral might encourage a breach of the peace. See *Redmond-Bate v. D.P.P.* [2000] H.R.L.R. 249. Nonetheless, mere foresight that one might encourage another to commit a criminal offence cannot make one liable as an accomplice for that person's crime.

3 *R. v. Deemal-Hall* [2005] Q.C.A. 206.

4 [2004] 2 Cr. App. R. 593 at 611.

(c) that *D* at the time of doing the act contemplated the commission of the offence by A, i.e. he foresaw it as a 'real or substantial risk' or 'real possibility', and
(d) that *D* when doing the act intended to assist A in what he was doing.

B. The mental element in common purpose complicity

In *R. v. Powell*,[5] Lord Hutton expounded:

> I consider that the test of foresight is a simpler and more practicable test for a jury to apply than the test of whether the act causing the death goes beyond what had been tacitly agreed as part of the joint enterprise. Therefore, in cases where an issue arises as to whether an action was within the scope of the joint venture, I would suggest that it might be preferable for a trial judge in charging a jury to base his direction on the test of foresight.
>
> . . .
>
> There will be cases giving rise to a fine distinction as to whether or not the unforeseen use of a particular weapon or the manner in which a particular weapon is used will take a killing outside the scope of the joint venture, but this issue will be one of fact for the common sense of the jury to decide.

Later courts have interpreted Lord Hutton's passages as meaning that the current law covers reckless participation. It has been held that a secondary party's recklessness as to whether his or her assistance and/encouragement might assist and/or encourage the perpetrator is sufficient. In other words, *D* will be liable so long as she believes that *P* might perpetrate the anticipated target crime with her assistance and/or because of her encouragement. She need not intend or obliquely intend *P* to perpetrate the anticipated target crime with her assistance and/or encouragement, because the courts have held that mere recklessness is sufficient.

C. Roadmap for this chapter

In this chapter, I shall argue that the mental element in complicity requires nothing less than intention. There must be intentional assistance or encouragement. Furthermore, I shall argue that the conduct element in complicity is not inchoate – there must be causal participation in the anticipated target crime before the accessory can be held liable for that crime. I will re-examine the modern and ancient authorities to show that recklessness is not sufficient

5 [1999] 1 A.C. 1 at 30.

for establishing the mental element in complicity. I shall argue that the law of complicity as applied in the common purpose scenario and more generally shows that the mental element requires intention.

I also shall try to demonstrate that attempted encouragement, which the courts have frequently accepted as enough for establishing the conduct element in the common purpose complicity scenario, is not sufficient for establishing the conduct element under section 8 of the *Accessories and Abettors Act 1861*. The *Act of 1861* did not create an inchoate crime. That provision requires factual participation. Hence, it has to be shown that the accessory made a remote physical contribution to the perpetrator's crime.

I shall argue that the interpretation the Law Lords gave the common purpose complicity doctrine in *R. v. Powell*[6] cannot be reconciled with a consistent line of authorities going back 500 years. I shall show that common purpose complicity is not established unless the accessory has it as her purpose not only to jointly perpetrate the target crime (the underlying joint enterprise), but also that her accomplice perpetrate any collateral crime(s) that she is to be held jointly liable for. It is not enough to show that the accessory foresaw that the perpetrator might commit a non-target[7] crime during the commission of the target offence (the joint enterprise). It must be shown that the accessory intended the perpetrator to perpetrate the collateral crime (should the need for it arise) for the purpose of effecting their joint enterprise. The collateral crime[8] must at least be a conditional-target crime. If it is not conditionally intended as a target crime, then it is a non-target crime and thus does not come within the purview of their common intentions.

6 [1999] 1 A.C. 1.

7 It is a non-target crime rather than a conditional-target crime, because the accessories have not directly or conditionally authorised (encouraged) it for the purpose of effecting their joint enterprise. Some cases in the United States use the term 'non-target crime', but this is a misnomer if what is meant is a 'conditional-target crime'. The term non-target is suited for negligence liability, but that is all. See *People v. Valdez* (2012) 55 Cal.4th 82 at 152, where it was observed that under California's statutory negligence standard for common purpose complicity 'a person who aids and abets a confederate in the commission of a criminal act is liable not only for that crime (the target crime), but also for any other offence (non-target crime) committed by the confederate as a "natural and probable consequence" of the crime originally aided and abetted.' Obviously, if the accessory does not intend the crime to be committed to make the joint enterprise succeed, then it is a non-target crime for her. If a person is negligent, then she does not intend what follows. 'The natural and probable consequences rule extends accomplice liability to the perpetrator's *reasonably* foreseeable crimes regardless of whether the defendant personally harboured the *specific intent* required for commission of the charged, non-target offence.' See *People v. Pearson* (2012) 53 Cal.4th 306.

8 In this monograph, I use the term 'collateral crime' to refer to both collateral crimes that are conditionally intended (conditional-target crimes) and those that are not intended at all (non-target crimes).

Historically, the law was not designed to allow a person to be held jointly liable for a crime that was not jointly intended either directly or conditionally.[9] (The conditional intention is also direct even though it is conditional.) The entire concept of common purpose liability as a form of complicity liability rests on the participants' mutual intentions – that is, their common purpose.[10] The jury has to be able to infer that the common purpose extended to the particular collateral crime. It can do this by inferring that the accessory conditionally or directly intended the collateral crime to be perpetrated.

II. The conduct element's relation to the mental element within the concept of derivative liability

A. Common purpose complicity is conceptually derivative liability

The current law is in a state of flux. Common purpose complicity does not exist as an independent form of complicity.[11] Its conduct element covers only 'encouragement' and not 'assistance,' because if the joint perpetrator assists her associate to perpetrate the collateral crime, standard complicity is made out. Liability is derivative in both standard complicity and also in common purpose complicity. Likewise, in both cases the accomplice is held equally liable for the perpetrator's crime pursuant to the procedural mechanism found in section 8 of the *Accessories and Abettors Act 1861.*

While both forms of complicity are conceptually forms of derivative liability, common purpose complicity is different from standard complicity

9 This was the law in England for centuries until it was changed by judicial fiat by a solo judge in 1990. In *R. v. Hyde* [1991] 1 Q.B. 134 Lord Lane, C.J., who had long understood the law, changed his view of the law because he was left befuddled by a number of paradoxical statements in Sir Robin Cooke's judgment in *Chan Wing-Siu v. The Queen* [1985] A.C. 168. This led Lord Lane, C.J. to supplement the 'factual encouragement by authorisation' requirement with a *mens rea* requirement of recklessness. Lord Lane, C.J. failed to see that he was supplementing the *actus reus* element with a *mens rea* element. The ancient and modern authorities prior to 1990 made the accessory liable only where she had conditionally or directly intended to encourage the collateral crime for the *purpose* of effecting the joint enterprise. See *Le Seignior Dacre's Case* (1535) Moore K.B. 86; *Sir Charles Stanley's Case* (1662) Kelyng, J. 86; *The Three Soldiers Case* (1697) Fost. 353; *R. v. Plummer* (1706) Kelyng, J. 109; *The King v. Hodgson* (1730) 1 Leach 6; *R. v. Hawkins* (1828) 3 Car. & P. 392; *R. v. Collison* (1831) 4 Car. & P. 565; *R. v. Price* (1858) 8 Cox C.C. 96; *R. v. Skeet* (1866) 4 F. & F. 931; *R. v. Caton* (1874) 12 Cox C.C. 624; *R. v. Short* (1932) 23 Cr. App. R. 170 *per* Lord Hewart, C.J., MacKinnon and Hawke, J.J.; *R. v. Spraggett* [1960] Crim. L.R. 840; *R. v. Smith* [1963] 1 W.L.R. 1200; *R. v. Anderson* [1966] 2 Q.B. 110 at 118–119; *R. v. Barr* (1989) 88 Cr. App. R. 362; *R. v. Slack* [1989] Q.B. 775; *R. v. Wakely* [1990] Crim. L.R. 119.

10 *R. v. Johns* [1978] 1 N.S.W.L.R. 282 *per* Street, C.J., Begg and Lusher, J.J. Cf. *R. v. Petters* [1995] Crim. L.R. 501; *Mohan v. The Queen* [1967] 2 A.C. 187; *R. v. Bristow* [2013] E.W.C.A. Crim. 1540 at para. 38, Treacy, L.J. (Hamblen and Nicol, J.J. concurring).

11 Cf. Peter Gillies, *Criminal Law* (Sydney: Law Book, 1985) at 140; Graham Virgo, 'Joint Enterprise Liability is Dead: Long Live Accessorial Liability' [2012] *Crim. L.R.* 850 at 856.

because it rests not on the joint perpetrator assisting her associate to perpetrate the collateral target crime, but on her encouraging her associate to do so by impliedly authorising it to be perpetrated to make their underlying joint enterprise succeed. Participation rests on encouragement by authorisation, but that is just another way of encouraging another to perpetrate a crime. Standard complicity and common purpose complicity both include encouragement as a conduct element and they both have the same *actus reus* and *mens rea* requirements.[12] The only difference between them is that common purpose complicity does not include assistance as a conduct element. Once assistance is present, the conduct collapses back into the standard complicity category.

Per contra, Simester[13] asserts that they are doctrinally distinct and have different *actus reus* and *mens rea* requirements. If we accept the analysis put forward in this monograph, we will see that the conduct element in common purpose complicity requires an intentional act or omission of encouragement. Since encouragement also is a way to participate via standard complicity, there is no conceptual distinction. The perceived doctrinal distinction is superficial. The distinctions between the modes of complicity are conduct-specific not conceptual. In the case of common purpose complicity, the mode of participation is intentional encouragement either express or implied, which can be inferred from evidence showing that the accessory impliedly or expressly authorised the perpetrator's collateral offending for the purpose of effecting their unlawful joint enterprise.[14]

B. Knowledge's relevance to the inference of intention

It is argued in this chapter that both forms of complicity have the same *mens rea* requirement. Traditionally, both modes of complicity required intentional participation. In recent decades the courts have held that mere recklessness is sufficient *mens rea* for both modes of complicity.[15] There is a line of cases emphasising the role of knowledge for inferring intention.[16] The most straightforward application of the knowledge constraint is found

12 Dennis J. Baker, *Glanville Williams: Textbook of Criminal Law* (London: Sweet & Maxwell, 4th edn 2015) at Chapter 17.

13 A. P. Simester, 'The Mental Element in Complicity' (2006) 122 *L.Q.R.* 578 at 593.

14 *R. v. Johns* [1978] 1 N.S.W.L.R. 282 *per* Street, C.J., Begg and Lusher, J.J.

15 The current law is in a state of flux, because the courts seem to be applying a recklessness standard as a substitute for factual encouragement, which is a conduct element. See *R. v. Powell* [1999] 1 A.C. 1 at 12 (a common purpose complicity case). Cf. *R. v. Bryce* [2004] 2 Cr. App. R. 592; *R. v. O'Brien* [1995] 2 Cr. App. R. 649; *R. v. Reardon* [1999] Crim. L.R. 392 (standard complicity cases). *R. v. Readon* was a case where there was sufficient evidence for a jury to infer that *A*, at the very least, obliquely intended to assist the first murder. As for the second murder, the evidence was equivocal, which led the court to invoke recklessness as a substantive fault element for accessorial murder.

16 *Rosemond v. U.S.* (2014) 134 S.Ct. 1240.

in cases where the accessory assisted/encouraged *P* to perpetrate a crime that has a circumstance element. For example, a jury cannot infer that *A* intended to assist and/or encourage *P* to perpetrate rape, if *A* did not *know* or *intend* the circumstance that *V* would not consent.

The jury have to infer as a question of fact that the accessory knew the relevant circumstances that made the perpetrator's intended act criminal. A person cannot intentionally assist child rape, if she does not know that *P* intends his victim to be underage. Negligence or strict liability as to the circumstance of the victim's age is sufficient for convicting the perpetrator, but the jury have to be able to infer that the accessory had actual knowledge of the relevant circumstances before it can infer that the accessory intended to assist or encourage such a crime. If *A* thinks she is assisting *P* to take property that *A* mistakenly believes belongs to *P*, then her mistake prevents her from knowingly (*a fortiori* intentionally) assisting *P*'s act of theft.[17] In the case of common purpose complicity, knowledge plays an important role for determining whether *A* intended to assist or encourage *P* to perpetrate the anticipated target crime. If *A* has present knowledge of *P*'s conditional intention to perpetrate the anticipated target crime, but continues to participate in the underlying joint enterprise, a jury could infer that *A* by her conduct and with her knowledge intends to encourage *P* to perpetrate the conditional collateral crime.[18]

If *A* lets *P* borrow her car and both *A* and *P* know for a fact that the brakes are faulty, *A* will be liable as an accessory to *P*'s dangerous driving. If *A* merely suspects something might be wrong with the brakes, *A* cannot be liable as an accessory. In the latter situation, *A* might be reckless, but *A* does not intend to assist an act of dangerous driving. Here, *A* merely risks assisting an act of dangerous driving. Compare this with the situation where *A* gives *P* a gun believing as a matter of virtual certainty that *P* plans to use the gun to kill. As it turns out *A*'s belief is correct. In this situation, even though *A* cannot know the future for sure, *A* should be liable as an accessory because the jury could infer that *A* intended the gun to be used to kill.

Similarly, if *D* intends to receive the proceeds of crime on a future date and does in fact receive the proceeds of crime on that date, it is no defence for her to argue that she did not know for sure that she would receive the proceeds of crime on that date.[19] Since she *intended* to receive the proceeds of crime and received the proceeds of crime, the jury is likely to infer she

17 On similar facts, see *People v. Molano* (1967) 253 Cal. App. 2d 841; cf. *R. v. Soares* (1802) Russ. & Ry. 25. See also *R. v. Palmer* (1804) 1 Bos. & P. N.R. 96 *per* Rooke, J. (technically an innocent agent case).

18 *R. v. Cramp* (1880) 14 Cox C.C. 390 at 393 *per* Denman, J.; *R. v. Surridge* (1942) 42 S.R. (N.S.W.) 278 at 282 *per* Jordan, C.J.; *Phan v. R* (2001) 123 A. Crim. R. 30; *R. v. Chishimba* [2010] N.S.W.C.C.A. 228 at paragraph 148.

19 See *R. v. Saik* [2007] 1 A.C. 18.

knowingly and thus intentionally received the proceeds of crime.[20] It is submitted that the oblique intention doctrine also could be used to infer knowledge in such cases. It could be used as a substantive fault doctrine, if the jury find as a matter of fact that the defendant obliquely intended to receive the proceeds of crime. Alternatively, it could be used as evidence where the jury could infer oblique intention or direct intention. The substantive outcome would not be different.[21] (See the discussion *infra.*)

The accessory must have knowledge of what is contemplated as a conditional-target crime, because the accessory cannot know the future. Therefore, it should be proved that she had present knowledge of *P*'s criminal plans for perpetrating the collateral crime. The problem is one of conditional intention: it must be shown that *A* knows that *P* plans to perpetrate collateral crime *X*, if certain contingencies arise during the joint perpetration of the underlying joint enterprise. If *A*[22] and *P*[23] agree that *P* should use lethal force during the course of a robbery should a security guard confront them, *A* will be liable because she knew that lethal force was planned as a possible collateral crime. *A* encourages its use for the purpose of effecting the joint enterprise.

The courts have run into error by failing to see that contemplation or foresight of the potential collateral crime is a special requirement in complicity liability, because the accessory's liability is contingent on the perpetrator's future criminal choices. At the time when the common purpose is formed, the commission of the collateral crime is *in futuro.* Foresight or contemplation is an issue because the jury has to ascertain whether the accessory intended the perpetrator's future offending when she joined the underlying criminal enterprise. When the accessory joins the underlying criminal enterprise with full knowledge of what is planned, the jury is able to infer that the accessory intended to encourage *P* by participating with mutual knowledge of what was conditionally intended as a collateral crime.

C. Conditional intention and knowledge

Foresight of the possibility that a perpetrator might have to commit a conditional-target crime for the purpose of making the joint enterprise

20 See *R. v. Saik* [2007] 1 A.C. 18; *R. v. Gnango* [2012] 1 A.C. 827 *per* Lord Kerr. In relation to common purpose complicity, see the powerful dissenting judgment of Kirby, J. in *Clayton v. The Queen* (2006) 168 A. Crim. R. 174.

21 This is the approach adopted in §2.02(2)(b) of the Model Penal Code, which provides: 'A person acts knowingly with respect to a material element of an offense when: (i) if the element involves the nature of his conduct or the attendant circumstances, he is aware that his conduct is of that nature or that such circumstances exist; and (ii) if the element involves a result of his conduct, he is aware that it is practically certain that his conduct will cause such a result.'

22 '*A*' is used for 'accessory.'

23 '*P*' is used for 'perpetrator.'

succeed is not knowledge that she will commit it. It is only knowledge of what is contemplated and intended (planned) as a possible crime, should the need for it to be perpetrated arise. Knowledge is evidence that can be used for inferring intention.[24] A person cannot know the future for certain, but she can intend the future.[25] A person can also have a conditional intention.

In *D.P.P. for Northern Ireland v. Maxwell*,[26] Maxwell had actual knowledge of the alternative crimes that were planned and intended. Maxwell knew the options and it was inferable that he intended to assist the gang to commit one of the optional crimes even though he did not know for sure which option would be chosen on the day in question. Maxwell gave them a semi-blank cheque as far as his assistance was concerned. A person's intention is conditional when she consents to lethal force being used to effect a joint enterprise should the need arise for such force during the commission of the joint enterprise. She might hope that the need to use such force will not arise, but as long as she has consented to it being used to effect the underlying joint enterprise, the jury can infer that she conditionally intended such force to be used.

In the common purpose situation, the accessory ought be liable only if she knows what the planned (conditional) target crimes are. Since a person cannot know the future, it is sufficient to establish beyond reasonable doubt that even though the accessory did not know for sure that the conditional-target crime would be perpetrated, she intended it to be perpetrated should the need for it to be perpetrated arise. A variation of the conditional-target crime situation is where *A* knows that *P* will perpetrate a collateral crime for certain, but does not know which crime it will be out of the options that are on the table. *D.P.P. for Northern Ireland v. Maxwell*[27] was not a case of Maxwell not knowing for sure whether the range of anticipated target crimes would have to be perpetrated to make the criminal enterprise succeed, but a case of Maxwell not knowing which crime would be perpetrated out of the range of crimes that had been planned as possible options. More commonly, the conditional-target crime situation involves *A* not *knowing* whether *P* will have to use lethal force to make their robbery succeed, but *intending P* to use it should it be needed.[28] The accessory cannot know for sure that lethal force will be used, if she does not know whether they will be

24 *R. v. Saik* [2007] 1 A.C. 18 (a conspiracy case that adopts a logical conceptualisation of knowledge). See *Provencher v. R.* [1956] S.C.R. 95, where *A* clearly had full knowledge of *P*'s criminal plans and intended to assist with the ulterior intention that *P* perpetrate the anticipated target crime.

25 See Baker, *op. cit. supra*, note 12 at paras 6–014 *et seq.*

26 [1978] 1 W.L.R. 1350 at 1358–1359.

27 [1978] 1 W.L.R. 1350.

28 As was the case in *Johns v. The Queen* [1980] 143 C.L.R. 108; *R. v. Becerra* (1976) 62 Cr. App. R. 212.

confronted by a guard during the course of their joint underlying robbery, but she can intend it be used should that situation arise. The accessory's present knowledge of *P*'s plans allows the jury to infer that she intended to encourage *P*'s conditional crimes.

D. The role of foresight in establishing the conduct element

What is foreseen as a conditional-target crime also has to be in fact encouraged by the accessory impliedly or expressly authorising *P* to perpetrate it. The biggest error the courts have made in the last couple of decades has been to dispense with the conduct element required for derivative liability (i.e. the factual encouragement by authorisation requirement). The accessory's knowledge of the possibility that the target crime might have to be perpetrated by the perpetrator to effect their joint enterprise allows the jury to infer that the accessory intended[29] to encourage[30] its perpetration to effect their underlying joint enterprise.[31]

In *Giorgianni v. The Queen*,[32] Gibbs C.J. said:

> Section 351 of the *Crimes Act* is based on s. 8 of the *Accessories and Abettors Act 1861* (U.K.), which, it has often been said, was only declaratory of the common law on the subject . . . The very words used in s. 351, and the *synonyms* which express their meanings – e.g. *help*, *encourage*, advise, persuade, induce, bring about by effort – indicate that a particular state of mind is essential before a person can become liable as a secondary party for the commission of an offence, even if the offence is one of strict liability. In *United States v. Peoni*, Judge Learned Hand referred to various statutory and common law definitions of 'accessories', by which he meant secondary parties, and . . . went on to say: 'It will be observed that all these definitions have nothing whatever to do with the probability

29 The decision in *R. v. Barr* (1989) 88 Cr. App. R. 362 recognised as much; it is a great shame that it was not followed in later cases. See also the trial judge's direction on *mens rea* as quoted in *R. v. Smith* [1963] 1 W.L.R. 1200 at 1205–1206.

30 In *R. v. Wakely* [1990] Crim. L.R. 119 at 120, Lord Lane, C.J. observed: 'The suggestion that a mere foresight of the real or definite possibility of violence being used is sufficient to constitute the mental element of murder is *prima facie*, academically speaking at least, not sufficient . . . [O]n the facts of this particular case the distinction between *foresight* and *tacit agreement* is as fine as could possibly be imagined, if indeed a distinction exists at all.' Lord Lane, C.J. was stating that foresight could be used by a jury to infer that *D* tacitly agreed to the violence that was used and intended its use for the purpose of effecting the joint enterprise.

31 See *Parker's Case* (1559) 2 Dyer 186a; *Duffey's and Hunt's Case* (1830) 1 Lewin 194; *R. v. Cruse* (1838) 8 Car. & P. 541; and *Johnson v. Youden* [1950] 1 All E.R. 300 endorsed by the House of Lords in *R. v. Churchill (No. 2)* [1967] 2 A.C. 224 at 236 and again in *D.P.P. for Northern Ireland v Maxwell* [1978] 1 W.L.R. 1350 at 1357.

32 *Giorgianni v. The Queen* (1985) 156 C.L.R. 473 at 479–480.

> that the forbidden result would follow upon the accessory's conduct; and [that] they all demand that he in some sort associate himself with the venture, that he participate in it as in something that he wishes to bring about, that he seek by his action to make it succeed. All the words used – even the most colourless "abet" – carry an implication of purposive attitude towards it.' In other words, the person charged as a secondary party should in some way be 'linked in purpose with the person actually committing the crime'.[33]

In *Attorney-General v. Able*[34] Woolf J. said:

> The editor of *Russell on Crime* (London: Stevens & Sons, 12th edn 1964) also provides assistance as to what is the 'bare minimum' which is necessary to constitute a person an accessory before the fact. At p. 151, it is stated that: 'the conduct of an alleged accessory should indicate (a) that he *knew* the particular deed was *contemplated* [i.e. planned, either as an unconditional target crime or as a conditional-target crime], and (b) that he *approved* of or *assented* to it, and (c) that his *attitude in respect of it in fact encouraged* the principal offender to perform – and I would here add or attempt to perform – "the deed"' [emphasis added].

E. Inferring conditional intention from foresight

In the context of conditional collateral crimes, the words 'knew what was contemplated' simply mean that it must be proved that the accessory *knew which collateral crimes were planned* to make the joint enterprise succeed. *It is about looking at the evidence to infer that the accessory tacitly agreed to the conditional-target crime being committed for the purpose of making the joint enterprise succeed and to infer that this agreement or authorisation was an act of encouragement.*[35] The accomplice must not only have knowledge of what is planned, but must also approve or assent to those plans being carried out should the need arise.[36] The accessory encourages the perpetrator by voluntarily

33 Citing *Du Cros v. Lambourne* [1907] 1 K.B. 40 at 44; *D.P.P. of Northern Ireland v. Maxwell* [1978] 1 W.L.R. 1350 at 1359.

34 [1984] Q.B. 795 at 809. Also cited with approval in *Giorgianni v. The Queen* (1985) 156 C.L.R. 473 at 481.

35 The jury can infer from the evidence that the accessory intended and agreed to the conditional-target crime being committed and thus that it was within the common purpose of all parties that such a crime be committed to effect the unlawful joint enterprise. See *R. v. Pridmore* (1913) 8 Cr. App. R. 198.

36 'Intent is an ingredient of the offence of aiding and abetting or counselling and procuring and knowledge of the essential facts of the principal offence is necessary before there can be intent. It is actual knowledge which is required and the law does not presume knowledge or impute it to an accused person where possession of knowledge is necessary for the

agreeing to participate in the joint enterprise where there is a mutual expectation that certain conditional crimes will be perpetrated to make their enterprise succeed. If *A* intends to encourage *P*'s criminal act with the ulterior intention of making *P*'s act succeed, then her culpability and participation make her equally blameable.

'Contemplation' was only ever meant to refer to *A*'s knowledge of conditional-target crimes; it was not meant to supplant the requirement that any criminal response to the contingencies of the joint enterprise be intended and authorised.[37] It is wrong to hold that where *A* foresaw that *P* might perpetrate a particular collateral crime she knew P would perpetrate it.[38] An accessory cannot be said to 'know' that *P* will use the gun to kill, if she merely foresees it as a mere possibility.[39] All she knows in the latter situation is that *P might* use it to commit murder, not that she *will* use it to kill. Following the House of Lords decision in *R. v. Saik*[40] (a decision on conspiracy but one that adopts a general philosophical conceptualisation of knowledge) it can be said that the knowledge constraint can be satisfied only if the accessory has (genuine) present knowledge[41] or alternatively she intended *P* to perpetrate the conditional-target crime. Under this standard the prosecution must prove *A* knew *P* would commit the crime. Since an accessory cannot know in advance that *P* will commit

formation of a criminal intent.' *Giorgianni v. The Queen* (1985) 156 C.L.R. 473 at 504–505 *per* Wilson, Deane and Dawson, J.J. See also *R. v. Johns* [1978] 1 N.S.W.L.R. 282.

37 See *R. v. Caton* (1874) 12 Cox C.C. 624. See also *Williams v. State* (1887) 9 Crim. L. Mag. & Rep. 480 at 482; *R. v. Johns* [1978] 1 N.S.W.L.R. 282.

38 In *Giorgianni v. The Queen* (1985) 156 C.L.R. 473 at 506–507, Wilson, Deane and Dawson, J.J. said: 'The necessary intent is absent if the person alleged to be a secondary participant does not know or believe that what he is assisting or encouraging is something which goes to make up the facts which constitute the commission of the relevant criminal offence . . . It is not sufficient if his knowledge or belief extends only to the *possibility or even probability* that the acts which he is assisting or encouraging are such, whether he realises it or not, as to constitute the factual ingredients of a crime. If that were sufficient, a person might be guilty of aiding, abetting, counselling or procuring the commission of an offence which formed no part of his *design*' [emphasis added]. How can *A* intentionally assist *P*'s theft if she believes *P* is collecting her own property? See *People v. Molano* (1967) 253 Cal. App. 2d 841; *R. v. Palmer* (1804) 1 Bos. & P. N.R. 96 *per* Rooke, J. (technically an innocent agent case). Cf. *R. v. Soares* (1802) Russ. & Ry. 25.

39 Some judges have held it is enough that *A* believes that there is a risk that *P* will perpetrate the anticipated target crime in circumstances that make it criminal. See *R. v. Bryce* [2004] 2 Cr. App. R. 592; *R. v. Powell* [1999] 1 A.C. 1. Cf. *R. v. Cruse* (1838) 8 Car. & P. 541 at 546 *per* Patteson, J.; *Johnson v. Youden* [1950] 1 All E.R. 300; *R. v. Sterecki* [2002] EWCA Crim. 1662.

40 [2007] 1 A.C. 18.

41 *R. v. Saik* [2007] 1 A.C. 18 at 36, Lord Nicholls said: 'The phrase under consideration ("intend or know") is a provision of general application to all conspiracies. In this context the word "know" should be interpreted strictly and not watered down. In this context knowledge means true belief.' This is a fairly standard philosophical conceptualisation of knowledge and should apply in other cases as a matter of general principle.

a particular collateral crime for certain, she ought only to be liable in the alternative when it can be demonstrated that she (conditionally) intended *P* to commit it.[42]

In *R. v. Bainbridge*,[43] Lord Parker C.J. said, 'It is clear that there must be not merely suspicion but knowledge that a crime of the type in question was *intended*.' Meanwhile, in *D.P.P. of Northern Ireland v. Maxwell*,[44] Lord Dilhorne said: 'It is clear that a person cannot properly be convicted of aiding and abetting in the commission of acts which he does not know may be or are intended.' In respect to the words 'know may be . . . intended', arguably, Lord Dilhorne had conditionally intended crimes in mind. This applies not only to cases where alternative crimes are planned, but also to cases where certain conditional crimes are planned and authorised by the parties to a joint criminal enterprise.

If *A* joins *P* to rob a bank (the target crime) and tacitly or expressly agrees that *P* should kill the guard (the conditional-target crime) for the purpose of effecting their joint enterprise (should the need arise) the jury would be able to infer that *A* intended *P* to kill the guard. The intent is conditional on their being confronted by a guard, but if that contingency occurs the *accessory's intention* is that the perpetrator should use lethal force to deal with it. The accessory's knowledge of what was conditionally intended (or contemplated as a possible or probable collateral crime) is merely evidence from which a jury can infer that the common intention of the parties extended to the collateral crime. Knowledge that the collateral crime was a possibility

42 *R. v. Saik* [2007] 1 A.C. 18 at 36 *per* Lord Nicholls, it was held actual knowledge is true knowledge and that where it is not present the alternative is to establish that the defendant intended the future facts that made her conduct criminal. It is enough to establish that *D* 'knows or intends'. See also section 1(2) of *Criminal Law Act 1977*, where Parliament expressly included such a test in the provision dealing with conspiracy. At para. 56, Baroness Hale, in her dissenting judgment, said: 'I believe that we are also agreed that, at this stage of the inquiry, their intentions may be conditional. There are many different kinds of conditional intent. There may be factual circumstances necessary to the carrying out of the purpose: we will blow up the Palace of Westminster if the King comes to open Parliament. Or there may be preconditions which the conspirators have set themselves: we will use our bombs if the IRA cease-fire ends. No substantive crime will be committed unless the condition materialises, but it is now generally accepted that they are guilty of a conspiracy to commit that crime. Or there may be provision for contingencies which could arise in a necessarily uncertain future: we will shoot if we have to in order to accomplish our purpose; or we will assist a suicide if we think it appropriate . . . In all those examples, both parties are involved in the guilty intention . . . Therefore *B* is not guilty of conspiracy unless both he and *A* "intend or know" that the money is the proceeds of crime. *A* knows that it is. *B* does not. But does he intend that it will be? Is a conditional intent of the "even if" kind sufficient for the purpose of section 1(2) as many think that it is for the purpose of section 1(1)? My Lords, I cannot see why it should be sufficient for the one but not for the other.' It is submitted that Baroness Hale's reasoning is more sound than that of the majority.

43 [1960] 1 Q.B. 129 at 134.

44 [1978] 1 W.L.R. 1350 at 1355.

is merely evidence from which a common intention for it to be perpetrated to make the underlying enterprise succeed can be inferred.

F. Mutually foreseeable possibilities

The participants need not hold the mutual belief that during the robbery it is virtually certain that a guard will confront them; this need be only mutually contemplated as a possibility. Once the jury accepts that the parties did in fact mutually contemplate the possibility of a security guard confronting them during the course of the robbery, it then needs to determine how they intended to deal with the contemplated event. The jury needs to be able to infer that this possibility was not only mutually contemplated, but also, based on that contemplation, the participants had an agreement (tacit or express) that a conditional-target crime be perpetrated to deal with it. It is how the accessory intends the perpetrator to deal with contingencies such as a security guard confronting her and her accomplice during a joint robbery that makes her blameworthy.

G. The foresight rule is a maxim of evidence not a substantive fault doctrine

The foresight of possibility rule is no more than a maxim of evidence in the law of common purpose complicity. In *D.P.P. for Northern Ireland v. Maxwell*,[45] Lord Fraser said:

> In these circumstances, the answer to the question whether he was rightly convicted depends upon the extent of his *knowledge of the common plan* when he took part in it. If he had *known full details of the plan* – the time, place and nature of the *crimes intended* – he would unquestionably be guilty as a principal because he had aided and abetted their commission. Even if he had not known the *intended* time and place, but had *known the nature of the crimes* that were *planned [intended]*, there could be no question of his guilt . . . he must have *intended to assist* in any one or more of these types of operations, with all that it necessarily involved, while being content to leave the choice of the actual operation to others, perhaps members of the gang or some higher commander [my emphasis].

The older authorities on common purpose complicity are clearer than some of the recent decisions on standard complicity.[46] The older cases make it clear that 'foresight' (i.e. contemplation or foresight of the collateral crime as a possibility) is not a substitute for intention. Contemplation merely arose as an issue in the old cases because the accessory's complicity

45 [1978] 1 W.L.R. 1350 at 1360.
46 See for example the recklessness standard adopted in *R. v. Bryce* [2004] 2 Cr. App. R. 592.

liability is always contingent on the perpetrator's *future* choices and actions. It is about establishing whether or not the accessory intended the perpetrator's future acts. Liability is limited to cases where the accessory knew what was planned and authorised those plans for the purpose of making the joint enterprise succeed.

In *R. v. Borthwick*,[47] Willes, J. said:

> In *Lord Dacre's case*, all went with a *design to resist every opposition*. In Moore[48] it is stated, that they went under an *agreement to kill* all who should resist them, and it appears, by that report of the case, as well as by what is said in Foster, that they were all acting in the same pursuit at the time when the murder was committed. Foster says, 'It was sufficient that, at the instant the fact was committed, they were all of the same party, and upon the same pursuit, and under the same engagement and *expectation of mutual defence* and support with those that did the fact.'

In these cases *A*'s knowledge of the planned collateral crimes was taken as a conditional intention that those crimes be perpetrated to make the enterprise succeed.[49] The question is: did *A* and *P* conditionally intend *P* to perpetrate the contemplated collateral crime? It is not about demonstrating that *A* shared *P*'s *mens rea* for the substantive offence, but about showing that *A* conditionally intended *P* to commit the collateral target crime.

III. Factual encouragement v. foresight and association

Common purpose complicity cannot be a form of derivative liability, if the factual encouragement requirement is to be dispensed with. Long ago, Sir Michael Foster justified common purpose complicity by asserting that the

47 (1779) 1 Douglas 207 at 212. Hale adopted the doctrine laid down in *Le Seignior Dacre's Case* (1535) Moore K.B. 86 as the law. See Sir Matthew Hale, *The History of the Pleas of the Crown* (London: Printed by E. and R. Nutt *et al.*, 1736) Vol. I at 443–444. This rule was applied in common purpose complicity cases right up until 1990. See *R. v. Macklin* (1838) 2 Lewin C. C. 225; *R. v. Betts and Ridley* (1931) 22 Cr. App. R. 148 at 153–156; *R. v. Appleby* (1943) 28 Cr. App. R. 1; *R. v. Grant* (1954) 38 Cr. App. R. 107. The doctrine also applied in cases where the old felony murder rule was not applicable. See *The Three Soldiers Case* (1697) Fost. 353; *R. v. Short* (1932) 23 Cr. App. R. 170 *per* Lord Chief Justice Hewart, MacKinnon and Hawke, J.J.; *R. v. Spraggett* [1960] Crim. L.R. 840; *R. v. Smith* [1963] 1 W.L.R. 1200 at 1203, where Slade J. (Hilbery, Ashworth, Melford Stevenson and Veale, J.J. concurring) said: 'these four men were acting in concert to tear up the joint, or otherwise make an attack on the bar and, if necessary, on anyone, such as the barman, who attempted to prevent them doing so and tried to drive them out of the public house.'

48 (1535) Moore K.B. 86.

49 It is necessary to prove that *D* '[w]ith the requisite knowledge or state of mind . . . did an act for the purpose of encouraging or assisting another person or persons to commit the target offence'. *R. v. Jeffrey* [2003] 2 Qd. R. 306 at 310–311; *R. v. Roberts* [2012] QCA 82 para. 164.

accomplice participates in the collateral crime by encouraging the perpetrator, which she does by authorising her to perpetrate it for the purpose of making their underlying criminal enterprise succeed. Foster wrote:[50]

> So that if several persons set out together, or in small parties, upon one common design, be it murder or other felony, or for any other purpose unlawful in itself . . . they are all, provided the fact be committed, in the eye of the law [equally liable]; . . . for it was made a common cause with them, each man operated his station at one and the same instant, towards the same common end, and the part each man took *tended to give countenance, encouragement, and protection to the whole gang*, and to *insure the success of their common enterprise* [my emphasis].

Lord Toulson recently wrote: 'Thus explained, participation in a joint enterprise is an example of mutual assistance and encouragement. It is not a doctrinally separate basis of secondary liability.'[51] This only works if we accept authorisation is a form of encouragement, because there needs to be some factual involvement in the collateral crime. Unless the accessory has something more than mere foresight of the possibility that the perpetrator might commit a collateral crime during the course of their joint enterprise, common purpose complicity is not derivative.[52] Derivative liability requires

50 Sir Michael Foster, *Crown Law* (London: Printed by W. Strahan and M. Woodfall, 1776) at 354. The law always required active encouragement or assistance. Coke wrote: '*Nullus dicitur Felo principalis, nisi Actor, aut qui presens est abettans, aut auxilians actorem ad Feloniam faciendam.*' Sir Edward Coke, *The Institutes of the Laws of England: Third Part* (London: W. Lee, 1648) at 138. Wishful thinking and even deliberate presence *per se* were not enough. See *R. v. Royce* (1767) 4 Burr. 2073 at 2080–2083; *Messenger's Case* (1661) Kel. 70 at 78–79; cf. *R. v. Whithorne* (1828) 3 Car. & P. 394. Hale also asserts that there must be either active assistance/encouragement or otherwise consent. See Hale, *op. cit. supra*, note 47 at 441; 537. This was affirmed in *R. v. Coney* (1881–82) L.R. 8 Q.B.D. 534 *per* Denman, J., Huddleston, B., Manisty, Hawkins, Lopes, Stephen, Cave, and North, J.J. See also *Autry v. Coffman* (1869) 46 Tenn. 510; *Green v. U. S.* (1927) 21 F.2d 508; *National Life & Acc. Ins. Co. v. Yates* (1933) 16 Tenn.App. 344; *State v. Gomez* (1967) 432 P.2d 444; *State v. Hunter* (1906) 77 S.C. 119; *State v. Ham* (1953) 76 S.E.2d 346; *State v. Duran* (1974) 86 N.M. 594.

51 Lord Toulson, 'Sir Michael Foster, Professor Williams and Complicity in Murder' in Dennis J. Baker and Jeremy Horder (eds), *The Sanctity of Life and the Criminal Law: The Legacy of Glanville Williams* (Cambridge: Cambridge University Press, 2013) at 235.

52 See *R. v. Taylor* (1872–75) L.R. 2 C.C.R. 147 at 149, where Cockburn, C.J. (Mellor and Brett, J.J., Bramwell and Pollock, B.B. concurring) held: 'The prisoner was not present at the fight, and all that he did was that he agreed to act as stake-holder, and received one sovereign from each of the combatants, and consented to hold the two sovereigns until after the fight, and then to pay them to the winner. In order to render the defendant liable to the charge [manslaughter] there must be some active proceeding on his part; he must procure or incite them to fight or in some way encourage them to do so. In this case the defendant was perfectly passive, and it is enough to say that there is nothing to show such a participation in the fight on the part of the defendant as to make him an accessory before the fact to the manslaughter under the circumstances.'

remote physical contributions. A person having mere *thoughts* about what another autonomous adult might do wrong is not sufficient to causally involve that person in those wrongs.[53] Complicity's *raison d'être* is remote participation by factual assistance or encouragement. A person can make a remote contribution by persuading another to perpetrate a crime – but there must be evidence to demonstrate that the perpetrator was persuaded. Inchoate persuasion is not sufficient for complicity.

A. Mere association as a basis for liability

Mere association is not enough to establish complicity liability.[54] Accessorial liability derives from *A*'s *involvement* in *P*'s offending. On derivative principles the accessory is liable only if she in fact participates in the primary offending. A person cannot be derivatively involved in the crime of another merely because she associated with the perpetrator in circumstances where she foresaw she might commit a crime. She has to form an intention with respect to the crimes that are foreseen as possible collateral crimes and must factually assist or encourage. Virgo thinks otherwise.[55] He argues reckless association and foresight are sufficient to make the accomplice liable for a specific intent crime such as murder, which carries a mandatory life sentence. Virgo argues:[56]

> [I]t is not necessary to show that *D1* was encouraged to commit crime *B* by virtue of the joint venture to commit crime *A*, and because *D2* might not desire crime *B* to be committed, so cannot be considered to have intended to encourage it. By continuing with the joint venture, being

53 See *R. v. Jones* (1977) 65 Cr. App. R. 250 *per* Lawton, L.J.; *R. v. Allen* [1965] 1 Q.B. 130 *per* Edmund-Davies, J. (as he then was).

54 *R. v. Davis and Hall* (1806) Russ & Ry 113; *R. v. Reid* (1976) 62 Cr. App. R. 109 at 112.

55 See Virgo, *op. cit. supra*, note 11 at 860. Professor Virgo's line of reasoning cannot be reconciled with the authorities. For example, in *R. v. Davies* [1954] 1 W.L.R. 214 at 217, Sellers, J. said: 'These two men had been engaged with others in an assault or series of assaults which cannot be too strongly condemned, but the facts negatived any participation by them in the murder. The fact that they were making an attack with their fists, and perhaps by kicking too, does not in itself associate them with the attack by one of their number with a knife or other weapon which caused death.' See also the House of Lords decision in *Davies v. D.P.P.* [1954] A.C. 378 at 401 *per* Lord Simonds L.C. In *Lenzi v. Miller* [1965] S.A.S.R. 1, Bright, J. said: 'In some cases the prosecution may rely upon an association between accessory and main offender. *But the purpose of proving the association is to give foundation to an inference that there was some community of minds between the two persons. The main offender's act must be wholly or partly a consequence of the accessory's counselling or procuring*... "An accessory... is one who directly or indirectly counsels procures or commands any person to commit any [crime] which is committed in consequence of such counselling procuring or commanding." Instigation [participation] is necessary as well as association' [emphasis added]. See also *Scott v. Killian* (1984) 36 S.A.S.R. 438 at 447 *per* Bollen, J.

56 Virgo, *op. cit. supra*, note 11 at 860.

> aware that crime *B* might be committed, *D2* is sufficiently associated with that crime to be regarded as responsible for its commission.

Virgo seems to have been influenced by Hughes L.J.'s (as he then was) reasoning in *R. v. A*,[57] where his Lordship said:

> [A]s a matter of principle, the liability of *D2* . . . rests . . . on his having continued in the common venture of crime *A* when he realises (even if he does not desire) that crime *B* may be committed in the course of it. Where crime *B* is murder, that means that he can properly be held guilty if he foresees that *D1* will cause death by acting with murderous intent (viz either the intent to kill or the intent to do GBH). He has associated himself with a foreseen murder. If all he foresees is that death may be caused without either of those intentions, he has not associated himself with a foreseen murder; he has associated himself with foreseen manslaughter.

Mere association cannot be conceptualised as a form of derivative liability. Participation liability for the acts of associates is based on the premise that *A*'s implied or express authorisation of the collateral crime *influenced* (encouraged) her associate to commit the collateral crime. If there is no factual influence, there is no factual participation. Conceptually, association liability is akin to vicarious liability, which hinges on agency and delegation – not on factual participation and involvement – that is, remote contributions. Supplying a gun is a remote contribution because its contribution relies on the perpetrator choosing to use it.[58] Association combined with foresight is a very wide theory of liability. Under such a theory, if *A* knows her friend *P* is a kleptomaniac and foresees that *P* might shoplift

57 *R. v. A* [2011] Q.B. 841 at 850. Lord Hughes is not the first judge to overlook the importance of actual assistance and encouragement. See *R. v. Stewart* [1995] 3 All E.R. 159. Cf. vicarious liability as discussed in Baker, *op. cit. supra*, note 12 at Chapter 8. See also *Liwai-Ming v. The Queen* [1965] H.K.L.R. 631, where 'The 1st appellant was convicted of a charge under s.11 of the *Summary Offences Ordinance*, Cap. 228, with behaving indecently by dancing and exposing her naked body to public view in a public place. The 2nd appellant was convicted of aiding and abetting, in that as the manager of the establishment she controlled the activities of the 1st appellant.' If the manager had encouraged the girl to strip naked, then her act of encouragement would make her an accessory. It also might be argued that if she was present her failure to stop the dancer from removing her clothes was encouragement by omission (cf. *State v. Ainsworth* (1993) 426 S.E.2d 410 at 425; *R. c. Rochon* (2011) 357 D.L.R. (4th) 391). If the manager was strictly liable merely because of her role as the dancer's manager, that is a case of vicarious liability. In such a case, *D* is held liable for the actions of her employee, because they are deemed to be her own acts. Such a case might also be explained as a duty to control case. (Compare the brief discussion in Chapter 1 on this point.)

58 Dennis J. Baker, 'The Moral Limits of Criminalising Remote Harms' (2007) 10 *New Crim. L. Rev.* 370 at 371–391.

every time she is in a shopping centre, *A* would be liable for *P*'s thefts if she associates with *P* while she steals. *A fortiori* if *A* assists *P* by driving her to the shopping centre in circumstances where she contemplates that *P* might steal some goods.

Such a theory of liability would be too restrictive of liberty and too great an extension of criminal law. The accessory should be liable for the shoplifting only when she drives *P* to the shopping centre with the intention of making *P*'s theft succeed.[59] *A* might drive *P* with foresight of *P*'s potential for thieving, but *A* might also intend to keep an eye on *P* to prevent her from stealing. Why should *A* be liable if she fails to prevent *P* from stealing even though she genuinely tried to stop her from stealing? In such circumstances it would be unjust to hold *A* liable for *P*'s shoplifting simply because *A* had foresight of *P*'s criminal propensities and was associating with *P* when *P* offended.

B. Association per se is not encouragement

Analytically, it can be seen that association *per se* is not encouragement, if we contrast mere association in the context of a lawful joint enterprise with that in an unlawful joint enterprise. (The association theory raises this question: why does association and foresight not count when the joint enterprise is lawful?) Let us assume that *A*, *B*, *C* and *D* attend a lawful (public) protest. Also, let us assume that these four have been on many public protests together in the past and on each occasion *D* has used aerosol paint to spray messages of protest on public monuments during the course of their joint lawful protest. Since the protest is lawful, they cannot be said to be engaging in an unlawful joint enterprise together.[60] If a group

59 As much was recognised in *Trial of Lord Mohun* (1692) Holt K.B. 479 at 479–480. See also the persuasive reasoning in *Mumford v. State* (1974) 313 A.2d 563 at 566; *U.S. v. Ramos-Rascon* (1993) 8 F.3d 704 at 711; *Wong Hoi v. The Queen* [1966] H.K.L.R. 386 at 397–398; *R. v. Beck* [1990] 1 Qd. R. 30 at 37 *per* Macrossan, C.J.; *R. v. Golding* (2008) 100 S.A.S.R. 216 at 227–230 *per* Gray, J. (Doyle, C.J. and David, J. concurring). See also the decision of the Supreme Court of Tasmania in *Truman v. Buxton* (2009) 198 A. Crim. R. 58, where Tennent, J. held that mere presence, knowledge and association were not enough to make the passenger in a car an accomplice for several acts of shoplifting that had been perpetrated by the other passengers in the car. However, Tennent, J. upheld *D*'s conviction, because there was sufficient evidence for the magistrate to infer that *D* had actively encouraged his associates to steal. In *R. v. Fred* [2001] Q.C.A. 561 *per* McPherson J.A., Mackenzie and Mullins J.J., the Supreme Court of Queensland held mere knowledge of another's criminal plans was not sufficient to establish participation. See further *R. v. Dick* [1947] 2 D.L.R. 213; *R. v. Cruise et al.* (1970) 9 C.R.N.S. 225; R. *v. Roy et al.* (1970) 9 C.R.N.S. 137; *R. v. Dunlop* [1979] 2 S.C.R. 881.

60 Nor would the flawed 'change of normative position' theory apply in such cases. *Per contra*, Simester, *op. cit. supra*, note 13 at 598–599, asserts: 'Through entering into a joint enterprise, S changes her normative position. She becomes, by her deliberate choice, a participant in a group action to commit a crime. Moreover, her new status has moral

of people have it as their common purpose to participate in a *lawful* public protest, the common purpose complicity doctrine cannot be used to make them all liable merely because they foresaw the possibility of their associate perpetrating an act of criminal damage with aerosol paint.

What's more, it would not matter whether it could be shown that *A* assisted *P* by driving *P* to the lawful protest in *A*'s car. Merely driving someone to a lawful activity is not an act capable of encouraging her to make an autonomous and fully informed decision to commit a crime once she gets to that location. *A* would be liable only where she does something extra to encourage *P* to offend after arriving at that location.[61] For example, *A* might in the heat of the lawful protest say to *P*, 'Spray a peace sign on the Cenotaph.' (*A* also might be liable if her intention was to *assist P* by driving her to the location of the crime, but for present purposes we will assume the protestors used public transport to travel to the crime scene with each paying his or her own fare.)

A, *B* and *C* can be liable for standard complicity only if they do something extra to encourage the act of criminal damage such as authorise it to be done in furtherance of their lawful protest. Merely associating with *D* would not be an act capable of encouraging her to commit criminal damage. In the hypothetical, *A*, *B*, and *C* had full knowledge of the fact *D* was carrying aerosol paint and that *D* had used such paint to spray messages of protest on public monuments at past protests. While the joint enterprise remains lawful (that is, while it remains a lawful protest), under Virgo's association theory mere foresight and association are not enough to ground a conviction. There is no duty for a person to police her fellow citizens.[62]

Compare the above scenario with the scenario where the parties jointly engage in an unlawful joint enterprise. Let's assume the four protestors engage in a nude protest involving public copulation to protest against war

significance: she associates herself with the conduct of the other members of the group in a way that the mere aider or abettor, who remains an independent character throughout the episode, does not. Whereas aiding and abetting doctrines are grounded in S's contribution to another's crime, joint enterprise is grounded in affiliation.' Others also think it is fair to dispense with the intentional encouragement (conduct) constraint to allow secondary parties to be liable for any bad results that flow from a joint criminal enterprise that they have chosen to join, as long as they had foresight of *P*'s potential collateral crimes. Horder and Hughes assert: 'The normative rule could be expressed as "do not join in a criminal venture that may give rise to the commission by the participants of crimes connected to the venture".' See Jeremy Horder and David Hughes, 'Joint Criminal Ventures and Murder: The Prospects for Law Reform' (2009) 20 *King's L.J.* 379 at 398. Horder and Hughes fail to conceptualise the problem properly. There is a big difference between a person taking the *consequences* of her personal acts and in her taking the *autonomous culpable acts (crimes)* of another as her own.

61 *R. v. Cruise* [1970] 4 C.C.C. 338; *Savard v. R.* [1946] S.C.R. 20; cf. *Allen v. Ireland* [1984] 1 W.L.R. 903 at 910 *per* Kerr, L.J.

62 Baker, *op. cit. supra*, note 12 at Chapter 17. See also *Com. v. Rega* (2007) 593 Pa. 65; *Com. v. Kimbrough* (2005) 872 A.2d 1244.

and agree to commit acts of indecency contrary to section 66 of the *Sexual Offences Act 2003* and section 5 of the *Public Order Act 1986*. Let's also assume that from past experience they believe there is a possibility that *D* might commit an act of criminal damage during the course of their nude protest. They know that *D* has a can of aerosol paint with him and that on past occasions he has used this type of paint to write messages of protest on public monuments such as the Cenotaph. Under Virgo's association theory they would be liable for *D*'s collateral criminal damage, because their association was via an unlawful joint enterprise (a joint act of public indecency). In both cases, there has been no act of encouragement apropos the collateral crime of criminal damage.

C. The unlawfulness of the joint enterprise is evidentially valuable only

The *unlawfulness* of the underlying joint enterprise adds nothing. It is conceptually hollow. It is merely of evidential value.[63] It allows the jury to

63 See for example *Miller v. The Queen* (1980) 32 A.L.R. 321, where the High Court of Australia invoked common purpose complicity, even though there was no underlying criminal enterprise. In that case *A* drove *P* around so that he could pick up girls to have consensual sexual intercourse with them. There was nothing unlawful about this conduct. However, *A* knew that *P* had killed a girl on one occasion and would do so again were *P* to form the desire to kill. In ancient times an 'unlawful purpose' was used to support an evidential presumption of mutual intention apropos the collateral crime. As Hale put it: 'But if, when they had come to steal the deer, or throw down the enclosure, any had opposed them in it either by words or actual resistance, and A. had killed him, it had been murder in all the rest of the company, that came with the intent to do that unlawful act, though there were no express intention to kill any person in the first enterprise, because the law presumes they come to make good their design against all opposition.' Hale, *op. cit. supra*, note 47 at 444. 'This was in application of the presumption that a person intends the natural and probable consequences of acts intentionally done, and that an unlawful act implies an unlawful intent.' See *Agnew v. U.S.* (1897) 165 U.S. 36 at 50 *per* Fuller, C.J. *Per contra*, if people plan to participate in a lawful joint enterprise, they would have no reason for believing that there would be acts of opposition against their lawful conduct. This will not always be the case. Cf. *Beatty v. Gillbanks* [1882] 9 Q.B.D. 308; *Redmond-Bate v. D.P.P.* [2000] H.R.L.R. 249). No doubt Hale's reasoning was influenced by the use of unlawfulness in constructive liability. In ancient times, common purpose liability was glued to constructive liability. See Henry de Bracton, *De legibus et consuetudinibus Angliae* (London: Longman, 1879), Vol. II, at 277. (Consequently, it is easy to understand why Hale took the view that unlawfulness gave rise to a presumption of mutual intention with respect to any crimes of opposition. However, there was a move away from using this sort of crude presumption long before *Woolmington v. D.P.P.* [1935] A.C. 462 changed the law with respect to presumptions of guilt.) See *R. v. Franz* (1861) 2 F. & F. 580, where the case reporters, Foster and Finlason, expound that: 'Blackburn, J. held that the prisoner must either actively or passively have been a party, not only to the burglary, but to the personal injury, and did not put the case on the old doctrine laid down in Hale (vol. i. 439)'. Coupled with this, the 'opposition to unlawful enterprise' doctrine is not too helpful in cases where the collateral crime has no relation to opposition, such as where *P* rapes *V* during a robbery (*People v. Nguyen* (2003) 26 Cal. Rptr. 2d. 323; *R. v. Kalinowski* (1930) 31 S.R. (N.S.W.) 377 at 380 *per* Davidson, J.) or

draw inferences as to what might have been planned as a collateral crime and also to infer that the common purpose extended to the collateral crime. The jury could infer the same where the underlying joint enterprise is lawful. In the above scenarios, *A*, *B* and *C* are not liable for *D*'s independent act of criminal damage, because they did nothing extra to encourage *D*. To repeat the words of Megaw, L.J. 'It is not enough, then, that the presence of the accused has, *in fact, given encouragement*. It must be proved that the accused intended to give encouragement; that he wilfully encouraged.'[64]

Encouragement by implied or express authorisation of the collateral crime is the fulcrum for derivative liability when the joint enterprise is unlawful. Encouragement by authorisation also can apply when the enterprise is lawful, because there would be no bar to invoking the doctrine of standard complicity to ground a conviction. Let us change the facts of the abovementioned hypothetical. Suppose *A*, *B*, *C* and *D* attend a lawful protest. It is agreed by all four that should the media provide coverage of the protest, *D* should spray paint a peace sign on a public monument to draw more attention to their protest. While none of them know for sure whether the media will attend their protest, they all conditionally intend that *D* should commit an act of criminal damage should the media arrive.

Agreeing (tacitly or expressly) that *D* should spray paint a peace sign on a public monument if the media arrives is more than mere association and foresight; it is an act of (conditional) intentional encouragement. By authorising and consenting to *D* spray painting a peace sign on a public monument, *A*, *B*, and *C* provide *D* with encouragement. *D* knows he has the support of the group and that his acts are their acts in the sense that they authorise them for the purpose of making their joint protest more successful. The oddity of the example is that the underlying enterprise is lawful – they set out to protest in a lawful way. Nonetheless, there is no reason in principle why intentional encouragement by authorisation cannot be dealt with as a standard case of complicity. They intended to encourage their associate to break the law, should it be necessary to attract media attention for their joint cause. Liability is derivative because by their act

burglary (*Mumford v. State* (1974) 313 A.2d 563 at 566), or where *P* commits an act of criminal damage while attending a lawful protest. See also *Watkins v. State* (1999) 125 Md.App. 555 at 569–570 citing *R. v. Plummer* (1700) 84 E.R. 1103; and *Commonwealth v. Waters* (1980) 491 Pa. 85.

64 *R. v. Clarkson* [1971] 1 W.L.R. 1402 at 1406; *R. v. Coney* (1881–82) L.R. 8 Q.B.D. 534 *per* Denman, J., Huddleston, B., Manisty, Hawkins, Lopes, Stephen, Cave, and North, J.J. In *Hopewell v. State* (1998) 122 Md.App. 207 at 218–219, Thieme, J. said: '[The mere presence doctrine] has arguably been developed in order to protect a defendant from what is in common terms referred to as "guilt by association." That is, an individual should not be condemned merely because of the company he keeps and because he may have been at the wrong place at the wrong time.'

of encouragement by authorisation they make a remote factual contribution to the perpetrator's act of criminal damage. This is also the active ingredient in common purpose complicity where there is an unlawful joint enterprise.

The core flaw in the reckless association model is that people can be roped in even when they have not done anything to encourage the defendant, and even when they have done something to discourage her. Let's assume in both the unlawful joint enterprise and lawful joint enterprise scenarios given above, that *A*, *B*, and *C* have expressly instructed (in categorical terms) *D* that he must not commit criminal damage this time. Let us assume they have not only told him not to commit any acts of criminal damage, but have also told him that they will have nothing more do to with him if he lets them down and engages in such conduct. In the case of the lawful joint enterprise, Virgo would not deem the association to be sufficient to make the secondary parties liable, because there are no acts of assistance or encouragement. However, in the case of the unlawful joint enterprise, Virgo would invoke association and recklessness to ground a conviction.

Arguably, complicity liability cannot be made out in either the lawful enterprise scenario or the unlawful enterprise scenario, because derivative liability requires a culpability link and a conduct link. The culpability link is not made out in either case because *A*, *B*, and *C* do not intend to encourage *D* to commit the non-target crime (criminal damage). Nor have they done anything to intentionally encourage him to commit the non-target crime. On the contrary, they have threatened to have nothing more to do with him should he commit the non-target crime. The latter is an intentional act of discouragement, not one of encouragement.

D may very well gain great comfort from the fact that his friends are willing to go with him, but this alone cannot be enough to satisfy the concept of factual participation by encouragement. Their presence might be sufficient to embolden *D* to damage property to make his protest more apparent, but their presence alone is not an act of encouragement.[65] There has to be something more.[66] In the hypothetical, *A*, *B* and *C* failed to do an act capable of encouraging *D* to commit the non-target crime of criminal damage. Joining an unlawful enterprise in circumstances where it has been made clear that no one should commit any non-target crime cannot be an act of encouragement, simply because the parties to the enterprise foresaw there was a possibility that one of them might depart from what was agreed and authorised as a part of the joint enterprise. It is for this reason that the

65 *R. v. Coney* (1881–82) L.R. 8 Q.B.D. 534 *per* Denman, J., Huddleston, B., Manisty, Hawkins, Lopes, Stephen, Cave, and North, J.J. See also *R. v. Clarkson* [1971] 1 W.L.R. 1402 at 1406 where Megaw, L.J. said: 'It is not enough, then, that the presence of the accused has, in fact, given encouragement. It must be proved that the accused *intended to give encouragement*; that *he wilfully encouraged*' [emphasis added].

66 *R. v. Coney* (1881–82) L.R. 8 Q.B.D. 534.

ancient law was right to require that the common purpose extend to any collateral crimes.[67]

To impose complicity liability on the basis that *A* foresaw that there was a possibility that *P* might commit some *non-target* crime (non-target in that it has not been directly or conditionally agreed as a target crime) during the course of their joint enterprise, is to base liability on recklessness and a nanogram of unintentional influence. Unintentional encouragement ought not be enough. There are many innocent acts that a person can do that risk encouraging others to perpetrate a crime. Reckless encouragement should not be enough to make all parties equally liable as perpetrators under section 8 of the *Accessories and Abettors Act 1861. A fortiori* where the putative accessory has warned the perpetrator not to commit a crime that the accessory has foreseen the perpetrator might commit as a possible incident of the lawful or unlawful joint enterprise. The accessory's desire and express command that the perpetrator not commit a crime in these circumstances cannot be deemed to be an act of positive encouragement.[68]

D. Reckless association v. reckless encouragement

If there is no doctrinal difference between standard complicity and common purpose complicity, as Virgo accepts,[69] then the intentional encouragement/assistance requirement applies in both cases. It applies in both cases, because in both situations liability *derives* from *factual participation* – that is, from *D* making a remote (participation) contribution to *P*'s crime. Virgo[70] dispenses with the conduct requirement in the common purpose complicity cases, but at the same time argues that it is not doctrinally distinct from standard complicity. He takes the view that reckless association is sufficient for grounding liability in common purpose complicity cases, but not in standard complicity cases. The core problem with this argument is that mere association cannot be conceptualised as factual participation in the collateral crime. Bare association will not always be encouragement.

Derivative liability requires the accessory to have factually participated in the perpetrator's crime. If there is no factual participation, then liability is not derivative. The best interpretation that can be given to Virgo's theory is that the act of association is an act of reckless encouragement,

67 *The Three Soldiers Case* (1697) Fost. 353; *R. v. Plummer* (1706) Kelyng, J. 109; *R. v. Hawkins* (1828) 3 Car. & P. 392; *R. v. Collison* (1831) 4 Car. & P. 565; *R. v. Price* (1858) 8 Cox C.C. 96; *R. v. Skeet* (1866) 4 F. & F. 931; *R. v. Caton* (1874) 12 Cox C.C. 624; *R. v. Short* (1932) 23 Cr. App. R. 170 *per* Lord Chief Justice Hewart, MacKinnon and Hawke, J.J.; *R. v. Smith* [1963] 1 W.L.R. 1200 at 1205–1207; *R. v. Anderson* [1966] 2 Q.B. 110 at 118–119.

68 See *R. v. Jones* (1977) 65 Cr. App. R. 250 *per* Lawton, L.J.; *R. v. Allen* [1965] 1 Q.B. 130 *per* Edmund-Davies, J. (as he then was).

69 Virgo, *op. cit. supra*, note 11 at 860 *et seq.*

70 *Ibid.*

because *A* foresees the risk of this association encouraging *P* to perpetrate the collateral crime, but this sort of reckless[71] factual encouragement is best prosecuted as a new independent offence, which could be achieved by amending the *Serious Crime Act 2007*'s offences to cover reckless encouragement. The level of foresight involved in the cases given by Virgo would not be sufficient to satisfy the oblique intention requirement found in section 45 of the *Serious Crime Act 2007* (see Chapter 4). Section 50 of the *Serious Crime Act 2007* provides a defence for reasonable encouragement, which might protect lawful protestors who foresee there is a risk that they might be encouraging an associate to perpetrate a crime.

E. Factual participation: the conduct element in derivative liability

Where there is no factual encouragement it is difficult to justify liability on derivative principles. 'To be guilty of aiding and abetting is to be guilty as if one were a principal of the underlying offence. Aiding and abetting is not a separate crime but rather is linked to the underlying offence and shares the requisite intent of that offence.'[72] Nonetheless, the mental element for an accessory differs from that for a perpetrator, because what the accessory intends to do personally is to assist or encourage. Personally, the accessory does not intend to perpetrate the conditional-target crime; instead she intends that the conditional-target crime be perpetrated by another.[73] Centuries ago, Hawkins expounded:[74]

71 Section 45 seems to criminalise only oblique intentional assistance or encouragement.

72 *U.S. v. Roan Eagle* (1989) 867 F.2d 436 at 445. 'The mental state of one participant in a criminal enterprise will not be imputed to another. In criminal cases involving multiple participants, with the potential for each to have a differing state of mind, the liability of each participant for any ensuing crime is dependent upon his or her own state of mind, and not upon that of anyone else. Thus, although an aider and abettor shares the guilt of the actual perpetrator, the mental state necessary for conviction as an aider and abettor is different from the mental state necessary for conviction as the actual perpetrator; the actual perpetrator must have whatever mental state is required for each crime charged, while the aider and abettor must act with knowledge of the perpetrator's criminal purpose and with an intent or purpose either to commit, or to encourage or facilitate commission of, the offence. The jury must find the intent to encourage and bring about conduct that is criminal, not the specific intent that is an element of the target offence.' See (2013) 21 Am. Jur. 2d Criminal Law § 176. See also *R. v. Jeffrey* [2003] 2 Qd. R. 306 at 310–311 *per* McPherson, J.A. Kirby, J. seems to overlook this distinction in *Clayton v. The Queen* (2006) 168 A. Crim. R. 174 at 216–217, when he insists on equal fault for equal blame. Fault will never be entirely equal, since a person who is willing to perpetrate a hideous crime such as murder is morally more evil (even if only slightly so) than one who is only willing to assist or encourage murder. See *United States v. Church* (1989) 29 M.J. 679.

73 The accessory is deemed to have intended to perpetrate the crime herself on the basis that she intended the perpetrator to perpetrate it. It is never a question of whether the accessory intended to kill (or cause GBH to) *V* herself, but merely whether she intended the perpetrator to kill *V*. Cf. Glanville Williams, *Criminal Law: The General Part* (London: Stevens & Sons, 2nd edn 1961) at 404.

74 William Hawkins, *A Treatise of the Pleas of the Crown* (London: Printed by E and R Nutt *et al.*, 1734), Vol. I, Chap. 29, Sect. 10. Hawkins asserts that partaking or participation involves:

Also those who by accident are barely present when a felony is committed, and *are merely passive*, and *neither any way encourage it* . . . shall neither be adjudged principals nor accessories . . . And if they any way showed an *assent* to the felony, it seems that they may be punished as principals in it; because the *showing such an assent* could not but give encouragement to it' [emphasis added].

Similarly, in *The Queen v Coney*,[75] Hawkins, J. said:

In my opinion, to constitute an aider and abettor some active steps must be taken by word, or action, with the intent to instigate the principal, or principals. Encouragement does not of necessity amount to aiding and abetting, it may be intentional or unintentional, a man may unwittingly encourage another in fact by his presence, by misinterpreted words, or gestures, or by his silence, or non-interference, or he may encourage intentionally by expressions, gestures, or actions intended to signify approval. In the latter case he aids and abets, in the former he does not.

More significantly, section 8 of the *Accessories and Abettors Act 1861* requires actual participation: Section 8 provides:

Whosoever shall aid, abet, counsel, or procure the commission of any indictable offence, whether the same be an offence at common law or by virtue of any Act passed or to be passed, shall be liable to be tried, indicted, and punished as a principal offender.

Section 8 does not include mere association as a form of participation. It requires participatory conduct involving aiding, abetting, counselling or procuring. The illogicality of attempting to ground derivative liability on non-participation, association and foresight is superlatively exemplified

hiring, commanding, conspiring, and showing 'an express liking, approbation, or assent to another's felonious design.' *Id.* at Sect. 16. Dalton wrote that accessories before the fact are 'such as command, hire, procure, move, conspire, counsel, abet, incourage or set on, or consent to commit any' crime. Michael Dalton, *The Country Justice* (London: Printed by William Rawlins *et al.*, 1697) at 396. Hale took the view that the accessory was the person who procured, counselled, commanded or abetted. Hale, *op. cit. supra*, note 47 at 615. None of the institutional writers used mere association to justify complicity liability!

75 (1881–82) L.R. 8 Q.B.D. 534 at 557. Cave, J. (at 539) said: 'Now it is a general rule in the case of principals in the second degree that there must be participation in the act, and that, although a man is present whilst a felony is being committed, if he takes no part in it, and does not act in concert with those who commit it, he will not be a principal in the second degree merely because he does not endeavour to prevent the felony, or apprehend the felon.' Foster was of the view that association and presence would be nothing more than evidence to be considered with all the other evidence to establish concurrence and consent. Foster, *op. cit. supra*, note 50 at 350. See also *R. v. Vanderstein* (1865) 10 Cox C.C. 177.

by the decision of *R. v. Willett.*[76] In that case, *A* was a passenger in a car driven by his brother, *P*. Both were seeking to escape from a car park where they had been attempting to steal from *V*'s van. *V* tried to prevent their escape from the car park by standing in its only exit. *P* killed *V* by driving over him and thus was convicted of murder. The issue in that case was whether there was any factual encouragement. It was held that the conduct element for complicity was not made out because there was no factual encouragement.

The issue was whether the accessory by his mere presence in the car had participated in the collateral murder that had been perpetrated in pursuance of their escape from the scene of the attempted theft. Moses, L.J. found on the evidence that 'the circumstances of the escape demonstrated that there can have been no advance plan to injure, let alone kill, anyone during the course of the theft. True it was part of the plan to escape but it does not follow that it was part of the plan to cause anyone injury.'[77] It was found that the evidence of mere presence did not support a finding that *A* had foreseen and authorised his brother to drive over a person to effect their escape. More importantly, it was held that without evidence demonstrating that *A* had encouraged *P* to drive the car at *V* in order to escape, complicity liability could not be established.[78] The Court of Appeal, in effect, held that foresight and association without factual encouragement was not enough to establish complicity liability. It was held that *A* continuing to sit in the passenger seat of the car was not an act of positive encouragement. Nor did it matter that *A* had a chance to try to persuade his brother not to run over *V*.[79]

There was other evidence that suggested that although *A* did not foresee the murder as an incident of the joint theft, he encouraged *P* after he realised *P* was intending to run over *V* for the purpose of making their escape succeed. On these facts, the case was one of encouragement *simpliciter*, rather than encouragement via advance authorisation of a conditional collateral crime. Witness testimony suggested that *A* did not authorise *P*'s offending in advance, because neither party anticipated such offending would be necessary to effect their joint theft, but on the evidence it was inferable that *A* told *P* to run over *V* when *V* blocked their escape.

76 [2010] EWCA Crim. 1620.

77 *R. v. Willett* [2010] E.W.C.A. Crim. 1620 at para. 14. At para. 18 is was said: 'It is difficult to see that merely continuing to sit in the passenger seat of the Mondeo amounted to any encouragement to the driver to run over Mr. Matharu. Events happened fast. There was an opportunity, at the last minute, we suppose, for the appellant to get out of the vehicle and remonstrate with Mr. Matharu. But his failure to do so cannot, we think, be said to be an encouragement to the driver to run him over. The speed and turn of events makes such a suggestion unrealistic.'

78 *R. v. Willett* [2010] E.W.C.A. Crim. 1620 at para. 16.

79 See *R. v. Willett* [2010] E.W.C.A. Crim. 1620 at paras. 17–31.

The common purpose doctrine would not be needed to obtain a conviction on such facts.[80] Such a case is best dealt with as standard complicity, because the encouragement is direct.

F. Advanced encouragement implied from conduct of joining enterprise

There is no need to show that a party to an unlawful joint enterprise encouraged the perpetrator at the scene of the crime. Normally, there will be no encouragement at that stage. The encouragement is implied from what was agreed (either tacitly or expressly) in advance. If *A* and *P* have agreed that *P* should use a gun to effect their escape should they be confronted by a security guard during the course of a robbery, *A*'s *authorisation* of *P* using the gun is an act of *encouragement.* Both parties must have foresight of the possible collateral crimes to be able to form a mutual conditional intention that those crimes be committed (if the need arises) for the purpose of effecting their joint enterprise. Normally the accessory will deny that there was a mutual conditional intention that the perpetrator commit the collateral crime. When there is a denial there has to be sufficient evidence for the jury to draw reasonable inferences. The jury will have to start by considering (1) whether the accessory contemplated that such a crime might be committed to effect the joint enterprise; and (2) whether the accessory had full advance knowledge of the collateral crimes that might have to be committed to effect the joint enterprise. If the evidence shows that the accessory not only contemplated the potential collateral crimes, but also knew that the perpetrator conditionally intended to perpetrate them, then a jury could infer that the accessory joined the unlawful enterprise conditionally intending to encourage the perpetrator to perpetrate the conditional-target crime.

There need be no express agreement, because a mutual conditional intention can be implied from the conduct of the participants.[81] It does not matter that the accessory to the unlawful joint enterprise really hoped that the need to commit the conditional-target crime would not arise, because the jury can infer that the accessory knew what was conditionally intended

80 See *R. v. Willett* [2010] E.W.C.A. Crim. 1620 at paras. 17–31.

81 *R. v. Johns* [1978] 1 N.S.W.L.R. 282 *per* Street, C.J., Begg and Lusher, J.J. 'The existence of an "intention in common" can be inferred from the actions of the accused and the other parties. As the Supreme Court of Canada observed in *R. v. Suchan* (1952), 104 C.C.C. 193 (S.C.C.): 'Common intention is seldom expressed and rarely reduced to writing and must, therefore, in general, be found from conduct of the parties. That which takes place at the scene of the offence is material, but also relevant is the conduct of the parties leading up to and subsequent thereto.' *R. v. M* [2011] M.J. No. 107 at para. 9 *per* Stewart, Prov. J. See also *R. v. Woodcock* (2008) 2008 O.N.C.J. 123 at para. 322 *per* Lipson, J.; *R. v. Briscoe* [2012] 100 W.C.B. (2d) 810at para. 442 *per* Yamauchi, J.

and authorised it.[82] 'The ascertainment of a common purpose is generally a matter of inference from the circumstances.'[83] If a person participates in a robbery *knowing* that her accomplice intends to use lethal force should it be needed to make the robbery succeed, this would be sufficient for the jury to infer that she authorised such force being used and also conditionally intended that it be used.

Common purpose complicity is often a consummated conspiracy, but there is no need to establish an agreement with respect to the collateral crime.[84] Learned Hand, J. said: 'Once some kind of criminal *concert*[85] is established, all parties are liable for everything anyone of the original participants does.'[86] The parties have a common purpose, they breathe together.[87] If the accessory and perpetrator conditionally and mutually intend that the perpetrator perpetrate the anticipated collateral crime, should the need for it to be perpetrated arise, then that is effectively an agreement.[88] The foresight of possibility formula is merely a maxim: it holds that evidence of foresight can be used for inferring conditional intention. From *A*'s knowledge and all the

82 *R. v. Penfold* (1980) 71 Cr. App. R. 4 at 8 *per* Shaw, L.J.
83 Williams, *op. cit. supra,* note 73 at 399.
84 As far as complicity and common purpose are concerned, there are common elements such as encouragement by implied agreement (authorisation – i.e. a common plan about how they will deal with contingencies such as being confronted by a security guard during the course of a robbery and so on) and intent can be inferred from knowledge: cf. *R. v. Saik* [2007] 1 A.C. 18; *R. v. Churchill (No. 2)* [1967] 2 A.C. 224 at 236; *D.P.P. for Northern Ireland v Maxwell* [1978] 1 W.L.R. 1350. The overlap has led to many jurisdictions in the United States combining complicity and conspiracy offences. See for example the provisions discussed by John F. Decker, 'The Mental State Requirement for Accomplice Liability in American Criminal Law' (2009) 60 *S.C.L. Rev.* 237 at 260–261. However, complicity will not necessarily involve a conspiracy. See *R. v. Kupferberg* (1919) 13 Cr. App. R. 166.
85 'Concert' means 'by mutual agreement': it is a term frequently used in the old authorities on common purpose complicity. In *Osland v. The Queen* (1998) 197 C.L.R. 316 at 343, McHugh, J. said: '[E]ven if only one participant performed the acts constituting the crime, each will be guilty as principals in the first degree if the acts were performed in the presence of all and pursuant to a preconceived plan. In this case, the parties are said to be acting in concert.' See also *R. v. Collison* (1831) 4 Car. & P. 565 where Garrow B. held that there had to be *prior concert* between the perpetrator and accessory with respect to any collateral crime. *R. v. Bolster* (1910) 3 Cr. App. R. 81; *R. v. Warner* (1833) 5 Car. & P. 525 at 529; *R. v. Bingley* (1821) Russ. & Ry. 446; *Williams v. State* (1887) 9 Crim. L. Mag. & Rep. 480 at 482.
86 *U.S. v. Peoni* (1938) 100 F.2d 401 at 403.
87 The word 'conspire' comes from two Latin words, *con* and *spirare,* which translate as 'to breathe together'. The old conspiracy writs referred to principals and accessories: see Anthony FitzHerbert, *La Novelle Natura Brevium* (London: Printed by George Sawbridge *et al.*, 1677) at 262. See also *R. v. Plummer* [1902] 2 K.B. 339 at 348.
88 It is doubtful that such remote and passive encouragement would have any causal impact on *P*'s autonomous choice to perpetrate the collateral crime. *A*'s influence must not only influence *P*'s decision, but must also be aimed at influencing *P*'s decision. In *R. v. Kennedy (No. 2)* [2008] 1 A.C. 269 at 275, Lord Bingham said: 'Thus *D* is not to be treated as causing *V* to act in a certain way if *V* makes a voluntary and informed decision to act in that way rather than another.' Cf. *R. v. Fretwell* (1862) Le. & Ca. 161.

other evidence, the jury is able to infer that *A* authorised and conditionally intended *P* to perpetrate the conditional-target crime.[89]

The jury can infer conditional intention where the evidence shows there was 'a precedent common purpose (agreement) to carry out the object (the conditional-target crime), if necessary'.[90] If it cannot be established that the accessory agreed, at least tacitly, to the conditional-target crime being perpetrated for the purpose of effecting the joint enterprise, then the fault element is not made out. Coupled with that, where there is no agreement there is no encouragement by authorisation, which is needed to satisfy the conduct requirement for complicity liability.[91]

If there is no evidence of an express agreement, then tacit agreement should not be presumed. There needs to be strong evidence to demonstrate that the accomplice tacitly authorised the perpetrator to commit the collateral crime. In most cases the collateral crime(s) will be planned and will have been discussed in advance. The defendant might deny that there was mutual conditional intention apropos the collateral crime, but the circumstantial evidence will normally be sufficient for the jury to determine one way or the other whether the accessory (conditionally) intended the perpetrator to commit the collateral crime. For example, if *A* and *P* have done several burglaries in the past and *P* has killed or caused serious injury in the past to effect one of their burglaries, this would provide clear evidence of a tacit agreement that lethal force was to be used if needed.[92] Similarly, if the accessory knows that the perpetrator is armed with a lethal weapon, has a bad temper, has been in prison before and will do anything to avoid going back to prison, then the jury could infer that the accessory knew that the perpetrator conditionally intended to use lethal force and intended to encourage it by joining the underlying joint enterprise.

89 See for example, *U.S. v. Ramos-Rascon* (1993) 8 F.3d 704 at 711 where it was held: '[M]ere participation in a criminal venture is not enough to constitute aiding and abetting; the government must also show that the defendant intentionally assisted in the joint venture's illegal purpose.' The United States Court of Appeals (Ninth Circuit) held that intentional assistance could not be inferred, because the 'evidence was insufficient to show that the defendants, who followed a truck containing cocaine to a hotel where the transaction was to take place, were guilty of possession with intent to distribute narcotics based on aiding and abetting theory, since the government presented no evidence that the defendants knew that transaction was taking place or that either defendant knew there was an illegal venture to aid and abet.' See also *Trial of Lord Mohun* (1692) Holt K.B. 479 at 479–480; *Mumford v. State* (1974) 313 A.2d 563 at 566.

90 *R. v. Skeet* (1866) 4 F. & F. 931 at 933 citing *R. v. Howell* (1839) 9 Car. & P. 437 at 450.

91 On remote harms, see Baker, *supra loc. cit.* note 58. It was for this reason that Williams asserted: 'I would say that in influencing the perpetrator he must act purposely.' See Glanville Williams, 'Complicity, Purpose and the Draft Code: Part 2' [1990] *Crim. L.R.* 98 at 99.

92 See for example, *Millar v. The Queen* (1980) 32 A.L.R. 321 at 326, where the accessory had full knowledge of the fact that the perpetrator had murdered a woman on an earlier occasion.

G. The degree of encouragement needed for establishing the conduct element

Factual encouragement involves an act or omission that persuades the perpetrator to act. It need not be the perpetrator's sole motivation for committing the collateral crime, but it must be a sufficient motivator to be conceptualised as positive encouragement for the purposes of establishing that *A* made a remote factual contribution to *P*'s crime. It must not only be capable of encouraging, but should also play on the perpetrator's mind when she commits the crime. It should be demonstrated that it in fact provided the perpetrator with a reason or motivation for committing the crime.[93]

Whether or not the encouragement was one of the reasons why *P* chose to perpetrate the collateral crime is a question of fact to be inferred from all the evidence. In common purpose cases where it is established that the accomplice authorised (tacitly or expressly) the perpetrator to commit the conditional-target crime (e.g. the killing of a security guard) for the purpose of effecting their joint enterprise (e.g. a bank robbery), the jury will be able to infer that the accomplice's authorisation of and assent to the criminal plan did in fact encourage the perpetrator, even if it was not the perpetrator's sole motivation for offending. Under the *Serious Crime Act 2007,* the act of encouragement need not be the perpetrator's sole motivation for perpetrating the anticipated target offence, but the jury needs to be able to infer that the act of encouragement was capable of motivating the perpetrator.[94]

IV. The doctrinal history: inferring conditional intention

A. Foresight is evidence of conditional intention

In the first section, I argued that there must be intentional encouragement for common purpose complicity to be made out. In this section,

93 *R. v. Clarkson* [1971] 1 W.L.R. 1402 *per* Megaw L.J. (Geoffrey Lane and Kilner Brown J.J. concurring); *R. v. Jones* (1977) 65 Cr. App. R. 250 at 252. In *Hutt v. R.* [1989] T.A.S.S.C. 27 at paragraph 53, Cox, J. (Underwood, Crawford, J.J. concurring) said: 'In the circumstances of this case an error of law occurred by reason of the omission to tell the jury that . . . there had to be proof to the requisite degree that the principal offender was in fact encouraged by the conduct of the accused to commit the crime.'

94 *State v. King* (1898) 104 Iowa, 727. In *R. v. Mendez* [2011] Q.B. 876 at 882–883, Toulson, L.J. said: 'At its most basic level, secondary liability is founded on a principle of causation, that a defendant (*D*) is liable for an offence committed by a principal actor (*P*) if by his conduct he has caused or materially contributed to the commission of the offence (with the requisite mental element); and a person who knowingly assists or encourages another to commit an offence is taken to have contributed to its commission.' See the discussion in Chapter 4 of this book. See also Williams, *op. cit. supra,* note 73 at 381–382; Joshua Dressler, 'Reassessing The Theoretical Underpinnings of Accomplice Liability: New Solutions to an Old Problem' (1985) 37 *Hastings L.J.* 91 at 131–134. Where there is no factual influence and *P* acts for her own reasons, *P* cannot be liable for encouraging *P* to offend, because there is no factual participation. Cf. *R. v. Calhaem* [1985] Q.B. 808; *R. v. Young* (1838) 8 Car. & P. 644.

I shall try to demonstrate that the authorities ancient and modern support this interpretation of the law. The *foresight of possibility* maxim proposed by the High Court of Australia in *Johns v The Queen*[95] was not proposed as a substantive fault doctrine for complicity liability, but as an evidential maxim. The judges made it clear that they were referring to the standard as an evidentiary maxim, not as a substantive fault element for establishing complicity liability.

In *Johns v. The Queen*,[96] it was held that the maxim could be used to direct a jury that from *A*'s foresight it could infer that *A* conditionally intended the collateral crimes that resulted from the unlawful joint enterprise. In other words, it can infer that *A* intended *P* to perpetrate the collateral crime, if it can be demonstrated that *A* knew that certain conditions might arise that would make the collateral crime necessary and that under those conditions her accomplice intended to perpetrate the collateral crime. Mason, Murphy and Wilson, J.J. said:

> Suppose a plan made by *A*, the principal offender, and *B*, the accessory before the fact, to rob premises, according to which *A* is to carry out the robbery. It is agreed that *A* will carry a loaded revolver and use it to overcome resistance in the unlikely event that the premises are attended, previous surveillance having established that the premises are invariably unattended at the time when the robbery is to be carried out. As it happens, a security officer is in attendance when *A* enters the premises and is shot by *A*. It would make nonsense to say that *B* is not guilty merely because it was an unlikely or improbable contingency that the premises would be attended at the time of the robbery, when we know that *B* assented to the shooting in the event that occurred . . . In the present case there was ample evidence from which the jury could infer that the applicant gave his assent to a criminal enterprise which involved the use, that is the discharge, of a loaded gun, in the event that Morriss resisted or sought to summon assistance.

95 [1980] 143 C.L.R. 108.

96 [1980] 143 C.L.R. 108 at 131–132 *per* (the majority) Mason, Murphy, and Wilson, J.J. See also *R. v. Johns* [1978] 1 N.S.W.L.R. 282. The same approach had been taken in all the Australian cases that preceded the High Court of Australia's decision in *Johns v. The Queen*; however, those earlier cases were much clearer on the point. See *R. v. Dunn* (1930) 30 S.R. (N.S.W.) 210 at 214 *per* Ferguson, J. (Street, C.J. concurred in a separate judgment) (James, J. also concurred.) {The Chief Justice Street in *R. v. Dunn* was the grandfather of the Chief Justice Street in *R. v. Johns* – three generations of Streets sat on the Supreme Court of N.S.W.}; *R. v. Dorrey & Gage* [1970] 3 N.S.W.L.R. 351 at 353; *R. v. Adams* (1932) V.L.R. 222 at 223–224 *per* Mann, J.; *R. v. Kalinowski* (1930) 31 S.R. (N.S.W.) 377 at 380–381 *per* Davidson, J.; *R. v. Dowdle* (1901) 26 V.L.R. 637 at 639–641 *per* Williams, J.; *R. v. Surridge* (1942) 42 S.R. (N.S.W.) 278 at 282–283 *per* Jordan, C.J.; *R. v. Grand* (1903) 3 S.R. (N.S.W.) 216 *per* Stephen, A.C.J., Owen and Simpson, J.J.

The High Court of Australia held that if the accomplice has tacitly or expressly authorised (agreed) *P*'s conditional-target crime for the purpose of effecting the unlawful joint enterprise (or to it being a part of the joint enterprise), it is no defence for her to assert that it was only probable that the collateral offence would be necessary for the purpose of effecting their joint enterprise. There was no dispensation with the fundamental requirement of factual encouragement by intentional authorisation. Mason, Murphy and Wilson, J.J. held that the accessory would be liable only if the collateral crime 'was contemplated as a possibility by the parties *in arriving at* their common purpose or design'.[97] Note the words 'in arriving at', because those words make it clear that the judges had nothing more than conditional intention in mind. The judges were asserting that the parties to the unlawful joint enterprise would have to contemplate any conditional crimes and authorise them when arriving at their common purpose, before defendants could be liable as accessories. If the possible collateral crimes have not been contemplated, then how can a jury infer that they were encouraged as a part of the common purpose of *A* and *P*? If *P* does not receive a message of authorisation from *A*, then how does *A* in fact encourage *P* to perpetrate the conditional collateral crime? What was contemplated forms a part of the wider enquiry in complicity, because the perpetrator's collateral crime is contingent on future events.

In *R. v. Smith*,[98] Slade, J. also recognises that the 'contemplation' or 'foresight' maxim is a rule for inferring conditional intention. Conditional intention can be implied from *A*'s own actions in relation to the collateral crime. Slade, J. said:

> The term 'agreement', 'confederacy', 'acting in concert', and 'conspiracy' all pre-suppose an agreement express or by implication to achieve a common purpose, and so long as the act done is within the ambit of that common purpose anyone who takes part in it, if it is an unlawful killing, is guilty of manslaughter. That does not mean that one cannot hypothesise a case in which there is an act which is wholly outside the scope of the agreement, in which case no doubt different considerations might apply . . . It must have been clearly within the contemplation of a man like Smith who, to use one expression, had almost gone berserk himself to have left the public-house only to get bricks to tear up the joint, that if the bar tender did his duty to quell the disturbance and picked up the night stick, anyone whom he knew had a knife in his possession, like Atkinson, might use it on the barman, as Atkinson did.

97 *Johns v. The Queen* [1980] 143 C.L.R. 108 at 125; *R. v. Kirkness* [1990] 3 S.C.R. 74, where the Supreme Court of Canada held that where there was only a common intention to break and enter, there was no liability for conduct beyond common intention.

98 [1963] 1 W.L.R. 1200 at 1205–1207.

> By no stretch of imagination, in the opinion of this court, can that be said to be outside the scope of the concerted action in this case. In a case of this kind it is difficult to imagine what would have been outside the scope of the concerted action, possibly the use of a loaded revolver, the presence of which was unknown to the other parties; but that is not this case, and I am expressing no opinion about that. *The court is satisfied that anything which is within the ambit of the concerted arrangement is the responsibility of each party who chooses to enter into the criminal purpose* [emphasis added].

In *R. v. Dunn*,[99] in the Supreme Court of New South Wales, Ferguson, J., drawing on a line of old poaching cases, said:

> [W]hen one person commits an offence the fact that he is at the time in company with another person is not enough to justify an inference that the offence was committed in pursuance of a common intent. Even if, at the time when the offence was committed, they are engaged in the joint commission of another offence, that of itself is not enough to prove common intent to commit the offence in question . . . That, I think, is the effect of the poaching cases. But when it is clear that there is a joint purpose of committing an offence, while the commission of it is to be the act of one only, in that case all those who share in the common purpose are guilty of the act done by his hand.

It needs to be proved that the accessory and the perpetrator had a mutual (conditional) intention with respect to the possible collateral crimes.[100] It has been the failure of the courts in the last couple of decades to conceptualise the problem as one of conditional intention that has led them to reduce the requirement of *intentional encouragement of the collateral crime* to one of *mere reckless foresight of the collateral crime.* This has caused gross

99 (1930) 30 S.R. (N.S.W.) 210 at 214 (Street, C.J. concurred in a separate judgment) (James, J. also concurred). The leading modern poaching case is *R. v. Pearce* (1930) 21 Cr App. R. 79. See also *Au Keng and Wong Wai Hung v. The Crown* (1954) 38 H.K.L.R. 142 at 159 *per* Gould, J. (Reece, J. concurring); Cf. the recent decision of the Supreme Court of Western Australia in *Sweeney v. Western Australia* [2006] W.A.S.C.A. 118 at paragraph 183, where Roberts-Smith, J.A. (Pullin, Buss, J.J.A.A. concurring) held 'a person charged as doing an act for the purpose of aiding, or aiding the commission of an offence, is not liable for anything other than what they expressly agreed to,' or conditionally intended. See also *Borg v. The Queen* [1972] W.A.R. 194 at 197 *per* Jackson, J.

100 The Court of Appeal also endorsed this approach in *R. v. Dunbar* [1988] Crim. L.R. 693, where was held: 'The jury's verdict meant that D did not contemplate the use of violence involving killing or grievous bodily harm. Accordingly, *X* or *Y* or both must have gone beyond the scope of *D*'s design and she could not be guilty of manslaughter.' Likewise, in *R. v. Gamble* [1989] N.I. 268, Carswell, J. said the question is whether collateral crimes 'go beyond the contemplation of the accessories *and* the authority given by them.'

injustices, because many of the common purpose cases involve specific intent crimes such as murder. Most of the errors in the modern cases stem from judges being bamboozled by Sir Robin Cooke's paradoxical statements in *Chan Wing-Siu v. The Queen.*[101] In that case, Sir Robin Cooke seemed to struggle to conceptualise the problem as one of conditional intention. Sir Robin Cooke's judgment is a labyrinth of statements concerning evidential maxims and rules of substantive law. His Honour seems to conflate the evidential maxim of foresight of possibility (i.e. *A*'s foresight of the possible collateral crimes that *P* might have to perpetrate to effect the joint enterprise) with the substantive rule of common purpose complicity liability (i.e. *A* must intentionally encourage, tacitly or expressly, the conditional collateral crimes.)

Sir Robin Cooke left some readers of his judgment uncertain as to whether he was proposing a substantive rule of complicity liability or an evidentiary maxim. His Honour seems to hold that encouragement by authorisation is a substantive requirement for the purposes of establishing common purpose complicity, but also seems to state the opposite. Nevertheless, careful analysis shows that Sir Robin Cooke, ultimately, not only insisted on authorisation, but also viewed the problem as one of conditional intention. In *Chan Wing-Siu v. The Queen*, Sir Robin Cooke said:[102]

> [T]aking the risk should not make that accused a party to such a crime of intention as murder or wounding with intent to cause grievous bodily harm. The judge is entitled to warn the jury to be cautious before reaching that conclusion; but the law can do no more by way of definition; it can only be for the jury to determine any issue of that kind on the facts of the particular case.

It is fairly clear that Sir Robin Cooke was trying to lay down a formula for inferring conditional intention with respect to collateral crimes committed during the course of an unlawful joint enterprise. The learned judge proposes foresight of possibility and alternatively foresight of a substantial risk as possible tests, but concludes 'no one formula is exclusively preferable; indeed it may be advantageous in a summing up to use more than one.'[103] Sir Robin Cooke was not proposing that intention and recklessness

101 [1985] A.C. 168 at 177.

102 [1985] A.C. 168 at 177.

103 *Chan Wing-Siu v. The Queen* [1985] A.C. 168 at 179. In *R. v. Britten* (1988) 40 S.A.S.R. 47 at 53 King, C.J. said: '[I]n many cases the proper basis of criminal liability in such circumstances would not be adequately explained by use of the *Chan Wing-Siu* formula.' In *Clayton v. The Queen* (2006) 168 A. Crim. R. 174 at 208 Kirby J. said: 'On the other hand, both in the New Zealand and Privy Council decisions (unsurprising because of the common author, Sir Robin Cooke) a series of formulae, expressed otherwise than in terms of "possibility", are advanced, including "substantial risk", "real risk", and "a risk

are alternative fault elements for complicity; rather he had maxims of evidence in mind.[104] The authorities Sir Robin Cooke cites require express or tacit encouragement by intentional authorisation. The learned judge does not suggest that the substantive law of complicity no longer requires factual (participation) encouragement – that is, remote factual contributions from the putative accessory.[105]

Sir Robin Cooke was not trying to abrogate the fundamental encouragement by authorisation requirement found in a long line of English authorities.[106] Sir Robin Cooke said: 'It turns on contemplation or, putting the same idea in other words, authorisation, which may be express but is more usually implied.'[107] This sentence would make more sense if it simply read: *It turns on encouragement by authorisation, which may be express but is more usually implied.* The learned judge created a source of confusion by stating: 'The criminal culpability lies in participating in the venture with that foresight.'[108] This suggests that foresight is a substantive fault requirement, rather than mere evidence for inferring conditional intention. Later courts have read too much into Sir Robin Cooke's terse statements, because the judges involved failed to examine the authorities predating *Chan Wing-Siu v. The Queen.*

The loose paradoxical statements found in *Chan Wing-Siu v. The Queen* are a consequence of Sir Robin Cooke being led astray by the *then* recent decision of the High Court of Australia in *Johns v. The Queen.*[109] In *Johns v. The Queen* the foresight maxim was invoked only because counsel for the appellant framed their defence as one where the defendant should not be liable unless the conditionally intended collateral crime was foreseen as a *probable* necessity for effecting the joint enterprise.[110] It is not clear why it

that something might well happen", revealing a degree of ambivalence in the foregoing authority about the test to be applied.' Sir Robin Cooke was clearly influenced by the confused discussion in McMullin V.P.'s judgment in the Hong Kong Court of Appeal in *Chan Wing-Siu* [1982] H.K.L.R. 280.

104 In *Chan Wing-Siu v. The Queen* [1985] A.C. 168 at 177, Sir Robin Cooke cites *Davies v. Director of Public Prosecutions* [1954] A.C. 378 at 401 *per* Lord Simonds L.C.

105 The words 'foresight of possibility' do not appear in any of the leading authorities of the modern period. See *R. v. Smith* [1963] 1 W.L.R. 1200; *R. v. Betty* (1964) 48 Cr. App. R. 6; *R. v. Anderson* [1966] 2 Q.B. 110.

106 See *R. v. Britten* (1988) 40 S.A.S.R. 47 at 53 *per* King, C.J.

107 *Chan Wing-Siu v. The Queen* [1985] A.C. 168 at 175.

108 *Chan Wing-Siu v. The Queen* [1985] A.C. 168 at 175.

109 (1980) 143 C.L.R. 108.

110 The leading case in Australia before *Johns v. The Queen* 1980) 143 C.L.R. 108 was *Brennan v. The King* (1936) 55 C.L.R. 153. The 1936 decision was a decision dealing with section 8 of the *Criminal Code of Western Australia*, which has a negligence (substantive) fault element. In that jurisdiction, a person is held liable for any collateral crime that was a natural *probable* consequence of the joint enterprise, regardless of intention and encouragement. It is a statutory offence that criminalises negligent encouragement. In many of these cases, there will be no factual encouragement because negligent participation

mattered whether the parties contemplated that it was probable that they might have to use lethal force to make their robbery succeed, rather than possible, if the parties agreed that it should be used should the need for it to be used arise. *A* and *P* might contemplate that there is only a 10 per cent chance that a security guard will be present on the night when they intend to burglarise a jewellery store, but if they mutually and conditionally intend that *P* should kill the guard should one be present on the night in question, then it hardly matters that there was only a 10 per cent chance that *P* would have to perpetrate the collateral crime (murder the guard).

The majority in *Johns v. The Queen* held that an accessory should be liable only for collateral crimes that fell within the parties' common purpose. Stephen, J. said accessorial liability applies where *A* 'knows what is contemplated, and both approves of it and in some way encourages it'.[111] The conditional crime 'is one which falls within the parties' own purpose and design precisely because it is within their contemplation and is foreseen as a possible [requirement] of the execution of their planned enterprise'.[112] Mason, Murphy and Wilson, J.J. said: 'A person is an accomplice in the crime charged if he took part in its commission, and was *privy* to the criminal intent of the thing done.'[113] Furthermore, it was said:[114]

> [I]f the collateral crime is a probable consequence of the execution of the common purpose, there is evidence from which the jury can conclude that it was within the parties' conditional intentions . . . The jury could therefore conclude that the common purpose involved resorting to the violence of this kind, should the occasion arise, and that the violence conditionally intended and authorised amounted to grievous bodily harm or homicide.

The above passage strongly supports the arguments that have been presented throughout the earlier parts of this chapter. Sir Robin Cooke held that 'the contingency in which the crime is committed need not itself be

in the underlying joint enterprise might not be sufficient to send any sort of message of encouragement to the perpetrator, so liability hinges on negligent association only. Under these offences, even if *P* is not encouraged by *A*'s acts, *A* will be liable if a reasonable person would have realised that *P* might perpetrate the collateral crime as a result of the joint enterprise: *a fortiori* if a reasonable person would have realised that *P* might be encouraged to perpetrate the collateral crime. If the negligent factual participation requirement is removed, then the offence becomes one of negligent attempted encouragement and thus is not a form of derivative liability.

111 *Johns v. The Queen* [1980] 143 C.L.R. 108 at 118.

112 *Johns v. The Queen* [1980] 143 C.L.R. 108 at 131 *per* Mason, Murphy and Wilson, J.J.

113 *Johns v. The Queen* [1980] 143 C.L.R. 108 at 130 *per* Mason, Murphy and Wilson, J.J. citing *R. v. Surridge* (1942) 42 S.R. (N.S.W.) 278 at 282 *per* Jordan C.J. and also *R. v. Cramp* (1880) 14 Cox C.C. 390 at 393 *per* Denman J.

114 *Johns v. The Queen* [1980] 143 C.L.R. 108 at 131 *per* Mason, Murphy and Wilson, J.J.

foreseen as more probable than not . . . [the accessory] should not escape the consequences by reliance upon a nuance of prior assessment, only too likely to have been optimistic.'[115] In other words, the accessory might be hopeful and optimistic in believing that the conditions that will make the collateral crime necessary might not arise, but her optimism cannot annul her conditional intention.

Mere recklessness as the substantive fault element in common purpose complicity is not consistent with the idea that there be encouragement by authorisation. A person does not recklessly authorise. Nor do two parties recklessly form a common purpose. Encouragement by authorisation is about the secondary party intending that the perpetrator commit the conditional-target crime should the need for it to be committed arise. When the secondary party is privy to the fact that the need might arise for the conditional-target crime to be perpetrated and is privy to the fact that the perpetrator intends to perpetrate it if the need arises, her continued participation in the joint venture with such knowledge is evidence from which the jury can infer she intended the perpetrator to perpetrate the conditional-target crime. *An inference of authorisation is just another way of inferring that the defendant knew what was planned as an option and agreed to be involved in it and thus provided encouragement by her act of authorisation/participation.*[116]

B. The old common purpose cases

A line of old authorities going back 500 years suggest that nothing less than factual encouragement by authorisation is required for common purpose complicity. In *Le Seignior Dacre's Case,*[117] Lord Dacre and his associates agreed to enter a park as trespassers to hunt. They also agreed to kill anyone who might oppose them and thus had a common intention that extended to killing opposers. Lord Dacre was on the other side of the park when a member of his group killed a gamekeeper who confronted them. The gamekeeper confronted them while they were in the park as unlawful trespassers. Lord Dacre and his associates were found to be guilty of murder, because they had jointly agreed to perpetrate an unlawful hunt (the target crime) in the course of which an opposing gamekeeper was killed (the conditional-target crime – it was conditioned on them being opposed). The nub of the case for present purposes is that Lord Dacre was liable for murder, because he had previously agreed with his associates that anyone who might oppose them should be

115 *Chan Wing-Siu v. The Queen* [1985] A.C. 168 at 177.

116 In *Johns v. The Queen* (1980) 143 C.L.R. 108 at 131 *per* Mason, Murphy and Wilson, J.J. See also *R. v. Wakely* [1990] Crim. L.R. 119 at 120, where Lord Lane, C.J. noted that 'the distinction between foresight and tacit agreement is as fine as could possibly be imagined, if indeed a distinction exists at all.'

117 *Le Seignior Dacre's Case* (1535) Moore K.B. 86.

killed or seriously injured.[118] All the members of the group shared in the *mens rea* of the crime. This case involved mutual (conditional) intention.

This view also was expressed in the leading treatises of criminal law of the day. The leading case is *The Three Soldiers Case*, reported in Foster's *Crown Law*.[119] Foster, J. reports:

> Three soldiers went together to rob an orchard, two got upon a pear tree and the third stood at the gate with a drawn sword in his hand. The owner's son coming collared the man at the gate and asked him what business he had there, and thereupon the soldier stabbed him. It was ruled by *Holt* to be murder in him, but that those on the tree were innocent. They came to commit a small inconsiderable trespass, and the man was killed upon a sudden affray without their *knowledge*. 'It would', said he, 'have been otherwise if they had all by, come together *with a general resolution against all opposers*' [original emphasis].

The passage from Foster is the *locus classicus* of this doctrine. This doctrine was upheld by Widgery, L.J. (Karminski, L.J. and Geoffrey Lane, J. concurring) in *R. v. Lovesey*.[120] Widgery, L.J. said:[121]

> There was clearly a common design to rob, but that would not suffice to convict of murder unless the common design included the use of whatever force was necessary to achieve the robbers' object (or to permit escape without fear of subsequent identification), even if this involved killing, or the infliction of grievous bodily harm on the victim . . . If the scope of the common design had been left to the jury in this way they might still have concluded that it extended to the use of extreme force. It is clear that the plan *envisaged* that the victim's resistance should be

118 The entire judgment is one paragraph: '*Le Seignor Dacre & auters accord de enter en un pke & de hunter la, & de tuer touts que eux resisteront: & accordant al ceo ils entront en le Park, & un vient al un de eux, Et demand, que il avoit de faire la; & l'auter luy occide, le seignor esteant un quarter dun mile de cest leiu, & rien scavoit de ceo: uncore ceo fuit adjudge murder en luy, & en touts ses companions. Et auxi un auter vient en un Orchard, pur gatherer pears & un a luy vient & rebuke luy, & il luy tua, le quel fuit adjudge murder.*' *Le Seignior Dacre's Case* (1535) Moore K.B. 86. See also *People v. Aaron* (1980) 409 Mich. 672 *per* Fitzgerald, J. Similarly, in *R. v. Hodgson* (1730) 1 Leach 6 it was held: '[A]s the boy was found to be unconcerned in the affray, his having been killed by one of the company could not possibly affect the rest; for the homicide did not happen in prosecution [furtherance] of the illegal act; and therefore the persons, though constructively present, could not be said to be aiding and abetting the death of one who was totally unconcerned in the design for which the parties had assembled.' See also Hawkins, *op. cit., supra*, note 74 at 312; *Mansell and Herbert's Case* (1555) 2 Dyer 128b.

119 See Foster, *op. cit. supra*, note 50 at 353. See also *R. v. Short* (1932) 23 Cr. App. R. 170 *per* Lord Chief Justice Hewart, MacKinnon and Hawke, J.J.

120 [1970] 1 Q.B. 352.

121 *R. v. Lovesey* [1970] 1 Q.B. 352 at 356 applying *R. v. Anderson* [1966] 2 Q.B. 110.

> rapidly overcome . . . There must, in our view, be many cases of this kind where the jury feel driven to the conclusion that the raiders' common design *extended to everything which in fact occurred in the course of the raid*, but the question must be left to the jury because it is a matter for them to decide . . . Where, however, the victim's death is not a product of the common design but is attributable to one of the co-adventurers going beyond the scope of that design, by using violence which is intended to cause grievous bodily harm, the others are not responsible for that *unauthorised act* [emphasis added].

Widgery, L.J. used the word 'envisaged' rather than the word 'contemplated,' but it is clear that the learned judge was referring to the issue of conditional intention apropos the collateral crime. This passage, like the one from Foster, has been overlooked in the recent common purpose complicity cases. Foster, J.[122] also asserted that the joint participants' common intention to carry out various crimes against any opposers might be proved by evidence showing that it was their common intention that they would kill, maim, wound or assault any opposers should the need for such opposition arise. According to Foster, where there is no evidence of an *express* agreement to commit collateral crimes of opposition, a general agreement to commit such crimes could be inferred from evidence such as the number of people involved in the joint enterprise, whether they were armed and so on.[123] Foster was of the view that evidence of the behaviour of the individual participants before and at the scene of the crime also would be helpful for drawing an inference of conditional intention.[124]

Similarly, Sir Matthew Hale, writing before the time of Foster, wrote:[125]

> But suppose, that *A. B.* and *C.* and divers others come together to commit a riot, as to steal deer, or pull down inclosures, and in their march upon their design, *A.* meets with *D.* or some other, *with whom he had a former quarrel*, or that by reason of some collateral provocation given by *D.* to *A. A.* kills him without any abetting by any of the rest of his company, this doth not make all the party of *A.* though present, to be therefore aiding and abetting, and consequently principal in this murder or manslaughter, which was . . . *not within the compass of their original intention* [emphasis added].

122 Foster, *op. cit. supra*, note 50 at 353.

123 'A general resolution [mutual intention] against all opposers, whether such resolution appeareth upon evidence to have been actually and explicitly entered into by the confederates, or may be reasonably collected from their number, arms, or behaviour at or before the scene of action, such resolutions so proved have always been considered as strong ingredients in cases of this kind.' *Ibid.* See also *R. v. Tattersal* (1801) 2 Leach 984.

124 Foster, *op. cit. supra*, note 50 at 353.

125 Hale, *op. cit., supra*, note 47 at 443–444.

This approach has been affirmed in many cases since.[126] In *R. v. Collison*,[127] Garrow B. was of the view that an accessory could be liable only for the perpetrator's collateral crime if the jury were satisfied that she joined the unlawful joint enterprise sharing the perpetrator's intention of 'resisting to death, or with extreme violence, any persons who might endeavour to apprehend them'. Garrow B. also said: 'but if they had only the common purpose of stealing apples, and the violence of the prisoner's companion was merely the result of the situation in which he found himself, and proceeded from the impulse of the moment, without any previous concert, the prisoner will be entitled to an acquittal.'

C. Constructive and complicity liability under the rule of felony murder

Notwithstanding that both Foster and Hale were writing in the heyday of constructive malice, even in felony murder cases, they limited liability to those who had encouraged the collateral act (constructive liability would cover any unintended consequences of the authorised act, but that is all) by authorising it. Common purpose complicity operated independently of the felony murder rule,[128] but many of the old common purpose cases also rested on constructive malice where the authorised collateral act had unintended consequences.[129] The most notorious use of constructive malice was in the felony murder cases.[130] When the target crime was a felony such as robbery,

126 See in particular, *R. v. Borthwick* (1779) 1 Doug. K.B. 207 at 212. In *R. v. White* (1806) Russ. & Ry. 99 at 101 where it was held: 'that if the prisoners came with the same illegal purpose, and both determined to resist, the act of one would fix guilt upon both, and that it might have been part of the plan to take different ways, in order to divide the force against them.' This head of liability was independent of the rule of felony murder head of liability. See *People v. Aaron* (1980) 409 Mich. 672 *per* Fitzgerald, J., See also *R. v. Howell* (1839) 9 Car. & P. 437 at 450–451; *R. v. Rubens* (1909) 2 Cr. App. R. 163; *R. v. Hawkins* (1828) 3 Car. & P. 392 *per* Park, J.; *R. v. Bingley* (1821) Russ. & Ry. 446; *R. v. Luck* (1862) 3 F. & F. 483. Cf. *R. v. Faulknor* (1887) 13 Cox C.C. 550. See further, William Oldnall Russell, *A Treatise on Crimes and Indictable Misdemeanours* (Boston: Lilly and Wait, 1831) at paras. 24–25. A similar rule applies in some U.S. jurisdictions, see *State v. Lucas* (1880) 55 Iowa 321; *State v. Craft* (1936) 338 Mo. 831; *Roy v. U.S.* (1995) 652 A.2d 1098.

127 (1831) 4 Car. & P. 565.

128 In *People v. Aaron* (1980) 409 Mich. 672, Fitzgerald, J., in the Supreme Court of Michigan, expounded: 'Moreover, because they had agreed previously to kill anyone who might resist them, all the members of the group shared in the *mens rea* of the crime. Thus, because *Lord Dacre's* case involved express malice, no doctrine finding malice from the intention to commit an unlawful act was necessary or in fact utilised.'

129 Cf. *Thody's Case* (1673) Freem. K.B. 514 where *D1* was guilty of murder and *D2* only of manslaughter. See also *Salisbury's Case* (1553) 1 Plow. 97; *R. v. Pridmore* (1913) 8 Cr. App. R. 198. On constructive malice more generally, see J.W.C., Turner, 'The Mental Element in Crimes at Common Law' in L. Radzinowicz and J.W. Cecil Turner (ed.), *The Modern Approach To Criminal Law* (London: Macmillan & Co. Ltd., 1945) at 195 *et seq.*; J.W. Cecil Turner, 'Malice Implied and Constructive' [1958] *Crim. L.R.* 15. 'Constructive malice' was abolished for murder by section 1 of the *Homicide Act 1957*.

130 See *Anonymous case* (1585) Godbolt 64 at 66 where it was said: 'for if many come together to make an assault, *ex malitia præcogitata*; and one of them only strikes the partie mortally,

all the parties were strictly and collectively[131] liable for any unintended consequences following from the authorised collateral crime. Basically, the felony murder rule was one of strict liability for unintended consequences. Once a group embarked on a felony, all the group members were strictly liable for any criminal consequences resulting from the authorised collateral crimes that were done in furtherance of the felony.[132]

However, there were limits. The underlying felony had to come within the participants' common purpose.[133] Once this was established, all the participants had to take the consequences of the felony. Because it was not necessary to prove that the perpetrator intended to kill the victim in felony murder cases, the intention requirement was met where the accessory's purpose was to promote or facilitate the commission of the underlying felony.[134] Suppose *A* and *P* agree that *P* should hit a night watchman over the head with a batten to knock him unconscious, because this will facilitate their joint robbery of a warehouse. Suppose also that *V* dies from the blow to his head. In this scenario, both *A* and *P* would have been liable under the old

and he dieth, it is murder in them all.' See also *Ashton's Case* (1703) 12 Mod. 256; *Domina R. v. Wallis* (1703) 1 Salk. 334. Dalton held that unlawful-act-murder required a violent act: see Dalton, *op. cit. supra*, note 74 at 342 *et seq.* It has been said that Coke extended constructive murder to cover non-violent acts (see Coke, *op. cit., supra*, note 50 at 56), but this is not correct. The rule had been applied to non-violent acts pre-Coke. See for example, Sir William Staunford, *Les Plees del Coron* (London: by Rychard Tottel, 1567) at 21; cf. William Lambarde, *Eirenarcha* (London: Printed by Ralph Newbery, 1588) at 243–244. Stephen asserts that Coke extended the constructive murder rule. See James Fitzjames Stephen, *A History of the Criminal Law of England* (London: Macmillan, 1883) Vol. III, at 57–58. In *R. v. Keate* (1702) Comb. 406 at 409, Holt, Ch. J. converted the constructive murder rule into the felony murder rule. Hence, from that point in time, strict liability for an unintended killing applied only if the defendant accidentally killed while committing a 'felony' as opposed to a lesser crime. Holt, Ch. J. said: 'In the case of killing the hen, my Lord Coke is too large, there must be a design of mischief to the person, or to commit a *felony or great riot*.'

131 For example, it was said in *R. v. Goodfellow* (1845) 1 Car. & K. 724, 'if any one of the defendants had a gun, all were armed.' Some commentators have argued that 'felony murder . . . operates in practice as a conclusive presumption: the *mens rea* required for murder is irrebuttably presumed from the defendant's *mens rea* in committing the felony'. See Nelson E. Roth and Scott E. Sundby, 'The Felony-Murder Rule: A Doctrine at Constitutional Crossroads' (1985) 70 *Cornell L. Rev.* 446 at 460. See also, Lambarde, *id.* at 243–244.

132 The felony did not have to involve violence. Felonies against property also counted. See *R. v. Standley* (1816) Russ. & Ry. 305; *Joshua Cornwall's Case* (1730) 2 Str. 881. Cf. *Anonymous* (1703) 8 Mod. 165.

133 *R. v. Edmeads* (1828) 3 Car. & P. 390; *R. v. Collison* (1831) 4 Car. & P. 565; *Mohammed v. Trinidad and Tobago* [2001] U.K.P.C. 21 *per* Lord Bingham; East, *op. cit. infra*, note 152 at 298–299; *State v. Bacon* (1995) 658 A.2d 54.

134 Hale, *op. cit. supra*, note 47 at 443–444. *R. v. Betts and Ridley* (1931) 22 Cr. App. R. 148 at 153–156. The act of violence leading to *V*'s death has to be 'done in the course of or in the furtherance of the . . . felony'. See also *The King v. Beard* [1920] A.C. 479. Most jurisdictions in the United States still invoke this rule. In *Campbell v. State* (1982) 293 Md. 438 at 447, it was said: 'Although the homicide itself need not be within the common design, the act which results in death must be in furtherance of the unlawful purpose.'

rule of felony murder for the unintended consequence of their assault,[135] because the assault *per se* was intended for the purpose of effecting the robbery.[136]

Per contra, under the rule of felony murder, if *A* and *P* agree that should a night watchmen be present, they should not proceed with their planned burglary, *A* is liable for the collateral crime (murder), if *P* discovers the guard is an old enemy and impulsively inflicts GBH upon the guard with that having the unintended consequence of causing the guard's death. *P* acts to serve her personal animus. Since *A* did not encourage *P* to use any force whatsoever in furtherance of the burglary, she would not have been liable for *P*'s independent autonomous choice to kill. In the latter situation, *P*'s act of murder coincides with the joint felony/burglary, but it was not in furtherance of the joint felony.[137] Coincidence is not encouragement by authorisation.[138] *P*'s assault during the burglary would be treated as a standalone crime committed against the express agreement of the parties and thus stands outside the reach of rule of felony murder and also the law of complicity.[139] Norval Morris has remarked that without such a doctrine, 'if one of two burglars ransacking a home glances out of a window, sees his enemy for whom he has long been searching and shoots him, the unarmed accomplice, party only to the burglary, will be guilty of murder in the first degree.'[140]

Accidental *killings* that were causally linked to *acts* that were done in furtherance of the joint felony were caught by the rule of felony murder, but the accidental consequences of deliberate acts that were outside the common purpose were not. The evidence had to be sufficient to demonstrate that the collateral crime did not serve only the perpetrator's personal

135 See *R. v. Grant* (1954) 38 Cr. App. R. 107, where the parties had a preconceived intention to use violence to overcome any resistance they encountered during the course of their joint enterprise.

136 *Anonymous case* (1585) Godbolt 64 at 66.

137 *Le Seignior Dacre's Case* (1535) Moore K.B. 86. As shown in the dense footnotes in this chapter, the *Le Seignior Dacre's* doctrine was accepted as the law for centuries. See *R. v. Borthwick* (1779) 1 Doug. K.B. 207 at 212; *The King v. Hodgson* (1730) 1 Leach 6; *R. v. Plummer* (1706) 12 Mod. 627; *R. v. White* (1806) Russ. & Ry. 99. For a discussion of *Le Seignior Dacre's Case*, see Hale, *op. cit. supra*, note 47 at 439; 443–445.

138 In *Stouffer v. State* (1997) 118 Md. App. 590 at 615–616, it was held: '[I]n order to convict for felony-murder, the killing must have been done by the defendant or by an accomplice or confederate or by one acting in furtherance of the felonious undertaking . . . it is clear that the felony must be more than incidental to the homicide.' In *Mumford v. State* (1974) 313 A.2d 563 at 566, Thompson, J. said: 'There is no criminal liability on the part of the others when the homicide was a fresh and independent product of the mind of one of the confederates, outside of, or foreign to, the common design . . . In sum, there must be a direct causal connection between the homicide and the [underlying joint crime]. Something more than mere coincidence in time and place between the two must be shown.'

139 *The King v. Hodgson* (1730) 1 Leach 6; *R. v. Plummer* (1706) 12 Mod. 627.

140 Norval Morris, 'The Felon's Responsibility for the Lethal Act of Others' (1956) 105 *U. Pa. L. Rev.* 50 at 73. Hale gives a similar example, see Hale, *op. cit. supra*, note 47 at 443–444.

animus. In cases where the doctrine of constructive malice continued to be part of English law, there was no need for the courts to consider whether the accessories intended the accidental consequences that resulted from an act that was within their common felonious design. It did not matter whether the parties intended the consequences of their common purpose, because they were constructively and derivatively liable for the consequences of acts that were within their common purpose.[141] If a joint felony caused the death of the victim, the fact that all the parties acted with a felonious intent, the intention to commit the felony that caused the victim's death, was sufficient to make them all constructively liable for that death.

In *R. v. Skeet*,[142] Pollock, C.B. said:

> That doctrine arose from the desire on the part of the old lawyers to render all parties who are jointly engaged in the commission of a *felony* responsible for deadly violence committed in the course of its execution. But that doctrine has been much limited in later times, and only applies in cases of felony, where there is . . . *evidence of a felonious design to carry out the unlawful purpose at all hazards, and whatever may be the consequences* [emphasis added].

Pollock C.B. seems to overlook the fact that the culpability constraint he refers to dates back to *Le Seignior Dacre's Case*[143] and has been applied in many leading cases since that time.[144]

V. Evidential maxims in practice: the way they mirror substantive fault doctrines

A. The natural probable consequence maxim

The process of inferring intention from outward acts was at one time expounded in the Latin maxim: *acta exteriora indicant interiora secreta*[145]

141 Hale, *op. cit. supra*, note 47 at 443–444; *R. v. Betts and Ridley* (1931) 22 Cr. App. R. 148 at 153–156.

142 (1866) 4 F. & F. 931 at 936–937.

143 (1535) Moore K.B. 86.

144 See *Sir Charles Stanley's Case* (1662) Kelyng, J. 86; *The Three Soldiers Case* (1697) Fost. 353; *R. v. Plummer* (1706) Kelyng, J. 109; *R. v. Hawkins* (1828) 3 Car. & P. 392; *R. v. Collison* (1831) 4 Car. & P. 565; *R. v. Borthwick* (1779) 1 Doug. K.B. 207 at 212; *R. v. White* (1806) Russ. & Ry. 99 at 101; *R. v. Howell* (1839) 9 Car. & P. 437 at 450–451; *R. v. Rubens* (1909) 2 Cr. App. R. 163; *R. v. Hawkins* (1828) 3 Car. & P. 392 *per* Park, J.; *R. v. Bingley* (1821) Russ. & Ry. 446; *R. v. Luck* (1862) 176 E.R. 217; *Thornhill v. State of Alabama* (1940) 310 U.S. 88 at 101; See also Staunford, *op. cit. supra*, note 130 at Li.I, Cap. 43; Ca. 44; Hale, *op. cit., supra*, note 47 at 443.

145 *The Six Carpenters' Case* (1610) 8 Coke Reports 146a at 146b where it was said: 'the law adjudges by the subsequent act, *quo animo*, or to what intent, he entered; for *acta exteriora indicant interiora secreta*.'

(outward acts indicate the thoughts hidden within). This was replaced in later times by the maxim that: 'Every man is supposed to intend the natural and probable consequences of his own acts, unless it can be shown from circumstances that he acted upon some other motives.'[146] Proof that the common purpose extended to the collateral crime was normally demonstrated by nothing more than a crude application of the evidential maxim that a person is presumed to have intended the natural and probable consequences of her actions.[147] Liability in many of the old cases rested on the natural probable consequence maxim.[148] This was applied for centuries, not only in civil cases, but also in criminal cases.[149] Long ago, Plowden wrote:[150]

> As if I command a man to rob such a one, and he attempts to rob him, and the other defends himself, and a combat ensues between them, and the person attempted to be robbed is killed, I shall be accessary to this murder, because when he attempted to rob him, he pursued my command, and then when he pursued my command, and in the execution thereof another thing happened, I ought in reason to be deemed

146 *Edwards v. Harben* (1788) 2 Term Rep. 587 at 589.

147 See *R. v. Beard* (1837) 8 Car. & P. 143 at 148 *per* Coleridge, J.; *R. v. Horsey* (1862) 3 F. & F. 287; *R. v. Jones* (1840) 9 Car. & P. 258; cf. *Flower v. Marten* (1837) 2 My. & C. 459 at 469, where it was clearly used as a maxim of evidence. In jurisdictions where the natural probable consequences doctrine has been adopted as a substantive fault element for complicity and where the rule of felony murder remains on the statute books, the courts have observed: '[G]iven that the natural and probable consequences doctrine looks to the reasonable likelihood that the non-target murder will result from the target offence, it would appear that applying the label "felony murder" rule to the target offence is not talismanic in deciding whether the aider and abettor can be convicted of a non-target murder. The key factor is the ability to anticipate the likelihood that the non-target offence will result from the target offence . . . The requirement that the non-target offence be reasonably foreseeable from the nature of the target offence ensures that in most circumstances, aiding and abetting a misdemeanour will not have murder as its natural and probable consequence, but it does not mandate it.' *People v. Canizalez* (2011) 197 Cal. App. 4th 832 at 854; cf. *Fitzpatrick v. U.S.* (1900) 178 U.S. 304 at 310.

148 Riot is an example of an offence where the courts were ready to infer that the parties to the riot mutually intended to assist and encourage each other not only to riot, but also to commit (conditional) crimes of opposition. In earlier times, riot was defined to be 'where three or more persons assemble and confederate themselves together, of their own authority, for some common object, either lawful or unlawful, and with the *intent mutually* supporting each other against opposition in execution of it.' See 'On The Law Respecting Riots, Routs and Unlawful Assembles' (1841) 9 *Monthly L. Mag.* 210.

149 See *National Coal Board v. Gamble* [1959] 1 Q.B. 11 at 23 *per* Devlin, J.; *D.P.P. v. Smith* 1961] A.C. 290. Cf. *R. v. Hyam* [1973] 3 W.L.R. 475; *R. v. Hancock* [1986] A.C. 455.

150 See Plowden's notes accompanying his report of *The Queen v. Saunders & Archer* (1575) 2 Plow. 473 at 475.

> a party therein, because my command was the cause of it. So if I command one to beat another, and he beats him so that he dies thereof, I shall be accessary to this murder, for it is a consequence of my command, which was the original foundation thereof, and which naturally tended to endanger the life of the other.

The natural probable consequence doctrine was applied more often than not in the early common purpose cases. Blackstone wrote:[151]

> And, if two or more come together to do an unlawful act against the king's peace, of which the probable consequence might be bloodshed – as to beat a man, to commit a riot, or to rob a park; and one of them kills a man; it is murder in them all, because of the unlawful act, the *malitia praecogitata*, or evil intended beforehand.

Likewise, East wrote:[152]

> The above rule governs all cases where divers persons resolve generally to resist all opposers in the commission of any breach of the peace, and to execute it with violence, in such a manner as *naturally tends to raise tumults and affrays*; as by committing a violent disseisin with great numbers, or going to beat a man, or rob a park, or standing in opposition to the sheriff's poste. For they must at their peril abide the event of their actions who wilfully engage in such bold disturbances of the public peace. In such cases the law adopts the presumption of fact that they came with intent to oppose all who should hinder them in their design [emphasis added].

151 William Blackstone, *Commentaries on the Laws of England* (Oxford: Clarendon Press, 1769) Vol. IV at 200. Hale was of the view that the *unlawfulness* of the joint enterprise gave rise to the presumption that the participants intended any collateral crimes of opposition to make their joint enterprise succeed 'against all opposition.' Hale, *op. cit., supra*, note 47 at 443–444. 'Henry of Bracton relied on theologians like Aquinas for the principle *versari in re illicita*. This principle, which means that an accused is responsible for the natural and probable consequences of his or her behaviour, has many nuances which passed from the moral theologians into Henry of Bracton's treatise on criminal responsibility and thence into the common law.' See 38 *Am. J. Juris.* 395. See Bracton, *op. cit. supra*, note 66 at 277. The rationale for criminalisation under the *versari in re illicita* maxim is that the offender has been reckless or negligent in placing herself in an unlawful position that had the potential to result in unintended criminal harm (e.g. felony murder). The maxim also was used to justify criminalising those who joined a criminal enterprise that had the potential to result in an accomplice perpetrating some collateral crime. Liability hinged on the notion of prior or antecedent negligence or recklessness: the accessory was reckless in joining the 'illicit' (criminal) enterprise etc. For a critique of this kind of antecedent fault see George P. Fletcher, *The Grammar of Criminal Law* (New York: Oxford University Press, 2007) Volume 1 at 277.

152 Sir Edward Hyde East, *A Treatise of the Pleas of the Crown* (London: Printed by A. Strahan, 1803) Vol. I., at 257.

All the parties to the unlawful joint enterprise were often presumed to have mutually intended any conditional crimes of opposition etc., if such crimes were the natural probable consequences of the unlawful joint enterprise.[153] The natural probable consequence doctrine has had a lasting impact in the law of common purpose complicity in some jurisdictions. In seven states in the United States and in four states in Australia, the evidential maxim was converted into a substantive mental element for common purpose complicity.[154] English law never adopted the natural probable consequence rule as a substantive fault element for common purpose complicity,[155] but it was used more generally as an evidential maxim for inferring intention in criminal cases.[156] In 1880 the *Criminal Code Bill* commissioners[157]

153 Cf. *R. v. Franz* (1861) 2 F. & F. 580, where there was a clear move away from the 'presumption' approach.

154 The seven states are Wisconsin, Minnesota, Kansas, Arizona, Iowa, California and Maine. The statutory provisions are: Wis. Stat. Ann. §939.05(2)(c) (West 2005); Minn. Stat. Ann. §609.05(2) (West 2003 & Supp. 2008); Kan. Stat. Ann. §21–3205(2) (2007); Ariz. Rev. Stat. Ann. § 13–303(A)(3) (2008); Iowa Code Ann. §703.2 (West 2003); Me. Rev. Stat. Ann. tit. 17-A, §57(3)(A) (Supp. 2007). The sort of negligence standard that is found in these provisions is exemplified in the wording of the Minnesota provision, which provides: 'Expansive liability. A person liable under subdivision 1 is also liable for any other crime committed in pursuance of the intended crime if *reasonably foreseeable* by the person as a probable consequence of committing or attempting to commit the crime intended.' In *Coston v. State* (1939) 190 So. 520 at 523 it was said: 'And a general intent to do evil, such as to cover all the natural probable consequences of the act, may be inferred from the circumstances of the case.' See also *People v. Kerrick* (1927) 86 Cal.App. 542 at 547; *State v. Nash* (1858) 7 Clarke 347; *Stephens v. State* (1884) 42 Ohio St. 150; *Brown v. Com.* (1921) 130 Va. 733; *Rollston v. Com.* (1991) 399 S.E.2d 823; *Shaikh v. Johnson* (2008) 276 Va. 537; *People v. Feagans* (1985) 480 N.E.2d 153; *People v. Campbell* (1979) 396 N.E.2d 607. For an overview of the provisions in the states that have criminal codes within Australia, see Andrew Hemming, 'In Search of a Model Code Provision for Complicity and Common Purpose in Australia' (2011) 30 *U. Tas. L. Rev.* 53.

155 *R. v. Hazel* (1785) 1 Leach 368 at 375–376.

156 See *R. v. Hazel* (1785) 1 Leach 368 at 375–376; *R. v. Harvey* (1823) 2 B. & C. 257 at 260; *R. v. Horsey* (1862) 3 F. & F. 287 at 289–90; *The Queen v. Aspinall* (1876) 2 Q.B.D. 48; *D.P.P. v Beard* [1920] A.C. 479; *Smyth v. R.* (1958) 98 C.L.R. 163; *National Coal Board v. Gamble* [1959] 1 Q.B. 11 at 23 *per* Devlin, J.; *D.P.P. v. Smith* [1961] A.C. 290; *R. v. Singh* [1962] A.C. 188; *R. v. Governor of Brixton Prison* [1963] 2 Q.B. 243; *R. v. Clark (No. 2)* [1964] 2 Q.B. 315 at 320 *per* Lord Parker, C.J. Cf. *R. v. Hyam* [1973] 3 W.L.R. 475; *R. v. Hancock* [1986] A.C. 455.

157 See section 72 of the *Criminal Code Bill 1880*, which provides: 'Every one is a party to and guilty of an offence who (a) Actually commits it; (b) Does or omits an act for the purpose of aiding any person to commit the offence; (c) Abets any person in the commission of the offence; (d) Counsels or procures any person to commit the offence . . . If several persons form a common intention to prosecute any unlawful purpose, and to assist each other therein, each of them is a party to every offence committed by any one of them in the prosecution of such common purpose, the commission of which offence was or ought to have been known to be a probable consequence of the prosecution of such common purpose.' Alas, Sir Samuel Griffith, the drafter of the *Queensland Criminal Code 1899*, was persuaded by section 72 of the *Criminal Code Bill 1880* when he created the

recommended that the natural probable consequences rule be enacted as a substantive fault element for common purpose complicity, but this recommendation was never enacted into law. Sir James Fitzjames Stephen, one of the commissioners, rejected it in his own writings on the subject. Stephen[158] proposed that the common purpose complicity doctrine be limited as follows.

> When several persons take part in the execution of a common criminal purpose, each is a principal in the second degree, in respect of every crime committed by any one of them in the execution of that purpose.
>
> If any of the offenders commits a crime foreign to the common criminal purpose, the others are neither principals in the second degree, nor accessories unless they actually instigate or assist in its commission.

Under the heading: 'Where Crime Committed is Probable Consequence of Crime Suggested,' Stephen[159] goes on to write:

> If a person instigates another to commit a crime, and the person so instigated commits a crime different from the one which he was instigated to commit, but likely to be caused by such instigation, the instigator is an accessory before the fact.

The *Criminal Code Bill 1880* was the work of Colin Blackburn, Charles R. Barry, Robert Lush and Sir James Fitzjames Stephen. However, it is widely acknowledged that Stephen, the greatest criminal lawyer of the nineteenth century, was its primary author.[160] Stephen, aware of the judiciary's and the bar's opposition to codification, made concessions in the *Draft Code* that he was not willing to make in his own writings on the subject. It is no coincidence that

substantive fault element for common purpose complicity in the *Queensland Criminal Code*. The *Queensland Criminal Code* was the first successful codification of the bulk of English criminal law. A substantive fault element of negligence was also adopted in Western Australia and a number of other Australian states. The drafters of the *Canadian Criminal Code 1892* and the *New Zealand Criminal Code 1893* also were influenced by the *Criminal Code Bill 1880* and thus adopted the negligence approach. For a discussion of the *Bill of 1880*'s influence in the colonies, see *Edmonds v. The Queen* [2011] N.Z.S.C. 159 at para. 22; see also J. Barry Wright, 'Self-Governing Codifications of English Criminal Law and Empire: The Queensland and Canadian Examples' (2007) 26 *The University of Queensland Law Journal* 39.

158 James Fitzjames Stephen, *A Digest of Criminal Law: Crimes and Punishments* (London: Macmillan and Co. Ltd., 4th edn 1887) at 32.

159 *Id.* at 34.

160 See Leon Radzinowicz, *Sir James Fitzjames Stephen, 1829–1894: and His Contribution to the Development of Criminal Law* (London: B. Quaritch, 1957).

Stephen dropped the natural probable consequences approach in his own proposals in his *Digest of Criminal Law.* The natural probable consequence doctrine was a general evidential maxim and it appears Stephen could see no justification for having a negligence standard as a substantive fault element in the law of complicity. Once it had become apparent that the *Criminal Code Bill 1880* was not going to get through Parliament, Stephen argued that the more principled approach laid down in *The Three Soldiers Case*[161] and *R. v. Plummer*[162] should be the law.

At common law, the natural probable consequence rule was nothing more than an evidential maxim for inferring intention.[163] It was not meant to stand as a substantive fault element either in complicity or elsewhere. Coupled with this, the maxim was only ever mentioned with reference to the standard mode of complicity, that is, complicity involving direct encouragement (i.e. commandment/instigation).[164] Neither the institutional writers nor Stephen mentioned it with reference to common purpose complicity. For instance, Coke wrote:

> But where death ensueth upon that act which is *commanded,* though death it self be not *commanded,* there he is accessory to it, for there the *commandment* is the cause of death. As if *A command B* to beat *C,* and he beat him, whereof he dieth; the *commander* is accessory: and thereof. . . . But where death ensueth upon another distinct cause, there the *consent* of the accessory cannot be drawn to it.[165]

161 (1697) Fost. 353.

162 (1706) Kelyng, J. 109. In that case, *P,* a gang member, fired a gun and killed not the police, but another member of the gang. It was held that the other gang members were not criminally liable for the murder, because the gun was not fired in furtherance of the gang's joint criminal purpose. Instead, *P* killed *V* because it was believed that *V* had informed the police of the gang's criminal plan.

163 *R. v. Hazel* (1785) 1 Leach 368 at 375–376.

164 In *Brennan v. The King* (1936) 55 C.L.R. 253 at 263, Dixon and Evatt, J.J. in the High Court of Australia took the view that the insertion of the 'natural probable consequence' test in section 8 of the *Criminal Code of Western Australia* was influenced by Foster's analysis of *direct solicitation* complicity, rather than any reference he made to common purpose complicity. Foster writes: 'So where the principal goeth beyond the terms of the *solicitation,* if in the event the *felony* committed was a *probable consequence* of what was ordered or advised, the person giving such orders or advice will be an accessary to that felony. *A.,* upon some affront given by *B.* ordereth his servant to way-lay him and give him a sound beating; the servant doth so, and *B.* dieth of this beating. *A.* is accessary to this murder.' See also Foster, *op. cit. supra,* note 50 at 370. Foster also wrote: 'If the principal totally and substantially varieth, if being s*olicited* to commit a felony of one kind he wilfully and knowingly committeth a felony of another, he will stand single in that offence, and the person *soliciting* will not be involved in his guilt.' *Id.* at 369.

165 Coke, *loc. cit. supra,* note 50. See also Hale, *op. cit. supra,* note 47 at 616–617; Russell, *op. cit. supra,* note 128 at para. 32.

The common purpose cases were dealt with by applying either the constructive malice doctrine where the unintended consequence was the result of an authorised/encouraged collateral crime, or alternatively, the doctrine laid down in *Le Seignior Dacre's Case*.[166] Stephen, like Coke, Hale, Foster and Hawkins before him, was referring to standard complicity involving direct solicitation/encouragement.[167] The natural probable consequences test was never applied to common purpose encouragement and the law has moved on with respect to general complicity.[168]

The reason the natural probable consequence maxim was only ever invoked in the standard complicity cases is that those cases did not involve the problem of conditional intention, but rather the distinct problem of imputing blame to the accessory for the accidental consequences of the perpetrator's acts – the acts that the accessory had purposively encouraged. In those cases, the accessory was already liable for purposively encouraging (commanding) the perpetrator to commit the particular crime such as assault. The only issue was whether she also could be liable for an unintended consequence (i.e. *V*'s death) that was the result of the assault that she had purposively commanded.

The courts seemed to have used the natural probable consequence doctrine to justify constructive (strict) liability for unintended consequences. If the accessory had encouraged (commanded) the perpetrator to expose someone to serious injury, then she also can be taken as having intended any greater harm that was a natural probable consequence of that serious injury.

166 (1535) Moore K.B. 86.

167 Hale wrote: 'If *A.* counsel or command *B.* to beat *C.* with a small wand or rod, which could not in all human reason cause death, if *B.* beat *C.* with a great club, or wound him with a sword, whereof he dies, it seems, that A. is not accessary, because there was no command of death, nor of any thing, that could probably cause death, and B. hath varied from the command in substance, and not in circumstance.' Hale, *op. cit. supra*, note 47 at 436. Likewise, Hawkins writes: '[I]f I command another to beat a man, and he beat him in such a manner that he dies thereof, I am an accessary before to the felony, because it happened in the execution of a command which naturally tended to endanger the life of the other. And *a fortiori* therefore it follows, that if a man command another to rob a man, and he in robbing him kill him; or to burn the house of *J. S.* and he by burning it, burn also the house of *J. N.*; the commander is as much an accessary to the subsequent felony as to that which was directly commanded . . . Also it is said, that if I command a man to rob another, and he kills him in the attempt, but does not rob him, I am guilty of the murder, because it was the direct and immediate effect of an act done in execution of my command to commit a felony. [But I am not liable where the consequence] was not the direct and immediate effect of the act done in pursuance of my command, but happened accidentally through the act or B. to which I being no way privy, cannot be made accessary by reason.' See Hawkins, *op cit. supra*, note 74 at 315–316.

168 *Johnson v. Youden* [1950] 1 All E.R. 300 was endorsed by the House of Lords in *R. v. Churchill (No. 2)* [1967] 2 A.C. 224 at 236 *et passim* and again in *D.P.P. for Northern Ireland v Maxwell* [1978] 1 W.L.R. 1350 at 1357 *et passim*.

Hence, the rule was not an application of the joint enterprise doctrine, because it did not hold that *A* was liable for unintended *autonomous human acts* that were foreseen as a possible incident of engaging in an unlawful joint enterprise: instead, it held that *A* must have intended the *consequences* of the *act* she intentionally (commanded) encouraged *P* to perpetrate.

The natural probable consequence doctrine was only ever invoked as a maxim of evidence to infer intention[169] or to rationalise constructive liability. Negligence was never treated as a substantive fault requirement for complicity. Lord Diplock has observed: 'It was the actual intention of the offender himself that the objective test was designed to ascertain.'[170] It has since been accepted that the maxim that every person is supposed to intend the natural and probable consequences of her own acts is unacceptable, because it incorrectly holds that the probability of the outcome is always sufficient to justify the conclusion that the outcome was intended.

The maxim was phased out of use, because it confused one kind of evidence of the mental state with the mental state itself.[171] The probability of the alleged non-target crime following the target crime is a kind of evidence and nothing more.[172] If the probability of the collateral crime following the target crime was a virtual certainty, then the jury can infer from this evidence that the defendant's claim that she did not intend the perpetrator to perpetrate the collateral crime is a lie. Often one can only judge whether the defendant intended a conditional-target crime by asking whether anyone in her shoes would have realised that the collateral crime was a virtual

169 In *R. v. Hazel* (1785) 1 Leach 368 at 375–376, it was said: 'All the cases in which the homicide has been deemed murder, though the primary intent was not to kill, have been decided on this ground, that where a man intends to do an act, he intends all the probable consequences of it; but it cannot be conceived that in throwing the stool at the child the prisoner intended her death; for it was not a probable consequence . . . In the present case there is not the appearance of any intention to kill, for every intent is an act of the mind, and can only be discovered externally by the fact which it occasions. Of these facts the Jury are to judge, and as they have declared that the intent of killing did not exist, the Court cannot infer that it did.' What was meant by probability is teased out further towards the end of the judgment. At pages 380–381 it was said: 'Suppose one of several persons playing at cricket throw the ball, which is much more likely to give a mortal blow than a small stool, at another, and the ball by accidentally hitting him in a mortal part occasion his death, could it be thought that the man who threw the ball merely in play, would be deemed guilty of so atrocious a crime as murder? . . . [I]t is not found that the prisoner had any preconceived malice, or that she intended to correct the deceased; or that the stool was so thrown as probably to hit; nor that it was by hitting likely to kill.'

170 Lord Diplock also said: 'the objective test did not define the relevant intention as to the consequences of a voluntary act. It was no more than one means of ascertaining the relevant intention, to which the *Criminal Evidence Act 1898* added another – the defendant's own evidence of what his actual intention was.' See *Hyam v. D.P.P.* [1975] A.C. 55 at 94 *per* Lord Diplock. Before the enactment of the *Criminal Evidence Act 1898*, *D* was not allowed to testify as to what his or her intention was.

171 Baker, *op. cit. supra*, note 12 at paras. at 4–035 *et seq.*

172 *Johns v. The Queen* [1980] 143 C.L.R. 108 at 131 *per* Mason, Murphy and Wilson, J.J.

certainty upon certain conditions arising (such as a confrontation with a guard during a robbery) and whether there is any reasonable interpretation of her actions other than the hypothesis that the conditional-target crime was within the common purpose she shared with the perpetrator.

B. Substantive oblique intention v. the evidential maxim for inferring direct intention

Even though a person's knowledge that a particular consequence will probably result from her act is an insufficient basis for saying that she intends it, there are strong reasons for holding that intention can be inferred when she foresaw the end consequence as a virtually certain consequence of her act.[173] This is called 'oblique' intent or 'indirect' intent – not the result that is in the straight line of the defendant's purpose, but a side-effect that she accepts as inevitable. Conceptually, indirect intention is not intention at all, but rather is a genus of 'extreme subjective recklessness.' The defendant intends to do *X* but does not intend it to result in *Y*, but knows that if she does *X* it will be virtually impossible for *Y* not to occur. Since her state of mind is such that she as good as intended to bring about *Y*,[174] she is deemed to have intended *Y*. The natural probable consequence maxim is no longer used to infer intention.[175] The courts now require nothing short of foresight of a virtual certainty.[176] A 99 out of 100 probability of a consequence/event/crime occurring as a result of *D*'s conduct is a virtual certainty, but a virtual certainty might be inferred when the probability is lower than this, if it is extremely high.

An inference of indirect intention is a finding of indirect intention rather than direct intention. For example, suppose *X* throws her own child from the fourth floor of a burning building as it is the only escape route, but her direct purpose is to save her child, whom she loves dearly, from being killed by the fire. *X* foresees the child's death as a virtually certain consequence of throwing her from the fourth floor. In this scenario direct intention cannot be inferred from her conduct, as the evidence clearly shows that she only obliquely intended to kill the child. *X*'s direct intention (purpose/desire)

173 To the extent that the probability is so low as to make the defendant only subjectively reckless, it would provide only evidence of recklessness. Similarly, if the probability of the consequence is very low and the defendant had no foresight of the probability that would be only evidence of negligence. Cf. *R. v. Hancock* [1986] A.C. 455 at 473F *per* Lord Scarman. See also the discussion in *People v. Smith* (1997) 57 Cal. App. 4th 1470 at 1473 where it was said: 'A person acts with an oblique intention when he or she knows that the result is practically certain to follow from his or her conduct, regardless of the desired result. This rules out the natural and probable consequences test as a measure of an oblique intention.'

174 Joshua Dressler, *Understanding Criminal Law* (Newark NJ: Lexis Nexis, 2006) at 130.

175 Section 8 of the *Criminal Justice Act 1967* was enacted to prevent it being used for such purposes.

176 *R. v. Woollin* [1999] 1 A.C. 82 at 96G *per* Lord Steyn.

was not to kill her child. Instead, *X*'s direct intention was to save the child's life, but the only option available was to throw the child from the burning building. She obliquely intended to kill the child, if she foresaw the death of the child as a virtually certain consequence of her actions. Even though duress of circumstances is not a defence to murder, the defence of necessity might be in these circumstances.[177]

Furthermore, it is very unlikely that a prosecution would be brought against someone who has done all she could to save a life, even though she obliquely intended to kill. (This treatise works from the premise that oblique intention exists in English law as a substantive fault doctrine separate from the substantive fault doctrine of direct intention. As we will see, there is also a maxim of evidence that uses foresight of virtual certainty as a yardstick, but it should not be confused with the substantive doctrine of oblique intention/indirect intention.)

If the jury infer that *X* did in fact foresee the death as a virtually certain consequence of her actions, then the substantive doctrine of oblique intention could be invoked to ground a conviction.[178] The oblique intention doctrine applies, because oblique intention is a substantive fault element for the crime of murder.[179] This is different from using evidence of foresight of virtual certainty to infer direct intention. In the latter situation, evidence that the defendant foresaw the consequence as a virtual certainty could be used only to infer direct intention, if it was clear that the defendant did not directly intend the opposite. In the hypothetical above, it was clear that the mother, *X*, directly intended to save her child's life, although she obliquely (indirectly) intended to kill the child, because she foresaw its death as a virtually certain consequence of throwing it from the fourth floor.

177 *A (Children) (Conjoined Twins: Medical Treatment) (No.2)* [2001] 1 F.L.R. 267; cf. *Gillick v. West Norfolk and Wisbech AHA* [1986] A.C. 112; *R. v. Fretwell* (1862) Le. & Ca. 161; *R. v. Salford HA Ex p. Janaway* [1989] A.C. 537.

178 *R. v. Howe* [1987] A.C. 417; *R. v. Ryan* [2013] S.C.C. 3.

179 See *Hyam v. D.P.P.* [1975] A.C. 55 at 75 *per* Lord Hailsham; *In re Stonewall F.* (1989) 208 Cal.App.3d 1054 at 1062 fn. 7 where the court said: 'Some legal theorists, Bentham among them, have recorded this divergence by distinguishing (as "oblique" intention), mere foresight of consequences from "direct intention" where the consequences must have been contemplated by the accused not merely as a foreseen outcome but as an end when he set out to achieve, or as a means to an end, and constituted at least part of his reason for doing what he did . . . The paradigm arson case exemplifying an "oblique" intention occurs when the culpable party burns his own house knowing, by virtue of its proximity, that his neighbour's house is also certain to burn.' (See *People v. George* (1941) 42 Cal.App.2d 568, 571–572 and the discussion of it in the text; cf. *People v. Hiltel* (1901) 131 Cal. 577.) See also *Mata-Medina v. People* (2003) 71 P. 3d. 973 at 978, where it was held that the *mens rea* for second-degree murder required it be proved that *D* be 'aware that his conduct is practically certain to cause the result'. See also *People v. Fabris* (1995) 31 Cal. App. 4th 685 at 698; Glanville Williams, 'Oblique Intention' (1987) 46 *Cambridge L.J.* 417 at 420; Glanville Williams, 'The Mens Rea for Murder: Leave it Alone' (1989) 105 *L.Q.R.* 387.

The grey area is where it can be shown that the defendant at the very least foresaw the consequence as a virtual certainty; but it is not clear whether she directly intended the consequence.[180] In this situation, the jury can use the evidence that *D* foresaw the consequence as virtually certain to infer either direct or indirect intention. Take the case where *Y* decides to burn down her terrace house to collect the insurance. If the objective facts show that it was virtually certain that the neighbouring houses also would be burnt down and that *Y* foresaw this as a virtual certainty, the jury can infer that *Y* obliquely intended to burn down those houses. However, the jury might, instead, infer that *Y* directly intended to burn the neighbouring houses down. *Y* might argue that she did not intend to burn the neighbouring houses, but merely intended to burn her own. Nonetheless, the jury need not accept her story. It can infer that *Y* not only foresaw that the other houses would be damaged, but directly intended the consequence. In this situation, the jury uses evidence of foresight of virtual certainty to infer direct intention, because the evidence does not strongly suggest that *Y*'s direct intention was merely to burn her own house.

Similarly, if an enraged man throws his three-month-old son down a flight of stairs, he would not be able to use anger to displace the inference that he directly intended to kill his son.[181] The judge would most likely tell the jury that they are entitled to find that the acts done in so-called blind rage can be found to be purposive, the anger overcoming the defendant's inhibitions rather than his direct intention to kill. The defendant might argue that he obliquely intended to kill his son only and that is direct intention was to release his anger, but such an argument would not help him because it would be an admission of oblique intention. Since oblique intention is an alternative substantive fault element for murder,[182] he would be found guilty in either case.

C. Evidential maxims v. substantive fault doctrines

Let us revert to the distinction between substantive fault elements and evidence. It is one thing to say that there was a 99 per cent chance of the baby dying when it was thrown from the fourth floor of a burning building and

180 See the facts in *R. v. Matthews* [2003] 2 Cr. App. R. 462 at 476, where the objective evidence showed that the defendants at least obliquely intended to kill. However, in that case it was not clear whether they obliquely intended to kill only or whether they in fact directly intended to kill. The Court of Appeal held: 'We think that, once what is required is an appreciation of virtual certainty of death, and not some lesser foresight of merely probable consequences, there is very little to choose between a rule of evidence and one of substantive law.' In such a case, because there is no evidence strongly supporting one finding over the other, the jury can use the evidence that *D* foresaw the consequence of her action as a virtual certainty to infer either direct or oblique intention.

181 See the facts in *R. v. Woollin* [1999] 1 A.C. 82.

182 Baker, *op. cit. supra*, note 12 at Chapter 4.

another to use this evidence to infer either direct or indirect intention. An expert might be called to attest that it was a virtual certainty that the child would die, if thrown from the fourth floor. Nonetheless, this virtual certainty is only a type of evidence – it does not mean that the defendant herself foresaw this virtual certainty. Nor does it mean she directly intended to kill the child.[183] The objective fact that the death was a virtual certainty is evidence of that fact alone. The jury have to infer whether or not the defendant's mental state was one where she foresaw that the virtually certain consequence of throwing the child from the fourth floor was that it would die. Similarly, the jury have to infer whether the defendant directly intended to kill. If the evidence strongly demonstrates that the defendant obliquely intended the consequence, the jury is free to infer either oblique intention or direct intention. The substantive result is the same either way. A person found guilty of oblique intention murder, barring some defence, will be convicted of murder and be subject to a mandatory life sentence. In the case where a person burns a terrace house that shares walls with adjoining terrace houses, the objective (evidential) facts are such that the jury is likely to infer, not only that she foresaw that the other houses would be damaged as a virtual certainty, but that she directly intended to damage them.

The maxim that a person intended the natural probable consequences of her actions meant *a fortiori* she intended the foreseen consequences of her actions. Coupled with this, in many older cases a finding of foresight itself was held to be enough to infer intention.[184] The law of common purpose complicity took a wrong turn, because maxims of evidence such as foresight of probable and possible consequences not only mirror substantive criminal law fault elements, but also have been blurred with them for centuries. A further problem is that recklessness took a long time to emerge as a substantive form of fault wholly distinct from intention and negligence.[185]

183 The surgeons in *A (Children) (Conjoined Twins: Medical Treatment) (No.2)* [2001] 1 F.L.R. 267 did not directly intend to kill the weaker twin, but they did indirectly intend to kill her. In that case, the defence of necessity provided a defence. See Baker, *op. cit. supra*, note 12 at Chapter 27.

184 For example, in *Williams v. Bayley* (1866) L.R. 1 H.L. 200 at 221, Lord Westbury said: 'But if a man does an act which is attended necessarily with an inevitable consequence, he must be taken in law to have foreseen that consequence, and, in point of fact, to have deliberately intended that it should be the result of his action.'

185 See the confused discussion in McMullin V.P.'s judgment in the Hong Kong Court of Appeal in *Chan Wing-Siu* [1982] H.K.L.R. 280. In *R. v. Moloney* [1985] A.C. 905 at 913, Lord Hailsham said: 'I conclude with the pious hope that your Lordships will not again have to decide that foresight and foreseeability are not the same thing as intention although either may give rise to an irresistible inference of such, and that matters which are essentially to be treated as matters of inference for a jury as to a subjective state of mind will not once again be erected into a legal presumption. They should remain, what they always *should have been*, part of the law of evidence and inference to be left to the

Since the evidential maxims now mirror the fault elements of recklessness and negligence more closely, evidence that *D* foresaw the consequences of her actions as a possibility, or as more probable than not, can only be used to infer recklessness. Similarly, in most cases where direct intention is required, the objective evidence will have to be such that the jury are able to infer that the defendant did in fact intend the consequences of her actions. If *D* kills *V* by firing a gun at *V* who is standing within a metre of *D*, the jury might infer that she must have intended to kill *V*. However, there may be other evidence to allow a jury to draw the opposite conclusion, such as witness testimony stating that *D* and *V* were police officers on duty together and that *D* was cleaning her gun at the police station when it accidentally fired and killed *V*. The jury might infer that *D* was grossly negligent in cleaning her gun in the confines of the police station without checking to see whether it was loaded, but on the objective facts the jurors would not be able to infer that *D* intended to kill *V*. The jury have to consider all the evidence, witness testimony, the defendant's testimony and then infer what *D*'s state of mind was. Since only *D* knows for sure what she intended or was thinking when she killed, the jury have to infer her intention from the objective evidence.[186]

jury after a proper direction as to their weight, and not part of the substantive law.' In *Hyam v. D.P.P.* [1975] A.C. 55 at 82, Lord Dilhorne said: 'Whether or not it be that the doing of the act with the knowledge that certain consequences are highly probable is to be treated as establishing the intent to bring about those consequences, I think it is clear that for at least 100 years such knowledge has been recognised as amounting to malice aforethought.' Glanville Williams writes: 'A statement much nearer to the truth is that the law frequently – though not invariably – treats as *intentional* all consequences due to that form of negligence which is distinguished as [subjective] recklessness – all consequences, that is to say, which the actor *foresees* as the probable results of this wrongful act.' Glanville Williams, *Salmond on Jurisprudence* (London: Steven & Sons, 1957) at 413. See also Williams, *op. cit. supra*, note 73 at 45 *et seq.*; Turner, *op. cit. supra*, note 129; J. W. Cecil Turner, *Russell on Crime* (London: Stevens & Sons, 1958) Vol. I, at 35–36; 43–44; Rollin M. Perkins, 'A Re-Examination of Malice Aforethought' (1934) 43 *Yale L.J.* 537. On the conflation of negligence with recklessness, see Jerome Hall, *Principles of Criminal Law* (Indianapolis: Bobbs-Merrill Co. Inc., 1960) at 122 *et seq.* See also *R. v. Mowatt* [1967] 3 W.L.R. 1192, *R. v. G* [2004] 1 A.C. 1034 and the authorities cited therein.

186 'Before parting with the question of intent and recklessness, I would observe that the expressions "subjective test" and "objective test" that were used in the argument, and which have recently come somewhat into favour, are, I think, unfortunate. A man's own intention is for him a subjective state, just as are his sensations of pleasure or of pain. But the state of another man's mind, or of his digestion, is an objective fact. When it has to be proved, it is to be proved in the same way as other objective facts are proved. A jury must consider the whole of the evidence relevant to it as a fact in issue. If an accused gives evidence of what his intentions were, the jury must weigh his testimony along with whatever inference as to his intentions can be drawn from his conduct or from other relevant facts . . . Whatever [*D*] says, [the jurors] may be able to conclude from the whole of the evidence that beyond doubt he had a guilty mind and a guilty purpose. But always the questions are what did [*D*] in fact know, foresee, expect, intend.' *Vallance v. The Queen* (1963) 108 C.L.R. 56 at 83 *per* Windeyer, J.

Likewise, a person can intend to kill even though the means she uses make her chances of succeeding a remote possibility. For example, *D* might use an airgun that she knows has a maximum firing range of about 500 yards to try to kill *V* who is standing 1,500 yards away. Even though *D* foresees that the likelihood of killing *V* with the airgun in these circumstances is a remote possibility, the jury could infer that she intended to kill *V*, unless there is evidence to the contrary. *D* might even confess that her intention was indeed to kill. There would have to be objective evidence to show that *D* intended to kill. To reiterate the point, unless a defendant has confessed, her intention has to be determined from the objective facts.

If the jury find that *D* did not intend the criminal consequences of her conduct and only foresaw those consequences as probable or possible, then it cannot infer that *D* directly intended those consequences. The objective facts might demonstrate that *D* thought about the risks involved and made a conscious choice to run the risk. Nonetheless, recklessness can only be inferred where the objective facts show that *D* was conscious of the risks involved in acting the way she did. As I said above, the maxims of foresight of possibility or foresight of probability mirror the substantive fault element of recklessness. To the extent that these evidential maxims were used in the past to infer direct intention[187] (and also to uphold a presumption of intention), they did not mirror the substantive fault doctrine of direct intention.

The evidential maxim of foresight of virtual certainty mirrors the substantive fault doctrine of oblique intention, but it does not mirror the substantive fault doctrine of direct intention in a purely conceptual sense.[188] Nonetheless, evidence of foresight of virtual certainty can be used to infer either oblique intention or direct intention.[189] So in a case where it is clear that the defendant obliquely intended to kill but did not directly intend to kill, the jury would be bound to infer that she obliquely intended to kill only. In *A (Children) (Conjoined Twins: Medical Treatment) (No. 2)*,[190] the objective evidence demonstrated that the surgeons did not directly intend to kill the weaker twin. However, they foresaw that the virtually certain consequence of separating the twins was that the weaker one would die. It was not their desire to kill the weaker twin, but they did obliquely intend to kill her. The fact that the court provided the surgeons with a declaration that the defence of necessity applied to their proposed conduct demonstrates that oblique intention without a defence is sufficient for grounding a murder conviction. (Hence, it is not a defence to assert that there was only indirect intention rather than direct intention.)

187 In *D.P.P v. Hyam* [1975] 1 A.C. 55 at 65, Lord Hailsham said: 'Knowledge or foresight is at the best material which entitles or compels a jury to draw the necessary inference as to intention.'

188 John Finnis, 'Intention and Side-Effects' in R.G. Frey and Christopher W. Morris (eds.) *Liability and Responsibility: Essays in Law and Morals* (Cambridge: Cambridge University Press, 1991) at 32 *et seq.*

189 *R. v. Matthews* [2003] 2 Cr. App. R. 462.

190 [2001] 1 F.L.R. 267.

Similarly, in the hypothetical above where the mother was forced to throw her young child from the fourth floor of a burning building, it was clear that she did not directly intend to kill her child. The objective evidence demonstrated exactly the opposite: that is, that she was trying to save the life her child who was about to be burnt to death. In such a case, the jury could not use evidence of her oblique intention to infer direct intention, because the objective evidence shows that she did not directly intend to kill her child. This might be a hollow victory for the mother, because the doctrine of oblique intention is a substantive fault element in itself. The mother could be convicted of murder; not that she is likely to be prosecuted. The House of Lords has held that in cases where it is clear that there was no direct intention, but where there is evidence of oblique intention, the jury should be directed to consider whether oblique intention was present.[191] This clearly demonstrates that foresight of virtual certainty is not only an evidential maxim for guiding juries, but also a substantive fault doctrine. In other words, if the jury have found that *D* did not directly intend, it can still infer oblique intention and convict on that basis – the jury cannot be inferring direct intention, if it has already accepted that *D* did not directly intend, as was the case in *R. v. Woollin*.[192]

Now that we can see the difference between the roles that foresight plays in evidential maxims and the role it plays in substantive fault doctrines, we can see how courts blurring evidential maxims (maxims that did not always mirror the substantive fault elements) with substantive law resulted in the factual encouragement requirement (a 'conduct element') being collapsed into a 'fault element' requiring no more than recklessness.[193]

D. Modern judicial statements concerning inferences of intentional encouragement

The authorities demonstrate that foresight was used to infer intentional encouragement in cases where the perpetrator's collateral crime was

191 In *R. v. Woollin* [1999] 1 A.C. 82 at 95E, Lord Steyn said: 'It may be appropriate to give a direction in accordance with *Nedrick* in any case in which the defendant may not have desired the result of his act.'

192 [1999] 1 A.C. 82. Cf. *R. v. Matthews* [2003] 2 Cr. App. R. 462, where it was not clear on the facts whether the defendants directly intended to kill *V* or merely obliquely intended to kill *V*. Since there was ample evidence for the jury to infer that they at least obliquely intended to kill him, not much turned on the question of whether it was one or the other.

193 See the commentary for *R. v. Smith* [1988] Crim. L.R. 616, where it is observed that the Court of Appeal held: 'The present case concerned a specific intent and it was incumbent upon the judge to direct in the plainest terms that the appellant could only be convicted if the jury were sure that he had the requisite intent to cause grievous bodily harm and that the foresight the judge referred to was not of itself to be regarded as an intent, though it could properly be regarded as evidence supporting the existence of the intent necessary to establish the offence.' Cf. *R. v. Barr* (1989) 88 Cr. App. R. 362.

conditioned on future events. Recall, in *Johns v. The Queen*[194] the majority said: 'if the act is a probable consequence of the execution of the common purpose, there is evidence from which the jury can conclude that it was within the parties' mutual conditional intentions.' In *Chan Wing-Siu v The Queen,*[195] Sir Robin Cooke held that the test for inferring conditional intention had to be at least a subjective test of foresight of possibility. In light of *R. v. Woollin,*[196] nothing short of foresight of virtual certainty can be used for inferring (conditional) intention.

A foreseeing *P*'s collateral offending as a virtual certainty is not necessarily conclusive evidence that *A* conditionally intended the collateral crime.[197] In *D.P.P. of Northern Ireland v. Maxwell,*[198] Lord Hailsham said:

> The fact that, in the event, the offence committed by the principals crystallised into one rather than the other of the [planned and authorised] possible alternatives within his contemplation [of the crimes that had been planned and agreed as possible alternatives] only means that in the event he was accessory to that specific offence rather than one of the others which in the event was not the offence committed.

Lord Hailsham held that it could be inferred from the evidence that Maxwell agreed to assist whichever crime was chosen out of the range of crimes that had been agreed as possible alternatives. Maxwell knew the alternative crimes that his accomplices conditionally intended to perpetrate. The only thing he did not know for certain was which crime out of the alternatives would be carried out on the day. Maxwell's conditional intention extended to all the possible alternatives that had not only been contemplated as necessary for their criminal purpose, but also agreed upon. It was agreed that one or the other would be perpetrated. There was ample evidence for the jury to infer that Maxwell intended to assist the perpetrator to commit one of the planned crimes. That case did not rest on mere recklessness being established.

Similarly, in *R. v. Bristow*[199] Treacy, L.J. (Hamblen and Nicol, J.J. concurring) adopted the trial judge's statement of the law, which was:

194 [1980] 143 C.L.R. 108 at 131 *per* Mason, Murphy and Wilson, J.J.
195 [1985] A.C. 168.
196 [1999] 1 A.C. 82.
197 In some cases, *A*'s foresight of the virtual certainty of *P* perpetrating the collateral crime will not be conclusive, because *A* may have expressly commanded *P* not to commit any collateral crimes. See the discussion *infra.*
198 [1978] 1 W.L.R. 1350 at 1359.
199 [2013] E.W.C.A. Crim. 1540 at para. 38. Likewise, in *R. v. Penfold* (1980) 71 Cr. App. R. 4 at 8, Shaw, L.J. said: 'Robbers who burst into a house can hardly fail to contemplate the possible necessity of some degree of force to overcome or silence the occupants. While they may not desire to inflict any real harm, they do agree, by implication, to put themselves under the dictates of any arising necessity. It would be absurd and nonsensical to assume that they agreed to go so far and not a whit further to achieve their objective.'

> [T]he jury could safely conclude that the team, on being confronted by JG, shared an immediate intention to get away, as planned, and carried that intention forward. It is open for the jury therefore, to conclude that each burglar intended the vehicular escape, should it arise in those circumstances, that that escape should be achieved at speed and with determination and, if necessary with no respect for property or person that might get in the way. On the evidence it is open for the jury to conclude that that intention was in the mind of each member of the team, each having the foresight to realise the risk of harm to a person who was trying to prevent the escape.

It is clear that the court below was allowing the jury to infer conditional intention with respect to the dangerous escape. In other words, not all the contingencies need to be expressly agreed or thought about deeply. In cases where people are planning to burglarise a house, it would not be unreasonable for the jury to infer that they thought about the possibility of being caught, about the possibility of stumbling upon an occupant and so on. In addition, the jury could infer that they had a common purpose that extended to the collateral crimes that were necessary for dealing with such contingencies.

Likewise, if one of the parties is armed with lethal weapons to the knowledge of all the participants, it would not be unreasonable for the jury to infer that they all intended the arms be used to inflict a certain level of injury or to facilitate their escape and so on. Of course, the accessory's bare knowledge of the fact that the perpetrator was armed does not demonstrate conclusively that the accessory authorised *P* to use those arms. As we will see below, the dangerous weapon doctrine is not much more than an evidential maxim.[200] It holds that because *A* knew that *P* was carrying a lethal weapon, the jury can infer that both parties conditionally intended serious or lethal violence to be used.[201] It allows the jury to infer that *acts* of a certain kind (e.g. inherently lethal acts) were within their common purpose.

200 See *Gray's Case* (1661) Kel. 24 at 64; *Halloway's Case* (1628) Cro. Car. 131; *R. v. Macklin* (1838) 2 Lewin 225; *R. v. Eagle* (1862) 2 F. & F. 827 *per* Erle, C. J.; Foster, *op. cit. supra*, note 50 at 271. These sorts of strong conclusions are no longer drawn, but inferences can be drawn from the lethality of any weapon possessed by the perpetrator. In *R. v. Ried* (1976) 62 Cr. App. R. 109 at 112, Lawton, L.J. said: 'When two or more men go out together in joint possession of offensive weapons such as revolvers and knives and the circumstances are such as to justify an inference that the very least they intend to do with them is to use them to cause fear in another, there is, in our judgment, always a likelihood that in the excitement and tensions of the occasion, one of them will use his weapon in some way which will cause death or serious injury.' See also *R. v. Garvey* [2002] EWCA Crim. 1481 at para. 8.

201 The lethality of the weapon would not be conclusive. There also would have to be other evidence. In *R. v. O'Flaherty* [2004] 2 Cr. App. R. 20 at para. 65, Mantell, L.J said: 'In a case of spontaneous violence such as this where there has been no prior agreement the jury will usually have to make inferences as to the scope of the joint enterprise from the knowledge and actions of the individual participants.'

In *R. v. Tyler*, Lord Denman, C.J. said:[202]

> [I]f they were aware [had knowledge] of the malignant purpose entertained by Thom [the perpetrator], and shared in that purpose with him, and were present aiding and abetting, and assisting him in the commission of acts fatal to life, in the course of accomplishing this purpose, then no doubt they are guilty as principals on this second count . . . If they contemplated a resistance to the lawfully constituted authorities of the country, in case any should come against them while they were so banded together, there would be a common purpose, and they would be answerable for anything which they did in the execution of it. If any man is found aiding another, of whose ill intentions he is thoroughly apprised, he is responsible. It will be for you to say whether, from what was done by these men both before and after the killing of Nicholas Meares, they did not intend this general resistance to the law . . . You will, therefore, say whether these two men were so far cognisant of an illegal purpose in Thom, and joined in his acts, that they are guilty of the murder which the hand of Thom committed . . . If you think that they kept together with the knowledge of any general purpose of resistance to the law, then they are guilty.

In *R. v. Pearce*, Avory, J. said:[203]

> The question which ought to have been put to the jury was: was there any evidence that Pearce was a party to the assault with the gun, in the sense of having arranged with Humphreys that, if they were interrupted in their poaching, they would assault a bailiff or anyone else who interrupted them with a gun or other weapon? And further, was there any evidence from which the jury would properly infer that Pearce and Humphreys went out with a common purpose, not merely to poach, but also to resist apprehension at all costs, even by violence if necessary.

In *R. v. Slack*,[204] Lord Lane, C.J. (Kennedy and Hutchison, J.J. concurring), held:

> If, however, as part of their joint plan it was understood between them expressly or tacitly that if necessary one of them would kill or do serious harm as part of their common enterprise, then B is guilty of murder . . . As appears from the cases we have cited, the direction

202 (1838) 8 Car. & P. 616 at 618–619; 620–621. See also *R. v. Pridmore* (1913) 8 Cr. App. R. 198 at 203 where Phillimore, J. held that conditional intention as to the collateral offence might be inferred from the conduct of the parties to the joint enterprise.

203 (1930) 21 Cr. App. R. 79 at 80–81.

204 [1989] Q.B. 775 at 781–782.

> may be in a variety of different forms. Provided that it is made clear to the jury that B to be guilty must be proved to have lent himself to a criminal enterprise involving the infliction, if necessary, of serious harm or death or to have had an *express or tacit understanding* with A that such harm or death should, *if necessary*, be inflicted, the precise form of words in which the jury are directed is not important [emphasis added].

There are plenty of other judicial statements to this effect. However, I think I have quoted more than enough doctrine to support the thesis presented in this chapter. *Right through the ancient and modern authorities is the fundamental factual encouragement by intentional authorisation constraint. The intentional encouragement constraint means that an accessory is not liable unless she authorises the criminal acts that result from the unlawful enterprise.* Acts and consequences are not the same thing. A consequence can be accidental, but a criminal act depends on the conscious autonomous choice of a human agent. (There may be the rare case where the accessory assists an excused agent such as where she gives an insane person a gun to assist a murder, but these cases do not affect the general principle.)[205]

A person can only be criminally liable for the acts of another, if she is involved in that person's act. The accessory has to participate with the requisite culpability. It is not enough that she commits a thought crime by taking great delight in hearing that *P* plans to rob her old enemy.

The accessory can only be linked to the perpetrator's act if she is physically and culpably involved. Physical involvement might not be anything more than verbal encouragement, but the accessory has to utter the words of encouragement to become involved in *P*'s crime. Factual encouragement might also be implied by her omissions. A security guard working in store has a duty to ensure that customers do not shoplift. If by chance, *A*, a security guard, sees her sister, *P*, shoplifting and fails to tell *P* to stop, or fails to report *P*, and *P* continues because of *A*'s omission, *A* encourages by omission. Similarly, let us assume *P* steals even more goods than she originally intended to steal because she sees *A* is failing to take action. On these facts, it could be argued that the shoplifter is encouraged to steal more, not only because of the circumstantial fact that the security guard on duty happens to be her sister, but also because of her sister's intentional omission.

It must be shown that the collateral crimes are not only within the conditional intentions of the perpetrator, but also within the conditional

205 *R. v. Manley* (1844) 1 Cox C.C. 104; *People v. Hallett* (1979) 419 NYS2d 397 (perpetrator's youth); *State v. Lord* (1938) 42 N.M. 638, 84 P.2d 80; *State v. McAllister* (1978) 366 So. 2d 1340 (perpetrator provoked). See also Hale, *op. cit., supra*, note 47 at 334; Hawkins, *op. cit. supra*, note 74 at Chap. 29, Sect. 11. Cf. *Eden v. Whally's Case* (1553) 1 Dyer 88.

intentions of the accessory. In *Johns v. The Queen*[206] the High Court of Australia emphatically endorsed the requirement that the accessory be proved to have encouraged the collateral crimes of her accomplice. Likewise, Sir Robin Cooke in *Chan Wing-Siu v The Queen*[207] recognised that the key ingredient in common purpose complicity liability is *factual encouragement by authorisation.* Coupled with this, all the old cases held that there had to be a general (implied or express[208]) encouragement with respect to collateral crimes of opposition resulting from unlawful joint enterprises. Mere association is not enough to satisfy the conduct element set out in section 8 of the *Accessories and Abettors Act 1861.*

E. Obliquely intended encouragement

Obliquely intended encouragement is probably enough for complicity liability under section 8 of the *Accessories and Abettors Act 1861,* but nothing less will do. In *R. v. Barr*[209] the court took the view that a conditional intention could be inferred where it could be shown that the accomplice foresaw as a matter of virtual certainty that the perpetrator would commit the collateral crime for the purpose of making the joint enterprise succeed. It was held that in light of *R. v. Hancock,*[210] and the *dicta* of Lord Lane, C.J. in *R. v. Nedrick,*[211] that foresight of virtual certainty was required to satisfy the conditional intention requirement. This is the preferable view. If we accept that the foresight rule was only ever applied in the complicity cases as an evidential maxim, then it is possible to limit complicity liability to cases where the accessory conditionally intended or intended *simpliciter* to encourage *P* to perpetrate the collateral crimes. Alternatively, complicity liability could be made out where *A*'s oblique conditional intention was to encourage *P* to perpetrate the collateral crime. In the case of oblique intention, the accomplice's culpability (oblique intention that the perpetrator commit the conditional-target crime for the purpose of effecting the joint enterprise) is almost equivalent[212] to that of the perpetrator's and thus there is no great injustice in holding her equally liable for a collateral crime even if it is a specific intent crime such as murder.

206 (1980) 143 C.L.R. 108.
207 [1985] A.C. 168.
208 In ancient times authorisation was sometimes implied or presumed on the basis that the parties had embarked on an unlawful joint enterprise where they could expect opposition. See Foster, *op. cit. supra,* note 50 at 353; Hale, *loc. cit. supra,* note 47.
209 (1989) 88 Cr. App. R. 362.
210 (1986) 82 Cr. App. R. 264.
211 (1986) 83 Cr. App. R. 267.
212 Even though both parties might specifically intend the non-target crime such as killing the security guard to effect their robbery, it is arguable that the party who is willing to perpetrate killing is morally more evil than a person who is only willing to rely on another to do the perpetration.

When an accomplice agrees (expressly or tacitly) that a perpetrator should commit a conditional-target crime for the purpose of making their underlying joint enterprise succeed, she manifests a high level of culpability. She does not share the perpetrator's specific intent to kill etc., because she does not intend to perpetrate a killing herself (and might be the type of person who could never bring herself to actually perpetrate a murder), but she has encouraged the perpetrator to kill for the purpose of effecting their joint enterprise. Such a state of culpability is only marginally less evil in moral terms than that manifested by the actual perpetrator. It is true that such a party does not do anything to assist the perpetrator, but her encouragement by authorisation of the conditional-target crime is an intentional act of participation in that collateral crime.

The English decisions before *R. v. Hyde*[213] included a factual participation constraint – i.e. a factual encouragement constraint. Lord Parker, C.J. asserted that the substantive law of complicity applied only where it could be demonstrated that the accessory encouraged the perpetrator's collateral crime by authorising it.[214] Alas, in *R. v. Hyde*,[215] Lord Lane, C.J. decided to change the law to supplement the substantive fault requirement based on intentional encouragement by authorisation with a fault requirement of a reckless encouragement. After reading a commentary on his own decision in *R. v. Wakely*,[216] Lord Lane, C.J. seems to have confused the roles that the evidential maxim of 'foresight of possibility', direct intention and factual participation play. This was very unfortunate, because over the decades Lord Lane, C.J. was one of the few judges who insisted that the substantive test was one of intentional encouragement by authorisation. Lord Lane, C.J. summed up the law correctly when he appeared as a young barrister in *R. v. Anderson*:[217]

> Mr Lane submits that that was a clear misdirection. He would put the principle of law to be invoked in this form: that where two persons embark on a joint enterprise, each is liable for the acts done in pursuance of that joint enterprise, that that includes liability for unusual consequences *if they arise from the execution of the agreed joint enterprise* but (and this is *the crux of the matter*) that, if one of the adventurers goes beyond what has been *tacitly agreed* as part of the common enterprise, his co-adventurer is not liable for the consequences of that *unauthorised*

213 Under the influence of *Chan Wing-Siu v. The Queen* [1985] A.C. 168, Lord Lane, C.J. in *R. v. Hyde* [1990] 3 W.L.R. 1115 was persuaded to supplement the authorisation requirement with a recklessness requirement. This was a stark departure from his earlier reasoning on this point. See his thoughtful judgment in *R. v. Slack* [1989] 3 W.L.R. 513.

214 *R. v. Anderson* [1966] 2 Q.B. 110 at 118–119.

215 [1991] 1 Q.B. 134 at 139.

216 [1990] Crim. L.R. 119.

217 [1966] 2 Q.B. 110 at 118–119.

> act. Finally, he says it is for the jury in every case to decide whether what was done was part of the joint enterprise, or went beyond it and was in fact an act *unauthorised* by that joint enterprise [emphasis added].

Mr Lane's (as he then was) submission was not only approved by a very strong court of five judges (the judges were Lord Parker, C.J.; Edmund-Davies, Marshall, Roskill and James, J.J.) siting in the Court of Criminal Appeal in *R. v. Anderson*,[218] but was also applied in numerous subsequent decisions.

The most powerful judicial statement I could find to support my interpretation of the law is that given by King, C.J., the former Chief Justice of the Supreme Court of South Australia. The statement is particularly authoritative, because Chief Justice King was not only one of the greatest jurists of the twentieth century,[219] but also a judge who had superlative skills in the field of criminal law. In *R. v. Britten*,[220] King, C.J. said:

> The judgment, delivered by Sir Robin Cooke in *Chan Wing-Siu v. The Queen* [1985] A.C. 168, discussed the authorities, including *Johns v The Queen* (1980) 143 C.L.R. 108 which lay down the well-established principles governing liability of participants in a joint criminal enterprise. *The judgment gives no indication of any intention to break new legal ground or to extend the grounds upon which criminal liability arises in such cases* . . . In *Mills v. The Queen* (1986) 61 A.L.J.R. 59 the High Court of Australia . . . said that 'in many cases it will be sufficient to direct the jury by adapting to the circumstances the simple formula mentioned by Sir Robin Cooke'.
>
> . . .
>
> I do not take the Privy Council in *Chan Wing-Siu v. The Queen* or the High Court in *Mills v. The Queen* to be abandoning the established principles upon which the criminal liability of participants in a joint enterprise for crimes actually perpetrated by other participants, is based. *The fundamental notion is that by participating in the enterprise, each participant impliedly authorises all criminal acts which are in his contemplation [mutual conditional intentions] as being part of the common design or as being*

218 [1966] 2 Q.B. 110 at 118–119. See also *R. v. LLM (A Juvenile)* [2002] EWCA Crim. 183 at para. 21; *R. v. Roberts* [2001] E.W.C.A. Crim. 1594 at para. 44; *R. v. Crooks* [1999] N.I. 226; *R. v. Greatrex* [1999] 1 Cr. App. R. 126 at 138; *R. v. Slack* [1989] Q.B. 775 at 780; *R. v. Ward* (1987) 85 Cr. App. R. 71. Even in *Chan Wing-Siu v. The Queen* [1985] A.C. 168 at 175, Sir Robin Cooke said: 'That there is such a principle is not in doubt. It turns on . . . intentional authorisation, which may be express but is more usually implied.'

219 King, C.J. was the Attorney-General for South Australia and thereafter the Chief Justice of South Australia for nearly twenty years.

220 (1988) 49 S.A.S.R. 47 at 53–54. See also *R. v. Cruise et al.* (1970) 9 C.R.N.S. 225; R. *v. Roy et al.* (1970) 9 C.R.N.S. 137.

> *a substantial risk [a virtual certainty] associated with its implementation.*[221] The concept of *authorisation is endorsed* by the Privy Council in *Chan Wing-Siu* (at 175) and the expression 'substantial risk' is taken from the judgment of Stephen, J. in *Johns v. The Queen* (at 117). That fundamental notion is sufficiently explained to the jury in many cases by some adaptation of the *Chan Wing-Siu* formula. It would be a mistake, however, in my opinion, to treat the use of that formula, as was done in argument on this appeal, as involving a new legal test differing from the established principles of the law of joint enterprise. Those principles are unaffected and there may be many cases in which they would not be sufficiently explained by use of the formula. Both *Chan Wing-Siu* and *Johns v. The Queen* were cases of persons going to premises armed with lethal weapons. In other cases different directions may be necessary. I take the example of a mass political demonstration, perhaps in a highly charged atmosphere, in which all participants might contemplate that there was a substantial risk that some hotheads might commit violent offences quite outside the common peaceful purpose of the demonstration. I think that if such offences were committed and peaceful participants were charged, the proper basis of criminal liability in such circumstances would not be adequately explained by use of the *Chan Wing-Siu* formula. The same might be said of a case of a joint enterprise to rob in which there was an express or tacit understanding that weapons would not be used. I doubt whether mere contemplation of a substantial risk that one of the participants might act in contravention of the common agreement would of itself be a sufficient basis of criminal liability. *One must not lose sight of the fundamental ground of liability which is the implied authorisation of what is contemplated as part of, or incidental to the implementation of, the common purpose. To do so would be to court the risk of substituting a formula which is a valuable tool for the explanation to the jury of the fundamental legal principle, for the principle itself, and of applying the formula indiscriminately to cases to which it is not appropriate.* The result might be a distortion of the true [derivative] principles underlying the criminal liability of participants in a joint enterprise for crimes of which they are not the actual perpetrators, and the unjust conviction of persons of crimes of which they could not be said, in any true sense, to be guilty [emphasis added].

If a person foresaw that the virtually certain consequence of joining with others to protest was that some of the protestors would be encouraged by her participation to commit acts of criminal damage, she should still

221 Virtual certainty or substantial risk is being used as a maxim to allow the jury to infer that the secondary party knew what was planned and thus encouraged it by approving in advance that it be perpetrated should the need for it to be perpetrated arise.

be liable unless some public interest defence applies (cf. section 50 of the *Serious Crime Act 2007*) or some other protection such as freedom of expression. But if a person has expressly told the perpetrator not to perpetrate the collateral crime, her express dissent annuls any implied encouragement that might be inferred from joining the underlying enterprise. Her oblique intention alone will not be enough to infer an act of encouragement.

In *Rosemond v. U.S.*,[222] Kagan, J. said:

> And the canonical formulation of that needed state of mind – is Judge Learned Hand's: To aid and abet a crime, a defendant must not just 'in some sort associate himself with the venture,' but also 'participate in it as in something that he wishes to bring about' and 'seek by his action to make it succeed' . . . We have previously found that intent requirement satisfied when a person actively participates in a criminal venture with full knowledge of the circumstances constituting the charged offence . . . So for purposes of aiding and abetting law, a person who actively participates in a criminal scheme knowing its extent and character intends that scheme's commission.
>
> . . .
>
> For all that to be true, though, the § 924(c) defendant's knowledge of a firearm must be advance knowledge – or otherwise said, knowledge that enables him to make the relevant legal (and indeed, moral) choice. When an accomplice knows beforehand of a confederate's design to carry a gun, he can attempt to alter that plan or, if unsuccessful, withdraw from the enterprise; it is deciding instead to go ahead with his role in the venture that shows his intent to aid an armed offence.

In the above quoted passages, the Supreme Court of the United States made it clear that direct intention is required. It drew this conclusion by drawing on the judgment of Learned Hand, J, which Hand, J. formulated by drawing on almost 500 years of English common law precedents. The Supreme Court of the United States also made it clear that intention can be inferred from the participator's knowledge of what was planned and her knowledge of the relevant circumstances. In *Rosemond v. U.S.*,[223] Kagan, J. rejects recklessness as the substantive fault element for complicity liability

222 (2014) 134 S.Ct. 1240, Kagan, J., delivered the opinion of the Court, in which Roberts, C. J., and Kennedy, Ginsburg, Breyer, and Sotomayor, J.J. joined, and in which Scalia, J., joined in all but footnotes 7 and 8. Alito, J., filed an opinion concurring in part and dissenting in part, in which Thomas, J., joined.

223 (2014) 134 S.Ct. 1240.

and seems to hold that the secondary party's advanced knowledge of the perpetrator's plan to use a gun is sufficient for a jury to infer that the secondary party intended the perpetrator to go armed.

When *A* and *P* carry out a joint criminal enterprise both believing as a matter of virtual certainty that *P* will perpetrate a collateral crime should condition *X* arise, a jury could infer that *A* intended to encourage *P*'s collateral crime. Since both parties had mutual expectations and full knowledge of what was planned, *A*'s continued participation with this mutual knowledge is an act of encouragement apropos the collateral crime. In such a case, even if *A* has expressly ordered *P* not to commit the collateral crime, evidence showing that *A* participated in the unlawful joint enterprise in circumstances where both *A* and *P* mutually believed *P* would commit the collateral crime as a matter of virtual certainty, would make it almost impossible for *A* to demonstrate that her continued participation did not annul her express order (act of discouragement) that *P* should not to perpetrate the collateral crime. *A*'s continued participation would allow the jury to infer that she is lying and in fact intended to authorise *P* to perpetrate the collateral crime.

Authorisation by its very nature seems to require purposive conduct on the accessory's part, but the virtual certainty maxim could be used to infer direct intention. If there is a mutual expectation that the collateral crime is a virtual certainty should a guard confront them during their joint robbery, the jury could draw the inference that *P* believed that she had *A*'s support and authorisation and that this in fact encouraged *P* in circumstances where *A* intended to encourage *P*. When the facts are as just given, *A* would find it almost impossible to convince a jury that she did not share *P*'s conditional intention with respect to the collateral crime. On evidence this strong the jury is likely infer that *A* intends to encourage by implied authorisation and this would be enough to make her liable. *A*'s direct intention is to send *P* a message of encouragement. Evidence demonstrating that *A* foresaw that it was virtually certain that *P* would be encouraged to perpetrate the collateral crime because of *A*'s participation in the underlying joint enterprise would not be conclusive evidence of intentional encouragement.[224] Derivative

224 See *R. v. Edmeads* (1828) 3 Car. & P. 390 at 392 where Vaughan, B. said whether the accessories authorised and thus encouraged the collateral crime 'is . . . a question for the Jury; but still, on this evidence, it is quite clear what the common purpose was. They all draw up in lines, and point their guns at the game-keepers, and they are all giving their countenance and assistance to the one of them who actually fires the gun. If it could be shewn that either of them separated himself from the rest, and shewed distinctly that he would have no hand in what they were doing, the objection would have much weight in it.' If *A* has withdrawn from the common design well in advance of it being perpetrated, then she will be able to raise withdrawal as a defence. Hale held that a person was not liable where she has withdrawn from the joint enterprise. Hale, *op. cit. supra*, note 47 at 537. Cf. *R. v. Fretwell* (1862) Le. & Ca. 161, where *A* assisted *P*'s self-murder (which at the time was a crime) by supplying her with an abortifacient. The facts in the report suggests that *A* believed *P* would use the

liability hinges on an act of *factual encouragement*,[225] not on an act of *discouragement*[226] combined with association and foresight.

F. Should reckless participation be criminalised independently of the common purpose doctrine?

This leaves one question: is reckless foresight sufficient to send a message of encouragement to the perpetrator of a collateral crime? Hence, can reckless participation in the underlying joint enterprise in fact encourage the perpetrator to perpetrate a crime that the accessory does not intend her to perpetrate? Encouragement in standard complicity cases is normally purposive,[227] but it may result from reckless conduct.[228] It also might result when *A* obliquely intends to encourage *P* to perpetrate the anticipated target crime.[229] However, the problem is more complex when we are considering encouragement by authorisation in the common purpose complicity cases.

We need factual encouragement for the purposes of establishing the conduct element for complicity. Clearly, a person cannot authorise recklessly. A person might know that by participating in the underlying criminal enterprise she is risking sending the perpetrator a message of encouragement. If so then the *conduct element* in common purpose complicity could be made out, even in cases where the accessory merely foresees there is a possibility that her unintended act of encouragement might have the effect of encouraging the perpetrator to perpetrate a contemplated collateral

abortifacient as a matter of virtual certainty, but the facts show that *A* commanded *P* not to use it and that *A* supplied *P* only because she threatened suicide.

225 *Hutt v. R.* [1989] T.A.S.S.C. 27 at paragraph 53, Cox, J. (Underwood, Crawford, J.J. concurring); *R. v. Coney* (1881–82) L.R. 8 Q.B.D. 534; *R. v. Clarkson* [1971] 1 W.L.R. 1402 at 1406; *Allen v. Ireland* [1984] 1 W.L.R. 903; *Charnley. v. R.* [2013] N.Z.C.A. 226.

226 In *Hicks v. United States* (1893) 150 U.S. 442 at 146, it was noted that: '[T]he words may have been used for a different purpose, and yet have had the actual effect of inciting Rowe to commit the murderous act . . . Hicks . . . testified that the expressions used by him were intended to dissuade Rowe from shooting.' The Supreme Court of the United States held: '[W]e do not think . . . that the mere use of certain words would suffice to warrant the jury in finding Hicks guilty, regardless of the intention with which they were used.'

227 In *People v. Terman* (1935) 4 Cal.App.2d 345 at 347, Pullen, J. said: '"Abet" is a French word combined of two words "a" and "beter"–to bait or excite an animal. The word "aid" does not imply guilty knowledge or felonious intent, whereas the word "abet" includes knowledge of the wrongful purpose of the perpetrator and counsel and encouragement in the crime.' See further, Glanville Williams, 'Complicity, Purpose and the Draft Code: Part 1' [1990] Crim. L.R. 4.

228 *R. v. Young* (1838) 8 Car. & P. 644; *R. v. Swindall* (1846) 2 Car. & K. 230; *Allen v. Ireland* [1984] 1 W.L.R. 903.

229 *R. v. Gnango* [2012] 1 A.C. 827, where *D2* by his conduct obliquely intended to encourage *D1* to try to kill him.

crime. However, since the *mental element* requires nothing less than oblique intention, reckless participation was not covered under the law before the courts reinterpreted in the 1990s.

It is true that many joint criminal enterprises can involve reckless acts of encouragement, because the joint perpetrator of the underlying crime might believe that by joining that underlying criminal joint enterprise, she might send a message to the perpetrator that she also supports him perpetrating foreseeable collateral crimes. Nonetheless, this sort of reckless encouragement should be criminalised in an independent offence that allows for fair labelling and proportionate punishment. Given the oblique intention requirement found in section 45 of the *Serious Crime Act 2007*, law reform might be necessary to ensure that reckless participation in the crimes of others is criminalised. The *Accessories and Abettors Act 1861* does not include any defence of reasonable encouragement, nor does it have any mechanism for allowing for fair labelling or proportionate punishment, when the collateral crime is a specific intent crime such as murder, which carries a mandatory life sentence. Reckless encouragement ought not to be enough to hold people liable for specific intent crimes that carry mandatory life sentences.

Cases of reckless encouragement by participating in an underlying joint enterprise are likely to be common, but are different from cases involving intentional implied or express authorisation. If fair labelling and proportionate punishment require the reckless encourager to be criminalised not only as a joint perpetrator of the underlying joint enterprise, but also as a participant in the collateral crime, then a special offence should be enacted to achieve such a penal end.

Since the bulk of the authorities going back 500 years require intentional encouragement, using recklessness as the fault element in common purpose complicity is not appropriate. Since section 44 of the *Serious Crime Act 2007* covers only intentional participation and section 45 covers only obliquely intended participation, a new offence is needed to plug the gap that would be left by reinterpreting complicity under section 8 of the *Accessories and Abettors Act 1861* as not covering reckless participation. Such a change, in practical terms, could raise concern that it would remove protection for society. However, this concern could be addressed by amending the *Serious Crime Act 2007* to criminalise reckless participation. The advantage of amendment to the *2007 Act*'s offences is that it allows for fair labelling and proportionate punishment.

VI. Dangerous weapons as evidence of common intention

The fundamentally different act rule or variation rule has been an issue mainly in homicide cases. In particular, it has been used to show that the accessory did not encourage the perpetrator's collateral crime, because the act perpetrated was fundamentally different to anything the parties agreed should be done.[230] The luminous statement of Sir Matthew Hale in his treatise has long been considered the *locus classicus* on the 'fundamentally different act' rule:

> If *A.* counsel or command *B.* to beat *C.* with a small wand or rod, which could not in all human reason cause death, if *B.* beat *C.* with a great club, or wound him with a sword, whereof he dies, it seems, that *A.* is not accessary, because there was no command of death, nor of any thing, that could probably cause death, and *B.* hath varied from the command in substance, and not in circumstance.[231]

Referring to Hale's example of a fundamentally different act, the court in *R. v. Hazel* said:

> Now in both these cases there was a clear intent in the accessary, yet in the first case, because his intent was not to kill the person who was killed, and because, in the second case, his intent was only to beat the person killed [in a way that posed little to no risk of death], the accessary was not guilty of murder.[232]

If *B* had used the small wand or rod to beat *C* and this had caused *C*'s death,[233] *A* would have been liable for constructive manslaughter because the act *A* commands is the cause of *C*'s death.[234]

The fundamentally different act rule does not allow the accessory to avoid a conviction as a participant in constructive crime, but it must be

230 See *The Three Soldiers Case* (1697) Fost. 353; *R. v. Plummer* (1706) Kelyng, J. 109; *R. v. Hawkins* (1828) 3 Car. & P. 392; *R. v. Collison* (1831) 4 Car. & P. 565; *R. v. Skeet* (1866) 4 F. & F. 931; *R. v. Caton* (1874) 12 Cox C.C. 624; *R. v. Short* (1932) 23 Cr. App. R. 170 *per* Lord Chief Justice Hewart, MacKinnon and Hawke, J.J.; *R. v. Spraggett* [1960] Crim. L.R. 840; *R. v. Smith* [1963] 1 W.L.R. 1200 at 1205–1207; *R. v. Anderson* [1966] 2 Q.B. 110 at 118–119; *R. v. Lovesey* [1970] 1 Q.B. 352; *R. v. Wan* [1995] Crim. L.R. 296; *R. v. Dunbar* [1988] Crim. L.R. 693.

231 Hale, *op. cit. supra*, note 47 at 436; 454. See also *R. v. Saunders and Archer* (1577) 2 Plow. 473.

232 *R. v. Hazel* (1785) 1 Leach 368 at 375–376.

233 *R. v. Bristow* [2013] E.W.C.A. Crim. 1540; *R. v. Creamer* [1966] 1 Q.B. 72; *R. v. Buck* (1960) 44 Cr. App. R. 213; *R. v. Gaylor* (1857) Dears. & B. 288 at 291 *per* Bramwell B.; *R. v. Smith* (1847) 2 Cox C.C. 233; see also Blackstone, *op. cit., supra*, note 151 at 37. The thin skull rule would apply. See *R. v. Blaue* [1975] 1 W.L.R. 1411. The exceptions recognised in the old law for voluntary manslaughter have no bearing on liability for involuntary manslaughter. See for example, *Johnson v. State* (1956) 91 So. 2d 185; *Hammon v. U.S.* (1997) 695 A.2d 97; *Thomas v. State* (1987) 510 N.E.2d 651; *Stacy v. State* (1957) 228 Ark. 260. *Mutatis mutandis*: compare the law as stated in *Bibithe's Case* (1598) 4 Co.Rep. 43b; *Goff v. Byby* (1596) Cro. Eliz. 540; *Goose's Case* (1597) Moore K.B. 461; *Trial of Lord Mohun* (1692) Holt, K.B. 479; *Thody's Case* (1673) Freem. K.B. 514. See also Hale, *op. cit. supra*, note 47 at 437; Hawkins, *op. cit. supra*, note 74 at Chap. 29, Sect. 24; *Moore v. Lowe* (1935) 116 W. Va. 165.

234 *R. v. Anderson* [1966] 2 Q.B. 110 at 120; *R. v. Gamble* [1989] N.I. 268.

demonstrated she encouraged/authorised the criminal act that is the basis of the constructive liability charge. In common purpose complicity, the dangerous weapon doctrine has been used to allow the jury to decide whether or not *A* intended to encourage *P*'s collateral crime. In *Williams v. State*,[235] it was said:

> If . . . two combine to fight a third with fists, and death accidentally results from a blow intended by one, the other also is responsible for the homicide. But if one resorts to a deadly weapon without the other's knowledge or consent, he only is thus liable. . . . The implied agreement here is evidently not to resort to the use of a deadly weapon, and the use of such a weapon is therefore foreign to the [intentions] of the parties, and a departure from the common design.

The rule itself seems to have evolved from the rule that one must take the unintended consequences of intentional acts. In the past when a person used a dangerous weapon or excessive force to inflict bodily harm that resulted in a death, the courts held the wrongdoer constructively liable for murder.[236] However, where the force was mild or the weapon not dangerous, the courts tended to invoke constructive manslaughter instead.[237] The dangerous weapon rule was used to determine whether *D* intended a certain kind act. If she did, then she had to accept liability for the unintended consequences of the act. The potential consequences of the given act would

235 (1887) 9 Crim. L. Mag. & Rep. 480 at 483 citing *R. v. Caton* (1874) 12 Cox C.C. 624.

236 See *The King v. Keat* (1701) 5 Mod. 287, where it was said: '[T]he defendant might not have intended to kill his servant when he first corrected him with a sword; but that being a very *improper instrument for correction*, shows that he had some ill intent; and death ensuing, it is murder.' In *R. v. Oneby* (1727) 2 Ld. Raym. 1485 at 1488–1489, it was said: 'If *A* strikes at *B* with any dangerous weapon, as a pistol, hammer, large stone, &c. which in probability might kill B. or do him some great bodily hurt . . . and *A.* kills *B.* this will be murder; for the act was voluntary, and it appears from the nature of it, that it was done with an intent to do mischief; and therefore since in all probability it might have occasioned *B.*'s death, or done him some great bodily harm, the law implies malice prepense.' See also *Halloway's Case* (1628) Cro. Car. 131. Bracton asserted: 'But here it is to be distinguished whether a person is employed upon a lawful or unlawful work, as if a person has projected a stone towards a place across which men are accustomed to pass, or whilst a person pursues a horse or an ox, and some one has been struck by the horse or the ox, and such like, this is imputed to his account. But if he was employed in a lawful work, as if a master is flogging his scholar for the sake of discipline, or if when a person was casting down hay from a cart, or cutting into a tree and such like, if he had taken as diligent care as he could, by looking out and by calling out, or the master not exceeding moderation in flogging his scholar, blame is not imputable to him.' Bracton, *op. cit. supra*, note 63 at 277.

237 *John Royley's Case* (1611) Cro. Jac. 296. Cf. the modern approach taken in *R. v. Creamer* [1966] 1 Q.B. 72; *D.P.P. v. Newbury* [1977] A.C. 500, where it was held that the unlawful act itself must be objectively dangerous.

depend on the act's nature. If the defendant intended trivial harm, then this was taken into consideration by allowing for a manslaughter conviction in homicide cases.[238] If a person beats another with a hammer, it is inferable that she must have intended to cause the victim serious injury.

In *Duffey's and Hunt's Case*, it was held that:[239] 'A party not cognizant of the intention of his companion to commit murder, is not liable, though in his company, to do an unlawful act.' Hence, *A* will not be liable for a collateral murder committed by *P* unless *A* intended to encourage *P*, at the very least, to inflict grievous bodily harm.[240] In *Duffey's and Hunt's Case*, the dangerous weapon doctrine was invoked to determine 'how far the accessory was cognizant of the intent and concurring in the act.' It was held that:

> if three persons go out to commit a felony, and one of them, unknown to the other, puts a pistol in his pocket and commits a felony of another kind, such as murder, the two who did not concur in this second felony will not be guilty thereof, notwithstanding it happened while they were engaged with him in the felonious act for which they went out.

The court used the dangerous weapon doctrine to infer that the accessories had not concurred in its use and thus had not intentionally authorised *P*'s fundamentally different act. A fundamentally different act is merely evidence from which it can be inferred the parties' common intention did not extend to the collateral offence.

The accessory's knowledge of the fact that *P* was carrying a lethal weapon is evidence from which a jury might infer that all the participants mutually intended the level of violence used by *P*. In *Macklin, Murphy, and Others' Case*,[241] Alderson, B. said:

> If the weapon used were a deadly weapon, it is reasonable to infer that the party intended death; and if he intended death, and death was

238 See generally, Walter E. Oberer, 'The Deadly Weapon Doctrine – Common Law Origin' (1962) 75 *Harv. L. Rev.* 1565; Julian P. Alexander, 'Presumptions in Criminal Cases' (1945–1946) 17 *Miss. L.J.* 45 at 49–55. The felony-murder rule was developed in some jurisdictions to limit its reach to dangerous felonies. See *R. v. Whitemarsh* (1898) 62 Just. P. 711; *R. v. Lumley* (1911) 22 Cox C.C. 635; *R. v. Jarmain* (1945) 2 All E.R. 613 at 616. For a list of the felonies that some U.S. courts deem to be inherently dangerous to human life, see 'What Felonies are Inherently or Foreseeably Dangerous to Human Life For Purposes of Felony-murder doctrine' (updated 2014) 50 A.L.R.3d 397.

239 (1830) 1 Lewin 194.

240 The Lords, following the fallacious reasoning in *R. v. Powell*, have now dispensed with the intentional factual encouragement by authorisation requirement. Therefore, if *P* causes *V* grievous bodily harm and this results in *V*'s death, *A* will be equally liable for murder as long as she foresaw that *P* might cause *V* grievous bodily harm. See *R. v. Rahman* [2009] 1 A.C. 129.

241 (1838) 2 Lewin 225 at 226.

> the consequence of his act, it is murder. If no weapon was used, then the question usually is, was there excessive violence? . . . Again, it is a principle of law, that if several persons act together in pursuance of a common intent, every act done in furtherance of such intent by each of them is, in law, done by all. The act, however, must be in pursuance of the common intent. Thus, if several were to intend and agree together to frighten a constable, and one were to shoot him through the head, such an act would affect the individual only by whom it was done.

A's knowledge of the fact that *P* possessed a dangerous weapon is mere evidence for inferring that *A* not only knew *P* would use it to effect the joint enterprise, but also that *A* intended *P* to use it for that purpose. The dangerousness of the weapon is considered for the purpose of determining whether *P*'s collateral crime was of an entirely different nature to any crime *A* had impliedly authorised. In other cases, there will be no weapon so the enquiry will turn on other evidence. To take an example from Hawkins's treatise,[242] '[I]f the joint enterprise intended, though unlawful, were a bare trespass, and one of the company be guilty of larceny, it is a crime in such offender only, because it is a crime of a *nature entirely different* from that *intended,* and not caused by the execution of it.' The words 'not caused by the execution of it' again refer to doctrine of constructive liability, which covers both the perpetrator and accessory when they both have the requisite fault for the underlying crime.[243]

The kind of weapon itself will never provide conclusive evidence of what *A* intended to encourage *P* to perpetrate.[244] The jury has to determine whether *A* intentionally authorised the collateral crime by considering all the evidence. Evidence showing that *A* knew that *P* was carrying a lethal weapon will be fairly compelling in circumstances where that weapon has

242 Hawkins, *op. cit. supra, note* 74 at Chap. 29, Sect. 9. See also Dalton, *op. cit. supra,* note 74 at 396.

243 *R. v. Creamer* [1966] 1 Q.B. 72; *R. v. Buck* (1960) 44 Cr. App. R. 213; *R. v. Gaylor* (1857) Dears. & B. 288 at 291 *per* Bramwell B.; *R. v. Smith* (1847) 2 Cox C.C. 233.

244 'The knowledge on the part of one criminal that his companion is carrying a weapon is strong evidence of a common intent to use [a certain level] of violence, but is not conclusive.' Williams, *op. cit. supra,* note 73 at 397 citing *R. v. Bannister* [1936] 4 D.L.R. 417. See also *R. v. Cramp* (1880) 14 Cox C.C. 390 at 393 *per* Denman, J.; and *R. v. Vandine* (1970) 1 N.S.W.R. 252 at 256, where Herron, C.J. said: 'It seems to me to have been a matter for a common-sense jury to decide whether or not a wounding of the victim with the bar was a consequence of the conspiracy to rob. It seems to me that there was evidence fit for the jury to consider that the appellant knew that McCoy had the bar and must have known that it was intended to be used as a natural consequence if the occasion presented itself to McCoy as necessary to effect their purpose.' Herron, C.J. was referring to inferences that might be used for imputing mutual conditional intention to *P* and *A* apropos the collateral crime. See also *Rosemond v. U.S.* (2014) 134 S.Ct. 1240; *State v. McClain* (2013) 827 N.W.2d 814; *R. v. George* (1936) 66 C.C.C. 365.

been used to kill. In addition, if it can be shown that *A* knew that *P* had a bad temper and was a violent type, the jury is likely to infer that *A* not only knew what was planned as a potential collateral crime, but also authorised it.[245] It will be very difficult for *A* to deny that she authorised the collateral crime when it is established that she believed that *P*'s collateral offending was a virtual certainty and participated with such a belief. Such evidence would allow a jury infer that *A* conditionally intended *P*'s collateral crime. If *A*, in circumstances where *P* has killed to make their joint enterprise (such as a robbery) succeed, knew that *P* was armed with weapons such as a knife or firearm and was a violent and bad-tempered character, the irresistible inference for the jury will be that there was a mutual intention that those weapons be used to cause the sort of violence that was in fact caused.

In *Davies v. Director of Public Prosecutions* [1954] A.C. 378 at 401, Lord Simonds L.C. said:

> In particular, I can see no reason why, if half a dozen boys fight another crowd, and one of them produces a knife and stabs one of the opponents to death, all the rest of his group should be treated as accomplices in the use of a knife and the infliction of mortal injury by that means, unless there is evidence that the rest intended or concerted . . . an attack with a knife by one of their number, as opposed to a common assault. If all that was designed or envisaged was in fact a common assault, and there was no evidence that Lawson, a party to that common assault, knew that any of his companions had a knife, then Lawson was not an accomplice in the crime consisting in its felonious use.

The dangerous weapon doctrine has since been used to infer that *A* was subjectively reckless[246] apropos the particular collateral crime. Under the *R. v. Powell* foresight rule, *A* is liable for *P*'s acts if they are of a kind that she foresaw *P* might perpetrate with the particular dangerous weapon. If *P* possesses a gun, then depending on all the evidence, *A* might foresee it being used to kill *V*, to kneecap *V* or merely to threaten *V*.[247] The jurors probably

245 This is essentially what happened in *Johns v. The Queen* (1980) 143 C.L.R. 108 at 111.

246 See *R. v. Powell* [1999] 1 A.C. 1; *R. v. Uddin* [1999] Q.B. 431 at 440; *R. v. Rahman* [2009] 1 A.C. 129. Cf. the aberrant decision in *R. v. Williams* (1973) 21 W.I.R. 329 *per* Smith, J.A. (Henriques P., and Hercules, J.A. concurring).

247 If *A* and *P* agree to threaten violence, that alone is not conclusive evidence of a mutual intention to use actual violence. It is merely a piece of evidence that has to be considered with all the other evidence. The courts have tended to overstate Professor Glanville Williams' proposition that: 'it seems that a common intent to threaten violence is equivalent to a common intent to use violence, for the one so easily leads to the other.' See Williams, *op. cit. supra*, note 73 at 397–398. Compare its use in *R. v. Powell* [1999] 1 A.C. 1 at 27. Professor Williams was merely asserting that if there was strong evidence showing that there was a common intention to threaten violence of a particular degree, the jury might infer that the parties also mutually intended to use actual violence of that degree.

have to visualise some sort of scale in their heads for the purpose of categorising the impact that the particular weapon was likely to have, if used in a particular way. The jury might conclude as a question of fact, that *P*'s possession of a small pair of nail clippers on a scale from 0 to 10 had only a negligibly small chance of causing serious injury and so on. *Per contra*, a jury would conclude the opposite were *P* possessing a high-powered gun. Also thrown into the equation is *A*'s knowledge of *P*'s (conditional) intention of using the weapon and of the *way* in which *P* conditionally intends to use it.

Spontaneity also adds little.[248] Usually *A* will have sufficient advance knowledge[249] of *P*'s conditional intentions to be in a position to authorise them. *A* would not need a great deal of notice. If during a gang fight *P* produces a knife, *A*'s continued participation with knowledge of the fact that a knife has been produced would be more than sufficient for the jury to infer that *A* encouraged *P* to use the knife to inflict the sort of violence that a knife is normally used to inflict in the context of an aggressive and heated gang fight.[250] Mutual intentions can be formed in an instance and they need not be expressed.[251] The participants in gang violence usually have sufficient background information not only to foresee the consequences of inflicting joint violence upon another human being, but also to foresee the possible contingencies such as opposition from the victim, and from this

None the less, evidence of a common intention to threaten violence would not be conclusive evidence of a common intention to use actual violence. There are numerous factors that could be raised to rebut an inference that there was a common intention to use violence, rather than merely to threaten it. See *R. v. Reid* (1976) 62 Cr. App. R. 109 at 112, where Lawton, L.J. said: 'The intent with which the appellant was in joint possession of the weapons with the others has to be inferred from the circumstances . . . If men carrying offensive – indeed deadly – weapons go to a man's house in the early hours of the morning for no discernible lawful purpose, they must, in our judgment, intend to do him harm of some kind . . . If such injury [that is, GBH or death caused by the perpetrator] was not *intended* by the accessories, they must be acquitted of murder . . .' [emphasis added].

248 Cf. *Savard v. R.* [1946] S.C.R. 20.

249 On advance knowledge, see the recent decision of the Supreme Court of the United States in *Rosemond v. U.S.* (2014) 134 S.Ct. 1240.

250 In *R. v. Rahman* [2009] 1 A.C. 129 there was no need to rely on the foresight rule, because there was ample evidence for a properly directed jury to infer that Rahman authorised the knife being used to stab the combatant. The knife also was used in a *way* that was mutually intended. The intention might have been formed only on the spot but it was formed. The fact that Rahman made no attempt to withdraw from the joint enterprise after the knife had been produced was evidence from which the jury could infer that he tacitly authorised its use there an then.

251 The substantive fault element requires the accessory to *know or intend* the relevant circumstances of *P*'s target crime or alternatively that *P* will perpetrate a particular collateral crime: see *The Queen v. Coney* (1881–82) L.R. 8 Q.B.D. 534 at 557 *per* Hawkins, J.; *R. v. Clarkson* [1971] 1 W.L.R. 1402 at 1406 *per* Megaw L.J.; *R. v. Churchill (No. 2)* [1967] 2 A.C. 224; *D.P.P. for Northern Ireland v. Maxwell* [1978] 1 W.L.R. 1350; *R. v. Saik* [2007] 1 A.C. 18; *R. v. Powell* [1999] 1 A.C. 1 at 12–13. See also *R. v. Uddin* [1999] Q.B. 431 at 441.

knowledge are able to form mutual intentions about how to respond to the expected contingencies.[252]

In many of these cases the dangerousness of the weapon will add little. The focus has to be on the dangerousness of the intended acts involved. A weapon's dangerousness is contingent on how *P* intends to use it. If a gang intends to inflict serious injury upon *V* by kicking *V* in the head, it seems neither here nor there that *P* used a batten to hit *V* in the head, because a kick to a head from a boot is as lethal as a blow from a batten. The *method* adopted to inflict the mutually intended grievous bodily harm is neither here nor there. (However, compare the discussion in the next section.)

VII. The limits of manslaughter as an alternative to murder

If the collateral crime that results in *V* being killed is fundamentally different from what the participants authorised they should not be liable for either murder or manslaughter.[253] However, if *A* and *P* agree that *P* should punch *V* to cause *V* grievous bodily harm and *P*'s punch kills *V*, both will be liable for murder.[254] *P* is constructively liable because she intends to cause *V* grievous bodily harm and as a result (accidentally) kills *V*. *A* is constructively liable for the consequences of the act that she participated in through her encouragement by authorisation. *A* authorised *P*'s aggravated assault and thus encouraged it, so she is jointly and constructively liable for the consequences of the assault. Constructive liability covers both the accessory and perpetrator, because they are both culpably involved in the act that causes *V*'s death. The Supreme Court of Canada[255] has held:

> In the case of an accused who aids or abets in the killing of another, the requisite intent that the aider or abettor must have in order to warrant a conviction for murder must be the same as that required of the person who actually does the killing. That is to say, the person aiding or abetting the crime must intend that death ensue or intend that he or the perpetrator cause bodily harm of a kind likely to result in death, and be reckless whether death ensues or not. If the intent of the aiding party is insufficient to support a conviction for murder, then that party might still be convicted of [constructive] manslaughter if the unlawful act which was aided or abetted is one he or she knows is likely to cause some harm short of death. Neither intent was demonstrated by the appellant in the present case.

252 *Miller v. The Queen* (1980) 32 A.L.R. 321 at 326.

253 This is the view endorsed by the majority in *R. v. Rahman* [2009] 1 A.C. 129.

254 *R. v. Reid* (1976) 62 Cr. App. R. 109 at 112 *per* Lawton, L.J.

255 [1990] 3 S.C.R. 74 *per* Cory, J. (Lamer C.J.C., La Forest, Sopinka and Gonthier, J.J. concurring).

A. Acts perpetrated in a fundamentally different way

However, if both *A* and *P* intend to cause *V* grievous bodily harm by means that are not inherently lethal with *P* departing from their common purpose by using inherently lethal means to cause the harm, *P* alone will be liable for killing *V*. *A* will not be liable for *P*'s departure from their plan. Suppose *A* and *P* agree to burglarise a wealthy heiress, *V*, and to use torture to force *V* to reveal where her safe is located and to reveal its combination. *A* agrees that *P* should use his gun to kneecap *V* if she does not reveal the safe's location and combination. *V* refuses to reveal the safe's location and combination and in frustration and anger *P* shoots *V* in the head at point-blank range. *V* dies instantly. Even though both parties conditionally intended to cause *V* grievous bodily harm, only *P* will be liable for murder.[256] *A* is not liable for murder or manslaughter, because the death was not a consequence of the particular act of grievous bodily harm that was encouraged by *A*. The grievous bodily harm encouraged by *A* was not inherently lethal; it only carried a high risk of death. The grievous bodily harm caused by *P* was of a fundamentally different nature, because the virtually certain consequence of that act was *V*'s death.

In homicide cases the court will need to determine whether the collateral crime carried a risk of death within the range of what *A* had encouraged by implied authorisation.[257] If *A* encourages *P* to inflict grievous bodily harm as a part of their joint enterprise, *A* should not be liable for unintended consequences such as *V*'s death, if that consequence is a result of *P* using means that were inherently more dangerous than the means *A* authorised. *A* might authorise means that pose little to no risk of *V* being killed. If the means used carry a much higher risk of killing *V*, then *A* could argue that the act was of a fundamentally different nature to anything she intended to encourage *P* to perpetrate. For instance, *A* might authorise *P* to use his bare fists to cause *V* serious injury, but instead *P* uses a hammer and as a result accidentally kills *V*. Even though *A* intended *P* to cause *V* grievous bodily harm and thus authorised such harm being caused to *V*, *A* did not authorise *P* to use means that were inherently lethal.

This problem arises because constructive liability allows a person to be held responsible for unintended consequences. In the hammer example, neither party intended the consequence of death, but constructive liability means *P* is criminally liable for the unintended consequence of her personal wrongdoing. The putative accessory is not liable unless it can be shown she participated in *P*'s wrongdoing. The constraint against collective constructive liability in such cases is *A*'s lack of intentional authorisation with respect

256 *R. v. Gamble* [1989] N.I. 268. Cf. *R. v. Stevenson* (1984) 62 N.S.R. (2d) 193.

257 *R. v. Gamble* [1989] 268; *Mumford v. State* (1974) 313 A.2d 563 at 566 *per* Thompson, J.; *Scott v. State* (1981) 49 Md.App. 70 at 81 *per* MacDaniel, J. (Moore and Lowe, J.J. concurring).

to the means used to inflict the grievous bodily harm.[258] The means used make *P*'s infliction of grievous bodily harm an act that is fundamentally different to the kind of act *A* authorised. *A* does not authorise *P* to use means that carry a very high risk of death for *V*. The act that causes *V*'s death must be encouraged by *A*.[259] *P* using a *hammer* to cause *V* serious injury, when it has been agreed *P* should use his bare fists only, is 'an overwhelming supervening event which is of such a character that it will relegate into history matters which would otherwise be looked on as causative factors'.[260]

> It is clear that a common design to use unlawful violence, short of the infliction of grievous bodily harm, renders all the co-adventurers guilty of manslaughter if the victim's death is an unexpected consequence of the carrying-out of that design. Where, however, the victim's death is not a product of the common design but is attributable to one of the co-adventurers going beyond the scope of that design, by using violence which is intended to cause grievous bodily harm, the others are not responsible for that unauthorised act.[261]

Consequently, *P* will be liable for murder but *A* will not be liable for manslaughter. *A* is not liable for manslaughter because the criminal act she encouraged *P* to perpetrate did not cause *V*'s death. Accidental consequences resulting from factually encouraged criminal acts have to be taken both constructively and collectively by both *A* and *P*. *Per contra*, accidental

258 *R. v. Taylor* (1872–75) L.R. 2 C.C.R. 147 at 149 *per* Cockburn, C.J.; *R. v. Crooks* [1999] N.I. 226 *per* Carswell, L.C.J.; *R. v. Reid* (1976) 62 Cr. App. R. 109 at 112 *per* Lawton, L.J.

259 *R. v. Taylor* (1872–75) L.R. 2 C.C.R. 147 at 149 *per* Cockburn, C.J.

260 [1966] 2 Q.B. 110 at 120. Lord Parker, C.J. goes on to observe: '[I]f one of them . . . had in a moment of passion decided to kill, [the other participants] would be acquitted altogether . . . There is nothing . . . illogical in such a result, in that it could well be said as a matter of common sense that in the latter circumstances the death resulted or was caused by the sudden action of the adventurer who decided to kill and killed.' In *R. v. Powell* [1999] 1 A.C. 1 at 30, Lord Hutton held: 'As the unforeseen use of the knife would take the killing outside the scope of the joint venture the jury should also have been directed, as the Court of Criminal Appeal held in *R. v. Anderson*, that A should not be found guilty of manslaughter.'

261 *R. v. Lovesey* [1970] 1 Q.B. 352 at 356 *per* Widgery, L.J.; *R. v. Reid* (1976) 62 Cr. App. R. 109 at 112 *per* Lawton, L.J. Cf. the facts in *Williams v. State* (2011) 94 So. 3d 324, a felony-murder case, that under English law would also result in a murder conviction for the accessory, because the acts of GBH that caused *V*'s death were authorised by accessory for the purpose of making the robbery succeed. See also *R. v. Cribbin* (1994) 21 C.R.R. (2d) 161 where it was held: 'The jury should have been instructed that the accused would be guilty as an accessory to *D*'s murder if he knew of *D*'s intention to kill or to cause bodily harm that he knew was likely to cause death and if he intended to aid and abet *D*.' Cf. *R. v. Kerr* (1921) 15 Cr. App. Rep. 165; *R. v. Harrington* (1851) 5 Cox C.C. 231; *R. v. Skeet* (1866) 4 F. & F. 931; R. *v. Caton* (1874) 12 Cox C.C. 624; *R. v. Lumley* (1911) 22 Cox C.C. 635; *R. v. Gross* (1913) 23 Cox C.C. 455.

consequences resulting from unauthorised criminal acts that are fundamentally different to the act that was intentionally authorised and encouraged by *A* can be linked only to the perpetrator's personal wrongdoing.

It would not be fair to hold a person liable for manslaughter when her associate has made an autonomous choice to cause grievous bodily harm by means that were much more likely to kill, since she has not factually participated in the more dangerous act. In such circumstances, the accessory does not participate in the act that causes *V*'s death. In *R. v. Anderson,* Lord Parker, C.J. said:

> It seems to this court that to say that adventurers are guilty of manslaughter when one of them has departed completely from the concerted action of the common design and has suddenly formed an intent to kill and has used a weapon and acted in a way which no party to that common design could suspect is something which would revolt the conscience of people today.[262]

B. Moral bad luck and intended consequences

The fact that *P* has used different means to commit a crime will not relieve *A* of liability if *A* has authorised the end harm. If *A* authorises *P* to use a knife to kill a security guard for the purpose of making their joint robbery succeed, it would be no defence for *A* to argue that *P* instead used a gun to kill the guard. Nor would it matter that *A* did not know *P* was carrying a gun, because *A* has encouraged the end result – the murder of the guard. This important distinction was overlooked in *R. v. Williams,*[263] where Smith, J.A. said:

> If the object or purpose of the counselling is achieved in substance the means used by the principal to achieve it is usually irrelevant on the question of the liability of the accessory . . . The act committed is not usually relevant in determining the scope of the common purpose contained in the counselling. And in order to ascertain the common purpose what must be identified in the counselling is the crime which the principal was counselled, procured and commanded to commit, not the means by which it was to be committed . . . If it was found that what was desired and expressed was that serious bodily injury should be inflicted, then whatever means were employed by Blackwood to effect that desired end would be within the ambit and scope of the counselling.

262 *R. v. Anderson* [1966] 2 Q.B. 110 at 120.

263 (1973) 21 W.I.R. 329 at 338; 340 *per* Smith, J.A. (Henriques, P., and Hercules, J.A. concurring). This runs counter to Hale's fundamentally different act rule. Cf. Hale, *op. cit. supra,* note 47 at 436.

This reasoning is fallacious in the context of constructive crimes, because the end crime depends on moral bad luck. One can encourage an act that is not likely to be morally as unlucky as some other act. Williams had only encouraged Blackwood to cause *V* serious injury by beating *V*. Williams had not asked Blackwood to use means that posed a real risk of causing the victim's death. Blackwood stabbed *V* in the neck, which is an act that is fundamentally different from beating a person with bare fists. It is one thing to encourage a wounding (a stabbing in a delicate place such as a neck) and another to encourage a beating with bare fists.

If Williams had encouraged Blackwood to use a knife to wound *V*, then both should have been liable for the consequences of the authorised act. Furthermore, if the beating by bare fists alone had killed *V*, then both should have been liable for murder.[264] On the facts of the case, Williams should have been liable only for the aggravated assault that preceded the wounding. If Williams had asked Blackwood to murder *V*, then the means used would have been irrelevant, because Williams would have encouraged Blackwood to perpetrate a particular result crime. If *A* intentionally authorises *P*'s act she has to take (collectively and constructively) the consequences of the act; therefore, foresight does not enter the equation as far as the unintended consequences are concerned. Foresight was used in *R. v. Powell* to impute *P*'s acts to *A*, not to impute the consequences of acts authorised by *A* to *A*.

C. The perpetrator's hidden agenda and the accessory's liability for a lesser offence

Even though an accessory cannot be convicted of manslaughter where death results from an act that she did not encourage,[265] in some cases the facts will be such that she will be liable for participating in some lesser offence. *A* should not be liable simply because some lesser (authorised)

264 If the beating was only intended to cause *V* actual bodily harm, then the conviction would be for manslaughter. *R. v. Creamer* [1966] 1 Q.B. 72; *R. v. Buck* (1960) 44 Cr. App. R. 213; *R. v. Gaylor* (1857) Dears. & B. 288 at 291 *per* Bramwell B.; *R. v. Smith* (1847) 2 Cox C.C. 233.

265 *R. v. Gamble* [1989] N.I. 268; *R. v. Rahman* [2009] 1 A.C. 129. In *R. v. Kirkness* [1990] 3 S.C.R. 74 at para. 39, it was noted that: 'In keeping with this spirit of reform, several courts have held that it is possible to find a party liable of the lesser included offence of manslaughter where the principal has committed an act of murder.' See *R. v. Kent* (1986) 40 Man. R. (2d) 160; see also R. *v. Hartford* (1980) 51 C.C.C. (2d) 462 (B.C. C.A.), and *R. v. Trudeau* (1985) 49 C.R. (3d) 234. Other common law jurisdictions have adopted the same approach: see *Murray v. R.* [1962] Tas. S.R. 170 (C. C. A.). At paragraph 41 it is observed: '[I]n the murder context, it is open to a jury to find an accused guilty of the lesser included offence of manslaughter where he or she aided or abetted a principal who is found guilty of murder. When dealing with crimes of personal violence, the *mens rea* for manslaughter will often be present in a party who has assisted.' See also *R. v. Lange* (2011) 276 C.C.C. (3d) 137.

act (e.g. intentional bodily harm) comes within the purview of the greater *unauthorised* harm (e.g. intentional killing). If *P* kills with a single shot from a gun and *A* has only authorised *P* to cause grievous bodily harm with her fists, then there is only one criminal act and one criminal consequence. *A fortiori* death is grievous bodily harm, but since *A* did not factually encourage *P* to deliberately kill *V*, *A* cannot be liable for murder. *P*'s intentional killing (a departure from what was authorised by *A*) breaks the chain of causation between *A*'s factual encouragement and *P*'s ultimate act. Since *P* will be convicted of murder only, on derivative principles, *A* cannot be liable for the independent offence of wounding with intent to commit grievous bodily harm.[266]

If there is an act of grievous bodily harm that is separate from the act that kills *V*, then *A* might be liable for wounding with intent to commit grievous bodily harm.[267] In *R. v. Gamble*,[268] *A1* (Douglas) and *A2* (McKee) were liable for wounding with intent to commit grievous bodily harm, because they participated in an act causing grievous bodily harm that preceded *P1*'s (Gamble) and *P2*'s (Boyd) deliberate killing of *V*. In that case *A1* and *A2* participated in a criminal joint enterprise where they agreed that *P1* and *P2* should inflict GBH upon *V*, but it was agreed that the means used to inflict the GBH would include only a beating and a kneecapping. They agreed that a firearm should be discharged into *V*'s limb for the purpose of kneecapping *V*.[269] The beating and kneecapping were complete before *V* was killed and therefore were separate crimes that preceded *V* being murdered. Douglas and McKee were involved in the precedent wounding with intent to commit grievous bodily harm, so as accessories they were jointly liable for it.

Douglas and McKee were not involved in the murder of *V*, because they had not authorised the act that caused *V*'s death. *P* either suddenly formed an intention to kill or secretly harboured such an intention prior to embarking on the punishment exercise. *P* used a knife to cut *V*'s throat

266 Cf. *R. v. Grant* [2014] E.W.C.A. Crim. 143, where it is noted that when a more serious crime such as attempted murder has been perpetrated, this would allow for inferences as to lesser included crimes such as aggravated assaults involving wounding. Hence, the lesser crime might be subsumed into the greater, but not vice versa.

267 'An assault is not less an assault because it is intended to be the first step towards murder, or rape, or robbery.' See James Fitzjames Stephen, *A History of the Criminal Law of England* (London: Macmillan, 1883) Vol. II, at 221.

268 [1989] N.I. 268. See also *R. v. Michaud* (2000) 144 C.C.C. (3d) 62.

269 Kneecapping is a punishment exercise practised by underworld figures. The gunshot is fired into the fleshy back part of the thigh, where it shatters bones and also severs arteries. There were hundreds of victims during the late 1970s and early 1980s. The I.R.A. carried out so many kneecappings that surgeons at Belfast's Royal Victoria Hospital developed a special treatment to deal with the arterial damage inflicted. See generally, L.E. Graham and R.C. Parke, 'The Northern Ireland Troubles and Limb Loss: A Retrospective Study' (2004) 28(3) *Prosthetics and Orthotics International* 225.

and did so with such force as to cause *V* to die instantly. *P*'s act was fundamentally different from any act authorised by Douglas and McKee. *V* most likely would not have died from the punishment exercise, even though there was a risk that it could be fatal.[270] Hence, the chain of causation was broken by *P*'s deliberate act of cutting *V*'s throat with ferocious force.[271] If the punishment exercise had killed *V*, then all four participants would have been liable for murder. The punishment exercise did not get a chance to cause *V*'s death, because *P* broke the chain of causation with his deliberate act of cutting *V*'s throat. There was a deliberate departure from what had been mutually and conditionally intended. Lord Bingham has observed that: 'Gamble and Boyd went beyond what was expressly or tacitly agreed as part of the common enterprise, with the consequence that their acts went beyond the contemplation of Douglas and McKee and the authority given by them.'[272] Lord Bingham in effect uses 'contemplation' to infer intentional encouragement by authorisation, which runs counter to the *R. v. Powell* test, and supports the thesis advocated in this book.[273]

270 See the observations of Lords Bingham and Roger in *R. v. Rahman* [2009] 1 A.C. 129 at 147; 157 respectively.

271 The distinction is overlooked by Lords Brown and Neuberger in *R. v. Rahman* [2009] 1 A.C. 129 at 167; 169H respectively. Lord Neuberger (at 169H) said: 'However, the actions foreseen and intended by Douglas and McKee plainly involved serious injury to the victim, and it is hard to say that a knife is more lethal than a gun. Indeed the two weapons were specifically equated in terms of potential lethalness by Lord Hutton in *R. v. Powell* [1999] 1 A.C. 1 at 30F-G, and in the passage cited by Lord Brown, at para 60 [where his Lordship observed: 'In a case of this kind it is difficult to imagine what would have been outside the scope of the concerted action, possibly the use of a loaded revolver, the presence of which was unknown to the other parties . . .'], from *R. v. Smith* [1963] 1 W.L.R. 1200 at 1206–1207, it was, to my mind correctly, implied that by using "a loaded revolver" *A* could (not, I emphasise, would) render the murder of *V* "outside the scope of the concerted action", if *B* foresaw only the use of a knife. Accordingly, while the actual decision in *R. v. Gamble* [1989] N.I. 268 can be justified in theory, it seems to me to have been a rather generous outcome for Douglas and McKee on the facts.' The straightforward response to Lord Neuberger's query is: the accessory must be involved in the actual act that causes *V*'s death. The knife attack in *R. v. Gamble* caused *V*'s death, not the kneecapping. Coupled with this, the *manner* in which the weapon is used is crucial. Cutting a person's throat in the *way* that *P* did in *R. v. Gamble* is fundamentally different from a kneecapping, because death is a virtually certain consequence of cutting a human's throat in this way. It also was an intended killing. *Per contra*, death is a probable consequence only of a kneecapping; its probability would depend in part on timely treatment being made available. I do not agree with Lord Neuberger's suggestion (at 171C-F) that shooting a person in the knee is as lethal as shooting her in the head.

272 *R. v. Rahman* [2009] 1 A.C. 129 at 148.

273 With respect to the defendant at issue in that case, Rahman, Lord Bingham expounds: 'In consequence, it was strongly arguable that the principal's intention to kill, if found by the jury, took his (the principal's) action outside the scope of the common design and rendered it fundamentally different from anything the appellants had foreseen or contemplated. These were not inferences which the jury would necessarily draw, but inferences which, properly directed, they might draw.' *R. v. Rahman* [2009] 1 A.C. 129 at 151.

The perpetrator's intentions are bound up with the act that she perpetrates. Consequently, evidence of her intentions can shed light on whether or not a given act was conditionally intended as a part of the joint enterprise.[274] *P* causing *V* grievous bodily harm in circumstances where *P* intends to cause grievous bodily harm that is *not* likely to cause *V*'s death is an intentional act that is fundamentally different from *P* intentionally inflicting grievous bodily harm for the purpose of killing *V*. There is no escaping the fact that purposive killing is different from purposively causing grievous bodily harm. Nonetheless, *P*'s secret intention to kill will not always relieve *A* of liability. In *R. v. Gamble*[275] all four participants intended to subject *V* to a punishment exercise that included a kneecapping. If the kneecapping had killed *V*, then it would not have mattered that the perpetrator of the kneecapping secretly desired the kneecapping to kill *V*. The kneecapping was intended and encouraged by all the participants and they all had *mens rea* for murder, because they all at least intended the kneecapping to result in grievous bodily harm. If the kneecapping had been the cause of *V*'s death, there would have been no 'justification for . . . requiring [the jury] to consider and decide whether the principal's intent when killing the victim was the full intent to kill or the usual lesser intent to cause grievous bodily harm.'[276] It would not have mattered in the least that some of the participants had only intended the kneecapping to cause grievous bodily harm, because that is enough to make them constructively liable for murder.[277] In such circumstances, the perpetrator's hidden agenda (fault) has no bearing on the factually encouraged (authorised) act and its causal consequences. Nor does it have any bearing on the culpability manifested by the other participants who have *mens rea* for murder, because they intend the perpetrator(s) to cause grievous bodily harm.

274 See *R. v. A* [2011] Q.B. 841; *R. v. Gilmour* [2000] 2 Cr. App. R. 407; *Attorney General's Reference (No 3 of 2004)* [2005] EWCA Crim. 1882; *per contra R. v. Rahman* [2009] 1 A.C. 129 at 152F; 153F, where Lord Bingham said the question does not turn on the intention with which the weapon was used but on its foreseen production and use.

275 [1989] N.I. 268.

276 *R. v. Rahman* [2009] 1 A.C. 129 at 164 *per* Lord Brown.

277 See *R. v. Rahman* [2009] 1 A.C. 129 at 167G, where Lord Neuberger said: 'an intention to kill, at least without more, should not be regarded as a "complete departure", or as being "entirely" or "fundamentally" different, from an intention to cause serious injury. In other words, given the definition of murder as established in *R. v. Cunningham* [1982] A.C. 566, it appears to me that it would be somewhat illogical if [an accessory] could avoid liability for murder merely because he believed that [the perpetrator] intended to cause really serious injury to *V* rather than to kill him.' And at 168D-E, Lord Neuberger said: 'The essence of the matter is that *B* joined with *A* in attacking *V* with a view to causing *V* serious injury, and *B* knew that *P* had a knife for that purpose. It would seem unrealistic and over-indulgent to *B*, at least in the absence of other facts, if he were acquitted of murder on the ground that a jury concludes that he may have thought that *A* was bent on causing *V* serious injury (with the obvious risk of death) rather than killing him.'

A final decision that sheds further light on the above discussion is that of the Court of Appeal in *R. v. A*,[278] where it was held that for *D* to be an accessory to murder she would have to have known that *P* would act with the intent either to kill or to do grievous bodily harm. Consequently, if *A* mistakenly assists *P* to kill she will not be liable. Take the example where *X* knocks *Y* unconscious and thereafter asks *S* to help her to dispose of *Y*'s (live) body by driving her and the (live) body to a nearby cliff so that *X* can throw it over the cliff.[279] *X* does not tell *S* that *Y* is merely unconscious. Instead, she tells *S* that *Y* is dead and that she needs to dispose of *Y*'s body before her murderous act is discovered. *S* helps *X* to dispose of *Y* by driving *X* to the cliff so that *X* can throw *Y* over the cliff. It is the act of *X* that causes *Y*'s death; she kills her by dropping her body from a cliff onto the rocks below. *X* intends to commit murder while *S* merely intends to help *X* dispose of what she believes is a corpse. Since *S* has no knowledge of the fact that *X* intends to kill or cause grievous bodily harm to *V*, she cannot be liable as an accessory to *X*'s murder. Unlike the defendants in *R. v. Gamble*, *S* authorises the act that causes *V*'s death. Nonetheless, *S* does not authorise murder as *S* assumes *X* intends to dispose of a putative corpse, not kill a human being.

In certain cases, it will be permissible to convict one party of murder and the other of manslaughter.[280] *S* would not be liable for unlawful dangerous manslaughter, as a reasonable person would not believe dropping a supposed corpse over a cliff is an objectively dangerous unlawful act. It is not objectively dangerous in the sense that *Y* is putatively dead. Nonetheless, it might be argued that it is grossly negligent to drop a human over a cliff without knowing for certain that she is dead, if a reasonable person would foresee that she might be alive and that such an act is highly likely to kill her.[281]

Suppose *A* gives *P* a pin to assist her to inflict actual bodily harm upon *V*. *A* believes that the pinprick will merely cause *V* to suffer actual bodily harm, but *P* believes it will cause *V* grievous bodily harm because *P* knows that *V* suffers from haemophilia.[282] *P* also intends the pinprick to kill *V*. *P* pinpricks *V* and *V* bleeds to death. On these facts, *P* should be liable for murder and *A* should be liable for unlawful dangerous act manslaughter.[283]

278 [2011] Q.B. 841.

279 *S* would be liable for her personal fault, which involves her putatively perpetrating offences relating to the disposal of corpses and so on. See the offences listed in Baker, *op. cit. supra*, note 12 at 32–023 and notes.

280 *R. v. Kirkness* [1990] 3 S.C.R. 74 at para. 39. Cf. *R. v. Kent* (1986) 40 Man. R. (2d) 160; R. *v. Hartford* (1980) 51 C.C.C. (2d) 462 (B.C. C.A.), *R. v. Trudeau* (1985), 49 C.R. (3d) 234; *Murray v. R.* [1962] Tas. S.R. 170 (C. C. A.).

281 *Attorney-General's Reference (No.4 of 1980)* [1981] 1 W.L.R. 705; cf. *R. v. Adomako* [1995] 1 A.C. 171.

282 *State v. Frazier* (1936) 339 Mo. 966; *Burrage v. U.S.* (2014) 134 S.Ct. 881 at 888.

283 Cf. *R. v. Carpenter* [2012] Q.B. 722 at 733 *per* Richards, L.J.; *People v. Flayhart* (1988) 72 N.Y.2d 737. However, this would be a very wide theory of criminal liability and thus should

VIII. The unfairness of constructive liability for another's crimes

'It is a precept of justice that punishment for crime should be graduated and proportioned to the offence.'[284] To subject an accessory to a mandatory life sentence for recklessness is contrary to justice. A murder conviction should be made out only where a person personally intends death or really serious bodily harm or where an accessory assists and encourages a perpetrator intending the perpetrator's murder to succeed. It is remarkable that the Law Commission for England and Wales has endorsed the decision given in *R. v. Powell.*[285] In *Clayton v. The Queen,*[286] Kirby, J. described the Law Commission's proposals[287] concerning common purpose complicity as unconvincing and lacking. Kirby, J. said:

> [W]ith respect to the conclusion expressed in the recent report of the Law Commission of England and Wales, I am not convinced by its reasoning and I note that it has proved controversial in its own jurisdiction . . . The flaw in the reasoning of those who have defended the current law is that the legal fiction they endorse can operate with a serious lack of proportionality. Culpability is too easily trumped by the desire for criminalisation. That may not concern those who live in a world of theory. It should, however, concern judges of the common law whose orders often result in multiple cases of very prolonged imprisonment for wrongdoing where individual culpability does not warrant that course.

My own criticism of the Law Commission's interpretation of the current law is that the authorities going back 500 years do not support it. Thorough research would have made this apparent to the Law Commission. Horder has defended the Law Commission's proposals and argues that without a mere recklessness requirement for common purpose complicity, some reckless people would get off.[288] But does that mean it is fair to hold them liable for murder when they were merely reckless?

be resisted. On gross negligence manslaughter, see Dennis J. Baker, 'Omissions Liability for Homicide Offences: Reconciling R. *v. Kennedy* with *R. v Evans*' (2010) 74(4) *J. Crim. L.* 310; *Burns v. The Queen* (2012) 246 C.L.R. 334.

284 *Atkins v. Virginia* (2002) 536 U.S. 304 at 311–12 *per* Stevens, J. (with O'Connor, Kennedy, Souter, Ginsburg and Breyer, J.J. concurring).

285 [1999] 1 A.C. 1.

286 (2006) 168 A. Crim. R. 174 at 224–225.

287 The Law Commission, *Inchoate Liability for Assisting and Encouraging Crime* (London: H.M.S.O., Law Com No 300 (July 2006) Cm. 6878).

288 'Jeremy Horder, Criminal Law Commissioner in 2007, told us that he believed the retention of the principle was sound because it was needed to ensure convictions of guilty parties: "[recklessness] is enough to make me liable, even though I did not intend it."' House of Commons Justice Committee, *Joint Enterprise*, Eleventh Report of Session 2010–2012, (London: London Stationery Office Limited, H.C. 1597, 2012) at para. 38.

Professor Sullivan also has provided a compelling critique of the Law Commission's proposals. Sullivan writes: 'It might have been hoped that a twenty-first-century law reform body would take a less punitive turn, but it is not to be.'[289] Sullivan also argues:

> Undeniably, when *D* involves himself with *P* in the commission of crime *A*, he may increase the risk that *P* will also commit a further offence, crime *B*, and maybe other offences too. It follows that *D* bears some moral responsibility for these further offences, assuming foresight of the possibility of further offences and a sufficient connection with the baseline offence.

Sullivan argues that recklessly increasing the risk of *P* committing the collateral offence would warrant *A* receiving an increased sentence for the underlying crime that *A* has jointly perpetrated with *P*. I disagree for the reasons given above. It is true that recklessness[290] could be used to grade some complicity offences as less serious forms of wrongdoing, but recklessness should not be used to establish complicity liability under section 8 of the *Accessories and Abettors Act 1861*. The *Act of 1861* can only meet the requirements of fair labelling and proportionate punishment, if is applied to intentional participation.

Sullivan's risk theory is that *A* increased the risk of *P* killing a security guard during the course of a robbery, because if they had not been robbing a bank *P* would not have been in a position where she could make such a criminal choice. This is problematic, because the act of jointly perpetrating the robbery alone does not encourage *P* to make the autonomous choice to kill a guard. That is a dramatic decision that is personal to *P* and is a result of *P*'s own independent deliberation. Any causal link based on risk is broken when *P* makes her informed choice to depart from the common purpose, which was merely to rob the bank without using lethal force.

Some argue that liability should hinge on the fact that *A* was already doing something wrong. In recent times theorists have labelled this as the 'change of normative position' theory,[291] but its traditional name is constructive liability theory. It is an utterly flawed theory that is better termed as constructive malice or constructive fault theory, because that is all it is. Such a theory is flawed even when we are talking about unintended consequences

289 G. R. Sullivan, 'Participating in Crime: Law Com No.305 – Joint Criminal Ventures' [2008] *Crim. L.R.* 19 at 30.

290 This is the approach taken in sections 45 and 46 of the *Serious Crime Act 2007*.

291 See John Gardner, *Offences and Defences* (Oxford: Oxford University Press, 2007) at 41–42. Cf. Andrew Ashworth, 'A Change of Normative Position: Determining the Contours of Culpability in Criminal Law' (2008) 11 *New Crim. L. Rev.* 232; Alan Norrie, 'Between Orthodox Subjectivism and Moral Contextualism: Intention and the Consultation Paper' [2006] *Crim. L.R.* 484 at 493.

that are causally connected to a secondary party's personal wrongdoing,[292] let alone when we are talking about independent autonomous criminal acts that are merely coincidentally and temporally connected to the putative accessory's wrongful conduct. There is a big difference between a person taking the *consequences* of her personal *acts* and in her taking the autonomous *culpable acts* of another as her own.

Consequences resulting from a person's personal *acts* have a direct causal relation with her personal wrongdoing, even if they are contingent on moral bad luck. For instance, *D* punches *V* intending nothing more than to cause *V* to suffer actual bodily harm. Alas, the punch causes *V* to fall and hit her head with *V* suffering a fractured skull and dying. *D* only intended actual bodily harm, but her personal act has caused much greater harm. It is unfair to hold her responsible for the death, because she only intended actual bodily harm. Nonetheless, the current law allows for constructive liability, so *D* would be liable for manslaughter.[293] Likewise, where *A* encourages *P* to inflict grievous bodily harm and it accidentally kills *V*, she has to take the consequences of the act that she intentionally encouraged *P* to perpetrate.[294] *P* does as *A* requests.

Constructive liability (or change of normative position theory) is even more draconian when it does not hinge on the causal consequences of personal wrongdoing, or on an act that *A* has encouraged, but is contingent on the independent, free and informed criminal choices of others. Criminal acts resulting from the acts of another are contingent on that other person's fully informed and autonomous criminal choices – if there is no culpable factual encouragement of those choices, then there is no conduct element to establish derivative liability. Change of normative position liability applies only in complicity where *A* culpably encourages or assists *P* to perpetrate some criminal act and that act has greater consequences than they both anticipated. As we have seen, if *A* encourages *P* to cause *V* grievous bodily harm and as a result *V* dies, both *A* and *P* are constructively liable for murder. *A* is equally liable, because she participated in the actual act that caused *V*'s death. *A* is liable for her personal wrongdoing, because she was derivatively involved in that act.

A. Proportional punishment

Reverting to Kirby J.'s observation about proportionality, it is clear that the Law Commission's interpretation of the law cannot be reconciled with the normative right to fair punishment[295] and the fundamental normative

292 See Baker, *op. cit. supra*, note 12 at paras. 12–036 *et seq.*

293 *Id.* at 15–021 *et seq.*

294 *The Queen v. Saunders & Archer* (1575) 2 Plow. 473 at 475.

295 Article 49(3) of the *Charter of Fundamental Rights of the European Union* provides: 'The severity of penalties must not be disproportionate to the criminal offence.' Section 143 of the *Criminal Justice Act 2003* provides: '(1) In considering the seriousness of any

right not to be unfairly criminalised.[296] In *R. v. Powell*,[297] Lord Mustill recognised that the Lords' interpretation of the law created a grave injustice. His Lordship said: 'Once again, an appeal to this House has shown how badly our country needs a new law of homicide, or a new law of punishment for homicide, or preferably both.' Nonetheless, as we have seen, a fairer result could have been achieved if the Lords had not dispensed with the intentional encouragement by authorisation requirement. Greater sentence parity and fairer criminalisation could be achieved by allowing for equal punishment and criminalisation only in cases where the accessory intentionally authorises the particular collateral crime for the purpose of making the underlying joint enterprise succeed. If the accessory intends the collateral crime to be committed to serve a common purpose she shares with the perpetrator, then making her equally liable for the collateral crime causes no injustice.

The accessory is only marginally less culpable than the perpetrator, because intending another to perpetrate a crime to serve her personal purpose is not much better than her intending to perpetrate it herself to serve her personal purpose. It is true that a person who is willing to perpetrate a crime as grave as murder is morally more culpable and evil than a person who only intends to rely on another's act of murder for her own purposes, but this would not justify a significant sentence discount and would not necessarily require the accessory's wrong to be labelled as something other than murder.

If a person could never form the moral courage to personally kill another or to personally commit a similarly horrendous crime, she would not pose the same danger to society as a willing perpetrator.[298] Accessorial acts do seem to justify a lighter sentence than acts of perpetration, even when the accessory's culpability is in the exact range as that of the perpetrator. A common mistake is to assume that both parties are required to have *mens rea* for the collateral crime. The accomplice will never have *mens rea*

offence, the court must consider the offender's culpability in committing the offence and any harm which the offence caused, was intended to cause or might foreseeably have caused.' On the constitutional right to not be unfairly punished, see Dennis J. Baker, 'Constitutionalizing the Harm Principle' (2008) *Criminal Justice Ethics* 3; Ronald Dworkin, *Freedom's Law: The Moral Reading of the American Constitution* (Cambridge MA: Harvard University Press, 1997). In the United States, the Eighth Amendment to the Constitution of the United States enshrines the right not to be unfairly punished. On the theory of proportionate punishment, see Andrew von Hirsch, *Censure and Sanctions* (Oxford: Clarendon Press, 1996).

296 See generally, Dennis J. Baker, *The Right Not to Be Criminalized: Demarcating Criminal Law's Authority* (Farnham: Ashgate, 2011).

297 [1999] 1 A.C. 1 at 12.

298 'Yet sometimes he may be the guiltier, as Lady Macbeth was. The master mind and guiding spirit of a crime ring will probably receive a heavier sentence than his tools.' Williams, *op. cit. supra*, note 73 at 404.

for the collateral crime, because she does not intend to perpetrate it; she merely intends to benefit from someone else perpetrating it for her benefit: she benefits in that the collateral crime is perpetrated with her factual encouragement by authorisation for the purpose of effecting the joint enterprise.

The adoption of the foresight of possibility maxim as a substantive fault element for common purpose complicity, as the Lords did in *R. v. Powell*,[299] has the effect of permitting a conviction of an accessory whose culpability as to the collateral crime is less than is required to prove the guilt of the perpetrator. In view of the relative roles of the perpetrator and accessory, an accomplice should not be convicted of the collateral crime unless she has the same or higher degree of culpability than is required to convict the perpetrator. To use recklessness to convict an accessory of a specific intent crime such as murder when the perpetrator can only be convicted if she intended or obliquely intended to kill or cause GBH is contrary to justice, because it fails to punish the accessory proportionately for her personal wrongdoing.

Kirby, J. would have liked to have struck down the foresight doctrine, but could not find a constitutional ground for doing so. In England and Wales there is a legal ground for declaring the doctrine incompatible with our fundamental human rights, because it is incompatible with the right not to be unfairly punished. It is also contrary to the fundamental normative human right not to be unfairly criminalised. The latter right is recognised in many of the specific rights found in the European Convention. It is a fundamental right that a person only be punished in proportion with the level of culpability she manifested when she offended and in accordance with the harmfulness of her offending. The basic formula is fault *x* harm = crime label and ultimately crime sentence.[300] This does not refer merely to the crime label, but to the substance of what is labelled.[301]

Hence, it will not do to argue that a mandatory life sentence is proportionate because the given conduct has been labelled as murder; it must be shown that in substance the conduct is an act of murder and therefore the sentence and crime label is proportionately applied. It would be grossly unfair to use a mandatory life sentence and the crime label of murder to punish a person who has not perpetrated a murder, but has merely foreseen

299 [1999] 1 A.C. 1.

300 This right is enshrined in the newly enacted Article 49 of the *Charter of Fundamental Rights of the European Union*, and section 143 of the *Criminal Justice Act 2003*, *supra* note 295. On the constitutional right to not be unfairly punished, see Baker, *op. cit. supra*, note 296 at Chapter 2. Article 49 is likely to be used at some point in the future to challenge the constructive fault doctrine that is used to elevate an intention to cause GBH into an intention to kill. Likewise, the constructive fault element found in unlawful act manslaughter should be declared as incompatible with Article 49.

301 *R. v. Winmill* (2008) 63 C.R. (6th) 224; cf. *R. v. Young* (2009) 246 C.C.C. (3d) 417.

that her associate might kill.[302] Unless *A* intends *P* to kill in furtherance of effecting their criminal joint enterprise, *A* should not be labelled and punished as a murderer. If *A* joins a robbery intending *P* to use lethal force to kill a security guard to effect their joint enterprise, then it would not be unfair to label *A* as a murderer and to subject *A* to the mandatory life sentence. A does not intend to perpetrate murder herself, but she intends her associate to perpetrate murder for the (common) purpose of effecting their joint enterprise (the robbery). There is equivalence between the culpability of the accessory and perpetrator in such cases, although a further discount might be warranted because one is an active killer while the other is an accomplice who merely benefits indirectly from the killing. In the case of murder both parties could still be given a mandatory life sentence, because the sentencing judge has the discretion to set different release dates for the various parties. The accessory may be eligible for earlier release than the perpetrator.[303] The difference in sentence is likely to be minimal where the accessory has authorised the murder.

When the accessory has not authorised a murder or other specific intent crime, she should be given a lighter sentence. In addition, she should be charged with some lesser offence.[304] In *Enmund v. Florida*,[305] the Supreme Court of the United States held that co-defendants who had 'plainly different' levels of culpability for a joint enterprise killing could not all receive the same sentence. It was held that sentencing the perpetrator and the other participants alike where they had different degrees of responsibility contravened the Eighth and Fourteenth Amendments to the United States Constitution.

> In determining whether a sentence is proportionate, and therefore, not arbitrary, the Supreme Court directs reviewing courts to not only evaluate the defendant's culpability individually, but also relative to his co-defendants and accomplices in the same case . . . Whether the issue is that of 'plainly different' defendants receiving the same sentence of death, or that of similarly-culpable defendants receiving different

302 Analogously, Hawkins expounds: 'Whether the offence of the accessary can ever rise higher than that of the principal. I take it to be an uncontroverted rule, that it never shall; it seeming incongruous and absurd that he who is only as a partaker of the guilt of another, should be adjudged guilty of a higher crime than the other.' Hawkins, *op. cit. supra*, 74 at Chap. 29, Sect. 15. Similarly, the ancient law provided that accessories after the fact be open to lesser punitive remedies than the perpetrator or accessory before the fact. See Ferdinando Pulton, *De pace Regis et regni* (London: Printed for the Companie of Stationers, 1610) at 137.

303 See the *Criminal Justice Act 2003*.

304 For limits of charging alternatives such as 45 and 46 of the *Serious Criminal Act 2007*, see the discussion in Chapter 4.

305 (1982) 458 U.S. 782 at 788; 798.

> sentences, the inquiry remains the same: whether the sentences are arbitrarily or unreasonably disparate.[306]

Such an inquiry is pertinent in the United States with respect to the capital sentences,[307] as it is in the United Kingdom with respect to the mandatory life sentence.

The mandatory life sentence is disproportionate punishment for the non-perpetrator[308] who did not intend anyone to be seriously injured or killed.[309] Such punishment contravenes the proportionate punishment right enshrined in Article 49(3) of the *Charter of Fundamental Rights of the European Union*. Some might argue that the right to not be unfairly criminalised or punished is more normative than constitutional, but given the evolution of human rights in the last decade,[310] it is not implausible to envisage the courts recognising such an interpretation within the next fifteen years. After all, the American precedents persuasively support the argument that Article 49(3) requires a person convicted of a specific intent crime to be punished proportionately for her personal wrongdoing.[311] Especially where the crime carries a mandatory life sentence.[312] It is clear that the utilitarian justifications for using common purpose complicity to tackle gang violence ought not be used to override a person's rights to be criminalised fairly and

306 *State v. Gamble* (2010) 63 So.3d 707 at 723. In *Larzelere v. State* (1996) 676 So.2d 394 at 406, it was held: 'When a co-defendant . . . is equally as culpable or more culpable than the defendant, disparate treatment of the co-defendant may render the defendant's punishment disproportionate.'

307 When England and Wales had capital punishment, '[a]ll were liable to the same punishment, except murder was capital only for a party who himself killed or used force.' See Williams, *op. cit. supra*, note 73 at 404 citing the repealed section 5 of the *Homicide Act 1957*. See also *State v. Cruz* (2002) 794 A.2d 165.

308 *Williams v. State* (1983) 461 So.2d 834; *Gavin v. State* (2003) 891 So.2d 907; *Hamm v. State* (1989) 564 So.2d 453.

309 Cf. *Tison v. Arizona* (1987) 481 U.S. 137 at 107; *People v. Taylor* (2010) 48 Cal.4th 574 at 661; *People v. Letner* (2010) 50 Cal.4th 99 at 193.

310 For example, in *Carter v. Canada (Attorney General)* [2015] S.C.C 5 at para. 126, the Supreme Court of Canada held: 'We have concluded that the laws prohibiting a physician's assistance in terminating life (*Criminal Code*, s. 241 (b) and s. 14) infringe Ms. Taylor's s. 7 rights to life, liberty and security of the person in a manner that is not in accordance with the principles of fundamental justice, and that the infringement is not justified under s. 1 of the Charter. To the extent that the impugned laws deny the s. 7 rights of people like Ms. Taylor they are void by operation of s. 52 of the *Constitution Act, 1982*.'

311 Astonishingly, Horder and Hughes argue that disproportionate punishment is fair in common purpose complicity cases because the formulations of common purpose complicity in English, New Zealand and Australian law already allow for unfair punishment. See Horder and Hughes, *op. cit. supra*, note 60 at 396–397. Such an argument is tautological, since it holds that injustices in the current law provide a justification for incorporating the same injustices in new laws.

312 Cf. *Getsy v. Mitchell* (2007) 495 F.3d 295; *Farina v. State* (2006) 937 So.2d 612.

to be punished fairly, when the crime at issue carries a lengthy jail term and often a mandatory life sentence.[313]

In *People v. Kliner*[314] it was held: '[S]imilarly situated co-defendants should not be given arbitrarily or unreasonably disparate sentences.' However, there is no requirement that both parties receive the exact same sentence. If *A* gives *P*, an insane person, a gun so that she can kill another person, it would not be disproportionate to sentence *A* to life imprisonment, even though *P* is sent to a psychiatric hospital for treatment. *A*'s personal fault and her derivative harm-doing are sufficient to warrant a life sentence for a murder that she intended to assist and desired *P* to perpetrate.[315] Similarly, if the co-defendants manifest an almost identical level of culpability it does not matter that the accessory is only derivatively linked to the end harm.[316]

The Supreme Court of the United States has held:[317]

> A claim that punishment is excessive is judged not by the standards that prevailed . . . when the Bill of Rights was adopted, but rather by those that currently prevail. As Chief Justice Warren explained in his opinion in *Trop v. Dulles,* 356 U.S. 86 (1958): 'The basic concept underlying the Eighth Amendment is nothing less than the dignity of man . . . The Amendment must draw its meaning from the evolving standards of decency that mark the progress of a maturing society' . . . Proportionality review under those evolving standards should be informed by 'objective factors to the maximum possible extent.' We have pinpointed that the 'clearest and most reliable objective evidence of contemporary values is the legislation enacted by the country's legislatures.

313 Dennis J. Baker, 'Collective Criminalization and the Constitutional Right to Endanger Others' (2009) 28 *Crim. Just. Ethics* 168.

314 (1998) 705 N.E.2d 850 at 897.

315 The crucial factors for an individualised determination are the wrongdoer's personal culpability and the circumstances of her harm-doing. See *Zant v. Stephens* (1983) 462 U.S. 862 at 879; *Atkins v. Virginia* (2002) 536 U.S. 304 *per* Stevens, J. (with O'Connor, Kennedy, Souter, Ginsburg and Breyer, J.J. concurring). 'Proportionality as defined by the Supreme Court evaluates a particular defendant's culpability for his crime in relation to the punishment that he has received.' *State v. Gamble* (2010) 63 So.3d 707 at 724. See also *Graham v. Florida* (2010) 130 S.Ct. 2011 at 2022 *per* Kennedy, J. delivering the opinion for the Supreme Court.

316 'With respect to retribution – the interest in seeing that the offender gets his "just deserts" – the severity of the appropriate punishment necessarily depends on the culpability of the offender.' *Atkins v. Virginia* (2002) 536 U.S. 304 at 319 *per* Stevens J. (with O'Connor, Kennedy, Souter, Ginsburg and Breyer, J.J. concurring).

317 *Atkins v. Virginia* (2002) 536 U.S. 304 at 311–312 *per* Stevens, J. (with O'Connor, Kennedy, Souter, Ginsburg and Breyer J.J. concurring).

Current legislation cannot provide conclusive guidance when judicial review is involved, but it is an objective factor to be considered.[318] Given that Parliament went to the trouble of enacting the *Serious Crime Act 2007*, which not only grades and labels offences according to the level of fault involved, but also gives the sentencing judge the discretion to determine an appropriate sentence in all cases including murder, contemporary standards demonstrate that a mandatory life sentence is not appropriate when the accessory has been reckless only.

Kirby, J. asserts that the courts have a duty to take corrective steps.[319] In this chapter, I have demonstrated that this can be achieved without judges engaging in judicial activism. The solution lies in the judges reinterpreting the law so that it can be reconciled with the ancient and modern authorities. It was judicial laxness that led to the evidential maxim of foresight of possibility being developed into a substantive fault doctrine for complicity in England and Wales from 1999.[320] In this chapter, I have traced the doctrine's roots with the aim of demonstrating that it requires the defendant to have directly or obliquely intended that the perpetrator commit the collateral crime for the purpose of making their joint enterprise succeed.

R. v. Powell[321] decided a new rule of substantive criminal law, which is not supported by the authorities. Nor can it be reconciled with the fundamental right to fair punishment enshrined in Article 49 of the *Charter of Fundamental Rights of the European Union*. Article 49[322] means the *R. v. Powell* doctrine is not legally sound. In *R. v. Powell*,[323] Lord Steyn was unable to see that he was supplementing a substantive fault element with an

318 '[O]bjective evidence, though of great importance, does not "wholly determine" the controversy, for the Constitution contemplates that in the end our own judgment will be brought to bear on the question of the acceptability of the penalty under the Eighth Amendment . . . For example, in *Enmund*, we concluded by expressing our own judgment about the issue: . . . Enmund's criminal culpability must be limited to his participation in the robbery, and his punishment must be tailored to his personal responsibility and moral guilt. Putting Enmund to death to avenge two killings that he did not commit and had no intention of committing or causing does not measurably contribute to the retributive end of ensuring that the criminal gets his just deserts.' *Atkins v. Virginia* (2002) 536 U.S. 304 at 312–313 *per* Stevens, J. (with O'Connor, Kennedy, Souter, Ginsburg and Breyer, J.J. concurring). See also the opinion of the Supreme Court of the United States in *Graham v. Florida* (2010) 130 S.Ct. 2011 at 2022–2023.

319 (2006) 168 A. Crim. R. 174 at 189.

320 *R. v. Powell* [1999] 1 A.C. 1.

321 [1999] 1 A.C. 1.

322 By and large, Britain is bound by the Charter. See Ingolf Pernice, 'The Treaty of Lisbon and Fundamental Rights' in Stefan Griller and Jacques Ziller (eds), *The Lisbon Treaty: E.U. Constitutionalism without a Constitutional Treaty?* (New York: Springer Wein, 2008) at 235 *et seq.*

323 [1999] 1 A.C. 1 at 13.

evidential maxim, but he could see that the end result was injustice. The apparent injustice led Lord Steyn to conclude: 'That does not mean that the established principle cannot be re-examined and, if found to be flawed, reformulated.' Lord Hutton also recognised the injustice:

> My Lords, I recognise that as a matter of logic there is force in the argument advanced on behalf of the appellants, and that on one view it is anomalous that if foreseeability of death or really serious harm is not sufficient to constitute *mens rea* for murder in the party who actually carries out the killing, but it is sufficient to constitute *mens rea* in a secondary party. But the rules of the common law are not based solely on logic but relate to practical concerns and, in relation to crimes committed in the course of joint enterprises, to the need to give effective protection to the public against criminals operating in gangs.[324]

The Supreme Court can be guided by policy considerations when it is engaging in judicial review, but it cannot use policy considerations to expand criminal offences.[325] Judges have no power to create new offences or extend existing offences for policy reasons.[326] Judges have to interpret the law in accordance with the precedents[327] and should only depart from the precedents when adhering to them would cause an injustice.[328] The 'danger of gang crime' justification for dispensing with fundamental principles of justice is totally unconvincing.[329] The danger of gang crime rationale does not provide a justification for dispensing with the requirement that the prosecution establish equal personal fault both in the perpetrator and accessory, if they are to receive equal punishment and be convicted of the same crime. Blame and punishment have to rest on personal fault. If the various parties manifested different levels of personal fault, then they have to be blamed and punished differently. Coupled with this, there is often enough leeway in the sentence for crime that is the underlying joint enterprise preceding the collateral crime to punish gang members sufficiently to deter them.

The Supreme Court not only has the power to overrule its previous decisions concerning common purpose complicity,[330] but also is legally bound

324 *R. v. Powell* [1999] 1 A.C. 1 at 25.

325 *R. v. Rimmington* [2006] 1 A.C. 459.

326 'As to constitutionality, it is one thing for the courts to adapt and develop the principles of the common law incrementally in order to keep up with the requirements of justice in a changing society, but major changes involving matters of controversial social policy are for Parliament.' *R. (on the application of Nicklinson) v. Ministry of Justice* [2012] E.W.H.C. 2381 at para. 79 *per* Toulson, L.J.

327 *R. v. Rimmington* [2006] 1 A.C. 459.

328 *Practice Statement (Judicial Precedent)* [1966] 1 W.L.R. 1234.

329 See *Clayton v. The Queen* (2006) 168 A. Crim. R. 174 at 271 *per* Kirby, J.

330 'Their Lordships nevertheless recognise that too rigid adherence to precedent may lead to injustice in a particular case and also unduly restrict the proper development of the

to do so should the matter come before it.[331] The Supreme Court could overrule its previous decisions either because it is clear that they are wrong in law given the authorities going back 500 years, or alternatively because they cause 'injustice and offend concepts of what is right and what is wrong' when measured against contemporary standards of justice. Contemporary standards of justice require the highest court of review to ensure that the criminal laws of England and Wales comply with the fundamental rights not to be unfairly punished and not to be unfairly criminalised. Parliament should not offload its law-making responsibilities on the Supreme Court of the United Kingdom, but nor should the Supreme Court offload its legal interpreting and judicial review responsibilities on Parliament. What I propose is a radical narrowing of the law to rid the law of the doctrine of reckless complicity, because section 8 of the *Accessories and Abettors Act 1861* is a procedural mechanism that only allows for each party to be labelled and punished as a perpetrator. If reckless complicity is to be criminalised, then the *Serious Crime Act 2007* should be amended to create a new offence of reckless participation. An independent offence would allow for fair labelling and proportionate punishment.

law. They propose, therefore, to modify their present practice and, while treating former decisions of this House as normally binding, to depart from a previous decision when it appears right to do so.' *Practice Statement (Judicial Precedent)* [1966] 1 W.L.R. 1234. See also *Miliangos v. George Frank (Textiles) Ltd.* [1976] A.C. 443; *A v. Hoare* [2008] 1 A.C. 844 at 871.

331 This right is enshrined in the newly enacted Article 49 of the *Charter of Fundamental Rights of the European Union*, which provides: 'The severity of penalties must not be disproportionate to the criminal offence.' See also 143 of the *Criminal Justice Act 2003*.

3 Mutual encouragement and parties exempt from complicity liability

Abstract

In Chapter 2, I argued that the mental element in complicity requires nothing less than intention including oblique intention. In this chapter, I shall explore the role of oblique intention in the law of complicity. I shall use the recent Supreme Court decision in R. v. Gnango *to argue the case for recognising oblique intention as an alternative mental element in complicity.* R. v. Gnango *also raises the issue of transferred intention and transferred defences, so I will explore those doctrines in the context of the law of complicity. A further issue raised in* R. v. Gnango *is the scope of the victim rule. Since the victim rule has implications for the transferred intention and transferred defence doctrines and ultimately for the fault and conduct elements for complicity, I examine it in the third part of this chapter.*

In this chapter, it is argued that the victim rule applies in all cases apart from where an innocent third party is harmed. Coupled with this, it is argued that when a person forces another to kill in lawful and justified defence (i.e., where D holds innocent V hostage and open fires on armed police) D is liable for the harm caused to V when the police return fire and kill V. Per contra, *if the police kill a co-perpetrator of a crime, there is no residual wrongful harm and thus D is not liable for the death of his co-perpetrator. The co-perpetrator's death is the result of the police acting lawfully and justifiably, as is the death of the innocent third party, but the aggressor who is killed by police is not wrongfully harmed by her co-perpetrator because the victim herself forces the police's hand. The police do not wrong an aggressor who is killed by them acting in lawful defence.* Per contra, *when the police kill an innocent hostage while trying to lawfully arrest the hostage taker, the hostage is wrongfully harmed. The hostage taker who culpably causes the police to harm her by forcing the police to shoot at him while he holds the hostage directly wrongs the innocent hostage.*

I. Introduction

'Of misadventures in turnaments, in courts and lists, King Henry II. ordained, that because at such duels happen many mischances, That each of them take an oath that he beareth no deadly hatred against

> the other, but only that he endeavoureth with him in love to try his strength in those common places of lists and duels, that he might the better know how to defend himself against his enemies; and therefore such mischances are not supposed felony, nor the coroners have not to do with such mischances which happen in such common meetings, where there is no intent to commit any felony.[1]

> At a time when society was less secure and less settled in its habits, when the carrying of swords was as common as the use of a walking stick at the present day, and when duelling was regarded as involving no moral stigma if fairly conducted, it is not surprising that the courts took a view more lenient towards provocation than is taken to-day when life and property are guarded by an efficient police force and social habits have changed.[2]

The decision in *National Coal Board v. Gamble*[3] was a turning point in the law of complicity. The dissenting judgment of Slade J. shows that it was still possible at that date to hold the opinion that the prosecution had to prove that the accessory intended to assist or encourage the perpetrator's offending.[4] Since that time, the courts have tended to hold that the mental element in complicity requires no more than recklessness.[5] The arguments presented in this chapter rest on the argument made earlier in this monograph that the mental element in complicity requires intention.[6] In Chapter 2, it was argued that complicity liability under section 8 of the *Accessories and Abettors Act 1861* ought only be made out where the accessory intentionally encourages and/or assists the perpetrator with the ulterior direct/oblique intention of making the perpetrator's crime succeed, because such an approach would allow for fair labelling and

1 Andrew Horne, *The Mirrour of Justices* (London: Imprinted for Matthew Walbanke, 1646) (translated into English by W.H. of Gray's Inn) at Ch. I., Sc. 13. *The Mirrour of Justices* was first published in 1328 in old French: the original manuscript is in the Parker Library, Corpus Christi College, Cambridge (manuscript identifier CCCC MS 258)).

2 *R. v. Semini* [1949] 1 K.B. 405.

3 [1959] 1 Q.B. 11. See *U.S. v. Peoni* (1938) 100 F.2d 401 citing *The Case of Macdaniel* (1748) Fost. 125, Coke, Hale, Blackstone and Bracton. See also *No Accessary in Treason, Petit Larceny, and Trespass* (1611) 12 Co. Rep. 81.

4 See also *R. v. Passey* (1836) 7 Car. & P. 282, where Alderson, B. said: 'if you think that [*D*] remained out of the wood for any innocent purpose, and not for the purpose of aiding those who were in it, then you will acquit him.' See also *R. v. Manners* (1837) 7 Car. & P. 801; *R. v. Lockett* (1836) 7 Car. & P. 300; *R. v. Fretwell* (1862) Le. & Ca. 161.

5 *R. v. Bryce* [2004] 2 Cr. App. R. 592 at 611 *per* Potter, L.J (Hooper and Astill, J.J. concurring.); *R. v. Powell* [1999] 1 A.C. 1.

6 See the unanimous decision of the High Court of Australia in *Giorgianni v. The Queen* (1985) 156 C.L.R. 473; see also *State v. Green* (2001) 774 A.2d 157, where it was held that the accessory to a gunfight was liable only if he intended to assist or encourage the perpetrator. See also *State v. Liebowitz* (2001) 65 Conn. App. 788.

proportionate punishment in cases where the perpetrator has committed a specific intent crime such as murder, which carries a mandatory life sentence.[7]

This chapter considers three major issues in standard complicity cases: (1) the role of oblique intention in complicity; (2) complicity liability for those who engage in mutual gunfights in public streets; and (3) the scope of the exempt party/victim rule. All of these issues arose in *R. v. Gnango*,[8] but unfortunately the Supreme Court's treatment of those issues was wholly unsatisfactory. Nonetheless, that decision provides us with a perfect backdrop for exploring these issues. I aim to demonstrate that the Supreme Court got the law wrong. I will put forward an alternative interpretation of the law. I rely on American law, but I am not aiming to carry out a full comparative study. Instead, the aim is to shed light on how the law might be reformed, interpreted and developed in Britain. The American case law is useful for highlighting some of the legal misconceptions drawn by the Lords in *R. v. Gnango*. The three issues mentioned above are of utmost importance, because gunfights in public streets are becoming more common.[9]

7 *R. v. Clarkson* [1971] 1 W.L.R. 1402 *per* Megaw, L.J. (Geoffrey Lane and Kilner Brown, J.J. concurring); *R. v. Coney* (1881–82) L.R. 8 Q.B.D. 534 *per* Denman, J., Huddleston, B., Manisty, Hawkins, Lopes, Stephen, Cave, and North, J.J. *R. v. Russell* [1933] V.L.R. 59 at 67 *per* Sir Leo Cussen A.C.J.; *R. v. Fretwell* (1862) Le. & Ca. 161; *United States v. Peoni* (2d Cir.1938) 100 F.2d 401 at 402 *per* Hand, J. In *Wilson-Bey v. U.S.* (2006) 903 A. 2d 818 at 831–832 it was said: 'Although *United States v. Peoni* was decided sixty-eight years ago, it remains the prevailing authority defining accomplice liability. In 1949 the Supreme Court explicitly adopted *Peoni*'s purpose-based formulation. *Nye & Nissen v. United States*, 336 U.S. 613 . . . Every United States Circuit Court of Appeals has adopted *Peoni*'s requirement that the accomplice be shown to have intended that the principal succeed in committing the charged offence, and the federal appellate courts have thus rejected, explicitly or implicitly, a standard that would permit the conviction of an accomplice without the requisite showing of intent. The majority of state courts have also adopted a purpose-based standard.' Affirmed in the recent decision of the Supreme Court of the United States in *Rosemond v. U.S.* (2014) 134 S.Ct. 1240. Williams wrote: 'A person cannot be a principal in the second degree to a crime requiring a specific intent unless he knew of the intent of the principal in the first degree.' Glanville Williams, *Criminal Law: The General Part* (London: Stevens & Sons, 1953) at 45 citing *R. v. Cruse* (1838) 8 Car. & P. 541. See also *Parker*'s *Case* (1559) 2 Dyer 186a; *No Accessary in Treason, Petit Larceny, and Trespass* (1611) 12 Co. Rep. 81.

8 [2012] 2 W.L.R. 17.

9 The latest case involved a Russian banker who was gunned down in a London street. See 'Russian Banker Shot Six Times had Testified over Murder Plot', *Telegraph* (London), 24 March 2012. As gang members tend to arm themselves with guns rather than other weapons these days, it is likely that similar cases will occur in the future. In the United States mutual gunfights in public places are common. See *State v. Spates* (2010) 779 N.W. 2d 770 and cases cited within.

A. Mutual gunfights v. joint criminal enterprises

Let us start by considering *R. v. Gnango.* The facts of that case were fairly straightforward, but the case raised a number of complex legal issues. As we will see, the Lords applied doctrines and principles that were not applicable to the facts. The facts were that Gnango and a man called Bandana Man[10] (hereinafter BM) engaged in a gunfight in a public car park in a densely populated residential area in London. Tragically, while they were attempting to kill each other a stray bullet struck and killed an innocent passer-by. It was clear that Gnango and BM had 'mutually intended'[11] to engage in the gunfight. They had voluntarily armed themselves before seeking each other out. The gunfight was not a chance encounter, but was anticipated by both parties.[12] Each party could have avoided being involved in the gunfight, because neither party was physically forced or psychologically pressured to turn up for the gunfight. 'When there is a mutual consent to go to a place, and there to perform the fight, where they come not for their defence, but to fight; each of them carries malice along with him, the one of them is killed, this is clearly murder in the other.'[13] The question relating to the issue of whether they mutually intended to have a gunfight is separate to the question of whether they intended to kill each other.[14] Likewise, it is separate from the question of whether they foresaw that the virtually certain side effect of the gunfight would be the death of a passer-by. Homicide law is concerned with whether *D* intended to kill or cause serious injury to a human being, not with whether she intended to engage in a gunfight.

Gnango went to find BM in the car park where he expected BM to be present. When Gnango arrived at the car park he could not find BM. Gnango

10 Bandana Man was also identified as TC, but his real name is not given in the judgment. It appears that even though he was alleged to have perpetrated the murder, he was not charged with any crime.

11 The question is simply: did each party intend (or tacitly consent) to engage in the particular gunfight? An express or tacit agreement to engage in violence, while sufficient, is not required; it is enough that 'there was a concurrent or mutual expectation that a street battle would ensue'. See *State v. Spates* (2010) 779 N.W. 2d 770 at 776. For more sophisticated sociological and philosophical analyses of 'mutual intention', see Raimo Tuomela, 'Joint Intention, We-Mode and I-Mode' (2006) 30(1) *Midwest Studies in Philosophy* 35; Brook J. Sadler, 'Shared Intentions and Shared Responsibility' (2006) 30(1) *Midwest Studies in Philosophy* 115; Richard Power, 'Mutual Intention' (1984) 14(1) *Journal for the Theory of Social Behaviour* 85.

12 See *R. v. Taverner* (1616) 3 Bulst. 171 *per* Coke, C.J.

13 *R. v. Taverner* (1616) 3 Bulst. 171 at 172 *per* Haughton, J. Cf. *R. v. Kirk* (1704) 12 Mod. 304 at 305 *per* Holt, C.J. See also the decision of the Court of Appeals of Texas in *Lay v. State* (2012) 359 S.W.3d 291 at 298.

14 Arguably, a public gunfight will also be mutual where *D* believes that the virtually certain consequence of doing *X* (voluntarily seeking out an armed rival in a public place) is that it will result in *Y* (a mutual gunfight with his armed and willing rival).

asked the occupants of a car that was parked in the car park whether they had seen a man wearing a red bandana. According to two of the witnesses from the car, Gnango told them 'he had come to *meet* someone to handle some business'. Not long after, the occupants of the car saw someone enter the car park. This man's face was covered with a red bandana. Bandana Man immediately pulled out a gun and started to shoot at Gnango. BM started the gunfight by firing the first bullet, but it was clear that both parties had attended a common location with the full expectation that a gunfight would take place. (That is why it was a mutual gunfight rather than a case of necessary self-defence arising from an unexpected attack from one party on the other.) Gnango hid behind the occupied car and then jumped up and started to fire bullets over the roof of the car. Thereafter, he went to the front of the car and fired more bullets over the bonnet while BM shot back. Magda Pniewska was walking home from work through the car park when one of the bullets hit her in the head and killed her. The forensic evidence showed that the bullet did not come from Gnango's gun.

Gnango was convicted of a firearms offence, the attempted murder of BM, and the murder of Magda Pniewska. He appealed against his murder conviction. His conviction for murder was grounded on the theory that the gunfight between Gnango and BM was a joint enterprise to commit the crime of affray, and that each foresaw that the other might kill a passer-by.[15] The trial judge accepted this as a basis for convicting him of murder. Gnango's conviction for murder was quashed by the Court of Appeal, because Gnango and BM were not engaged in a joint enterprise when BM killed Magda Pniewska.

The Supreme Court restored Gnango's conviction for murder on the basis that he had aided, abetted, counselled and procured BM's murderous act. The court did not distinguish between aiding and abetting (assisting) and counselling and procuring (encouraging or causing), but it is fairly clear that it must have had encouragement only in mind, because on the facts there was no factual assistance given. The majority judgment seems to rest on the assumption that it was not a case of common purpose complicity, but a standard case of encouraging murder.[16] It is argued below that the majority judgment is problematic, because it misinterprets several important doctrines.

B. Oblique intention as an alternative mental element in complicity

In *R. v. Gnango*, the majority were wrong to hold that Gnango had it as his purpose that BM should kill him, because clearly that was not the case. Nonetheless, that finding was moot, because the Supreme Court also referred

15 See the authorities as discussed in Dennis J. Baker, *Glanville Williams: Textbook of Criminal Law* (London: Sweet & Maxwell, 4th edn 2015) at para. 17–084 *et seq.*

16 *R. v. Gnango* [2012] 2 W.L.R. 17 *per* Lords Phillips and Judge, C.J. (with Lord Wilson concurring); and *per* Lord Dyson in a separate judgment.

to recklessness as an alternative mental element in complicity. Since I am arguing that the mental element in complicity requires nothing less than intention including oblique intention, I shall use the *Gnango* case to argue the case for recognising oblique intention as an alternative mental element in complicity.

Gnango did not desire to be killed, but he did obliquely intend to be killed. His direct intention was not to encourage BM to try to kill him, but he did obliquely intend to encourage BM to kill him. There is a substantive difference.[17] The decision of the majority in *R. v. Gnango* could be grounded on oblique intention, but it appears to be grounded on recklessness, which runs counter to a line of authorities requiring intention as the mental element in complicity;[18] but it is understandable that the Supreme Court was led astray given the recent move towards recklessness as the mental element in complicity.[19] Nonetheless, I adhere to the view that complicity liability ought only be made out under section 8 of the *Accessories and Abettors Act 1861* when the accessory intends (either directly or obliquely) to assist or encourage the perpetrator to perpetrate a crime with the ulterior intention (the ulterior intention may be either direct or oblique intention) that the perpetrator succeed in perpetrating the target crime.[20]

It is argued below that *R. v. Gnango* was a case where oblique intention was relevant. Therefore, an appropriate direction should have been given to the jury with respect to oblique intention. The jury should have been asked to consider whether Gnango obliquely intended to encourage BM to kill him. Furthermore, it is argued that the jury should have been given a clear direction with respect to the issue of whether or not the gunfight was mutual or whether it was a mere chance encounter where Gnango was forced to defend himself against BM's deadly attack.

C. Joint perpetration theory

In *R. v. Gnango*, Lords Clarke and Brown also restored the conviction, but provided an alternative basis for doing so. They held that Gnango and BM were joint perpetrators of Magda Pniewska's murder. Lord Dyson also

17 Direct intention refers to purposive intention – that is, to cases where *D*'s purpose for doing *X* (shooting *V*) is to bring about consequence *Y* (*V*'s death). Oblique/indirect intention covers what is conceptually extreme subjective recklessness (see Baker, *op. cit. supra*, note 15 at 4–021 paras. *et seq.*

18 *United States v. Peoni* (2d Cir.1938) 100 F.2d 401 at 402 *per* Learned Hand, J. (Swan and Chase, J.J. concurring). Learned Hand, J. drew on a long line of English authorities and the writings of the institutional writers as far back as Bracton. See also *R. v. Passey* (1836) 7 Car. & P. 282; *R. v. Manners* (1837) 7 Car. & P. 801; *R. v. Lockett* (1836) 7 Car. & P. 300; *R. v. Fretwell* (1862) Le. & Ca. 161; *No Accessary in Treason, Petit Larceny, and Trespass* (1611) 12 Co. Rep. 81.

19 The position was still unclear until the decisions in *R. v. Bryce* [2004] 2 Cr. App. R. 592; *R. v. Powell* [1999] 1 A.C. 1, where there was a move towards adopting recklessness as the mental element in complicity.

20 Direct intention was affirmed as the mental element in complicity in the recent decision of the Supreme Court of the United States in *Rosemond v. U.S.* (2014) 134 S.Ct. 1240.

presented the joint perpetration theory as an alternative basis for upholding the conviction. It is argued below that the joint perpetration theory is not an appropriate means for obtaining a conviction in cases where there is no factual joint perpetration. The facts clearly show that the direct cause of Magda Pniewska's death was BM's act of shooting her, and that the indirect cause was Gnango encouraging BM to shoot at him. An indirect cause and a direct cause do not combine to form a *joint* direct cause – and thus, there was no joint perpetration on the facts. Lord Clarke also referred to something akin to 'provocative act' murder[21] as a possible basis for upholding a conviction in such a case, but this approach also is unavailable on the facts of this case. It is unavailable because Gnango did not pressure BM into firing the fatal shot. BM's choice to engage in the lethal gunfight was fully unfettered. Lord Kerr refused to restore the conviction, because he was of the view that an alternative form of complicity could not be introduced to restore the conviction at the Supreme Court level, because the jury had not been given appropriate directions at the trial to make such a finding safe. Lord Kerr also rejected the joint perpetration theory. It is argued below that the joint perpetration and joint causation theories referred to by Lords Clarke and Brown are not suitable for obtaining a conviction in such a case. It is conceptually more feasible to use the law of complicity and the doctrines of oblique intention and transferred intention to obtain a conviction.

D. The victim rule

The victim rule/exempt party rule also was an issue in *R. v. Gnango.* Since the rule as it was addressed in *R. v. Gnango* raised issues with respect to transferred malice and with respect to the conduct element in complicity, it is convenient to address that rule in this chapter. (However, in a different book it would be tempting to dedicate a separate chapter to the victim rule.) I shall argue that the Supreme Court's narrow reading of the 'exempt party' rule is less than convincing. Under this rule, two general exemptions from complicity liability exist at common law: (1) A party to a crime cannot be an accomplice if she was the victim of the offence.[22] For example, a child

21 Provocative act murder is shorthand used 'for that category of intervening-act causation cases in which, during the commission of a crime, the intermediary (i.e. a police officer or crime victim) is provoked by the defendant's conduct into a response that results in someone's death.' See *People v. Concha* (2009) 47 Cal. 4th 653 at 663. This mode of murder is recognised in California and a few other U.S. states. A form of it also has been recognised in England in *R. v. Pagett* (1983) 76 Cr. App. R. 279. (However in the latter case, the jury decided that Pagett was guilty of unlawful dangerous act manslaughter rather than murder.)

22 This rule is commonly referred to as the victim rule. See Glanville Williams, 'Victims and Other Exempt Parties in Crime' (1990) 10 *Legal Studies* 245. The rule was first expounded in *R. v. Tyrrell* [1894] 1 QB 710. The *Tyrrell* decision has been drawn upon in numerous

cannot be held liable as an accomplice of child rape where she (putatively) consents and encourages an adult to have sexual intercourse with her. (2) A party cannot be an accomplice if her conduct was 'inevitably incidental'[23] to the commission of the offence.[24] For example, a prostitute cannot be an accomplice to the offence of soliciting[25] a prostitute.[26] Nor can an assault victim be an accomplice to an assault against her. Similarly, *D* receiving stolen goods does not make *D* an accomplice to the seller's theft.[27] Coupled with the above rules, legislation may expressly exclude certain parties from being liable as accomplices for other reasons.[28] Does that mean that a defendant is exempt from complicity liability only when the statute

cases in the United States to develop the victim rule (and also the 'inevitably incidental conduct' rule). See *In re Meagan R.* (1996) 42 Cal. App. 4th 17 at 23; and *City of Auburn v. Hedlund* (2009) 165 Wash. 2d 645 at 652, where it was said: 'The statute appears to be a codification of a much older common law rule dating at least back to an 1893 English statutory rape case, where the court reasoned that a law intended to protect young girls could not also hold them responsible as accomplices.' See also *People v. Tobias* (1999) 91 Cal. Rptr. 2d 396 at 412; *U.S. v. Williamson* (1964) 235 F Supp. 836 at 838; *Application of Balucan* (1960) 44 Haw. 271 at 281; *Gebardi v. U.S.* (1932) 287 U.S. 112 at 122 (a decision of the Supreme Court of the United States); and *U.S. v. Annunziato* (1961) 293 F 2d 373 at 379 where it was said: 'It is quite true that mere yielding to the commission of a crime against one's self does not render a complying person a co-conspirator.'

23 *R. v. Titley* (1880) 14 Cox C.C. 502; *Ex parte Barker* (1891) 30 N.B.R. 406.

24 At least one English case has recognised the 'inevitably incidental conduct' rule: *R. v. Congdon* [1990] N.L.J.R. 1221. The rule is widely recognised in the United States. In *U.S. v. Daniels* (201) 653 F. 3d 399 at 413 it was stated: 'When a crime inherently requires "two to tango", but the statute is not intended to punish the victim of the crime – as is the case in prostitution or the manufacture of pornography – federal courts regularly apply a common-law exception to conspiratorial or accomplice liability. See generally Model Penal Code § 2.06(6)(b) (stating that "a person is not an accomplice in an offence' if 'he is a victim' or 'the offence is so defined that his conduct is inevitably incident to its commission").' In *Club 35, LLC v. Borough of Sayreville*, (2011) 420 N.J. Super 231 it was said: '[C]onduct "inevitably incident" to the conduct constituting an offence is not punishable unless the offence is *defined to include it*' [emphasis added]. These are a couple of recent decisions, but the U.S. reports contain hundreds of similar decisions covering a wide range of conduct.

25 Section 51A of the *Sexual Offences Act 2003*.

26 See *R. v. Congdon* [1990] N.L.J.R. 1221. In the United States, *R. v. Tyrrell* [1894] 1 Q.B. 710 also has been raised in support of the inevitably incident rule. See *Williams v. Superior Court* (1973) 30 Cal. App. 3d 8 at 13.

27 This is a bilateral transaction, even though there can be no participation in the theft by the receiver since the theft was completed beforehand without her participation. See Baker, *op. cit. supra*, note 15 at para 36–015; *R. v. Ready* [1942] V.L.R. 85. See also *State v. Lee* (2004) 683 N.W. 2d 309 at 314–315; and *Scott v. Killian* (1984) 36 S.A.S.R. 438 at 447, where a man attended a brothel and paid for sexual intercourse with a woman. It was held that he was not an accomplice to prostitution.

28 Cf. section 47(8)(c) of the *Serious Crime Act 2007*, which provides that a participant whose act of encouragement is also an attempt to commit an independent crime is not also convictable of an offence under the *Act of 2007*. See also the express exemptions mentioned in *Giorgianni v. R.* (1985) 156 C.L.R. 473 at 491; *Maroney v. R.* (2004) 216 C.L.R. 31 at 42–43; and *Mallan v. Lee* (1949) 80 C.L.R. 198 at 216 *per* Dixon, J. (as he then was).

identifies her as a victim or where the statute expressly exempts her for some other reason? It is argued below that where a statute is silent as to whether a victim or an inevitably incidental party is liable as an accessory,[29] there is a presumption of no complicity liability.[30] I also argue that the *obiter* statements of Lords Phillips and Lord Judge C.J. in *R. v. Gnango*,[31] that the consenting masochists in *R. v. Brown*[32] could have been convicted as accessories to their own assaults, rests on an erroneous interpretation of the exempt party rule. The masochists were not only incidental parties to the assaults against them, but were also victims of the assaults that were perpetrated against them. They were members of the protected class (human beings) that the *Offences against the Person Act 1861* aims to protect from bodily harm.

There was no need for the Supreme Court to dilute the exempt party/victim rule to uphold Gnango's murder conviction, since it could have held that the rule did not apply because Gnango was not the actual victim. It is argued below that when a person engages in conduct that risks the lives of third parties, she cannot rely on the victim rule to evade justice because she is not the actual victim. She cannot consent on behalf of the real victim. The victim rule was only ever intended to apply to the factual victim who invited harm against herself and only when she did so without exposing innocent others to a risk of being victimised. For instance, it would protect a masochist, but it would not protect a *sado*masochist, because the latter is both a victim and a harm-doer.[33]

II. Oblique intention and mutual gunfights

In *R. v. Gnango* the Supreme Court was confronted with the following problem:

> If (1) *D1* and *D2* voluntarily engage in fighting each other, each intending to kill or cause grievous bodily harm to the other and each foreseeing that the other has the reciprocal intention, and if (2) *D1* mistakenly kills *V* in the course of the fight, in what circumstances, if any, is *D2* guilty of the offence of murdering *V*?

29 For example, section 5 of the *Sexual Offences Act 2003* does not expressly exempt a child victim from accomplice liability, but clearly a child would be exempt (even where *D* is also a child) because the act aims to protect children. Cf. section 51 of the *Serious Crime Act 2007*.

30 In *R. v. Tyrrell* [1894] 1 Q.B. 710, Lord Coleridge, C.J. said: 'it is impossible to say that the *Act*, which is absolutely silent about aiding or abetting, or soliciting or inciting, can have intended that the girls for whose protection it was passed should be punishable under it for the offences committed upon themselves.'

31 [2012] 2 W.L.R. 17 at 33G.

32 [1994] 1 A.C. 212.

33 Nonetheless, if the masochist does not also act as a sadist and reciprocate the harm the victim rule should apply.

The court had to consider the law of complicity and the exempt party/victim rule. I will start by discussing the court's findings in relation to the law of complicity. In the following sections, I shall consider joint perpetration theory, provocative act murder and the exempt party/victim rule. The first issue that the court had to determine was whether it was a case of common purpose complicity or a straightforward case of aiding, abetting, counselling and procuring murder. Common purpose complicity and complicity in the pure sense are both forms of derivative liability. The secondary party's liability derives from the perpetrator's (or, if you like, principal's) criminal act. As we saw in Chapter 2, under both heads of complicity liability the secondary party is derivatively liable for involving herself in the criminal act of another. It is only the *mode* of participation that differs.[34] In the case of common purpose complicity, the conduct element (the act of participation/involvement) is made out when it is established that *A* encouraged *P* by an implied or express act of authorisation. (The elements of common purpose complicity were discussed in detail in the last chapter, so I will not reiterate them here.) In the case of standard complicity, the conduct element is established by proving that *A*'s act encouraged or assisted *P*.

The first argument based on the law of complicity put forward by the Crown[35] was that Gnango and BM had jointly perpetrated the offence of

34 The court used the term parasitic liability to refer to common purpose complicity, but this term is somewhat superfluous. It merely suggests that liability for the collateral offence is parasitic because it derives from a host offence. For example, the host or underlying crime might be robbery with the collateral (or parasitic) offence being a murder of a security guard that has occurred during the robbery. All that is being said here is that the accomplice's liability derives from his *active* participation in the collateral offence, if she encouraged the perpetrator's murder for the purpose of effecting the robbery. She is already a joint perpetrator of the underlying robbery and is liable as such. As we saw in the last chapter, there can be only factual participation in the collateral crime as opposed to some sort of fictitious constructive participation.

35 *R. v. Gnango* [2012] 2 W.L.R.17 at 26C. The trial judge's direction to the jury sums up the argument as follows: 'If you are sure that Bandana Man and the defendant joined together to commit such unlawful violence by having a gunfight, whether pre-planned or whether on the spur of the moment on the top of the steps and the side of the car, and that this joint enterprise came into being before Magda was killed by a shot from Bandana Man, then the defendant would be guilty of murder also, along with Bandana Man, provided the other requirements are satisfied. So if you are sure that Bandana Man and the defendant were in a joint enterprise to cause an affray, to use unlawful violence against each other by having a gunfight and by firing at each other, whether this joint enterprise was the result of a pre-planned meeting or arose on the spur of the moment when they saw each other, and that in the course of that joint enterprise fight, Magda was murdered by Bandana Man on the basis of transferred malice, as I have explained it to you, and that the defendant realised – and the prosecution say that he must have realised – that in the course of their joint enterprise gunfight, Bandana Man might kill with the requisite intention for murder, then the defendant would also be guilty of murder.'

affray (the underlying offence),[36] and therefore Gnango was liable for BM's collateral crime (the murder of the passer-by), because he foresaw it as a possible incident of jointly perpetrating the affray. The Supreme Court of the United Kingdom rightly dismissed that argument.[37] There was no evidence to support the claim that Gnango and BM had it as their common purpose to perpetrate the offence of affray. There need not be a formal agreement, but there would have to be some evidence to suggest that they had it as their common purpose to commit the offence of affray.

Lords Phillips and Judge C.J. (with Lord Wilson concurring) said:[38]

> [A]n affray need not involve any common enterprise or common purpose. The Court of Appeal rightly held that [common purpose] accessory liability must be founded on a common unlawful enterprise or purpose. It is joining in this common enterprise that renders the conduct of the accomplice an encouragement to the principal to commit the additional offence, thereby justifying the conviction of the accomplice. Because affray does not necessarily involve any common purpose it cannot automatically constitute a foundation for parasitic [common purpose] accessory liability . . . The Court of Appeal left open, however, the possibility that, on the facts of an individual case, affray may be the product of a common purpose or enterprise capable of providing a foundation for parasitic accessory liability. A duel was given as an example of such a situation.
>
> . . .
>
> The fallacy of this argument is that, if there was a joint intention to have an affray, that intention was to have an affray by shooting at each other with homicidal intent. It is artificial to treat the intention to have an affray as a separate intention from the intention to have a potentially homicidal shooting match.[39]

Since it was clear that Gnango and BM were not engaged in a joint enterprise to commit affray, an alternative mode of complicity had to be considered. Rather than ground the case on common purpose complicity,

36 Section 3 of the *Public Order Act 1986*. For them to have jointly committed affray they would had to have acted jointly for the common purpose of causing fear, but it was held that it was 'not realistic to say that they acted in concert to cause fear; they acted independently and antagonistically in a manner which did so'. *R. v. Gnango* [2012] 2 W.L.R. 17 at 27B *per* Lord Phillips and Lord Judge, C.J. (with Lord Wilson concurring).

37 This argument was not only dismissed by the Lords in the majority, but also by Lord Kerr in his dissenting judgment. See *R. v. Gnango* [2012] 2 W.L.R. 17 at 48G.

38 *R. v. Gnango* [2012] 2 W.L.R. 17 at 31A.

39 *R. v. Gnango* [2012] 2 W.L.R. 17 at 32A.

Lords Phillips and Judge, C.J. (with Lord Wilson concurring)[40] took the view that it was a standard case of aiding, abetting, counselling and procuring murder. This left their Lordships with the following question: can *X* be liable as an accessory for encouraging *Y* to murder *X*? Their Lordships held that a person can be liable for murder for intentionally encouraging (counselling and procuring) another to kill her. The only reason why the Crown had sought to ground its case of murder on the common purpose complicity doctrine was that it thought that would allow it to bypass the potential barrier posed by the victim rule. Their Lordships held that the standard form of complicity could provide a direct route to conviction, because the victim rule posed no barrier. The direct route to conviction was explained as follows:

(i) Bandana Man attempted to kill the defendant.
(ii) By agreeing to the shoot-out, the defendant aided and abetted[41] Bandana Man in this attempted murder.
(iii) Bandana Man accidentally killed Miss Pniewska instead of the defendant. Under the doctrine of transferred malice he was guilty of her murder.
(iv) The doctrine of transferred malice applied equally to the defendant as aider and abetter of Bandana Man's attempted murder. He also was guilty of Miss Pniewska's murder.[42]

A. When the victim is a third (untended transferred) party

As we will see, the victim rule is not relevant in a case like *R. v. Gnango*, but not for the reasons given by their Lordships. It is not available because Gnango was not the actual victim. The real victim was Magda Pniewska and she did not consent to being the victim. The victim rule cannot be applied beyond pure cases where the consenting victim is in fact the victim. It applies only when the intended victim is the only factual victim of what she risked or encouraged. If Gnango had been wounded by BM's gunfire without any passer-by being injured, he would not have been

40 Lord Dyson (*R. v. Gnango* [2012] 2 W.L.R. 17 at 46B) supported this view, but also held that the conviction could be upheld on the alternative basis that BM and Gnango were joint perpetrators. Lords Brown and Clarke also prefer the joint principal alternative.

41 Here, their Lordships truncated the words 'aid, abet, counsel, and procure' to 'aid and abet'. Elsewhere, they have used all four words. Presumably, their Lordships were not suggesting that it was a case of aiding, because there was no aiding on the facts. Gnango's actions provided factual encouragement, but that is all. Gnango did not supply BM with a gun, nor did he assist him to pull the trigger. All he did was encourage BM to shoot, as this was the certain result of him approaching Gnango with full knowledge of the fact that both he and BM were armed for battle.

42 *R. v. Gnango* [2012] 2 W.L.R. 17 at 32.

charged with encouraging BM to wound him. Instead, he would have been charged with attempted murder of BM and of a firearms offence and nothing more. If Magda Pniewska had been killed with one bullet from BM's gun, with Gnango being wounded with a different bullet, Gnango would have been liable for the murder of Magda Pniewska, but not for encouraging BM to wound him. As a general rule, the victim rule will not apply as far as any third party (transferred victim) is concerned. We will leave the victim rule aside for now, as it needs to be discussed separately.

B. Complicity liability

Let us turn our focus to the way the majority[43] in *R. v. Gnango* used complicity to restore Gnango's conviction for murder. Could it really be said that Gnango's purpose was to encourage BM to murder him? Lords Phillips, Judge C.J., Wilson and Dyson did not bother to state one way or the other whether intention is the mental element in complicity or whether it is recklessness. As I noted at the outset, the accessory ought to be liable only when she has intentionally (directly or obliquely) encouraged (or assisted) the perpetrator to commit a crime with the ulterior intention that the perpetrator succeed in perpetrating the crime. Even if we accept the foresight rule that has been invoked in a number of standard complicity cases,[44] there would still have to be an intentional act of encouragement.

The foresight rule has been invoked only as a substitute *vis-à-vis A*'s ulterior intention that *P* succeed in perpetrating the crime that both *A* and *P* knows *P* plans to perpetrate. There still has to be intentional conduct with respect to any prior assistance or encouragement. (The defences of duress, insanity, automatism and so on would apply in the normal way with respect to unintentional assistance or encouragement.) Thus, if *A* robotically assists *P* while in a state of automatism, she will not be liable because her act of assistance is not volitional and thus intentional.[45] If the act of assistance is an unintentional act, then there is no need to consider whether the putative accessory realised her act of assistance was capable of assisting the perpetrator to perpetrate the anticipated target offence or whether she believed that there was a 'real or substantial risk' that the perpetrator would perpetrate the anticipated target crime.

43 This includes Lord Dyson, as his primary legal argument for upholding the conviction is the same as that given by Lords Phillips and Judge, C.J. (with Lord Wilson concurring).

44 *R. v. Bryce* [2004] 2 Cr. App. R. 592; *R. v. O'Brien* [1995] 2 Cr. App. R. 649; *R. v. Reardon* [1999] Crim. L.R. 392.

45 *R. v. Fraser* (1984) 13 C.C.C. (3d) 292; *R. v. Chapin* (1978) 41 C.C.C. (2d) 300; *R. v. Cosgrove* (1975) 29 C.C.C. (2d) 169; *R. v.* Waterfield (1974) 18 C.C.C. (2d) 140. Cf. the situation where the perpetrator, instead of the accessory, suffers automatism: *R. v. Quick* [1973] Q.B. 910 at 923; *State v. Price* (1982) 294 SE2d 426; *Sellers v. State* (1991) 809 P.2d 676.

Reckless acts of assistance and encouragement do not give rise to complicity liability. Suppose there has been a spate of burglaries in *A*'s neighbourhood and *A* recklessly leaves her ladder unsecured in her front garden where a burglar finds it and uses it to commit a burglary. Let us assume that *A* does not intend to assist any burglars, but she foresees the possibility of her ladder being used by a burglar. If *A*'s assistance is reckless, then *a fortiori* she does not intend that *P*'s crime succeed. A putative accessory should not be liable merely because she foresees someone might use her ladder to burglarise a house. Nor should it matter that the putative accessory foresaw that her unsecured ladder might be used to burglarise a neighbour whom she despises. In the latter context, the putative accessory might genuinely desire that a burglar succeed should the burglar target her despised neighbour, but any assistance on the putative accessory's part is reckless assistance. The putative accessory's act of assistance was unintentional, even though she might have desired that should *P* take her ladder without her permission that *P* succeed in burglarising her neighbour. (The case would be different if *A* intentionally omits to secure the ladder with the ulterior intention of assisting a burglar.)

Being reckless with a ladder is hardly sufficient to make a person a participant in a burglary merely because she foresaw it might facilitate a burglary against someone whom she hoped any burglar would be successful in burglarising. However, if *A* gives (an intentional act) *P* her ladder in circumstances where she foresees that *P* might use it to burglarise a particular house, she would be liable under the *R. v. Bryce*[46] doctrine. The *R. v. Bryce* doctrine does not require *A* to intentionally give *P* a ladder with the ulterior intention that *P* use it to succeed in perpetrating a burglary, it merely requires *A* to do the intentional act of assistance (give *P* the ladder) with ulterior reckless foresight of the possibility that *P* might use it to perpetrate a burglary. Hereinafter, I work from the premise that the mental element in complicity requires intention or oblique intention and thus I will not discuss the *R. v. Bryce* doctrine further.

C. The role of oblique intention in mutual combats

Gnango did not intend to commit suicide. It was not his purpose or desire to have BM kill him; if it had been, Gnango would have stood still when BM fired at him so that BM might succeed. Why avoid a bullet if you desire that it hit you? Gnango was not consenting to be killed, nor was he desiring or directly intending to encourage BM to kill him. Nonetheless, Gnango took a conscious risk with his own life. He did not directly intend to be killed by BM, but he indirectly intended to be killed and was willing to risk the lives of proximate passers-by. A jury could infer from the facts that Gnango

46 [2004] 2 Cr. App. R. 592 at 611 *per* Potter, L.J (Hooper and Astill, J.J. concurring).

foresaw that by shooting at BM with the direct intention of killing him it was virtually certain that BM would shoot back with the same direct intention. And from this it could be inferred that he obliquely intended to encourage BM to kill him.[47]

The jury might have greater difficulty trying to infer that Gnango obliquely intended to kill passers-by. He took a risk with their lives, but he was not obliquely intending to shoot them, nor was he obliquely intending to encourage BM to attempt to kill them. The virtually certain consequence of him going armed to confront BM, who he believed would be armed and ready for battle, was that BM would try to shoot him dead. The death of the passer-by was not necessarily foreseen as a virtual certainty. If the gunfight had been in a crowded rush-hour underground carriage, then it would be inferable that he foresaw the death of a fellow passenger as a virtual certainty. Even though the gun battle took place in a densely populated part of London, it took place in an almost empty car park on a Sunday morning. The focus in such cases should not be on whether *D* saw the victim's death as a virtual certainty, but simply on whether *D* foresaw the attempt on his own life as a virtual certainty. The oblique intention doctrine applies because Gnango obliquely intended to encourage BM to kill him, and the transferred intention doctrine applies because BM missed his intended human target (Gnango) and hit an unintended human target (Miss Pniewska). Hence, the complicity doctrine, oblique intention and transferred intention can be invoked to ground a murder conviction.

D. Comparing depraved-indifference murder in the United States

In United States law, depraved-indifference murder applies when *D* acts with a depraved indifference to human life and when her conduct results in a death. Depraved-indifference murder applies when *D* perpetrates an act knowing it is extremely likely that the act will kill or cause serious bodily harm to someone else. 'It involves rather the deliberate perpetration of a knowingly dangerous act with reckless and wanton unconcern and indifference as to whether anyone is harmed or not.'[48] (In most states, depraved-heart murders are labelled as second-degree murder.)

47 This argument rests on the premise that oblique intention is a substantive fault element in itself in criminal law. It was argued in the last chapter that foresight of virtual certainty is both a substantive fault element and also a maxim of evidence. Evidence that *D* had foreseen a criminal consequence as a virtually certain consequence of her actions can be used to infer either direct intention or indirect (oblique) intention. It was clear that Gnango did not have it as his direct or purposive intention that he be killed by BM, but clearly he had foresight of the virtual certainty that an attempt to kill him would be made by BM. To infer direct intention from foresight of virtual certainty in such a case would be to fictitiously infer direct intention where there was none.

48 *Stouffer v. State* (1997) 118 Md.App. 590 at 609.

There is a line of cases in the United States that have upheld murder convictions by focusing on the direct risk that the secondary party creates for her victim by participating in dangerous conduct such as a gunfight, which in turn encourages others also to participate in the gunfight.[49] In most of these cases, the 'depraved-indifference murder' doctrine[50] (also known as 'depraved-heart murder') was invoked on the basis that *D*, by participating in a gunfight with the perpetrator, took an extreme risk with the lives of those who got hit in the crossfire. Such defendants know that they are directly risking the lives of passers-by and that they are also encouraging their fellow participants to take a similar risk. In *Alston v. State*,[51] Judge Moylan explained the rationale for invoking the depraved-indifference doctrine in such cases. His Honour said:

> The 'bottom line' is that when a group, or two groups, of hoodlums deliberately engage in a gang-war style of shoot-out in a crowded urban area, they collectively trigger an escalating chain reaction creating a high risk to human life. When instead of taking their gunslinging vendetta to an uninhabited island or some remote spot in the desert, they arrogantly indulge in their homicidal insanity in the middle of a crowded block of residences, each participant in such collective madness displays a wanton and depraved indifference to any human life that might randomly fall within their overlapping and deadly enfilades. Should death to one of the innocent bystanders or homeowners ensue, each participant in the lethal encounter has exhibited the *mens rea* that qualifies him for depraved-heart murder.
>
> . . .

49 In the 'depraved heart' situation the jury is not inferring that there was an actual intent to kill, because there is none in such cases. Rather it is inferring that *D* as good as intended to kill *V*, because she foresaw *V*'s death (or her own death for that matter) as a practically certain consequence of engaging in the gunfight in the presence of proximate passers-by.

50 'The doctrine of universal malice, depraved heart murder, or reckless homicide manifesting extreme indifference to human life is intended to embrace those cases where a person has no deliberate intent to kill or injure any particular individual . . . The difference between culpable negligence manslaughter and depraved heart murder is the degree of mental state of culpability; depraved heart murder requires a higher degree of recklessness from which malice or deliberate design might be implied.' Christine Gimeno *et al.*, 'Depraved or Extreme Indifference to Human Life' (2014) 40 *C.J.S.: Homicide* § 42. Depraved heart murder is a form of reckless murder: it covers cases where the risk *D* takes with *V*'s life is extreme. But the subjective recklessness required seems to be a shade less than that required for oblique intention in England and Wales. See *People v Sanchez* (2002) 777 N.E. 2d 204 at 217, where it was observed by the Court of Appeals of New York that 'we have found depraved indifference where the defendant indulged in behaviour evidencing a grave risk of death, but again it is behaviour that falls short of a certainty of death'.

51 (1994) 662 A. 2d 247 (Court of Appeals of Maryland), quoting Judge Moylan's reasoning in his decision in the Court of Special Appeals. See also *People v. Russell* (1998) 91 N.Y. 2d 280 (Court of Appeals of New York). This approach has long history in the United States: see *Commonwealth v. Hare* (1844) 2 Clark 467.

> In terms of the *actus reus* of this particular depraved-heart murder, the deadly homicidal force was not a bullet. Such an analytic approach would commit us to the trivializing foolishness of seeking to establish the trajectory and provenance of each of forty or fifty bullets fired in the course of a single wild exchange. The deadly homicidal force, rather, was a collective hail of bullets, a collective fusillade, with no further parsing required. Which bullet came from which gun is inconsequential. One does not anguish over which member of the firing squad killed the prisoner.

Britain does not have a form of murder akin to depraved-indifference murder.[52] Instead, the question is: did *D* obliquely intend to encourage *P* to kill *D*? The question is not: did the defendant obliquely intend to kill the passers-by by engaging in the gunfight? (The latter might be difficult to establish, because the passer-by's death was more likely to have been foreseen as highly probable rather than as virtually certain.) Nothing less than oblique intention is sufficient for grounding a murder conviction in Britain. It is one thing to assert that Gnango believed that by confronting BM the virtually certain consequence would be that BM would try to kill him; it is something entirely different to assert that he foresaw a passer-by's death as a virtually certain consequence of his encouraging BM to kill him. The latter would be highly probable, but not necessarily a virtual certainty. In such a situation it might be said that Gnango obliquely intended to encourage BM to take an extreme risk with the lives of passers-by, but not that he obliquely intended to encourage him to kill them.

An alternative route to liability might be to charge both parties with reckless manslaughter[53] or unlawful dangerous act manslaughter, one as a perpetrator and the other as an accessory. (Presumably reckless manslaughter still exists in English law, because there is no authority abrogating it. However, the convention is for the prosecutor to charge unlawful dangerous act manslaughter.) Gnango encouraged BM to perpetrate an unlawful and objectively dangerous act, since he encouraged him to discharge a firearm in a public place and also to attempt to murder him.[54] A person who

52 For a fuller account of the 'depraved heart' doctrine, see the leading American treatises including Joshua Dressler, *Understanding Criminal Law* (Newark NJ: LexisNexis, 2006) at 554 *et seq.*; Wayne LaFave, *Substantive Criminal Law* (St. Paul MN: West Publishing, 3rd edn 2003) Vol. II, at §14.4. The doctrine has a long history in one variant or another. See Francis Wharton, *American Criminal Law* (Philadelphia: Kay and Brother, 3rd edn 1855) at 435. Cf. Sir Michael Foster, *Crown Cases* (Oxford: Clarendon Press, 1762) at 261, where Foster said: 'If action unlawful in itself be done . . . *indiscriminately*, fall where it may, and death ensure against the original intention of the party, it will be murder.'

53 See *R. v. Lidar* [2000] 4 Archbold News 3, CA. See also *R. v. Pike* [1961] Crim. L.R. 547; *Gray v. Barr* [1971] 2 Q.B. 554 at 557.

54 *R. v. Creamer* [1966] 1 Q.B. 72; *R. v. Buck* (1960) 44 Cr. App. R. 213. Cf. *R. v. Fretwell* (1862) Le. & Ca. 161.

intentionally encourages another to perpetrate an unlawful and dangerous act that causes another's death is guilty of being accessory to manslaughter.[55] Nonetheless in *R. v. Gnango*, a murder conviction seemed more appropriate because *A* obliquely intended to encourage *P* to kill.

Using complicity, oblique intention and transferred intention to ground a murder conviction means that the jury only have to consider whether the secondary party believed that the virtually certain consequence of him confronting an armed gangster to participate in a gunfight was that the armed gangster would attempt to kill him. It is not necessary to consider whether Gnango also foresaw the death of the passer-by as a virtual certainty: it is only necessary to determine that he obliquely intended to encourage the perpetrator to kill him. It would be almost impossible for the jury to infer that Gnango obliquely intended to encourage BM to kill a passer-by.[56] The latter would require the jury to determine whether Miss Pniewska's 'death or serious bodily harm had been a virtual certainty (barring some unforeseen intervention) as a result of [BM's] actions and that the defendant had appreciated that such was the case'.[57]

In such a case, a jury is likely to infer that *A* did not foresee *V*'s death as a virtually certain consequence of him encouraging *P* to try to kill *A*, because *V* only strayed in the path of the bullet by chance. Given that it was a densely populated part of London, there was a reasonably high chance that a passer-by would be caught in the crossfire, but the car park was almost empty. A high probability is not a virtual certainty. Gnango encouraged BM to risk the lives of passers-by, but he did not encourage him to try to kill them.

Lords Phillips, Judge, C.J., Wilson and Dyson would have done well to invoke the doctrine of oblique intention, because it would have made their application of complicity and transferred intention watertight. There is a substantive distinction between direct intention and oblique intention. The jury should have been directed on the issue of oblique intention, because it was clear that Gnango did not directly intend to encourage BM to kill Gnango himself. If the jury had determined that it was a case of oblique intention, then that would have allowed it to return a guilty verdict. Lord Kerr in his dissenting judgment held that the

55 See *R. v. Creamer* [1966] 1 Q.B. 72 at 82, where Lord Parker, C.J. said: 'A man is guilty of involuntary manslaughter when he intends an unlawful act and one likely to do harm to the person and death results which was neither foreseen nor intended. It is the accident of death resulting which makes him guilty of manslaughter as opposed to some lesser offence such as assault, or, in the present case, abortion . . . Bearing that in mind, it is quite consistent that a man who has counselled and procured such an illegal and dangerous act from which death, unintended, results should be guilty of being accessory before the fact to manslaughter.' See also *R. v. Law* [1987] 10 N.I.J.B. 72; *R. v. Chai* (2002) 128 A. Crim. R. 101. Cf. *Goff v. Byby* (1596) Cro. Eliz. 540.

56 He only encouraged BM to expose the passers-by to a high risk of being killed, whereas he encouraged BM to try to kill him.

57 *R. v. Woollin* [1999] 1 A.C. 82.

conviction could not be restored, because the jury had not been given clear directions as far as the issue of intentional encouragement was concerned. Lord Kerr said: 'Before . . . oblique intention could form the basis of a jury's verdict, of course, precise directions to this effect would have to be given.'[58] Lord Kerr thought the question should have been framed in terms of direct intention,[59] rather than in terms of oblique intention, but as I have already noted, the facts show that neither party directly intended to be killed. It appears that the jury was satisfied that Gnango and BM did in fact directly intend to kill each other, but it should have been asked to consider whether Gnango also obliquely intended to encourage BM to kill Gnango himself.

III. Mutual combats and transferred defences

In a case like *R. v. Gnango*, it also would be necessary to give the jury crisp directions concerning the question of whether the gunfight was mutual. This sort of direction is required to ensure that the defence of self-defence is considered in appropriate cases. A clear direction on whether or not the gunfight was voluntary and mutual allows the court to pay due attention to the issue of self-defence. It also allows the court to consider whether the participant in a mutual gunfight was grossly negligent in not retreating before being forced to kill in self-defence.

In *R. v. Gnango* the jury should have been asked to determine whether Gnango's encouragement did in fact encourage BM to try to kill Gnango.[60] Given that BM started shooting first, the jury might have concluded that BM acted without any factual encouragement. However, it seems that there was plenty of evidence for the jury to conclude that they had in fact encouraged each other by their mutual and voluntary participation in the gunfight. Since the participation in the gunfight was mutual and voluntary, Gnango's encouragement started before he arrived at the scene of the gunfight.[61]

58 *R. v. Gnango* [2012] 2 W.L.R. 17 at 52B.

59 *R. v. Gnango* [2012] 2 W.L.R. 17 at 49.

60 *The Queen v. Coney* (1881–82) L.R. 8 Q.B.D. 534 at 557 *per* Hawkins, J.; *R. v. Clarkson* [1971] 1 W.L.R. 1402 at 1406 *per* Megaw L.J.; *R. v. Allen* [1965] 1 Q.B. 130. In *Hutt v. R.* [1989] T.A.S.S.C. 27 at paragraph 53, Cox, J. (Underwood, Crawford, J.J. concurring) said: 'In the circumstances of this case an error of law occurred by reason of the omission to tell the jury that . . . there had to be proof to the requisite degree that the principal offender was in fact encouraged by the conduct of the accused to commit the crime.' See also *Roughley v. The Queen* (1995) 78 A. Crim. R. 160 at 162 *per* Cox, J.; *R. v. Phan* (2001) 123 A. Crim. R. 30 at paragraph 69; *Randall v. The Queen* (2004) 146 A. Crim. R. 197.

61 'This I say for law, that if one only do give the cause and provocation, and send the challenge, and the other accepts of it, and upon this they enter combat, and he which sends the challenge is killed, this is clearly murder in the other; for it is not material in the law who begins the quarrel, (so as there was a former quarrel) and the malice still continuing until the last stroke given; for the difference will be this, if they are once

BM's core reason for attempting to kill Gnango might have been that he was attempting a pre-emptive strike to prevent Gnango getting him first, but it was inferable from the evidence that one of the events that motivated or moved[62] BM to try to kill Gnango in the car park was Gnango's return fire.[63] Lord Kerr said:

reconciled for the first matter, and afterwards they happen to fall out again suddenly, and do fight, and the one kills the other, this is but a manslaughter.' *R. v. Taverner* (1616) 3 Bulst. 171 *per* Coke, C.J. On the second point, it is worth noting that a murder following a sudden falling out is no longer deemed manslaughter. The old chance-medley doctrine has been abrogated. See *R. v. Semini* [1949] 1 K.B. 405 at 406. The chance-medley rule worked almost as a presumption of no direct intent in cases where the killing resulted from a chance killing during a combat. When it was in force, the chance-medley doctrine held it to be only manslaughter 'where one man upon a sudden occasion kills another without malice in fact, or malice implied by law.' See *Raven's Case* (1661) Kelyng, J. 24 at 67. See also Sir Edward Coke, *The Institutes of the Laws of England: Third Part* (London: W. Lee, 1648) at 57.

62 Dalton uses the word 'mover' with respect to encourager. Dalton writes that a person is an accessory to a crime 'if he were either a Procurer, or Mover or Aider, Comforter or Consenter thereto.' He goes on to use the words: 'command, procure, move, aid, or consent thereto'. See Michael Dalton, *The Country Justice* (London: Printed by William Rawlins *et al.*, 1697) at 396. It is arguable that the concept of move requires the encouragement to have been a motivator. It need not be the sole motivator, but it must be a motivator. Hale also refers to 'movers and procurers'. See Sir Matthew Hale, *The History of the Pleas of the Crown* (London: Printed by R. Nutt *et al.*, 1736) at 145; 293; 312–313; 337–338; 376; 613; 625. The term mover also was used in the law of complicity: see R. *v. Fuller* (1797) 1 Bos. & P. 180 at 185, where the court said: 'The form of charging an accessory before the fact is, 'that he did incite, move, procure, aid, and abet'.' In *The Lord Sanchar's Case* (1612) 9 Co. Rep. 116, it was held that the accessory was liable for murder because he did 'stir up, move, abet, counsel, and procure' the perpetrator. See also *R. v. Caspar* (1839) 9 Car. & P. 289; *R. v. Watson* (1817) 2 Stark. 116; *R. v. Winifred* (1789) 1 Leach 515; *R. v. Pow* (1754) 1 Leach 45. *Mutatis mutandis,* Dalton referring to a barrator, describes a common mover as a 'stirrer up'. *Id.* at 31. The old crime of barratry was essentially one of encouragement. 'If a counsellor at law *encourage* a man to bring false actions through malice, and for the purposes of oppression, he may be indicted as a common barrator.' Likewise, it has been said: 'A barrator is defined to be a common mover, exciter, or maintainer of suits or quarrels in Courts of Record, or otherwise, as the County Court, and the like . . . ' *R. v. Urlyn* (1670) 2 Saund. 308. See also *R. v. Anonymous* (1685) 3 Mod. 97. In *R. v. Thomson* (1675) 3 Keb. 735, the barrator was referred to as an accessory. In *Francis Throgmorton's Case* (1596) Cro. Eliz. 563, the court referred to barratry as involving 'causation' and 'procurement': 'An action . . . will lie against one person for *causing* another to be maliciously prosecuted . . . where two or more conspire together to *procure* one to be indicted of felony or trespass, and he is afterwards acquitted, it shall be intended by law to be maliciously done, for which conspiracy lies . . . for it would be in hindrance of justice' [emphasis added]. Cf. section 3 of the *Treason Felony Act 1848,* which makes it an offence 'to move or stir any foreigner or stranger with force to invade the United Kingdom . . . '.

63 Cf. the inchoate offences found in sections 44–46 of the *Serious Crime Act 2007,* where it is enough that the encouragement was capable of encouraging the perpetrator to perpetrate the crime. It need not be shown that the perpetrator was in fact encouraged to perpetrate it. See Dennis J Baker, 'Complicity, Proportionality and the *Serious Crime Act*' (2011) 14(3) *New Crim. L. Rev.* 403.

> Can it be said that solely because there was an exchange of fire, this must be on foot of a plan? Agreement to shoot it out with an opponent, if reached in advance, would be such a plan although there is no evidence that this is what happened here.[64] But where there has been what has been described as a 'spontaneous agreement' to engage in a shoot-out, the question arises whether this can truly be said to be the product of an agreement in any real sense.

Lord Kerr does not focus on the agreement involved in entering a mutual combat, but on the fact that the Court of Appeal rejected the idea that there could be a common purpose when the purpose was to shoot at each other. As I pointed out above, it is necessary only to demonstrate that there was tacit consent or a mutual intention to engage in a gunfight.[65] This issue is relevant to whether the accessory can revive the right to act in self-defence after voluntarily entering a mutual combat, but has no relevance on the issue of whether there was a common purpose for the purposes of invoking the law of complicity.

A. Reviving the right to self-defence after entering a mutual combat

It was clear that the meeting between Gnango and BM was not a chance meeting. The jury found that the defendants had voluntarily met in circumstances where they believed the opposing party would be armed and ready for battle. If Gnango did not believe BM was armed and ready for battle, then why did he arm himself? Why did Gnango attend the same car park at the same point in time?

In *State v. Spates*,[66] Ternus, C.J. (sitting in the Supreme Court of Iowa) said:

> To constitute 'mutual combat' there must exist a mutual intent and willingness to fight and this may be manifested by the acts and conduct of the parties and the circumstances attending the leading up to the combat.[67]
>
> . . .
>
> Thus, an express or tacit agreement to engage in violence, while sufficient, is not required; it is enough that 'there was a concurrent or mutual expectation that a street battle would ensue'.[68]

Gnango armed himself and went to the particular car park to find BM. It was reasonable for the jury to infer that they were meeting for the purpose of conducting a gunfight. Normal citizens do not carry lethal weapons around

64 *R. v. Gnango* [2012] 2 W.L.R. 17 at 50B.
65 *R. v. Taverner* (1616) 3 Bulst. 171 *per* Coke, C.J.
66 *State v. Spates* (2010) 779 N.W. 2d 770.
67 *State v. Spates* (2010) 779 N.W. 2d 770 at 776.
68 *State v. Spates* (2010) 779 N.W. 2d 770 at 776.

London. Nor do they take them to resolve a dispute. They had both prepared for a gunfight by arming themselves before meeting. Coupled with this, BM wore a red bandana to hide his face and started to fire at Gnango as soon as he caught sight of him. This evidence would be sufficient for a jury to infer that BM believed that Gnango was armed and ready to kill him. The evidence was strong enough for the jury to infer that they had engaged in a mutual gunfight. Notwithstanding the clear evidence, juries in future cases of this kind should be asked to consider whether the armed combat was mutual or merely a chance encounter involving an attacker and a self-defender.

The jury would have to consider self-defence in cases where a mutual combatant has effectively withdrawn from the combat. In *R. v. Gnango*[69] the trial judge's directions included a direction in the following terms:

> If you are sure that Bandana Man and the defendant joined together to commit such unlawful violence by having a gunfight, whether preplanned or whether on the spur of the moment on the top of the steps and the side of the car, and that this joint enterprise came into being before Magda was killed by a shot from Bandana Man, then the defendant would be guilty of murder also, along with Bandana Man, provided the other requirements are satisfied.

This direction is inadequate as far as the issue of whether the combat was mutual is concerned. The direction given by the Supreme Court of Iowa provides an example of the type of mutual combat direction that would be adequate. The direction in *R. v. Gnango* was bound up as a part of the direction concerning whether or not BM and Gnango intended to engage in a joint enterprise and thus it was not sufficient for focusing the jury on the question of whether or not the gunfight was mutual.

It is important to ensure that the jury determine as a matter of fact that the gunfight was mutual and not a *chance* encounter where a gangster was pressured to defend himself from a *surprise* attack. If the encounter had been a chance one, then self-defence might have applied. The old law of chance-medley no longer applies to reduce murder to manslaughter in a case where a person is taken by surprise in a mutual combat,[70] but the normal rules of

69 [2012] 2 W.L.R. 17 at 27.

70 In *R. v. Semini* [1949] 1 K.B. 405 at 406, Lord Goddard, C.J, provided the following explanation of the abrogated chance-medley rule: 'If two men quarrel and fight, and either or both of them are armed with a lethal weapon, and in the heat of the fight one draws and uses the weapon with fatal results, that is causing death by chance medley and amounts to manslaughter, unless the jury find that from the commencement he intended to use the lethal weapon and was armed for that purpose.' Even if this rule were still in force, it would not help Gnango since he intended to use lethal force from the commencement of the gunfight. See *Raven's Case* (1661) Kelyng, J. 24, 67; see also Hale, *op. cit. supra*, note 62 at 483.

self-defence could apply in appropriate cases.[71] Self-defence cannot be made out in cases where the participants in a mutual gunfight have sought each other out for the purpose of killing each other.[72]

The defence of self-defence was not available to Gnango not only because he was armed and expecting to do battle, but because it was not necessary for him to kill to save his own life. The necessity requirement was not made out on the facts.[73] Where two men seek each other out to kill each other they do not act in self-defence as a matter of necessity. The necessity for self-defence can be avoided simply by avoiding the gunfight.[74] Even in situations where a mutual combatant has made a genuine attempt to withdraw from the gunfight, it will be very difficult for her to convince a jury that she made such a retreat and therefore is entitled to rely on the defence of self-defence. The very nature of a voluntary and mutual gunfight means that it will be difficult for a combatant to communicate a sufficient withdrawal for the purposes of reviving the right of self-defence.

In the ancient law, a death resulting from a fight was treated as manslaughter under the chance-medley doctrine. That doctrine presumed that a killing by chance in the heat of an argument was not premeditated and

71 See e.g., *U.S. v. Jenkins* (2004) 59 M.J. 893; cf. *State v. Meyers* (1989) 245 Kan. 471; *People v. Hecker* (1985) 109 Cal. 451 at 462.

72 *Dakin's Case* (1828) 1 Lewin 166; *R. v. Ayes* (1810) Russ. & Ry. 166; *R. v. Walters* (1688) 12 State Tr. 113. In B.E. Witkin and Norman L. Epstein, *California Criminal Law* (St Paul MN: Thomson/West, 3rd edn 2000) Vol. I, at 409 it is noted that: 'The person . . . who voluntarily engages in a fight, and is met by a counter-attack, has no privilege to stand his ground and defend. If the defendant "was the assailant or engaged in mutual combat", he or she "must really and in good faith have endeavoured to decline any further struggle before the homicide was committed".' Citing, among other authorities, *People v. Duchon* (1958) 165 C.A. 2d 690; *People v. Smith* (1973) 33 C.A. 3d 51. Tinsley asserts that the 'doctrine of self-defence cannot be invoked to excuse killing done in mutual combat willingly entered into. An individual who willingly provoked mutual combat is not justified or excused in taking life unless he has withdrawn in good faith, has communicated that withdrawal to his opponent, and had done all in his power to avert necessity of killing.' Jimmie E. Tinsley, 'Withdrawal by Aggressor Reviving Right of Self-Defence' (2014) 3 *Am. Jur. Proof of Facts* 2d 705 at § 2.5 citing *U.S. v. Jenkins* (2004) 59 M.J. 893; *State v. Meyers* (1989) 245 Kan. 471.

73 For a full discussion of the requirement of necessity in self-defence, see Baker, *op. cit. supra*, note 15 at Chapter 24.

74 Stroud observes: 'The allowance of this excuse of self-defence upon chance-medley, coupled with the condition which requires a retreat before the delivery of the mortal stroke, is a remarkable instance of the subtlety with which, in times of greater violence than our own, the rigour of the law was tempered by considerations of expediency. Where two persons fight upon a sudden quarrel, one killing the other is guilty of murder or manslaughter, according to the degree of provocation or the circumstances of the case. But it is obviously in the interests of peace to allow either party, even in the heat of combat, a *locus poenitentiae* before homicide is actually perpetrated. If the fighting were prearranged between the parties, it would be different, for in that case they would both have had their *locus poenitentiae*.' See Douglas Aikenhead Stroud, *Mens Rea* (London: Sweet & Maxwell, 1924) at 286.

thus was partially excusable. Chance-medley was only available if the defendant had killed in self-defence. The defensive killing had to be both necessary and proportionate, which meant that the killer had to effectively withdraw from the combat before killing her opponent. Withdrawal from the mutual combat is required to demonstrate that the necessity for self-defence is independent of the mutual combat. With reference to chance-medley, Blackstone wrote:[75]

> But the self-defence, which we are now speaking of, is that whereby a man may protect himself from an assault, or the like, in the course of a sudden brawl or quarrel, by killing him who assaults him. And this is what the law expresses by the word chance-medley . . . which in its etymology signifies a casual affray, the latter an affray in the heat of blood or passion: it appears properly applied to such killings, as happens in self-defence upon a sudden re-counter. This right of natural defence does not imply a right of attacking: for, instead of attacking one another for injuries past or impending, men need only have recourse to the proper tribunals of justice. They cannot therefore legally exercise this right of preventive defence, but in sudden and violent cases; when certain and immediate suffering would be the consequence of waiting for the assistance of the law. Wherefore, to excuse homicide by the plea of self-defence, it must appear that the slayer had no other possible means of escaping from his assailant . . . For which reason the law requires, that the person, who kills another in his own defence should have retreated as far as he conveniently or safely can, to avoid the violence of the assault, before he turns upon his assailant; and that, not fictitiously, or in order to watch his opportunity, but from a real tenderness of (bedding his brother's blood).

The chance-medley rule seemed to rest on both excuse and justification.[76] The partial excuse of chance-medley combined with the justificatory defence of self-defence only reduced a murder conviction to manslaughter,[77] because the defendant was deemed blameworthy for entering into the fight

75 Sir William Blackstone, *Commentaries on the Laws of England* (Oxford: Clarendon Press, 1769) Vol. IV at 184–185; Sir William Staunford, *Les Plees del Coron* (London: by Rychard Tottel, 1567) at 16. East writes: 'To reduce the crime to self-defence upon chance-medley, the party must decline the combat before a mortal stroke, and afterwards kill his adversary through necessity to avoid death.' Sir Edward Hyde East, *A Treatise of the Pleas of the Crown* (London: printed by A. Strahan, 1803) Vol. I., at 201; 279.

76 See *R. v. Kirkham* (1837) 8 Car. & P. 115 *per* Coleridge, J.; *Mancini v. D.P.P.* [1942] A.C. 1 at 10–11 *per* Lord Simon; *D.P.P. v. Camplin* [1978] A.C. 705 at 713 *per* Lord Diplock. See also James Fitzjames Stephen, *A Digest of Criminal Law* (London: Macmillan & Co., Ltd., 1904) at 190.

77 See *R. v. Kessal* (1824) 1 Car. & P. 437; *R. v. Snow* (1776) 1 Leach 151; *R. v. Lord Byron* (1765) 19 State Tr. 1177.

or combat to start with.[78] Hence, those engaged in a mutual combat were only entitled to a partial (imperfect) defence of self-defence.[79]

B. Imperfect (partial) self-defence v. perfect self-defence in mutual combats

Some U.S. states continue to have a doctrine of imperfect or partial self-defence, which applies in cases where the defender was the original aggressor or was originally a mutual combatant. In those states the partial or imperfect self-defence doctrine allows murder to be reduced to manslaughter only.[80] The doctrine of imperfect self-defence in those states is analogous to the old English chance-medley doctrine. Such an approach seems to rest on something akin to the change of normative position rationale for criminalisation,[81] because *D* is denied a full defence on the basis that her own wrongdoing was an indirect cause of her having to act in self-defence. This rationale for reducing self-defence to a partial defence is flawed, because *D*'s withdrawal from the combat breaks the causal chain between her prior wrongdoing and her necessary self-defence. It is *V*'s continued aggression after *D*'s withdrawal that gives rise to the necessity for self-defence.

As we have seen, in early English law self-defence in the context of a mutual combat provided the defendant with a partial defence only. The law was changed in 1828 when the chance-medley doctrine was abrogated by statute.[82] Since that time the defendant's independent prior wrongdoing has not been used to make self-defence a partial defence. There is no such defence as partial self-defence in our current law. Consequently, on the facts given by Blackstone, self-defence would now provide a full justificatory

78 Kenny expounded: 'Where in any chance-medley (i.e. "sudden combat") one of the combatants desisted from fighting, but the other continued his assault, and then the former one, having no other probable means of escape open to him, killed his assailant, the necessity of self-defence prevented the homicide from being a felony. But, as at first he was to blame for his share in the affray, the case was distinguished from the strictly "justifiable" homicide in which a person, who had been assaulted when entirely passive, slew his assailant in self-defence. On the other hand, if the chance-medley had been continued by both the combatants down to the time when the fatal blow was struck, the homicide would have nothing even to excuse it, and would be felonious possibly even a murder.' Courtney Stanhope Kenny, *Outlines of Criminal Law* (London: Macmillan, 1907) at 99.

79 'The two essential conditions of the plea of self-defence, in whatever circumstances and against whatever charge that plea may be set up (whether upon chance-medley or not) are, that the force used must have been necessary, and that it must have been proportionate.' Stroud, *op. cit. supra*, note 74 at 288.

80 See *State v. Wood* (2002) 561 S.E.2d 304; *Middleton v. McNeil* (2004) 124 S. Ct. 1830; *State v. Chavez* (1983) 661 P.2d 887 at 889. Cf. *Christian v. State* (2008) 405 Md. 306.

81 For a general overview of the 'change of normative position' rationale for criminalisation, see Andrew Ashworth, 'A Change of Normative Position: Determining the Contours of Culpability in Criminal Law' (2008) 11 *New Crim. L. Rev.* 232.

82 *R. v. Semini* [1949] 1 K.B. 405 at 407–409 *per* Lord Goddard, C.J.

defence. The fact that the defendant was engaged in a fight prior to acting in self-defence would not prevent her from successfully raising self-defence as a full justificatory defence to murder.[83] However, she would be liable for the assault and any other criminal conduct that was independent of and prior to her act of killing in self-defence. The main challenge for the defendant will be to establish that she had effectively withdrawn from the fight and was therefore acting purely in self-defence.

C. The mutual combatant's duty to retreat

This leaves us with a final question: does a mutual combatant have a duty to retreat? It is submitted that the duty to retreat identified by the institutional writers has survived as far as mutual combats are concerned. It has survived for this reason: a mutual combatant has to retreat sufficiently to be able to demonstrate that she has withdrawn or dissociated herself from the combat. Self-defence is only available as a defence where the defendant's defensive killing is subsequent to and independent of the mutual combat. An integral component of a mutual gunfight is defensive action on the part of the participants. The participants intend to take defensive action because their ulterior aim is to preserve their own lives.[84] Continuing participation in a gunfight is by its very nature a defensive act. Gnango might have been motivated by a number of factors such as revenge or a desire to take pre-emptive action to thwart a future attack from BM, but one of the motivators for his return fire was self-defence. Once the gunfight had commenced every shot from Gnango was partly motivated by self-defence. In this context, *D*'s defensive shots are integral to the mutual combat and therefore *D* should be denied a defence. A person is not a lawful and justifiable self-defender when she is a voluntary participant in a violent

83 See Baker, *op. cit. supra*, note 15 at 699–700. *Per contra*, *R. v. Browne* [1973] N.I. 96 at 107, where Lowry, L.C.J. said: 'The need to act must not have been created by conduct of the accused in the immediate context of the incident which was likely or was intended to give rise to that need.' Lowry, L.C.J.'s statement of the law seems wrong on this point. The better view is that a mutual aggressor in a combat has a full defence of self-defence where he 'withdraws from the conflict in good faith and in such a manner that his adversary knows or should know that he desires to withdraw and discontinue the conflict'. This is the approach adopted in most U.S. jurisdictions. See *State v. Wright* (2008) 978 So. 2d 1062; *State v. Nailor* (2011) 78 So. 3d 816; *State v. Barnes* (2012) 100 So. 3d 926; *Lay v. State* (2012) 359 S.W.3d 291; *State v. Jackson* (2009) 681 S.E.2d 17; *State v. Jackson* (1963) 94 Ariz. 117. Cf. *Richard Mason's Case* (1748) Fost. 132, where the evidence allowed the court to infer that *D* was acting in revenge and was not motivated by self-defence alone. Compare also the decision of the Supreme Court of New Mexico in *State v. Lucero* (1998) 126 N.M. 552, where Serna, J. held that: '*D*'s discharge of gun into air after following a rival gang member to a vacant lot created a substantial risk of death or great bodily harm that precluded him, as instigator of the conflict, from claiming self defence for the shooting of a rival's companions during a gun battle that resulted when a rival responded with gunfire.'

84 See Baker, *op. cit. supra*, note 15 at para. 4–013.

gunfight in a public street.[85] However, where *D* clearly communicates her withdrawal from the combat she might be able to revive her lawful right to self-defence.

Take the following hypothetical change of the facts of *R. v. Gnango*. Suppose Gnango shelters behind cars in the car park from where he shouts to BM: 'I am going to disarm myself as I do not want to continue with this battle. I am going to throw my gun into the open so that you can see that I have disarmed myself. Let us go our own ways without harming anyone.' After Gnango throws his gun into the open, BM continues to fire bullets at the cars where Gnango is sheltering. The bullets are penetrating the cars and one nicks Gnango's leg. Gnango believes (correctly) that he will be killed if he does not get out of the car park, so he hotwires a car to escape from the car park. When Gnango attempts to drive out of the car park BM jumps from behind a column and starts shooting at him. Gnango drives directly at BM to stop him from shooting him. BM is killed. On these facts, it is arguable that the mutual combat was over when Gnango used the car to kill BM as a matter of necessity to save his own life. On these facts, Gnango should have a full defence because he disarmed himself, withdrew from the mutual combat and communicated his withdrawal. Hence, a person does not continue to be a participant in a mutual gunfight after she has disarmed herself and has communicated her withdrawal.

The duty of retreat applies because a mutual combatant has to withdraw from a combat before she can revive the right of self-defence. Such an onerous duty of retreat would not apply in a normal case of self-defence,[86] but it is essential to impose such a duty in the context of a mutual combat. It is the only way for the combatant to dissociate with the combat. A further reason for imposing a strict duty of retreat on a mutual combatant in a public place, before allowing self-defence as a full defence, is that it would be grossly negligent for her not to retreat when she can do so safely. If a person has helped to create a dangerous situation such as a gunfight in a public street, she has a duty to take reasonable steps to reduce the danger that gunfight poses to innocent pedestrians, because she has set that danger in motion.[87] A combatant that becomes a participant in the gunfight should

85 *State v. Abeyta* (1995) 901 P.2d 164 at 174; *Davis v. State* (2011) 268 P.3d 86; *People v. Hill* (2000) 315 Ill. App. 3d 1005.

86 Baker, *op. cit. supra*, note 15 at Chapter 24.

87 Hence, it would be grossly negligent to use lethal force that was not absolutely necessary where such force posed a risk to the lives of innocent others. *D* could be liable for gross negligence manslaughter. See *R. v. Salmon* (1880–81) L.R. 6 Q.B.D. 79, *R. v. Miller* [1983] 2 A.C. 161; cf. *Attorney General for Northern Ireland's Reference No. 1* [1977] A.C.105 at 137. See *State v. Zumwalt* (1998) 973 S.W.2d 504, where it was held: 'If the killing or injury of a person intended to be hit would, under all the circumstances, have been excusable or justifiable on the theory of self-defence, then the unintended killing or injury of a bystander by a random shot fired in the proper and prudent exercise of such self-defence is also excusable or justifiable.' This approach has been adopted in a number of U.S. states. See

retreat when she has a reasonable chance to retreat, because this would allow her to avoid unnecessarily endangering innocent passers-by.

If the defender has failed to retreat when there was a reasonable chance for her to retreat, she should be liable if she accidentally kills an innocent passer-by while she is attempting to kill her aggressor in self-defence. Likewise, where the defender kills her aggressor. Hence, the defender has a duty to retreat when she has contributed to the creation of the necessity for her own self-defence. When the defender has retreated as far as she possibly could and is forced to kill in self-defence, she should have a full defence. Self-defence is available where a defendant accidentally kills a bystander while defending herself from an unwarranted attack as long as she retreated as far as she safely could retreat. Defences transfer to an unintended human target in the same way that fault transfers to an unintended human target.[88]

D. Transferred intention and transferred defences

The doctrines of transferred intention and transferred defence are legal fictions,[89] but they work well in practice. Invoking the transferred intention doctrine or transferred defence doctrine may be a cumbersome way of inculpating or exculpating a particular defendant, but jurists find this approach easy to apply.[90] Coupled with this, the 'transfer' doctrines allow for a penal result that has moral equivalence with the defendant's moral culpability. There are some aberrant decisions where courts have convicted

People v. Adams (1972) 9 Ill. App. 3d 61; *People v. Jackson* (1973) 390 Mich. 621; *Foreman v. State* (1950) 47 So 2d 308; *State v. Stevenson* (1936) 38 Del 105; *State v. Williams* (1981) 2 Ohio App.3d 289; *People v. Riva* (2003) 5 Cal.Rptr.3d 649; *Banks v. State* (1997) 955 S.W.2d 116.

88 *The King v. Brown* (1776) 1 Leach 148; *R. v. Gross* (1913) 23 Cox C.C. 455 *per* Darling, J.; *Shalto v. The State* (1988) 42 W.I.R. 374; *Poe v. State* (1966) 341 Md. 523 at 537. See also Glanville Williams, *Criminal Law: The General Part* (London: Stevens & Sons, 2nd edn 1961) at 132; Stroud, *op. cit. supra*, note 74 at 301–302. This is the approach adopted in nearly every state in the United States. See for example, *People v. Levitt* (1984) 156 Cal. App.3d 500 at 507; *People v. Browning* (1991) 233 Cal.App.3d 1410 at 1413; *State v. Robinson* (1999) 132 Ohio App.3d 830; *Minix v. Commonwealth* (1937) 100 S.W.2d 825; *Gettings v. State* (1947) 32 Ala. App. 644; *Henley v. State* (1946) 210 Ark. 759; *Mayweather v. State* (1926) 29 Ariz. 460; *Henwood v. People* (1913) 54 Colo. 188; *Smith v. State* (1991) 204 Ga.App. 173; *People v. Adams* (1972) 9 Ill.App.3d 61; *Bowman v. Commonwealth* (1940) 284 Ky. 103; *People v. Jackson* (1973) 390 Mich. 621; *Dykes v. State* (1957) 99 SW2d 602; *Pittman v. State* (1954) 272 P.2d 458; *State v. Castillo* (1969) 23 Utah 2d 70; *People v. Blue* (2003) 799 N.E.2d 804; *McCraney v. State* (1994) 871 P2d 922; *Gray v. Commonwealth* (1933) 57 S.W.2d 6; *Gladden v. State* (1974) 273 Md. 383.

89 See Peter Westen, 'The Significance of Transferred Intent' (2013) 7(2) *Crim. Law and Philos.* 321.

90 For a logical and clear-cut judicial schema of the doctrine, see *Harvey v. State* (1996) 681 A.2d 628.

an offender of a more serious offence, because the transferred victim (such as a child or a police officer) was within a special category covered by a more serious offence. See for example *Palafox v. State*,[91] where it was said: 'When the only difference between what the actor desired or intended and the actual result is that a different offence was committed, the actor is responsible for causing the result that actually occurs.' The better view is that a person cannot be liable for a greater crime than she intended simply because the transferred victim falls within some protected group.

The normal rules of constructive liability would apply when unintended consequences flow from an intended act. In *U.S. v. Fornes-Espinoza*,[92] following *U.S. v. Montoya*,[93] it was held: 'If the theory of transferred intent were applied under 18 U.S.C. § 111, an assault not intentionally directed at a federal officer would become subject to the augmented penalties of section 111 merely because the blow happened by chance to strike a federal officer. We do not believe that Congress intended this result.' To hold an offender strictly liable for a more serious offence than she intended or would have been constructively liable for, simply because she harmed a victim that has been deemed worthy of greater protection, is contrary to justice.

E. The limits of double transferred intention

Can a transferred intention be used to justify convictions for two direct intent crimes? Where there is a single intention and a single consequence, there should be only one conviction based on direct intention. But it is not clear that is the position the courts will take. Suppose *X* shoots at *Y* with an intention of killing *Y*. *X*'s bullet travels through *Y* and also kills *Yy* (*Y*'s baby) who unbeknown to *X* was strapped on *Y*'s back. The logical solution in a case like this would be to convict *X* of murder for killing *Y* and of gross negligence manslaughter for killing *Yy*, if a reasonable person would have known of *Yy*'s presence. Similarly, if *X* fires a gun at *Y* intending to kill *Y* and the bullet travels through *Y* and into a nearby house and kills a second victim, *Y2*. The facts would have to support both a murder conviction and a gross negligence conviction.

If *X* fires a gun at *Y* intending to kill *Y* who is standing in Trafalgar Square, then oblique intention might apply as far as any second or third victim is concerned, because a jury might infer that *X* foresaw for certain that his bullet might travel through *Y* and kill others in such a busy square. Suppose *X* is in a deserted part of the Snowdonia National Park where she

91 (1997) 949 S.W.2d 48 at 49. See also *State v. Rodriguez-Gonzales* (2003) 790 P.2d 287 at 289; *State v. Higgins* (2003) 826 A.2d 1126 at 1143; *State v. Phillips* (2002) 842 So.2d 27; *Com. v. Melton* (2002) 763 N.E.2d 1092.

92 (2007) 241 Fed.Appx. 398.

93 (1984) 739 F.2d 1437 at 1438.

sees her old enemy *Y* hiking up a hill towards her. *X* has her hunting gun with her and fires at *Y* and kills her. Unbeknown to *X*, *Y* has her baby, *Yy*, strapped to her back. The bullet travels through *Y* and kills both *Y* and *Yy*. In this situation the evidence would not be sufficient to allow a jury to infer that *X* intended to kill *Y* and obliquely intended to kill *Yy*, because *X* did not know of the existence of *Yy*. It is doubtful that even a reasonable person would have known of the existence of *Yy*, so it appears *X* would not be liable even for gross negligence manslaughter for killing *Yy*.

The question that remains is whether transferred intention can transfer from *Y* to *Yy*, when the intention has been extinguished on *Y*. Suppose *X* fires a bullet at *Y* and the bullet hits *Y*'s belt buckle and ricochets off and kills *Z*, without *Y* being harmed at all. *X*'s fault is not extinguished on *Y* so it can transfer to *Z*. The transferred intention doctrine allows *X*'s intention to be transferred to the unintended victim in this case and there is no need to ask whether *X* foresaw the death of the intended victim as a virtual certainty or whether *X* was grossly negligent in killing *Z*, because the transferred intention doctrine works from the premise that *X* was acting with an intention to kill when she killed so it does not matter who she killed. However, when there are two victims this does not work, because it would hold *X* liable for two crimes when she only had fault for one crime. Intending to murder one person is different from intending to murder two people. When a person intends double murder and kills two people she deserves two life sentences, not one.

The transferred malice doctrine allows for a conviction based on the fiction of transferring intention to the harm that occurs, but it does not allow intention to be transferred over and over culminating in convictions for *several* harms when only a single harm was intended. In some cases, oblique intention and gross negligence will apply where *D* has killed *V1* and also *V2*, but in other cases *D* should not be liable at all for accidentally killing innocent others if she had no fault with respect to those victims. Otherwise, we would have a form of constructive fault distorting the transferred intention doctrine. The change of normative position theory should not be used to make people liable for greater harm than they intended. If *D* intends harm *f* then she should only be held liable for harm equal to $f\ (f(x) \propto g(x))$.

Compare *People v. Watson*,[94] where it was held that the offender was liable for two specific intent crimes even though his specific intent only extended to one potential victim. Moreno, J. said: '[A] person maliciously intending to kill is guilty of the murder of all persons actually killed.' It is true that if *D* takes a shot at *V1* who is standing right next to *V2*, *D* risks killing *V2* by aiming her shot at *V1*, but she does not intend to kill both. *D* intends to kill *V1* and risks killing *V2*,[95] but by chance kills *V2* and only risks killing

94 (2008) 43 Cal.4th 652 at 689. Cf. *Brady v. State* (1997) 700 So.2d 471.

95 The state of being endangered is a consequence in itself, but intending to endanger a person is different from intending to kill her. See Baker, *op. cit. supra*, note 15 at Chapters

V1. (Risk + specific intention does not = specific intention + specific intention.)[96] Coupled with that, a person cannot recklessly attempt.[97] The same problem arises when *D* attempts to murder *V1* but accidentally kills *V2*, if *D*'s fault is extinguished on *V2*, then it seems *D* should not be liable for both murdering *V2* and also for attempting to murder *V1*. Justice would be served by convicting *D* of murdering *V2* without any need to use some sort of constructive fault theory to make *D* liable also for an attempt. (If *D* had been acting innocently when she accidentally killed another, there would be no intention to transfer. Similarly, when *D*'s fault is extinguished on one victim it cannot then be transferred to another victim and then another and so on simply because *D* was acting wrongly when she accidentally killed those later victims.)

The doctrine of transferred intent does not apply to crimes of recklessness or negligence, because they are general intent crimes and thus there is no intent to transfer. For the purpose of crimes of recklessness and gross negligence, the defendant need not intend to strike a particular person. Thus, when *D* shoots into a group of persons with the aim of killing one of them, she can be convicted of gross negligence manslaughter for any others she kills, because a reasonable person would foresee the risk. In some cases, oblique intention might be made out. Since oblique intention is conceptually and philosophically a form of extreme subjective recklessness, there would be no barrier to *D* being charged with intending to kill *V1* and obliquely intending to kill *V2*, where *D* intends to kill *V1* and foresees that it is a virtual certainty that her bullet will travel through *V1* and kill *V2* too.

Alternatively, if *D* uses a high-powered gun to kill *V1* with the bullet travelling through *V1* and also hitting and killing *V2*, *D* could be liable for the murder of *V1* (the person she specifically intends to kill) and the manslaughter of *V2* (the person she does not intend to kill but recklessly kills through her unlawful dangerous act – assuming recklessness is made out on the particular facts).[98] However, double transfers or multiple transfers of intention to many victims when there was only an intention to kill one person would be unjust and impossible to reconcile with *D*'s actual culpability.[99] In *R. v. Gnango*, BM's intention to kill Gnango transferred to the victim and Gnango was simply liable as an accessory for encouraging BM to try to murder him.

10 and 11. See also *People v. Riva* (2003) 112 Cal.App.4th 981 at 999; *People v. Lee* (1994) 28 Cal.App.4th 1724 at 1736–1737.

96 Some courts have failed to grasp this notion. See for example, *People v. Gomez* (2003) 107 Cal.App.4th 328 at 335; *Henry v. State* (2011) 419 Md. 588.

97 Baker, *op. cit. supra*, note 15 at 537 *et seq.* See also *People v. Bland* (2002) 28 Cal.4th 313.

98 There are also non-fatal offences against the person that might apply where *D* recklessly injures a bystander while successfully killing *V*.

99 See generally, Dennis J. Baker, *The Right Not to Be Criminalized: Demarcating Criminal Law's Authority* (Farnham: Ashgate, 2011).

IV. The joint perpetration theory

In *R. v. Gnango*, Lords Clarke and Brown held that Gnango was liable as a joint perpetrator, rather than as an accomplice. Lord Dyson cited the joint perpetrator theory as an alternative basis for restoring the conviction. It is submitted that this approach should be resisted. The joint perpetration theory will be available only where there is joint acting accompanied by joint fault. When *D1* and *D2* rob a bank with *D1* putting a gun to the bank teller's head and *D2* putting the money in a bag, they jointly perpetrate robbery. It does not matter that they take different roles, because they jointly perpetrate the robbery with a common intention. If *D2* merely operates as a lookout, then she would only participate as an assister. However, when *D2* perpetrates one part of the *actus reus* (i.e. the theft element in robbery) while *P* perpetrates the other part (i.e. the assault element in robbery), their combined acts are a joint perpetration of the offence of robbery – one act without the other would make their acts independent crimes of assault and theft. There contributions to the robbery are direct causes of the robbery. Compare this with the case where *D1* merely lends *D2* her car or merely acts as a lookout believing as a matter of virtual certainty that *D2* will use her assistance to rob a bank. In the latter case there is a remote contribution by way of assistance, but there is no direct contribution and thus no joint perpetration.[100] Joint perpetration requires each party to make a direct causal contribution to the perpetration of the *actus reus*.

Gnango and BM were not joint perpetrators. It is best to avoid the fiction of deeming parties to a crime to be joint perpetrators when the facts clearly show that one was a perpetrator (a doer) and the other was an accomplice (an encourager). Gnango was not a joint perpetrator, because he did not physically help BM to fire the bullet that killed Magda Pniewska. There was no direct joint causal contribution. BM's act of firing the gun was the direct cause of *V*'s death and Gnango's encouragement was an indirect cause. An indirect cause does not combine with a direct cause to form a joint direct

100 Joint perpetration requires concurrent (co-existing) causation and action aimed at a particular criminal target. Take the example provided in *Hook v. M'Callum* (1905) 7 F. 528 at 532, where The Lord Justice-Clerk said: 'The illustration was suggested of a joint assault. If two men attack a third, one hitting him on the head and the other on the shins, they may both be jointly and severally liable for the whole injuries, although it may be quite certain what specific part of the injuries was due to each, yet as the whole *res gestæ* come together when both are present, each is responsible for the whole; but if *A* is assaulted by *B* and is subsequently assaulted by *C*, then plainly there are two separate wrongs, for one of which B is alone responsible, and for the other of which *C* is alone responsible, and this even although the two assaults are separated by an interval of only ten minutes, and although *B* and *C* have the same ground, or supposed ground, of quarrel against *A*. It would be different if *B* and *C* were acting in conspiracy, but there must be specific averments of that.'

cause. The transferred intention doctrine cannot be used to convert a solo perpetration into a joint perpetration. Problems arise not only because of a lack of joint doing,[101] but also because of a lack of joint fault. The individual *mentes reae* of the joint perpetrators have to be considered separately. Their fault cannot be bound together.

If two people jointly perpetrate an offence, they must not only jointly do the conduct element, but also must have joint fault. This is what distinguishes perpetration from participation. Take the example where *X* knocks *Y* unconscious and thereafter asks *S* to help him to dispose of her body by throwing it over a cliff. *X* does not tell *S* that *Y* is merely unconscious. Instead, she tells *S* that *Y* is dead and that she needs to dispose of her body before her murderous act is discovered. *S* helps *X* to dispose of *Y* by physically helping her to throw her putative corpse over a cliff. It is the joint act of *X* and *S* that causes *Y*'s death; they jointly kill her by dropping her body from a cliff onto the rocks below. They jointly perpetrate the *act* that kills her, but their individual *mentes reae* are different.[102] *X* intends to commit murder while *S* merely intends to help *X* dispose of what she believes is a corpse. There may be several criminal acts (e.g. putative disposal of a corpse; an act of killing and so on) and one of these acts might jointly and concurrently cause a particular result, but the joint act that causes *V*'s death must also be jointly intended if both parties are to be convicted of murder.[103] Alternatively, homicide liability might apply to both parties if the death was the result of joint gross negligence or the result of a joint unlawful and dangerous act.

The individual *mentes reae* of the joint perpetrators must relate to a joint purpose. If *X* and *S* intend to kill *Y* by dropping her from a cliff, then they are joint perpetrators of murder. They not only jointly do the act that kills her, but both intend to do that act for the purpose of killing her. *Per contra,* it would be incongruous to argue that because Gnango obliquely intended to encourage BM to kill him, and *vice versa,* that they obliquely intended to *jointly* kill each other. They did not act jointly and nor did they have a joint purpose; they merely had a mutual intention to engage in a gunfight. Gnango would have jointly perpetrated the attempt of murder against himself if he had tried to jointly pull the trigger of BM's gun while

101 To satisfy the *actus reus* element of murder, the joint perpetrators' joint act must be the cause of death.

102 *S* might be liable for gross negligence manslaughter if a reasonable person would have believed that *Y* could still be alive, but *X* would still be liable for murder. Unlike *Ds* in *R. v. Gamble* (1989) N.I. 268, *S* authorises the act that causes *V*'s death. Nonetheless, *S* does not authorise murder because *S* assumes *X* intends to dispose of a corpse, not kill a human being.

103 *S* commits the offence of preventing a corpse from being buried. See *R. v. Hunter* [1974] Q.B. 95. But the fault for that act does not combine with *X*'s fault to form a single act of murder.

it was aimed at his own head. But Gnango and BM did not have it as their joint purpose that Gnango should be killed by a joint *act* on their part, nor did they have a joint purpose that BM should be killed by a joint act on their part.

Furthermore, Gnango and BM did not intend to jointly perpetrate the double murder of themselves; they might have done if they had tied themselves together and jointly jumped from a cliff to kill themselves.[104] It was not a case of joint perpetration, because each party acted independently to try to perpetrate the killing of the other. There is no reason why the transferred intention doctrine cannot be invoked in a genuine case of joint perpetration, but this was not such a case. Take the example where *X* and *Y* are on a 20th-floor balcony when they notice a rival gangster walking below. Suppose that they decide to kill him by throwing a large object down to hit him. They jointly grab a large television set and jointly throw it from the balcony to hit him. It turns out that they miss him and instead hit another passer-by. Clearly, the transferred intention doctrine will apply, because they jointly intended to kill a human being and in fact jointly killed a human being. It does not matter that they missed their intended human target.

A. General intent and the proximate cause approach

Some American courts have invoked a theory of 'proximate causation' to ground murder convictions in cases where it is not possible to ascertain who fired the shot that killed the passer-by.[105] However, in English law a substantial *indirect* causal contribution would not count as a *direct* causal contribution and therefore the law of complicity would still be required to obtain a conviction.

> [These] jurisdictions have extended proximate cause liability to participants in gun battles, finding that an individual's participation in such a battle represents a depraved indifference to human life such that he or she meets the *mens rea* for second-degree depraved heart murder. Further, courts have determined that the combined hail of bullets that result from such a battle are jointly responsible for the fatal injury, such that a determination of which the defendant's bullet 'actually' caused the death is unnecessary. Finally, courts have found

104 On suicide pacts, see Dennis J. Baker, *Glanville Williams: Textbook of Criminal Law* (London: Sweet & Maxwell, 2015) at Chapter 26. Cf. section 2 of the *Suicide Act 1961*. With respect to sequential perpetration as opposed to concurrent joint perpetration in a suicide pact, see section 4 of the *Homicide Act 1957*; *R. v. Russell* (1832) 1 Mood. C.C. 356; *R. v. Croft* [1944] K.B. 295.

105 See *Com. v. Santiago* (1997) 425 Mass. 491; cf. *Roy v. United States* (2005) 871 A. 2d 498.

> that a death which results from the shower of bullets created during this type of battle is more than reasonably foreseeable, i.e. conscious awareness of danger.[106]

These sorts of joint causal claims are dubious, because often the 'direct causer' (e.g. the person who fired the gun and killed *V*) has acted voluntarily and in circumstances where she could have avoided having to act at all. Consequently, holding indirect causal contributions as proximate causes without invoking the law of complicity would not be sufficient to justify a conviction for a specific intention crime such as murder in England and Wales. Many of the American cases rest on subjective recklessness and on deeming indirect causation to be a proximate cause. Additionally, in many of the U.S. cases the proximate causation doctrine is invoked with the medieval felony murder rule. Remarkably, the felony murder rule is still invoked in many jurisdictions in America, even though it is a draconian rule that cannot be reconciled with the requirements of fair criminalisation and proportionate punishment.[107]

Under the proximate (indirect) causation theory *D1* is deemed to be independently liable (not derivatively liable, but in many U.S. cases derivative liability is invoked as well) for *D2*'s criminal acts when *D1* made an indirect causal contribution to *D2*'s act. *D1*'s participation in a mutual gunfight has been held to be a substantial and proximate cause of a passer-by's death, even when her bullet was not the direct cause of the victim's death, because *D1*'s participation in the gunfight is a contributory cause of the gunfight itself. This is conceptually different from labelling *D1* as a joint perpetrator. The indirect cause theory merely provides a causal link between *D1*'s participation in the gunfight and the end consequences of *D2*'s participation in the gunfight. Conceptually, these cases simply rely on the concept of complicity, even if that is not the doctrine that is used to label it in some U.S. cases. Indirect causation is derivative liability's *raison d'être*.

The criminal consequence of *D2*'s participation in the gunfight is that a bullet from her gun has killed an innocent passer-by. *D1* was one of the indirect causes of *D2*'s fatal shot, because she provoked *D2* into shooting at her. If *D1* had not been shooting at *D2*, *D2* would not have been shooting at *D1* and thus would not have killed an innocent bystander. If *D1*, *D2* and their associates had not participated in the mutual gunfight, there would have been no gunfight. This type of substantial causal contribution to a gunfight that causes a passer-by's death has been held to be a proximate cause in many U.S. jurisdictions, but this approach does not present a theory of joint perpetration; it is joint participation with one being a perpetrator and the

106 *State v. Spates* (2010) 779 N.W. 2d 770 at 777.
107 Baker, *op. cit. supra*, note 99.

other a secondary party.[108] In these jurisdictions, *D*'s independent recklessness combined with her indirect causal contribution to the direct cause of *V*'s death has been used to make her liable for second-degree murder/reckless (depraved-heart) manslaughter, but the same result can be achieved by invoking complicity.[109] If the mental element in complicity is intention, then reckless participation would have to be dealt with through some other legal mechanism.

Liability in these cases is not based on joint perpetration, which would require concurrent direct causation. Some courts have mistaken prior indirect causation for concurrent direct causation.[110] Instead, liability is based on the fact that the participants encouraged the perpetrator by participating in the mutual gunfight. It is in effect a case of obliquely intentional (or perhaps only reckless complicity) complicity liability based on transferred intention.[111] The participants in the gunfight do not jointly perpetrate a murder merely by participating in a gunfight; nor do they jointly cause it in a direct sense. Instead, they make a factual contribution (if we accept that this sort of encouragement is capable of causing another to act) to the act that in fact causes *V*'s death. This sort of encouragement is a cause of *P* being motivated.[112] The perpetrator's participation is voluntary. It would be enough to establish complicity liability since *D1* shooting at *D2* would be at least one of the motivators (encouragements) of *D2*'s act of perpetration.

It is not a direct cause, because *D2* makes a fully informed and voluntary choice to participate in the gunfight, but it is conduct that is capable of encouraging *D2* to perpetrate the fatal shooting. *D1*'s *mens rea* for murder cannot derive from *D2*'s *mens rea* for murder unless we invoke both the

108 *State v. Spates* (2010) 779 N.W. 2d 770 at 777 and the authorities cited therein.

109 Cf. *In re Aurelio R.* (1985) 167 Cal. App. 3d 52.

110 See *People v. Sanchez* (2001) 29 P. 3d 209 at 219, where it was held: 'If a jury finds that a defendant proximately caused a death, either solely through his own conduct or through the actions of others where his conduct is shown to be a *substantial concurrent cause* of the death, and the defendant did so with a premeditated intent to kill, then the defendant is guilty of first degree murder' [emphasis added].

111 Cf. *R. v. Creamer* [1966] 1 Q.B. 72; *R. v. Buck* (1960) 44 Cr. App. R. 213; *R. v. Gaylor* (1857) Dears. & B. 288 at 291 *per* Bramwell, B.; *R. v. Smith* (1847) 2 Cox C.C. 233.

112 It would also mean that *P* was acting under duress, but duress would not be available as a defence because of *P*'s prior fault in subjecting herself to duress. See *State v. Edwards* (2006) 717 N.W.2d 405 at 412, where in the Supreme Court of Minnesota, Anderson, C.J. (citing Model Penal Code § 3.04 cmt. 4(b)), said: 'There is, however, much authority, both common law and statutory, demanding that a person claiming self-defence be free from fault in bringing on the difficulty.' See also *State v. Carridine* (2012) 812 N.W.2d 130 at 145 *per* Anderson, J.; *Young v. Scales* (2005) 873 A.2d 337; *Com. v. Vives* (2006) 447 Mass. 537; *Rasley v. State* (2004) 878 So. 2d 473; *State v. Urena* (2006) 899 A.2d 1281. For a fuller discussion of the underlying principles, see Paul H. Robinson, 'Causing the Conditions of One's Own Defence: A Study in the Limits of Theory in Criminal Law Doctrine' (1985) 71 *Va. L.Rev.* 1 at 27; Donald A. Dripps, 'Fundamental Retribution Error: Criminal Justice and the Social Psychology of Blame' (2003) 56 *Vand. L. Rev.* 1383 at 1413.

transferred malice and complicity doctrines. It is true that in the case of depraved-indifference murder the fault element can be made out by pointing to the fact that *D1* was risking lives by participating in the gunfight and one of the consequences of the joint gunfight was the death of a passer-by, but it cannot be said that *D1* had it as her purpose to kill the passer-by. However, once *D2*'s intention is transferred from her intended victim to the victim that was actually killed, she would be liable for murder. *D1*'s murder conviction could then hinge on *D2*'s perpetration via the law of complicity.

To establish joint perpetration as opposed to complicity, it is necessary to show that each party had the requisite *mens rea* for murder or for whatever crime she is charged with. This will be easier to establish in cases where the participants in a mutual gunfight are charged with reckless manslaughter rather than with murder, because it can be said that each participant subjectively risks the lives of pedestrians by jointly creating a hail of bullets.[113] Any conviction without the assistance of derivative liability would rest on a legal fiction, since *D1*'s act is not the direct cause of *V*'s death. It would be better to invoke the law of complicity and the transferred malice doctrine in such cases.[114] If the law of complicity is used in cases like those mentioned above, the perpetrator would be deemed to be the direct cause of *V*'s death, which in fact she was, and the encourager would be treated as making an indirect causal contribution, which she in fact did.

B. Unknown perpetrator

When it is not known whose bullet killed *V*, English law provides an apt solution. If it is not possible to ascertain who the perpetrator was, then all the parties are treated as accomplices and perpetrators. As Lords Phillips and Judge C.J. observe, 'in *R. v. Giannetto*[115] the appellant was convicted of murdering his wife. The Crown was unable to say whether he had inflicted the fatal injuries himself or, at the very least, had arranged for someone else to do so. On this basis however he was guilty of her murder either as a principal or as an accessory.' This is far preferable to trying to elevate the concept of indirect causation to one of direct concurrent causation and then to one of joint perpetration. Section 8 of the *Abettors and Accessories Act 1861* is a procedural provision whereby accessories can be charged and

113 Cf. *Roy v. United States* (2005) 871 A. 2d 498.

114 Even in cases where it was not possible to identify the perpetrator, the U.S. courts have tended to rely on the law of complicity to ground a conviction, if it was clear that one of the participants was the perpetrator. See *Alston v. State* (1995) 339 Md. 306; *Reyes v. State* (2001) 783 So. 2d 1129; *State v. Garza* (1996) 259 Kan. 826; *People v. Russell* (1998) 91 N.Y. 2d 280.

115 [1997] 1 Cr. App. R. 1.

convicted as perpetrators, and *vice versa*.[116] It is not necessary to prove which party was the perpetrator and which was the accessory, as long as it can be proved that one had to be the perpetrator and the other the accessory.[117] The complicity provisions are of assistance only if there is sufficient evidence for the jury to infer that it was one or the other.[118] If it cannot be proved that it had to be one of them, then neither can be charged.

C. Excluding change of normative position (constructive) liability

In some U.S. jurisdictions, proximate cause has been applied too widely when it has been applied in conjunction with the all-embracing felony murder rule.[119] Most states limit the felony murder rule to acts that are perpetrated by a co-perpetrator in furtherance of the underlying felony,[120] but some states have extended it to cover any foreseeable death whether it be perpetrated in furtherance of the felony or not.[121] Extreme cases have gone unchecked in the U.S. In some cases a co-felon has been held liable for the death of an accomplice who was killed by the target victim (*PV*: putative victim) of the felony.[122] For example, in *People v. Klebanowski*,

116 Baker, *op. cit. supra*, note 15 at para 14–009. See also section 44 of the *Magistrates' Courts Act 1980.*

117 *R. v. Giannetto* [1997] 1 Cr. App. R. 1; *Smith v. Mellors* (1987) 84 Cr. App. R. 279; *R. v. Swindall* (1864) 175 E.R. 95.

118 See Glanville Williams, 'Which of You Did It?' (1989) 52 *Mod. L. Rev.*179; cf. Lissa Griffin, 'Which One of You Did It? Criminal Liability for Causing or Allowing the Death of a Child' (2005) 15 *Ind. Int'l & Comp. L. Rev.* 89.

119 In *Berkeley v. Com.* (1995) 19 Va.App. 279 at 291–292, it was held that a conviction required that 'the killing must have been done by the defendant or an accomplice or confederate or one acting in furtherance of the felonious undertaking . . . In other words . . . a felon may not be convicted of felony-murder if the actual killing was committed by the police or the victim or by some other person not acting in concert with the felons.'

120 See *State v. Carothers* (1974) 84 Wash.2d 256; *People v. Robinson* (2006) 475 Mich. 1; *People v. Fisher* (2000) 9 P.3d 1189 at 1191; *Watkins v. State* (2000) 357 Md. 258 at 270; *King v. Com.* (1988) 6 Va.App. 351; *Barnes v. Com.* (2000) 33 Va.App. 619 at 631; *Government of Virgin Islands v. Albert* (2000) 89 F.Supp.2d 658 at 666; *Commonwealth v. Redline* (1958) 391 Pa. 486 at 495–496; *Rivers v. Com.* (1995) 21 Va.App. 416 at 423; *People v. Washington* (1965) 62 Cal.2d 777; *Alvarez v. District Court In and For City and County of Denver* (1974) 186 Colo. 37; *Comer v. State* (2009) 977 A.2d 334 at 340; *State v. Pina* (2010) 233 P.3d 71 at 78; *State v. Sophophone* (2001) 19 P.3d 70 at 77; *Campbell v. State* (1982) 293 Md. 438; *Com. v. Balliro* (1965) 349 Mass. 505; *State v. Branson* (1992) 487 N.W.2d 880; *State v. Rust* (1977) 197 Neb. 528; *Sheriff, Clark County v. Hicks* (1973) 506 P.2d 766 at 768; *State v. Bonner* (1992) 411 S.E.2d 598 at 603; *Com. v. Redline* (1958) 391 Pa. 486; *State v. Severs* (1988) 759 S.W.2d 935 at 938; *Wooden v. Com* (1981) 284 S.E.2d 811 at 816. Cf. *People v. Mejia* (2012) 211 Cal.App.4th 586 at 613, where it was held that the provocative conduct of a provocateur was sufficient for upholding a provocative act murder conviction where it was 'intended to further the activities of the gang'.

121 *People v. Klebanowski* (2006) 852 N.E.2d 813; *Dickens v. State* (2005) 106 P.3d 599; cf. *Lattimore v. State* (1998) 720 So. 2d 1000.

122 *People v. Klebanowski* (2006) 852 N.E.2d 813; *People v. Gillis* (2006) 474 Mich. 105, where *D* was held liable for felony murder after he accidentally hit another car 10 minutes

P1 and *P2* perpetrated a robbery against an off-duty police officer. When *P1* and *P2* were escaping from the robbery *PV* shot at *P1* and killed him. The court invoked the proximate cause theory and the felony murder rule to convict *P2* of the murder of *P1* on the basis that *P1* and *P2* caused *PV* to kill *P1*.

However, on the facts of that case, *PV* was not forced to kill *P1*. *P1* and *P2* were fleeing from the robbery and posed no danger to *PV*. A person's life is worth more than property and since *PV*'s life and limb was not in any danger he was not caused to shoot the fleeing robber in the back. The decision is contrary to our contemporary standards of justice. It is unjust to deem that the surviving co-perpetrator of the underlying robbery caused *PV* to kill *P1*, when there was no necessity for *PV*'s murderous act. Similarly, in England and Wales murder would not be made out under the *R. v. Gnango* doctrine (i.e. complicity plus transferred intention), when a third party/putative victim acts unreasonably in killing a fleeing robber. Similarly if a third party/putative victim accidentally kills a bystander while using excessive force to try to apprehend fleeing burglars, the surviving burglar should not be liable for the killer's autonomous decision to use excessive force.[123] *These cases do not involve a simple application of transferred malice doctrine to an unintended victim, but involve a third party acting unjustifiably in killing an* intended *victim.*

D. The felony murder rule, complicity and justifiable defence

The felony murder rule means that if *P1* and *P2* perpetrate a robbery with *P1* accidently killing the security guard as a consequence of a minor assault, both *P1* and *P2* will be liable for murder. This is much wider than complicity liability, which would only allow for manslaughter convictions where the perpetrator intended minor harm only. In England and Wales, if *P1* and *P2* perpetrate an *unarmed* robbery of a convenience store with

into his escape from a burglary. The felony-murder rule aside, this approach stretches causation theory to breaking point. Surely the appropriate solution in a modern age would be to charge such a defendant with (1) burglary and (2) gross negligence manslaughter or causing death by dangerous driving. The facts show that *D* drove in the wrong direction up a freeway ramp at speed. In England and Wales, such a defendant could be charged with (1) burglary and (2) with causing death by dangerous driving contrary to section 1 of the *Road Traffic Act 1988*. The subsequent dangerous driving is an independent crime that is best treated as such. It is either causing death by dangerous driving or alternatively gross negligence manslaughter. Cf. *Montague v. Com.* (1999) 31 Va. App. 187, where it was held that a death resulting from a motor car accident was not causally connected to a felony that had been completed 11 hours before the accident.

123 See *R. v. Martin* [2003] Q.B. 1, where D shot two fleeing burglars in the back. The surviving victim was not deemed to be the cause of Martin's autonomous actions. Nor would it have been possible to deem that he was Martin's accomplice.

P1 being killed by *SG*, a security guard, as they flee from the scene of the robbery, *P2* would not be liable for homicide. Common purpose complicity does not apply because *P2* (the surviving co-perpetrator has not encouraged *SG*'s lethal act) nor were *P2* and *SG* joint participants in an unlawful joint enterprise.[124] Similarly, it would be absurd to argue that the act of fleeing with goods from a convenience store was an act capable of encouraging a reasonable security guard with appropriate training to use lethal force. No doubt the unarmed robbers' act of fleeing from a robbery was a reason for the guard's actions, but *P2* does not have *mens rea* for the purposes of complicity liability.[125] Although, in a technical sense it might be said that they obliquely intended to encourage the guard to pursue them, it is doubtful any jury would infer that they obliquely intended to encourage the guard to try to kill them while unarmed and while running from the guard.

If the guard successfully raised public defence,[126] which is not likely given that the level of force used was disproportionate,[127] *a fortiori P2* would not be an accomplice. On complicity principles, a person cannot be derivatively liable[128] for another's lawfully justifiable act.[129] Liability derives from another's crime, not from her lawful conduct. Nor would a person be an accessory where a perpetrator's actions are putatively justifiable only, unless she has done something to assist or encourage the perpetrator. The case might be different with respect to putatively justifiable actions, when the court relies solely on the proximate cause theory.

The proximate causation (indirect causation without *mens rea*) theory combined with the felony murder rule is a grossly unjust basis for criminal liability, because it would mean that if two unarmed robbers were fleeing a robbery and both were shot in the back of the leg by a police officer with them both surviving, they both would be liable for wounding themselves

124 See *State v. Small* (2012) 100 So.3d 797; *Davis v. Fox* (2012) 229 W.Va. 662; *State v. Myers* (2000) 760 So. 2d 310; *State v. Kalathakis* (1990) 563 So.2d 228; *Commonwealth v. Redline* (1958) 391 Pa. 486; *Butler v. People* (1888) 18 N.E. 338; *People v. Garippo* (1920) 292 Ill. 293. See also *State v. Garner* (1959) 238 La. 563 at 577, where it was held that: '*A* attempts to rob *B*. *B*, while resisting the attempted robbery, shoots at *A* and accidentally kills *C* who is an innocent third party. *A* cannot be convicted of the murder of *C*.'

125 The fault element would not be made out under either the *Accessories and Abettors Act 1861*, nor under the *Serious Crime Act 2007*.

126 See section 3 of the *Criminal Law Act 1967*.

127 Property is worth less than a life and thus killing to save property would be unreasonable. Likewise, it would be unreasonable to use lethal force to arrest a person who is not posing a danger to the lives of others. See Baker, *op. cit. supra*, note 15 at Chapter 24.

128 That is why *R. v. Pagett* (1983) 76 Cr. App. R. 279 rests on the provocative act murder doctrine, rather than the law of complicity.

129 However, an accomplice may be liable for an excused perpetrator's criminal acts. See *R. v. Manley* (1844) 1 Cox C.C. 104; *People v. Hallett* (1979) 419 NYS2d 397; *State v. Lord* (1938) 42 N.M. 638; *State v. McAllister* (1978) 366 So. 2d 1340.

with intent to do grievous bodily harm to themselves (or for wounding each other with intent to do GBH) contrary to the *Offences against the Person Act 1861*, even though the police officer was perhaps acting lawfully in using that level of force to apprehend them.[130]

Complicity liability requires actual assistance or encouragement. The fleeing robbers would have to assist or encourage the officer to wound. Clearly that is not the case on the above facts; reckless and negligent influence is not sufficient to impose complicity liability. (Coupled with this, the victim rule should apply in such cases. See the discussion below.)

V. The provocative act murder doctrine

The provocative act murder doctrine operates in a few U.S. states[131] and has effectively been recognised in the common law of murder in England and Wales.[132] '"Provocative act murder" is not an independent crime with a fixed level of liability. It is simply a type of murder. The words "provocative act murder" are merely shorthand, used for that category of intervening-act causation case in which, during the commission of a crime, the intermediary (i.e. a police officer or crime victim) is provoked by the defendant's conduct into a response that results in someone's death.'[133] It is simply a way of committing murder. However, it has its own *actus reus* and *mens rea* requirements. In *Sisson v. Superior Court*[134] it was said that:

130 Cf. the discussion in *People v. Washington* (1965) 402 P.2d 130; *State ex rel. Painter v. Zakaib* (1991) 411 S.E.2d 25.

131 It operates primarily in California.

132 *R. v. Pagett* (1983) 76 Cr. App. R. 279. In *Com. v. Moyer* (1947) 53 A.2d 736 at 744–745, Maxey, C.J. observed: 'This same principle is illustrated in the so-called "Squib Case" of *Scott v. Shepherd* (1772) 2 Wm. Bl. 892. In that case . . . the defendant threw a lighted squib made of gunpowder from the street into the market house. A large concourse of people were assembled there. One Willis to prevent injury to himself and to the goods of one Yates, grasped the lighted squib and threw it across the market house where it fell upon one Ryal. The latter, to save his own goods from being injured, took up the lighted squib and threw it to another part of the market house and struck the plaintiff in the face, putting out one of his eyes. In that case, Justice Gould said, the defendant may be considered in the same view as if he himself had personally thrown the squib in the plaintiff's face. The terror impressed upon Willis and Ryal excited self-defence, and deprived them of the power of recollection. What they did therefore was the inevitable consequence of the defendant's unlawful act.' Chief Justice DeGrey said, 'The throwing the squib was an act unlawful and tending to affright the bystanders. So far, mischief was originally intended; not any particular mischief, but mischief indiscriminate and wanton. Whatever mischief therefore follows, he is the author of it; – *Egreditur personam*, as the phrase is in criminal cases. And though criminal cases are no rule for civil ones, yet in trespass I think there is an analogy.'

133 See *People v. Concha* (2009) 47 Cal. 4th 653 at 663; cf. *State v. Wilson* (2009) 912 N.E.2d 133; *Taylor v. State* (1900) 41 Tex.Crim. 564.

134 16 Cal.App.4th 24.

> A provocative act murder has both a physical and a mental element that the prosecution must establish. To constitute the *actus reus* of provocative act murder, the defendant must commit an act that provokes a third party to fire a fatal shot. The *mens rea* element is satisfied if the defendant knows that his or her provocative act has a high probability – not merely a foreseeable possibility – of eliciting a [lawfully justifiable] life-threatening response from the person who actually fires the fatal bullet.

I have inserted the words 'lawfully justifiable', because the provocateur cannot be held liable for murder when the victim was killed as a result of the perpetrator's gross negligence or excessive force.[135] Where there has been gross negligence the chain of causation would be broken and the grossly negligent perpetrator alone should be liable for the death that is a direct cause of her gross negligence.[136] (Problems may arise in cases where *P* makes an unreasonable mistake about the necessity for self-defence.)[137] Provocative act murder is not a form of complicity liability; rather it is a form of innocent agency liability.[138] *D* is liable for provoking a lawful response from *P*: because *D*'s *mens rea* is combined with the consequences of *P*'s lawful actions to produce a crime. *P* is treated as a mere instrument in *D*'s hands.

In *People v. Garcia*,[139] Vartabedian, A.J. said:

> Liability is not based on a felony-murder theory because '[w]hen a killing is not committed by a robber [felon] or by his accomplice but by

135 Cf. *R. v. Martin* [2003] Q.B. 1, where *D* killed two fleeing burglars. Even if *D* had been acting lawfully, it would have been too great an extension of criminal liability to invoke the provocative act murder doctrine to make an accomplice liable for the murder of his co-perpetrator.

136 *R. v. Jordan* (1956) 40 Cr. App. R. 152; *People v. Cervantes* (2001) 26 Cal.4th 860; see also section 3 of the *Criminal Law Act 1967*. Compare, *People v. Hansen* (1997) 68 Cal.Rptr.2d 897 at 899–900, where the chain of causation was held not to be broken, because *D*, a 35-year-old man, instituted Russian roulette and encouraged a minor victim (a 14-year-old child) to participate. The minor's negligence was not sufficient to break the chain of causation. '[N]egligence on the part of the victim is not a defence to criminal liability . . . A defendant may be criminally liable for a result directly caused by his act even if there is another contributing cause. If an intervening cause is a normal and reasonably foreseeable result of the defendant's original act the intervening act is "dependent" and not a superseding cause, and will not relieve defendant of liability . . . "(1) The consequence need not have been a strong probability; a possible consequence which might reasonably have been contemplated is enough. (2) The precise consequence need not have been foreseen; it is enough that the defendant should have foreseen the possibility of some harm of the kind which might result from his act."'

137 An unreasonable genuine mistake about the necessity for defensive action does not bar the defendant from raising the defence of self-defence. However, an unreasonable genuine mistake as to the amount of force that is required to thwart an attack is a bar to the defendant raising the defence. See Baker, *op. cit. supra*, note 15 at Chapter 24.

138 [1999] 1 A.C. 82.

139 (1999) 69 Cal. App. 4th 1324 at 1329.

> his victim, malice aforethought is not attributable to the robber, for the killing is not committed by him in the perpetration or attempt to perpetrate robbery.' Murder liability in such cases is based upon proof of malice and vicarious liability.

Vartabedian, A.J.'s statement of the theoretical basis of the law is helpful, but it is not entirely correct. His Honour runs into error by mistakenly combining malice with vicarious liability theory to explain the basis of the law. The basis of the law has nothing to do with vicarious liability; rather *D* is liable for provocative act murder because she has intentionally (either directly or obliquely) provoked *P* to kill: *P* is essentially a justified or excused agent because she acts under duress and also acts in lawful defence. Thus, the doctrine is based on a form of justified or excused agency theory. *P* is not an innocent agent in the pure sense, because she knows what she is doing and could sacrifice herself, but the involuntariness of her actions is sufficient to treat her as a non-responsible justified/excused agent.

A. The fault element for provocative act murder

In light of *R. v. Woollin*,[140] a murder conviction in England and Wales would depend on the prosecution proving beyond reasonable doubt that the defendant believed that his or her provocative act would as a matter of virtual certainty, not merely as a matter of high probability, elicit a life-threatening response from the person who actually fired the fatal bullet.[141] Hence, *D* must do her provocative act intending or obliquely intending *V* to be killed or suffer grievous bodily harm as a result of it.

This doctrine was essentially recognised by the Court of Appeal in *R. v. Pagett*,[142] but it does not apply where the party who was allegedly caused to kill made a free choice to kill. It only applies when the defendant has caused a person to be psychologically pressured to kill as a matter of justifiable necessity. The psychological pressure would need to be extreme. In *R. v. Pagett*, *D* used his ex-girlfriend as a human shield as he fired shots at the police officers who were trying to arrest him for the abduction of his

140 Under the *Serious Crime Act 2007*, there is an alternative mental element for the section 44–46 offences found in section 47(5)(a)(iii). That subsection holds that *D* will be liable for trying to encourage or assist *P*'s crime, if '[*D*'s] state of mind was such that, were he to do it, it would be done with that fault.' The subsection has to be read in conjunction with section 47(6) which provides: 'For the purposes of subsection (5)(a)(iii), *D* is to be assumed to be able to do the act in question.'

141 *Sisson v. Superior Court* (2013) 216 Cal.App.4th 24. See also *People v. Gallegos* (1997) 54 Cal. App.4th 453 at 461.

142 (1983) 76 Cr. App. R. 279. For other cases where defendants caused people to be killed by using them as human shields see *Jackson v. State* (1979) 286 Md. 430; *Pizano v. Superior Court* (1978) 21 Cal.3d 128; *State v. Kress* (1969) 105 N.J.Super. 514, *Wilson v. State* (1934) 188 Ark. 846.

girlfriend and for an attempted murder that he had perpetrated about an hour earlier. Pagett was holding his ex-girlfriend hostage in his flat, which had been surrounded by police officers. One of the officers asked Pagett to surrender. Pagett said that 'there was no way he would come out alive, he would shoot the girl and himself . . . He fired his gun twice at the police cars. They were hit but not badly damaged; some police officers were hit by pellets but not injured.'[143] Pagett's hostage shouted out: 'Please move or he will shoot me.' *D* was convicted of unlawful act manslaughter for causing the police to kill *V*. In *R. v. Pagett*,[144] Goff L.J. said:

> In our judgment, the question whether an accused person can be held guilty of homicide, either murder or manslaughter, of a victim the immediate cause of whose death is the act of another person must be determined on the ordinary principles of causation . . . [145]
>
> . . .
>
> There can, we consider, be no doubt that a reasonable act performed for the purpose of self-preservation, being of course itself an act caused by the accused's own act, does not operate as a *novus actus interveniens.* If authority is needed for this almost self-evident proposition, it is to be found in such cases as *R. v. Pitts* (1842) C. & M. 284, and *R. v. Curley* (1909) 2 Cr.App.R. 96. In both these cases, the act performed for the purpose of self-preservation consisted of an act by the victim in attempting to escape from the violence of the accused, which in fact resulted in the victim's death. In each case it was held as a matter of law that, if the victim acted in a reasonable attempt to escape the violence of the accused, the death of the victim was caused by the act of the accused. Now one form of self-preservation is self-defence; for present purposes, we can see no distinction in principle between an attempt to escape the consequences of the accused's act, and a response which takes the form of self-defence. Furthermore, in our judgment, if a reasonable act of self-defence against the act of the accused causes the death of a third party, we can see no reason in principle why the act of self-defence, being an *involuntary act* caused by the act of the accused, should relieve the accused from criminal responsibility for the death of the third party. Of course, it does not necessarily follow that the accused will be guilty

143 *R. v. Pagett* (1983) 76 Cr. App. R. 279 at 281. See also *People v. Lima* (2004) 118 Cal. App. 4th 259, where it was held: 'Provocative act doctrine for murder, which applies when a defendant or his accomplice commits provocative act and his victim or police officer kills a third party in *reasonable response* to that act, is not limited in application only to deaths by gunfire' [emphasis added]. In that case, a third party was killed during a high-speed police chase.

144 *R. v. Pagett* (1983) 76 Cr. App. R. 279 at 283–284.

145 *R. v. Pagett* (1983) 76 Cr. App. R. 279 at 287.

> of the murder, or even of the manslaughter, of the third party; though in the majority of cases he is likely to be guilty at least of manslaughter. Whether he is guilty of murder or manslaughter will depend upon the question whether all the ingredients of the relevant offence have been proved; in particular, on a charge of murder, it will be necessary that *the accused had the necessary intent* [emphasis added].[146]

Compare *R. v. Pagett* with the decision in *Sisson v. Superior Court*,[147] where the court held that gross negligence by way of unnecessary and excessive force from police officers would not break the chain of causation. In *Sisson v. Superior Court*,[148] Elias, J., sitting on his own in a state intermediate appellate court in California, held that an 'application of the provocative act murder doctrine does not require the killing to result from the reasonable response by the actual shooter. . . . Thus, whether the officers in this case used reasonable force in firing at Sisson's vehicle is immaterial to Sisson's defence of the murder charge.' As this is a decision from a single judge sitting in an intermediate court, and runs counter to the authorities of the Supreme Court of California,[149] other courts are not likely to follow it.

In *Sisson v. Superior Court*, a group of police officers fired 26 bullets into the passenger side of a car that was fleeing from a potential arrest. The police shot an innocent passenger in the head. It is arguable that the police obliquely intended to kill the passenger, because they must have foreseen that the virtually certain consequence of firing 26 bullets from high-powered guns into the passenger side of the vehicle would be that the passenger would be fatally wounded. Transferred self-defence or transferred public defence[150] would provide a defence, but only if it was

146 *R. v. Pagett* (1983) 76 Cr. App. R. 279 at 289 *per* Goff, L.J. citing *R. v. Pitts* (1842) C. & M. 284, and *R. v. Curley* (1909) 2 Cr. App. R. 96.

147 (2013) 216 Cal.App.4th 24.

148 (2013) 216 Cal.App.4th 24.

149 *People v. Gilbert* (1966) 63 Cal.2d 690 at 704–705, where Traynor, C.J. said: 'When the defendant or his accomplice, with a conscious disregard for life, intentionally commits an act that is likely to cause death, and his victim or a police officer kills in reasonable response to such act, the defendant is guilty of murder. In such a case, the killing is attributable, not merely to the commission of a felony, but to the intentional act of the defendant or his accomplice committed with conscious disregard for life. Thus, the victim's self-defensive killing or the police officer's killing in the performance of his duty cannot be considered an independent intervening cause for which the defendant is not liable, for it is a reasonable response to the dilemma thrust upon the victim or the policeman be the intentional act of the defendant or his accomplice.' See also *People v. Lima* (2004) 118 Cal. App. 4th 259.

150 In England and Wales section 3 of the *Criminal Law Act 1967* provides: '(1) A person may use such *force as is reasonable in the circumstances* in the prevention of crime, or in effecting or assisting in the lawful arrest of offenders or suspected offenders or of persons unlawfully at large. (2) Subsection (1) above shall replace the rules of the common law on the question when force used for a purpose mentioned in the subsection is justified by that purpose' [emphasis added].

necessary for the police to use such force. The sort of disproportionate force used in *Sisson v. Superior Court* was not necessary or proportionate force, because the police were merely attempting to arrest an unarmed man who posed no immediate threat to the police officers or the public. Sisson was merely wanted for questioning on identity theft charges and for questioning on a historical allegation that he once took his child without permission. Sisson acted unlawfully when he drove away from the police to evade arrest, but he was unarmed and was not being arrested for offences of serious violence.

The driver had no history of violence and it was clear that he had a passenger in his car. The police could have stopped the car by shooting at its tyres or radiator, if they felt it so urgent to arrest Sisson. Unlike Pagett, Sisson had not taken a hostage, was unarmed, was not wanted for serious offences of violence, and thus he could have been apprehended by non-lethal means at a later point in time. Police officers should not be able to use unreasonable force to arrest a person when that person poses no immediate danger to others and when they foresee that such force is virtually certain to cause the death of innocent others. Elias, J.'s conclusion that unreasonable excessive force from the perpetrator does not break the chain of causation between *D*'s provocation and the consequences of *P*'s act is erroneous.[151] It certainly cannot be reconciled with the fundamental principle that a person is not responsible for wrongs that are directly caused by the independent autonomous choice of another. The sort of gross negligence demonstrated in *Sisson v. Superior Court* broke the chain of causation between Sisson's act of evading arrest and the police officers' acts of firing 26 bullets into his car.[152] (The police did not make a mistake about the necessity for force, because Sisson was escaping. Instead, they made an unreasonable mistake about the level of force that was required to arrest Sisson.) A person evading arrest for non-violent crimes would not foresee that the virtually certain consequence of his act of evading arrest in a non-violent way would be that a group of police officers would fire 26 bullets from high-powered guns at him and an innocent passenger in his car. The voluntary independent acts of the police officers broke the chain of causation.[153] On the facts of this case, it was clear that the police were not forced to take such drastic actions. Nor can it be said that he was encouraging the police to kill him or his passenger.

It was held in Californian law that the mental element for provocative act murder is satisfied if *D* knew that her provocative act had a high probability of eliciting a life-threatening response from the person who actually fires the fatal bullet. In English law, *D* would have to obliquely intend to force the police to use lethal force. Californian law also holds that liability

151 *Sisson v. Superior Court* (2013) 216 Cal.App.4th 24.
152 *R. v. Jordan* (1956) 40 Cr. App. R. 152.
153 *R. v. Kennedy (No 2)*[2008] 1 A.C. 269.

for provocative act murder is determined by whether the killing was a natural and probable consequence of *D*'s provocative act, not by whether the actual perpetrator's use of force was reasonable, but under either test the decision in *Sisson v. Superior Court* seems wrong. The natural and probable consequence test also is objective and a jury would have no difficulty inferring that the natural probable consequence of *D* driving away from police while they are trying to arrest *D* for allegedly perpetrating a non-violent crime such as identify theft, would not be that the police would bombard *D* and an innocent third party in a hail of lethal bullets. The natural probable consequence test seems to be used to justify transferring liability for the direct cause of death to the person who only made an indirect causal contribution, because the intervening part was not a fully innocent agent, but was in fact a reckless agent who should have been directly liable for her intervening recklessness.

B. Transferred intention, provocative act theory

In a case like *R. v. Pagett* could it be argued that it would be sufficient for *P* to intend the police to suffer at least GBH, after which there is a transfer of malice to the victim, just as there would be if *D* fired at *V*, missing but causing an avalanche which then killed *V*? So even if *D* did not have the requisite direct intent to kill his girlfriend *V*, it might be sufficient if he had had direct or oblique intent regarding the police officers. This cannot work for obvious reasons. *P* intends to kill or cause GBH to the police officers, but that intention does not transfer to the victim, because the police are autonomous interveners. Their intervention is justifiable, but it cannot be said that *P*'s intention transfers back to his girlfriend on the basis that he was intending to kill the police when he caused them to make an independent, but justified, choice to attempt to kill him – because the missing link is not *mens rea*, but an act of perpetration. Since the police were acting lawfully and justifiably, no liability could derive from their actions. The police were trying to kill Pagett in lawful self-defence and accidentally killed an innocent third party, so their defence of lawful public defence transferred to the innocent third party. Without a transfer of defence and without accepting that their hands had been forced, the police would have been personally liable. A bullet ricocheting from an object and thereafter causing *V*'s death or a bullet causing an avalanche and thereafter causing *V*'s death is different, because this is simply a matter of physical causation being achieved in an unintended way, but in circumstances where *D*'s *mens rea* for murder is concurrent with event that causes *V*'s death.

Reverting to a case like *R. v. Pagett*, as far as the fault element is concerned, it is more plausible to argue that *P* is liable for the actions of the police, because he forced their hand and obliquely intended to kill himself and/or his girlfriend by making the decision to force their hand. When a person takes a hostage and thereafter fires bullets at armed police who try to rescue the hostage, that is evidence upon which a reasonable jury could infer that he obliquely intended to kill his hostage by forcing the police to respond in justifiable defence.

Let us apply these principles to the facts of *R. v. Gnango.* BM was not pressured to attempt to kill Gnango. He was not psychologically pressured or physically forced to turn up for the gun battle, nor was he psychologically pressured or physically forced to carry a lethal weapon. When Gnango started to fire back at BM, BM had two choices: he could have continued to shoot at Gnango or he could have withdrawn and run for safety. The provocative act murder doctrine should only be invoked in cases where the killer had no real choice but to kill[154] or where the police are pressured to kill as a matter of necessity to preserve their own lives or to protect the lives of others. If the police are under immense psychological pressure, because they have to choose whether or not to kill a suicide bomber to prevent her from blowing up a crowded train full of innocent passengers, they could hardly be said to have killed willingly. They make a choice that they do not want to make because they are pressured by *the necessity of the circumstances* to act to save the innocent passengers on the train.[155] Thus, if they miss their target, the terrorist, and instead shoot dead an innocent passenger, the terrorist (if she is apprehended alive) could be held liable for the murder of the passenger under the rule laid down in *R. v. Pagett.*[156] In such a case the terrorist obliquely intends to use the police to perpetrate murder.

An unreasonable mistake about the necessity for defensive action ought to be sufficient to break the chain of causation between *D*'s provocative act and *P*'s act of perpetration. So too ought an unreasonable mistake about the amount of force that is required to arrest *D.*[157] The subjective mistake test for the necessity element in self-defence might be sufficient for exculpating the police,[158] but that should not mean that an innocent person who is mistaken as a provoker of a lethal response is liable for the mistaken justified harms of the police. Take the killing of Jean Charles de Menezes on the London Tube as an example. The police mistakenly believed de Menezes was a terrorist. Many have argued their mistaken belief was unreasonable, but even if it was reasonable there is no way that de Menezes, had he survived, should have been liable for any harm caused by the police. The police mistakenly believed killing him was a necessity to protect the public and believed he was forcing their hands, but had they missed de Menezes and killed some other innocent passenger in the train coach, de Menezes

154 *People v. Concha* (2009) 47 Cal. 4th 653.

155 It is akin to the sort of moral involuntariness that is used to underwrite the duress of circumstances defence. See generally, Baker, *op. cit. supra,* note 15 at Chapter 28.

156 (1983) 76 Cr. App. R. 279. See also *Jackson v. State* (1979) 286 Md. 430; *Palmer v. State* (1999) 704 N.E.2d 124, where the necessity for action was clear on the facts.

157 *R. v. Roberts* (1971) 56 Cr. App. R. 95.

158 *R. v. Williams* (1984) 78 Cr. App. R. 276.

would not have been liable for provocative act murder. The case might be different when a person deliberately poses as a terrorist to cause the police to make a mistake about the necessity for lethal force.

C. Psychological duress and physical involuntariness

It might help to distinguish mere encouragement from psychological pressure or moral involuntariness.[159] If a person is forced to jump from a skyscraper to her death because a terrorist has set the lower 50 floors alight by crashing a passenger aeroplane into them, it could not be said that she freely chose to jump. She has no real choice. Moral involuntariness can vary in degrees, so the caused party's intervening choice must be morally involuntary. If it can be established that the intervening party's act was not reasonably foreseeable[160] or was totally unreasonable,[161] then it is likely that the court will hold that the intervening party was not caused to kill and so on. In *Pagett D* was armed and was shooting at the police while using his ex-girlfriend as a human shield. The police were under extreme psychological pressure to act and had reasonable grounds for believing that it was necessary to stop Pagett before he attempted to kill more people, including his ex-girlfriend. More importantly, lethal force seemed to be a proportionate response given that Pagett was shooting at the police officers and was wanted for violent crimes including attempted murder. Pagett created the conditions that led to the police response.[162]

If Pagett had not been armed with a gun and had not been firing bullets at the police while using his ex-girlfriend as a human shield, the court most likely would have held that he had not caused the police to kill his ex-girlfriend. If Pagett had merely been armed with a small knife and thus posed no danger to the police or passers-by, then it would have been unreasonable for the police to shoot at him while he was using his girlfriend as a human shield. If the intervening party's response to *D*'s provocative act is unreasonable and disproportionate, *D* will not be held to be the cause of the intervening party's personal actions.

159 For a good judicial discussion of moral involuntariness, see *R. v. Ruzic* [2001] S.C.C. 24 (Can.) *per* LeBel, J.

160 *R. v. Roberts* (1971) 56 Cr. App. R. 95. See also *People v. Concha* (2009) 47 Cal 4th 653 at 662, where it was said: 'When the defendant or his accomplice, with a conscious disregard for life, intentionally commits an act that is likely to cause death, and his victim or a police officer kills in reasonable response to such act, the defendant is guilty of murder.'

161 *Royall v. R.* (1991) 172 C.L.R. 378 at 398 *per* Brennan, J. in the High Court of Australia, citing the following English precedents as authority for this statement of the law: *R. v. Pitts* (1842) Car. & M. 284; *R. v. Curley* (1909) 2 Cr. App. R. 109; *Director of Public Prosecutions v. Daley* [1980] A.C. 237.

162 As was the case in *R. v. Pagett* (1983) 76 Cr. App. R. 279. See also *Com. V. Askew* (1989) 404 Mass. 532, where *V* was killed when *X* intervened to remove a loaded gun from *Y*. *X* was under pressure to act, as *Y* was wielding a loaded gun and had his hand on the trigger.

There is a cardinal difference between providing a person with an incentive to do something and psychologically pressuring her to do it as a matter of necessity. Take the example where a gangster offers an assassin £100,000 to kill her arch-enemy. The gangster will be liable as an accessory to murder if the assassin goes ahead with the murder, because she has encouraged the assassin to commit murder. But the gangster has not caused the assassin to kill; she has not put a gun to the assassin's head and demanded that she kill. All she has done is provide the assassin with a strong incentive to kill. If the assassin kills for the money, she makes a voluntary choice to kill. She has been incentivised, but she makes a voluntary choice. The assassin can only cause herself to do it, her will is not overborne and she has other options. Most law-abiding citizens would not choose to perpetrate an assassination, not even for a million pounds. They might decide otherwise where there is a gun pointed at their heads. If a police constable is pressured to kill a terrorist on a crowded London train, she does not make a voluntary choice. Her freedom is not unfettered; she is under enormous psychological pressure because she is morally compelled to act as a matter of necessity to take reasonable and proportionate action to save the passengers.

The causation requirement will not be satisfied unless the victim's will is overborne or she is physically forced to kill as a matter of necessity.[163] It should be shown that the intervening party had no reasonable alternative but to kill. Otherwise any encouragement will count. Thus, *R. v. Gnango* is not an appropriate case for invoking the provocative act murder doctrine. BM was not forced to try to kill Gnango; Gnango's encouragement did not cause BM to act with moral involuntariness. A person can hardly engage in a mutual gunfight and argue that he was forced to kill, because he voluntarily joined the gunfight for that very purpose.[164] *Per contra*, a genuine victim's self-defensive killing 'or the police officer's killing in the performance of his duty cannot be considered an independent intervening cause for which the defendant is not liable, for it is a *reasonable response* to the dilemma *thrust upon the victim or the policeman* by the intentional act of the defendant or his accomplice'.[165]

163 In *People v. Garcia* (1999) 69 Cal. App. 4th 1324 at 1329, Vartabedian, A.J. said: '[M]ere participation in an armed robbery is not sufficient to invoke murder liability, direct or vicarious, when the victim resists and kills . . . The life-threatening acts must be other than those implicit in the crime of armed robbery.'

164 Cf. *People v. Slaughter* (2002) 27 Cal. 4th 1187 at 1203.

165 Cf. *People v. Gardner* (1995) 37 Cal.App.4th 473 at 481 (holding that the response need not be reasonable, but need only be a proximate cause. Such a statement of the law seems to be tautological, since a grossly unreasonable response cannot be a proximate cause. In *People v. Concha* (2009) 47 Cal. 4th 653 at 661, the Supreme Court of California said: '"[I]f the eventual victim's death is not the natural and probable consequence of a defendant's act, then liability cannot attach." Our prior decisions make clear that, where the defendant perpetrates an inherently dangerous felony, the victim's self-defensive killing is a natural and probable response . . . '.

D. Intentional encourager and non-responsible instruments

In *R. v. Gnango,* BM was not forced to continue the gunfight once it had commenced. The defences of duress (duress is no defence to murder)[166] and self-defence would not have been available to BM if he had been caught and prosecuted for murder, and nor should the provocative act murder doctrine have been invoked to treat him as a non-responsible instrument (quasi innocent agent) of Gnango's criminal encouragement. Lord Clarke suggested that something akin to the provocative act murder doctrine could provide an alternative basis for convicting Gnango, but as we have seen it would have the effect of treating BM as not being responsible for shooting Magda Pniewska dead. BM did not kill Magda Pniewska as a matter of lawful defence or necessity. BM had not withdrawn from the gunfight and thus had not revived his right to self-defence, so transferred self-defence was not available to him. BM's act was the direct cause of Magda Pniewska's death and he acted with the requisite fault for murder. Hence, BM was not a non-responsible (excused or justified) agent[167] who was used by Gnango to kill. Instead, BM's actions were informed, voluntary, autonomous and lawfully unjustified and inexcusable.

E. Extinguished defences v. transferred defences

A more problematic case is where a police officer or a victim kills a participant in an unlawful joint enterprise. In *People v. Concha,*[168] Concha, Hernandez and Sanchez attempted to murder Harris. During the attempt, Harris responded in self-defence by stabbing Sanchez to death. The provocative act murder doctrine was invoked to convict Concha and Hernandez of murder for the death of their accomplice, Sanchez. Basically, they were held jointly liable for causing (encouraging/provoking) Harris to kill their accomplice. It is true that the joint act of the three including the dead accomplice (Sanchez) caused/provoked the intended victim (Harris) to defend himself by killing Sanchez. It is also true that they must have foreseen this as a possibility if not as a virtual certainty. If a person tries to kill another she must foresee lethal self-defence as a very high probability, if not a virtual certainty.

Nonetheless, it is submitted that there should be no liability in such cases. This is not a case of defendants using a non-culpable (excused or

166 Baker, *op. cit. supra,* note 15 at Chapter 28.

167 Cf. *People v. Slaughter* (2002) 27 Cal. 4th 1187 at 1203, where *D,* in effect, tried to shift his responsibility for murder by arguing that he was a mere instrument that had been provoked to kill. The court rejected his claim, because the evidence showed he intended to kill for his own purposes.

168 *People v. Concha* (2009) 47 Cal. 4th 653 at 663; cf. *R. v. Martin* [2003] Q.B. 1, where *D* was acting unlawfully and unjustifiably because his lethal force was not a necessary and proportionate response.

justified) agent to kill an innocent third party. The joint participants of the unlawful enterprise were jointly risking becoming the victim of their target victim's *lawful* actions. A normal risk of engaging in violent crime is that the victim might retaliate with lawfully justifiable force. If Harris had only wounded Sanchez, Sanchez would not have been liable for causing Harris to wound him or for causing Harris to attempt to kill him. Sanchez would have been treated as a victim and thus would have been prosecuted only for his attempted murder of Harris. Therefore, the joint perpetrators (Concha and Hernandez) of the attempt on Harris's life should not have been held liable for Harris's lawful killing of Sanchez. Harris acted lawfully and against the right party and therefore there was no residual liability flowing from acting through a justified and innocent intervening party. Compare *R. v. Pagett* where there was residual liability that rested in Pagett, because an innocent third party was killed as a result of Pagett's wrongdoing. If Pagett had been injured by the police and no other party had been hurt, then *all the unjustified and inexcusable* wrongdoing and harm-doing would have been extinguished, because the police would have acted lawfully and justifiably in harming Pagett himself. If no third party had been harmed because of Pagett's wrongdoing, then there would have been no outstanding wrongdoing and *harm-doing* to attribute to Pagett.

In *Commonwealth v. Redline*, Jones, C.J. said:[169]

> In the present instance, the victim of the homicide was one of the robbers who, while resisting apprehension in his effort to escape, was shot and killed by a policeman in the performance of his duty. Thus, the homicide was justifiable and, obviously, could not be availed of, on any rational legal theory, to support a charge of murder. How can anyone, no matter how much of an outlaw he may be, have a criminal charge lodged against him for the consequences of the lawful conduct of another person? The mere statement of the question carries with it its own answer.

The above case can be explained as a case where the police office's defence was not transferred to an innocent third party, but was extinguished on the right party. That is, the party they lawfully killed in public defence. *Therefore, there was no residual harm-doing or wrongdoing to attribute to the co-perpetrators.* Pagett did not wrong himself by encouraging the police to use lawful force against him, even though he risked physical harm.

It is little wonder that no state in the U.S. apart from California uses the provocative act murder doctrine to convict accomplices of crimes that have been perpetrated against a fellow accomplice during the commission of a crime. In such cases there is no residual *wrongful* harm to attribute the

169 (1958) 391 Pa. 486 at 509.

putative wrongdoers. Coupled with this, a person ought not to be criminally liable for her own victimisation simply because it was a result of her trying to criminally victimise the victimiser or someone else.[170] In *People v. Concha,*[171] the Supreme Court of California held:

> In the present case, although it is apparent that defendants Concha and Hernandez did not intend to kill their accomplice, they had the intent to kill a person when they attacked their intended victim, and therefore are guilty of murder as to any killing either of them proximately caused while acting together pursuant to their intent to kill.

This reasoning is fallacious, because the transferred intention doctrine only covers the accidental consequences of the perpetrator's acts. The perpetrators (Concha and Hernandez) did not accidentally kill the wrong victim (Sanchez instead of Harris) as a result of their joint attack on Harris.

The transferred intention doctrine would have applied if either Concha and Hernandez had accidentally killed Sanchez while trying to kill Harris, but it cannot be applied where the victim or a police officer intervenes, unless this results in an innocent third party being killed in a transferred defence situation.[172] The defence transfers for the justifiable/excused intervener, but this leaves a residue of *wrongful* harm, which combines with the provocateur's fault for *causing* the perpetrator to directly bring about the harm. More generally, Parliament should enact a statutory defence of 'joint enterprise participant victimisation' to prevent accomplices being held criminally liable for the lawful and justifiable injuries and deaths caused by third parties to their fellow participants in a joint enterprise.[173] In *R. v. Pagett* the killing

170 See *State v. Small* (2012) 100 So.3d 797; *Davis v. Fox* (2012) 229 W.Va. 662; *State v. Myers* (2000) 760 So. 2d 310; *State v. Kalathakis* (1990) 563 So.2d 228; *Commonwealth v. Redline* (1958) 391 Pa. 486; *Butler v. People* (1888) 18 N.E. 338; *People v. Garippo* (1920) 292 Ill. 293, 127 N.E. 75. See also *State v. Garner* (1959 238 La. 563 at 577.

171 (2009) 47 Cal. 4th 653 at 661.

172 The core difference in a case such as *R. v. Pagett* (1983) 76 Cr. App. R. 279 is that an innocent third party died as a result of the lawful defensive actions of another (the police). The defendant in *R. v. Pagett* provoked the police to take defensive action, which resulted in an innocent third party being killed.

173 For example, Connecticut General Statutes provide such a defence for felony murder. The Connecticut Penal Code, C.G.S.A. § 53a-54c, provides: 'A person is guilty of murder when, acting either alone or with one or more persons, he commits or attempts to commit robbery, burglary, kidnapping, sexual assault in the first degree, aggravated sexual assault in the first degree, sexual assault in the third degree, sexual assault in the third degree with a firearm, escape in the first degree, or escape in the second degree and, in the course of and in furtherance of such crime or of flight therefrom, he, or another participant, if any, causes the *death of a person other than one of the participants* . . . ' [emphasis added]. Similarly, N.Y. Penal Law § 150.20 provides: 'A person is guilty of arson in the first degree when he intentionally damages a building . . . and when (b) another person *who is not a participant* in the crime is present in such building or motor vehicle at the time; and (c) the defendant

was only lawful based on the notion of transferred public defence – but the wrong person was killed and thus harm was caused. The person killed was not an aggressor so the police would have had no right to use lethal force against her. However, it was Pagett that caused the police to shoot at him and *V* and thus cause *V*'s death and Pagett obliquely intended that result.

F. Co-defendant as a victim of a jointly perpetrated wrong

Compare this sort of case with cases where the contributory conduct of the victim played a role and where the direct cause of the victim's death was a joint act of the victim and perpetrator rather than a lawfully justifiable act of a third party. In *R. v. Willoughby*,[174] Rose, L.J. held that accomplices engaged in a criminal joint enterprise owe each other a duty of care and that when a joint act of the accomplices directly causes one of the accomplices to be injured or killed, the other accomplice is criminally liable for his direct causal contribution to the joint criminal act that caused the other accomplice's death. The *ex turpi causa* doctrine does not apply in criminal cases. *R. v. Willoughby* can be distinguished from the abovementioned cases, because the perpetrator in that case was not a justified or excused third party, but rather was Willoughby himself.[175] Coupled with this, Willoughby's own joint act was a joint concurrent and direct cause of his accomplice's death. In *State v. Pellegrino*,[176] Shea, A.J., in the Supreme Court of Connecticut, said: 'the fact that [the accomplice also] may have been negligent with respect to his own safety can no more relieve the defendant of criminal liability than if [the accomplice] had been an innocent victim who was contributorily negligent.'

The provocative act murder doctrine in combination with the transferred defence doctrine works differently from the transferred intention doctrine, because it more or less deems the police officer or target victim to be an innocent agent. It works on the defendant intending or obliquely intending to use the provoked party to kill another. It is arguable that Concha and Hernandez (and also Sanchez) obliquely intended to encourage Harris to kill them. Nonetheless there was no residue harm or wrongdoing to be attributed to them.

knows that fact or the circumstances are such as to render the presence of such person therein a reasonable possibility' [emphasis added]. See *State v. Hansen* (1986) 734 P.2d 421 at 427; *Davis v. Fox* (2012) 735 S.E.2d 259 at 263 and the cases cited therein.

174 [2005] 1 W.L.R. 1880.

175 Compare the civil law position as set out in *Joyce v. O'Brien* [2013] P.I.Q.R. P23.

176 (1984) 194 Conn. 279 at 296. In that case, the defendant's conduct was a substantial and direct cause of the accomplice's death. The defendant was convicted of committing manslaughter in the first degree by causing the death of his accomplice, and convicted of arson for starting a fire with the intent to destroy a building while aware that his accomplice was inside the building.

Coupled with the above, since their joint voluntary aim was to risk being a victim, the victim rule should apply to exclude them from being held liable for their own joint (putative) victimisation. The victim rule excludes accomplices from being held criminally liable for the victimisation of their accomplice, when the victimisation results from the lawful intervention of a third party. In such cases, the law deems all the accomplices to be joint victims.[177] The dominant cause of the accomplice's injury or death in such cases is the accomplice's own voluntary choice to engage in a crime where the accomplice knows the victim is likely to try to injure or kill the accomplice to defend herself from the accomplice's joint unlawful attack. Such cases are clearly distinguishable from cases where an accomplice is harmed as a result of the gross negligence of her fellow accomplice while jointly perpetrating a criminal offence such as arson.

VI. The scope of the exempt party (victim) rule

The current law as far as the victim rule is concerned in England and Wales is to be found in two court decisions, section 2 of the *Criminal Law Act 1977* and section 51 of the *Serious Crime Act 2007*. The leading decision was *R. v. Tyrrell*,[178] where it was held that a 16-year-old girl could not be an accessory to her own sexual violation even though she consented, because the statute was designed to protect young girls even against themselves. In *R. v. Gnango*,[179] Lords Phillips and Judge said: 'there is no common law rule that precludes conviction of a defendant of being party to a crime of which he was the actual or intended victim.' Their Lordships took the view that the victim rule was limited to cases where the statute was intended to protect people from their own foolish decisions such as is the case where minors consent to engage in sexual intercourse. They seem to take the view that the victim rule can be applied at the discretion of judges when they are able to draw from a statute a legislative policy in support of applying the victim rule.

A. The victim rule: a common law doctrine

The statute discussed in *R. v. Tyrrell* did not expressly contain an exemption for victims, but the court felt it was able to imply that such an exemption

177 Cf. the decision of the Supreme Court of Washington in *City of Auburn v. Hedlund* (2009) 165 Wash.2d 645 at 650–651, where *D* was charged with driving under the influence and with reckless driving as an accomplice and with furnishing alcohol to minors. Chambers, J. said: 'Under Washington law, "[u]nless otherwise provided by this title or by the law defining the crime, a person is not an accomplice in a crime committed by another person if: (a) He is a victim of that crime."' See RCW 9A.08.020(5).

178 [1894] 1 Q.B. 710.

179 [2012] 1 A.C. 827 at 846.

was applicable to the given statute. The victim rule looks more like a common law creation[180] than a statutory provision, because it seems to be a rule of general application that can be applied to any statute that requires the victim rule to be implied as a matter of policy. Glanville Williams wrote: '[I]t seems to be a general principle that the victim of an offence is not punishable. Where, for example, the law aims at the protection of the person, her consent to the crime does not implicate her.'[181] The offences in the *Sexual Offences Act 2003* deem that a minor is incapable of giving a valid consent and therefore the offences are needed to protect them not only from non-consensual sexual relations, but also from sexual relations where they putatively consent. However, Lords Phillips and Judge overlooked the fact that *R. v. Brown*[182] held that the *Offences against the Person Act 1861* is also needed to protect people against themselves.[183] They also seem to run into error by holding that the victim rule does not exist at common law. It certainly was not a statutory creation.

The victim rule is implied when a statute on its face seems to be aimed at protecting the particular class of victim. Long after the decision in *R. v. Tyrrell*, the victim rule was recognised in two statutory provisions. For

180 The American courts have interpreted *R. v. Tyrrell* as creating a victim rule at common law. '[It is a] common law rule dating at least back to an 1893 English statutory rape case, where the court reasoned that a law intended to protect young girls could not also hold them responsible as accomplices.' *City of Auburn v. Hedlund* (2009) 165 Wash.2d 645 at 653 *per* Chambers, J. citing Professor Wayne R. LaFave, *Substantive Criminal Law* (St Paul MN: West Publishing, 2003) at 369–370. Blakey and Roddy (at note 359) write that the decision in *Gebardi v. U.S.* (1932) 287 U.S. 112 at 123 involving an appeal against the conviction of a female defendant for conspiring to violate the *Mann Act* was allowed 'where she willingly crossed state lines to have sex with the other defendant, a man who was not then her husband'. In that case, the Supreme Court of the United States cited 'the common law rule of *Queen v. Tyrrell* (1894) 1 Q.B. 710 . . . Incorporating the common law tradition into the interpretation of the *Mann Act*, and reading an exception into the *Act* that limited liability for women'. At note 219, Blakey and Roddy write: 'The victim exclusion rule, however, is not followed in all cases; its application remains in each instance a question of policy.' G. Robert Blakey and Kevin P. Roddy, 'Reflections on *Reves v. Ernst & Young*: Its Meaning and Impact on Substantive, Accessory, Aiding, Abetting, and Conspiracy Liability Under RICO' (1996) 33 *Am. Crim. L. Rev.* 1345. In *Giorgianni v. The Queen* (1985) 156 C.L.R. 473 (a decision of the High Court of Australia) Mason, J. said: 'In *Mallan v. Lee* (1949) 80 C.L.R. 198 at 216, Dixon J. observed that "the application of sections dealing with aiding and abetting may be excluded by the nature of the substantive offence or the general tenor or policy of the provisions by which it is created". A similar approach must be taken to apply to the exclusion of the doctrine of secondary participation at common law. It may, therefore, be inapplicable to a person of a class whom the substantive offence is designed to protect (*R. v. Tyrrell* [1894] 1 Q.B. 710; *R. v. Whitehouse* [1977] Q.B. 868).' See also Ross E. Davies, 'A Public Trust Exception to the Rule of Lenity' (1996) 63 *U. Chi. L. Rev.* 1175 at 1201–1202.

181 Williams, *op. cit. supra*, note 88 at 357.

182 [1994] 1 A.C. 212.

183 See Dennis J. Baker, 'Should Unnecessary Harmful Nontherapeutic Cosmetic Surgery Be Criminalized' (2014) 17 *New Crim. L. Rev.* 587.

example, section 2 of the *Criminal Law Act 1977* provides some exemptions from liability for conspiracy:

> (1) A person shall not by virtue of section 1 above be guilty of conspiracy to commit any offence if he is an intended victim of that offence.
> (2) A person shall not by virtue of section 1 above be guilty of conspiracy to commit any offence or offences if the only other person or persons with whom he agrees are (both initially and at all times during the currency of the agreement) persons of any one or more of the following descriptions, that is to say –
>
> (a) his spouse [or civil partner];
> (b) a person under the age of criminal responsibility; and
> (c) an intended victim of that offence or of each of those offences.
>
> (3) A person is under the age of criminal responsibility for the purposes of subsection (2)(b) above so long as it is conclusively presumed, by virtue of section 50 of the *Children and Young Persons Act 1933*, that he cannot be guilty of any offence.

This would protect a person who conspires to perpetrate a fraud without realising that she is the intended victim of the fraud. For example, in *Stewart v. Wright*,[184] *V* attempted to participate in a fraud, but was unwittingly the victim of the fraud in which he tried to participate. The facts of *Stewart v. Wright* (a civil case in the Circuit Court of Appeals, Eighth Circuit) are succinctly stated in the headnote to the judgment as follows:

> *B.* and his associates, who were confidence men engaged in enticing others to their city and swindling them out of their money by means of pretended foot races, induced the plaintiff to come and while there to wager money represented as belonging to *B.* upon the result of such a race upon promise of a percentage of the expected winnings. It was falsely represented to plaintiff that the foot race had been fixed so that *B.* would certainly win. It was also represented that the men with whom the wagers were made were wealthy miners, whereas in fact they were not miners, but were secretly associated with *B.*, and were members of his band of swindlers, as were also the foot racers. *B.* pretended to act as stakeholder, and to secretly withdraw moneys from the stakes from time to time, and to pass them to plaintiff to be again wagered. Plaintiff was also induced to wager his own money upon the pretended foot race. Plaintiff did not win, and it was never intended by the swindlers that he should win. All of the acts and pretences of *B.* and his associates were

184 (1906) 147 F. 321.

> false and fraudulent, and were part of a prearranged and frequently practiced scheme to defraud.

In *Stewart v. Wright*[185] Hook, J. said:

> It would seem anomalous if Wright were held to be *particeps criminis* [an equal participant] to a larceny of his own money, and equally so if he were held to be *in pari delicto* [equally at fault] with those who stole it. Conduct similar to that under consideration has been held to constitute larceny, even though the fraud or pretence practiced on the victim, and by which he was despoiled of his money, assumed the simulated form of a violation of the law, in which he participated.

It was held that Wright was not deprived of a remedy by the maxim *ex dolo malo non oritur actio*.

Nonetheless, if a case like this were to be tried in the England in the twenty-first century, the inchoate offences found in the *Serious Crime Act 2007* would allow the victim, Wright, to be prosecuted for his attempted participation in the frauds against third parties. Wright would be exempt from the conspiracy against himself, but not for the factually impossible attempt to defraud others. He would not be exempt from his attempt to participate in a fraud against third parties. After all, Wright was attempting to participate in a fraud (Wright attempted to encourage the fraudsters to make false representations to other potential victims because he mistakenly believed he would profit from their lies) for the purpose of making a property gain for himself.

Below I argue that even if the victim rule applies more broadly, it does not apply to the facts of a case such as *R. v. Gnango* because the actual victim was a third party. Arguably, the same applies when a person intends a third party to be the victim of a fraud that he or she attempts to encourage or assist. Section 51 of the *Serious Crime Act 2007* also provides a fairly general victim exemption. Section 51 provides:

> (1) In the case of protective offences, a person does not commit an offence under this Part by reference to such an offence if –
>
> (a) he falls within the protected category; and
> (b) he is the person in respect of whom the protective offence was committed or would have been if it had been committed.
>
> (2) 'Protective offence' means an offence that exists (wholly or in part) for the protection of a particular category of persons ('the protected category').

185 (1906) 147 F. 321 at 333.

B. Consenting to victimisation for the ulterior purpose of perpetrating a crime

Before we examine the victim rule in detail, it is worth noting that the old case of *R. v. Wright*[186] did not settle English case law to the effect that there is no general exemption from accessorial liability for victims. In *R. v. Wright*[187] it was held that: '[A] person who . . . maims himself, or procures another to maim him, that he may have more colour to beg; or disables himself to prevent being pressed for a soldier is subject to fine and imprisonment at common law; and so is the party by whom it was effected at the other's desire.' Almost seven hundred years ago, Horne said: 'Mayhem is the want of member, or the enfeebling of it by breaking, or cutting the bones of a man, whereby he is less able to combat.'[188] A person who allowed himself to be disabled deprived 'the King of the aid and assistance of his subjects.'[189] In the context of consensual combats, the courts have excluded the victims from being held liable as accessories of their own maiming. It has been held that '[t]he assailant in a fight not by consent may be convicted of the principal crime; that one not the assailant in a fight not by consent may be convicted of the principal crime for maiming only if his assailant has in good faith declined further combat.'[190] In *Foster v. People*[191] consent was held to be a partial defence. Hallett, C.J. said: '[T]he only effect of consent, then, is to reduce the offence in certain specified cases, from a higher to a lower grade. Whether the higher offence is a felony, appears to be an open question.' His Honour went on to expound:[192] 'this act is criminal in a high or low degree, according to the relations of the parties, as whether they were in combat, etc., at the time of the injury.'

186 *R. v. Wright* (1603) Co. Lit. 127b. It is worth noting that maiming is now dealt with via the offences found in the *Offences against the Person Act 1861*. Maiming is still prosecuted as a distinct crime in some U.S. jurisdictions. See for example, *Goodman v. Superior Court* (1978) 84 Cal.App.3d 621 at 623, where it was said: 'Mayhem in early common law was committable only by infliction of an injury which substantially reduced the victim's formidability in combat . . . Thus, "if the injury be such as disfigures him only, without diminishing his corporeal abilities, it does not fall within the crime of mayhem".' See also *People v. Sekona* (1994) 32 Cal.Rptr.2d 606; *People v. Nunes* (1920) 47 Cal.App. 346 at 348; *People v. Sears* (1965) 62 Cal.2d 737 at 745; *People v. Wright* (1892) 93 Cal. 564 at 566.

187 This is the text of the case as reported in East, *op. cit. supra*, note 75 at 396; see also Hale, *op. cit. supra*, note 62 at 412.

188 Horne, *op. cit. supra*, note 1 at Ch. I., Sc. 10. Cf. *R. v. Tickner* (1778) 1 Leach 187; *R. v. Lee* (1763) 1 Leach 51; *R. v. Mills* (1783) 1 Leach 259; *R. v. Hunt* (1825) 1 Mood. C.C. 93.

189 Blackstone, *loc. cit. supra*, note 75.

190 *Carpenter v. People* (1903) 31 Colo. 284 at 288 *per* Steele, J.

191 (1871) 1 Colo. 293 at 296. *Henry v. State* (1916) 188 S.W. 539 at 540, Kirby, J. said that: 'If the testimony had only shown that the injury occurred while the parties were fighting by mutual agreement, it would not have constituted the offence of maiming.' See also *Godfrey v. People* (1875) 2 Cow.Cr.Rep. 209.

192 *Foster v. People* (1871) 1 Colo. 293 at 297–298.

Consent does not provide any kind of defence to the offences found in sections 18, 20 and 47 of the *Offences against the Person Act 1861* unless one of the exceptions applies,[193] but this does not weigh on the independent issue of whether a consenting victim can be an accessory to her own victimisation. Third parties can be liable as accessories even when the victim has consented to the assault, but there is no precedent[194] in the common law world that holds that a person can be liable as an accessory to her own assault. The harm that the crime of mayhem was aimed at preventing was that caused to the King by the loss of a potentially able soldier.[195] It was not aimed at protecting the dignity and personhood of the subject for the subject's own benefit. The state was not concerned about the harm that the consenter might endure, but about the harm that his disablement might cause the state. It also was concerned about how the consenter might use her self-harm to perpetrate some ulterior crime, as was the case in *R. v. Wright*.

A case such as *R. v. Brown*[196] is distinguishable from cases involving those who consent to harm with the ulterior motive of using the inflicted injury to commit some ulterior fraud or crime. *R. v. Brown* was a case of *V* consenting to harm *X* for the purpose of receiving harm *X* in itself – there was no ulterior crime or fraud in view. The only ulterior aim of defendants in *R. v. Brown* was to receive sexual pleasure, which is not a wrong or a crime *per se*. *R. v. Wright* covers only cases where *V* consents to *Y* inflicting harm *X* upon her, because harm *X* will help her to commit some ulterior crime.

Similarly, in *State v. Bass*,[197] Bryson told Bass (a physician) that he was going to cut off his fingers to get insurance money. The physician refused

193 *R. v. Brown* [1994] 1 A.C. 212. See also Dennis J. Baker, 'Moral Limits of Consent as a Defence in the Criminal Law' (2009) 12 *New Crim. L. Rev.* 93.

194 The exception being the *obiter* statements in *R. v. Gnango* [2012] 1 A.C. 827 *per* Lords Phillips and Judge, C.J.

195 'Note, the life and members of every subject are under the safeguard and protection of the king to the end that they may serve the king and their countrie, when occasion shall be offered . . . Nay, the lord of the villiene, for the cause aforesaid, cannot mayhem the villiene, but the king shall punish him for mayheming of his subject (for that hereby he hath disabled him to do the king service) by fine, ransome, and imprisonment, until the fine and ransome be paid.' Sir Edward Coke, *The first part of the Institutes of the laws of England* (London: Printed for the Society of Stationers, Anno Domini, 1670.) at 127a; 288a. 'Mayhem signifies a corporal hurt, by which a man loseth the use of any member that is or might be any defence unto him in time of battle.' Jacob Giles, *The Complete Court-keeper, Or, Land-steward's Assistant* (London: His Majesty's Law-Printers, 1764) at 65. See also *R. v. Russell* (1832) 1 Mood. C.C. 356 at 367, where it was said: 'That case is mentioned in Co. Lit. 127b, *Wright's case*: he was indicted for maiming himself for the purpose of begging, and punished. It is there put as the principle, that the life and members of every subject of the king are under the safeguard and protection of the king, and may be called in for the service of the state.'

196 [1994] 1 A.C. 212. See also *State v. Ashley* (1997) 701 So. 2d 338; *Gaines v. Wolcott* (1969) 119 Ga.App. 313.

197 (1961) 120 SE2d 580.

to amputate Bryson's fingers, but accepted payment to inject his fingers with procaine so that he would not feel pain when the attempt was made to cut off his fingers. Bass also gave Bryson a rubber tourniquet to stop the likely bleeding, and showed him how to apply and use it. Thereafter, a third party, Tryson, at Bryson's request, used an electric saw to cut off four fingers. Moore, J. took the view that Bass was criminally liable as an accessory to the maiming because he assisted the perpetrator and instigator of the maiming. It also was held that consent provided no defence, because of the level of harm inflicted. Moore, J. was not only concerned about the ulterior attempted fraud that Bass knowingly facilitated, but also about the harm posed to society where a person disables him or herself. Moore, J. said:[198]

> Our government is deeply concerned, financially and otherwise, for the health of its citizens and that they not become a public charge. Likewise our Commonwealth needs the services of its citizens quite as much as the kings of England needed the services of theirs.[199]

It was once a crime to commit suicide or self-maim oneself, but that is no longer the law. The *Offences against the Person Act 1861* replaced the old offence of maiming and did not replace it with any offence that criminalises self-harm. Self-harm requires a medical response, not a criminal law response. In cases where the self-harm is perpetrated to facilitate some ulterior crime such as insurance fraud, the appropriate criminal law response is to convict the self-harmer of the ulterior crime alone. What's more, a person should not be liable as an accessory for allowing another to harm her. In *State v. Carey*[200] it was said:

> *Ordinarily, a man may injure his own body by his own hand or the hand of an agent, without himself violating the criminal law.* And the person who injures his body with such assent may commit a crime of which the injured party is not guilty . . . This distinction between a man's injuring his own body himself, or through assent to such injury from another, and the crime that may be committed by another in inflicting such injury, has been strongly drawn in crimes akin to the one under discussion [emphasis added].

As I noted at the outset of this chapter, the exempt party rule exempts certain parties from complicity liability. In particular, it exempts (1) victims;

198 *Bass v. State* (1961) 120 SE2d 580 at 586.

199 This sort of remote harm rationale for accessorial criminalisation is not convincing. See Dennis J. Baker, 'The Moral Limits of Criminalising Remote Harms' 10 *New Crim. L. Rev.* 370. For a more detailed discussion, see Baker, *op. cit. supra*, note 15 at Chapter 3.

200 (1904) 56 A. 632 at 636.

and (2) inevitably incidental parties[201] such as a non-married party who marries a bigamist, a consenting masochist, a purchaser of drugs when the offence only criminalises distribution,[202] a prostitute who has been solicited for prostitution,[203] a blackmail victim,[204] a bribe-taker where the legislation merely covers bribe giving – and the list goes on.

C. Bilateral transactions and the presumption of no complicity

Professor Wharton asserts: 'Thus, a man who purchases liquor by the retail, from one who by selling the same makes himself liable to the statutory penalty, does not become involved in the transaction as a particeps.'[205] In *State v. Merida-Medina*,[206] it was said that the exempt party rule

> extends the same concept to situations wherein the person may not be characterised exactly as a 'victim' . . . Exclusion of the victim does not wholly meet the problems that arise. Should a woman be deemed an accomplice when an abortion is performed upon her? Should the man who has intercourse with a prostitute be viewed as an accomplice in the act of prostitution, the purchaser an accomplice in the unlawful sale, the unmarried party to a bigamous marriage an accomplice of the bigamist, the bribe-giver an accomplice of the taker?
>
> . . .
>
> No one can draft a prohibition of adultery without awareness that two parties to the conduct necessarily will be involved. It is proposed,

201 That is, those whose conduct is inevitably incident to the offence. See also the penetrating arguments given in decision of the Supreme Court of Canada in *Ex parte Barker* (1891) 30 N.B.R. 406.

202 There is a plethora of U.S. cases accepting that a person who receives drugs cannot be an accomplice of a person convicted of distributing drugs. One should be convicted of possession and the other of distribution/supply. See *Rodriguez v. State* (2003) 104 S.W. 3d 87; *Robinson v. State* (1991) 815 S.W. 2d 361 at 363–364 and the cases cited therein. See also the cases discussed in Leslie Reagan, 'Victim or Accomplice? Crime, Medical Malpractice, and the Construction of the Aborting Woman in American Case Law, 1860s–1970' (2001) 10(2) *10 Colum. J. Gender & L.* 311.

203 For the offence of soliciting prostitution, see section 51A of the *Sexual Offences Act 2003*.

204 *U.S. v. Castle* (1991) 925 F. 2d 831; *U.S. v. Spitler* (1986) 800 F. 2d 1267 at 1276; *U.S. v. Nelson* (1980) 486 F. Supp. 464 at 490.

205 Francis Wharton, *Treatise of the Criminal Law of the United States* (Philadelphia: Kay & Brother, 3rd edn 1855) at 873. See also the related Wharton Rule, which applies to conspiracies, as discussed in Baker, *op. cit. supra* 15 at para. 17–198 *et seq.*; LaFave, *op. cit. supra*, note 52 at 318 *et seq.*

206 (2008) 221 Or. App. 614 at 618–619. Parliament has enacted special assistance offences (see section 2 of the *Suicide Act 1961*; sections 2 and 3 of the *Female Genital Mutilation Act 2003*) and has purposely not made the consenting victim liable either directly or as an accessory.

> therefore, that in such cases the general section on complicity be made inapplicable, leaving to the definition of the crime itself the selective judgment that must be made. If legislators know that buyers will not be viewed as accomplices in sales unless the statute indicates that this behaviour is included in the prohibition, they will focus on the problem as they frame the definition of the crime. And since the exception is confined to behaviour 'inevitably incident to' the commission of the crime, the problem, we repeat, inescapably presents itself in defining the crime.

The exemption for victims and inevitably incidental parties should apply where the statute is silent on complicity liability. If the statute is silent on complicity liability, that should be taken as a presumption of no complicity liability. Merely pointing out that Parliament has taken the trouble to impose criminal penalties to protect a specific class of victim in certain statutes[207] is not enough to rebut the presumption of no complicity for victims and inevitably incidental parties in other cases where the statute is silent on the matter. If Parliament wants to criminalise both parties, then it should define the substantive offence to make both parties to the transaction directly liable. For example, sections 1 and 2 of the *Bribery Act 2010* make both parties to bribery directly liable by separately proscribing bribe giving and bribe receiving.[208] *Per contra*, since section 57 of the *Offences against the Person Act 1861* does not make both the married and non-married party to a bigamous marriage directly liable, it must be presumed that Parliament intended that the non-married party not be criminalised either as a bigamist or as an accomplice to bigamy.[209] This interpretation is supported by

207 Section 51 of the *Serious Crime Act 2007*.

208 *U.S. v. Blondek* (1990) 741 F Supp. 116 at 118. The rule has been accepted by English courts: see *R. v. Congdon* [1990] N.L.J.R. 1221; *R. v. Titley* (1880) 14 Cox C.C. 502. See also the decision of the Supreme Court of Canada in *Ex parte Barker* (1891) 30 N.B.R. 406 at para. 22, where King, J. said: 'In common understanding a buyer does not assist the seller in making the sale to him. To constitute a sale there must be a seller and a purchaser; but their interests are distinct and to some extent opposite, and to call one of the parties to the contract an aider or abettor of the other is to confuse things that are essentially distinct. The difficulty, as often happens, arises from too much learning. A plain man's view would be that a buyer is a buyer and a seller a seller, and nothing more, and that one is not an abettor of the other; and that, as the Legislature (with the buyer distinctly and necessarily in its mind, as he is in every conception of a sale) did not make him punishable as buyer, it could hardly have intended to punish him as being what he and most other people never knew that he was, viz., an abettor of the seller. But, in my opinion, he is nothing of the sort . . . It only confirms me in the opinion that in the common understanding of men, legislators as well as others, a buyer does not in any proper and legal sense aid, abet, counsel, or procure the seller to sell to him.' Cf. *Fairburn v. Evans* [1916] 1 K.B. 218; *Sayce v. Coupe* [1953] 1 Q.B. 1; *R. v. MacKenzie* (1911) 6 Cr. App. R. 64. See also the decision on bribery in *The Queen v. Mok Wei-Tak and Another* [1986] H.K.L.R. 1054.

209 See e.g. *Ex parte Cooper* (1912) 162 Cal. 81.

the empirical statistic that there has never been a prosecution of a non-married party to bigamy as an accomplice in England and Wales.

Lords Phillips and Judge, C.J. unhelpfully suggest in an *obiter* statement that the exempt party/victim rule is much narrower than this. Their Lordships asserted that section 51 of the *Serious Crime Act 2007*

> is cogent indication that there is no common law rule that precludes conviction of a defendant of being party to a crime of which he was the actual or intended victim. We are satisfied that there is no such rule. This is evident from the fact that, under common law, attempted suicide was a crime, as was aiding and abetting suicide.[210]

Their Lordships seem to overlook the fact that Parliament went to the trouble of decriminalising suicide because it felt that self-harm was not a justification for criminalisation.[211] Coupled with that, suicide was never criminalised simply to serve paternalistic ends.[212] It is not a crime for *B* to encourage *A* to kill *B*. The *Suicide Act 1961* targets harm to others; it tries to prevent people from relying on the consent of a suicidal person to assist her to harm herself.[213] If *A* assists *B* in harming herself, *A* is inflicting harm upon *B*, even though *B* is using *A* to essentially self-harm.

It is doubtful whether much can be read into the fact that the *Serious Crime Act 2007* did not incorporate a more general and robust *inevitably incidental conduct* rule. That it did not can be attributed to the fact that the Law Commission failed to consider the victim rule fully.

210 *R. v. Gnango* [2012] 2 W.L.R. 17 at 33G.

211 'According to the common law, a person could not rightfully take his own life. If he did so, he became guilty of murder. The law also prohibited self-maiming. Consequently, the consent of one given to another, either to kill or maim, was ineffective to prevent criminal liability on the part of the latter.' See *State v. Bass* (1961) 120 S.E.2d 580 at 584. However, suicide has been decriminalised. Coupled with this, consensual maiming was only ever intended to criminalise the ulterior harm suffered by the King in losing potentially able soldiers. The victim of maiming, wounding, assault and so on should not be criminalised as an accomplice to her own victimisation. Those who assist suicide are still criminalised, as would those who assist someone to self-harm (as the physician did in *State v. Bass* by injecting procaine into *V*'s fingers so he would not feel pain when he got his brother to cut them off with the aim of defrauding his insurer), but the receiver of the harm should not be criminalised on complicity principles. Cf. *R. v. Nbakwa* (1956) S.A. 557 (S.R.) where *D* was not an accessory because suicide was not a crime in Rhodesia. See also *Blackburn v. State* (1872) 23 Ohio St. 146; *Com. v. Bowen* (1815) 13 Mass. 356; *State v. Willis* (1961) 255 N.C. 473.

212 Richard R. Cherry, *Lectures on the Growth of Criminal Law in Ancient Communities* (London: Macmillan & Co., 1890) at 106; Blackstone, *op. cit. supra*, note 75 at 190–191; Glanville Williams, *The Sanctity of Life and the Criminal Law* (London: Faber and Faber Ltd., 1958) at 224–264. *Felo de se* has a long history: see *Harleston's Case* (1354) Cro. Eliz. 371.

213 In *R. v. Brown* [1994] 1 A.C. 212 at 235D, Lord Templeman said: 'In any event the appellants in this case did not mutilate their own bodies. They inflicted bodily harm on willing victims.'

The politicians who pass criminal laws often have little to no understanding of the laws they are dealing with. Consequently, it could hardly be said that Parliament considered the victim rule in general terms in 2007 and decided it should be abrogated at common law. Clearly this was not the case. If that were the case, then why has the Crown Prosecution Service not been prosecuting inevitably incidental parties as accomplices? The rule was not considered in general terms. Parliament blindly adopted the rule from *R. v. Tyrrell* without giving the matter any serious consideration, because the Law Commission did not research the issue properly. Notwithstanding this, the American cases show that *Tyrrell* has a much wider scope than merely excluding accomplice liability where the accomplice is in a categorised victim class. The courts in England and Wales could adopt the wider American interpretation of *Tyrrell* (an English decision) without inventing any new defence, which they are not empowered to do.[214]

D. The protective class rule

In *R. v. Gnango*, Lords Phillips and Judge C.J. also said:

> In *R. v. Brown* [1994] 1 A.C. 212 sadomasochists were held to have been rightly convicted of causing injury to others who willingly consented to the injuries that they received. There would have been no bar to conviction of the latter of having aided and abetted the infliction of those injuries upon themselves.[215]

Conceptually, masochists are in a protective class because they are in the class of people that are protected by the *Offences against the Person Act 1861*. In the headnote to *R. v. Tyrrell*,[216] it was noted that: 'At common law a person cannot be convicted of a misdemeanour committed upon himself, except the offence of maiming himself so as to render him unfit for military service. It follows that he cannot be convicted of aiding and abetting such a misdemeanour.' The masochist is not only an inevitably incidental party to her own assault, but also a victim of it. She is an incidental party to it because without a human victim there can be no assault. She is also a victim of her assault, since the offences found in sections 18, 20 and 47 of the *Offences against the Person Act 1861* exist (wholly or in part) for the protection of humans regardless of their age, gender, etc. The wording of the offences found in the *Act of 1861* make it clear that those offences do not target self-harm through the hands of another. That would be the effect of making the victim an accessory.

214 If the courts have no power to create or extend criminal offences, *R. v. Rimmington* [2006] 1 A.C. 459, then they also have no power to create or extend defences.

215 [2012] 2 W.L.R. 17 at 33G.

216 [1894] 1 Q.B. 710.

There is nothing in the *Serious Crime Act 2007 Act* or in *R. v. Tyrrell* to suggest that sections 18, 20 and 47 of the *Offences against the Person Act 1861* apply only to certain classes of people (children, women, etc.). Rather, the victim rule covers those within the protective class whom the particular legislation aims to protect. In the case of physical assault, the class is any human being whether child or adult, whether female or male. There is nothing in the *Offences against the Person Act 1861* that singles a minor out for special protection. Thus, if a 15-year-old encourages and consents[217] to an adult physically assaulting her in a non-sexual way, the victim rule will apply because she falls within the general class of people protected by sections 18, 20 and 47 of the *Offences against the Person Act 1861* (i.e. she is a human being). Thus, if the victim rule does not exempt adult masochists from accomplice liability for non-sexual assaults involving actual bodily harm and greater harm, it cannot exempt a 15-year-old masochist either (masochist for present purposes refers to children under the age of 16 who consent to non-sexual harm),[218] because the *Offences against the Person Act* offences do not aim to give children any greater protection than it aims to give adults.

E. Criminalising victims

Criminalising consenting harm-receiving masochists[219] would contravene the general right not to be unfairly criminalised, since 'victimisation' does not provide a legitimate justification for criminalisation.[220] This probably explains why the masochists in *R. v. Brown* were not prosecuted as accessories to their own victimisation. What cannot be ignored is that the strong policy has always been not to criminalise as accessories those who encourage others to harm. This explains why it is impossible to find a single case in the law reports where a person has been convicted of encouraging her own victimisation. Even *R. v. Gnango* rests on an innocent third party being victimised.

A further absurdity would arise if we were to try to exclude the exemption for incidental parties who are not victims as such. For example, if a person is directly liable for an offence under section 2 of the *Bribery Act*

217 On when minors can consent to harm that is less than actual bodily harm, and is of a non-sexual nature, see Dennis J. Baker, 'Should Unnecessary Harmful Nontherapeutic Cosmetic Surgery Be Criminalized' (2014) 17 *New Crim. L. Rev.* 587.

218 Such as the harm involved in receiving a tattoo. See section 1 of the *Tattooing of Minors Act 1969*, applied in *Harvie v. Stewart* (2010) G.W.D. 27–533. Oddly, a child under the age of 16 can consent to an abortion, but not to having a tattoo. See *Gillick v. West Norfolk and Wisbech AHA* [1986] A.C. 112. See also *Reed v. State* (1999) 991 S.W.2d 354.

219 It would not exclude direct liability for a sadomasochist, because the latter is both a victim and a harm-doer. However, the latter would be criminalised directly for committing assault, rather than as an accomplice when assault is reciprocated against her.

220 See Baker, *op. cit. supra*, note 15 at Chapter 2.

2010, there will be no bar to also holding her derivatively liable for encouraging *D* to commit the offence under section 1 of the *Act of 2010*, as long as it can be shown that her act of requesting a bribe, or agreeing to receive or accept a financial or other advantage, constituted an act of encouragement. Similarly, those who are directly liable under section 1 of the *Bribery Act 2010* for offering a bribe to induce a person 'to perform improperly a relevant function or activity' could also be held derivatively liable for the section 2 offence where it can be shown that their act of bribery encouraged another person to commit the section 2 offence. This would be the result if the Supreme Court is right in suggesting that there is no common law rule that precludes a person from being convicted of a crime when she was an incidental party or victim of that crime.[221]

F. Non-consenting third parties and the victim rule

The victim rule was an issue in *R. v. Gnango*, because it was thought that the victim of a crime could not be held liable for encouraging another to victimise her. The following questions were posed by the Supreme Court:[222]

> (i) Does the victim rule preclude the conviction of a defendant for aiding and abetting a crime in respect of which he is the victim, even where the crime is not designed to protect a particular class of which the victim is a member? If yes, (ii) does the victim rule preclude the conviction of a defendant for aiding and abetting a crime in respect of which he was the intended victim, but where the actual victim is a third party?

A literal application of the rule would have meant that Gnango could not be liable for encouraging his own murder. As a general rule, a person cannot aid, abet, counsel or procure attempted murder against herself.[223] Nor can she aid, abet, counsel or procure an assault against herself involving actual bodily harm. However, this was a case where a third party was victimised because of the encourager's encouragement. In *R. v. Gnango* the victim rule would have

221 Their Lordships thought it would be safe enough to leave the exempt party/victim exemption to the discretion of the prosecution. They said: 'It is no doubt appropriate for prosecuting authorities to consider carefully whether there is justification for prosecuting anyone as party to a crime where he is the victim, or intended victim of that crime, but that is not to say that the actual or intended victim of a crime should on that ground alone be absolved from criminal responsibility in relation to it.' *R. v. Gnango* [2012] 2 W.L.R. 17 at 33G.

222 *R. v. Gnango* [2012] 2 W.L.R. 17 at 32C.

223 It is not a crime for *X* to kill herself; nor is it a crime for *X* to encourage *Y* to kill *X*. It is a crime for *Y* to encourage or assist *X* to kill herself. See sections 1 and 2 of *the Suicide Act 1961*.

applied if Gnango had been the only victim of what he was encouraging. For instance, if Gnango had survived being shot in the leg by BM, he would not have been liable for counselling or procuring an attempted murder against himself. Nor would he have been liable for counselling or procuring his own wounding. Gnango was liable because an innocent third party was killed as a result of his encouragement.

Once the transferred malice rule comes into play, the exempt party/victim rule goes out the door. A person cannot consent on behalf of a non-consenting victim in a transferred intention situation. It was not a case of Gnango merely consenting to the risk of being killed, but a case of him encouraging BM to risk the lives of passers-by. Thus, where a person consents to being harmed in a situation where he foresees that others may be harmed by the conduct that he is encouraging, then the victim rule is excluded to the extent that a non-consenting third party is harmed. Coupled with this, it is clear that Gnango was not consenting to be victimised; he was merely risking being victimised. If he had been consenting to be killed, he would have stood still so that BM would have been able to succeed.

Since Gnango was not victimised, he was not covered by the victim rule. The actual victim was a non-consenting passer-by. When a person engages in conduct that risks the health and safety of others, she cannot say: 'Because *I* consented to the risk of being a victim, they did too.' It does not matter that he only obliquely intended to encourage BM to kill him, because he also took an extreme risk with the lives of the passers-by. The victim rule does not apply in cases where the victim is not the encourager of the harm (is not the consenter), but an innocent third party. The putative victim cannot transfer the actual victim's victimisation to herself for the purposes of invoking the victim rule as a defence against complicity liability. It is arguable that the victim rule applies only to an actual victim and only when she is the only victim of what she has encouraged and consented to have done to her.

Keane v. Police[224] provides a good example of the kinds of policy arguments that might be raised to exclude the victim rule where the victim falls within a protective class. In that case, the appellant was charged with and found guilty of aiding, abetting, counselling or procuring a breach of a domestic violence restraining order. The perpetrator, Smith, was the appellant's former domestic partner. Smith had been made the subject of a restraining order pursuant to section 4 of the *Domestic Violence Act 1994* (S.A.). During the currency of the restraining order, the appellant telephoned Smith, asking him to take care of their two infant children. Smith agreed. Smith went to the appellant's home and she let him in. The appellant knew full well that Smith's presence was in breach of the restraining order that had been taken out against him. When Smith's suggestion that he and his estranged

224 (1997) 69 S.A.S.R. 481.

partner should reconcile their relationship was rejected he became violent. The police were called to remove him. Thereafter, Smith was convicted of an offence for breaching the restraining order. The appellant was charged with counselling and procuring the breach. The appellant contended that she could not be liable for counselling and procuring, because the restraining order was designed specifically to protect her. The court did not accept this argument, because 'the appellant's actions, in addition to *causing distress to the children*, resulted in the police having to come to the house to remove the offender'.[225]

Generally, people should be criminalised only for harming others,[226] not for harming themselves. The justification for not applying the victim rule when third parties are not harmed is that paternalism is not a good reason for punishing people.[227] If a person harms herself by consenting to be harmed by another and she is the only person harmed, then it would be unfair and senseless to harm her further by subjecting her to the criminal justice system and penal punishment. It is not a case of a person being less culpable when she perpetrates a self-harm such as attempting suicide or self-maiming herself, but a case of the harm being less wrong. Its wrongness is less, because it does not involve a non-consenting victim and it does not involve harm to others as opposed to harm to self.[228] Hence, to be complicit in a crime against oneself is not to exhibit a fundamentally different level of culpability, because the *mens rea* is the same either way. Intention is intention. Instead, it is not as wrong, because the violation is aimed at oneself, even though that person uses another to inflict the harm. Hence, suicide is a fundamentally different act from murder, because it only involves self-harm. Similarly, *V* allowing another to kill her is fundamentally different from *V* murdering another non-consenting person, because *V* does not violate the rights of others by allowing another person

225 *Keane v. Police* (1997) 69 S.A.S.R. 481 at 484. See also the cases discussed in Marya K. Lucas, 'An Invitation to Liability? Attempts at Holding Victims of Domestic Violence Liable as Accomplices When They Invite Violations of Their Own Protective Orders' (2004) 5 *Geo. J. Gender & L.* 763.

226 Dennis J. Baker, 'Constitutionalizing the Harm Principle' (2008) 27 *Crim. Just. Ethics* 3; Dennis J. Baker, 'The Impossibility of a Critically Objective Criminal Law' (2011) 56(2) *McGill L.J.* 349; Dennis J. Baker, 'The Harm Principle vs Kantian Criteria for Ensuring Fair, Principled and Just Criminalisation' (2008) 33 *Australian Journal of Legal Philosophy* 66; Joel Feinberg, *Harm to Others: The Moral Limits of the Criminal Law* (New York: Oxford University Press, 1984).

227 Dennis J. Baker, 'Collective Criminalization and the Constitutional Right to Endanger Others' (2009) 28(2) *Criminal Justice Ethics* 168; Andrew von Hirsch, 'Extending the Harm Principle: "Remote" Harms and Fair Imputation' in Andrew P. Simester and A.T.H. Smith (eds.), *Harm and Culpability* (Oxford: Clarendon Press, 1996) at 261 *et seq.*

228 For a very detailed and penetrating discussion of the moral case against paternalistic criminalization, see Joel Feinberg, *The Moral Limits of the Criminal Law: Harm to Self* (New York: Oxford University Press, 1986); John Kleinig, *Paternalism* (Manchester: Manchester University Press, 1983).

to kill her. The conceptual divide between harm to others and harm to self is important. Of course, the nature of the harm has normative implications for the nature of the moral culpability manifested. It is one thing to intend to expose a third party to the risk of being a victim of petty theft, and something very different to intend to expose an innocent third party to the risk of being murdered.

It is true that the consenting victim is harmed by another, but the criminal law aims to criminalise the harm-doer only, not the harm receiver. The harm receiver falls into the same category as a self-harmer, because from her perspective allowing another to harm her is no different than if she inflicted the harm upon herself. The consenting victim (*CV*) allowing another to cut off her finger is no more violative of the rights of others than if *CV* were to chop off her own finger. In both cases, *CV* ends up being the only person harmed. The harm-doer goes to jail for harming others, but *CV* should not be criminalised because *CV* did not violate the rights of others. *CV* did not wrong another person, nor did *CV* harm another person.

In *Keane v. Police*, Keane not only wasted police resources, but also exposed non-consenting third parties (her children) to the risk of being subjected to violence. She was not merely risking violence to herself, she was also risking violence to her children. I do not think the waste of police resources argument is strong enough on its own to exclude the victim rule, since the perpetrators have to be dealt with anyway. However, Keane *exposed her children to a risk of violence* and this provided a strong policy argument for excluding the victim rule. She was encouraging another to engage in conduct that could have resulted in harm to other non-consenting parties. It was not a pure case of consenting to harm to self. In *R. v. Gnango*, the victim exemption was not inapplicable merely because an unintended victim was killed, but because Gnango encouraged another to engage in conduct that resulted in harm to a non-consenting third party.

4 The problem of making participation inchoate

Abstract

This monograph tries to identify the limits of derivative liability and its alternatives in an attempt to build a case for reinterpreting the mental element in complicity so that it requires nothing less than intention. If the courts accept the interpretation of complicity under section 8 of the Accessories and Abettors Act 1861 *as presented in this monograph, then it is necessary to find a law that can deal with reckless participation. In this chapter, I provide a doctrinal and theoretical analysis of the new independent direct liability offences found in sections 44–46 of the* Serious Crime Act 2007 *to ascertain whether they cover reckless participation and reckless inchoate participation. I also examine the conduct element for these offences to determine whether it is apt for catching the sort of reckless encouragement that is often present in the joint enterprise (common purpose) complicity cases and conclude that it is. The main shortfall of the offences found in the* Serious Crime Act 2007 *is that they do not cover reckless participation. I conclude that section 44 covers only intentional (inchoate) participation and that section 45 covers only oblique intentional (inchoate) participation. Consequently, interpreting the mental element in complicity as requiring nothing less than intention will leave a* lacuna *in the law. It is submitted that section 45 of the* Act of 2007 *should be supplemented with a section 45A offence criminalising reckless (inchoate) participation. Section 45 is an independent offence that criminalises personal wrongdoing and as it is not a form of derivative liability, but rather personal liability, it allows for fair labelling and proportionate punishment for the independent wrong involved in encouraging and assisting another to perpetrate a crime. Therefore, a variant of the section 45 offence with recklessness as its mental element would also allow for fair labelling and proportionate punishment.*

I. Introduction

> I shall form these conclusions, first, that all endeavour, is an offence against the Common-wealth: though nothing follow thereupon.[1]

1 George Mackenzie, *The Laws and Customs of Scotland in Matters Criminal* (Edinburgh: Andrew Anderson, 2nd edn 1699) at 5–6.

> Abetting is only encouraging: it may be innocent: for it may be without effect. Aiding, indeed, cannot be innocent: but abetting may.[2]

A. Act capability and impossibility

The second statement above is partly true only, since assisting too may be innocent (i.e. not wrongful). A person may accidentally or mistakenly assist another to perpetrate a crime. For example, *R*[3] (the *remote party* – that is the party who is remotely involved in that she assists or encourages or is the party that at least *tries* to assist or encourage a putative crime) might drive *P*[4] (the *perpetrator* of the anticipated target offence) to a house believing that she is assisting *P* to collect her own property, when in fact, unbeknown to *R*, *P* is using *R* to get to the location of her next burglary (the anticipated target crime).[5] On these facts, *R*'s act of driving *P* to the house that *P* burglarises is not done with the aim of assisting *P*'s burglary. *R* believes she is assisting *P* to engage in non-criminal conduct. Thus aiding too may be innocent. Under the *Serious Crime Act 2007* both assisting and encouraging are deemed criminal conduct regardless of whether the attempt to aid or encourage is with effect.

However, the second of the two quotations above draws attention to a more fundamental point. That is the issue of *putative* causation. The new inchoate offences require the remote party's act to be an act that is *capable* of assisting or encouraging *P*. It is likely to be more difficult to establish a putative casual connexion when the remote party's *encouragement* is without effect than when her *assistance* is without effect. Proof of a putative causal connection is not difficult to establish for assistance, since an act that is factually *capable* or *putatively capable* of assisting will not be difficult to define and prove. A determination of whether or not the remote party's conduct was factually *capable* of *assisting* the perpetrator to perpetrate the target crime is not likely to be as difficult as a factual determination that attempts to determine whether the remote party's conduct was capable of *encouraging* the perpetrator to offend.

In this chapter, I shall try to provide an interpretation of the provisions that can be reconciled with the fundamental requirements of justice including fair labelling and fair criminalisation and also the right to freedom of

2 *R. v. Royce* (1767) 4 Burr. 2073 at 2081 *per* Lord Mansfield.

3 In this chapter I use '*R*' to refer to the 'remote party'. In the earlier chapters I used '*A*' for 'accessory'. I use the term remote party in this chapter, because in cases where *P* has not even attempted the anticipated target crime the remote party, *R*, is not an accessory/derivative participant. *R* cannot participate in a crime that *P* does not even attempt, because a person cannot participate in a non-existent crime. Thus, *R* will be used in this chapter in all references to the remote party, both for those remote parties who are accessories in the normal sense and for those remote parties who *try* to participate in the potential crime of another.

4 '*P*' refers to the perpetrator of the anticipated target crime, not to the assistor or encourager who perpetrates a crime of her own under the *Serious Crime Act 2007*.

5 See *People v. Molano* (1967) 253 Cal. App. 2d 841. See further Sir James Fitzjames Stephen, *A Digest of the Criminal Law* (London: Macmillan, 6th edn 1904) at 399–400.

expression. I shall also consider the defence of impossibility. The new provisions could deal with joint enterprise complicity cases where it is proved that *P* was in fact encouraged to perpetrate the anticipated collateral crime because of *R*'s participation in the underlying criminal joint enterprise, but the inchoate form of the offences found in the *Act of 2007* should not be applied to joint enterprises where no collateral crime has been perpetrated, simply because it was foreseeable that a collateral crime might be perpetrated, unless there is strong evidence that *R*'s reckless participation in the underlying joint enterprise was capable of encouraging *P* to perpetrate the anticipated target crime. The offences in the *Act of 2007* do not cover reckless participation, so unless the law is amended to cover reckless participation including reckless encouragement via participating in an underlying criminal enterprise, those who recklessly encourage the perpetration of a collateral crime by participating in an underlying criminal enterprise will not be caught.

II. History and doctrine

It is important to have a clear view of the new statutory provisions and the history that underlies them before we can analyse the core doctrinal and conceptual problems these provisions pose. At common law the offence of incitement[6] (or solicitation) was committed when a person 'counselled, procured or commanded' another to commit a crime, whether as perpetrator or as accessory, and whether or not the person incited did what she was urged to do.[7] This was an inchoate crime that covered encouragement only. If *P* had in fact been encouraged by the inciter's incitement, the inciter would of course have been an accomplice and would normally have been charged as such under section 8 of the *Accessories and Abettors Act 1861* and its predecessors; but on a charge of incitement it was no defence to show that the crime was actually committed.[8] Incitement covered acts of encouragement only, so it did not cover attempts to *assist* another to commit a crime.

The person who attempted to assist crime did not commit an offence at common law if her assistance was not used. After supplying assistance an accomplice can make quite strenuous attempts to prevent it being *used* and

6 This offence had ancient roots. See *R. v. Bacon* (1663) 1 Keb. 809, where it was said that Bacon 'was indicted for offering 100l. in a bagg to Parry to murder Sir Harbottle Grimston the Master of the Rolls'. In *R. v. Turvy* (1708) Holt K.B. 364 at 365, Holt, C.J., said: 'To persuade and solicit is a crime, but that is not the crime laid here. He is found guilty of the whole; but if he had been found guilty of the persuasion, it may be that would have helped it.' *Contra, R. v. Collingwood* (1704) 6 Mod. 288. See also *R. v. Scofield* (1784) Cald. M.C. 397. See also *R. v. Higgins* (1801) 102 E.R. 341; *R. v. Vaughn* (1769) 4 Burr. 2494.

7 *R. v. Gregory* (1865–72) L.R. 1 C.C.R. 77.

8 See section 6(3) of the *Criminal Law Act 1967*; *R. v. Curr* [1967] 2 W.L.R. 595; *R. (on the application of Saveljeys) v. Poland* [2012] E.W.H.C. 206 (Admin) at para. 18; see also *Gawen v. Hussee and Gibbes* (1537) 1 Dyer 38a.

thus might evade criminal liability, but under the *Serious Crime Act 2007* she will be liable even if she prevents her assistance from facilitating *P*'s criminal conduct. Lawmakers thought that a new inchoate offence was needed to criminalise inchoate participation by assistance. The old common law offence of incitement already criminalised attempted participation by encouragement,[9] so the lawmakers decided to reform the law to catch assistance.[10]

A. Personal liability not derivative liability

The core difference between sections 44–46 of the *Serious Crime Act 2007* and section 8 of the *Accessories and Abettors Act 1861* is that the former are offences of personal liability, whereas section 8 is merely a procedural mechanism for holding a person derivatively liable for a crime perpetrated by another person. What is criminalised under the new law? An old evidential maxim

9 See *R. v. Higgins* (1801) 2 East 5 at 22–23, where Le Blanc, J. said: 'This is a charge of an act done; namely, an actual solicitation of a servant to rob his master, and not merely a wish or desire that he should do so. A solicitation or inciting of another, by whatever means it is attempted, is an act done; and that such an act done with a criminal intent is punishable by indictment . . .'. Cf. *Eaton v. Allen* (1598) 4 Co. Rep. 16 where incitement is contradistinguished from conspiracy. (See also *R. v. Best* (1705) 2 Ld. Raym. 1167; *R. v. Johnson* (1678) 2 Show. 1; *R. v. Brown* (1899) 63 J.P. 790; *R. v. Roberts* (1855) Dears. 539.) There also were cases concerning the subornation of perjury. For some early examples see *Partridge v. Strange* (1552) 1 Plow. 77; *Prowse v. Cary* (1587) Cro. Eliz. 93. The concept of solicitation/encouragement also arose in the ecclesiastical cases concerning the spiritual offence of solicitation of chastity (for some examples, see *R. v. Peirson* (1705) 2 Ld. Raym. 1197; *Rigaut v. Gallisard* (1702) 7 Mod. 78; cf. *Hicks v. Gore* (1685) 3 Mod. 84).

10 'Parliament has enacted a considerable number of statutory offences that criminalise particular instances of inchoate assistance. However, there are no statutory inchoate offences of assisting some of the most serious crimes, including murder, robbery, blackmail or burglary . . . We agree with Professor Spencer that there is a general problem, and it needs a general solution.' Law Commissioner, *Inchoate Liability for Assisting and Encouraging Crime*, Report 300 (London: H.M.S.O., 2006) at para. 3.7. In his early work Professor John Spencer proposed that unused assistance be criminalised. J.R. Spencer, 'Trying to Help Another Person Commit a Crime' in Peter Smith, *Criminal Law: Essays in Honour of J.C. Smith* (London: Butterworths, 1987) at 148. Kadish thought about the same issue a couple of years before Spencer penned his paper. See Sanford H. Kadish, 'Complicity, Cause and Blame: A Study in the Interpretation of Doctrine' (1985) 73 *Cal. L. Rev.* 323 at 359. And prior to that, Richard Buxton argued that attempted assistance warranted a criminal response. See Richard Buxton, 'Complicity in the Criminal Code' (1969) 85 *Law Q. Rev.* 252 at 268. Some jurisdictions in the United States adopted such an approach many decades ago. See §2.06(3)(a)(ii) of the A.L.I.'s Model Penal Code. The *Kentucky Penal Code KRS* § 506.010(3) provides: 'A person is guilty of criminal attempt to commit a crime when he engages in conduct intended to aid another person to commit that crime, although the crime is not committed or attempted by the other person, provided that his conduct would establish complicity under KRS 502.020 if the crime were committed by the other person.' Similar provisions can be found in about ten other statutes in the United States. See for example, Ariz. Rev. Stat. Ann. § 13–1001(A)(3) (West 1989); N.J. Stat. Ann. § 2C:5–1(c) (West 1995) as discussed in *State v. Sunzar* (1999) 331 N.J.Super. 248 at 255; *State v. Jovanovic* (1980) 174 N.J.Super. 435.

was *voluntas reputabatur pro facto* (the will is to be taken for the deed), but a thought crime is no crime at all.[11] Under the new law there must be an *act* that could be *capable* of assisting the perpetrator to perpetrate the anticipated target crime should the perpetrator try to perpetrate it. *R*'s *act* should be such that it would establish complicity liability under section 8 of the *Accessories and Abettors Act 1861*, were *P* to perpetrate the anticipated target crime. The new offence of encouragement like the old common law offence of incitement criminalises conduct that *attempts* to move another to perpetrate a crime or does in fact move that person to perpetrate the anticipated target crime. Consequently, the offence of encouragement like the old common law offence of incitement has to be proved by some *apertum factum*.[12]

R's act might be the fact that *R* has posted a message on a social media website to encourage her followers to riot and commit criminal damage.[13] The encouragement might be proved even by omission. If *R* is a security guard in a department store, she has a contractual duty to ensure that customers do not shoplift.[14] If by chance[15] *R* sees her sister, *P*, shoplifting and fails to tell *P* to stop, or fails to report *P* and *P* continues because of

11 *Sir Harbert Crofts v. Brown* (1616) 3 Bulst. 167; *Eaton v. Allen* (1598) 4 Co. Rep. 16.

12 *R. v. Nichols* (1676) 3 Keb. 803.

13 *R. v. Blackshaw* [2012] 1 W.L.R. 1126.

14 *R. v. Pittwood* 1902) 19 T.L.R. 37. In the thoroughly shocking case of *State v. Ainsworth* (1993) 426 S.E.2d 410 at 425, a parent failed in her duty to protect her son from being sexually violated. A legal issue that arose in *State v. Ainsworth* was whether 'a mother may be found guilty of rape on a theory of aiding and abetting when her twelve-year-old child engaged in intercourse with an adult woman in her presence and the mother did not take any reasonable steps to prevent the intercourse'. In *State v. Walden* (1982) 293 S.E.2d 780 at 786 (a decision from the Supreme Court of North Carolina), Mitchell, J. said: '[W]e believe that to require a parent as a matter of law to take affirmative action to prevent harm to his or her child or be held criminally liable imposes a reasonable duty upon the parent. Further we believe this duty is and has always been inherent in the duty of parents to provide for the safety and welfare of their children, which duty has long been recognised by the common law and by statute. This is not to say that parents have the legal duty to place themselves in danger of death or great bodily harm in coming to the aid of their children. To require such, would require every parent to exhibit courage and heroism which, although commendable in the extreme, cannot realistically be expected or required of all people. But parents do have the duty to take every step reasonably possible under the circumstances of a given situation to prevent harm to their children.' Cf. *R. v. Dytham* [1979] 3 W.L.R. 467. See also *R. c. Rochon* (2011) 357 D.L.R. (4th) 391, where *D* discovered that her son had been growing marijuana on her property. The Quebec Court of Appeal (*per* Duval Hesler, C.J.Q., Dalphond, and Kasirer, JJ.A.) held that *D* had no duty to report her son to the police or to control his criminal activities on her property. Compare also *Sneddon v. Stevenson* [1967] 1 W.L.R. 1051, where it was suggested that mere presence for the purposes of entrapping the defendant was not an act of solicitation.

15 In this hypothetical there is no prearrangement/agreement (conspiracy to steal) and no positive encouragement from *R*.

R's omission, *R* encourages by omission. Similarly, let us assume *P* steals more goods than she originally intended to steal because she sees that *R* is failing to take action. On these facts it could be argued that the shoplifter is encouraged to continue stealing, not only because of the circumstantial fact that the security guard on duty happens to be her sister, but also because of her sister's intentional omission.[16]

The core offences are now found in sections 44–46 of the *Serious Crime Act 2007*. The *Act of 2007* targets acts that are 'capable' of encouraging or assisting people to commit crimes.[17] There is no normative difference between encouragement and assistance; both can be used to participate in the crime of another or to participate in the crimes of many others.[18] A person could stand on a podium and use speech to incite thousands to riot and perpetrate acts of criminal damage. Such a person could also use social media to encourage thousands to riot and to commit criminal damage, as some did during the 2011 England riots.[19] Encouragement has the potential to move thousands of people.[20] Many of the incitement offences prior to the decision in *R. v. Higgins*[21] were concerned with conduct that was likely to incite the masses to engage in public disorder offences such as treason.[22] The early incitement statutes seemed to focus on conduct that

16 See sections 65(1) and 65(2)(b) of the *Serious Crime Act 2007*, which provides: 'A reference in this Part to a person's doing an act that is capable of encouraging the commission of an offence includes . . . failing to take reasonable steps to discharge a duty.'

17 I use the label 'anticipated offence' (as used in the *Act of 2007*), because the inchoate offences are substantive offences *per se*.

18 'Attempted participation' because that is what the encourager does, if her attempt to participate has no effect.

19 *R. v. Blackshaw* [2012] 1 W.L.R. 1126, where it was held that *D*'s tweets inciting thousands to riot were in fact capable of encouraging some of those who received the tweets to riot.

20 See for example, *R. v. Badger* (1843) 4 Q.B. 468 at 469–470, where Lord Denman, C.J., observed: 'Large meetings of such persons were held, whose passions were inflamed by seditious harangues addressed to them by strangers travelling about the country under the name of chartists; there was imminent danger that the peace would be broken and anarchy become universal.' See also *R. v. Blackshaw* [2012] 1 W.L.R. 1126.

21 (1801) 2 East 5 at 9.

22 There are numerous modern statutes that target conduct that has the potential to incite collectives of people to engage in criminal conduct. See for example, sections 1 and 2 of the *Terrorism Act 2006*; sections 18–22 of the *Public Order Act 1986*; section 1 of the *Incitement to Disaffection Act 1934*; section 6 of the *Ministry of Defence Police Act 1987*; section 27 of the *Cable and Broadcasting Act 1984*; section 3 of the *Aliens Restriction (Amendment) Act 1919*. See also *R. v. Abu Hamza* [2007] Q.B. 659; *O'Connell v. R.* (1844) 11 Cl. & F. 155; *R. v. Murphy* (1837) 8 Car. & P. 297; *R. v. Carlile* (1831) 4 Car. & P. 415; and *R. v. Shipley* (1784) 21 St. Tr. 847 where *D* was charged with criminal libel for publishing material that had the potential to 'incite the subjects of our lord the King to attempt by force and violence, and with arms, to make alterations in the Government, state, and constitution of this kingdom'. (Calls for non-violent protests to bring about constitutional change would be protected by the freedom of expression right: *Lehideux v. France* (2000) 30 E.H.R.R. 665.) Section 239(1) of the *Communications Act 2003* provides: 'OFCOM must serve a notice under subsection

had the potential to incite the masses to rise up against the state. Of course there were some exceptions.

Likewise, assistance can facilitate the crimes of many. Those who set up webpages to assist people to download pirated movies assist thousands, if not millions, to illegally download movies.

> Secondary liability for copyright infringement may be imposed on a party that has not directly infringed a copyright, but has played a significant role in direct infringement committed by others, for example by providing direct infringers with a product that enables infringement . . . The rationale for secondary liability is that a party who distributes infringement-enabling products or services may facilitate direct infringement on a massive scale, making it 'impossible to enforce [copyright protection] effectively against all direct infringers.' In such circumstances, 'the only practical alternative is to go against the distributor of the copying device for secondary liability'.[23]

B. Do we need liability for attempted participation?

Is it necessary to criminalise the attempt to assist and encourage? Is it not enough to prosecute the webpage creators when someone actually uses their page to download an illegal movie? This sort of conduct could be tackled as a case of personal liability by making it a crime to operate pirate websites etc. or to sell items that can be used in fraud (i.e. section 6 of the *Fraud Act 2006* criminalises those who possess articles that can be used in fraud, and liability is personal for the personal choice to possess).

There are situations where particularly vulnerable victims need special protection from being encouraged to engage in conduct that victimises them, but these sorts of cases are best dealt with by enacting narrowly tailored incitement offences similar to those found in the *Sexual Offences Act 2003*, which aim to protect children and vulnerable adults. Also, there are narrowly tailored incitement offences that deal with particularly heinous conduct such as inciting murder.[24] In addition, there are incitement offences

(2) on the holder of a licence to provide a television licensable content service if they are satisfied – (a) that the holder of the licence has included in the service one or more programmes containing material likely to encourage or to incite the commission of crime, or to lead to disorder.' See further, Sir Matthew Hale, *The History of the Pleas of the Crown* (London: Printed by R. Nutt *et al.*, 1736) at 339; Sir Edward Hyde East, *A Treatise of the Pleas of the Crown* (London: Printed by A. Strahan, 1803) Vol. I., at 100. See also *R. v. Casement* [1917] 1 K.B. 98; *Story's Case* (1570) 3 Dyer 298; *R. v. Fuller* (1797) 1 Bos. & P. 180; *Johnson v. Wicherley* (1674) Pollex. 449; *R. v. Count de Castlemain* (1679) T. Raym. 379; *Crosby's Case* (1700) Skin. 578.

23 *Arista Records LLC v. Lime Group LLC* (2011) 784 F.Supp.2d 398 at para. 37.

24 See section 4 of the *Offences against the Person Act 1861*; *R. v. Winter* [2007] E.W.C.A. Crim. 3493.

that target those who incite individuals rather than collectives of people to commit offences against the state.[25] The advantage of the *Serious Crime Act 2007* is that it plugs any gaps that might be left by relying on *ad hoc* laws. It provides catchall provisions that cover all facilitation and incitement.

Nonetheless, the person who merely attempts to assist or encourage a single person to commit a crime poses little danger to society. It is true that a person who attempts to assist an act of terrorism poses a greater danger to society than one who attempts to assist an act of shoplifting, but that is a different conceptual point. Deterrence at this level does not require inchoate offences, rather it requires terrorism to be labelled and punished more severely than shoplifting and it requires those who consummate their assistance of terrorism to be punished more severely than if they have consummated their assistance of shoplifting. There seems no pressing case for criminalising attempted participation by assistance or encouragement.

Greater harm is risked when the assistance or encouragement is aimed at many potential offenders,[26] but the new offences make no distinction between attempted participation in a single crime and attempted participation in the crimes of many. Nonetheless, any criminal harm is contingent on the third party making the choice to offend. When the third party offends or attempts to offend,[27] complicity liability is sufficient for criminalising both her and the encourager or assister. There was no pressing case for a new layer of attempted participation liability. Generally, people should be punished for their past wrongdoing and harm-doing, not for what others *might have done* with their assistance or because of their encouragement.[28] It would be enough to criminalise encouragement that actually moves a perpetrator (or in part moves her to act) to perpetrate or attempt to perpetrate a crime, or assistance that actually assists a perpetrator to either consummate or attempt to consummate a crime. In the case of those who set up pirate movie websites, the assistance will nearly always be consummated since a user somewhere will have made use of the website. Similarly, where a person uses social media to encourage many to riot, the encouragement, if capable

25 See section 91 of the *Police Act 1996*; section 40 of the *Armed Forces Act 2006*; section 7 of the *Official Secrets Act 1920*; section 7(2) of the *Perjury Act 1911*. There are a few offences that target those who incite individuals to commit specific offences that are not against the state. See for example, section 19 of the *Misuse of Drugs Act 1971*; section 4 of the *Offences against the Person Act 1861* (inciting murder); section 52(2)(a) of the *Criminal Justice Act 1993* (encouraging insider trading); section 2(1) of the *Suicide Act 1961* (encouraging or assisting suicide).

26 Cf. *Arista Records LLC v. Lime Group LLC* (2011) 784 F.Supp.2d 398. Cf. *R. v. Most* (1881) 7 Q.B.D. 244 apropos incitement.

27 *R. v. Dunnington* [1984] Q.B. 472; *R. v. Crangle* (1987) (Northern Ireland unreported judgments); *R. v. Hapgood* (1870) L.R. 1 C.C.R. 221; *R. v. Clayton* (1843) 1 Car. & K. 128; *R. v. Williams* (1844) 1 Car. & K. 589.

28 Dennis J. Baker, 'Punishment Without a Crime: Is Preventive Detention Reconcilable with Justice?' (2009) 34 *Aust. J. L. Phil.* 120.

of encouraging, will reach someone somewhere and thus will nearly always be consummated by participation in the riot.

Even if the *acts that have the potential for assisting or encouraging great numbers of people to perpetrate crime* argument provides a good justification for this sort of inchoate liability, it was not one given as a special justification by the Government or the Law Commission.

III. The letter of the law under the *Serious Crime Act 2007*

The common law offence of incitement was abolished and three new offences were enacted. Those offences target those who:

(1) Intentionally do an act that is capable of encouraging or assisting another person's putative or actual offending intending to assist or encourage that offending (section 44).
(2) Do an act that is capable of encouraging or assisting another person's putative or actual offending *believing* that person *will* perpetrate the target crime (section 45).
(3) Do an act that is capable of encouraging or assisting another person's putative or actual offending *believing* she *will* perpetrate an anticipated target crime within a certain range of crimes (section 46).

A. Deciding which offence to charge

The Law Commission recommended that these new offences, along with five other proposed offences, replace the old law of complicity,[29] but the Government enacted only some of the Commission's proposed offences and left the old law of complicity in place. As a consequence, complicity law as provided for in the *Accessories and Abettors Act 1861* stands side-by-side with the new independent offences. The overlap is apparent. The problem with this approach is that it allows the Crown Prosecution Service to cherry-pick: if the encouraged or assisted perpetrator actually attempts or consummates the anticipated substantive crime, the prosecutor will be able to charge under the *Accessories and Abettors Act 1861*, which in effect allows the defendant to be convicted and sentenced as a perpetrator of the target crime. If the perpetrator is not encouraged or assisted by the remote party's act of assistance or encouragement, the prosecutor can go for one of the offences found in sections 44–46 of the *Serious Crime Act 2007*.[30] However, sections 44–46 can also be invoked where the assistance or encouragement is consummated.

29 See Law Commission, *Participating in Crime*, Report 305 (London: H.M.S.O., 2007).
30 Cf. Dennis J. Baker, 'Complicity, Proportionality, and the *Serious Crime Act*' (2011) 14 *New Crim. L. Rev.* 403.

B. Sentencing and labelling

Under the *Act of 2007* the assister/encourager is not labelled as a perpetrator of the anticipated target offence. For example, if a person is convicted of assisting or attempting to assist murder under the *Act of 2007*, she will not be labelled as a murderer as she would be under the section 8 of the *Act of 1861*. Instead, the crime label would be for one of the offences found in sections 44–46 of the *Act of 2007*. Therefore, she will be convicted of assisting or encouraging (or attempting to assist or encourage) contrary to section 44 of the *Serious Crime Act 2007* and so on. Similarly, under the new *Act of 2007*, the sentencing judge has the discretion not to impose a life sentence for murder, because none of the new offences carry a mandatory life sentence. The sentencing judge might give a light sentence where the remote party has provided trivial or ineffectual assistance and encouragement and where she did not intend *P* to perpetrate a murder. Likewise, the sentencing judge could impose a life sentence under the *Act of 2007*, where *R* has provided *P* with major assistance and where *R* intended *P* to use her assistance for the purpose of perpetrating murder and where *P* has in fact killed.[31] Where *P* has not killed or attempted to kill *V*, a life sentence for *R* would be disproportionate punishment.[32] *R* should not be given a life sentence merely for trying to persuade *P* to kill *V*.

However, section 58(3) of the *Serious Crime Act 2007* provides that in any case other than murder the remote party 'is liable to any penalty for which she would be liable on conviction of the anticipated or reference offence'. This provision allows for fair sentencing, but at one level seems to allow for unfair crime labelling. The provision allows for fair sentencing, because the defendant's sentence is calibrated with the gravity of the crime she attempted to participate in. However, the crime labels are somewhat asymmetrical, because sections 44–46 criminalise both inchoate participation and consummated participation and use the same label for both forms of participation.

A person who supplies a gun that is used by *P* to kill is labelled the same under sections 44–46 as a person who attempts to supply a gun that is not used to kill. Hence, under the *Serious Crime Act*, consummated participation is labelled the same as attempted participation. However, the sentencing judge does have the discretion to punish consummated participation more severely than inchoate participation as long as the sentence is calibrated with the anticipated target crime.[33] Where the anticipated target crime has

31 See section 58(1) of the *Serious Crime Act 2007*.

32 See generally, Dennis J. Baker, *The Right Not to Be Criminalized: Demarcating Criminal Law's Authority* (Farnham: Ashgate, 2011); Andrew von Hirsch, *Censure and Sanctions* (Oxford: Clarendon Press, 1996).

33 Nonetheless, some would argue that results do not matter and that attempts should be labelled and punished the same as consummated offences. For a fuller discussion, see

been perpetrated or attempted, it is likely that the prosecution will invoke section 8 of the *Accessories and Abettors Act 1861.* Where the encourager and the perpetrator agree that *P* should perpetrate the crime, the prosecution is likely to charge them with conspiracy.[34]

C. The mental element for section 44

Let us start by examining the section 44 offence. Section 44 provides:

> (1) A person commits an offence if –
>
> (a) he does an act capable of encouraging or assisting the commission of an offence; and
> (b) he intends to encourage or assist its commission.
>
> (2) But he is not to be taken to have intended to encourage or assist the commission of an offence merely because such encouragement or assistance was a foreseeable consequence of his act.

The fault element for the new offences has been set out in a convoluted set of provisions. The mental element for the section 44 offence is set out in both section 44 and in section 47. The assister/encourager is liable under section 44 if she intends to encourage and/or assist *P* to commit the anticipated target crime. Intention does not include oblique intention. It is not enough that *R* intends to assist *P* in circumstances where she foresees that it is virtually certain that *P* will use her assistance to commit the anticipated target crime. *R* is caught by section 44 if she shares the perpetrator's purpose that the 'anticipated or reference' offence be committed. *R* must intend to assist/encourage *P* to perpetrate the particular anticipated crime. This means that *R* must by her assistance and/or encouragement seek to bring about the perpetrator's offending.[35] A clear example is where *R* gives *P* a gun to assist *P* to kill *V*, because *R* hates *V* and wants to see *P* succeed in

Joel Feinberg, 'Criminal Attempts: Equal Punishment for Failed Attempts' in J. Feinberg, *Problems at the Roots of Law* (New York: Oxford University Press, 2003) at 100. Cf. Lawrence Crocker, 'Justice in Criminal Liability: Decriminalizing Harmless Attempts' (1992) 53 *Ohio St. L.J.* 1057. For an interesting account of the wrongness of attempts, see Stephen P. Garvey, 'Are Attempts Like Treason' (2011) 14 *New Crim. L. Rev.* 173.

34 In many cases the prosecution's use of the *Serious Crime Act 2007* will be for inchoate liability where *R* has *attempted to participate* in the inchoate crimes of others. See the discussion *infra.*

35 The intention requirement found in section 44 of the *Act of 2007* seems to impose a fault standard akin to that expounded by Judge Learned Hand in *United States v. Peoni*, 100 F.2d 401 at 402 (2d Cir.1938), where he said: '[I]t [is] . . . nothing whatever to do with the probability that the forbidden result would follow upon the [assister's/encourager's] conduct . . . he must in some sort associate himself with the venture, in that he participates in it as in something that he wishes to bring about, that he seek by his action to make it succeed.'

killing *V*. Since *R* provides the gun to *P* and has it as her ulterior purpose that *P* use that assistance to unlawfully[36] kill *V*, her conduct is caught by section 44. This is a straightforward case.

Section 44(2) holds that D 'is not to be taken to have intended to encourage or assist the commission of an offence merely because such encouragement or assistance was a *foreseeable consequence* of his' intentional act of assistance or encouragement. Parliament was aiming to exclude 'oblique intention' from section 44.[37] Coupled with this, section 45 is an offence of oblique intention. We can safely interpret section 44 as an offence of intention. Under section 44, it is not enough to demonstrate that the encourager or assister obliquely intended to assist or encourage *P*'s act of perpetration. A literal interpretation of the section suggests that the prosecution is required to prove beyond reasonable doubt that the assister/encourager intended to assist and/or encourage *P* to perpetrate the anticipated target crime. A person does not necessarily intend to assist or encourage a crime merely because she sees its perpetration as a virtually certain consequence of her intentional assistance/encouragement. *R* must intentionally do some act of assistance and/or encouragement with the ulterior direct intention that the assistance/encouragement be used by *P* to perpetrate the anticipated target crime.

The act of assistance or encouragement has to be the product of voluntary action. Automatism might provide a defence in rare cases. Similarly, the defence of duress might also apply in some cases. Nonetheless, it is difficult to image a case where *R* will have formed the ulterior direct intention that her assistance be used to facilitate *P*'s anticipated target crime, if her initial act of assistance or encouragement was involuntary or unintended. *R* will not be liable if she intended to assist *P* to kill in self-defence. Injustices may arise in problematic double-effect cases where there is no legal defence for the perpetrator's morally excusable/justifiable conduct, such as where *R* assists *P* to kill as a matter of necessity or under duress of circumstances.

Take the example where a group is stranded in an overloaded lifeboat in icy waters. Suppose one of the passengers, *V*, weights 150 kilograms.

36 On defences, see Dennis J. Baker, *Glanville Williams Textbook of Criminal Law* (London: Sweet & Maxwell, 4th edn 2015). See also *Gillick v. West Norfolk and Wisbech AHA* [1986] A.C. 112; Joshua Dressler, 'Reflections on *Dudley and Stephens* and Killing the Innocent: Taking a Wrong Conceptual Path' in Dennis J. Baker *et al.*, *The Sanctity of Life and the Criminal Law: The Legacy of Glanville Williams* (Cambridge: Cambridge University Press, 2013) at 126 *et seq.*

37 When the relevant Bill was introduced, the Parliamentary Under-Secretary of State for Justice said: 'The notion of intention is given a particular meaning by subsection (2) . . . I hope that it assists the Hon. Member for Hornchurch if I say that what we are trying to get at is that intention should be interpreted in a narrow way, and should exclude the concept of *virtual certainty*. It is equivalent to meaning that D's *purpose must be to assist or encourage the offence*.' (Hansard, HC Public Bill Committee, 6th Sitting, July 3, 2007, col.211.) *Pepper v. Hart* [1993] A.C. 593 means that courts should look at Parliamentary proceedings in Hansard 'for the purpose of resolving ambiguity in the construction of statutes'.

P asks *V* to get off the boat to save the lives of five children weighting 30 kilograms each. *V* refuses so *P* asks *R* for her gun so that she can force *V* off the boat. *P* uses the gun to force *V* to jump from the boat into the icy waters where she drowns to death. Since three of the children belong to *R*, *R* is psychologically compelled to assist *P*. Here *R* has assisted *P* to kill *V* in circumstances where necessity and duress of circumstances are not defences to *murder*. Necessity and duress of circumstances *could* provide *R* with a defence under section 44, because it is not murder but an independent offence.[38] However, if the prosecution were to charge *R* with murder via the procedural mechanism found in section 8 of the *Accessories and Abettors Act 1861*, she would be liable for murder.[39] Since section 8 is a mechanism for deeming that the accessory also was a perpetrator of the target crime, *R* would not be able to raise duress as a defence where the charge is murder.

D. The mental element for section 45

Let us start by examining the section 45 offence. Section 45 provides:

> A person commits an offence if –
>
> (a) he does an act capable of encouraging or assisting the commission of an offence; and
> (b) he believes –
>
> (i) that the offence will be committed; and
> (ii) that his act will encourage or assist its commission.

Section 45 covers obliquely intended (inchoate) participation. Section 45 requires the remote party to 'believe' that her encouragement or assistance

38 Cf. *Miller v. Com.* (2013) 391 S.W.3d 801 at 804 where Noble, J. said: 'But Miller was actually convicted of criminal attempt to commit that crime. This is a separate, inchoate offense created by KRS 506.010. Unlike complicity to a crime, which is simply a means to commit the other crime and results in conviction for the other crime, criminal attempt is a separate crime.' The new offences found in the *Serious Crime Act 2007* work in a similar fashion, because they are offences *per se*. See also *McMillan v. State* (2008) 181 Md.App. 298 at 328 where Hollander, J. said: 'At common law, the rationale for barring the duress defence in a prosecution for murder was that a person "ought rather to die himself than escape by the murder of an innocent" . . . This rationale disappears when the sole ground for the murder charge is that the defendant participated in an underlying felony, under duress, and the defendant's co-felons unexpectedly killed the victim, thereby elevating the charge to felony-murder. We conclude that if duress would serve as a defence to the underlying felony, it is also available as a defence to a felony-murder arising from that felony, assuming the criteria for such a defence are otherwise satisfied. Therefore, we shall proceed to consider whether, under the circumstances of this case, appellant was entitled to a jury instruction as to the defence of duress.'

39 *R. v. Howe* [1987] A.C. 417.

'will' assist or encourage the perpetrator and that the perpetrator 'will' commit the anticipated offence. This requires oblique intention. Obviously there is a point at which foresight (recklessness) becomes foresight of virtual certainty (oblique intent), but foreseeing that something will, rather than could or might happen, is to see the certainty of its happening. At least the conduct element of the offence must be obliquely intended for either section 45 or 46 of the *Act of 2007*. The wording of the provision seems to leave the courts no option but to hold that the 'believe will' test requires oblique intention, even though this will produce absurd results in practice.

It will have absurd results in practice, because reckless (inchoate) participation will not be caught by the *Serious Crime Act 2007*. This has implications for the theory presented in this book, because I have argued that the law under section 8 of the *Accessories and Abettors Act 1861* covers intentional participation only. The oblique intention offence found in section 45 of the *Serious Crime Act 2007* leaves a gap in the law, because it leaves reckless (inchoate) participation outside the reach of the criminal law. Coupled with that, it is not clear that the oblique intention offence found in section 45 will add much to the direct intention offence found in section 44, because in many cases the jury will infer direct intention from foresight of virtual certainty.

E. A practical application of sections 44 and 45

In *R. v. Fretwell*,[40] Fretwell (hereinafter *F*) was induced by *P*, who was pregnant by him, to obtain a substance for the purpose of producing an abortion, which *F* did with full knowledge of the fact that *P* would use it for that purpose. *P* took the abortifacient when *F* was not present and against his wishes. There was ample evidence for a jury to infer that *F* believed that *P* would use the abortifacient, but the evidence also showed that *F* commanded *P* not to use it and that he hoped she would not use it. The question was whether *F* assisted *P*'s self-murder (which at the time was a crime)[41] by supplying her with an abortifacient. Erle, C.J. (Martin, B.,

40 (1862) Le. & Ca. 161.

41 The crime of suicide was summed up in the Latin term *Felonia de se* or *felo de se*: 'felon of himself'. In our ancient common law an adult who committed suicide was deemed to be a felon, and the crime was punishable by forfeiture of property to the king. See *Lady Margaret Hales v. Petit* (1561) 1 Plow. 253 at 258–260; *Foxley's Case* (1600) 5 Co. Rep. 109 at 110b; *Anonymous Case* (1397) Jenk. 65. The offence was made out when the perpetrator intended to kill herself or when she did some unlawful act that resulted in her own death. *R. v. Russell* (1832) 1 Mood. 356; see also William Blackstone, *Commentaries on the Laws of England* (Oxford: Clarendon Press, 1769) Vol. IV at 189. This was in a time when the felony murder rule played a role. Cf. *R. v. Buck* (1960) 44 Cr. App. R. 213; *R. v. Creamer* [1966] 1 Q.B. 72 at 82; *R. v. Gaylor* (1857) Dears. & B. 288.

Channell, B., Blackburn, J. and Keating, J. concurring) held that, even if *P* were *felo de se*, *F* could not be convicted of murder, either as a principal or as an accessory because he had not administered the poison to *P*, nor had he caused *P* to take it. Hence, it was held in that case that nothing but ulterior direct intention was sufficient for accessorial liability. Fretwell's act of assistance was intentional: he intended to supply the abortifacient.[42] It was not his ulterior direct intention that the drug be used to procure an abortion, but it was his ulterior *oblique* intention[43] that it be used for such a purpose. On such facts, the jury could have inferred that *F* believed that *P* would use the abortifacient.

If a person is threatening suicide to get an abortifacient, then it seems that that person will use the abortifacient. Fretwell did not intend to assist *P* to perpetrate self-murder, but he must have believed *P* would perpetrate an offence contrary to section 58 of the *Offences against the Person Act 1861*.[44] If these facts arose under the *Serious Crime Act 2007*, Fretwell would be liable for the oblique intention offence found in section 45, but not for the direct intention offence found in section 44.[45]

We have seen that the law of complicity under section 8 of the *Accessories and Abettors Act 1861* has been held to no longer require direct ulterior intention as far as the anticipated target crime is concerned. As I have pointed out in earlier chapters, in recent decades judges have held that mere recklessness is sufficient.[46] Nonetheless, it is clear that section 44 of the *Serious Crime Act 2007* requires a direct ulterior intention.

42 *P* tried to obtain an abortifacient, but the pharmacist refused to sell it to her. Thereafter, she asked Fretwell to obtain it for her and told him that she would commit suicide if he did not assist her. Fretwell was under duress (compare *Louth v. Diprose* (1991) 175 C.L.R. 621; *R. v. Steane* [1947] K.B. 997). Fretwell's act of supply was voluntary, even though he did not act willingly. Fretwell's freedom was not fully unfettered. Duress is not a defence to murder (*R. v. Howe* [1987] A.C. 417), but it would provide a defence where the remote party is convicted of one of the offences found in the *Serious Crime Act 2007*.

43 I shall use the term 'ulterior oblique intention,' even though it is not the most apt term. Conceptually, such a term is problematic as oblique intention is a species of recklessness. It is a very high degree of recklessness, but it is recklessness. It is about risking a virtually certain consequence/state of affairs. Cf. the discussion in John Finnis, 'Intention and Side-Effects' in R.G. Frey and Christopher W. Morris (eds), *Liability and Responsibility: Essays in Law and Morals* (Cambridge: Cambridge University Press, 1991) at 32 *et seq.*

44 Cf. the discussion in *R. v. Buck* (1960) 44 Cr. App. R. 213 *per* Edmund Davies J.

45 If *R. v. Fretwell* were decided today, Fretwell would not be liable under section 2 of the *Suicide Act 1961*, because his act of assistance was not 'intended to encourage or assist suicide or an attempt at suicide'. Instead, Fretwell by his assistance obliquely intended to assist abortion or attempted abortion. This sort of illegal abortion risks the life of its recipient, but the aim is not to kill her. The aim is to abort the foetus.

46 In *R. v. Bryce* [2004] 2 Cr. App. R. 35, it was held that the mental element in complicity requires no more than reckless foresight.

F. What does section 47 add to the mental element in section 44?

To ascertain whether the assister/encourager is liable for assisting or encouraging a crime that has unintended consequences, or takes place in unintended circumstances, we need to examine the rules set out in sections 47(5), (6) and (7) of the *Serious Crime Act 2007*. Subsection 47(5) provides:

> In proving for the purposes of this section whether an act is one which, if done, would amount to the commission of an offence –
>
> (a) if the offence is one requiring proof of fault, it must be proved that –
>
> (i) D *believed* that, were the act to be done, it *would* be done with that fault;
> (ii) D was *reckless* as to whether or not it would be done with that fault; or
> (iii) D's state of mind was such that, were he to do it, it *would* be done with that fault; and
>
> (b) if the offence is one requiring proof of particular circumstances or consequences (or both), it must be proved that –
>
> (i) D *believed* that, were the act to be done, it *would* be done in those circumstances or with those consequences; or
> (ii) D was *reckless* as to whether or not it would be done in those circumstances or with those consequences.

Let us apply section 44 and 47 to an offence where fault as to circumstances is an issue. In English law the offence of rape is made out when it is proved beyond reasonable doubt that *D* intentionally penetrated the vagina, anus or mouth of *V* with his penis in circumstances where *V* did not consent to the penetration, and where *D* did not reasonably believe that *V* consented.[47] The perpetrator need only be negligent as to the circumstance of whether or not the woman is consenting. Let us look at the facts of a couple of cases to ascertain where a person who assists or encourages another to have (non-consensual) sexual intercourse stands under section 44. The case is straightforward where the remote party intends to assist or encourage the perpetrator to have non-consensual sexual intercourse as opposed to consensual sexual intercourse. For example, in *R. v. Baltimore*,[48] Harvey and

47 See section 1 of the *Sexual Offences Act 2003*.

48 (1768) 1 Wm. Bl. 648. In Barrow's report of the case, he reports: 'They were committed as being charged upon the oath of the said Sarah Woodcock, for being feloniously assisting aiding and abetting him in feloniously ravishing and carnally knowing her against her will and consent, against the form of the statute. But they were not charged, either by the oath or warrant of commitment, with being present: and therefore they were agreed to be only accessary before the fact.' See *R. v. Lord Baltimore* (1768) 4 Burr. 2179. Cf. *R. v. Ram* (1893) 17 Cox C.C. 609.

Griffenburg were charged with being accessories to rape. The victim had been inveigled into Lord Baltimore's house, '[w]here she was confined for five days, during which she neither ate nor drank; and upon her still refusing to comply with his lordship's will . . . two women forcibly lifted her into his bed' where he raped her.

In *R. v. Baltimore* the evidence showed that the accessories intended to assist Baltimore to have non-consensual sexual intercourse. The accessories knew that the young woman had refused to have sexual intercourse with Baltimore for five days when they physically forced her into his bed. Similarly, there are numerous cases where gang members have taken it in turns to rape a woman, each helping the others by taking turns in holding her down.[49] If *R* rapes *V* and thereafter holds her down so that his fellow gang member, *P*, can also have sexual intercourse with her, a jury would have no difficulty inferring that *R* knew for a fact that *V* was not consenting and thus intended to assist *P* to rape her.

To *intend* to assist or encourage the offence of rape, the assister/encourager has to have present knowledge of the relevant circumstance that the intercourse is non-consensual. If all the assister/encourager believed was that there was a chance that *V* might not have been consenting, then she cannot be said to have intended to assist or encourage rape. The knowledge that is required for a person to be able to intend the relevant circumstances has to be of the circumstances that are present at the time when the assister or encourager forms the intention to assist or encourage.[50] A *belief* in future circumstances is not actual knowledge

49 Where gang members jointly hold down (or abduct) a woman so that a fellow gang member can have sexual intercourse with her in circumstances where she is screaming and trying to escape, a jury could infer that they knew for a fact she was not consenting and intended to assist non-consensual intercourse. See *R. v. Dunlop* [1979] 2 S.C.R. 881, where two men held down a girl while 18 other men from their motorcycle gang raped her. For similar cases see *R. v. Salajko* [1970] 1 C.C.C. 352; *Waters v. Kassulke* (1990) 916 F.2d 329; *State v. Fortner* (1990) 387 S.E.2d 812; *Com. v. Medeiros* (2009) 899 N.E.2d 905. Similarly, if *R* drives a van while *V* is imprisoned in the back and is being raped by *R*'s fellow gang members, *R* clearly assists the gang members' acts of rape in circumstances where *R* has present knowledge of the fact that *V* is not consenting. See *State v. Adams* (2008) 958 A.2d 295, where the driver's continuing act of driving a van assisted the perpetrator's continuing act of non-consensual intercourse in the back of the moving van. See also *State v. Eker* (1985) 697 P.2d 273.

50 The Law Lords in a conspiracy case (*R. v. Saik* [2007] 1 A.C. 18) termed 'actual knowledge' as 'true knowledge' – but both terms simply mean knowledge of the present facts. Cf. *Cook v. Stockwell* (1915) 79 J.P. 394, where there was sufficient evidence for a jury to infer that *D* had knowledge of the fact that he was assisting *Ps* to perpetrate an offence. Cf. *Cafferata v. Wilson* [1936] 3 All E.R. 149, which, on the facts, seemed more borderline. There is no such thing as reckless knowledge. Knowing there is a risk that circumstance *X* might exist when *P* does act *Y* is not the same as knowing circumstance *X* presently exists. A person either knows the facts or she does not. Recklessness refers to a belief that the facts might be *X*, *Y*, *Z* and so on, not to present knowledge of those facts. *D* risks assisting *P* to perpetrate

of those circumstances – because no one can know the future. A person can intend future facts or intend to operate in certain circumstances *in futuro*, but she does not know for a fact that those future circumstances will exist. She desires that they will exist, but that is different from knowing that they will exist.

The only substitute for knowledge of the present facts is intention. If *R* intends to assist/encourage *P* to have sexual intercourse with *V* and intends that the sexual intercourse take place in circumstances where *V* is not consenting, then it does not matter that she does not know for sure whether *V* will be consenting or not. In this situation, *R*'s fault rests on what she intends the circumstances to be. Hence, if *R* intends to assist *P* to rape *V*, *R* will be liable even if at the time when the sexual intercourse takes place, *V*, by pure chance, consents. *R*'s mistaken belief about what the future circumstances would be does not negative her intention to assist the rape. *R* intended to assist/encourage a rape and her fault for the inchoate offence found in section 44 is set in stone from the time when she formed the intention to assist/encourage the rape and did an act capable of assisting or encouraging it.

R tried to assist *P* to rape *V*, even though it was impossible for *P* to succeed, because unbeknown to *P* and *R*, *V* was willing to consent to the sexual intercourse and did in fact consent to it when it took place. On these facts, it is no defence for the assister/encourager to argue that her knowledge of the circumstantial facts was incorrect; that is, for her to argue that she wrongly believed that *V* would not consent. It is true that the assister/encourager was only guessing that *V* would not consent, but in the hypothetical she *intended* to assist or encourage non-consensual intercourse.

The sort of direct intention requirement that is found in section 44 is satisfied when the offender assists or encourages a rape (or other offence where fault as to circumstances or consequences is relevant) intending the relevant circumstances to exist.[51] Alternatively, the direct intention requirement would be satisfied where the relevant circumstances already exist and *R* has full (present) knowledge of those circumstances. The jury can infer

an offence when she believes that *P*'s act might take place in circumstances that make it criminal, but this does not mean that *D* intends *P*'s act to take place in circumstances that make it criminal. In some cases, *D*'s recklessness will be so extreme that the jury might infer that *D* was not merely reckless, but in fact had present knowledge of the relevant circumstances or alternatively intended those circumstances to exist. It is worth bearing in mind that in *Johnson v. Youden* [1950] 1 K.B. 544 at 546, Lord Goddard C.J. said: 'Before a person can be convicted of aiding and abetting the commission of an offence he must at least know the essential matters which constitute that offence. He need not actually know that an offence has been committed because he may not know that the facts constitute an offence and ignorance of the law is no defence'.

51 This is encapsulated in the 'intends or knows' test recognised by the Lords in a conspiracy case: see *R. v. Saik* [2007] 1 A.C. 18. See also section 2 of the *Conspiracy Act 1977*, which provides: 'intend or know that that fact or circumstance shall or will exist at the time when the conduct constituting the offence is to take place'.

from the evidence that *R* had present knowledge of the fact that *V* was not consenting and thus intended to assist or encourage *P* to rape.[52]

If the remote party is present and can see that the victim is protesting and is physically fighting to escape from the sexual encounter, then clearly she has full knowledge of facts that would allow her to determine there and then that the victim is not consenting. In *D.P.P. v. K*[53] the accessories had present knowledge of the fact that the victim was not consenting when they encouraged a boy to rape her. Similarly, if *R* encourages *P* to have sexual intercourse with his 12-year-old son (knowing for a fact his son is aged 12, because he was in the hospital 12 years before when his son was born), *R* could hardly claim he did not have present knowledge of the fact that his son was only 12.[54] *R*'s knowledge of the relevant circumstances would allow a jury to infer that *R* intentionally encouraged *P* to commit a sexual offence against his child.[55] In these sorts of cases it is not a question of ascertaining whether the assister or encourager intended or knew that the fact or circumstance would exist, because their assistance or encouragement is given in a situation where they have present knowledge of the existence of the relevant circumstance.

A literal interpretation of section 44 in isolation from section 47 requires the prosecution to prove that the assister or encourager directly intended to do the act that was capable of assisting and encouraging *P* and had an ulterior direct intention that her intentional act of assistance or encouragement would assist or encourage *P* to perpetrate the anticipated target crime. A person can only directly intend in this sense if she knows the present circumstantial facts or intends that the perpetrator's *conduct* (such as sexual intercourse) take place in certain circumstances (such as where the woman is not consenting). A literal interpretation

52 Cf. *Sanders v. State* (1976) 348 N.E.2d 642 at 644, where Hunter, J. said: 'the evidence contained in the record discloses more than negative acquiescence on the appellant's part. It discloses that the appellant agreed to drive the car away after the robbery and continued driving the vehicle while his accomplice was forcefully fondling the victim in the back seat. It discloses that the appellant went inside the house to check on its suitability for the rape, reported that it was o.k., and that the appellant remained in voice contact with the accomplice while the accomplice was raping the victim. These actions represent affirmative conduct from which the jury could reasonably find the appellant guilty of rape as an accessory.' See also *State v. Adrian* (1974) 522 P.2d 1091; *Suber v. State* (1933) 168 S.E. 585.

53 [1997] 1 Cr. App. R. 36.

54 See *State v. Ainsworth* (1993) 426 S.E.2d 410, where the encourager/assister (*A* assisted *P* by encouraging the child (*V*) to have sexual intercourse with *P*) had present knowledge of the fact that the child was underage and thus was not providing legal consent. The encourager was not merely negligent or reckless as to the circumstances (that is, that the sexual intercourse that he was encouraging was taking place in circumstances where *V* was underage and thus incapable of consenting), because *A* knew for a fact that the child was aged only 12. *A* had present knowledge of the relevant circumstances – *A* was not merely trying to guess what the circumstances might be in the future.

55 See the various offences in the *Sexual Offences Act 2003*.

of section 44 also would mean the same as far as consequences are concerned. Likewise, with respect to *P*'s *mens rea* for the anticipated target offence. A person cannot know the consequences of another's actions that are to take place in the future. Nonetheless, she can intend the consequences of another's actions. *R* could give *P* a gun intending not only that *P* use it to shoot *V*, but also that *V* be killed as a result of *P* firing the gun at *V*. Under section 44, *R* must at least intend to encourage or assist *P* to do the relevant act that forms the conduct element of the anticipated target crime, even though *R* need not intend the consequences of *P*'s act, nor need she intend the circumstances of *P*'s act. Furthermore, she need only be reckless as to whether *P* will have the requisite fault for the anticipated target crime.

G. Recklessness as to P's fault and consequences and circumstances of P's act

The corollary of the literal interpretation of section 44 in isolation from section 47 is that it would allow the remote party to evade liability in cases where she did not intend the relevant consequences of *P*'s act and where she did not intend *P*'s act to take place in the particular circumstances. What's more, it would exclude liability where the remote party was only reckless as to whether *P* would act with the requisite fault for the anticipated target offence. Section 47 broadens the section 44 offence so that it criminalises *R*'s recklessness as to *P*'s fault for the anticipated target crime and *R*'s recklessness as to the circumstances and consequences of *P*'s act.

Let us start by considering an example of constructive liability. A perpetrator can be held constructively liable for murder where she intends to inflict grievous bodily harm upon *V*, if the intended non-fatal harm accidentally causes *V*'s death. However, if *R* gives *P* a cricket bat intending to assist *P* to inflict grievous bodily harm upon *V* with the harm resulting in *V*'s death, *R* would not be liable under section 44 for assisting *P*'s constructive murder, because she did not intend to assist *P* to commit murder. Nonetheless, since *R* intended to assist *P* to perpetrate an offence contrary to section 20 of the *Offences against the Person Act 1861*, she would be liable for the inchoate form of the offence found in section 44. Hence, section 47 adds nothing with respect to consequences when the act that *R* intends to assist or encourage is criminal *per se*.

Section 47 seems to do more work when the remote party intends to assist or encourage *P* to do an act and is reckless as to the circumstances in which that act will be done. If *R* intends to help her friend have sexual intercourse with *V*, and is reckless as to whether she will be helping *P* have non-consensual sexual intercourse, then section 47 could be invoked to obtain a conviction under the *Serious Crime Act 2007*. Generally, when *R* is reckless as to the relevant circumstances that make *P*'s conduct criminal there will be sufficient evidence to demonstrate that she was reckless as to whether *P* would act with the requisite fault for the anticipated target crime.

It is important to note that section 47 does not convert section 44 into a crime of reckless (inchoate) participation. Section 47(2) provides: 'If it is alleged under section 44(1)(b) that a person (D) intended to encourage or assist the commission of an offence, it is sufficient to prove that he intended to encourage or assist the doing of an *act* which would amount to the commission of that offence.'[56] Section 44 means that *R* will be liable only if she *intended* to assist or encourage *P*'s *act* of sexual intercourse. If *R* is reckless as to whether she is assisting or encouraging *P* to have sexual intercourse, then section 44 is not satisfied and there is no need to consider section 47. But if it can be proved beyond reasonable doubt that *R* intended to assist and/or encourage *P* to have sexual intercourse with *V*, then the Crown need only demonstrate that *R* was reckless as to whether that intercourse would be non-consensual and was reckless as to whether *P* would have the intercourse in circumstances where a reasonable person would have realised *V* was not consenting. Hence, *R* would be liable where she *intends* to assist and/or encourage *P* to have sexual intercourse with *V* (*P*'s act) and is *reckless* as to whether *V* will consent (the circumstances of *P*'s act).

Section 47 introduces a recklessness element into the section 44 offence, but it is still an offence of direct intention. *R* must intend to assist and/or encourage *P*'s act. If *R* does not intend to assist and/or encourage *P*'s act as required by section 44, then there is no need to consider whether *R* was reckless as to the circumstances in which it took place. Suppose *P* (a 17-year-old) asks *R* for the use of her flat because *P* wants somewhere private to have a date with his new girlfriend, *V*. *R* has heard a rumour that *V* is aged 15, but she has no way of confirming *V*'s age. *R* lets *P* use her flat, but tells *P* she does not want him having sexual intercourse in her flat and that he is to use it merely to cook dinner for *V*. However, *R* suspects *V* might ignore her and have sexual intercourse in her flat, because she has heard from her 16-year-old daughter, *X* (who attends the same school as *P* and *V* and knows them both socially) that *P* and *V* are already in a sexual relationship. As it turns out, *P* and *V* have sexual intercourse in *R*'s flat and *P* is arrested because *V* turns out to be aged only 15.

R would not be liable under section 44, because she does not intend to assist *P* to have sexual intercourse with *V*. *R* only intends to assist *P* to have a dinner date with *V*. *R* recklessly assists the intercourse, because she suspected *V* might use her assistance (the use of her flat) to have sexual intercourse with *V*, but section 44 requires intentional assistance as far as *P*'s *act* is concerned. It is true that *R* is also reckless as to whether *V* is of the age of consent (an issue for section 47 as consent is a circumstance), but

56 *Serious Crime Act 2007*.

since *R* did not intend to assist *P*'s *act* of intercourse we do not get to the question of whether *R* was reckless as to the relevant circumstances of that act. Hence, while section 47 incorporates a recklessness element into the section 44 offence, it does not make that offence a crime of recklessness.

H. What does section 47 add to the mental element in section 45?

The remote party must obliquely intend to assist and/or encourage *P*'s act, even though she need not obliquely intend the consequences of that act or the circumstances of that act for either section 45 or section 46. Additionally, *R* need not obliquely intend that *P* act with the requisite fault for the anticipated target crime. *R* need only be reckless as to whether *P* will perpetrate the anticipated target crime with the requisite fault for that crime. Under section 45 the defendant need not intend to assist and/or encourage the perpetrator's offending.

Section 47(5)(b)(ii) does not dilute the fault element found in section 45 as far as *P*'s 'act' is concerned, but it does with respect to whether *P* will act with the requisite fault for the anticipated target offence. Likewise, it is enough to show that *R* was reckless as to whether *P*'s act would have certain consequences or would take place in circumstances that would make it a criminal act. Mere recklessness as to the unintended consequences and circumstances of *P*'s act is sufficient for making *R* liable where *R* oblique intentionally participated in *P*'s act. Let us start with an example of unintended circumstances. Consider the crime of rape again. A person might assist (or encourage) conduct that takes place in circumstances that make it criminal, even though she does not intend to assist or encourage the conduct in those circumstances. Sexual intercourse between unrelated adults is not criminal conduct, but it is if it takes place in circumstances where there is no consent. Consequently, if *R* obliquely intends to assist and/or encourage *P* to engage in the *act* of sexual intercourse with *V* and is reckless as to whether *V* is consenting, *R* can be liable for encouraging/assisting *P* to perpetrate rape, if *V* does not consent. It need be shown only that *R* suspected that *P* would have the requisite fault and that the sexual intercourse might take place in circumstances where *V* was not consenting.

Since recklessness as to consequences and circumstances is sufficient for making a remote party criminally liable, *R*'s lack of oblique intention *vis-à-vis* circumstances and consequences will provide no defence. Nonetheless, *R* will not be liable for assisting or encouraging *P*'s act of sexual intercourse, if she did not suspect that *V* might not consent and if she did not suspect that *P* might act with the requisite fault for rape. Under the *Act of 2007*, it has to be shown that *R* at least suspected that *P* would act (or was acting) with the requisite fault for the anticipated target offence (section 47(5)(a)), and that *R* was personally reckless as to whether circumstances existed (or would exist) that made the conduct criminal or would have made it criminal (section 47(5)(b)).

It will not be enough to show that *R* was negligent in not foreseeing that *P*'s conduct would take place in particular circumstances. *R* will not be liable for assisting or encouraging *P* to engage in apparently innocuous conduct such as consensual sexual intercourse merely because a reasonable person would have foreseen that the conduct might take place in circumstances that would make it criminal conduct.[57] Suppose *P* and *V* attend *R*'s pharmacy to purchase prophylactics to assist them to have protected sexual intercourse; *P* is aged 30 and *V* is aged 14. *V* looks underage and a reasonable person would have suspected that she was underage and thus unable to engage in sexual relations with a 30-year-old. Suppose *R* does not suspect *V* is underage and gives it no real thought. (Where the victim of rape is over the age of 13 but under the age of 16, section 9 of the *Sexual Offences Act 2003* uses a negligence standard. The perpetrator would be liable for an offence under section 9 of the *Sexual Offences Act 2003* where he has sexual intercourse with a 14-year-old girl and 'does not reasonably believe that [*V*] is 16 or over.' *R* at least obliquely intends to assist *P* to do the act; that is, have sexual intercourse.) Since *R* is not reckless as to whether the act of intercourse will take place in circumstances where *V* is under the age of 16, she is not reckless as to the relevant circumstances. Negligence as to the relevant circumstances is sufficient for making the perpetrator liable, but the remote party will be liable only where she is subjectively reckless as to the relevant circumstances.[58]

It is important to note that section 47 does not make section 45 an offence of reckless participation. Recklessness will be sufficient for core components of the offence, but the initial assistance or encouragement

57 Compare the example of the lawful act that was used to ground a conviction under section 46 in *Sadique v. R.* [2013] E.W.C.A. Crim. 1150, where 'The case against the appellant was that his national distribution business was used to supply cutting agents like benzocaine and lignocaine to drug dealers and to distributors of cutting agents. These were misused for the purposes of criminal drug supply. Of itself possession of these chemicals was not unlawful, and they could be lawfully sold.'

58 Compare *R. v. Skaf* (2004) 60 N.S.W.L.R. 86, a case involving Australia's worst ever serial gang rapists, where *R*'s part in *P*'s rape was to entice *V* to accompany him in a car, then take her to a park, '[t]o persuade her to remain in the park until *P* and the other men, with whom he had been in constant communication by mobile phone, arrived in the park to seize her. On the Crown case, his part in the crime was complete when he left *V* in the company of *P* (and *P*'s other accomplices) and then he left the vicinity . . . There was little or no dispute as to Skaf's conduct. The critical issue was his state of knowledge and his intent in bringing *V* to the park and leaving her (at least temporarily) shortly before she was sexually assaulted. Before they could convict [under the law of N.S.W.], the jury had to be satisfied beyond reasonable doubt that Skaf's intention was to make *V* available to *P* (his brother) and that he was doing this so that his brother could have non-consensual sexual intercourse.' In that case, there was ample evidence for the jury to infer that Skaf's ulterior direct intention was that *P* rape *V*. Skaf was reckless as to whether or not the sexual intercourse would take place in circumstances where *V* would not be consenting and where *P* would act with the requisite fault for rape.

of *P*'s act must be obliquely intended. The remote party must obliquely intend to assist/encourage the act of sexual intercourse before she can be held liable for assisting or encouraging the crime of rape. If *R* lets 17-year-old *P* use her flat for a dinner date believing *P* might use it to have sexual intercourse with 15-year-old *V*, she is not liable under section 45. For section 45 to apply *R* would have to believe that *P* will use her flat to have sexual intercourse with *V*. If it is proved that *R* believed that *P* would use the flat for that purpose, then the issue of *R*'s recklessness as to the circumstances of that act of intercourse can be addressed under section 47. The same rule applies with respect to whether *R* suspects *P* will act with the requisite fault for the anticipated target offence.

Similarly, the same rule applies with respect to consequences. Suppose *R* gives *P* a croquet mallet believing *P might* use it to inflict grievous bodily harm upon *V*. *P* uses it to beat *V* to a pulp and as a result *P* accidentally kills *V*. In this scenario, *R* is not liable for either the section 44 or 45 offence, because she does not intend or obliquely intend to assist the aggravated assault. If *R* had believed that *P* would use the mallet to inflict GBH upon *V*, then section 45 would apply. Section 47 might also be relevant as far as the question of whether *P* would act with the requisite fault for section 18 or 20 of the *Offences against the Person Act 1861* is concerned. Since *R* would be liable for assisting and encouraging aggravated assault, it seems her recklessness as to the consequences of *P*'s act would have no bearing on her liability for the section 45 offence, but it might have some influence on the sentence. The sentencing judge might give a higher sentence where it can be shown that *R* suspected that the assault might kill *V*.[59]

I. Why do consequences matter?

In the case of murder a conviction under sections 44–45 does not carry a mandatory life sentence. In extreme cases a life sentence might be justifiable, but in other cases a more lenient sentence will be appropriate. Where the remote party intended to assist/encourage an offence contrary to section 20 of the *Offences against the Person Act 1861*, rather than assist/encourage murder, a life sentence should not be invoked. If it can be proved that *R* suspected that *P*'s aggravated assault might kill *V*, then the

59 Section 57 of the *Serious Crime Act 2007* does not apply, because the offences found in section 18 and 20 of the *Offences against the Person Act 1861*, unlike manslaughter, are not lesser included offences for murder. Notwithstanding this, the inchoate nature of the offences found in sections 44 and 45 mean that once a person encourages or assists another to commit an aggravated assault, she is liable for the section 44 or 45 offence regardless of whether the assault is perpetrated and regardless of whether the assault results in *V*'s death. Liability hinges on her intention at the time when she provided her assistance/encouragement and on the fact she did an act that was capable of encouraging and assisting *P* to perpetrate an aggravated assault.

sentencing judge would have the discretion to impose a life sentence, but it is not likely that the judge would impose such a sentence.

Similarly, where *P* perpetrates unlawful dangerous act manslaughter, *R* will not be sentenced for encouraging or assisting manslaughter, unless she suspected that *P*'s unlawful dangerous act might cause *V*'s death.[60] When *R* encourages *P* to inflict minor harm upon *V*, *R* will not be sentenced on the basis that she assisted or encouraged manslaughter, if it is proved that she did not suspect *V* would be killed by *P*'s unlawful harm-doing. Where the unlawful and dangerous act that *R* has assisted or encouraged *P* to perpetrate ends up as constructive manslaughter, *R* will be liable for manslaughter as an accessory under section 8 of the *Accessories and Abettors Act 1861* regardless of whether she suspected that *P*'s unlawful act might kill *V*.[61]

Section 47 does not make the sections 44 and 45 offences of reckless participation. Therefore, reinterpreting the mental element in complicity under section 8 of the *Accessories and Abettors Act 1861* as requiring nothing less than intention would leave a *lacuna* in the law. Reckless participation ought to be criminalised under the *Serious Crime Act 2007*, not under the *Accessories and Abettors Act 1861*, because the former allows for fair labelling and proportionate punishment. The *Serious Crime Act 2007* should be amended to include a new section 45A. The new provision should read:

> A person commits an offence if –
>
> (a) he does an act capable of encouraging or assisting the commission of an offence; and
> (b) he believes –
>
> (i) that the offence *might* be committed; and
> (ii) that his act *might* encourage or assist its commission.

Such a provision would allow those who recklessly participate or recklessly attempt to participate in the crimes of others to be tried and convicted of an independent facilitation/encouragement offence and be punished for their personal wrongdoing for that offence. Such a provision would catch many of the joint enterprise cases, thereby ensuring that those who recklessly participate in collateral crimes as a result of joining some underlying joint enterprise will not be held liable as perpetrators of the collateral crimes under section 8 of the *Accessories and Abettors Act 1861*. This is particularly

60 A person 'is guilty of involuntary manslaughter when he intends an unlawful act and one likely to do harm to the person and death results which was neither foreseen nor intended. It is the accident of death resulting which makes him guilty of manslaughter as opposed to some lesser offence such as assault . . .' *R. v. Creamer* [1966] 1 Q.B. 72 at 82 *per* Lord Parker, C.J.

61 *R. v. Buck* (1960) 44 Cr. App. R. 213; *R. v. Creamer* [1966] 1 Q.B. 72; *R. v. Smith* (1847) 2 Cox C.C. 233.

important when the collateral crime is a specific intention crime such as murder, which carries a mandatory life sentence. As we will see, section 46 of the *Serious Crime Act 2007* also requires a supplementary crime of reckless participation.

IV. Recklessly encouraging and assisting several and alternative crimes

Section 46 of the *Serious Crime Act 2007* provides:

> (1) A person commits an offence if – (a) he does an act capable of encouraging or assisting the commission of one or more of a number of offences; and (b) he believes –
>
> (i) that one or more of those offences will be committed (but has no belief as to which); and (ii) that his act will encourage or assist the commission of one or more of them.
>
> (2) It is immaterial for the purposes of subsection (1)(b)(ii) whether the person has any belief as to which offence will be encouraged or assisted.
>
> (3) If a person is charged with an offence under subsection (1) – (a) the indictment must specify the offences alleged to be the 'number of offences' mentioned in paragraph (a) of that subsection; but (b) nothing in paragraph (a) requires all the offences potentially comprised in that number to be specified.

The *actus reus* for this offence is the same as for the section 44 and section 45 offence. The defendant must do some act which is capable of encouraging or assisting another to commit one or more offences within a certain range. For example, if *R* gives *P* a gun, she does an act that is capable of assisting a number of offences. *P* might use it to commit murder, or to commit robbery, or to commit rape, or to abduct a child, or to commit criminal damage etc.

Under section 46 the assister/encourager need not intend to assist or encourage the perpetrator's offending. It is enough that she believes her intentional act of encouragement or assistance will assist or encourage the perpetrator to commit one or more offences and that the perpetrator will commit one or more of the anticipated offences. Section 46 requires the defendant to *believe* not only that the perpetrator *will* commit one of the anticipated offences, but also that her assistance/encouragement will assist or encourage the perpetrator to do so. The section requires oblique intention as far as these elements are concerned.

This offence could deal with three situations. First, there are cases where the defendant believes she is assisting or encouraging the defendant to commit more than one offence. *R* might give *P* a jemmy bar so that she can burglarise houses *X*, *Y* and *Z*. If *R* believes that *P* will burglarise those houses and that the jemmy bar will assist *P* to do so, then she is liable. But if *P* uses the jemmy bar to burglarise a fourth house, *R* should not be liable, unless she believed *P* would also burglarise that house. (In this case, it seems better to charge *R* with three counts under section 45.)[62]

Second, *R* might supply the perpetrator with oxyacetylene cutting equipment, which *R* believes will be used to commit some kind of property offence, such as melting down stolen goods, or burglary and so on.[63] In this situation, *P*'s offending is not conditional on contingencies; it is a case of *P* believing that one of the crimes within a certain range will be perpetrated with her assistance. As long as it can be shown that the crime that *P* perpetrated was one within the range that *R* believed *P* would perpetrate with her assistance or encouragement, section 46 can be invoked.[64] In *Sadique v. R.*,[65] Lord Judge, C.J. summed the law up nicely:

> Before the appellant in the present case could be convicted, the jury had to be satisfied that (a) he was involved in the supply of the relevant chemicals and (b) that, if misused criminally, the chemicals were capable of misuse by others to commit offences of supplying or being concerned in the supply of, or being in possession with intent to supply class A and/or class B drugs. None of this would be criminal unless it was also proved (c) that at the time when the relevant chemicals were being supplied, the appellant believed that what he was doing would encourage or assist the commission of one or more of these drug-related offences and (d) that he also believed that this was the purpose, or one of the purposes, for which the chemicals would be used by those to whom he supplied them. If those ingredients were established, as the chemicals could be used for cutting agents for class A drugs or class B drugs, or both, it was not necessary for the Crown to prove that he had a specific belief about the particular drug-related offence which those he was encouraging or assisting would or did commit.

The scenario in *Sadique v. R.* is a situation where the section is likely to be very useful. In this sense, section 46 is designed to deal with a case like *D.P.P. of Northern Ireland v. Maxwell*,[66] where Maxwell was a member of a terrorist organisation that used firearms and bombs to carry out attacks against Roman Catholics and their property. Maxwell was told by a member of the organisation to act as an escort for another car containing a

62 See sections 49(2) and 57 of the *Serious Crime Act 2007*.
63 Cf. *R. v. Bainbridge* [1960] 1 Q.B. 129.
64 *Sadique v. R.* [2013] E.W.C.A. Crim. 1150. Cf. the *obiter* in *R. v. Sadique* [2012] 1 W.L.R. 1700.
65 [2013] E.W.C.A. Crim. 1150 at para. 34.
66 [1978] 1 W.L.R. 1350. See also *R. v. Yanover (No. 1)* (1985) 20 C.C.C. (3d) 300.

number of men. Maxwell was asked to lead them to a particular inn. After Maxwell reached the inn he drove off, but after he left one of the men he had led to the inn attempted to bomb it. Maxwell was charged and convicted of unlawfully and maliciously doing an act with intent to cause an explosion likely to endanger life, contrary to section 3(a) of the *Explosive Substances Act 1883* and possession of the bomb, contrary to section 3(b) of the *Act of 1883*. Maxwell's defence was that he did not know which crime would be committed out of the range of crimes that he believed the terrorists would commit.

What if *R* believes that the possible offences include murder, aggravated assault, abduction, robbery and so on? Under section 46, it would be necessary to demonstrate that she believed the perpetrator would commit any one of those offences. It is not necessary to demonstrate that she believed that a particular alternative was more likely than the others,[67] but it must be proved she believed any offence she is being held liable for attempting to assist or encourage would have been committed. It is not enough to show that *R* believed crime *X would* be committed and that crimes *Y* and *Z might* be committed. It has to be shown that *R* believed *X*, *Y* and *Z* would be committed; or that *R* believed *X* would be committed, or alternatively *Y* would be committed, or alternatively *Z* would be committed; or that *R* believed that *X* and *Y* or *Z* would be committed and so on. The remote party is liable only for encouraging the offences she believed would be committed. The question will always be: did the defendant believe that the perpetrator would commit the particular offence(s), which she is now being held liable for encouraging and assisting? Therefore, if *R* believes she is assisting *P* to produce both Class A and Class B drugs, it does not matter that she does not believe that *P* will produce Class A drugs instead of Class B drugs, as long as she believes *P* will produce either both or one of them. If *R* believes *P* will produce only the Class A drug, then she should be charged under section 45 rather than 46. Section 46 is available only where *R* believes that *P* will commit either offence *A* or an alternative offence. The law under the *Accessories and Abettors Act 1861* has been given a wider interpretation. Under that *Act*, the courts have held that the restriction to crimes foreseen by *R* means *kind of crime* rather than incidence of a specific crime or specific alternative crime.

Third, there are cases where *P* conditionally intends to perpetrate crimes in alternative of each other depending on the contingencies that arise one the day in question. The offence found in section 46 is well suited for dealing with the conditional intention cases. Suppose *R*'s intentional act of assistance or encouragement is intended to facilitate *P* to perpetrate

67 Section 46(1)(b)(i) of the *Serious Crime Act 2007 provides*: '(1) A person commits an offence if – (b) he believes – (i) that one or more of those offences will be committed (but has no belief as to which) . . .'

alternative offences. *P* might conditionally intend to perpetrate offences in alternative to each other depending on the contingencies that arise on the day. When *R* assists or encourages *P*, *P*'s potential crimes are *in futuro*, but *P* may have formulated in her own mind an intention to perpetrate more than one crime depending on the contingencies – or one crime instead of the other depending on the contingencies. At this stage *P* has no belief as to which crime she will perpetrate, so it does not matter that the remote party has no belief as to which crime *P* will perpetrate. *P* intends to perpetrate one of the crimes within a range of crimes depending on the contingencies, and if *R* has knowledge of *P*'s plans and has formed a belief that *P* will perpetrate robbery instead of burglary should *P* be confronted during the burglary, section 46 could be invoked. It is irrelevant that *R* had no belief as to which crime *P* would perpetrate, as long as *R* believed *P* would perpetrate burglary, or alternatively robbery should the need for robbery arise. It would have to be shown that *R* believed that *P* would perpetrate robbery instead of burglary should the contingencies make robbery necessary. Another example is where *R* gives *P* a gun believing she will use it to commit a robbery and that it will assist her to do so, but also believing that if the robbery goes wrong *P* will use it to kill.[68]

The section 46 offence, like the section 44 and section 45 offences, is governed by section 47. If the anticipated offence is one requiring proof of fault, section 47(5)(a)(i) and (ii) applies. *R* will only be liable if she believed or suspected the perpetrator had the requisite fault for the anticipated offence. If not, it will be sufficient to show that if *R* were to do the offence herself that she would have the requisite fault for the anticipated offence: section 47(5)(a)(iii). (The latter provision catches a situation where an innocent agent is used to perpetrate an offence.) Like sections 44 and 45, if the anticipated offence is one requiring proof of particular circumstances or consequences (or both), section 46 is governed by section 47(5)(b)(i) and (ii). It must be shown that *R* believed that the perpetrator would commit one of the anticipated offences, and also believed or suspected that 'it would be done in those circumstances or with those consequences'.

Again, the oblique intention requirement excludes liability for reckless participation. Given that section 46 allows for fair labelling and proportionate punishment, it should be supplemented with a new section 46A. The new provision should provide:

68 *R* need only encourage or assist acts, which would amount to offences. Section 47(4) of the *Serious Crime Act 2007* provides: 'If it is alleged under section 46(1)(b) that a person (D) believed that one or more of a number of offences would be committed and that his act would encourage or assist the commission of one or more of them, it is sufficient to prove that he believed – (a) that one or more of a number of acts would be done which would amount to the commission of one or more of those offences; and (b) that his act would encourage or assist the doing of one or more of those acts.'

(1) A person commits an offence if – (a) he does an act capable of encouraging or assisting the commission of one or more of a number of offences; and (b) he believes –

(i) that one or more of those offences *might* be committed (but has no belief as to which); and (ii) that his act *might* encourage or assist the commission of one or more of them.

(2) It is immaterial for the purposes of subsection (1)(b)(ii) whether the person has any belief as to which offence will be encouraged or assisted.

Conditional intention will be difficult to prove in practice. Therefore, an offence of reckless participation seems better suited for many of the situations targeted by section 46.

A. Sentencing

Section 58(6) of the *Serious Crime Act 2007* provides: 'If none of the reference offences is murder but one or more of them is punishable with imprisonment, he is liable – (a) to imprisonment for a term not exceeding the maximum term provided for any one of those offences (taking the longer or the longest term as the limit for the purposes of this paragraph where the terms provided differ); or (b) to a fine.'

V. Encouraging and assisting an innocent agent

This requires a discussion of the rationale for the alternative mental element found in section 47(5)(a)(iii). That subsection holds that *R* will be liable for trying to encourage or assist the criminality of *P*, if '[*R*'s] state of mind was such that, were he to do it, it would be done with that fault'. The subsection has to be read in conjunction with section 47(6) which provides: 'For the purposes of subsection (5)(a)(iii), *D* is to be assumed to be able to do the act in question.' Under the *Act of 2007* it is irrelevant that the encouraged party lacks *mens rea* or is exempt from liability for some other reason. If *R* encourages an exempt party (a child under 10)[69] to steal a watch from a store, *R* will be caught by section 47(5)(a)(iii), because she intends the store to be permanently deprived of its property. *R* encourages the child (an innocent agent) to steal knowing that the child cannot be convicted of theft because she is exempt from criminal liability. *R* uses an innocent agent to bring about the *actus reus* of the offence. *R*'s state of mind is such that, if

69 Cf. *D.P.P. v. K & B* [1997] 1 Cr. App. R. 36; *Walters v. Lunt* [1951] 2 All E.R. 645; *McGregor v. Benyon* [1957] Crim.L.R. 608. See also Sir Michael Foster, *Crown Law* (London: Printed by W. Strahan and M. Woodfall, 1776) at 113; 349.

she were to steal the watch, she would intend to permanently deprive the store of it. It is irrelevant that *R* knew that the party she was encouraging or assisting could not in law commit the offence.

Section 47(5)(a)(iii) not only catches cases involving encouraged parties who are 'exempt'[70] from criminal liability, but also 'innocent agents' in the pure sense. In *R. v. A*,[71] the defendant took his non-English-speaking wife to an abortion clinic and asked the medical team to perform an abortion on her. *R* acted as her interpreter and falsely told the medical team that his wife wanted an abortion, when he knew she did not. *R* told his wife that she was having a minor operation to cure her blood.[72] *R*'s false representations were discovered before the abortion took place. If the abortion had been performed the doctors would not have been liable as they were acting lawfully.[73] *R* was effectively using the doctors as innocent agents. The doctors were being conned into performing an (illegal) abortion, as the pregnant patient was not consenting. If *R* had performed the abortion himself, he would have committed an offence contrary to section 58 of the *Offences against the Person Act 1861*. Additionally, *R*'s state of mind was such that, were he to do the abortion himself, it would have been done with the fault required by section 58 of the *Act of 1861*.

In *R. v. Cogan*,[74] the Court of Appeal took the step of applying the doctrine of innocent agency to an act of sexual intercourse. A husband compelled his wife to have sexual intercourse with Cogan, who believed that the wife was consenting. Cogan having had his conviction of rape quashed on appeal, the question arose whether a conviction of the husband as aider and abettor could stand. The Court of Appeal held that it could, since the defendant was liable as perpetrator and the form of the conviction did not matter. The decision was rendered possible by the fact that the defendant happened to be a man. Only a man can perpetrate rape; the statute says so. Parliament has now embraced the notion of sexually violating another by using the genitals of another, and thus has taken steps to make sure that those who cause another to be sexually violated come within the ambit of

70 Some exempt parties, of course, may also be innocent agents in that they do not understand that they are being used to commit a crime. A 15-year-old girl is not likely to be an innocent agent in this sense, if she realises that her stepfather is committing a crime by trying to sleep with her. Similarly, some children under the age of 10, who are exempt from criminal liability, will understand that they are being used to commit a crime.

71 [2010] E.W.C.A. Crim. 1949. For a cornucopia of other examples where section 47(5)(a)(iii) could be invoked (were those sorts of offences made out in England and Wales) see 'Criminal Responsibility of One Co-operating in Offence Which he is Incapable of Committing Personally' 131 A.L.R. 1322.

72 The wife was a young woman who was brought from Pakistan as a part of an arranged marriage and was forced to marry a man 20 years her senior.

73 It is assumed they were acting within the terms of the *Abortion Act 1967*.

74 [1976] Q.B. 217.

the criminal law.[75] Consequently, in the context of sexual offences the new inchoate offences are likely to add little.

Take the example where bordello madam *X* uses trafficked ladies from the Third World in her London brothel. Let us assume she takes their passports, locks them up, and forces them to have non-consensual sexual intercourse with non-suspecting customers. Suppose she encourages the customers to use the ladies by advertising her services on a website. The advertisements include rates and photos of scantily clad ladies. If the customers are innocent agents (mere instruments), because they have no idea that the women they use are not consenting, they cannot be liable for rape. (Since these women are forced to have sexual intercourse with non-suspecting customers they are effectively raped by innocent agents – the customers. The pimps and people traffickers cause them to be raped by the innocent and non-suspecting customers.)[76] If the customers use the non-consenting women for sexual purposes, the bordello madam would be liable under section 4 of the *Sexual Offences Act 2003*. If the offence found in section 4 of the *Sexual Offences Act 2003* is consummated, then it is best to charge the bordello madam with that offence. Nonetheless, her advertisements could count as attempts that are capable of encouraging the innocent agents (non-suspecting customers) to have non-consensual sexual intercourse with the ladies under her control. A jury could infer that the bordello madam believed that her encouragement would lead to her customers having non-consensual sexual intercourse with (virtually) imprisoned women under her control and that '[*R*'s] state of mind was such that, were she to do it, it would be done with that fault'.

R's encouragement of an innocent agent was not incitement at common law, since incitement presupposed a guilty incitee. Suppose that *R* has been 'working on' the innocent agent, trying to get her to agree to do the act, and much remains to be done by *R* by way of preparation if the agent does agree to do it. The encouragement may not be sufficiently proximate to be an attempt. The problem at common law was that it did not constitute incitement either. It had been held that one could only commit incitement of a guilty agent, so to speak, not of an innocent one. If, for instance, a person tried to encourage another to commit the *actus reus* of a crime requiring *mens rea*, concealing from her the facts that made the act

75 See section 4 of the *Sexual Offences Act 2003*.

76 Section 53A of the *Sexual Offences Act 2003* also criminalises the innocent agent, even though he lacks any fault. It is sufficient that the innocent agent 'ought' to have known that the prostitute was being forced into prostitution by a third party. These new offences cannot be reconciled with the constitutional principles of justice including the presumption of *mens rea*. See Dennis J. Baker, 'Collective Criminalisation and the Constitutional Right to Endanger Others' (2009) 28 *Crim. Just. Ethics* 168 at 189–190.

criminal, she would not have been guilty of incitement.[77] Under the *Serious Crime Act 2007*, it need only be shown that the encouragement was capable of encouraging *P* to perpetrate the anticipated target crime.

VI. Causation, act capableness and impossibility

A. Subjectivity v. objectivity

In this section the main focus will be on acts of encouragement with a minimum discussion of acts of assistance, because acts of encouragement seem to raise more complex conceptual questions. It will be argued below that putative encouragement/assistance is established only where it is capable of making a (indirect) causal contribution to the perpetrator's *putative* crime. The Court of Appeal has held that an objective standard is used to determine when an act is capable of assisting and encouraging the perpetrator.[78] Does this mean that *R* is guilty of the section 44 offence when she attempts to assist/encourage *P*, even though *P* does not commit or attempt to perpetrate the anticipated target crime, provided *R*'s act of assistance/encouragement would establish complicity under section 8 of the *Accessories and Abettors Act 1861* were *P* to perpetrate or attempt to perpetrate the anticipated target crime? The answer is not straightforward since we need to factor in mistakes, factual impossibility, context and circumstances.

The problem is more complex when we focus on acts of encouragement. Might it not be argued that a purely objective test would be too strict, because an unjustifiable[79] or inexcusable act would not be capable of encouraging a reasonable and prudent person to perpetrate a crime? Criminal conduct is unjustified conduct and therefore a reasonable person would not be persuaded by unjustifiable reasons to perpetrate a crime. A reasonable person

77 *R. v. Curr* [1968] 2 Q.B. 944. *Contra, D.P.P. v. Armstrong* [2000] Crim. L.R. 379; *R. v. C* [2006] 1 Cr. App. R. 20. Later courts have held that the knowledge of *mens rea* of the incitee was irrelevant. Section 47(5)(iii) and 47(6) of the *Serious Crime the 2007* also make it clear that the incitee's state of mind is irrelevant.

78 *R. v. Sadique* [2012] 1 W.L.R. 1700 at 1710G where Hooper, L.J., giving the judgment for the Court of Appeal, (Supperstone, J., Sir Geoffrey Grigson, concurring) said: 'D's act must objectively be capable of encouraging or assisting the commission of one or more of a number of offences.'

79 Gardner writes: 'Any attempt to justify oneself, in any context, is an attempt to show that one did not defy the balance of reasons. More precisely, it is an attempt to show that the following three conditions were met: first, that there were reasons for one to do as one did (or think as one thought, feel as one felt, etc.); secondly, that these reasons stood undefeated by conflicting reasons; and, thirdly, that one did as one did (thought as one thought, felt as one felt, etc.) for one of these undefeated reasons. This much is built into the very idea of justification. People who have different moral beliefs may disagree, of course, about which reasons stand undefeated in which conflicts of reasons.' See John Gardner, 'The Mysterious Case of the Reasonable Person' (2001) 51 *U. Toronto L.J.* 273.

might engage in crime when she is justified by self-defence or necessity, but she would not engage in crime without a legitimate justification. (The excused agent does not act reasonably, but is excused from criminal liability because she could not help her offending. This applies to defences such as insanity.) A reasonable and prudent person is someone we would assume would not commit a crime. When a hoodlum uses Twitter to incite riots, it can be assumed that such encouragement is not capable of inciting reasonable law-abiding citizens to riot. Would a message posted on a social media website be capable of encouraging priests, police officers, law professors, lawyers, retired schoolteachers and other professionals to riot? Is it capable of encouraging hard-working blue-collar workers to riot?[80] It might be capable of encouraging like-minded hoodlums, but the jury decide as a question of fact whether that was the case and whether the message was aimed at such an audience.

The question is more complex when *R* does not make a mistake, but knowingly targets an audience that she believes is impossible to encourage or assist. Suppose *R* emails a group of police officers to ask them to riot at a given place and time. The jury might conclude that the private emails to the police officers were not capable of encouraging such strong-willed and duty-bound citizens to join a criminal riot. The test is not whether the particular type of person who receives the encouragement could be encouraged. Rather the test works on objective generalities. The evaluative assessment of *R*'s *conduct* does not involve the jury hypothetically looking into the mind of the potential perpetrator(s) to determine whether as a question of fact they could have been encouraged by *R*'s act of encouragement. It is enough for the jury to infer from all the evidence that the act was capable of encouraging someone within the potential target audience.

In *People v. Duffy*,[81] *R* gave *P*[82] a loaded gun and taunted *P* to kill himself. A reasonable person would not be persuaded to kill herself merely because someone gives her a gun and tells her to kill herself. However, in *People v. Duffy*, *P*'s circumstances were that he 'had been drinking heavily and was in an extremely depressed and suicidal state'. It was in these circumstances that *R* taunted *P* to 'put the gun in his mouth and blow his head off'. *R* also gave *P* a rifle and ammunition knowing full well that *P* was intoxicated, depressed and suicidal. A jury would have no difficulty inferring that *R*'s acts were capable of encouraging a person in *P*'s circumstances to commit

80 It would depend on the context. See *R. v. Badger* (1843) 4 Q.B. 468 at 469–470.

81 (1992) 79 N.Y.2d 611. See also *State v. Lassiter* (1984) 484 A.2d 13, where *V* threatened to jump out of a window after being beaten badly by *D*. *D*'s response to *V*'s threat was: 'go ahead and jump'. *V* did, and *D*'s conviction for murder was upheld. See further *Persampieri v. Commonwealth* (1961) 175 NE2d 387. Cf. *Vaux's Case* (1592) 4 Co. Rep. 44a; *Yania v. Bigan* (1959) 397 Pa. 316, the latter being a civil case.

82 Suicide is not an offence, so technically it is better to think of the victim as the doer, rather than as a criminal perpetrator.

suicide. *R*'s act was not the only reason why *P* committed suicide, but it was enough to tip *P* over the edge. *R*'s act was capable of providing *P* with a more than negligible reason for acting as he did. Suicide itself is not a crime, but section 2 of the *Suicide Act 1961* provides: '(1) A person ('D') commits an offence if – (a) D does an act capable of encouraging or assisting the suicide or attempted suicide of another person, and (b) D's act was intended to encourage or assist suicide or an attempt at suicide.' Notably, section 2 of the *Act of 1961* requires nothing less than direct intention. The difficulty in this sort of case will be in establishing *mens rea* for the sections 44–45 offences, not in establishing the conduct element.

R's knowledge of the relevant circumstances is important for determining whether she intended or obliquely intended to encourage *P*. *P*'s circumstances would also provide evidence with respect to whether *R*'s act was capable of encouraging *P*. Circumstances and context are relevant factual matters for determining the evaluative question about whether the encouragement or assistance was objectively capable of encouraging or assisting in the particular situation. Clearly, if *R* is on Twitter encouraging riots while continuing mass riots are in progress, that is an evidential matter that is relevant, not only for determining *mens rea*, but also for determining whether the act was objectively capable of encouraging riots. If *R* is encouraging a suicidal person to commit suicide, then the fact that *P* was suicidal is an evidential matter that is relevant to the particular case. The jury has to consider all the evidence in a given case, but this does not collapse the objective standard into a subjective standard. Where *R* believes that her encouragement or assistance will not be taken up by the putative perpetrator, then she will lack *mens rea* for the section 45 offence, *a fortiori* for the section 44 offence.

B. Factual mistakes and the putative factual nexus

R might give *P* a gun and also offer *P* £500,000 to kill *V*. It turns out that *P* is an undercover police officer and therefore it is impossible for *P* to be persuaded on this occasion. The test for impossibility for attempt liability is that *D* is liable if her attempt would have succeeded had the facts been as she had believed.[83] If *D* tries to rape *V* believing *V* is alive, but *V* is in fact dead, then *D* is liable for attempted rape because if the facts had been as he

83 Cf. *R. v. Fitzmaurice* [1983] 2 W.L.R. 227; *D.P.P. v. Armstrong* [2000] Crim. L.R. 379; *R. v. Jones* [2008] Q.B. 460. See also *People v. Breton* (1992) 603 N.E.2d 1290; *People v. Pagliuca* (1983) 119 Ill. App. 3d 906. Cf. *R. v. McDonough* (1963) 47 Cr. App. R. 37. *P* is not liable where enforcement officers encourage her to perpetrate a crime that she would not have perpetrated but for their encouragement, but they may set a bait and may allow *P* to attempt to encourage them to commit a crime in order to obtain a conviction. Hence, law enforcement officers can take a passive role to obtain a conviction, but they cannot actively persuade a person to commit a crime. See *R. v. Looseley* [2001] 1 W.L.R. 2060; *Teixeira de Castro v. Portugal* (1999) 28 E.H.R.R. 101.

believed it would have been possible for her to perpetrate rape.[84] Similarly, if *D* tries to kill *V* by shooting her at point-blank range in the head, but fails because *V* is already dead, *D* will be liable for attempted murder because if the facts had been as *D* believed it would have been possible for *D* to kill *V* with her chosen methods.[85] The new offences found in sections 44–46 of the *Serious Crime Act 2007* criminalise both inchoate participation and consummated participation. Consequently, the issues of impossibility and mistake of fact raise issues for attempted participation under the *act capable of assisting or encouraging requirement.*

We are told that the *acts* of assistance/encouragement have to be capable of assisting or encouraging, but the new *Act* does not include a provision on impossibility. Suppose *R* gives *P* a gun and offers *P* £500,000 to kill *V*. *R* believes *P* is a professional assassin. Unbeknown to *R*, *P* is an undercover police officer who will not try to kill *V*, because *P* is undercover to protect *V*. These facts do not involve a situation where there is *inherent* factually impossibility,[86] rather the situation is a straightforward case of factual impossibility *simpliciter*. *R*'s act would have been capable of encouraging *P* had the facts been as *R* believed (i.e. had *P* been a professional assassin).

Suppose *R* gives a putative perpetrator *Pp* a gun knowing full well that *Pp* is a pacifist who will never kill. Following a subjective test, provision of a gun is only capable of assisting a murder if the person to whom it is given will use it to kill. If it is given to a pacifist then this is not an act capable of assisting murder. This is clearly not the law under the *Serious Crime Act 2007*. Supplying a gun is an act that is objectively capable of assisting the person supplied to perpetrate a murder. However, if *R* believes that *P* will not use that gun for that purpose, she lacks *mens rea* for the offences found in sections 44–46 of the *Act of 2007*. If she mistakenly believes that *Pp* is a professional assassin, then she will be liable since *P*'s mistake of fact does not negate *R*'s *mens rea*, nor does it change the nature of her physical act of assistance.

The word 'capable' means that it must be proved beyond reasonable doubt that *R*'s act of encouragement was capable of (*causing/moving*) encouraging *P* to perpetrate the anticipated target crime. In the case of inchoate participation it is a matter of establishing that the act was putatively capable of assisting the perpetrator. It is not too difficult to assess when the remote party's unused *assistance* could have factually assisted the perpetrator. For example, if the remote party, *R*, supplies the perpetrator,

84 Compare section 2A(2) of the *Suicide Act 1961* which provides: 'Where the facts are such that an act is not capable of encouraging or assisting suicide or attempted suicide, for the purposes of this *Act* it is to be treated as so capable if the act would have been so capable had the facts been as *D* believed them to be at the time of the act or had subsequent events happened in the manner *D* believed they would happen (or both).'

85 *State v. Santiago* (2012) 305 Conn. 101.

86 Inherent factual impossibility is discussed *infra.*

P, with a high-powered gun intending to assist *P* to commit murder in circumstances where *P* changes her mind and decides not to even attempt to perpetrate the murder, it would not be too controversial for a jury to infer that as a matter of fact *R*'s act of equipping *P* with a gun was objectively capable of assisting *P*'s putative murder.

Attempted assistance makes no causal contribution to the anticipated target crime, because the end crime, if perpetrated, is not perpetrated with assistance that is never supplied. Attempted assistance is no assistance at all. Likewise, if *P* does not even attempt to perpetrate the anticipated target crime, the remote party cannot be said to have made an indirect causal contribution to a crime that never takes place. Suppose *R* leaves a ladder in front of *V*'s house intending to assist *P* to burglarise *V*'s house. Suppose also that *P* decides not to go ahead with the burglary. *R* does not make an indirect causal contribution to the burglary, because it never takes place. *R* may have caused a ladder to be in a certain location, but it is not a crime *per se* to leave a ladder near another's house. Nonetheless, *R*'s act of leaving the ladder in front of the house is an act capable of assisting the putative burglary and she will be liable on the basis that it would have made a causal contribution had *P* used it to perpetrate or attempt[87] to perpetrate the burglary. Inchoate liability criminalises potential harm.

Compare this with the case of complicity under section 8 of the *Accessories and Abetters Act 1861* where *P* is burglarising a house with *A* assisting her by acting as a lookout. Suppose that the lookout for *P* does not need to warn *P* of someone approaching, because no one interrupts *P*'s burglary. On these facts, the accessory has provided factual assistance even though she did not need to warn *P*. The accessory not only assisted *P* by making it less risky for *P* to perpetrate the burglary, but also by encouraging her to perpetrate it. The accessory keeping lookout has the effect of encouraging *P* to perpetrate the burglary; it may not be the sole motivator for *P*'s burglary but the accessory reducing the risk of detection for *P* would provide *P* with a more than negligible motivation for perpetrating the particular burglary on the day in question. Similarly, suppose *R* supplies *P* with a gun hoping to assist *P* to kill *V*. *P* already has a knife in her possession, which equips her to kill with a single hit. When *P* goes to kill *V* she takes the gun supplied by *R* and also takes her own knife. *P* decides to use her knife to kill *V* and thus never uses the gun supplied by *R*. The inchoateness of the offences found in the *Act of 2007* means that it does not matter whether *P* uses her own knife rather than the gun supplied by *R*.[88]

The courts have to take care to identify sufficient (putative) indirect causation to satisfy the 'capable of' test. *R*'s encouragement need not be the predominant motivator for *P* perpetrating the anticipated target crime,

87 *R. v. Dunnington* [1984] Q.B. 472; *R. v. Crangle* (1987) (Northern Ireland unreported judgments); *R. v. Hapgood* (1870) L.R. 1 C.C.R. 221; *R. v. Clayton* (1843) 1 Car. & K. 128; *R. v. Williams* (1844) 1 Car. & K. 589.

88 The *Penal Code of Kentucky* has a provision that works in the same way. See KRS § 506.010(3).

but it must have the potential to be a more then negligible motivator, if the 'capable of' encouraging element is to be satisfied. When *P* has not attempted to consummate the anticipated target crime, the court might have great difficulty in deciding whether *R*'s encouragement would have been capable of providing the *particular perpetrator* with a more than negligible motivation (reason) for perpetrating the anticipated target crime.

C. Factual nexus in consummated participation v. inchoate participation

The common law offence of incitement was made out even when the encouragement was to the world at large,[89] but the encouragement had to reach the mind of the potential recipient. Glanville Williams wrote: 'Since incitement relates to incomplete criminal conduct, it is immaterial that the words had no effect on the person solicited; but they must have reached his mind. If they do not, there may be a conviction for attempt to incite.'[90] This differs from attempted participation by encouragement pursuant to the offences found in the *Serious Crime Act 2007*, because those offences require *R*'s act to be an act that is putatively capable of encouraging *P* to perpetrate the anticipated target crime.

The act need not in fact encourage *P* to offend, but it must be putatively capable of factually encouraging *P* to offend. If *P* has ignored the encouragement, then it has to be demonstrated that it could have influenced a person communally situated in contemporary Britain, in the same circumstances as *P*, to offend. This is an objective test, but the jury will have to consider all the evidence to determine whether the act was capable of encouraging *P* even though *P* ignored it.

Complicity at common law is made out only if the perpetrator is 'in fact . . . encouraged'[91] to perpetrate the anticipated target crime as a result of the accessory's encouragement. If there is no factual encouragement, then there is no factual participation. If there is no factual participation, then the secondary party's liability cannot be derivative. Derivative liability hinges on the 'derivative offender'[92] participating in the anticipated target crime. When *R*'s encouragement does not in fact encourage *P* to perpetrate the anticipated target crime, *R* only attempts to participate in the anticipated target crime. Attempted participation is not participation in fact; therefore, it cannot be used to convict a putative accomplice of the perpetrator's crime pursuant to section 8 of the *Accessories and Abettors Act 1861*.

89 *R. v. Most* (1881) 7 Q.B.D. 244; *R. v. Diamond* (1920) 84 J.P. 211; *Invicta Plastics Ltd. v. Clare* [1976] R.T.R. 251.

90 *R. v. Quail* (1866) 4 F. & F. 1076; *R. v. Krause* (1902) 66 J.P. 121.

91 *R. v. Schriek* [1997] 2 N.Z.L.R. 139 at 150; *Charnley. v. R.* [2013] N.Z.C.A. 226 at paragraph 46 *per* Arnold, J. (Simon, France and Dobson J.J. concurring). Cf. *R. v. Calhaem* [1985] Q.B. 808; *R. v. Mendez* [2011] Q.B. 876. Compare also *R. v. Welham* (1845) 1 Cox C.C. 192; R. *v. M'Inerney* (1886) 8 A.L.T. 71.

92 To use a term coined by Street, C.J. See *R. v. Johns* [1978] 1 N.S.W.L.R. 282 at 286.

D. Factual encouragement under section 8 of the Accessories and Abettors Act 1861

Under section 8 of the *Accessories and Abettors Act 1861* a person may take delight in witnessing a crime such as where she sees a rival's car being criminally damaged, but she has no duty to prevent the crime or to report it to the police.[93] Where a bystander approves of the crime she sees another perpetrating, she only becomes liable if she participates in that crime. It is not enough that she takes delight in seeing a rival's property being damaged; she has to provide intentional assistance and/or encouragement before she can be linked to that crime.[94] There is no need to demonstrate that *P* was aware of *R*'s act of *assistance*, if the assistance has in fact assisted *P* to perpetrate the anticipated target crime.[95] Where *R* has physically assisted *P*, factual participation will not be an issue; the focus will be on whether *R* acted with the requisite *mens rea*. It is necessary to establish only that *R* had the requisite fault for complicity liability when she in fact assisted *P*. The case is different when *R encourages P*, because factual encouragement cannot be present where *P* is unaware of it.[96] 'There must be an intention to encourage; and there must also be encouragement in fact.'[97] Acts of encouragement cannot be encouragement in fact, unless *P* is aware of them. A person cannot be encouraged by encouragement that never reaches her mind. Attempted encouragement is not consummated encouragement.

In *R. v. Lam*, in the Supreme Court of Victoria, Redlich, J. said:

> No causal connection is required between the act of aiding and abetting and the offence committed. The authors of Smith and Hogan

93 See Hale, *op. cit. supra*, note 22 at 439; *The Queen v. Coney* (1881–82) L.R. 8 Q.B.D. 534 at 557 *per* Hawkins, J.; *R. v. Clarkson* [1971] 1 W.L.R. 1402 at 1406 *per* Megaw, L.J.

94 *The Queen v. Coney* (1881–82) L.R. 8 Q.B.D. 534 at 557 *per* Hawkins, J.; *R. v. Clarkson* [1971] 1 W.L.R. 1402 at 1406; *R. v. Allen* [1965] 1 Q.B. 130; *R. v. Phan* (2001) 123 A. Crim. R. 30 at paragraph 69; *Randall v. The Queen* (2004) 146 A. Crim. R. 197; *Roughley v. The Queen* (1995) 78 A. Crim. R. 160 at 162 *per* Cox, J.; *State v. Walden* (1982) 306 N.C. 466 at 472, where Mitchell, J. said: 'It is necessary, in order to [be liable as an accomplice], that he should do or say something showing his consent to the felonious purpose and contributing to its execution, as an aider and abettor.' See also *Kirchner v. State* (2013) 322 Ga.App. 275; *State v. Birchfield* (1952) 235 N.C. 410; *Charnley. v. R.* [2013] N.Z.C.A. 226.

95 *State v. Tally* (1894) 102 Ala. 25 (to the extent that McClellan, J. suggests in his judgment in *State v. Tally*, that unused assistance is sufficient, his opinion is wrong. For *R* to be said to have factually participated in *P*'s crime, *P* must use *R*'s assistance. It is true that *P* need not be aware of factual assistance for *R* to factually participate, but unused assistance is no participation at all. The dissenting opinion of Head, J. in *State v. Tally* is the correct view as far as ineffectual assistance is concerned. Cf. *R. v. Fred* [2001] Q.C.A. 561, where there was no factual assistance, even though *R* knew that *P* planned to kill *V*. *R* also hoped *P* would kill *V*, but she did nothing to assist or encourage *P*. See also *Way v. State* (1908) 46 So. 273; *Commonwealth v. Kern* (1867) 1 Brewst. 350.

96 *Hall v. Com.* (1906) 29 Ky. L. Rep. 485, *per contra Bast v. Com.* (1907) 99 S.W. 978.

97 *R. v. Clarkson* [1971] 1 W.L.R. 1402 at 1407 *per* Megaw, L.J. (Geoffrey Lane and Kilner Brown, J.J. concurring).

> suggest that it is unnecessary that the principal offender be influenced in any way by the principal in the second degree. They argue that the natural meaning of the terms of aiding and abetting does not imply a causal element. If the acts of the secondary participant were ignored or if the offence would have been committed even if such acts had not been proffered, secondary participation would have been established.[98]
>
> . . .
>
> [I]t would be 'manifest nonsense' to require proof that the principal offenders were aware of the encouragement provided by each accused or that there had to be a causal connection between the acts of the secondary participant and the commission of the offence.[99]

I take the view that in the law of complicity it would be manifest nonsense not to prove factual participation beyond reasonable doubt. It would be manifest nonsense not to prove factual participation, because such an approach would conflate attempted participation with actual participation. It also would dispense with the *actus reus* requirement for derivative liability. Redlich, J.'s approach suggests that it is acceptable for the jury to infer factual participation, even when the evidence demonstrates that the remote party only attempted to participate in the perpetrator's crime. Such an approach would allow all attempted participation by encouragement to be prosecuted as complicity, when it should be dealt with as an inchoate offence.

The law of complicity deals with consummated participation, not with attempted participation. The law of complicity, unlike the *Serious Crime Act 2007*, requires factual influence[100] or assistance, even if that influence is of a minor nature.[101] The perpetrator has to be factually influenced, in part at least, by the encourager and must perpetrate or attempt to perpetrate the anticipated target crime.[102] (In cases where *P* does not even attempt

98 (2005) 159 A. Crim. R. 448 at paragraph 60 citing J. C. Smith and Brian Hogan, *Criminal Law* (London: Butterworths, 7th edn 1992) at 145.

99 *R. v. Lam* (2005) 159 A. Crim. R. 448 at paragraph 62.

100 Compare the discussion by Lord Toulson in his chapter entitled: 'Sir Michael Foster, Professor Williams and Complicity in Murder' in Dennis J. Baker *et al.* (eds), *The Sanctity of Life and the Criminal Law: The Legacy of Glanville Williams* (Cambridge: Cambridge University Press, 2013) at 230 *et seq.*

101 *R. v. Giannetto* (1997) 1 Cr. App. R. 1 at 13; *Wilcox v. Jeffery* [1951] 1 All E.R. 464 .

102 *The Queen v. Coney* (1881–82) L.R. 8 Q.B.D. 534, *per* Denman, J., Huddleston, B., Manisty, Hawkins, Lopes, Stephen, Cave, and North, JJ. (Lord Coleridge, C.J., Pollock, B., and Mathew, J., dissenting); *R. v. Allen* [1965] 1 Q.B. 130 *per* Edmund Davies, J. (Marshall and Lawton J.J. concurring); *R. v. Clarkson* [1971] 1 W.L.R. 1402 *per* Megaw L.J. (Geoffrey Lane and Kilner Brown J.J. concurring); *R. v. Jones* (1977) 65 Cr. App. R. 250 at 252. In *Hutt v. R.* [1989] T.A.S.S.C. 27 at paragraph 53, Cox, J. (Underwood, Crawford, J.J. concurring) said: 'In the circumstances of this case an error of law occurred by reason of the omission to tell the jury that . . . there had to be proof to the requisite degree that the principal offender was in fact encouraged by the conduct of the accused to commit the crime.' Drawing on a long line of precedents, a line of recent American cases hold that there must

to perpetrate the offence she was encouraged to perpetrate, *R* cannot be derivatively liable, because there is no target crime for her liability to derive from.)[103] The perpetrator must perpetrate the anticipated target crime partly 'in consequence'[104] of the remote party's encouragement. Where there is no influence, the remote party's liability has to be for inchoate participation rather than for derivative participation.

Take the example where *R* is standing on the balcony of her 50th-floor apartment when she observes, with the use of her binoculars, *P* on the street below with a gun pointed at *V*'s head (*V* is *R*'s old school enemy). *R* screams out to *P*, 'Kill her!' Thirty seconds later *P* pulls the trigger and kills *V*. When the evidence is presented in court, it emerges that *P* did not hear *R*. *P* had no awareness of the fact that *R* was watching from her balcony and had no idea that *R* was attempting to encourage her to kill *V*. *P* did not hear *R*'s words of encouragement, because *R* was too far away and there was too much traffic noise on the street. Nonetheless, CCTV footage shows that *R* did in fact attempt to encourage *P* to kill *V*. On these facts, *R* cannot be liable as an accessory to murder, because she did not in fact participate in *P*'s crime. Even though the encouragement did not in fact influence *P*, *R* could be liable for an inchoate offence under the *Serious Crime Act 2007*, because encouraging a person to kill when that person is already minded to kill is an act that is capable of encouraging such a person to kill. When *P* is already intent on killing *V*, minor encouragement could be the tipping point. If the encouragement had reached *P*'s mind, it would be no defence for *R* to assert that *P* was already intent on killing *V*, because a reasonable jury could infer that *R*'s encouragement was an additional factual influencer that pushed *P* over the edge.[105]

be intentional encouragement that influences the perpetrator. Influence is inferred from the evidence. See *People v. Nunez* (2013) 57 Cal.4th 1 at 46; *Hines v. State* (2013) 740 S.E.2d 786 at 794; *State v. James* (2013) 738 S.E.2d 420 at 424; *People v. Phillips* (2012) 972 N.E.2d 724; *State v. Gonzalez* (2012) 135 Conn.App. 101 at 107; *Davis v. Lafler* (2011) 658 F.3d 525 at 544; *Henderson v. State* (2002) 349 Ark. 701; *United States v. Heath* (1999) 188 F.3d 916; *Hopewell v. State* (1998) 122 Md.App. 207 at 215 *et passim*; *Ybarra v. Illinois* (1979) 444 U.S. 85; *People v. Durham* (1969) 70 Cal.2d 171 at 181; *United States v. Williams* (1951) 341 U.S. 58; *Hicks v. United States* (1893) 150 U.S. 442. In *State v. Bennett* (2013) 307 Conn. 758 at 770, Harper, J. said: 'Mere presence as an inactive companion, passive acquiescence, or the doing of innocent acts which may in fact aid the one who commits the crime must be distinguished from the criminal intent and community of unlawful purpose shared by one who knowingly and wilfully assists the perpetrator of the offence in the acts which prepare for, facilitate, or consummate it.'

103 *R. v. Dunnington* [1984] Q.B. 472; *R. v. Hapgood* (1870) L.R. 1 C.C.R. 221; *R. v. Clayton* (1843) 1 Car. & K. 128; *R. v. Williams* (1844) 1 Car. & K. 589.

104 Stephen, *op. cit. supra*, note 5.

105 Cf. *State v. Tally* (1894) 15 So. 722. Kadish writes: 'The secondary party may be liable if the principal is aware of the proffered aid, since knowledge of the efforts of another to give help may constitute sufficient encouragement to hold the secondary actor liable.' Kadish, *op. cit. supra*, note 10 at 359 citing *State v. Tazwell* (1878) 30 La.Ann. 884; George P. Fletcher, *Rethinking Criminal Law* (Boston: Little, Brown, 1978) at 677–682.

The jury might conclude that *R*'s encouragement was too trivial to have been capable of making any difference. If so, the encouragement will be deemed to have been incapable of encouraging *P* in the particular case. But it is no defence for *R* to assert that the offence would have been committed even if she had not assisted and encouraged *P*, if she has in fact encouraged or assisted *P*. If *R* supplies *P* with a gun to assist *P* to kill *V*, it is neither here nor there that *P* could have easily obtained a gun from another source. The fact is that *P* did not use a gun from another source; instead *P* used the gun *R* supplied and thus *R* has made a factual (indirect causal) contribution to *P*'s crime.

In *R. v. Lam*, Redlich, J. goes on to assert:[106]

> Gillies similarly submits that it would be irrelevant to establish that the principal did not see or hear or was indifferent to the act of the secondary participant. Legal texts recognise that in criminal trials in which the secondary participant is not said to be acting pursuant to an agreement with the principal offender, it would be unrealistic and most often impossible to establish that the principal offender knew of the secondary participant's act and was influenced by it to commit the crime. Gillies suggests *that it is sufficient if the accessory's act, viewed objectively, is considered by the jury to be reasonably capable of having encouraged or assisted the principal offender. It need not do so in fact* [emphasis added].

Gillies' assertion is incorrect as far as accessorial liability under section 8 of the *Accessories and Abetters Act 1861* is concerned. It may be difficult to prove factual encouragement, but that is no justification for treating attempted participation as consummated participation.

E. Presumption of factual encouragement and inchoate participation

A person cannot participate in an unattempted crime,[107] but she can attempt to participate in potential crimes.[108] In this section, the focus will be on the incredible breadth[109] of the concept of 'attempted participation

106 *R. v. Lam* (2005) 159 A. Crim. R. 448 at paragraph 61 citing Peter Gillies, *The Law of Criminal Complicity* (Sydney: Law Book Co., 1980) at 54–55.

107 Under section 8 of the *Accessories and Abettors Act 1861*, a person can be liable as an accessory for participating in the perpetrator's attempted crimes, but not for attempting to participate in the perpetrator's unattempted crimes. See *R. v. Dunnington* [1984] Q.B. 472; *R. v. Crangle* (1987) (Northern Ireland unreported judgments); *R. v. Hapgood* (1870) L.R. 1 C.C.R. 221; *R. v. Clayton* (1843) 1 Car. & K. 128; *R. v. Williams* (1844) 1 Car. & K. 589; cf. *R. v. Anderson* [1986] A.C. 27.

108 Cf. *State v. Jovanovic* (1980) 174 N.J.Super. 435.

109 For an example of its incredibly wide application, see *R. v. Blackshaw* [2012] 1 W.L.R. 1126, where it was not clear that Blackshaw's ostensibly childish acts of encouragement were *capable* of encouraging rational autonomous adults to riot and commit criminal damage.

by encouragement'.[110] Attempted participation by assistance is not more harmful or wrongful than attempted participation by encouragement, but the latter has porous boundaries. It is more difficult to define the cut-off point for determining when an act of encouragement is clearly capable of encouraging.

Any persuasion or encouragement (including a threat) is sufficient for the purposes of sections 44–46 of the *Serious Crime Act 2007.*[111] It need not be shown that the act of encouragement actually moved[112] the perpetrator to perpetrate the anticipated target offence, because it need be shown only that the encourager's act was capable of encouraging (psychologically moving) the perpetrator to offend. Not only does the adjective *capable* imply a causation requirement, but so too does the verb *encourage.* For an example of a statute that uses the verb 'move' instead of the verb 'encourage,' see section 3 of the *Treason Felony Act 1848,* which makes it an offence 'to move or stir any foreigner or stranger with force to invade the United Kingdom . . . '.

Dalton uses the noun 'mover', among others, to refer to the encourager. Dalton writes that a person is an accessory to a crime 'if he were either a Procurer, or Mover or Aider, Comforter or Consenter thereto'. Dalton goes on to use the verbs: 'command, procure, move, aid, or consent thereto'.[113] It is arguable that the concept of *move* requires the encouragement to have been a motivator. Putative indirect causation is a relevant consideration, because it must be shown that *R*'s act was capable of moving *P* to offend (i.e. that it was capable of having an indirect causal impact, even though on this occasion it did not). *R*'s encouragement need not be *P*'s sole motivator for acting, but it must be a motivator or a putative motivator. The causation requirement is satisfied when the jury is able to infer that the act of encouragement was in fact *capable* of putting the perpetrator in a state of being motivated to perpetrate the anticipated target crime. The remote party's act of encouragement is something that motivates; it has to be capable of providing the perpetrator with an inducement or incentive or reason for perpetrating the anticipated target crime.

It might be factually impossible for an act to be capable of encouraging (or assisting) in a given situation, but unless it is inherently factually

110 Of course, there is nothing new about this concept. The common law offence of incitement, in effect, criminalised attempted participation. For a discussion of that offence, see Glanville Williams, *Textbook of Criminal Law* (London: Stevens & Sons, 1983) at 334–336; see also Douglas Aikenhead Stroud, *Mens Rea* (London: Sweet & Maxwell, 1914) at 153.

111 Section 65 of the *Serious Crime Act 2007.*

112 See Michael Dalton, *The Country Justice* (London: Printed by William Rawlins *et al.*, 1697) at 396; Hale, *op. cit. supra,* note 22 at 145; 293; 312–313; 337–338; 376; 613; 625; R. *v. Fuller* (1797) 1 Bos. & P. 180 at 185; *The Lord Sanchar's Case* (1612) 9 Co. Rep. 116; *R. v. Caspar* (1839) 9 Car. & P. 289; *R. v. Watson* (1817) 2 Stark. 116; *R. v. Winifred* (1789) 1 Leach 515; *R. v. Pow* (1754) 1 Leach 45; R. *v. Urlyn* (1670) 2 Saund. 308; *R. v. Anonymous* (1685) 3 Mod. 97; *R. v. Thomson* (1675) 3 Keb. 735; *Francis Throgmorton's Case* (1596) Cro. Eliz. 563.

113 Dalton, *ibid.*

impossible for that act ever to encourage (or assist) *R* should be liable for attempting to encourage *P*. Similarly, if *R* sends *P* a letter offering *P* money if *P* kills *V*, but the letter never reaches *P* because it is discovered by the police before it arrives, *R* is liable for attempting the section 44 offence. Here, *R*'s act is not capable of encouraging *P*, since *P* does not receive the message. If the letter had reached *P*, it would have been an act capable of encouraging *P* and therefore *R* should be liable for attempting the section 44 offence. Compare the case where the message does reach *P* (a complete attempt), but *P* ignores it. In the latter situation, *R* is liable for the section 44 offence, not for attempting the section 44 offence since she has completed an act that was capable of encouraging *P*. When objectively judged[114] her act is capable of encouraging *P* even though it failed to have any effect. Similarly, when she attempts to send a message of encouragement, her incomplete act of encouragement when objectively judged would have been capable of encouraging *P* had it been complete.

There is no presumption of influence or assistance; the evidence must be sufficient for the jury to infer that *P* was in fact[115] influenced by *R*'s act or that *R*'s act was capable of encouraging or assisting *P*. In *The Queen v. Coney*,[116] Hawkins, J. said:

> Encouragement does not of necessity amount to aiding and abetting, it may be intentional or unintentional, a man may unwittingly encourage another in fact by his presence, by misinterpreted words, or gestures, or by his silence, on non-interference, or *he may encourage intentionally by expressions, gestures, or actions intended to signify approval. In the latter case he aids and abets, in the former he does not* [emphasis added].

In many cases the evidence of factual encouragement will be so strong that the issue will not be contested by defence counsel; it is only in this sense that factual encouragement might be (presumed) taken as a given.[117]

114 *R. v. Sadique* [2012] 1 WLR 1700 at 1710G where Hooper, L.J., giving the judgment for the Court of Appeal (Supperstone, J., Sir Geoffrey Grigson, concurring), said: 'D's act must objectively be capable of encouraging or assisting the commission of one or more of a number of offences.'

115 *Hutt v. R.* [1989] T.A.S.S.C. 27 at paragraph 53, Cox, J. (Underwood, Crawford, J.J. concurring.); *R. v. Clarkson* [1971] 1 W.L.R. 1402 at 1407 *per* Megaw L.J. (Geoffrey Lane and Kilner Brown J.J. concurring). See also *Charnley. v. R.* [2013] N.Z.C.A. 226 at paragraph 46 *per* Arnold, J. (Simon, France and Dobson J.J. concurring).

116 (1881–82) L.R. 8 Q.B.D. 534 at 557; *R. v. Chishimba* [2010] N.S.W.C.C.A. 228 at paragraph 148. Foster wrote: 'But the persons engaged with [D] will not be involved in his guilt, unless they *actually Aided and Abetted him in the Fact.* For They assembled for another purpose, which was lawful and consequently the guilt of the person actually killing cannot by any fiction of law be carried against them beyond their original Intention.' Foster, *op. cit. supra*, note 69 at 354.

117 Glanville Williams writes: '[I]s it necessary to show that the words of the accessory really had an effect on the mind of the principal, and played a part in bringing about the

Accessorial liability under section 8 of the *Accessories and Abettors Act 1861* is made out only when there has been factual participation. Where proof of factual encouragement is an issue, the jury will need to consider all the evidence to determine whether factual encouragement is inferable on the facts.[118] This is different from holding that factual encouragement is not required.[119] Under the *Serious Crime Act 2007* it will be enough to establish that the encouragement or assistance was capable of encouraging or assisting even though it had no effect in the given case.

VII. Impossibility and capability

Suppose *R* attempts to assist *P* to kill *V* by trying to send *P* a gun via the post. When *R*'s attempt to assist *P* fails, because the gun she tries to post to *P* is lost in the post, *R* is not liable under the *Serious Crime Act 2007,* because her ineffectual attempt to assist is not an act capable of assisting *P.* When *R* attempts to send *P* a gun to assist *P* to kill *V, R* can be liable only for attempting to commit one of the crimes found in sections 44–46 of the *Serious Crime Act 2007.* (Apart from the exception found in section 49 of the *Act of 2007,* to be discussed shortly, there is no limitation on charging *R* with attempting the crimes found in sections 44–46 crimes.)

If the words of encouragement do not reach their intended audience, then they cannot motivate or influence her. At common law, the prosecution used to charge the remote party with attempted incitement in such cases.[120] For example, in *R. v. Krause,*[121] *D* sent a letter soliciting *P* to murder *V.* The letter was sent to Johannesburg, but the solicited party never received it. Krause had not in fact encouraged *P,* because his message never reached *P.* Nonetheless, it was held that the defendant could be convicted of an attempt to commit the crime of incitement.

crime? . . . Usually the words directing another to commit a crime can, where the other actually commits the crime, be presumed to have had some effect upon his mind.' See Glanville Williams, *Criminal Law: The General Part* (London: Stevens & Sons, 1961) at 382. Williams suggests that in cases where the evidence is categorical, factual encouragement might be presumed. But this is just another way of saying that it would be pointless for defence counsel to contest the point where the evidence is very strong, because the jury will ultimately infer factual encouragement where the evidence of it is very strong.

118 *State v. Acker* (2013) 111 So.3d 535 at 441 *per* Picket, J. See also *State v. Anderson* (1998) 707 So.2d 1223.

119 *National Coal Board v. Gamble* [1959] 1 Q.B. 11 at 24 *per* Devlin, J.; *Allen v. Ireland* [1984] 1 W.L.R. 903; *Charnley. v. R.* [2013] N.Z.C.A. 226. at paragraph 46; *State v. Goodwin* (1978) 118 N.H. 862.

120 *R. v. Banks* (1873) 12 Cox C.C. 393; *R. v. Ransford* (1874) 13 Cox C.C. 9; *Hornton v. Mead* [1913] 1 K.B. 154 *per* Phillimore, J.; cf. *R. v. Vaughan* (1769) 4 Burr. 2494. See also *R. v. Giambalvo* (1982) 70 C.C.C. (2d) 324, where putative *P* refused to perpetrate the crime that *D* had asked her to perpetrate.

121 (1902) 66 J.P. 121.

What's more, factual impossibility would not provide *R* with a defence. It will not do for *R* to assert that her act was incapable of assisting and encouraging *P*, because the facts were not as *R* believed them to be.[122] Suppose *R* supplies *P* with what she believes is a teaspoon of cyanide salts for the purpose of assisting *P* to kill *V*. Unbeknown to *R*, the teaspoon of substance that she gives *P* is merely common cooking salt. *R* wrongly believes the cooking salt is cyanide. It is factually impossible to kill a person by putting a teaspoon of normal cooking salt in her food. *R*'s act of attempted assistance is factually incapable of assisting *P* to kill. Nonetheless, factual impossibility provides no defence for attempts.[123] If the facts had been as *R* believed them to be, then *R*'s act would have been capable of assisting *P* to kill *V*. It is possible to kill a person by putting a teaspoon of cyanide salts in her food. *R*'s act was an act that was more than merely preparatory to perpetrating one of the offences found in sections 44–46 of the *Serious Crime Act 2007*. *R*'s attempt to perpetrate one of the offences found in sections 44–46 was complete.

A. *Inherent factual impossibility*

Inherent factual impossibility would provide a defence, because inherent factual impossibility refers to acts that are not more than merely preparatory to attempted perpetration. When *R* uses means that make perpetration of the crime inherently (factually) impossible to achieve, she performs an innocuous lawful act, unless those means have been criminalised in themselves. Let me simplify by providing two examples. Suppose *R* tries to use telepathy in an attempt to encourage *P* (a professional assassin) to kill *V*.[124] Since it is inherently impossible to communicate with another human being via telepathy, *R* has not done an act that is capable of encouraging *P* to kill. Nor is *R*'s act a failed attempt: it is an act that is not even mere preparation for perpetrating one of the offences found in sections 44–46 of the *Serious*

122 Cf. the discussion in *State v. Jovanovic* (1980) 174 N.J.Super. 435.

123 Baker, *op. cit. supra*, note 36 at 18–043 *et passim*. Section 2 of the *Criminal Attempts Act 1981* provides: 'A person may be guilty of attempting to commit an offence to which this section applies even though the facts are such that the commission of the offence is impossible. (3) In any case where – (a) apart from this subsection a person's intention would not be regarded as having amounted to an intent to commit an offence; but (b) if the facts of the case had been as he believed them to be, his intention would be so regarded, then, for the purposes of subsection (1) above, he shall be regarded as having had an intent to commit that offence.'

124 It was said in *State v. Jones* (1994) 873 P.2d 122 at 142 that 'telepathy is "communication through means other than the senses, as by the exercise of mystical powers".' See also the bizarre facts in *People v. Anderson* (2001) 25 Cal.4th 543 at 597. Natural telepathy is impossible, but electronic devices might be used to facilitate other forms of telepathy. See L. Pawela *et al.*, 'Enhancing Pseudo-Telepathy in the Magic Square Game' (2013) 8(6) *PLoS ONE* 1.

Crime Act 2007.[125] Since it is not a crime to telepathize *per se*, there is no crime to charge *R* with.

In the hypothetical just mentioned, *R* herself used inherently ineffective means, but the defence would also apply where *R* encourages *P* to use means that make perpetration of the anticipated target crime inherently impossible. For example, *R* encourages *P*, a witch doctor, to kill *V* by putting a death spell on her.[126] On these facts, *R* encourages *P* to kill by means of a curse, but she encourages *P* to use means that are inherently incapable of killing a human being. If *R*'s act is limited to encouraging *P* to kill by curse, then she has encouraged *P* to perpetrate an act that is not even merely preparatory to murder and therefore *R* should not be liable under the *Serious Crime Act 2007.* If the encouragement was more general, such as to kill *V*

125 'If a statute simply made it a felony to attempt to kill any human being, or to conspire to do so, an attempt by means of witchcraft, or a conspiracy to kill by means of charms and incantations [*sic.*], would not be an offence within such a statute. The poverty of language compels one to say "an attempt to kill by means of witchcraft", but such an attempt is really no attempt at all to kill. It is true the sin or wickedness may be as great as an attempt or conspiracy by competent means; but human laws are made, not to punish sin, but to prevent crime and mischief.' *Attorney General v. Sillem* (1863) 2 Hurl. & C. 431 at 526–527 *per* Pollock, C.B. See also *U.S. v. Lundy* (2012) 676 F.3d 444 at 449 where Clement, J. said two elements must be proved when factual impossibility is raised as a defence: 'first, that the defendant acted with the kind of culpability otherwise required for the commission of the underlying substantive offence, and, second, that the defendant had engaged in conduct which constitutes a *substantial step* toward commission of the crime. The substantial step must be conduct which strongly corroborates the firmness of defendant's criminal attempt. *The Model Penal Code* endorses this approach. See Model Penal Code § 5.01 (1985)' [emphasis added]. Clearly, pinning a voodoo doll or casting a death spell would not be a substantial physical step in attempting to murder another human being.

126 As fanciful as the example sounds, I managed to find a case with similar facts. In *U.S. v. Francis* (1997) 131 F.3d 1452, 'Francis and Rendiff Green were arrested for selling crack cocaine. Shortly thereafter, Green and another inmate began making arrangements to have a Jamaican Obeah priest put a voodoo curse on Ernest Hardy, the informant to whom Green and Francis sold crack. Francis joined the voodoo plot.' Some people believe they can kill by curse. See *Bradshaw v. U.S.* [2012] 55 A.3d 394. Where a person genuinely believes in voodoo, such severe delusions, if medically verified, might be evidence of insanity or diminished responsibility. Cf. the discussion in *Conaway v. State* (1983) 663 S.W.2d 53; *Genius v. Pepe* (1998) 147 F.3d 64; *Outler v. State* (1975) 322 So.2d 623. The *Diagnostic and Statistical Manual of Mental Disorders* (Washington D.C.: American Psychiatric Association, 4th edn. 2000) at 697 states: 'The diagnostic criteria for Schizotypal Personality Disorder include: A pervasive pattern of social and interpersonal deficits marked by acute discomfort with, and reduced capacity for, close relationships as well as by cognitive or perceptual distortions and eccentricities of behaviour, beginning by early adulthood and present in a variety of contexts, as indicated by five (or more) or the following: (1) ideas of reference (excluding delusions of reference) (2) odd beliefs or magical thinking that influences behaviour and is inconsistent with subcultural norms (e.g. superstitiousness, belief in clairvoyance, telepathy, or "sixth sense"; in children and adolescents, bizarre fantasies . . .' For another case where black magic has been used to try to influence, see *Humber College v. O.P.S.E.U.* (1987) 31 L.A.C. (3d) 266.

either by using a curse or by using any other means you can conjure up, then the case would be different.[127]

R's encouragement should be that *P* do an act that in the normal course of events could result in a crime. Where *R1* and *R2* encourage *P* to cast a death spell on *V*, their belief that inherently ineffective means could be used to kill should be distinguished from the standard case of factual impossibility, where *R* is only mistaken about the relevant facts. There may be extreme cases where a victim is killed by fright[128] or commits suicide because of a spell,[129] but such cases are likely to fall outside the compass of the law of participatory and inchoate liability.[130] Factual impossibility as opposed to '*inherent* factual impossibility' is no defence in the law of attempts.[131]

Compare this to a case where *R* attempts to hypnotise *P* into perpetrating a criminal offence. Since it is possible to hypnotise people,[132] the latter would be factually possible and thus could be an attempt to perpetrate one of the offences found in the *Act of 2007*. *P* would act as an automaton and as an innocent agent and thus would be able to rely on the defence of automatism.[133] The defence of *inherent* factual impossibility has been recognised by some legislatures and courts in the United States. For instance, in the Supreme Court of Kansas. in *State v. Logan*,[134] McFarland, J. said:

127 Section 4 of the *Offences against the Person Act 1861* could also be invoked. Such threats are not protected by the freedom of expression right. See *U.S. v. Turner* (2013) 720 F.3d 411, where Turner discussed killing Judges Easterbrook, Bauer and Posner.

128 *R. v. Hayward* (1908) 21 Cox C.C. 692.

129 In primitive societies where beliefs in magic might be the norm, cursing could have a powerful psychological impact. See Glanville Williams, *Criminal Law: The General Part* (London: Stevens & Sons, 1953) at 502.

130 In such a case, *mens rea* and causation would have to be established. See Baker, *op. cit. supra*, note 36 Chapters 4 and 11. *P* would have to target a particular victim, and the victim would have to be aware of the curse for a causal connexion to be established.

131 See section 1 of the *Criminal Attempts Act 1981*; Glanville Williams, 'The Lords and Impossible Attempts, or *Quis Custodiet Ipsos Custodes*' (1986) 45 *Cambridge L.J.* 33. Cf. *R. v. McDonough* (1963) 47 Cr. App. R. 37; *R. v. Shephard* [1919] 2 K.B. 125; *R. v. Whitchurch* (1890) 24 Q.B.D. 420; *R. v. West* [1948] 1 K.B. 709; *R.* v. *Brown* (1899) 63 J.P. 790.

132 See *People v. Poplaski* (1994) 616 N.Y.S.2d 434 at 439, where it is observed that the 'defendant met children through a computer bulletin board, spoke to them over the phone, attempted to hypnotise them, and asked the victims to engage in the same sexual activity, to wit: masturbation'. Some medical studies suggest hypnosis is medically possible. See Gary Elkins *et al.*, 'Hypnotherapy for the Management of Chronic Pain' (2007) 55(3) *Int. J. Clin. Exp. Hypn.* 275; The British Psychological Society, *The Nature of Hypnosis* (Leicester: A report prepared by a Working Party at the request of The Professional Affairs Board of The British Psychological Society: March 2001).

133 Stroud, *op. cit. supra*, note 110 at 245.

134 656 P.2d 777 at 780. In *State v. Bird* (1979) 285 N.W.2d 481, Sheran, J. said: 'inherent impossibility (in which an actor uses means which a reasonable person would view as completely inappropriate to the objectives sought) [is a defence] to a charge of attempt.' See also *People v. Elmore* (1970) 261 N.E.2d 736; *Commonwealth v. Johnson* (1933) 167 A. 344 at 348.

> An example of inherent impossibility contained in the Minnesota statutory comment is trying 'to sink a battleship with a pop-gun' . . . [S]ubdivision 2 of the attempt statute (Minn.Stat. § 609.17 (1978)) provides that an act may be an attempt 'notwithstanding the circumstances under which it was performed or the means employed to commit the crime intended or the act itself were such that the commission of the crime was not possible, *unless such impossibility would have been clearly evident to a person of normal understanding* [emphasis added].

The same defence applies to inherently ineffectual assistance. Suppose *R* gives *P* a water pistol to assist *P* to shoot down a jumbo jet. Clearly, *R*'s act of assistance is inherently incapable of assisting *P* to shoot down the passenger jet. *R*'s act of assistance is incapable of assisting *P* because it is inherently impossible to shoot down a passenger jet with a water pistol.[135] Similarly, if *R* sells *P* a voodoo doll so that *P* can use it to cast a death spell upon *V*, she would not be liable for attempting to assist *P* to kill. There are physical limits to what a person can achieve with given assistance. Acts of encouragement also have their limits. 'Loyal and natural boy! I will work the *means* – To make thee capable.'[136] *R* should not be caught by the *Serious Crime Act 2007* when her attempted assistance or encouragement is inherently incapable of assisting or encouraging *P* (providing *P* with means) to perpetrate the anticipated target crime or where she encourages *P* to do the inherently impossible. If the act of assistance or encouragement could have no effect in any circumstances, then *R*'s fallacious belief that it could assist or encourage should not be enough to make her liable for one of the offences found in sections 44–46 of the *Serious Crime Act 2007*.

B. Legal impossibility

Legal impossibility would provide *R* with a defence where *P*'s anticipated target crime is in fact a lawful activity. It is important to note that since attempted participation is a form of attempts liability, the legal impossibility, factual impossibility and inherent factual impossibility rules apply. A person cannot be held liable for attempting to assist or encourage a non-existent crime, because it is impossible to charge a person with trying to encourage or assist a non-existent crime. *R* is liable under the *Serious Crime Act 2007* only when she attempts or is successful in encouraging another

135 Inherent factual impossibility would provide a defence under the *Serious Crime Act 2007*, because *R*'s assistance or encouragement has to pass a capability standard. On the 'inherent factual impossibility' defence, see Baker, *op. cit. supra*, note 36 at para. 18–043 *et seq.*

136 M. William Shake-speare, *His true chronicle historie of the life and death of King Lear and his three daughters* (London: Printed by Nicholas Okes for Nathaniel Butter, 1608) Act II, Scene 1.

person to perpetrate a criminal offence.[137] Suppose *R* and *P* go to the beach and *R* attempts to encourage *P* to take her bikini top off; both *R* and *P* believe that it is a crime in England and Wales for a woman to go topless on a public beach. Suppose also that *P* ignores *R*'s encouragement and keeps her top on. *R*'s ineffectual attempt is not conduct that would be caught by the *Serious Crime Act 2007*, because *R* does not attempt to encourage *P* to commit a crime. Rather, *R* encourages *P* to perpetrate a lawful and innocuous act. Some courts in the United States have mistaken legal impossibility for factual impossibility and thus have suggested a person could be liable for attempting a non-existent crime.[138]

C. The common law and impossibility

It is worth noting that the *Act of 2007* is silent on impossibility. There is nothing in the new *Act* that suggests the common law interpretation of impossibility should not apply. At common law a person could not attempt to conspire or do the impossible, unless the impossibility related solely to means and not to the end in view.[139] The rule was changed by statute for attempt and conspiracy,[140] but nothing was enacted for incitement, and it was held in *R. v. Fitzmaurice*[141] that the impossibility rule governed the common law offence of incitement. Many decades ago, the Law Commission,[142] in recommending the change for attempt and conspiracy, refrained from making any recommendation for incitement, chiefly because the Commission expressed the opinion that the courts might be able to declare that the law of incitement is in line with the law for the other offences, without statutory help. The suggestion was received with some scepticism, and has now been falsified by the decision in *R. v. Fitzmaurice.* However, the court made it clear that nothing but the most complete impossibility would exclude liability. If the projected

137 For a full discussion of the impossibility rules, see Baker, *op. cit. supra*, note 36 at para. 18–043 et *seq.*

138 See *In re Sealed Case* (2000) 223 F.3d 775 at 779, where Williams, J. said: 'Pure legal impossibility is always a defence. For example, a hunter cannot be convicted of attempting to shoot a deer if the law does not prohibit shooting deer in the first place.' See also *U.S. v. Fernandez* (2013) 722 F.3d 1 at 31 *per* Lipez, J.; *U.S. v. Hsu* (1998) 155 F.3d 189 at 199–203 *per* Rendell, J. Cf. *U.S. v. Lundy* (2012) 676 F.3d 444 at 449, where it was held that: 'Factual impossibility is not a defence if the crime could have been committed had the attendant circumstances been as the actor believed them to be.' Inherent factual impossibility is contradistinguishable, because it is impossible for the facts that the defendant believes to exist to ever exist in the real world: see Baker, *op. cit. supra*, note 36 at para. 18–043 *et seq.*

139 On the difficulty of the means–end distinction, see *R. v. Harris* (1979) 69 Cr. App. R. 122.

140 Section 1(2) and section 5 (1) of the *Criminal Attempts Act 1981.* See also *R. v. Hollinshead* [1985] A.C. 975.

141 [1983] 2 W.L.R. 227. See also Williams, *op. cit. supra*, note 129 at para. 194.

142 Law Commission, *Criminal Law: Attempt and Impossibility in Relation to Attempt, Conspiracy and Incitement*, Report 102 (London: H.M.S.O., 1980), Part IV.

crime, though impossible at the time, might become possible before it was expected to be committed, the encouragement would be an offence.[143]

When the Law Commission[144] revisited the issue in 2006, it thought that it was unnecessary 'for the Bill to include a clause expressly addressing the issue of [impossibility]'. The reason was that the inchoate nature of the offences means that they would catch the standard cases of factual impossibility – attempts to steal from an empty pocket, attempts to kill a person who is already dead, attempts to import drugs and so on. If *R* encourages *P* to steal from *V*'s pocket she is liable as soon as she utters her encouragement; it does not matter whether the pocket contains a wallet. Similarly, if *R* pays *P* to kill *V*, it is neither here nor there that *V* is killed in a car accident before *P* gets the chance to carry out the assassination.[145] *R*'s liability depends on whether her act was capable of encouraging *P* to kill and on her culpability for the inchoate offence. But none of this deals with the issue of inherent factual impossibility with respect to the means used by *R* to assist (e.g. *R* gives *P* a water pistol to sink a cruise liner) or to encourage *P* (e.g. *R* uses telepathy to encourage *P* to kill *V*).

VIII. When is trivial encouragement capable of encouraging?

Many acts of encouragement may seem trivial, but in certain circumstances they will be capable of encouraging others to offend.[146] Section 65 of the *Serious Crime Act 2007* provides:

> (1) A reference in this Part to a person's doing an act that is capable of encouraging the commission of an offence includes a reference to his doing so by threatening another person or otherwise putting pressure on another person to commit the offence.
> (2) A reference in this Part to a person's doing an act that is capable of encouraging or assisting the commission of an offence includes a reference to his doing so by –
>
> (a) taking steps to reduce the possibility of criminal proceedings being brought in respect of that offence;
> (b) failing to take reasonable steps to discharge a duty.
>
> (3) But a person is not to be regarded as doing an act that is capable of encouraging or assisting the commission of an offence merely because he fails to respond to a constable's request for assistance in preventing a breach of the peace.

143 See *R. v. Shepherd* [1919] 2 K.B. 125.

144 Law Commission, *Inchoate Liability for Assisting and Encouraging Crime*, Report 300 (London: H.M.S.O., 2006) at para. 6.62.

145 Cf. *D.P.P. v. Armstrong* [2000] Crim. L.R. 379.

146 *State v. Barnum* (2000) 14 S.W.3d 587 at 591 *per* Price, C.J.; *State v. Jackson* (2012) 385 S.W.3d 437 at 441–442.

In *R. v. Blackshaw*,[147] *R*'s acts of encouragement were trivial and remote, but the context in which they were done convinced the court that they were capable of encouraging the putative perpetrators to riot and perpetrate criminal damage. The decision was a sentencing decision, but it contains some useful observations. Blackshaw used social media to encourage people to riot and perpetrate criminal damage. Posts on Twitter may seem too trivial to encourage fully autonomous adults to go out rioting and smashing up buildings, but the context in which Blackshaw posted his messages of encouragement was as follows:

> At 00.45 on 9 August a police station in Handsworth in Birmingham was set on fire, and shortly afterwards Merseyside police confirmed that they were dealing with a number of incidents in South Liverpool, which included cars being set alight. Some 200 rioters hurled missiles at officers in Smithdown Road, Liverpool. A few minutes later BBC staff reported that hundreds of youths were ransacking a Panasonic store in West Ealing, and there were then disturbances and troubles in Derby . . . To underline one specific aspect of all these offences we mention that a friendly international soccer match between England and Holland was called off that morning because of the rioting in London. The story of the public disorder in this country had a vast international dimension. Television films of London burning were seen throughout the world. We have no doubt they were a source of incredulity abroad as they were at home, and of considerable dismay among those who retain affection for this country. The rioting also enabled a spokesman for a dictatorial regime abroad to equate those conducting demonstrations for greater civil liberties with the rioters here.[148]
>
> . . . .
>
> At 22.30 on 8 August 2011 [Blackshaw] used Facebook to set up and plan a public event called '*Smash Down in Northwich Town*'. It would start behind the premises of McDonalds at 13.00 next day. The riots were in full flow. The defendant knew perfectly well that they were. The purpose of his website was to wreak criminal damage and rioting in the centre of Northwich, and the event called for participants to meet in a restaurant in Northwich at lunchtime on 9 August. The website was aimed at his close associates, who he referred to as the 'Mob Hill Massive', and his friends, *but he also opened it to public view* and included in the website references to on-going rioting in London, Birmingham and Liverpool. He posted a message of encouragement on the website that read: 'we'll need to get on this, kicking off all over.' . . . Fortunately members of

147 [2012] 1 W.L.R. 1126.
148 *R. v. Blackshaw* [2012] 1 W.L.R. 1126 at 1137–1138.

> the community who saw the website were revolted by it and alerted the police. It addition, some of them left messages on the website expressing their disgust in no uncertain terms. The police infiltrated the website and posted messages on it, warning of the consequences if the website were followed. By the time it was closed down by the police, nine people had confirmed their intention to attend. In the result, the offence which the defendant was inciting did not take place [emphasis added].[149]

There was no doubt that Blackshaw's Facebook event was capable of encouraging like-minded people to participate in the continuing riots in the context of the 2011 England riots. The 2011 England riots were the worst riots in recent history, because they involved thousands of people from many London boroughs, as well as cities and towns across England, perpetrating arson and criminal damage. There were mass riots up and down the country.[150] One reputable publication called them 'The BlackBerry riots', because the organisers used mobile phones and social media to instigate and organise them.[151] There was a mass of unemployed and disadvantaged people rioting, because a supposedly unlawful police shooting of a notorious criminal enraged them. In this context, Blackshaw's post on social media had the potential to encourage further acts of rioting and criminal damage. When a mob is on the rampage, it does not need much prodding. The fault constraint offers such defendants some protection. Under section 45 of the *Serious Crime Act 2007, R* would need to know the relevant circumstances for the jury to infer that she *believed* her encouragement *would* encourage *Ps* to perpetrate the anticipated target crimes; *a fortiori* under section 44 of the *Act of 2007.*

Furthermore, *R*'s encouragement need not be the predominant motivator for *P* perpetrating the anticipated target crime, but it must be a more then negligible motivator, if the 'capable of' encouraging element is to be satisfied. *R*'s encouragement would not be capable of providing a *perpetrator* with a more than negligible motivation (reason) for perpetrating the anticipated target crime, if it is very trivial. All the circumstances would have to be considered, because in special cases trivial encouragement can tip the balance.

In order to establish a causal or factual nexus in the full sense, *R*'s encouragement would have to overbear the will of *P*.[152] Duress that overbears a person's will would make that person a quasi innocent agent.

149 *R. v. Blackshaw* [2012] 1 W.L.R. 1126 at 1142.

150 *R. v. Blackshaw* [2012] 1 W.L.R. 1126 at 1142.

151 'The Blackberry Riots', *The Economist*, 13 August 2011.

152 See the discussion in *R. v. v Kennedy (No. 2)* [2008] 1 A.C. 269; *Lewis v. State* (1985) 474 So.2d 766. See also Sue Woolf Brenner, 'Undue Influence in the Criminal Law: A Proposed Analysis of the Criminal Offence of "Causing Suicide"' (1982) 47 *Albany L. Rev.* 62; Luis E. Chiesa, 'Punishing Without Free Will' (2011) *Utah L. Rev.* 1403.

Fraud,[153] duress or undue influence could be used to encourage a person to perpetrate a crime or to commit suicide,[154] but lesser forms of persuasion also have a causal bearing. Causation for the purposes of establishing attempted participation does not require anything this strong. It is enough to establish that *R*'s encouragement provided *P* with a solid *extra* reason for perpetrating the anticipated target crime. *R*'s act need not be *P*'s predominant reason for perpetrating, but it must be one of the reasons behind *P*'s general reason for perpetrating the anticipated target crime. There may be many factors motivating *P* to perpetrate the anticipated target crime, but as long as *R*'s act of encouragement has some impact in that it tips the balance, *R* can be liable. In the headnote to *State v. Jones*,[155] it is asserted: 'In order for one who incites to suicide to be guilty of murder, a causal connection must exist between the incitement and the suicide; the incitement must be not necessarily the sole cause, but an inducing cause of the crime.'

If the encouragement when judged objectively in all the circumstances is too trivial to have been capable of influencing *P*'s decision to perpetrate the anticipated target crime, the jury should not infer that it did in fact influence *P*'s decision to perpetrate the anticipated target crime or that it would have been capable of influencing *P* to perpetrate the anticipated target crime. In *R. v. Giannetto*,[156] Kennedy, L.J. observed:

153 Such as where *R* tells *P* a lie that *V* has been sleeping with *P*'s wife and at the same time tells *P* that he should kill *V* to seek revenge. Or where *R* lies to *V* to convince her to commit suicide, such as where *R* uses undue influence and fraud to convince *V* that she is dying with cancer.

154 See *State v. Melchert-Dinkel* (2012) 816 N.W.2d 703, where 'Mark Drybrough hanged himself in England in 2005, and Nadia Kajouji drowned herself in Canada three years later, both shortly after 46-year-old William Melchert-Dinkel, who knew that Drybrough and Kajouji were contemplating suicide, sent each a series of Internet messages from his home in Faribault, prodding them to kill themselves. Melchert-Dinkel instructed Drybrough and Kajouji how to commit suicide by hanging, tried to persuade them to hang themselves, and convinced them that he was a distraught young woman who would commit suicide simultaneously with them or shortly afterward . . . [The evidence was that] *D* falsely presented himself as a woman, particularly as a "kind, sympathetic emergency room nurse" who "befriends his victims by pretending to be suicidal". Police linked Melchert–Dinkel to the described email addresses.' Cf. the now repealed Ga. Code Ann. § 16–5-5(c) (2003), which made a person liable for encouraging suicide when she 'knowingly and wilfully commits any act which destroys the volition of another, such as fraudulent practices upon such person's fears, affections, or sympathies; duress; or any undue influence . . . and thereby intentionally causes or induces such other person to commit or attempt to commit suicide.' This provision was repealed by Laws 2012, Act 639, § 1, eff. May 1, 2012.

155 (1910) 67 S.E. 160 at 162.

156 (1997) 1 Cr. App. R. 1 at 13. Similarly, it is doubtful that the conduct in *Wilcox v. Jeffery* [1951] 1 All E.R. 464, when objectively judged, could be said to have been an act capable of encouraging the fully autonomous perpetrator to perpetrate the relevant target offence.

> Supposing somebody came up to [D] and said, 'I am going to kill your wife', if [D] played any part, either in encouragement, as little as patting [P] on the back, nodding, saying, 'Oh goody', that would be sufficient to involve him in the murder, to make him guilty, because he is encouraging the murder.

It is doubtful that this sort of trivial indirect encouragement would be capable of influencing a person to perpetrate a very serious crime such as murder. However, the jury would have to consider all the circumstances. If a person is already intent on committing murder or on committing suicide, then very trivial encouragement could be the tipping point. In the hypothetical, 'Oh goody' is uttered to someone who is already intent on perpetrating a murder, so perhaps it is capable of influencing *P*'s final decision in a more than negligible way. Hence, the jury could infer that it was capable of tipping the balance, but it would need firm evidence demonstrating that *P* was very serious about perpetrating the anticipated target crime. The better view is that it would have made no causal difference and thus would be too trivial to count as an act that is capable of providing *P* with a more than negligible reason for perpetrating murder.

Kadish writes: 'It is often said that any amount of influence or aid suffices, no matter how slight. Is this evidence that a successful contribution is not required after all?'[157] A person who gives very minor encouragement ought not to be held as an accessory, because such assistance, unless there are special circumstances, would not be capable of influencing a fully autonomous adult to perpetrate a crime. Would mere suggestion be encouragement that is capable of having a more than negligible influence on a fully autonomous adult perpetrator's decision to perpetrate a crime? Shakespeare said: 'They'll take suggestion as a cat laps milk.'[158] Children and the very gullible might take suggestion as a cat laps milk, but this surely cannot be the case with respect to fully autonomous adult agents. It would be harsh to use trivial encouragement to convict a person of an offence under the *Serious Crime Act 2007*, especially if she allegedly had some minor influence on another's decision to perpetrate a very trivial crime. For example, in *State v. Butler*,[159] Scott, J. said:

157 Kadish, *op. cit. supra*, note 10 at 361–362.

158 M. William Shake-speare, *The Tempest*, (London: printed by J. M. for Henry Herringman, 1670).

159 (1894) 35 P. 1093 at 1094; cf. the discussion in *U.S. v. Bagdasarian* (2011) 652 F.3d 1113. 'It has been urged in strong terms that solicitation of adultery ought not to be criminal whether adultery is a felony or a misdemeanour, as it is feared that many innocent gestures, remarks, and innuendos will be interpreted as invitations to commit adultery. The danger of false charges, however, is not a problem limited to the adultery situation; it is a risk implicit in the punishment of almost all inchoate crimes.' See Herbert Wechsler, William Kenneth Jones and Harold L. Korn, 'Treatment of Inchoate Crimes in the Model Penal Code of the American Law Institute: Attempt, Solicitation, and Conspiracy' (1961) 61 *Colum. L. Rev.* 571 at 623.

> The reasons given in that case showing why solicitation should not be held an attempt to commit adultery apply with equal force whether adultery be a misdemeanour or a felony. These relate to the difficulty of determining what is a solicitation. 'What expressions of the face,' says the court, 'or double entendres of the tongue, are to be adjudged solicitation? What freedoms of manners amount to this crime? Is every Cyprian who nods or winks to the married men she meets upon the sidewalk indictable for soliciting to adultery? And could the law safely undertake to decide what recognitions in the street were chaste, and what were lewd? It would be a dangerous and difficult rule of criminal law to administer.

The offences found in sections 44–46 of the *Serious Crime Act 2007* seem to require the suggestion to be made in a context where it would be capable of making a more than negligible difference to *P*'s decision to perpetrate the anticipated target crime. When a person is not hypnotised she is able to make up her own mind. Merely suggesting something to a sane person is different from putting a gun to her head and demanding she do as suggested. If *R* provides information in a gardening book about growing cannabis, does she really encourage others to grow it? The courts think so.[160] Surely the autonomous agent is not so easily encouraged.[161] *R*'s act is capable of assisting, but it is a stretch to argue that it is capable of encouraging. It would be possible to convict her under section 45 of the *Act of 2007*, if she intends or believes that one of her customers 'will' be assisted. The encouragement may be directed to persons generally, as it was in *Invicta Plastics Ltd. v. Clare*,[162] and it may encourage a general course of crime.[163] If the person encouraged gives ear and assents to the plan proposed, she and the encourager become conspirators.

A. Inchoate participation by association and omission

Factual encouragement cannot be inferred from the remote party's mere presence at the scene of the crime; but mere presence considered along

160 *R. v. Marlow* [1998] 1 Cr. App. R. (S.) 273.

161 On at least one occasion, the court has held that selling articles (articles whose telos is to facilitate fraud) to a middleman who would then encourage others to use them was not sufficient for establishing incitement at common law. As the defendants had not encouraged the middleman personally to use the articles, they were able to evade justice. See *R. v. James* (1986) 82 Cr. App. R. 226. They would now be caught by section 66 of the *Serious Crime Act 2007*, which criminalises indirect encouragement. In addition, such defendants directly encourage the middleman to possess an article for use in fraud and thus encourage him to commit an offence contrary to section 6 of the *Fraud Act 2006*.

162 [1976] R.T.R. 251. See also *R. v. Jones* [2008] Q.B. 460; cf. *Baney v. State* (2009) 42 So.3d 170.

163 Section 66 of the *Serious Crime Act 2007*.

with the remote party's relation to the perpetrator and the remote party's actions before, during and after the commission of the crime might be enough to allow the jury to infer factual encouragement.[164] In *R. v. Salajko*,[165] a girl was raped by a gang of thugs. Three men were charged with rape. It was proved beyond reasonable double that two of these had in fact raped the victim. It had been established that the third accused, Salajko, had been present when the girl was raped, but that he had not had sexual intercourse with her. The evidence was that while *V* was being raped by *P*, Salajko stood nearby with his pants down and in a visible state of sexual excitement. It was clearly open to the jury to infer encouragement by conduct, but the Ontario Court of Appeal held otherwise. Gale C.J.O., delivering the judgment of the court, said:

> The accused gave an explanation as to the incident but quite apart from it we do not think that the evidence can be translated into a conclusion that the accused was aiding or abetting the others when they were ravaging the girl. Passive acquiescence is not sufficient to induce such a finding and [there was no] other evidence to suggest anything in the way of aiding or counselling or encouragement on the part of the accused with respect to that which was being done by the others.

It is arguable that Salajko did an act that was capable of encouraging the continuing act of rape, because standing naked in association with other gang members who are perpetrating a rape clearly sends a message of

164 In *Diggs v. State* (2013) 213 Md.App. 28 at 83 Kehoe, J. said: 'The mere presence of the defendant at the time and place of the commission of the crime is not enough to prove the defendant aided and abetted. But if presence is proven, it is a fact that may be considered, along with all the surrounding circumstances.' See also *State v. Novotny* (2013) 307 P.3d 1278 at 1286; *Maddox v. State* (2013) 746 S.E.2d 280; *State v. Merritt* (1999) 143 N.H. 714; *State v. Laudarowicz* (1997) 694 A.2d 980; *State v. Vaillancourt* (1982) 122 N.H. 1153. The court will need more than mere presence to prove that the remote party was a (inchoate) participator; other relevant factors might include companionship and conduct before and after the offence. See *People v. Miranda* (2011) 192 Cal.App.4th 398 at 407. Under the *Serious Crimes Act 2007* the Crown has to prove that the encourager's act was in fact capable of influencing the perpetrator, but in a joint enterprise/common purpose scenario it need not prove that there was a prearrangement or that the remote party had prior knowledge of the perpetrator's purpose, because a mutual intention (purpose) may be formed instantaneously at the time when the crime is perpetrated. Cf. *People v. Nguyen* (1993) 21 Cal.App.4th 518 at 532; *Powell v. State* (2012) 291 Ga. 743 at 745; *State v. Palubicki* (2005) 700 N.W.2d 476 at 486. See also *People v. Johnson* (1973) 33 Cal.App.3d 9 at 22; *People v. Boyer* (2006) 38 Cal.4th 412 at 467; *State v. Gonzalez* (2012) 283 P.3d 840. Cf. *U.S. v. Jones* (2013) 713 F.3d 336.

165 [1970] 1 O.R. 824.

encouragement.[166] (*R. v. Salajko*[167] is not likely to be followed in light of the decision of the Supreme Court of Canada in *R. v. Kirkness*.[168]) Not only can it be inferred that by attending the gang rape Salajko approved of it, but the fact he took his pants off and stood nearby in a visible state of lust sent a message of encouragement to the perpetrator. The message was that Salajko approved of the perpetrator's continuing rape. The fact that Salajko stood nearby in the nude sent the message that he also was waiting to rape *V*. That sort of sexual conduct in the context of a gang rape would allow a reasonable jury to infer encouragement by conduct.

The case of *R. v. McCarry*[169] is also troubling. In that case it was reasonable for the jury to infer that Waters had encouraged McCarry to rape *V*, but it was not reasonable for the jury to infer that Waters intended to encourage McCarry to murder *V*.[170] Waters and McCarry had taken *V* to a remote location to have sexual intercourse with her. McCarry raped *V* and Waters attempted to rape her. If Waters' attempt to rape *V* preceded McCarry's rape of *V*, then it was reasonable for the jury to infer that by his conduct he encouraged McCarry to rape *V*. However, it is not clear how attempting to rape a person encourages a fellow rapist to depart from the common purpose (gang rape) and murder *V*. It is arguable that there was encouragement of an unlawful dangerous act, because McCarry drove Waters to a remote location knowing that he 'had a long-established history of strangling during sexual intercourse'. Sir Anthony May said: 'It should be remembered that . . . Waters had given evidence that the strangling continued while he drove to a more secluded spot. This by itself could be seen as participating encouragement.'[171] If it had been established that Waters had encouraged the unlawful dangerous act of sexual strangulation (autoerotic asphyxiation, which is the intentional restriction of oxygen to the brain for sexual arousal),[172] then he would have been rightly convictable of manslaughter.

When a person encourages another to perform an unlawful dangerous act such as autoerotic asphyxiation (even if *V* had consented to the autoerotic

166 Section 67 of the *Serious Crime Act 2007* provides: 'A reference in this Part to an act includes a reference to a course of conduct, and a reference to doing an act is to be read accordingly.'

167 [1970] 1 O.R. 824 at para. 4. Cf. *R. v. Black* [1970] 4 C.C.C. 251.

168 [1990] 3 S.C.R. 74 at para. 50 where it was said: 'the decision in *R. v. Salajko* is anomalous and should not be followed.'

169 [2009] E.W.C.A. Crim. 1718.

170 See also *Miller v. The Queen* (1980) 32 A.L.R. 321.

171 *R. v. McCarry* [2009] E.W.C.A. Crim. 1718 at para. 26.

172 'Both the appellants told interviewing police officers that McCarry had had sexual intercourse with the deceased and that she had encouraged him to strangle her to increase her sexual pleasure. Her death, they said, was accidental.' *R. v. McCarry* [2009] E.W.C.A. Crim. 1718 at para. 6.

asphyxiation, consent is no defence to actual bodily harm)[173] and it causes *V*'s death, both can be held liable for manslaughter.[174] If *V* died as a result of McCarry forming a direct intention to kill her, Waters should not have been held liable for murder unless he encouraged murder.[175] McCarry was an asphyxiophiliac who had a history of engaging in autoerotic asphyxiation and Waters had full knowledge of this fact. There was ample evidence for the jury to infer that Waters, at the very least, knew that McCarry intended to take *V* to an isolated place to have sexual intercourse involving autoerotic asphyxiation. But it was not clear on the evidence that Waters intended to encourage McCarry to depart from the normal pattern of conduct (i.e. sexual intercourse involving autoerotic asphyxia) and kill *V*. The normal pattern of conduct involved sexual intercourse where McCarry would perform erotic asphyxiation. There was no pattern of conduct where McCarry had killed or had attempted to kill women.[176] The evidence suggests that Waters' intention was to encourage McCarry to have sexual intercourse involving autoerotic asphyxiation, but that is all. Since Waters authorised the unlawful dangerous act of autoerotic asphyxiation, a conviction for manslaughter would have been appropriate had that act accidentally killed *V*. Since that act did not cause *V*'s death, Waters should not have been liable for either murder or manslaughter. McCarry's deliberate act of murder broke the chain of causation between the act that Waters authorised and encouraged and *V*'s death.

I am assuming that McCarry's act of strangulation was more violent, involved greater pressure to the neck area etc. than was necessary for autoerotic asphyxiation. In other words, his act of strangulation was designed to kill rather than achieve autoerotic asphyxiation. If McCarry's act of strangulation was a standard act of autoerotic asphyxiation (whatever that may be) with him secretly intending to kill *V*, then it might have been argued that the unlawful dangerous act that was authorised by Waters was the cause of *V*'s death. There is a very fine line here. If a jury finds that the unlawful dangerous act encouraged by *R* caused *V*'s death, *R* can be liable for manslaughter even though *P* has the requisite *mens rea* for murder and is liable for murder.[177]

Lord Toulson[178] takes the view that *R. v. Rahman*[179] prevents an accomplice being convicted of manslaughter where the perpetrator has been convicted

173 *R. v. Brown* [1994] [1994] 1 A.C. 212.

174 Cf. *Miller v. The Queen* (1980) 32 A.L.R. 321.

175 *R. v. Creamer* [1966] 1 Q.B. 72; *R. v. Buck* (1960) 44 Cr. App. R. 213; *R. v. Gaylor* (1857) Dears. & B. 288 at 291 *per* Bramwell B.; *R. v. Smith* (1847) 2 Cox C.C. 233.

176 Cf. *Miller v. The Queen* (1980) 32 A.L.R. 321.

177 *R. v. Kirkness* [1990] 3 S.C.R. 74 at para. 39; *R. v. Kent* (1986) 40 Man. R. (2d) 160; R. *v. Hartford* (1980) 51 C.C.C. (2d) 462 (B.C. C.A.), and *R. v. Trudeau* (1985) 49 C.R. (3d) 234; *Murray v. R.* [1962] Tas. S.R. 170 (C. C. A.).

178 Toulson, *op. cit. supra*, note 100.

179 [2009] 1 A.C. 129.

of murder. But this is not correct. As I explained in Chapter 2 of this book, if the act that causes *V* death is authorised and encouraged by the accomplice, she is liable for the unintended consequences of that act. If the unintended consequence of an unlawful dangerous act is *V*'s death, *R* should be liable for constructive manslaughter or for one of the offences found in the *Serious Crime Act 2007*. If the *same* unlawful *act* kills *V* in circumstances where *P* (secretly or otherwise) intended to kill or cause *V* GBH, *P*'s *mens rea* is for murder and she should be convicted of murder. It is irrelevant that *R*'s *mens rea* was for assisting and encouraging manslaughter only, because the inchoate provisions apply to any crime that she attempted to encourage. The actual crime she intended to encourage is only relevant to her sentence. Under the *Act of 1861*, *R* will not be liable for constructive manslaughter when the unlawful act that causes *V*'s death is fundamentally different from the unlawful dangerous act that she encouraged *P* to perpetrate, because the act she authorised/encouraged did not get a chance to cause *V*'s death.[180] The chain of causation is broken by *P*'s fundamentally different and more lethal act.

Compare the *obiter dicta* comments in *Peppersharp v. D.P.P.*,[181] where it was stated that the fact that a protestor was passively 'wearing a black hat and hooded jacket' and 'was also carrying a banner' was sufficient to infer that he encouraged the other protestors to trespass and commit criminal damage. Alas, the court was influenced by the fallacious proposals put forward by the Law Commission. The assertion made by the Law Commission that a person can be liable for the crimes of another simply because she recklessly attended a place where she knew or believed the crime might be committed, is not supported by the authorities.[182] Peppersharp's dress in itself was not an act capable of encouraging protestors to trespass and engage in acts of criminal damage. One has the right to wear a black hat and a hooded jacket. Unless there were express messages on the banner encouraging the perpetrators to commit the crime in question, it is not clear how Peppersharp encouraged them. In any case, Peppersharp's conviction was personal rather than derivative; he was personally liable for his own act of trespass contrary to section 68 of the *Criminal Justice and Public Order Act 1994*.

IX. Attempts to attempt and the *Serious Crime Act 2007*

Let us now consider attempts to attempt with reference to section 47(8)(c) of the *Serious Crime Act 2007*, which provides: '(8) Reference in this section to the doing of an act includes reference to – an attempt to do an act (*except an act amounting to the commission of the offence of attempting to commit*

180 *R. v. Gamble* [1989] N.I. 268.
181 [2012] E.W.H.C. 474 at paras. 10; 24–25.
182 See Law Commission, *Participating in Crime* (Law Com. No. 305) (London: H.M.S.O., 2007) at para. 2.23.

another offence).' Since the perpetrator cannot be liable for an attempt to attempt, it is not clear why section 47(8)(c) was included in the new *Act*. If *P* cannot be liable for an attempt to attempt, then *R* cannot be liable for encouraging *P* to do an act that is an attempt to attempt perpetrating a crime. The focus of section 47(8)(c) is on the *act* that *R* attempts to encourage or assist *P* to perpetrate. The provision does not exclude liability for assisting or encouraging crimes that *P* fails to consummate. If *R* gives *P* a gun intending to assist *P* to murder *V* with *P* firing at *V* but missing, *R* will be liable for assisting *P*'s attempted murder of *V*. The provision seems to be limited to excluding liability for *R* where *R* has assisted or encouraged *P* (or attempted to assist or encourage *P*) to do an act that would be an attempt to attempt a crime.

It seems it is aimed at excluding liability for encouraging or assisting *P* to do an act that would only be criminal for *P* if double inchoate liability were invoked for *P*. The provision focuses on the inchoateness of the act that *R* assists or encourages (or attempts to assist or encourage), rather than on the inchoateness of *R*'s act of assistance or encouragement. The provision clearly excludes liability for assisting or encouraging (or attempting to assist or encourage), with the requisite section 44, 45 or 46 *mens rea*, acts that would amount to attempts to attempt to perpetrate a crime.

It does not preclude section 44, 45 or 46 liability for assisting or encouraging attempts or attempts to encourage or assist crimes that subsume attempts such as the abrogated offence of embracery.[183] Section 47(8)(c)'s *raison d'être* is to avoid participation and inchoate participation liability for encouraging and/or assisting conduct that would be criminal only if double inchoate liability were recognised as making the putative perpetrator liable for attempting to attempt the anticipated target crime.[184]

183 Closely related is the idea of *legal* impossibility: 'It is singular, but it is also true, that there are a large number of crimes which it is impossible to attempt to commit. For instance, high treason by imagining the king's death cannot be attempted, because the crime consists in displaying by an overt act a treasonable intention, but an attempt to do something (e.g. an attempt to fire a loaded pistol at the Queen) would be an overt act displaying a treasonable intention just as much as actual firing, indeed the actual murder of the Queen would (as appears from the case of the regicides) be no more than an overt act manifesting a treasonable intent to put Her Majesty to death. Similarly a man could hardly attempt to commit perjury, or riot, or libel, or to offer bad money, or to commit an assault, for an attempt to strike is an actual assault.' Sir James Fitzjames Stephen, *A History of the Criminal Law of England* (London: Macmillan, 1883) Vol. II at 227. On attempting perjury and libel compare *Miskovsky v. Jones* (2014) 559 Fed.Appx. 673; *State v. Espinoza* (2013) 233 Ariz. 176 at 181; cf. *R. v. Deller* (1952) 36 Cr. App. R. 184.

184 If *P* has consummated the offence, then that is what *R* should be charged with encouraging or assisting. Cf. Courtney Stanhope Kenny, *Outlines of Criminal Law* (London: Macmillan, 1907) at 75, citing *R. v. Meredith* (1838) 8 Car. & P. 589.

It is worth noting that section 1(4) of the *Criminal Attempts Act 1981* makes it an offence to attempt to perpetrate

> any offence which, if it were completed, would be triable in England and Wales as an indictable offence, *other than* – (a) conspiracy (at common law *or* under section 1 of the *Criminal Law Act 1977* or any other enactment); (b) aiding, abetting, counselling, procuring or suborning the commission of an offence; (ba) an offence under section 2(1) of the *Suicide Act 1961* (encouraging or assisting suicide . . .).

Before the enactment of the *Criminal Attempts Act 1981*, England and Wales had no general statute criminalising all attempts to perpetrate crimes.[185] There were numerous statutes criminalising crimes in the nature of specific attempts, but the rest was left to the common law. Section 1(4) of the *Criminal Attempts Act 1981* was not amended to include the *Serious Crime Act 2007* offences, because it aims to criminalise attempted participation.

Like the offences found in the *Serious Crime Act 2007*, many enactments criminalise both attempt and success. A person cannot be charged with an attempt to perpetrate a crime that is itself defined as an attempt or where the offence itself criminalises both attempt and success. Consequently, a person cannot be convicted of an offence for encouraging or assisting another to do an act that is an attempt to perpetrate an attempt crime. Numerous statutory offences make it an offence to do *X* or '*to attempt*' *X*.[186]

185 Stephen, *op. cit. supra*, note 183 at 224. See also J. W. Cecil Turner, *Russell on Crime* (London: Stevens & Sons, 1958) Vol. I, at 187–189; Jerome Hall, *General Principles of Criminal Law* (Indianapolis: Bobbs Merrill, 2nd edn., 1960) at 559–599.

186 For example, section 101(1) of the *Reserve Forces Act 1996* criminalises, 'A person who . . . by any means (a) procures or persuades, *or attempts to* procure or persuade, a member of a reserve force to commit an offence of desertion or absence without leave . . .'. There are many statutory offences that criminalise both the 'attempts to' as well as success. See section 120(4) of the *Fair Trading Act 1973*; sections 9(b) and 14 of the *Theft Act 1968*; section 5 of the *Farriers (Registration) Act 1975*; section 6 of the *Perjury Act 1911*; section 3(3) of the *Road Safety Act 2006*; section 47(1) of the *Wireless Telegraphy Act 2006*; section 49 of the *Courts Act 2003*; sections 136; 141–143; 149 and 157 of the *Licensing Act 2003*; section 95(3)(c) of the *Adoption and Children Act 2002*; section 246 of the *Merchant Shipping Act 1995*; section 11 of the *Official Secrets Act 1989*; section 5 of the *Road Traffic Act 1988*; section 3A of the *Crossbows Act 1987*; section 6 of the *Ministry of Defence Police Act 1987*; sections 208(2) and 356(2)(b) of the *Insolvency Act 1986*; section 92 of the *County Courts Act 1984*; section 3(2) of the *Submarine Telegraph Act 1885*; section 35A of the *Road Traffic Regulation Act 1984*; section 4(1)(b) of the *British Fishing Boats Act 1983*; section 65(1)(g) and 2(c) of the *Representation of the People Act 1983*; section 18 of the *Wildlife and Countryside Act 1981*; section 26 of the *Town Police Clauses Act 1847*; sections 68(b) and 71(b) of the *Animal Health Act 1981*; sections 26A(d) and (e) of the *Immigration Act 1971*. Other enactments have a general attempt provision; see section 40C(3) of the *Prison Act 1952*; section 7 of the *Official Secrets Act 1920*.

Similarly, other statutes criminalise certain incitements *per se*, as was the case with embracery and subornation of perjury.

In *State v. Davis*,[187] Lampron, J. said:

> [W]e recognise that if the essence of a certain crime is the attempt to do a certain act there cannot be an attempt to commit the crime because it is committed whether or not the [offence is consummated]. Such a crime is an attempt to induce prostitution. Embracery, which is an attempt to corrupt or influence a jury is another. As to crimes of this sort it is true as argued by defendant that 'there can be no crime of an attempt to commit an attempt'.

In *Rooks v. State*,[188] McMurray, J. said:

> We know of no law authorising the conviction for an attempt to commit a crime which itself is a particular type of attempt to commit a crime . . . The refinement and metaphysical acumen [*sic*] that can see a tangible idea in the words an attempt to attempt to act is too great for practical use. It is like conceiving of the beginning of eternity or the starting place of infinity.

It is not surprising that Spencer and Virgo, referring to section 48(8)(c) of the *Serious Crime Act of 2007*, asked: 'Can any reader of this paper make sense of the wording of subsection 47(8)(c)? The authors of this article cannot – and think that if anybody can, they deserve to win a prize.'[189] The provision is paradoxical as it serves no purpose whatsoever. Since an attempt to perpetrate an attempt is not a crime itself, a person could not be liable for encouraging another to perpetrate an act that is an attempt to attempt some other crime. Section 47(8)(c) is not needed as a safeguard here, because one cannot be liable for encouraging or assisting (or attempting to encourage or assist) a non-existent crime.

It is true that a person could be liable for attempting to encourage a person to perpetrate a crime such as the abrogated crime of embracery, but a person could not be liable for encouraging or assisting a person to attempt to perpetrate a crime like[190] the abrogated crime of embracery.[191]

187 (1967) 108 N.H. 158 at 162.

188 (1995) 217 Ga.App. 643 at 669.

189 John Spencer and Graham Virgo, 'Encouraging and Assisting Crime: Legislate in Haste, Repent at Leisure' (2008) *Arch. News*, 7–9.

190 A biased juror would perpetrate the offence of contempt of court were she to allow herself to be influenced. Cf. *Attorney General v. Fraill* [2011] 2 Cr. App. R. 21; *Attorney General v. Dallas* [2012] 1 W.L.R. 991.

191 Some jurisdictions in the United States expressly exclude criminal liability for attempted participation. See the discussion of the relevant statutory exclusion in *State v. Eames* (1978) 365 So.2d 1361. *Per contra*, the *Serious Crime Act 2007* aims to criminalise

Presumably, all the provision tries to do is to make sure that people are punished only for encouraging and/or assisting another's attempted crime rather than another's attempt to attempt another crime.

How does this work in practice? Let us use the abrogated common law crime of embracery to shed some light on the subject.[192] 'Embracery is a corrupt attempt to influence a jury in their verdict, although no verdict is given.'[193] If the definition of the attempt *crime* covers *P*'s *act* of attempting to encourage or assist *P* to perpetrate the anticipated target crime, then section 47(8)(c) means *R* will be liable for encouraging or assisting *P*'s crime of embracery.[194] However, if *R* only intends to encourage *P* to attempt to do an act that is an attempt to perpetrate embracery, *R* will not be liable under section 44 of the *Serious Crime Act 2007*. *R* will not be liable, because she has not encouraged *P* to do an act that is a crime in itself.[195] (The solicitation of embracery or contempt of court is complete when the request to commit the crime is made, regardless of whether the crime solicited is ever committed or attempted.) Since the abolition of the common law offence of embracery, *R*'s act is likely to be treated as contempt of court[196] or an attempt to pervert the course of justice.[197]

attempted and successful participation. Cf. *Stewart v. Wright* (1906) 147 F. 321, where *V* attempted to participate in a fraud, but was unwittingly the victim of the fraud he tried to participate in. In *Stewart v. Wright* (1906) 147 F. 321 at 333 (a civil case in the Circuit Court of Appeals, Eighth Circuit), Hook, J. said: 'It would seem anomalous if Wright were held to be *particeps criminis* [an equal participant] to a larceny of his own money, and equally so if he were held to be in *pari delicto* [equally at fault] with those who stole it. Conduct similar to that under consideration has been held to constitute larceny, even though the fraud or pretence practiced on the victim, and by which he was despoiled of his money, assumed the simulated form of a violation of the law, in which he participated.' It was held that Wright was not deprived of a remedy by the maxim *ex dolo malo non oritur action*. Nonetheless, if this case were to be tried in the U.K. in the twenty-first century, the inchoate offences found in the *Serious Crime Act 2007* would allow the victim, Wright, to be prosecuted for his attempted participation. After all, he was attempting to participate in a fraud (Wright attempted to encourage the fraudsters to make false representations to other potential victims because he mistakenly believed he would profit from their lies) for the purpose of making a property gain for himself.

192 This offence was abolished by section 17 of the *Bribery Act 2010*. Cf. *R. v. Roderick* (1837) 7 Car. & P. 795.

193 William Hawkins, *A Treatise of the Pleas of the Crown* (London: Printed by E and R Nutt, *et al.*, 1734), Vol. I at 773. See also *R. v. Owen* [1976] 1 W.L.R. 840; *Pomfreit v. Brownsal* (1599) Cro. Eliz. 735; *The King v. T. Mein* (1791) 4 Term Reports 480 at 483.

194 See *State v. Sales* (1866) 2 Nev. 268, where, in the Supreme Court of Nevada, Lewis, C.J., said: 'It is a general rule of the common law that an attempt to commit a crime is itself a crime, but, in our opinion, from the very nature of the crime of embracery, there can be no attempt to commit it.' See also *State v. Campbell* (1995) 657 So.2d 152 at 155 *per* Doucet, C.J.; *R. v. Darby* (1702) 7 Mod. 100; *R. v. Cole* (1901) 3 Ont. L. Rep. 389.

195 Cf. the discussion in *Patterson v. State* (1989) 192 Ga.App. 449.

196 *R. v. Owen* [1976] 1 W.L.R. 840.

197 'At common law, attempting to pervert the course of justice, like perverting the course of justice, is a substantive offence.' *R. v. Rogerson* (1992) 174 C.L.R. 268 at 279 *per* Mason, C.J.,

Hence, if *R* encourages *P1* to do some act that would only be an attempt to perpetrate some crime that is an attempt in itself, or is otherwise an act that is only an attempt to attempt to perpetrate a crime, then section 47(8)(c) would apply. This prevents *R* from being convicted of encouraging or assisting *P*'s attempt to attempt to commit a crime – a non-existent crime, meaning section 47(8)(c) is utterly superfluous. Another example of an attempt that is a crime *per se* is given in *People v. Jelke*,[198] where the relevant provision made it an offence for a person to 'attempt to induce, entice, procure or compel [a woman] to live a life of prostitution'.[199]

A. Double inchoate liability for the assister/encourager

The term 'double inchoate liability' seems to have been coined by Glanville Williams in 1978.[200] Section 49(3), (4) and (5) of the *Serious Crime Act 2007* seems be to be aimed at limiting liability for those who encourage certain inchoate forms of the offences found in sections 44–46. Liability is excluded for the section 45 and 46 offences where the crime encouraged and/or assisted is one of a number of statutory incitements, but there is no bar to invoking section 44.[201] An attempt to encourage and/or assist another to perpetrate an inchoate crime pushes liability too far back.

citing e.g. *R. v. Andrews* [1973] Q.B. 422 at 425; *R. v. Rowell* [1978] 1 W.L.R. 132 at 138; *R. v. Machin* (1980) 71 Cr. App. R. 166 at 170. See also *R. v. Vreones* [1891] 1 Q.B. 360; *R. v. Kellett* [1976] Q.B. 372; *R. v. Kenny* [2013] 3 W.L.R. 59.

198 (1956) 135 N.E.2d 213.

199 See *People v. Loocerello* (1962) 233 N.Y.S.2d 206; and *People v. Lupinos* (1998) 176 Misc.2d 852 at 854, where Garnett, J. said: '[W]here a certain crime is actually defined in terms of either doing or attempting a certain crime, then the argument that there is no crime of attempting this attempt is persuasive . . . These principles are easy of application when the penal statute includes the word "attempt" within its definition. For example, a defendant cannot be charged with Attempted Resisting Arrest, *People v. Howlett* (1973) 76 Misc.2d 801 or Attempted Obstruction of Governmental Administration, *People v. Schmidt* (1974) 76 Misc.2d 976, because the statutory definition explicitly includes an attempt. *Penal Law:* Sections 205.30, 195.05.' At 855, Garnett, J. said: 'The prosecution's argument that the statute is written in the disjunctive is not persuasive. If the word "or" permitted the District Attorney to choose one of the theories in the statute and charge an attempt, then those crimes such as Resisting Arrest and or Obstructing Governmental Administration, which include "or attempts" (Penal Law Sections 205.30, 195.05) could be charged as attempts under the alternate statutory theory' [emphasis added]. This reasoning applies to the English statutory offences referred to above.

200 See Glanville Williams, *Textbook of Criminal Law* (London: Steven & Sons, 1978) at 388. The first case to make reference to the term was *Northeast Women's Center, Inc. v. McMonagle* (1988) 689 F.Supp. 465, where: 'The defendants asserted error in the court's instructions that a person is guilty of extortion if they find any of the defendants "conspired to attempt extortion" in that a conspiracy to attempt a crime is a double inchoate crime and therefore no crime at all.' A year later, Robbins published a lengthy paper on the subject. See Ira P. Robbins, 'Double Inchoate Crimes' (1989) 26 *Harv. J. on Legis.* 1 at 91.

201 Section 49 of the *Serious Crime Act 2007* provides: '(3) A person may, in relation to the same act, commit an offence under more than one provision of this Part. (4) In reckoning

Section 49(4) and (5) is used to limit liability as follows.

> (3) A person may, in relation to the same act, commit an offence under more than one provision of this Part.
> (4) In reckoning whether –
>
> (a) for the purposes of section 45, an act is capable of encouraging or assisting the commission of an offence; or
> (b) for the purposes of section 46, an act is capable of encouraging or assisting the commission of one or more of a number of offences; offences under this Part and listed offences are to be disregarded.
>
> (5) 'Listed offence' means –
>
> (a) in England and Wales, an offence listed in Part 1, 2 or 3 of Schedule 3.[202]

Section 49 does not exclude section 44 from applying to sections 45 and 46 or to any of the statutory incitements and offences of preparation listed in Schedule 3.[203] Section 49 only limits the application of the offences found in sections 45 and 46, because it holds that those offences cannot be invoked where *R* attempts to encourage/assist or in fact encourages/assists *P* to perpetrate one of the offences found in sections 44, 45 or 46 or Schedule 3 of the *Serious Crime Act 2007*. However, the section 44 offence can be applied to any offence including itself.[204] Nor does the provision exclude liability for indirect assistance (see section 66) or for bilateral transactions under section 44. (For example, offering bribes is an offence in itself, but it is also an attempt to encourage another party to perpetrate the offence of taking a bribe.[205])

whether – (a) for the purposes of section 45, an act is capable of encouraging or assisting the commission of an offence; or (b) for the purposes of section 46, an act is capable of encouraging or assisting the commission of one or more of a number of offences; offences under this Part and listed offences are to be disregarded. (5) 'Listed offence' means – (a) in England and Wales, an offence listed in Part 1, 2 or 3 of Schedule 3.'

202 The listed offences mainly cover statutory incitements; see the list of offences in Schedule 3 of the *Act of 2007*. Corporate manslaughter is also excluded.

203 See also section 1 of *Forgery and Counterfeiting Act 1981*, where the offence of forgery is complete when the instrument is 'made' although it is never published or used. Similarly, section 1 of the *Bribery Act 2010* criminalises the 'offer to bribe' regardless of whether the offer succeeds at inducing the bribed party to improperly perform a function or activity. Bribery could be attempted, however: see *R. v. Smith* [1960] 2 W.L.R. 164; *R. v. Cassano* (1805) 5 Esp. 231; *R. v. Plympton* (1724) 2 Ld. Raym. 1377. Similarly, the offence of blackmail found in section 21 of the *Theft Act 1968* is perpetrated as soon as the demand is made; nothing need have been handed over. However, if *P* attempts to blackmail *V* but fails as her blackmail demand gets lost in the post, she could be convicted of the attempt. See for example, *State v. Austin* (1986) 105 Wash.2d 511.

204 The only exception is found in section 51A, which provides: 'Section 44 does not apply to an offence under section 2(1) of the *Suicide Act 1961*.'

205 See sections 1 and 2 of the *Bribery Act 2010*.

There is no bar to section 44 being applied to other facilitation offences such as the offence found in section 25 of the *Immigration Act 1971*, which makes it an offence to do 'an act which facilitates the commission of a breach of immigration law by an individual who is not a citizen of the European Union'. A person could be liable for attempting to encourage or assist another to facilitate a breach of immigration law. Section 44 has the potential to create a vast territory of inchoate liability. The section 45 and section 46 offences also have a wide reach, because Schedule 3 excludes only a narrow range of statutory incitements and offences of preparation from the reach of those offences. There are many statutory incitements and offences of preparation that are not listed in Schedule 3; therefore, sections 45 and 46 are not excluded from applying to those offences. The justice of allowing and the need to allow the law to reach such remote wrongs is questionable.[206] The operation of the law is pushed back into the realm of what (from the point of view of the ultimate criminal intent) is not much more than an overt manifestation of a 'thought crime'! It is true that in other areas of the law the line between inchoate and substantive offences is not firm, for a number of crimes are defined in such a way as to include what the person in the street might regard as an attempt. This is so with assault, abortion and blackmail. The full crime of burglary is committed as soon as the premises are trespassed upon with the requisite intent.

In addition, there also is a range of crimes that criminalise mere preparation. For example, there are statutes that create various offences of possessing prohibited articles, the object of which is frequently to prevent the articles from being used for criminal purposes. Examples are statutory offences of possessing explosives[207] or firearms,[208] and possessing implements for certain forgeries and counterfeiting,[209] articles for use in fraud,[210] and possessing anything with intent to commit an indictable offence against the person[211] or any damage to property.[212] The offences found in section 3A of the *Computer Misuse Act 1990* include:

> (1) A person is guilty of an offence if he makes, adapts, supplies or offers to supply any article intending it to be used to commit, or to assist in the commission of, an offence under section 1, 3 or 3ZA.

206 For a discussion of the reasonable limits of 'inchoate' criminalisation, see Douglas N. Husak, 'The Nature and Justifiability of Non-Consummate Offences' (1995) 37 *Ariz. L. Rev.* 151.

207 Section 4(1) of the *Explosive Substances Act 1883*.

208 Section 16 of the *Firearms Act 1968*.

209 Section 17 of the *Forgery and Counterfeiting Act 1981*.

210 Section 6 of the *Fraud Act 2006*. See also section 25(1) of the *Theft Act 1968*.

211 Section 64 of the *Offences against the Persons Act 1861* as amended by the *Criminal Law Act 1967*.

212 A conditional intent, namely to use the article if necessary, is sufficient, *R. v. Buckingham* (1976) 63 Cr. App. R. 159.

(2) A person is guilty of an offence if he supplies or offers to supply any article believing that it is likely to be used to commit, or to assist in the commission of, an offence under section 1, 3 or 3ZA.

(3) A person is guilty of an offence if he obtains any article (a) intending to use it to commit, or to assist in the commission of, an offence under section 1, 3 or 3ZA, or (b) with a view to its being supplied for use to commit, or to assist in the commission of, an offence under section 1, 3 or 3ZA.

As we have seen, subsections 49(4) and (5) of the *Serious Crime Act 2007* hold that a person cannot be guilty under section 45 or section 46 for oblique intentionally encouraging and/or assisting the offences found in sections 44, 45 or 46 or any of those offences listed in Schedule 3, because sections 45 and 46 do not apply to sections 44, 45 and 46 or to any of the offences that are listed in Schedule 3 of the *Act of 2007*. The list of excluded offences does not merely cover statutory incitements, but also preparatory and inchoate assistance-type offences. For example, the offences found in section 3A of the *Computer Misuse Act 1990* are listed in Schedule 3. It is difficult to fathom why Schedule 3 lists the offences found in section 3A of the *Computer Misuse Act 1990*, but ignores almost identical offences found in sections 6 and 7 of the *Fraud Act 2006*. It is an oversight to exclude sections 45 and 46 from applying to certain statutory incitements and offences of preparation, but not to others. A general exclusion would make more sense than using an *ad hoc* list. Coupled with this, section 44 also should be excluded from applying to itself, to statutory incitements, and to the section 45 and 46 offences.

The *Serious Crime Act 2007* should be amended to provide for a general exclusion. For example, the *Texas Penal Code* provides:[213] 'Attempt or conspiracy to commit, or solicitation of, a preparatory offence defined in this chapter is not an offence.' If the enactment of subsections 49(4) and (5) and section 47(8)(c) was aimed at excluding inchoate liability for attempting to encourage and/or assist a perpetrator to engage in independent inchoate crimes, then it was a very poor attempt. The exemptions are contradictory, narrow and self-defeating. It would have been far better to have a general provision. A little more research on the part of the Law Commission would have produced results, because there are jurisdictions in the common law world that have dealt with this problem. The *Maine Criminal Code*[214] provides: 'It shall not be a crime to conspire to commit, or to attempt, or solicit, any [inchoate] crime.' Similarly, the commentary on Construction with other Statutes annexed to § 14:27 of the *Louisiana Revised Statutes*[215] provides:

213 V.T.C.A., Penal Code § 15.05. Preparatory offences in the Texas Penal Code include criminal attempt, criminal conspiracy and criminal solicitation. As to preparatory offenses more generally, see §§ 78 to 148 of the *Texas Penal Code*.

214 ME ST T. 17-A § 154.

215 LSA-R.S. 14:27. The commentary quotes *State v. Eames*, (1978) 365 So.2d 1361 *per* Dixon, J.

'If the definition of another crime includes the attempt to do something, this section cannot be employed, for then a defendant would be charged with an attempt to attempt to do an illegal act.' In *R. v. Déry*,[216] Forget, J.C.A. said:

> There is some uncertainty about whether inchoate offences can be combined. On the one hand, there is long-standing English authority supporting some 'doubling-up'. For example, there are cases holding that it is an offence at common law to attempt to incite someone to commit an offence. In addition, before they were abolished by a 1977[217] statute, attempting to conspire and inciting to conspire were recognized as offences at common law in England. On the other hand, in the leading Canadian case, *R. v. Dungey*, the Ontario Court of Appeal refused to accept the idea of an attempt to conspire. The case originally involved a charge of conspiracy to defraud. There had been a request to enter into an agreement but the trial judge was not convinced that an agreement had actually been made. The Crown appealed the acquittal seeking a verdict of attempted conspiracy to defraud, but it was held that there is no such offence in Canadian law.
>
> In its reasoning the court emphasized the inchoate character of conspiracy and the analogy to attempt. It was stressed that the various inchoate offences are facets of an integrated scheme of liability for preparation which would be distorted if doubling-up were permitted. If the conduct of the respondent was not sufficiently proximate to the substantive offence to be an attempt to commit it, and if there was not a conspiracy to commit it, it would be inappropriate to push inchoate liability any further back. It was also said that an offence of attempting to conspire to defraud would be 'tantamount to convicting a person of an attempt to attempt to defraud.
>
> The reasoning in *Dungey*, together with the statutory abolition of the offence of attempting to conspire in England, is some evidence of a

(with two Justices concurring and one Justice concurring in result). See also *United States v. Riddle* (1996) 44 M.J. 282 at 288; *U.S. v. Awan* (2006) 459 F.Supp.2d 167 at 184; *U.S. v. Roeseler* (2001) 55 M.J. 286 at 298; *U.S. v. Ortiz* (1990) 738 F.Supp. 1394. In *U.S. v. Riddle* (1996) 44 M.J. 282 at 285, Sullivan, J. said: 'The double inchoate offence of attempt to conspire is unnecessary in those jurisdictions that have adopted either a solicitation statute or a conspiracy statute that embodies the unilateral theory of conspiracy, or both.' However, many jurisdictions in the U.S. do allow for double inchoate liability. See also *U.S. v. Lanzon* (2011) 639 F.3d 1293 at 1298.

216 [2005] 197 C.C.C. (3d) 534 at paragraph 93.

217 Section 5(1)(7) of the *Criminal Law Act 1977* provided: 'Incitement . . . to commit the offence of conspiracy (whether the conspiracy incited . . . would be an offence at common law or under section 1 above or any other enactment) shall cease to be offences.' Section 5(1)(7) was repealed by *Serious Crime Act 2007*, Sch.14 para.1 (October 1, 2008), because the common law offence of incitement was abrogated by section 59 of the *Act of 2007*. The governing provision is now section 49 of the *Act of 2007*.

trend against acceptance of doubling-up. This trend may be the result of increasing attention to the interrelationships between the inchoate offences and the common rationale of restraint which underlies their particular limitations.

B. Indirect (inchoate) participation

Section 66 of the *Serious Crime Act 2007* has a specific provision that targets indirect encouragement and/or assistance. Section 66 provides: 'If a person (D1) arranges for a person (D2) to do an act that is capable of encouraging or assisting the commission of an offence, and D2 does the act, D1 is also to be treated for the purposes of this Part as having done it.'[218] If *R1* encourages *R2* to encourage *P* (an assassin) to kill *V*, *R* will be liable for the section 44 offence even when *P* ignores *R2*'s encouragement.[219] Section 66 expressly states that the middle party must at least attempt to encourage the intended perpetrator, but she need not succeed. Hence, the words 'and D2 does the act' clearly require nothing less than an attempt from the middle party. If *P* kills or attempts[220] to kill *V* as a result of *R2*'s encouragement, both *R1* and *R2* will be liable for the section 44 offence, but the Crown is more likely to prosecute *R1* and *R2* as accessories to murder under section 8 of the *Accessories and Abettors Act 1861*.[221] There is nothing unfair about criminalising *R1*'s actions when *R2* attempts to encourage *P*, but it is appropriate that the law does not criminalise *R1*'s failed attempt to encourage *R2* to encourage *P*, especially when the putative crime could be as serious as murder.[222]

X. Remote encouragement

The new offences need to have some sort of defence, because they are so incredibly wide that they have the potential to chill free speech and also result in unfair and unnecessary criminalisation.[219] People can participate in an activity directly, indirectly, remotely and at various degrees.

218 See *Earl of Somerset's Case* (1616) 14 Jac. 1; 1 St. Tr. 334. This sort of case is also caught in some jurisdictions in the United States. For example, in *State v. Manthey* (1992) 169 Wis.2d 673 at 687, where Myse, J. said: 'Section 946.31(1), Stats., provides: "Whoever under oath or affirmation orally makes a false material statement which the person does not believe to be true, in any matter, cause, action or proceeding, before [a court] . . . is guilty of a Class D felony." The question presented here is whether one can be guilty of solicitation of perjury where "A" solicits "B" to solicit "A" to commit perjury. This phenomenon is referred to as a "double inchoate crime". There is no question that under current Wisconsin law, "A" is guilty of solicitation if "A" advises "B" to procure "C" to commit a felony.'

219 Western states are over-criminalised and more inchoate offences have the potential to add to the over-criminalisation crisis. For a discussion of the over-criminalisation crisis see Douglas N. Husak, *Overcriminalisation: The Limits of the Criminal Law* (New York: Oxford University Press, 2008). See also the classic paper by Sanford H. Kadish, 'The Crisis of Overcriminalisation' (1967) 374 *Annals Am. Acad. Pol. & Soc. Sci.*, 157.

Take a game of football in a public stadium. The direct participants are the football players. The spectators observe but they do not participate. The cheerleaders engage in an independent act of cheerleading, but they do not participate in the football game *per se*. The coach is a participant in the football game even though she does not play. She directly counsels and advises the players and thus is involved in their game. The coach shares some of the blame for any mistakes made by the players and the rewards when the game goes well. The spectators are not responsible for mistakes in the game, nor are they responsible for it being played well. Their presence gives the players a reason for playing at the particular location on the particular day, but it does not give the players a reason for breaking the rules or for criminally assaulting the other players. The players give the football organisation a reason for staging such games. The organisers give the football players a reason for playing, because they pay them to play and make them celebrities. It could be argued that it is the organisers and players that encourage the spectators to spectate the game in question, because they market the game to draw in spectators. The organisers host such games to make money from the spectators. Encouragement runs both ways here as the demand for such games also induces the organisers to supply such games. This sort of remote and collective encouragement is too diffuse to be measured as encouragement for the purpose of establishing participation.[220] There has to be some sort of direct encouragement/assistance aimed at an identifiable (putative) perpetrator.

A more individualised example of remote participation is provided in *Evans v. Jones*,[221] where Lord Abinger, C.B. said:

> A strong feeling at that time prevailed against Napoleon Bonaparte, who threatened an invasion of this kingdom; but it gave great satisfaction to myself, and all who took an interest in the administration of public justice, to hear the principle pronounced by Lord Ellenborough, and the first common law authorities, that a wager on the duration of his life was illegal, as being against public policy – as having a tendency to encourage his assassination, which, even in the instance of a public enemy, should receive no encouragement from the law.

This sort of encouragement is remote, as putting down a wager was not conduct that directly encouraged another to kill Napoleon Bonaparte.

220 *R. v. Clarkson* [1971] 1 W.L.R. 1402 at 1406; *R. v. Coney* (1881–82) L.R. 8 Q.B.D. 534 *per* Denman, J., Huddleston, B., Manisty, Hawkins, Lopes, Stephen, Cave, and North, J.J. Foster, *op. cit. supra*, note 69 at 350. See also *R. v. Vanderstein* (1865) 10 Cox C.C. 177.

221 (1839) 5 M. & W. 77 at 81. For the case discussing the wager against Napoleon Bonaparte, see *Gilbert v. Sykes* (1812) 16 East 150.

If a person in London had placed a wager on Muammar al-Gaddafi's life during the Arab Spring in 2011, it would have been a stretch to count the wager as tangible encouragement against his life. In such a case the perpetrator alone should be held responsible for the killing. This can be rationalised in psychological terms by saying that the intervention of the responsible actor diverts our retributive wrath from the remote encourager, who is not sufficiently connected to the end harm to warrant censure. It would not be right to make people responsible for the subsequent behaviour of others, merely because they foresaw or could have foreseen that behaviour as a consequence of their remote action. There is no pressing necessity to regard more remote authors as responsible for the harm itself, though they may well be prosecuted for other offences, such as attempt, or in appropriate circumstances for independent offences such as possession offences.

A. Remote (inchoate) participation and personal wrongs

A person who inadvertently provokes another to kill without encouraging him to do so does not become guilty of murder or manslaughter, even though she realised or should have realised what the effect of her conduct would be.[222] Unintentionally provoking another person to break the peace[223] or to drive recklessly[224] does not make the provoker criminally liable for that other person's personal wrongdoing. Generally, the courts have not held people liable where their lawful conduct has had the unintended effect of influencing another's criminal choices. Take the example of *X*, the owner of a corner store. *X* sells an ice cream to customer *Y*; *Y* subsequently walks out of *X*'s shop and throws the ice cream's packaging on the ground. Should *X* be held responsible for *Y*'s littering? The harm is contingent on *Y* making an intervening choice to throw the packet on the ground, but it would not have come about but for *X* selling the ice cream to *Y*. It is clear that *X* is not morally blameworthy (criminally condemnable) for this kind of remote harm. The appropriate measure is to punish those who actually throw papers on the street.[225]

In *Schneider v. State of New Jersey*,[226] Clara Schneider was a protestor who stood in the street and distributed handbills to passing pedestrians.

222 Cf. *R. v. Dubois* (1959) 32 C.R. 187 (Quebec).

223 *Beatty v. Gillbanks* (1882) 9 Q.B.D. 308; Cf. *Wise v. Dunning* [1902] 1 K.B. 167.

224 *R. v. Mastin* (1834) 172 E.R. 1292.

225 *Schneider v. New Jersey* (1939) 308 U.S. 147; *Martin v. City of Struthers* (1943) 319 U.S. 141; *Van Nuys Pub. Co. v. City of Thousand Oaks* (1971) 5 Cal.3d 817; *International Soc. for Krishna Consciousness of Berkeley, Inc. v. Kearnes* (1978) 454 F.Supp. 116; *Village of Schaumburg v. Citizens for a Better Environment* (1980) 444 U.S. 620; *Schad v. Borough of Mount Ephraim* (1981) 452 U.S. 61; *Jews for Jesus, Inc. v. Massachusetts Bay Transp. Authority* (1993) 984 F.2d 1319; *Miller v. City of Laramie* (1994) 880 P.2d 594.

226 (1939) 308 U.S. 147.

Schneider was convicted of canvassing without a permit as required by an ordinance of the Town of Irvington. The handbills contained information about a labour dispute with a meat market and outlined the position of the organised labour movement. The handbills were an attempt to persuade people to refrain from patronising the relevant meat market. Many of those who accepted the handbills threw them on the street either after reading them or without reading them at all. The end result was that the street and gutter was littered with the discarded handbills. The police arrested the petitioner instead of those who were responsible for discarding the handbills. The Milwaukee County convicted the petitioner under a local ordinance. The Supreme Court of New Jersey upheld the petitioner's conviction.[227] The petitioner appealed to the Supreme Court of the United States. Roberts, J. (delivering the opinion of the Court) said:[228]

> The motive of the legislation under attack . . . is held by the courts below to be the prevention of littering of the streets and, although the alleged offenders were not charged with themselves scattering paper in the streets, their convictions were sustained upon the theory that distribution by them *encouraged or resulted* in such littering. We are of opinion that the purpose to keep the streets clean and of good appearance is insufficient to justify an ordinance which prohibits a person rightfully on a public street from handing literature to one willing to receive it. Any burden imposed upon the city authorities in cleaning and caring for the streets as an indirect consequence of such distribution results from the constitutional protection of the freedom of speech and press. This constitutional protection does not deprive a city of all power to prevent street littering. There are obvious methods of preventing littering. *Amongst these is the punishment of those who actually throw papers on the streets* [emphasis added].

In *R. v. Goldman*,[229] Goldman was convicted of attempting to incite his potential supplier to distribute photographs of children under the age of 16.[230] As we saw above, an attempt to encourage is, by and large, caught by the *Act of 2007*.[231] Goldman responded to an advertisement placed by *X* (the potential supplier) by requesting pornographic videotapes of girls aged 7 to 13. Goldman sent *X* payment for the videotapes, but *X* did not supply them. Goldman was convicted because he had attempted to encourage *X* to

227 *Town of Irvington v. Schneider* (1938) 120 N.J.L. 460.

228 *Schneider v. New Jersey* (1939) 308 U.S. 147 at 162.

229 *R. v. Goldman* [2001] E.W.C.A. Crim. 1684.

230 Goldman attempted to commit a substantive offence. The substantive offence which he attempted to incite another to commit is set out in section 1 of the *Protection of Children Act 1978*.

231 Compare, *R. v. Jones* [2008] Q.B. 460; *Baney v. State* (2009) 42 So.3d 170.

distribute the illegal videos. Nevertheless, it would be wrong to leave *X* out of the equation, as she was the original instigator. Arguably, *X* was trying to encourage Goldman and his ilk to possess child pornography.[232] *X* might not have encouraged Goldman to distribute the videos, but his advertisement surely encouraged him to possess them.[233] *X* must have believed that by *encouraging* people to purchase child pornography those same people would commit the offence of possessing it. *X* must also have believed that by selling child pornography to certain people that she would *assist* them to possess it. If the supplier is the person who initiated the idea, then she encouraged the crime. But, if the would-be perpetrator goes to the supplier and asks for the supply, the fact of supply in itself should not be regarded as an encouragement, any more than it should be regarded as conspiracy.

When many paedophiles purchase child pornography they create the demand for the market in child pornography. This type of remote encouragement is not caught by the *Serious Crime Act 2007*. The *Act of 2007* does not criminalise paedophiles at large merely because they collectively encourage others to go into the business of producing and supplying child pornography. Rather, there has to be an individualised act of encouragement. The *Act of 2007* deals with individual requests (acts of encouragement) for such material when those requests are conveyed (or there is an attempt to convey such requests)[234] to a particular supplier/producer. (The producer/supplier would be liable when she places an advertisement to the world at large, because such an advertisement has the potential to encourage a paedophile within the general population to possess child pornography.)[235] It is true that paedophiles create the demand for self-service websites containing these ghastly materials, but if they serve themselves they have not encouraged another to serve them.[236] A supplier is encouraged to stay in business as the funds accumulate automatically into her account, but she is not encouraged to distribute to a particular individual. If the offending images and movies have been uploaded on a website three years before *R* purchases them, then it is difficult to see how *R* is responsible for encouraging *P*'s past uploading of the illegal images. Furthermore, it is difficult to see how *R* encourages

232 There were jurisdictional issues involved, however.

233 Section 1(c) of the *Protection of Children Act 1978* criminalises only those who possess the images for the purpose of distribution or for the purpose of showing others them. If the paedophile intends only to look at them himself, he is not caught by that provision.

234 Cf. *R. v. Jones* [2008] Q.B. 460; *Baney v. State* (2009) 42 So.3d 170.

235 See *Invicta Plastics Ltd. v. Clare* [1976] R.T.R. 251.

236 The court points out in *R. (on the Application of O'Shea) v. City of Coventry Magistrates' Court* [2004] E.W.H.C. 905 (Admin), that somewhere within the process a human agent will send a videotape or product. But this is not true with respect to websites where the images may be digital and may be posted in advance for anyone to download for payment without any further human action being required. In such cases, it appears that the encourager does not encourage an act of supply, but merely creates the demand for the supplier/producer to create an automated mechanism of supply via the Internet.

an act of supply, if all he has to do is pay a fee for the images and movies to automatically download to his computer. Similarly, if a person leaves a pile of melons and pumpkins on an old table on the side of a highway and leaves an honesty box on the table, she encourages the world at large to purchase her goods, but she herself is not encouraged by any particular individual to supply that individual. In the criminal law, responsibility is individual not collective; the criminal law targets individuals not collectives.[237]

There would be no justification for using the inchoate offences of encouragement found in the *Serious Crime Act 2007* to prosecute possessors of child pornography for creating the demand for producers and distributors to go into the business of producing these horrible materials. The encouragement is too remote. It would be enough to charge the possessor with a possession offence and the distributor with a distribution offence. There is nothing wrong with prohibiting people from possessing or distributing these sorts of materials. In *U.S. v. Stevens*,[238] Alito, J. observed that the underlying crime (sexually violating children) 'could not be effectively combated without targeting the distribution of child pornography'. Hence, it is necessary and justifiable to have possession, distribution and production offences. It is also necessary and justifiable to have offences that target those who *directly* encourage others to produce, distribute or possess such materials. The encouragement must be direct and proximate. It is worth noting that possessing child pornography is a remote harm, because those who merely purchase child pornography do not come into contact with the children. The possessors are not the people who directly harm the children; it is the producers who harm the children who are violated to produce such materials.

The majority decision in *U.S. v. Stevens*[239] is too indulgent in holding that *distributing* graphic films depicting dogfighting is protected speech.

237 Baker, *op. cit. supra*, note 36 at Chapter 9; Dennis J. Baker, 'Collective Criminalisation and the Constitutional Right to Endanger Others' (2009) 28 *Crim. Just. Ethics* 168.

238 *U.S. v. Stevens* (2010) 559 U.S. 460 at 494 citing *New York v. Ferber* (1982) 458 U.S. 747 at 759. Alito, J. also said: 'As the Court put it, "the distribution network for child pornography must be closed if the production of material which requires the sexual exploitation of children is to be effectively controlled" . . . [T]here is no serious contention that the legislature was unjustified in believing that it is difficult, if not impossible, to halt the exploitation of children by pursuing only those who produce the photographs and movies . . . The most expeditious if not the only practical method of law enforcement may be to dry up the market for this material by imposing severe criminal penalties on persons selling, advertising, or otherwise promoting the product.' Cf. also the discussion in *Reno v. American Civil Liberties Union* (1997) 521 U.S. 844; *Podracky v. Com.* (2008) 52 Va.App. 130. For a full survey of American law concerning the Internet and child pornography, see Lori J. Parker, 'Validity, Construction, and Application of Federal Enactments Proscribing Obscenity and Child Pornography or Access Thereto on the Internet' 7 A.L.R. Fed. 2d 1 (updated 2015, originally published in 2005).

239 (2010) 559 U.S. 460 where Roberts, C.J., delivered the opinion of the Court, in which Stevens, Scalia, Kennedy, Thomas, Ginsburg, Breyer and Sotomayor, J.J, concurred. Alito, J., filed a dissenting opinion. Alito, J.'s opinion is more convincing than that of the majority. A normative case can be made for criminalising distribution *per se*.

In that case, Stevens sold videotapes showing dogs viciously tearing each other apart. Stevens did not create the dogfights, nor did he incite others to do so, but he was given a 37-month prison sentence under a federal law (18 U.S.C. § 48) that banned dealing in depictions of animal cruelty. The Supreme Court of the United States held the law that was used to imprison him was substantially overbroad, and thus was invalid under the First Amendment to the U.S. Constitution. This sort of case satisfies the harm justification for criminalisation and punishment, even though a 37-month prison sentence was a disproportionate sentence. A six-week prison sentence might have been justified, since the speech was an unjustifiable and inexcusable remote harm. It was remotely harmful in a way that counts, because the defendant was culpable for benefiting from the original harm. This is a case where it would have been justifiable to criminalise the distribution itself.

The moral justification for criminalisation in such cases is not utilitarian. The justification for criminalisation is that the possessor/distributor chooses to benefit from the fruits of the underlying criminal harm. The case is analogous to the case where a person handles stolen goods. Such a person does not harm anyone directly by purchasing stolen goods at a discount, but she culpably benefits from the underlying criminal harm. It is the culpable extraction of a benefit from the criminal harm that makes it fair to criminalise her ancillary role.[240] The purchasers of ivory collectively form the lucrative ivory market that is poaching's *raison d'être.* It is also true that the purchases of child pornography form the lucrative market that is the *raison d'être* of child pornography distribution and production. The market for ivory increases the risk of harm to the endangered elephant population, because the market itself encourages production. The ivory possessor should be charged with a possession offence rather than with an encouragement offence, because her possession is a benefit that she receives as a result of the original harm. She receives the fruits of a criminal harm and thus perpetrates a personal wrong in itself. *X* does not kill the elephants or even come into contact with them, but she intends to benefit from the poacher's criminal harm. When a paedophile chooses to possess images of real children he chooses to take the benefit of a criminal harm. The possessor/purchaser intentionally and knowingly receives the fruits of a grave criminal harm. By receiving a product that can be produced only through wrongful harm, the possessor underwrites the wrongful harm. Her knowledge of the underlying harm-doing is certain and she chooses to benefit from the fruits of the harm. When *X* sells a gun to a potential killer she might not know for sure whether she will use it to kill, but when *Y* purchases ivory or child pornography she knows as a matter of fact that a harm has been committed to produce such products.

240 Baker, *op. cit. supra*, note 32 at Chapter 4.

Similarly, the gravamen of the offence of receiving stolen goods is the receiving of the goods with knowledge that they were stolen. It is wrong for a person to possess or receive goods that she knows are stolen, because she knows the goods have become available only because someone has committed a wrongful harm against an innocent other. In the aforementioned cases, liability is personal not derivative.

An example of unjust remote harm criminalisation can be found in section 53A of the *Sexual Offences Act 2003*, which provides:

> (1) A person (A) commits an offence if – (a) A makes or promises payment for the sexual services of a prostitute (B), (b) a third person (C) has engaged in exploitative conduct of a kind likely to induce or encourage B to provide the sexual services for which A has made or promised payment, and (c) C engaged in that conduct for or in the expectation of gain for C or another person (apart from A or B).
> (2) The following are irrelevant – (a) where in the world the sexual services are to be provided and whether those services are provided, (b) whether A is, or ought to be, aware that C has engaged in exploitative conduct.
> (3) C engages in exploitative conduct if – (a) C uses force, threats (whether or not relating to violence) or any other form of coercion, or (b) C practises any form of deception.
> (4) A person guilty of an offence under this section is liable on summary conviction to a fine not exceeding level 3 on the standard scale.

The problem with criminalising prostitution use on the basis that it creates the market for people-trafficking and forced prostitution is that the encouragement from the existence of the general market for prostitution is too remote. Furthermore, unlike ivory possession and child pornography possession, harm *per se* cannot be used to justify criminalisation, because the prostitute user does not necessarily benefit from harmful prostitution (i.e. non-consensual prostitution) as opposed to harmless prostitution (i.e. consensual prostitution involving consenting adults entering a valid contract for sexual services). In this sort of case, it is enough to criminalise those who traffic and force people to prostitute themselves.[241] If the punter

241 See section 4 of the *Sexual Offences Act 2003*, which makes it an offence to cause a person to engage in non-consensual sexual activity. The *Sexual Offences Act 2003* also criminalises trafficking: trafficking into the U.K. for sexual exploitation is covered by section 57; trafficking within the U.K. for sexual exploitation is covered by section 58; trafficking outside the U.K. for sexual exploitation is covered by section 58A; trafficking out of the U.K. for sexual exploitation is covered by section 59; and trafficking people for sexual exploitation is covered by section 59A.

has sexual intercourse with a woman he suspects is not consenting, then he would be liable for rape.[242] There is no need to criminalise those who have sexual intercourse with a prostitute when a reasonable person in his position would have believed that there was genuine consent.

Does a prostitute encourage prostitution use by merely standing in the street in a low cut mini-dress? Would this be an act that is capable of encouraging a kerb crawler to perpetrate an offence contrary to section 51A of the *Sexual Offences Act 2003*?[243] The kerb crawler is in that area cruising the kerb because he already intends to find a prostitute. It would be too much to prosecute the prostitute under section 44 or 45 of the *Serious Crime Act 2007* for encouraging the punter to kerb crawl, simply because she and other prostitutes create the demand for kerb crawlers. Prostitution results in kerb crawling, because the kerb crawler crawls where he knows he will find prostitutes. Vice versa the kerb crawlers create the demand for prostitution supply. To criminalise people merely for creating the demand for distributors/suppliers/producers to exist would result in unfair remote harm criminalisation.[244] The offences found in the *Serious Crime Act 2007* should be invoked only when there is proximate direct encouragement. After all, there are narrowly tailored offences that criminalise kerb crawling in itself and thus there is no need to use encouragement type offences to rope in the prostitutes as well.

B. The reasonable conduct defence

Section 50 of the *Serious Crime Act 2007* includes a reasonableness defence. The defence provides:

> (1) A person is not guilty of an offence under this Part if he proves –
>
> (a) that he knew certain circumstances existed; and
> (b) that it was reasonable for him to act as he did in those circumstances.

242 Negligence as to consent is sufficient for establishing rape under section 1 of the *Sexual Offences Act 2003*.

243 Section 51A of the *Sexual Offence Act 2003* provides: '(1) It is an offence for a person in a street or public place to solicit another (B) for the purpose of obtaining B's sexual services as a prostitute. (2) The reference to a person in a street or public place includes a person in a vehicle in a street or public place.'

244 Dennis J. Baker, 'The Moral Limits of Criminalizing Remote Harms' (2007) 10(3) *New Crim. L. Rev.* 371; Dennis J. Baker and Lucy X. Zhao, 'The Normativity of Using Prison to Control Hate Speech: The Hollowness of Waldron's Harm Theory' (2013) 14(4) *New Crim. L. Rev.* 621 at 627; Andrew von Hirsch, 'Extending the Harm Principle: "Remote" Harms and Fair Imputation' in Andrew P. Simester and A.T.H. Smith (eds), *Harm and Culpability* (Oxford: Clarendon Press, 1996) at 261 *et seq.* Of course, it is no longer a criminal offence to libel others.

(2) A person is not guilty of an offence under this Part if he proves –

(a) that he believed certain circumstances to exist;
(b) that his belief was reasonable; and
(c) that it was reasonable for him to act as he did in the circumstances as he believed them to be.

(3) Factors to be considered in determining whether it was reasonable for a person to act as he did include –

(a) the seriousness of the anticipated offence (or, in the case of an offence under section 46, the offences specified in the indictment);
(b) any purpose for which he claims to have been acting;
(c) any authority by which he claims to have been acting.

Long ago it was held that libellous allegations could incite violence and breaches of the peace. Is libel too remote? In *De Libellis Famosis Case*, it was said:

> Every libel (which is called *famosus libellus, seu infamatoria scriptura*), is made either against a private man, or against a magistrate or public person. If it be against a private man it deserves a severe punishment, for although the libel be made against one, yet it incites all those of the same family, kindred, or society to revenge, and so tends *per consequens* to quarrels and breach of the peace, and may be the cause of shedding of blood, and of great inconvenience: if it be against a magistrate, or other public person, it is a greater offence; for it concerns not only the breach of the peace.[245]
>
> . . .
>
> It is not material whether the libel be true,[246] or whether the party against whom it is made, be of good or ill fame; for in a settled state of Government the party grieved ought to complain for every injury done him in an ordinary course of law, and not by any means to revenge himself, either by the odious course of libelling, or otherwise . . .

This type of provocative conduct would not be caught by the *Serious Crime Act 2007*, because the libeller does not encourage the putative perpetrator to perpetrate a particular anticipated target crime. Nor would the libeller, apart from special facts, have the *mens rea* required for the offences found

245 (1606) 5 Co. Rep. 125. Cf. *Paris v. Levy* (1860) 9 C.B. N.S. 342 at 344–345.
246 These days Article 10 of the *European Convention for the Protection of Human Rights and Fundamental Freedoms*, 4 November 1950, 213 U.N.T.S. 222 (entered into force generally on 3 September 1953) could be invoked for *true* speech.

in the *Act of 2007*. In *Beatty v. Gillbanks*,[247] it was held that the Salvation Army had acted lawfully in congregating in a public place in Weston-super-Mare even though its officers believed from past experience that this would provoke an attack from an opposing organisation, the Skeleton Army. The Salvation Army believed that the Skeleton Army would behave unlawfully, but it was not its purpose to encourage it to behave unlawfully. Its aim was merely to congregate in public for the purposes of preaching its religion to followers. Field, J. (Cave, J. concurring) said:[248]

> The appellants have, with others, formed themselves into an association for religious exercises among themselves . . . No one imputes to this association any other object, and so far from wishing to carry that out with violence, their opinions seem to be opposed to such a course, and, at all events in the present case, they made no opposition to the authorities. That being their lawful object, they assembled as they had done before and marched in procession through the streets of Weston-super-Mare. No one can say that such an assembly is in itself an unlawful one. The appellants complain that in consequence of this assembly they have been found guilty of a crime of which there is no reasonable evidence that they have been guilty.
>
> . . .
>
> [T]he evidence set forth in the case . . . shews that the disturbances were caused by other people antagonistic to the appellants, and that no acts of violence were committed by them.

In *Redmond-Bate v. D.P.P*, Ms Redmond-Bate had been preaching on the steps of a cathedral when a police constable arrested her. A crowd of more than one hundred had gathered around Ms Redmond-Bate and some members of that crowd were becoming hostile. A police officer asked Redmond-Bate to stop preaching, because he feared that if she continued to preach it would result in a breach of the peace. Redmond-Bate refused to stop preaching and as a result the police officer arrested her for wilfully obstructing him in the execution of his duty under section 89(2) of the *Police Act 1996*. Sedley, L.J. (Collins J. concurring) said:[249] 'If the threat

247 (1882) 9 Q.B.D. 308. Cf. *Wise v. Dunning* [1902] 1 K.B. 167; *Duncan v. Jones* [1936] 1 K.B. 218.

248 *Beatty v. Gillbanks* (1882) 9 Q.B.D. 308 at 313–314. It is worth noting that the members of the Salvation Army were passive and were not inciting crime or hatred against themselves – nor where they threatening. If they have made true threats – or had engaged in conduct of a genuinely threatening nature – then they might have been liable for a breach of the peace. Cf. the discussion on free speech and threats in *U.S. v. Turner* (2013) 720 F.3d 411 at 420; *Virginia v. Black* (2003) 538 U.S. 343.

249 *Redmond-Bate v. D.P.P.* [2000] H.R.L.R. 249 at 259.

of disorder or violence was coming from passers-by who were taking the opportunity to react so as to cause trouble, then it was they and not the preachers who should be asked to desist and arrested if they would not.' Sedley, L.J. also said:[250]

> I am unable to see any lawful basis for the arrest or therefore the conviction . . . There was no suggestion of highway obstruction. Nobody had to stop and listen. If they did so, they were as free to express the view that the preachers should be locked up or silenced as the appellant and her companions were to preach.

In *R. (on the application of Laporte) v. Chief Constable of Gloucestershire*, Lord Brown said:

> Take Mr. Beatty, the Salvation Army captain,[251] or Ms Redmond-Bate,[252] the Wakefield preacher. The Divisional Court was in each case clearly right to have set aside their respective convictions. I repeat, the police's first duty is to protect the rights of the innocent rather than to compel the innocent to cease exercising them.[253]

The section 50 defence will require some sort of balancing of harm and public interest. It will be left to the jury to evaluate the social value of the

250 *Redmond-Bate v. D.P.P.* [2000] H.R.L.R. 249 at 260. Sedley, L.J. also said: 'Free speech includes not only the inoffensive but the irritating, the contentious, the eccentric, the heretical, the unwelcome and the provocative provided it does not tend to provoke violence. Freedom only to speak inoffensively is not worth having. What Speaker's Corner (where the law applies as fully as anywhere else) demonstrates is the tolerance which is both extended by the law to opinion of every kind and expected by the law in the conduct of those who disagree, even strongly, with what they hear. From the condemnation of Socrates to the persecution of modern writers and journalists, our world has seen too many examples of State control of unofficial ideas. A central purpose of the *European Convention on Human Rights* has been to set close limits to any such assumed power. We in this country continue to owe a debt to the jury which in 1670 refused to convict the Quakers William Penn and William Mead for preaching ideas which offended against State orthodoxy.' In *U.S. v. Polouizzi* (2010) 687 F.Supp.2d 133 at 169, Weinstein, J. observed: 'The Quakers, William Penn and William Mead, were prosecuted in London in 1670 for preaching to an unlawful assembly and for breach of the peace. After the jury acquitted Mead of all charges and found Penn not guilty of disturbing the peace, it was deprived of food, water and heat. Despite these coercive tactics, the jury still refused to find guilt, and was fined. Some jurors, including a man named Bushell, refused to pay; they were imprisoned, until ordered released by the Chief Justice on the ground that the jury in effect determines the law when deciding by general verdict.' See *Bushell's Case* (1670) 6 St. Tr. 999 and *Hamond v. Howell* (1677) 2 Mod. 218.

251 *Beatty v. Gillbanks* (1882) 9 Q.B.D. 308.

252 See *Redmond-Bate v. D.P.P.* [2000] H.R.L.R. 249.

253 [2007] 2 A.C. 105 at 155. See also *Austin v. Commissioner of Police of the Metropolis* [2008] Q.B. 660 at 680–681.

conduct involved. Feinberg has written: 'The more valuable (useful) the dangerous conduct . . . the more reasonable it is to take the risk . . . and for extremely valuable conduct it is reasonable to run risks up to the point of clear and present danger.'[254] Should the television crew be held criminally liable for creating the demand for nude and violent street protests? Would it not be an intolerable extension of criminal responsibility if television crews and others were held criminally liable for exercising their lawful rights and liberties, simply because it might encourage others to engage in criminal conduct to attract publicity for their cause?[255] The courts are likely to hold that media coverage of protests involves free speech and serves a highly valuable purpose – informing the public about what is going on in the world. This is the sort of valuable conduct that Parliament had in mind when it enacted section 50.

254 Joel Feinberg, *The Moral Limits of the Criminal Law: Harm to Others* (New York: Oxford University Press, Vol. I 1984) at 215–216.

255 See Glanville Williams, 'Complicity, Purpose and the Draft Code: Part 1' [1990] Crim. L.R. 4 at 10.

5 Defences, labelling and sentencing

Abstract

At common law withdrawal does not seem to have been recognised as a defence for inchoate offences such as conspiracy, attempt and incitement. The Serious Crime Act 2007 *also fails to incorporate a withdrawal defence. In this chapter, it is argued that withdrawal, renunciation and abandonment should provide defences. At the very least, they should go to mitigation in sentencing, if it is clear on the evidence that the defendant effectively neutralised her attempted assistance or encouragement and took firm steps to renounce her criminal intentions.*

I. Introduction

> But yet in some cases the time may be material; for if I command one to kill *J. S.* and before the fact done I go to him and tell him that I have repented, and expressly charge him not to kill *J. S.* and he afterwards kills him, there I shall not be accessary to this murder, because I have countermanded my first command, which in all reason shall discharge me, for the malicious mind of the accessary ought to continue to do ill until the time of the act done, or else he shall not be charged; but if he had killed *J. S.* before the time of my discharge or countermand given, I should have been accessary to the death, notwithstanding my private repentance.[1]
>
> To be effective as a defence, there must be an appreciable interval between the alleged abandonment of the criminal enterprise and the act for which responsibility is sought to be avoided. The co-conspirator must have a reasonable opportunity to follow the example and refrain from further action before the act in question is committed. A conspirator cannot escape responsibility for an act which is the natural result of a criminal scheme he has helped to devise and carry forward by running away at the instant when the act in question is

1 *R. v. Saunders and Archer* (1577) 2 Plow. 473 at 476.

about to be committed and the transaction which immediately begets it has actually been commenced.[2]

In this section, I shall consider some of the core defences for both complicity and inchoate (attempted) complicity. Section 2.06 of the American Law Institute's *Model Penal Code* provides:

> (6) Unless otherwise provided by the Code or by the law defining the offence, a person is not an accomplice in an offence committed by another person if:
>
> (a) he is a victim of that offence; or
> (b) the offence is so defined that his conduct is inevitably incident to its commission; or
> (c) he terminates his complicity prior to the commission of the offence and
>
> (i) wholly deprives it of effectiveness in the commission of the offence; or
> (ii) gives timely warning to the law enforcement authorities or otherwise makes proper effort to prevent the commission of the offense.

I examined the 'victim rule' defence and the 'inevitably incidental party' defence in Chapter 3. Therefore, I shall not reconsider them here. I considered the defence of 'impossibility' in relation to attempted complicity in Chapter 4 and thus shall not reconsider it here. My focus in this chapter will be on the defences of Withdrawal and Abandonment in relation to both consummated complicity and attempted complicity.

II. Withdrawal from complicity

A person who joins a criminal enterprise or otherwise assists or encourages another to commit a crime is not irrevocably liable for all the crimes committed by that other person. An accessory can terminate her participation as an accomplice in the crimes of others. If an accessory takes reasonable steps to try to neutralise her acts of assistance and encouragement, she may be able to raise the defence of withdrawal to avoid complicity liability. The accessory would have to withdraw her assistance or encouragement in a timely manner and demonstrate that the perpetrator was aware of her withdrawal.[3]

2 *State v. Banks* (2009) 771 N.W.2d 75 at 94 *per* Miller-Lerman, J. citing *State v. Wilson* (1974) 192 Neb. 435.

3 See generally, Dennis J. Baker, *Glanville Williams: Textbook of Criminal Law* (London: Sweet & Maxwell, 4th edn 2015) at paras. 17–174 *et seq.*

The accessory need not in fact neutralise her assistance or encouragement. If the putative accessory effectively neutralises her assistance or encouragement, she is not liable because the conduct element for complicity liability is not made out. The *actus reus* for complicity liability is factual participation. There must be factual encouragement or assistance. If *A* has managed to retrieve the gun she gave to *P* to assist *P* to kill *V* before *P* kills *V*, then *A* has not in fact assisted *P* to kill *V*. Similarly, if *A* neutralises her encouragement before *P* acts on it, then *A* has not in fact encouraged *P*.[4] A putative accessory who has only attempted to participate in the perpetrator's crime might be liable for an inchoate offence under the *Serious Crime Act 2007*, but she will not be liable as an accessory. A person who has encouraged a crime can still (in general) escape complicity in it if she expressly and unequivocally countermands the crime or withdraws her assent in due time before it is committed,[5] but she will remain liable for any previous attempt, encouragement or conspiracy, as an inchoate offence.

Similarly, in the context of joint enterprise complicity, it is important to observe that withdrawal is different from non-participation in an unauthorised collateral crime. Suppose *A* and *P* agree to burglarise a house. They also agree that they will not use guns or weapons and will flee without using violence, if they are disturbed. Suppose when they embark on the burglary, unbeknown to *A*, *P* is armed with a gun. When they arrive at the house they hear someone walking in the upstairs room. *A* says to *P*, 'We need to get out of here now, I can hear someone upstairs.' At that point *A* flees, but *P* remains and waits for the occupant to come down the stairs. When the occupant emerges, *P* discovers it is the woman who had an affair with her ex-husband some years before, so *P*, motivated by revenge, kills *V*. *A* is not liable for the collateral murder, because she did not in fact encourage it by authorising it as a conditional target crime. *P* departed from the common purpose for her own personal reasons. *A* did not encourage *P* to carry a gun or to use violence, let alone lethal violence. *A* would not raise withdrawal as a defence in such a case, because *A* did not in fact participate in the collateral crime. *A*'s defence is that the conduct element for complicity liability is not made out, because she did not provide factual encouragement *vis-à-vis* the collateral crime.[6]

4 In *R. v. Croft* [1944] K.B. 295, Lawrence, J. seems to have presumed that *A*'s factual encouragement was still playing on *P*'s mind, even though the evidence demonstrated that *P* had changed her mind. The evidence was that *P* had changed her mind and that her act of perpetration was accidental. Perhaps the court found the evidence unconvincing, because the defendant was the only witness. Cf. *State v. Webb* (1909) 216 Mo. 378.

5 *R. v. Richardson* (1795) 1 Leach 387; *R. v. Croft* [1944] K.B. 295; *R. v. Barnard* (1980) 70 Cr. App. R. 28; *R. v. Baker* [1994] Crim. L.R. 444; *R. v. Rook* [1993] 1 W.L.R. 1005; *R. v. Whitefield* (1984) 79 Cr. App. R. 36.

6 *R. v. Rafferty* [2007] E.W.C.A. Crim. 1846; *R. v. Perman* [1996] 1 Cr. App. R. 24. In *R. v. Rajakumar* [2014] 1 Cr. App. R. 168 at 178, Davis, L.J. said: 'Withdrawal is capable of being a separate issue from assessing the scope of a joint enterprise, even if there may well be significant elements of overlap.'

Compare this case with the case where the accessory participates in the collateral crime, because it is a crime that she conditionally intends to be perpetrated, if it has to be perpetrated to make the underlying criminal enterprise succeed.[7] Withdrawal can be raised as a defence in this type of case, because the accessory has in fact participated in the anticipated target crime by encouraging it via her authorisation of it. In this type of case, the withdrawal defence will be available only if steps have been taken that are reasonably capable of neutralising *A*'s encouragement by prior authorisation. As we will see, the accessory fleeing from the crime at the last minute, when *P* is in a heightened emotional state and is intent on consummating the anticipated target crime, is unlikely to have a reasonable prospect of neutralising or dampening *A*'s prior encouragement.[8]

A. Justifications for the withdrawal defence

Some of the reasons that have been given in support of the defence of withdrawal are that a person who is willing to take reasonable steps to try to neutralise her original assistance/encouragement is less dangerous than a person who does not have a change of heart. A person who tries to neutralise her past assistance or encouragement before any criminal harm eventuates is less blameworthy than one who is not willing to take such steps. Similarly, a person who takes reasonable steps to try to prevent a crime in which she has participated from escalating into a more serious crime is not as dangerous as a person who is willing to let it go to the next level.[9] When the crime is a continuing crime and the accessory is culpably linked to it in its entirety, she will not be able to use the fact that she withdrew after the crime commenced to avoid liability, because she has already participated in the crime.[10] The defence of withdrawal encourages the accessory to take

7 This was the case in *R. v. Becerra* (1976) 62 Cr. App. R. 212. See also *People v. Williams* (2001) 324 Ill. App. 3d 419.

8 *R. v. Becerra* (1976) 62 Cr. App. R. 212.

9 Cf. the facts in *R. v. Mitchell* (1998) 163 J.P. 75; *R. v. O'Flaherty* [2004] 2 Cr. App. R. 20. These cases will sometimes be defended on the basis that the crime committed was a collateral crime that was not authorised by the accessory. In other cases, it will be clear that the accessory authorised the collateral crime, so any avoidance of liability will hinge on the accessory successfully raising the withdrawal defence.

10 If *A* has already participated in a continuing act of violence, then her withdrawal from it is not possible post her factual participation. See *People v. Lykins* (1978) 65 Ill.App.3d 808 at 813, where Green, J. said: [T]he defendant attempted a withdrawal, if at all, after he had hit the victim and while [*P*] was clubbing the victim. Thus, the force which was an element of the underlying robbery was already being applied. The robbery had commenced. Furthermore, although the defendant testified that he screamed at [*P*] to stop the beating and refused to proceed with the robbery, he did not testify that he admonished others not to commit the robbery. In fact, he admitted that he later accepted a portion of the proceeds of the robbery.' See also *People v. De La Sancha* (2012) IL App (2d) 101262-*U*, where *D* did not attempt to stop the assault until after he had already participated in it.

reasonable steps to try to neutralise her participation, because this might persuade the perpetrator to desist as well. The defence aims to encourage not only the accessory to withdraw her participation, but also aims to have the indirect effect of encouraging the perpetrator to withdraw from her planned criminality.

The rationale for the withdrawal defence is in part deterrence, because it aims to provide the accessory with an incentive for desisting and also for trying to prevent the anticipated target crime from being perpetrated. The message is that it is worthwhile taking reasonable steps to try to neutralise encouragement and assistance that has been put in motion. If the encourager waits until it is too late to withdraw her participation, or withdraws only after the crime is virtually unstoppable,[11] as is often the case in spontaneous violence cases,[12] the deterrence and culpability justifications for allowing the defence are reduced to vanishing point,[13] because she seems to be no less culpable, and no less dangerous, than the person who does not withdraw at all. A person who does not withdraw in a way that allows her withdrawal to have a *reasonable prospect* of neutralising or *seriously dampening* her prior participation manifests a higher degree of culpability than a person who takes appropriate steps to try to annul her past participation. Such a person is more wavering in her decision to withdraw than a person who firmly draws the line at a point in time where there is still a reasonable prospect of preventing the end harm from transpiring.

B. Effective and timely withdrawals

An effective and timely withdrawal of participation can relieve the accessory of any liability for crimes that are perpetrated after she has withdrawn from the anticipated target crime. It is well established that the withdrawal must be timely. The accessory must take reasonable steps to try to neutralise her assistance or encouragement, but that she need not try to prevent the target crime from being perpetrated. The accessory need only do acts that are 'reasonably capable' of rendering her assistance or encouragement

See also *R. v. Perman* [1996] 1 Cr. App. R. 24; *R. v. Campbell* [2009] E.W.C.A. Crim. 50; cf. *Smith v. U.S.* (2013) 133 S. Ct. 714.

11 *R. v. Becerra* (1976) 62 Cr. App. R. 212; *R. v. Phillips* (1848) 3 Cox. C.C. 133; *People v. Brown* (1962) 26 Ill.2d 308. See also *People v. Jones* (2007) 876 N.E.2d 15.

12 See *R. v. Becerra* (1976) 62 Cr. App. R. 212; *R. v. O'Flaherty* [2004] 2 Cr. App. R. 20; *R. v. Mitchell* (1998) 163 J.P. 75. In these sorts of cases the accessory usually has not taken steps that are reasonably capable of neutralising her assistance or encouragement, because her withdrawal is not sufficiently timely to have any effect in the heat of the moment when *P* is on the brink of striking. See also the recent decision of the Supreme Court of Canada in *R. c. Gauthier* [2013] 2 S.C.R. 403.

13 Cf. *R. v. Sully* (2012) 112 S.A.S.R. 157.

ineffective.[14] She need not succeed in neutralising her assistance or encouragement, but her acts of withdrawal, when judged objectively, have to be sufficient for a jury to find as a question of fact that they had a reasonable prospect of neutralising her past participation.[15] It is for the jury to determine as a question of fact whether the accessory took reasonable steps to try to neutralise or dampen her past assistance or encouragement.

In *White v. Ridley*,[16] Gibbs, J. said:

> Professor Glanville Williams cites from the judgment in *Eldredge v. United States*[17]: 'A declared intent to withdraw from a conspiracy to dynamite a building is not enough, if the fuse has been set; he must step on the fuse.' It seems entirely reasonable to insist that a person who has counselled or procured another to commit a crime, or has conspired with others to commit a crime, should accompany his countermand or withdrawal with such action as he *can reasonably take*[18] to undo the effect of his previous encouragement or participation [emphasis added].

In *R. v. O'Flaherty*,[19] Mantell, L.J. said:

> To disengage from an incident a person must do enough to demonstrate that he or she is withdrawing the joint enterprise. This is ultimately a question of fact and degree for the jury. Account will be taken *inter alia* of the nature of the assistance and encouragement already given and how imminent the infliction of the fatal injury or injuries is, as well as the nature of the action said to constitute withdrawal. In cases of assistance it has sometimes been suggested that, for there to be an effective withdrawal, reasonable steps must have been taken to prevent the crime. It is clear, however, this is not necessary.

14 *R. v. Young* (1838) 8 Car. & P. 644.

15 *R. v. O'Flaherty* [2004] 2 Cr. App. R. 20; see also *R. v. Rajakumar* [2014] 1 Cr. App. R. 168. In *Croxford v. The Queen* (2011) 215 A. Crim. R. 297 at paras. 52–53 it was said: 'Whether the accused has taken all reasonable steps to undo the effect of his previous assistance or encouragement is a question for the jury . . . If withdrawal of the accused's assistance or encouragement is in issue then the prosecution must prove that the accused did not effectively withdraw his assistance or encouragement prior to the offence being committed.' *Croxford v. The Queen* (2011) 215 A. Crim. R. 297 at paras. 52–53.

16 *White v. Ridley* (1978) 140 C.L.R. 342 at 350. Cf. *R. v. Rook* [1993] 1 W.L.R. 1005 at 1012.

17 (1932) 62 F. (2d) 449 at 451.

18 By 'reasonably take', Gibbs, J. seems to be suggesting that if *A* has withdrawn her participation by telling *P* she is going to warn the police and the victim about the planned crime, that *A* need not take further unreasonable steps such as risk her own life by trying to disarm *P* who is armed with a lethal weapon that has been supplied at some earlier point in time by *A*.

19 [2004] 2 Cr. App. R. 20 at para. 60. See also *R. v. Rajakumar* (2014) 1 Cr. App. R. 168.

Statutory provisions in the United States require the defendant to make 'a reasonable effort'[20] or a 'substantial effort'[21] to try to prevent her participation from facilitating or encouraging the perpetrator. The English authorities seem to adopt an approach akin to the reasonable steps approach. It is arguable that the defence of withdrawal in English law hinges on the defendant taking reasonable steps to *try* to prevent her participation from having any effect.[22] 'Try' is the key word, because, as we have seen, if the crime is prevented there is no participation. Is there a higher standard for withdrawing assistance than there is for withdrawing encouragement? No, the standard is the same in both cases. In practice acts that are reasonably capable of neutralising assistance will be more onerous to perform. It will be easier for the putative accessory to demonstrate that her 'encouragement' was annulled. Dalton wrote:[23]

> *A.* counselleth or commandeth *B.* to kill *C.* and before he hath killed him, *A.* doth repent, and countermands it, charging *B.* not to kill *C.* and yet after *B.* doth kill *C.* Here *A.* shall not be adjudged accessary to the death of *C.* for the Law adjudgeth no man accessary to a felony before the fact, but such as continue in that mind at the time that the felony is done and executed.

When the putative accessory has withdrawn her encouragement by telling *P* in unequivocal terms that she no longer wants the crime to be perpetrated, the jury is likely to hold that *A*'s act of withdrawal was capable of neutralising

20 Cf. M.S.A. § 609.05 (Minnesota Statutes Annotated), where Subdivision 3 provides: 'Abandonment of criminal purpose. A person who intentionally aids, advises, hires, counsels, or conspires with or otherwise procures another to commit a crime and thereafter abandons that purpose and makes a *reasonable effort to prevent the commission of the crime prior to its commission* is not liable if the crime is thereafter committed' [emphasis added]. See also *Guevara v. State* (2003) 103 S.W.3d 549; *State v. Evans* (1984) 347 N.W.2d 813; *State v. Lemacks* (1999) 996 S.W.2d 166; and *State v. Dorantes* (2011) 331 S.W.3d 370 applying T. C. A. § 39–11–402(3) (West's Tennessee Code Annotated). A.R.S. § 13–1005 (Arizona Revised Statutes Annotated) provides: 'A. In a prosecution for . . . facilitation, it is a defence that the defendant, under circumstances manifesting a voluntary and complete renunciation of his criminal intent, gave timely warning to law enforcement authorities or otherwise made a reasonable effort to prevent the conduct or result which is the object of the attempt, conspiracy or facilitation.'

21 Cf. N.M.S.A. 1978, § 30–28–3B(2) (West's New Mexico Statutes Annotated).

22 None of the English authorities expressly stated that the accessory has to take 'reasonable steps' to prevent her participation from having effect, but the defence has been allowed only where 'reasonable steps' have been taken. See the cases as discussed in Baker, *loc. cit. supra*, note 3; *Croxford v. The Queen* (2011) 215 A. Crim. R. 297; *R. v. Duong* (2011) 110 S.A.S.R. 296 at 318. Cf. *R. v. Sully* (2012) 112 S.A.S.R. 157; *Miller v. Miller* (2011) 242 C.L.R. 446 at 489; 500; 510; *R. v. LK* (2010) 241 C.L.R. 177 at 240; *R. v. Evans* [2009] 1 W.L.R. 1999 at 2004.

23 Michael Dalton, *The Country Justice* (London: Printed by Henry Lintot, 1746) at 369.

her participation.[24] The jury is likely to accept that where an accessory has told the perpetrator not to go ahead with the crime, that such conduct is capable of preventing her earlier encouragement from continuing to influence *P*.

Per contra, if *A* has given *P* a gun, *A* phoning *P* over and over to beg *P* not to use the gun to kill *V* is not an act that is reasonably capable of neutralising the assistance *A* has already given *P*. If *P* was intent on using a gun to kill *V* when *A* gave *P* the gun, then *P* may not be willing to change her mind merely because *A* has asked *P* not to use the gun to kill *V*. If *A* has acted positively to assist the crime, she must do an act that is reasonably capable of neutralising her assistance such as warning the victim or notifying the police that the crime is planned. There is no requirement that the accessory report the crime to the police or the victim,[25] but reporting the crime to the police would provide fairly powerful evidence of her withdrawal from the criminal venture.[26]

If *A* has supplied *P* with a gun for the purpose of helping *P* kill *V*, then acts that would be reasonably capable of neutralising that assistance might include *A* recovering the gun;[27] *A* warning both the police and the victim about *P*'s planned murder etc. If, notwithstanding *A*'s warnings to the police and *V*, *P* manages to use *A*'s gun to kill *V*, *A* should be able to establish withdrawal, because judged objectively her timely warnings to both the victim and the police are reasonable attempts to try to render her past assistance ineffective. In normal circumstances, *A*'s acts (her timely warnings to both the victim and the police) would be reasonably capable of neutralising her past participation. Not only would such acts of withdrawal (the timely warnings) be reasonably capable of preventing *A*'s past participation (her supply of the gun) from assisting *P*, but they also have a reasonable prospect of neutralising her past participation.

An accessory would normally be able to avoid complicity liability by providing the police with timely notice of the intended crime, or by giving a timely warning to the intended victim. If *A* informed *P* of her intention to inform the police or the victim, this would be strong evidence that *A* did not want *P* to use the advice, encouragement or information which *A* provided

24 *R. v. Rook* [1993] 1 W.L.R. 1005.

25 David Lanham, 'Accomplices and Withdrawal' (1981) 97 *L.Q.R.* 575 at 579–585. Some American decisions suggest that a person who has given help must either withdraw the help or, if she cannot do that, must go to the police. But the American Law Institute's Modal Penal Code section 206(6) requires only that the defendant 'gives timely warning to law enforcement authorities or otherwise makes proper effort to prevent the commission of the offence'. Going to the police was not made a requirement in *R. v. Grundy* [1977] Crim. L.R. 543; *R. v. Whitefield* (1983) 79 Cr. App. R. 36. See also *R. v. O'Flaherty* [2004] 2 Cr. App. R. 20 at paras. 61–62.

26 *R. v. O'Flaherty* [2004] 2 Cr. App. R. 20.

27 *R. v. Becerra* (1976) 62 Cr. App. R. 212; *R. v. Bryce* [2004] 2 Cr. App. R. 35.

at some earlier point in time.[28] Similarly, if *A* phones or emails *P* over and over to tell him she does not want him to go through with the crime or use the information or advice she provided, this should be sufficient to establish withdrawal.[29] In a pre-planned joint enterprise *A* may communicate her withdrawal simply by telling her co-perpetrators that she has no intention of continuing with the plan, and that they too should abandon it. Not showing up on the day will not be sufficient; the accessory must communicate her withdrawal in unequivocal terms before the criminality is under way.

Where a person who, having given information enabling a burglary to be committed, repented and tried to stop his companion going on with the project for two weeks before the companion committed the crime, this was held to be sufficient to let him out of liability for the crime[30] (though he would remain liable for conspiracy). But where one burglar gave a knife to his companion to use against anyone who might interrupt them, but on someone approaching, said: 'Come on, let's go,' suiting the action to the word, this was held to be insufficient to exempt him from complicity in a stabbing that his companion proceeded to inflict with the knife; and the Court of Appeal seemed to indicate that the defendant could on the facts have dissociated himself from the crime only by physically intervening to prevent the use of the knife.[31]

C. Involuntary withdrawals

If a gang member is forced to withdraw from a crime because she is arrested, does this allow her to raise the withdrawal defence? In such a case *A*'s withdrawal is involuntary. The rationale for the withdrawal defence is that *A*'s voluntary choice to withdraw from the planned criminal enterprise makes her less dangerous and less blameworthy. Involuntary withdrawal does not demonstrate that *A* is less dangerous than a person who refuses to withdraw at all. In *R. v. Johnson*[32] *P* and *A* entered a house with intent to steal, *A* was apprehended, without *P* becoming aware of the fact, and *P* afterwards stole an article in the house. The trial judge, Maule J., ruled that *A* could be convicted as accessory. If the arrest is known to the others, it would seem that the arrest should be accounted an involuntary withdrawal from the plan, so that the party arrested should not be allowed to rely on the defence of voluntary withdrawal.[33]

28 *R. v. Grundy* [1977] Crim. L.R. 543.
29 *R. v. Grundy* [1977] Crim. L.R. 543.
30 *R. v. Grundy* [1977] Crim. L.R. 543.
31 *R. v. Becerra* (1976) 62 Cr. App. R. 212.
32 (1841) Car. & M. 218.
33 *Chennault v. State* (1984) 667 S.W.2d 299.

If a number of criminals make forcible resistance to arrest, and one of them is arrested, and ceases resistance and encouragement to her companions, it seems that she will not ordinarily be implicated in an act of force subsequently committed by another of the gang.[34] But that is not because she has withdrawn, but because she does not in fact participate in the subsequent crimes. When her accomplices see her being arrested, the encouragement she has given her companions by joining their forcible resistance comes to an end. But if she has supplied a companion with a weapon to be used in resisting, the arrest will not end her liability for the use of the weapon, any more than in the case of voluntary withdrawal, unless perhaps she offers to try to persuade her companion not to use the weapon. In the United States it has been held that 'incarceration does not create a rebuttable presumption of withdrawal' as far as the inchoate crime of conspiracy is concerned.[35] As we will see below, the requirements for abandoning inchoate crimes are more demanding.

D. Communicating a withdrawal

If the accessory does not withdraw before the crime becomes unstoppable, then the jury is likely to infer that she did not make a reasonable or timely effort to neutralise her participation.[36] There need not be an express withdrawal of advice and consent,[37] if the encourager has made

34 *R. v. Jackson* (1673) 1 Hale P.C. 464.

35 *U.S. v. Leslie* (2011) 658 F.3d 140 at 143–144 (Calabresi, Wesley, and Lynch, J.J. *per curiam*), where it was said: '[D] argues that imprisonment may be evidence of an affirmative act of withdrawal from a conspiracy; we agree. But "while arrest or incarceration may constitute a withdrawal from a conspiracy, it does not follow that in every instance it must." In the trial context, evidence of imprisonment during a conspiracy is merely a relevant fact that entitles the defendant to a jury instruction on withdrawal. The jury decides whether imprisonment constitutes a withdrawal "in light of the length and location of the internment, the nature of the conspiracy, and any other available evidence". We have never held that a jury must find a withdrawal if the government does not prove that the defendant continued in the conspiracy after imprisonment . . . the [evidential] burden remains on the defendant to present affirmative evidence that he withdrew from the conspiracy. The defendant's imprisonment is but one fact to consider in deciding whether withdrawal occurred.' See also *United States v. Massino* (2008) 546 F.3d 123 at 136 *per curiam.*

36 Cf. *People v. Brown* (1962) 26 Ill.2d 308. See also *People v. Jones* (2007) 876 N.E.2d 15; *State v. Pratt* (1994) 255 Kan. 767 at 772 *per* McFarland, J.; *State v. Bowen* (1993) 505 N.W.2d 682 at 691 *per* Caporale, J.; also see *Galan v. State* (1932) 44 Ohio App. 192 *per* Washburn, J.; *People v. Nichols* (1921) 129 N.E. 883 at 886 *per* Hiscock, C.J.

37 See Matthew Hale, *The History of the Pleas of the Crown* (London: Printed by E. and R. Nutt *et al.*, 1736) Vol. I at 436; 537; 618; *R. v. Mitchell* (1998) 163 J.P. 75 *per* Otton, L.J., Kay and Moses, J.J.; *R. v. Sully* [2012] 112 S.A.S.R. 157 at 176–178. The putative accessory could be caught by one of the inchoate offences found in sections 44–46 of the *Serious Crime Act 2007.*

her change of heart clear by conduct, as by quitting the gang.[38] She must make it clear that she is no longer in the game and wants no part of it. It is not enough that she does not turn up when it is time to perpetrate the crime, if she has already encouraged her confederates by promising to participate at some future date.[39] Merely running away because it looks as though it is getting too risky would not be enough.[40] In the case of spontaneous gang violence, often the defendant's attempt to withdraw will involve nothing more than her running off before the fatal blow is delivered to the victim. If a person participates in savage gang violence, it will be difficult for her to dissociate herself from the independent acts of her confederates.[41]

Some of the joint enterprise cases have been problematic where the enterprise was split into two events. Such cases raise two potential exculpation routes for the putative accessary: (1) The putative accessory will not be liable for complicity where she has not in fact participated in the second crime such as where she has done nothing to encourage the collateral offence;[42] (2) The accessory will not be liable where she has effectively withdrawn before the collateral crime is perpetrated.

In *R. v. Mitchell*, Thomas, L.J. (as he then was) observed said:

> If a group of men, in a spontaneous joint enterprise of violence are chasing another man armed with weapons, bottles and sticks through the streets of a town, and at a point when the man being chased and the remaining chasers turn a corner out of the sight of one of the attackers, and that one attacker then stops, puts down his weapon and walks back the way he had come, and does not go round the corner, he does not participate any further in the attack which culminates two streets later with the death of the man being chased. In such a case, a jury may well conclude that that one man, by stopping and acting as he did, had withdrawn from the joint enterprise of which he was at one stage a willing member. It is a question of fact and degree in every case.[43]

38 Sir Michael Foster, *Crown Law* (London: Printed by W. Strahan and M. Woodfall, 1776) at 354. In the case of spontaneous violence, it has been held that dropping one's weapons and walking off is sufficient to isolate one's early participation from acts which may transpire post withdrawal: *R. v. Mitchell* (1998) 163 J.P. 75; *R. v. O'Flaherty* [2004] 2 Cr. App. R. 20.

39 *R. v. Goodspeed* (1911) 6 Cr. App. R. 133; see also *R. v. Emelio* (2012) 222 A. Crim. R. 566; *Croxford v. The Queen* (2011) 215 A. Crim. R. 297.

40 *R. v. Perman* [1996] 1 Cr. App. R. 24 at 34.

41 *R. v. Mitchell* (1998) 163 J.P. 75.

42 See *R. v. Rafferty* [2007] E.W.C.A. Crim. 1846, where *D* had not participated in the collateral crime because it was fundamentally different from anything he had encouraged. In a nutshell, the collateral crime was not a part of the joint enterprise. The *actus reus* for complicity was not made out, because *D* had not in fact participated in the collateral crime.

43 *R. v. Mitchell* [2009] 1 Cr. App. R. 438 at 448.

The example given by Thomas, L.J. is one of non-participation, not withdrawal. If a person has not participated in the collateral crime, then she cannot raise the defence of withdrawal.[44] In *R. v. Mitchell*,[45] Mitchell and her co-defendants jointly attacked three victims in a car park following a dispute over a taxi. The violence was split into two incidents, because some of the co-defendants went to a nearby house to fetch weapons. Mitchell remained in the car park during both bouts of violence. It was argued on Mitchell's behalf that there had been two separate incidents of violence that led to the victim's death and that she had played no part in the second fatal incident. After the violence started there was a lull in the violence, because some members of Mitchell's group went to a nearby house to pick up a knuckleduster, a CS spray canister and a medieval mace. (It is worth noting that it was not the use of any of these weapons that caused the victim's death. Rather, a member of Mitchell's group killed the elderly victim by kicking him in the head and by stamping his head into the ground.) It was argued on Mitchell's behalf that she was only present during the second outbreak of violence because she wanted to find her shoes, which she had lost during the violence. Mitchell denied encouraging the perpetrator to kick the victim in the head, but she had inflicted similar violence on the victim during the earlier stages of the violence.

The evidence demonstrated that Mitchell was a party to a single joint enterprise from which she had not withdrawn at the time when the victim was killed. Mitchell was present during both parts of the attack, had instigated the attack and had herself kicked the victim in the head in the earlier part of the attack. There was plenty of evidence for the jury to infer that Mitchell had encouraged and authorised the lethal act of the perpetrator, because she started the fight and had already inflicted similar violence on the victim. If Mitchell wanted to withdraw her message of encouragement, then she should have take reasonable steps to do so. Mitchell hanging around a car park looking for shoes while a person was being trampled to death nearby as a result of violence she had initiated was hardly an act of withdrawal.[46] Mitchell should have called the police, tried to intervene, or at the very least have begged her accomplices to stop the violence.

It will be very difficult for a person to withdraw encouragement when there is no reasonable prospect of it being withdrawn by her particular

44 'Far from contradicting an element of the offence, withdrawal presupposes that the defendant committed the offence.' *U.S. v. Guevara* (2013) 706 F.3d 38 citing *Smith v. United States* (2013) 133 S.Ct. 714.

45 [2009] 1 Cr. App. R. 438.

46 *R. v. Mitchell* [2009] 1 Cr. App. R. 438 at 452.

acts of withdrawal. When a violent gang fight is under way, it will be almost unstoppable and more than mere words will be required to stop it.[47] Mere words are not likely to be held to be an act that is reasonably capable of withdrawing encouragement in the heat of gang violence. Coupled with this, withdrawing once the violence has commenced is not timely. Untimely withdrawal is not reasonable withdrawal. Mitchell made no attempt to withdraw and, even if she had, it would not have been sufficiently timely to have had a reasonable prospect of cancelling her participation.

E. Burden of proof

In a majority of states in the United States the withdrawal defence is treated as an affirmative defence,[48] which means the burden of proving withdrawal is on the defendant.[49] The defendant has to prove the defence by a preponderance of the evidence.[50] In some states, once the defendant has raised evidence to support her claim that withdrawal is an issue, the State is required to prove beyond reasonable doubt that the defence was not made out.[51] Buscemi observes that Kentucky has taken an intermediate stance. Section 500.070 of the new *Kentucky Penal Code* imposes the burden of disproving a defence on the Commonwealth only when 'evidence tending to support the defence is of such probative force that in the absence of countervailing evidence the defendant would be entitled to a directed verdict of acquittal'.[52]

47 See *People v. Jones* (2007) 876 N.E.2d 15, where Gordon, J. said: '[T]he defendant must timely communicate his intent to withdraw in such a manner so that it is possible for the trier of fact "to say that the accused had wholly and effectively detached himself from the criminal enterprise before the act with which he is charged is in the process of consummation or has become so inevitable that it cannot reasonably be stayed". Stated differently, "withdrawal may not be effectively made" from a felony murder when the "transaction which immediately begets it has actually been commenced".' Also see *State v. Pratt* (1994) 255 Kan. 767 at 772 *per* McFarland, J.; *State v. Bowen* (1993) 505 N.W.2d 682 at 691 *per* Caporale, J.; *Galan v. State* (1932) 44 Ohio App. 192 *per* Washburn, J.; *People v. Nichols* (1921) 129 N.E. 883 at 886 *per* Hiscock, C.J.

48 See section 1.12 of the American Law Institute's Model Penal Code. Also see *State v. Lynch* (2013) 309 P.3d 482 at 490. Cf. the discussion in *R. v. Rajakumar* (2014) 1 Cr. App. R. 168.

49 For a survey of the law in the various states, see Peter Buscemi, 'Conspiracy: Statutory Reform Since the Model Penal Code' (1975) 75 *Colum. L. Rev.* 1122 at 1172.

50 *Smith v. U.S.* (2013) 133 S.Ct. 714 at 718 *per* Scalia, J. The preponderance of evidence standard requires the relevant issue to be proved as more likely true than not. See *United States v. Ward* (1995) 68 F.3d 146.

51 Buscemi, *loc. cit. supra*, note 49.

52 *Id.* at 1173.

III. Cancelling attempted complicity

At common law withdrawal does not seem to have been recognised as a defence for inchoate offences such as conspiracy,[53] attempt[54] and incitement.[55] The *Serious Crime Act 2007* also fails to incorporate a withdrawal defence. Nonetheless, the sentencing judge is not likely to impose a custodial sentence, not even where the putative assister/encourager has attempted to encourage or assist a very serious crime, if it is clear on the evidence that the defendant effectively neutralised her assistance or encouragement and took firm steps to renounce her criminal intentions. Under the *Serious Crime Act 2007*, attempted complicity becomes a crime as soon as a secondary party does an act that is capable of encouraging or assisting the perpetrator to perpetrate a crime and, therefore, withdrawal is not a defence.

Even though withdrawal is not a defence, evidence of the secondary party's voluntary withdrawal can be used in mitigation of punishment.[56] That no defence of withdrawal or renunciation was included in the *Serious Crime Act 2007* was an oversight of the Law Commission and its researchers.

53 In *Mogul Steamship Co. Ltd. v. McGregor, Gow & Co.* (1888) 21 Q.B.D. 544 at 549, Lord Coleridge, C.J. said: 'In the *Bridgewater Case*, referred to at the bar, and in which I was counsel, nothing was done in fact; yet a gentleman was convicted because he had entered into an unlawful combination from which almost on the spot he withdrew, and withdrew altogether. No one was harmed, but the public offence was complete.' See also *R. v. De Berenger* (1814) 3 M. & S. 67 at 76 *per* Bayley, J.; and *R. v. Grundy* [1977] Crim. L.R. 543. In *R. v. LK* (2010) 241 C.L.R. 177 at 264, Gummow, Hayne, Crennan, Kiefel and Bell J.J., in a joint judgment, observe: 'At common law it was considered that as the offence of conspiracy is complete upon agreement there could be no defence of withdrawal.' See also *U.S. v. Read* (1981) 658 F.2d 1225. Hawkins said the defence also applied to conspiracies, but there is no modern authority in support of such an assertion. See William Hawkins, *A Treatise of the Pleas of the Crown* (London: Printed by E and R Nutt *et al.*, 1734), Vol. II. at 442. In the United States withdrawal is a defence to inchoate crimes, but in the case of conspiracy it has been held that a person does not effectively withdraw from a conspiracy merely because she ceases to participate. See *U.S. v. Schiro* (2012) 679 F.3d 521; *U.S. v. Heard* (2013) 709 F.3d 413.

54 Once the participation has reached the attempt stage, it is a crime *per se.* A person cannot withdraw from a crime that is over and done. See *R. v. Page* [1933] V.L.R. 351 at 354; *R. v. Collingridge* (1976) 16 S.A.S.R. 117 at 132, where Bright, J., referring to an example given by the trial judge, seems to suggest that a person cannot withdraw from an attempt, but the example he gives is not useful because the attempt was over and done. See also James Fitzjames Stephen, *A Digest of the Criminal Law* (London: Macmillan & Co. 1904) at 40. Cf. *R. v. Lankford* [1959] Crim. L.R. 209.

55 *People v. Gordon* (1975) 47 Cal. App. 3d 465.

56 Daniel L. Rotenberg, 'Withdrawal as a Defence to Relational Crimes' (1962) *Wis. L. Rev.* 596 at 600. See also Christopher Russell, 'Does Attempted Murder Deserve Greater Punishment than Murder – Moral Luck and the Duty to Prevent Harm' (2004) 18 *Notre Dame J.L. Ethics & Pub. Pol'y* 419; Kenneth W. Simons, 'Does Punishment for Culpable Indifference Simply Punish for Bad Character – Examining the Requisite Connection between *Mens Rea* and *Actus Reus*' (2002) 6 *Buff. Crim. L. Rev.* 219.

Offences and defences fell within the Law Commission's remit, but it failed to consider a full range of defences with respect to inchoate participation. In the United States, every state, but for a couple, has enacted a defence of renunciation or abandonment for inchoate crimes.[57]

In the United States the three interrelated defences are abandonment, withdrawal and renunciation. Withdrawal is a defence for complicity liability, whereas 'abandonment' and 'renunciation' are normally applied to inchoate crimes.[58] The defence is called the *abandonment* defence in some states,[59] but the terms *renunciation defence* and *abandonment defence* are frequently used interchangeably.[60] The proposed United States federal criminal code recommends that renunciation be included as a defence.[61] For example, section 541 of the *Delaware Penal Code* provides:[62]

> (a) In any prosecution for criminal solicitation or conspiracy in which the crime solicited or the crime contemplated by the conspiracy *was not in fact committed*, it is an affirmative defence that, under circumstances manifesting a voluntary and complete renunciation of the criminal purpose, *the accused prevented the commission of the crime.*

57 The renunciation defence normally covers conspiracy and attempts as well as solicitation. See for example, Ala.Code §13A-4–1(b) (1982); Alaska Stat. §11.31.110(b)(2) (Cum. Supp.1982); Ariz.Rev.Stat.Ann. §13–1005(B) (1978); Ark.Stat.Ann. §41–706 (1977); Colo.Rev.Stat.Ann. §18–2-301(4) (1978); Conn. Gen. Stat. Ann. § 53a-48(b) (West 1972); Ga. Code Ann., § 16–4-5 (West); Fla.Stat.Ann. §777.04(5)(b) (West 1976); Hawaii Rev. Stat. §705–530(2) (1976); Iowa Code Ann. §705.2 (West 1979); Ky.Rev.Stat. §506.060(1) (1975); Me.Rev.Stat.Ann. tit. 17-A, §154(2)(B) (1983); Mich.2d Proposed Rev. §1010(2) (1979); Minn.Stat.Ann. §609.05(Subd. 3) (West 1964); Mo. Ann. Stat. § 564.016 (Vernon 1979; N.H.Rev.Stat.Ann. §629:2(II) (1974); N.M.Stat.Ann. §30–28–3(B) (Cum. Supp.1983); N.Y.Penal Law § 40.10(4) (McKinney 1975); N.D.Cent.Code §12.1–06–05(3)(b) (1976); Ohio Rev.Code Ann. §2923.03(E) (Page 1982); Or.Rev.Stat. §161.440 (1981); 18 Pa.Cons.Stat.Ann. §902(b) (Purdon 1983); Tenn.Code Ann. §39–116 (1975); Tex. Penal Code Ann. tit. 4, §15.04(b) (Vernon 1974); Wyo.Stat. §6–1-302(b) (1983); Guam Crim. & Corr.Code §7.73(c) (1977).

58 See for example, *Matter of J.F., Jr.* (1997) 948 S.W.2d 807; *Hawkins v. State* (2007) 214 S.W.3d 668. See generally, Michael T. Cahill, 'Defining Inchoate Crime: An Incomplete Attempt,' (2012) 9 *Ohio St. J. Crim. L.* 751; Larry Alexander and Kimberly D. Kessler, '*Mens Rea* and Inchoate Crimes' (1997) 87 *J. Crim. L. & Criminology* 1138 at 1183; Paul R. Hoeber, 'The Abandonment Defence to Criminal Attempt and Other Problems of Temporal Individualisation' (1986) 74 *Cal. L. Rev.* 377.

59 See *Chrisman v. State* (2009) 910 N.E.2d 1290; *U.S. v. Smauley* (1994) 39 M.J. 853; *U.S. v. Schoof* (1992) 34 M.J. 811; *U.S. v. Dworken* (1998) 855 F.2d 12; *People v. Salazar* (1985) 140 Mich.App. 137.

60 See *U.S. v. Vasco* (2009) 564 F.3d 12 at 21; *Longval v. State* (2009) 914 So.2d 1098; *U.S. v. Wales* (2005) 127 Fed.Appx. 424 at 430.

61 S. 1630, 97th Cong., 2d Sess. § 1002(b) (1982). Model Penal Code § 5.02(3); S. 1437, 95th Cong., 1st Sess. § 1003(b) (1977) (federal).

62 Del. Code Ann. tit. 11, § 541 (1979).

(b) In any prosecution for an attempt to commit a crime it is an affirmative defence that, under circumstances manifesting a voluntary and complete renunciation of the criminal purpose, the accused *avoided the commission of the crime attempted by abandoning the criminal effort and*, if mere abandonment was insufficient to accomplish avoidance, *by taking further and affirmative steps which prevented the commission of the crime attempted.*

(c) A renunciation is not 'voluntary and complete' within the meaning of this section if it is motivated in whole or in part by:

(1) A belief that circumstances exist which increase the probability of detection or apprehension of the accused or another participant in the criminal enterprise, or which render more difficult the accomplishment of the criminal purpose; or

(2) A decision to postpone the criminal conduct until another time or to transfer the criminal effort to another victim or another but similar objective [emphasis added].

Similarly, the *Idaho Penal Code* provides:[63]

> It is an affirmative defence that the defendant, after soliciting another person to commit a crime, *persuaded him not to do so or otherwise prevented the commission of the crime*, under circumstances manifesting a complete and voluntary renunciation of his criminal purpose [emphasis added].

A. The justifications for an abandonment defence for inchoate participation

In *State v. Latraverse*,[64] a decision of the Supreme Court of Rhode Island, Kelleher, J. said: 'the sole motivation for our recognition of an abandonment defence is the hope that individuals will desist from pursuing their criminal designs, thereby reducing the risk that the intended substantive crime will be accomplished.' Meanwhile, Morse has argued that:

> [T]he renunciation defence is based upon primarily consequential considerations. The law wishes to give agents an incentive not to cause the prohibited harm, and perhaps renunciation indicates that the agent is not so dangerous after all and that no incapacitation is needed. Neither of these considerations bears on desert for the prior conduct, although the incentive effect is fully consistent with the action-guiding function.[65]

63 Idaho Code §18–2003 (Interim Supp.1983).

64 (1982) 443 A.2d 890 at 896. Fletcher also asserts that such a defence encourages desistence. George P. Fletcher, *Rethinking Criminal Law* (Boston: Little Brown, 1977) at 544.

65 Stephen J. Morse, 'Reason, Results, and Criminal Responsibility' (2004) *U. Ill. L. Rev.* 363 at 424.

The defence is deigned not only to encourage desistance, but also to recognise that those who renounce their encouragement or take positive steps[66] to ensure that it does not lead to another perpetrating a crime are not as dangerous as those who never desist.[67] Those who take burdensome and timely steps to cancel criminal wrongs they have attempted to set in motion are less blameworthy than those who take no such steps.[68]

In most states in the United States, the renunciation defence applies only if the perpetrator has not perpetrated or attempted to perpetrate the crime she has been encouraged to perpetrate. If the crime has been perpetrated or attempted, then the encourager/assister would be liable as an accessory and thus would need to invoke the withdrawal defence. In this respect, preventing the substantive harm is a primary aim of the renunciation defence.[69] The defence also recognises that those who are willing to change their minds and take steps to prevent the crime that they previously encouraged or assisted are less culpable. The renunciation of their prior criminal plans reduces their culpability. It is for this reason that the defence normally requires the renunciation to be voluntary and timely.

If the putative accessory renounces or abandons her participation in the anticipated target crime because the police are on her tail or because she thinks it is too risky for the crime to be perpetrated on a particular day, then her renunciation will not be voluntary.[70] She will manifest the same level of culpability as those who do not renounce their participation.[71] In *U.S. v. Buttrickit*,[72] Lynch, J. said:

> First, allowance of the defence recognises that the actor's conduct no longer poses a danger to society. Second, the availability of the defence provides actors with a 'motive for desisting from their criminal designs, thereby diminishing the risk that the substantive crime will be committed'.

The encourager/assister will often be in a better position than anyone else to prevent the crime and thus it makes sense to provide her with an incentive to try to cancel her past assistance or encouragement.

66 For a theoretical discussion of the stages of abandonment, see David O. Brink, 'First Acts, Last Acts, and Abandonment' (2013) 19(2) *Legal Theory* 114.

67 See generally, Daniel G. Moriarty, 'Extending the Defence of Renunciation' (1989) 62 *Temp. L. Rev.* 1; Evan Tsen Lee, 'Cancelling Crime' (1997) 30 *Conn. L. Rev.* 117.

68 In this sense, I have a wider view of culpability in mind, not mere *mens rea* in the strict legal sense. For a fuller discussion see Jean E. Hampton, '*Mens Rea*' (1990) 7(2) *Social Philosophy and Policy* 1; Jean E. Hampton, 'The Nature of Morality' (1989) 7(1) *Social Philosophy and Policy* 22 at 42.

69 Paul H. Robinson, 1 *Crim. L. Defence*, § 81.

70 *Chennault v. State* (1984) 667 S.W.2d 299.

71 Robinson, *loc. cit. supra*, note 69.

72 (2005) 432 F.3d 373.

The requirement in the renunciation defence that the defendant prevent the anticipated target crime from being attempted or perpetrated places a higher burden on the defendant than does the withdrawal defence in complicity.[73] It makes sense that the defence should not apply where the perpetrator has attempted or has consummated the anticipated target crime, because liability then rests on actual participation not on attempted participation. The defence applies to inchoate offences such as attempts and also conspiracy, but our focus is on attempted participation. When a person has attempted to commit a crime,[74] she can easily prevent that crime from being perpetrated because all she has to do is desist from consummating her attempt.[75] This also will be the case where the defendant has entered a conspiracy,[76] unless the agreement itself has the effect of encouraging the co-conspirator to perpetrate the offence on her own. If the agreement in itself results in encouragement, then the defendant might be caught by section 45 of the *Serious Crime Act 2007.*

Let us consider how such a defence might apply to the offences found in sections 44–46 of the *Serious Crime Act 2007.* Renunciation will be more

73 In *People v. Sisselman* (1989) 147 A.D.2d 261 at 263–264, Yesawich, J. said: 'Renunciation does not negate the commission of the inchoate crime . . . but rather offers those guilty of such crimes an incentive to take steps to prevent the object or substantive crime, in exchange for which the defendant is excused from liability. Unlike charges based upon accessorial conduct or criminal facilitation where only substantial efforts to prevent the object crime are required to invoke the renunciation defence . . . charges of conspiracy and solicitation give way to the renunciation defence only where "the defendant prevented the commission of such crime". The statute does not go so far as to say that defendant's efforts must be the "sole" reason that the object crime was not committed; indeed, such a reading would thwart the purpose of the provision where, for instance, two co-conspirators acted in concert to prevent the consummation of the object crime, and to that extent the pattern instruction is an overstatement of the law.' This is the position taken in most jurisdictions in the United States.

74 The defendant must have at least attempted to perpetrate the crime. Furthermore, the defence is available only if the defendant admits perpetrating the underlying inchoate crime, because otherwise there would be no crime for the defendant to defend. See *Falay v. State* (2013) 740 S.E.2d 738; *State v. Hughes* (1986) 521 A2d 1295.

75 The attempt would have to get past the more than merely preparatory stage before the abandonment defence would apply, because mere preparation (barring special statutory exceptions) *per se* is not criminal conduct. The defence seems to provide an escape route for those who stop at the attempt stage, because if they stopped at the mere preparation stage they would not be liable at all. See *Mullins v. Commonwealth* (1940) 5 S.E.2d 491, where *D* was about to rape *V* but desisted and released the girl. In that case, it appears *D*'s acts were still mere preparation and that he abandoned his plans before it constituted an attempt. See also *Commonwealth v. Peaslee* (1901) 177 Mass. 267, where *D* set up materials in a building for the purpose of committing arson. Compare *State v. Strommen* (2002) 648 N.W.2d 681; *Dale v. State* (1995) 535 N.W.2d 619; *State v. Gartlan* (1999) 132 N.C.App. 272; *State v. Cox* (1979) 278 N.W.2d 62.

76 *State v. Webb* (1909) 115 S.W. 998; *Smith v. U.S.* (2013) 133 S.Ct. 714; *State v. Liljedahl* (1982) 327 N.W.2d 27; *People v. Sisselman* (1989) 542 N.Y.S.2d 801; *People v. Denio* (1997) 454 Mich. 691.

difficult when a putative assister/encourager has attempted to participate in another's crime, because the encourager/assister will have to take voluntary steps to prevent the perpetrator from succeeding, if she is to raise the defence of renunciation.[77] Generally, the renunciation defence requires more than mere desistance; it requires the renouncer to have 'abandoned his effort to commit the crime or otherwise prevent its commission'.[78] This strict approach seems logical for inchoate offences.

The renunciation must also be voluntary; it is not enough that the defendant abandons her crime because it is too risky to proceed.[79] Suppose *D* posts a gun to *P* intending to assist *P* to kill *V*. *D* has a change of heart and goes to *P*'s house and waits for the postman and recovers the gun. Here, the defence would apply, because *P* prevented the crime from being perpetrated with her assistance and *D* in no other way encouraged *P* to perpetrate the murder. Similarly, if *D* has sent *P* a cheque for £100,000 to encourage her to kill *V*, *D* would have to cancel the cheque and make it clear to *P* that she is no longer going to pay her to kill. She would also have to make sure that *P* understood that message and thus was no longer under the influence of her original encouragement.[80]

In some contexts it will be difficult for *D* to annul encouragement, because she may not be able to change *P*'s mind. For instance, suppose *D* encourages *P* to kill *V* by telling *P* that *V* has been having an affair with *P*'s husband. *D* not only tells *P* about the affair, but also shows her explicit footage of *P*'s husband kissing and cuddling *V*. In addition, *V* is *P*'s best friend. Suppose also that *D* tells *P* that she should kill *V*, because *V* has destroyed *P*'s marriage. Thereafter, *D* changes her mind and tells *P* that her husband and his lover are not worth going to jail for. *D* tells *P* to get even by divorcing him and suing him for every penny she can get. Alas, *P* cannot get the explicit footage off her mind, nor can she come to terms with the fact that

77 *People v. Ozarowski* (1976) 38 N.Y.2d 481.

78 See *People v. Stevens* (2009) 884 N.Y.S.2d 283. Also see section 5.01(4) of the A.L.I.'s *Model Penal Code.*

79 See *People v. Stevens* (2009) 884 N.Y.S.2d 283, where Kavanagh, J. (Mercure, J.P., Rose, Kane and Garry, J.J. concurring) said: 'renunciation is available as an affirmative defence to a defendant who has been charged with attempting to commit a crime if "under circumstances manifesting a voluntary and complete renunciation of his [or her] criminal purpose, the defendant avoided the commission of the crime attempted by abandoning his [or her] criminal effort and, if mere abandonment was insufficient to accomplish such avoidance, by taking further and affirmative steps which prevented the commission thereof".' Also see *People v. Sisselman* (1989) 147 A.D.2d 261; *Wesbrook v. State* (2000) 29 S.W.3d 103 at 122.

80 See *State v. Webb* (1909) 216 Mo. 378, where it was held that the defendant must dissuade the other party from doing an act based on the defendant's encouragement; if the other party commits the crime of her own volition the defendant will still have a defence. See also *State v. Kinchen* (1910) 126 La. 39, where it was held that the defence applied to solicitation, if the defendant's encouragement on all the parties involved is in fact annulled.

the two people she loved and trusted the most, her best friend and her husband, would treat her so badly. The explicit footage and *D*'s message of encourage are still playing on *P*'s mind when the police pull her up for a routine traffic violation and find her with a high-powered gun in her car. When the police ask *P* why she has a high-powered gun in her car, she confesses that she is driving to *V*'s house to kill her for having an affair with her husband. *P* also tells the police that her friend *D* encouraged her to kill *V* and that *V* had showed her video footage on her iPad which proved her husband was having an affair with *V*. *P* tells the police she just could not get the video footage off her mind and thus decided to follow *D*'s original advice and kill *V*.

In this hypothetical, *P*'s act of driving to *V*'s place with a gun is mere preparation.[81] It is not attempted murder. In the hypothetical *D* did not assist *P* by supplying the gun. All *D* did was encourage *P* to kill by showing her the explicit footage while simultaneously telling her to kill *V*. *D* did all she could do to cancel her encouragement, but failed to succeed. To the extent that the American case law states that *D* has to prevent a crime that she has encouraged or assisted, that issue does not arise here since the police intercepted *P*. However, the question remains whether *D*'s failed attempt to cancel her encouragement is sufficient for establishing the renunciation defence.

Some cases suggest it would be,[82] but others suggest that the encouragement would have to be totally cancelled. In other words, *D* would have to convince *P* to abandon the murder.[83] (If in the hypothetical above, *P* had been intercepted by the police because of a timely tip-off from *D*, then that would be sufficient to constitute total cancellation, because *D* has prevented the crime from being perpetrated. Such actions would also evince

81 Cf. *Schemm v. State* (2007) 228 S.W.3d 844. If the crime gets to the attempt stage then *D*'s participation is no longer attempted participation, but instead is consummated participation. Consequently, the defence of renunciation would not be applicable. As we have seen above, withdrawal can provide a defence where *P* has attempted or consummated the crime that the accessory assisted or encouraged her to perpetrate, but only if withdrawal is timely and otherwise reasonable. See *People v. Sisselman* (1989) 147 A.D.2d 261 at 263–264; *Peacock v. State* (1986) 498 So.2d 545; *State v. Smith* (1980) 409 N.E.2d 1199; *State v. Peterman* (2005) 280 Kan. 56.

82 See *Forman v. State* (1954) 220 Miss. 276 at 287 where Hall, J. said: 'The attempted withdrawal about which appellant testified came just a moment before the shooting of Everett by Wheeler and we think it was entirely too late to absolve her of her part in the whole conspiracy.' See also *People v. King* (1938) 30 Cal. App. 2d 185 at 205 where it was said: 'It is not enough that he may have changed his mind, and tries when too late to avoid responsibility. He will be liable if he fails within time to let the other party know of his withdrawal, and does everything in his power to prevent the commission of the crime.'

83 Cf. 18 Pa. Cons. Stat. Ann. § 902(b). See also *State v. Kinchen* (1910) 126 La. 39 at 48 *per* Provosty, J.; *State v. Cromwell* (2009) 33 So.3d 31; *United States v. Buttrick* (2005) 432 F.3d 373 at 377; *U.S. v. Vasco* (2009) 564 F.3d 12 at 21; *Com. v. Joseph* (2004) 848 A.2d 934; *Schemm v. State* (2007) 228 S.W.3d 844; *Commonwealth v. Higley* (1975) 70 Pa. D. & C.2d 142.

a voluntary renunciation of her encouragement.) Even in the few jurisdictions in the United States that allow the defence of renunciation where the target crime has not been prevented, the defence will fail if the defendant's renunciation is not timely.[84]

Under the offences found in sections 44–46 of the *Serious Crime Act 2007*, the question is moot because renunciation is not recognised as a substantive defence. This is a shortcoming of the new *Act*, because it does not provide the defendant with any incentive to change her mind. It does not provide the defendant with an incentive to rethink her attempted participation. Given that inchoate crimes are designed to cut in before any harm is attempted, it would make sense to provide putative participators with an incentive to try to prevent the harm that they have tried to assist or encourage before it is brought about. Under the *Serious Crime Act 2007*, a lighter sentence is the only concession that is likely to be granted to a defendant who has cancelled her assistance or encouragement. The latter will be at the discretion of the sentencing judge.[85]

B. Proving cancellation

Proof will be problematic in cases where a defendant claims she has cancelled her encouragement. It is much easier to prove that assistance has been cancelled. For example, if *D* gives *P* a gun to kill *V*, but also retrieves the gun before *P* gets a chance to use it, then it is not difficult to prove she cancelled her assistance. But as we have just seen, it may be difficult to establish that prior encouragement was no longer playing on *P*'s mind when *P* was found preparing to perpetrate the crime she was encouraged to perpetrate. In some cases, it might be clear that some supervening encouragement has taken over and that *D*'s encouragement was no longer operating on *P*'s mind when *P* was preparing to perpetrate the particular target crime, but such cases are likely to be rare.

84 *State v. Cromwell* (2009) 33 So.3d 31 *per* McMillan, J.; also see *People v. Crawford* (1998) 232 Mich. App. 608 at 617, where Gage, J. said: 'It is an affirmative defence to a prosecution [for solicitation], under circumstances manifesting a voluntary and complete renunciation of his or her criminal purpose, the actor notified the person solicited of his or her renunciation and either gave timely warning and cooperation to appropriate law enforcement authorities or otherwise made a substantial effort to prevent the performance of the criminal conduct commanded or solicited, provided that conduct does not occur. The defendant shall establish by a preponderance of the evidence the affirmative defence under this subsection.'

85 See section 58 of the *Serious Crime Act 2007*.

6 Conclusion

I. Concluding remarks: common purpose complicity

A. The law as interpreted by the courts since 1999

(1) 'Where two parties embark on a joint enterprise to commit a crime, and one party foresees that in the course of the enterprise the other party may carry out, with the requisite *mens rea*, an act constituting another crime, the former is liable for that crime if committed by the latter in the course of the enterprise.'[1]

(2) If it is proved that the perpetrator's criminal acts were fundamentally different to those that the accessory anticipated as possibilities, she will not be liable for those acts. Lord Toulson has asserted that *R. v. Powell* changed the law. Lord Toulson writes:

> Aiding and abetting in the criminal law requires not only knowledge of the principal's objective but a desire to help him attain it. That principle is consistent with . . . earlier English authorities, but the law has become increasingly complex and potential liability wider.[2]

The Law Commission advocated that this version of the law be put into statutory form. It is a good thing the Government rejected the Law Commission's proposals, because this leaves the Supreme Court with an opportunity for reinterpreting the current law to bring it into line with the authorities going back 500 years. The Law Commission's proposals were nothing more than a restatement of the mistaken *R. v. Powell* doctrine.[3] Even if those proposals

1 *R. v. Powell* [1999] 1 A.C. 1.

2 Lord Toulson, 'Sir Michael Foster, Professor Williams and Complicity in Murder' in Dennis J. Baker *et al.* (eds), *The Sanctity of Life and the Criminal Law: The Legacy of Glanville Williams* (Cambridge: Cambridge University Press, 2013) at 241. In the same chapter, Lord Toulson writes: 'The Law changed with the decisions of the Privy Council in *Chan Wing-Sui* and the House of Lords in *Powell and English*.' *Id.* at 244.

3 The Law Commission, *Inchoate Liability for Assisting and Encouraging Crime* (London: H.M.S.O., Law Com No 300 (July 2006) Cm. 6878) at paras. 3.166–3.169.

had been put into the statutory form, the Supreme Court would have had the power to subject them to judicial review on human rights grounds.

B. The law according to a very long line of authorities

J.W. Cecil Turner summarised it in 1958:[4]

> [T]here must be participation; therefore if a verdict against a man as principal does not show that he did the act, or did some act at the time in aid which shows that he was present aiding and abetting, or that he was of the same party, in the same pursuit, and under the same expectation of *mutual defence and support*[5] with those who did the fact, the prisoner cannot be convicted. The law requires the accessory to intentionally encourage the collateral crimes before she can be convicted of those crimes.[6] To reiterate the words of Stephen, J., the accessory is liable, if she 'knows what is contemplated, and both approves of it and in some way encourages it'.[7]

When the Supreme Court revisits this issue it should interpret the law with the following factors in mind.

(1) There must be a mutual agreement that extends to the collateral crime. *A* must agree with *P* (either expressly or impliedly) that the collateral crime be perpetrated by *P*, if necessary, to make their joint enterprise[8] succeed.

(a) *Where there is no express agreement the jury will have to decide from the evidence whether* A *by her participation in the underlying enterprise intended to send* P *a message of encouragement. In other words, did* A *by her own actions or words intend to authorise* P*'s collateral crime.*[9] *It is not enough*

4 J.W. Cecil Turner, *Russell on Crime* (London: Stevens & Sons, 1958) Vol. I, at 147.

5 Sir Michael Foster, *Crown Law* (London: Printed by W. Strahan and M. Woodfall, 1776) at 350; for a modern example of mutual encouragement by such conduct, see *Allen v. Ireland* [1984] 1 W.L.R. 903.

6 *R. v. Lovesey* [1970] 1 Q.B. 352 at 356 applying *R. v. Anderson* [1966] 2 Q.B. 110; with both cases being applied by the Court of Appeal in *R. v. Dunbar* [1988] Crim. L.R. 693. See also *R. v. Spraggett* [1960] Crim. L.R. 840; *R. v. Smith* [1963] 1 W.L.R. 1200 at 1205–1207 *per* Slade, J. and the earlier authorities such as *The Three Soldiers Case* (1697) Fost. 353; *R. v. Plummer* (1706) Kelyng, J. 109; *R. v. Hawkins* (1828) 3 Car. & P. 392; *R. v. Collison* (1831) 4 Car. & P. 565; *R. v. Skeet* (1866) 4 F. & F. 931; *R. v. Caton* (1874) 12 Cox C.C. 624.

7 *Johns v. The Queen* [1980] 143 C.L.R. 108 at 118.

8 I see no compelling case for limiting complicity liability to 'unlawful' enterprises, but standard complicity would be as easy to apply to crimes flowing from lawful enterprises where there are acts of intentional encouragement.

9 Cf. some of the old tacit approval cases from the U.S.: *Omer v. Com.* (1894) 25 S.W. 594; *State v. Cox* (1877) 65 Mo. 29; *True v. Com.* (1890) 14 S. W 684; *Plummer v. Com.* (1866)

that A accidentally or recklessly conveyed a message of authorisation and encouragement. The jury has to be able to infer from all the evidence that A intended to encouraged the collateral crime. In addition, the jury will have to determine whether P was in fact encouraged because of A's implicit or explicit authorisation of P's criminal plans with respect to the collateral crime, because there must be factual participation. Derivative liability hinges on factual participation, so there needs to be sufficient evidence for the jury to infer that A's authorisation/encouragement was one of the reasons why P perpetrated the collateral crime. It need not be the sole reason or even the predominant reason, but it has to be one of the reasons for it.[10]

(b) *The corollary of agreement is intentional authorisation: A cannot agree that P should commit the collateral crime unless she intends to agree.*

A person cannot agree by mistake, accident or recklessly – because mistaken agreement is no agreement at all. Nor can one recklessly authorise: the result of *A*'s conduct might be that it sends a message of what seems like authorisation, but unintentional influence is not sufficient to form an implied common purpose.[11]

C. Proving encouragement by conduct

Intentional encouragement by authorisation can be implied from the conduct of the participants.[12] Similarly, the evidence might show that the agreement was spontaneous, but that will be sufficient.[13] The question is for the jury to determine as a question of fact. Some commentators have argued that the factual encouragement constraint should be dispensed with because it might be too difficult for the prosecution to prove that there

1 Bush (Ky.) 76; *Harper v. State* (1903) 35 So. 572; *Smith v. Com.* (1882) 4 Ky. L. Rep. 353; *Clem v. State* (1870) 33 Ind. 419.

10 *R. v. Clarkson* [1971] 1 W.L.R. 1402 *per* Megaw L.J. (Geoffrey Lane and Kilner Brown J.J. concurring); *R. v. Jones* (1977) 65 Cr. App. R. 250 at 252. In *Hutt v. R.* [1989] T.A.S.S.C. 27 at paragraph 53, Cox, J. (Underwood, Crawford, J.J. concurring). Cf. the inchoate offences in the *Serious Crime Act 2007*, where the encouragement need only be capable of supplying *P* with a motivation for offending. Since those offences are inchoate, there is no need to show that the particular act of encouragement was in fact one of the reasons that motivated *P* to offend.

11 Analogously a rape victim does not consent where she is mistaken as to the nature of the act she is authorising. If she believes she is authorising a medical procedure when in fact she is authorising sexual intercourse, then *D*'s deception means she does not agree to the sexual intercourse at all. For further examples, see Dennis J. Baker, *Glanville Williams: Textbook of Criminal Law* (London: Sweet & Maxwell, 2015) at Chapter 26.

12 *Miller v. The Queen* (1980) 32 A.L.R. 321 at 326; *R. v. Pridmore* (1913) 8 Cr. App. R. 198 at 203 *per* Phillimore, J.; *R. v. Bolster* (1910) 3 Cr. App. R. 81; *Stacey v. Whitehurst* (1865) 18 C.B. N.S. 344.

13 *Clarke v. Tasmania* [2013] T.A.S.C.C.A. 11 at para. 132; *R. v. Sully* (2012) 112 S.A.S.R. 157 at para. 64; *Johns v. The Queen* (1981) 143 C.L.R. 108 at 118; *R. v. Swindall* (1846) 2 Cox C.C. 141; *State v. Israel* (2002) 113 Wash.App. 243; *Gillard v. The Queen* (2003) 219 C.L.R. 1 at 66.

was factual encouragement.[14] Such an argument is fallacious. The prosecution would have no greater difficulty proving it than they do in proving encouragement in standard complicity cases. The foresight of virtual certainty maxim, the dangerous weapon maxim, and *A*'s knowledge of what was planned, *inter alia*, can be used to infer that *A* intended to encourage *P* to perpetrate the collateral crime. Similarly, all the circumstances can be considered to determine whether *A*'s conduct did in fact encourage *P*.

In many cases, it will be patently obvious that *A* not only anticipated *P*'s collateral crime, but also authorised it for the purpose of making the joint enterprise succeed. *Johns v. The Queen*,[15] *Millar v. The Queen*,[16] *Chan Wing-Siu v. The Queen*[17] and *R. v. Rahman*,[18] among others, are prime examples of cases where juries would have had no problem inferring factual encouragement (an advance or spontaneous meeting of the minds with respect to the collateral crime) from the circumstantial evidence and also from the defendant's own testimony. I could list plenty of similar cases too, but there is no need to for present purposes. Hence, these cases would not be decided differently were intentional encouragement required, as there was ample evidence for the juries to infer that there was in fact intentional encouragement in those cases.

There need not be an overt meeting of the minds; the evidence need only be sufficient to allow the jury to infer that there was a mutual intention with respect to the conditional collateral crime. In other words, the jury need to infer from the evidence that all the participants expected the same contingency, intended the same criminal response to that contingency, and knew that the other participants had the same expectations and intentions. See for example *Miller v. The Queen*,[19] where the accessory had full knowledge of the fact that the perpetrator had murdered a woman on an earlier occasion. Worrell was a sexual predator and Miller drove him around so that he could pick up women for sexual encounters. Worrell would pick up the women and then Miller would drive him to an isolated location so that he could copulate with them. Miller would leave the car while Worrell had sexual

14 Jeremy Horder and David Hughes, 'Joint Criminal Ventures and Murder: The Prospects for Law Reform' (2009) 20 *King's L.J.* 379.

15 (1980) 143 C.L.R. 108.

16 (1980) 32 A.L.R. 321.

17 [1985] A.C. 168.

18 [2009] 1 A.C. 129 at 159–160, where there was sufficient evidence for a jury to infer intentional encouragement by authorisation. *A* became aware of the fact that *P* had a knife during the course of their joint violence. *A* continued in the joint violence with full knowledge of the fact that *P* had produced a knife. The jury could infer that *A* tacitly agreed to its use by continuing the joint violence with such knowledge. *A* had knowledge not only of *P*'s possession of the knife, but of the fact that *P* had taken the knife out of his pocket and had it in his hand ready for use and that *P* was in a heightened emotional state and was already engaging in violence.

19 (1980) 32 A.L.R. 321 at 326.

relations with the women. On one occasion, Miller returned to the car to find that Worrell had killed the woman he had picked up. In the months following the first murder, Miller continued to drive Worrell around so that he could pick up more women for sexual relations. Worrell murdered a further six women. There were many occasions where Worrell did not harm the women, but merely had sex with them. Nonetheless, Miller continued to drive him even though he knew Worrell had started to randomly kill some of the women he was having sex with. Miller was charged with seven counts of murder and was found guilty on all counts but for the first count, because when Worrell first killed, Miller had no idea that Worrell intended to kill and thus did not encourage it by authorising it. The High Court of Australia held:

> It was open to the jury to conclude that after the first murder had occurred the scope of the common purpose had altered. Miller now knew that Worrell not only intended sexual intercourse with the girls but might also murder them, while Worrell knew that when Miller participated in further expeditions he was fully aware of the fatal outcome of earlier expeditions. Because of these additional elements the jury might conclude that the purpose common to them both on these subsequent expeditions had altered. Because of their knowledge of one another's state of mind a new factor would be present in the recurring common purpose of the pair: when Miller would leave Worrell and a girl together, he would no longer be leaving them merely so that they might have sexual intercourse but also so that, if the mood took him, Worrell might, in Miller's absence, murder the girl.

There was more than enough evidence for a jury to infer that Miller intended to send a message of encouragement as far as the later murders were concerned. Worrell and Miller knew the state of each other's minds and formed mutual intentions from their common knowledge of the conditional collateral crimes Worrell had perpetrated on past occasions. Similarly, the accessory in *Johns v. The Queen*[20] knew that the perpetrator was quick-tempered and violent. Coupled with this, on the way to the robbery, the perpetrator told Johns that he 'wouldn't stand for any nonsense' from the robbery victim. The perpetrator told Johns that the target victim was 'always armed and wouldn't stand any mucking round if it came to a showdown'.[21] The accessory also testified that he believed that the perpetrator 'wouldn't let a bloke like [*V*] get on top of him'. There was ample evidence in that case to allow a jury to infer that Johns intended to encourage the perpetrator's conditional collateral crime by making it

20 (1980) 143 C.L.R. 108.
21 *Johns v. The Queen* (1980) 143 C.L.R. 108 at 111.

clear that he approved of it as a conditional crime. There were mutual expectations, mutual knowledge and mutual (conditional) intentions apropos the collateral crime. That the 'contemplation' rule was being used as a rule of evidence was made clear in the Supreme Court of New South Wales, before the case was appealed to the High Court of Australia. In *R. v. Johns*,[22] Begg, J. (Street, C.J. concurring) said:

> In every case, therefore, it is necessary to determine what was the common design to which the parties assented expressly or tacitly to achieve some common purpose. If the features of that enterprise establish that it was within the contemplation of the parties [a test for inferring conditional intention apropos the collateral crime] that some act might be done by one of them in playing his role in pursuance of that enterprise, each of them is responsible for that act.
>
> . . .
>
> The basis for admitting evidence of the acts or statements of such persons against each other is that the prearrangement to commit the crime is taken as implying an authority to each to act on behalf of the others.[23]
>
> . . .
>
> This involves a consideration of what it was that Johns authorised, procured or assented to and what was foreseen, contemplated or intended by him to be involved in the performance.[24]

D. Looking back and the law going forward

Some of the greatest jurists of the last 150 years have made it clear that accessorial liability should rest on intention. More than 80 years ago, the great Australian jurist, Sir Leo Cussen, A.C.J., said:

> [T]he person charged as a principal in the second degree must in some way be linked in purpose with the person actually committing the crime; and by his words or conduct do something to bring about, or render more likely, such commission.[25]

A few years later, the leading American jurist, Learned Hand, J. (Swan and Chase, J.J. concurring) asserted that an accessory should only be liable for

22 [1978] 1 N.S.W.L.R. 282 at 295.

23 *R. v. Johns* [1978] 1 N.S.W.L.R. 282 at 301 *per* Lusher, J. citing *Tripodi v. The Queen* (1961) 104 C.L.R. 1.

24 *R. v. Johns* [1978] 1 N.S.W.L.R. 282 at 302 *per* Lusher, J.

25 *R. v. Russell* [1933] V.L.R. 59 at 67. Sir Leo Cussen's statement was endorsed by the High Court of Australia in *Giorgianni v. The Queen* (1985) 156 C.L.R. 473.

the perpetrator's criminal act when '[h]e wishes to bring it about, and he seeks by his action to make it succeed'.[26] In the United States, the passage from Learned Hand, J.'s judgment is regarded as the *locus classicus* on the subject.[27] Starke, J. siting in the High Court of Australia, said:[28]

> Aiders and abettors are only liable, according to English law, for such crimes committed by principals in the first degree as are done in execution of their common purpose. If any of the offenders commits a crime foreign to the common criminal purpose, the others are neither principals in the second degree, nor accessories, unless they actually instigate or assist in its commission.

Given that these statements were made almost 100 years ago, it is remarkable that the Law Commission in the twenty-first century has asserted that the foresight approach adopted in *R. v. Powell*, which can be justified only on the absurd 'change of normative position' theory, should be put into statutory form. Lords Steyn and Mustill[29] mistakenly thought they were bound to apply the evidential maxim of foresight of possibility as a substantive fault element in common purpose complicity, but unlike the law commissioners,[30] accepted doing so was grossly unfair.

In a couple of recent cases,[31] the High Court of Australia also has been led astray by Sir Robin Cooke's decision in *Chan Wing-Siu v. The Queen.*[32] These decisions, like *R. v. Powell*, rest on the fiction that foresight and participation in an underlying joint enterprise are sufficient to justify derivative

26 *United States v. Peoni* (2d Cir.1938) 100 F.2d 401 at 402. Justice Learned Hand's doctrine has been endorsed in nearly every state in the U.S.A. See *Wilson-Bey v. U.S.* (2006) 903 A. 2d 818 at 831–832. It also was endorsed by the High Court of Australia in *Giorgianni v. The Queen* (1985) 156 C.L.R. 473.

27 In a recent decision of the Supreme Court of the United States, Kagan, J., delivering the opinion of the Court, said: 'And the canonical formulation of that needed state of mind – later appropriated by this Court and oft-quoted in both parties' briefs – is Judge Learned Hand's: to aid and abet a crime, a defendant must not just "in some sort associate himself with the venture", but also "participate in it as in something that he wishes to bring about" and "seek by his action to make it succeed".' See *Rosemond v. U.S.* (2014) 134 S.Ct. 1240 at 1248.

28 *Brennan v. The King* (1936) 55 C.L.R. 253 at 259. Starke, J. also concluded that there was sufficient evidence for a properly directed jury to infer that Brennan had conditionally intended the collateral crime.

29 *R. v. Powell* [1999] 1 A.C. 1 at 12–13.

30 Horder and Hughes were a core part of the Law Commission's criminal law team at the time and were wholly in favour of statutory offences based on a form of constructive liability. See Horder and Hughes, *op. cit. supra*, note 14 at 398.

31 *McAuliffe v. The Queen* (1995) 183 C.L.R. 108 at 117–119; *contra*, *Clayton v. The Queen* (2006) 168 A. Crim. R. 174 (Kirby, J. dissenting). The foresight doctrine was not applied as a substantive fault element in Australia until the decision in *McAuliffe v. The Queen*; before that time it was used merely as an evidential maxim.

32 [1985] A.C. 168.

liability, even if *D* participates in the underlying joint enterprise without intending to encourage *P* to perpetrate the collateral crime.

E. Reinterpreting complicity so that it can be reconciled with justice

I have argued that the common purpose complicity doctrine as expounded by Sir Robin Cooke in *Chan Wing-Siu v. The Queen* (and since adopted by the Lords) cannot be reconciled with a consistent line of authorities going back 500 years. Historically it was necessary for *D2* to authorise *D1*'s actions. Thus *D2* could not be liable where she simply foresaw *D1*'s actions, especially when *D2* had expressly forbidden those actions. *D2* could only be liable if she had at least obliquely intended to encourage the perpetrator by impliedly authorising any collateral crimes. Collateral crimes are normally conditional – they depend on what happens while the joint enterprise is being carried out. 'Foresight' was only ever meant to pertain to *D2*'s knowledge of any planned collateral crime that would be perpetrated where necessary to make the underlying joint enterprise succeed. It was not meant to supplant the requirement that any criminal response to the contingencies of a joint enterprise be intended and authorised. (*D2*'s implied authorisation forms the conduct element because it is factual encouragement.) If lawmakers were to accept this interpretation, it would result in a radical narrowing of the doctrine as laid down in *Chan Wing-Siu v. The Queen.* Such a change, in practical terms, could raise concern that it would remove protection for society. I have argued, in Chapter 4, that this concern could be addressed by amending the *Serious Crime Act 2007* to criminalise reckless participation. The advantage of amendment to the *2007 Act*'s offences is that it allows for fair labelling and proportionate punishment.

Corrective steps await a decision coming before the Supreme Court of the United Kingdom. In *Clayton v. The Queen,* Kirby, J. said:[33]

> The question of law was originally expressed by judges. It therefore can be re-expressed by them . . . In the present age, waiting for a modern Parliament to grapple with issues of law reform of this kind is like waiting for the Greek Kalends. It will not happen. Eventually courts must accept this reality and shoulder their own responsibility for the state of the common law.

Should an appeal be brought, the Supreme Court of the United Kingdom has a legal duty to judicially review the law in light of Article 49(3) of the *Charter of Fundamental Rights of the European Union.* Coupled with this, while it is not the Supreme Court's role to abrogate unjust laws unless

33 (2006) 168 A. Crim. R. 174 at 225.

they contravene our recognised human rights, it has a duty to interpret current laws so that they accord with the authorities that underpin them. The Supreme Court of the United Kingdom would not be overstepping the mark were it to interpret the law of common purpose complicity to reconcile it with the authorities from *Le Seignior Dacre's Case*[34] through to *R. v. Anderson*[35] and beyond.[36] Judge Learned Hand relied on English authorities dating back to the mid-sixteenth century to support his finding that the law requires the accessory to in some way associate himself with the criminal enterprise, 'that he participate in it as in something that he wishes to bring about, that he seek by his action to make it succeed'.[37]

II. The shortfalls in the *Serious Crime Act 2007*

In this book I have tried to identify the limits of derivative liability and its alternatives in an attempt to build a case for reinterpreting the mental element in complicity so that it requires nothing less than intention. I have argued that if the courts accept the interpretation of complicity under section 8 of the *Accessories and Abettors Act 1861* as presented in this book, then it is necessary to find a law that can deal with reckless participation.

34 (1535) Moore K.B. 86. See also *Parker's Case* (1559) 2 Dyer 186a.

35 [1966] 2 Q.B. 110 at 118–119.

36 This was also accepted as the law in Hong Kong prior to Sir Robin Cooke's decision in *Chan Wing-Siu v. The Queen* [1985] A.C. 168; see *Au Keng and Wong Wai Hung The Crown* (1954) 38 H.K.L.R. 142 at 159, where Gould, J. (Reece, J. concurring) said: 'There was no reference to the evidence on the subject of common intention, one of the necessary ingredients of guilt in a principal in the second degree.' Many courts have held that implied or tacit agreement and conditional intention apropos any collateral offence is necessary to sustain a conviction. See the authorities cited throughout Chapter 2 of this book. The clearest examples can be found in *R. v. Lovesey* [1970] 1 Q.B. 352 at 356; *R. v. Spragget* [1960] Crim. L.R. 840; *R. v. Short* (1932) 23 Cr. App. R. 170; *R. v. Adams* (1932) V.L.R. 222 at 223–224 *per* Mann, J.; *R. v. Kalinowski* (1930) 31 S.R. (N.S.W.) 377 at 380–381 *per* Davidson, J.; *R. v. Dowdle* (1901) 26 V.L.R. 637 at 639–641 *per* Williams, J.; *R. v. Lowery (No 2)* [1972] V.R. 560 at 561–562 *per* Smith, J. In *R. v. Surridge* (1942) 42 S.R. (N.S.W.) 278 at 282–283, Jordan, C.J. said: 'Thus, if two persons agree that one of them shall kill or inflict grievous bodily harm on another party whilst the other stands by and keeps watch or otherwise assists, the latter is guilty of murder as an accomplice if the third party is killed, since he is a principal in the second degree. Again, if they agree that the active party shall commit a crime, and agree also, expressly or tacitly, that if resistance is offered any necessary violence may be used to overcome it, including killing or inflicting grievous bodily harm, then if the active party intentionally kills or inflicts grievous bodily harm which causes death, in order to overcome resistance, the other party is guilty of murder, because the killing was within the common purpose. If the killing amounted only to manslaughter by the active party, the other party is also guilty only of manslaughter.'

37 *United States v. Peoni* (2d Cir.1938) 100 F.2d 401 at 402 *per* Learned Hand, J. (Swan and Chase, J.J. concurring). Learned Hand, J. also held that the writings of the institutional writers as far back as Bracton, and more recently Coke, Hale, Foster, Hawkins and Blackstone, supported such an interpretation of the law.

In Chapter 4, I provided a doctrinal and theoretical analysis of the new personal liability offences found in section 44–46 of the *Serious Crime Act 2007* to ascertain whether they cover reckless participation and reckless inchoate participation. I also examined the conduct element for those offences to determine whether it is apt for catching the sort of reckless encouragement that is often present in the joint enterprise (common purpose) complicity cases and conclude that it is.

The main shortfall of the offences found in the *Serious Crime Act 2007* is that they do not cover reckless participation. I concluded that section 44 covers only intentional (inchoate) participation and that section 45 covers only oblique intentional (inchoate) participation. Consequently, interpreting the mental element in complicity as requiring nothing less than intention will leave a *lacuna* in the law. It is submitted that section 45 of the *Act of 2007* should be supplemented with a section 45A offence criminalising reckless (inchoate) participation. Section 45 is an independent offence that criminalises personal wrongdoing, and as it is not a form of derivative liability, but rather personal liability, it allows for fair labelling and proportionate punishment for the independent wrong involved in encouraging and assisting another to perpetrate a crime.

The House of Commons Justice Committee reviewed the offences found in sections 44–46 of the *Serious Crime Act 2007* and concluded:[38]

> In relation to the SCA, as stated above, we are concerned about the complexity of the provisions, and the difficulties that academics, lawyers and judges have found in interpreting the provisions. At the same time, we accept that there are, as yet, relatively few cases, and that the latest judgment in the case of *Sadique* may allow the legislation to settle into accepted use and interpretation. *We recommend that the Ministry conduct a further and full post-legislative assessment of Part 2 in 2016. If, in the meantime, the number of appeals on Part 2 increases, we expect the Ministry to consider bringing forward legislative proposals for revising, or even replacing, Part 2 to meet the purpose of the legislation in a less tortuous fashion* [emphasis in original].

I do not think the provisions are so difficult to interpret. The core problem with the *Serious Crime Act 2007* is that they do not criminalise reckless participation. Unless they are reformed to include a new offence of reckless participation, judges interpreting the law of complicity under section 8 of the *Accessories and Abettors Act 1861* will feel compelled to continue plugging

38 House of Commons Justice Committee, *Post-Legislative Scrutiny of Part 2 (Encouraging or Assisting Crime) of the Serious Crime Act 2007*, Sixth Report of Session 2013–2014 (London: London Stationery Office Limited, H.C. 639, 2013) at para. 31.

the gap by interpreting complicity as also covering reckless participation, when the ancient and modern authorities suggest otherwise.

III. Synthesis

A. *Reconciling complicity with fairness and justice*

The central theme in this book is to have a just and fair law of complicity. I have argued this can be best achieved by:

(1) Interpreting the mental element in complicity as requiring nothing less than oblique intention.
(2) Interpreting the victim rule so that it excludes actual victims as opposed to transferred victims from being criminalised.
(3) Enacting new personal liability offences of reckless participation as opposed to bringing reckless participation within the derivative liability provision found in section 8 of the *Accessories and Abettors Act 1981.*
(4) Recognising abandonment as a defence for inchoate participation.

A doctrine of joint criminal enterprise that allowed a person to be convicted for a collateral crime that she did not intend to assist or encourage simply because she participated in the underlying joint enterprise and foresaw that the collateral crime might be perpetrated by another member of her group would be unjust, because it is doubtful that a reasonable jury could infer factual encouragement in such a case.

It would be better to enact a section 45A in the *Serious Crime Act 2007* as a less serious offence of reckless participation, so that those who are merely reckless receive a more lenient sentence and are labelled as less serious wrongdoers. For example, the *New York Penal Code* (*McKinney's Penal Law* § 115.00(1)) provides:

> A person is guilty of criminal facilitation in the fourth degree when, believing it probable that he is rendering aid:
>
> 1. to a person who intends to commit a crime, he engages in conduct which provides such person with means or opportunity for the commission thereof and which in fact aids such person to commit a felony; or
> 2. to a person under sixteen years of age who intends to engage in conduct which would constitute a crime, he, being over eighteen years of age, engages in conduct which provides such person with means or opportunity for the commission thereof and which in fact aids such person to commit a crime.
>
> Criminal facilitation in the fourth degree is a class A misdemeanour.

Index

For legal cases please see separate table of legal cases.

For Product Safety Concerns and Information please contact our EU representative GPSR@taylorandfrancis.com
Taylor & Francis Verlag GmbH, Kaufingerstraße 24, 80331 München, Germany

www.ingramcontent.com/pod-product-compliance
Ingram Content Group UK Ltd.
Pitfield, Milton Keynes, MK11 3LW, UK
UKHW020022200926
475702UK00014B/2007
9781138614253